Pass It On!

How to Thrive in the Military Lifestyle

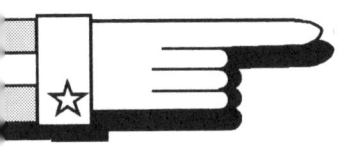

Pass It On!

How to Thrive in the Military Lifestyle

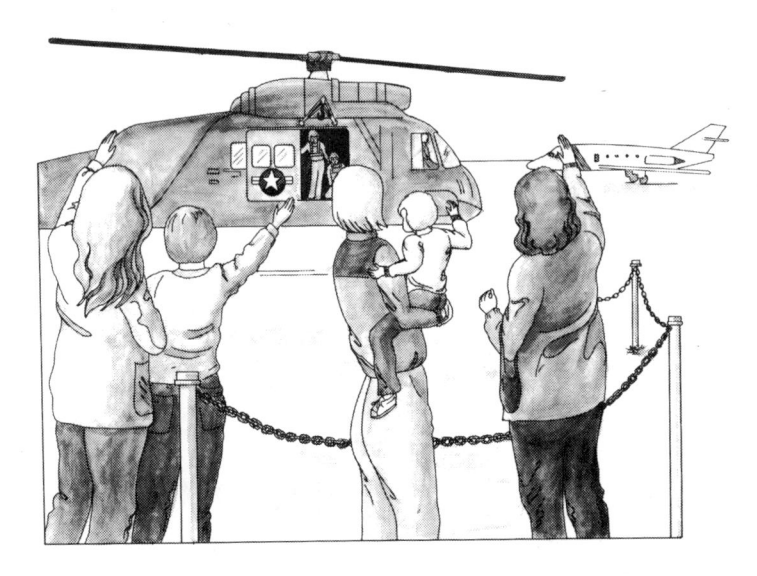

Kathleen P. O'Beirne

Lifescape Enterprises

These collected works have appeared previously under the author's copyright in *Family, G/C/T, Ladycom,* and *Let's Go Fly a Kite! Activities for Kids in NE Florida and SE Georgia* , and without copyright in *Florida Times-Union* , *Dolphin, Camden County Tribune, Savannah News-Press,* and *Army, Navy, Air Force Times.*

Additionally, portions of these works by the author have appeared in the U. S. Government publications: *Charting Your Life in the United States Coast Guard, Making a Home in the Navy: Ideas to Grow On,* and *Wifeline.*

Copyright (c) 1991 by Kathleen P. O'Beirne

Published by
Lifescape Enterprises
P. O. Box 218
West Mystic, CT 06388

All rights reserved, including the right to reproduce this book or portions thereof in any form or by any means, electronic or mechanical, including photocopying, recording, or by any information storage and retrieval system, without permission in writing from the author.
All inquiries should be addressed to Lifescape Enterprises, P. O. Box 218, West Mystic, Connecticut 06388.

Printed in the United States of America

10 9 8 7 6 5 4 3 2

First Edition

*Cover design and most illustrations by
Helen M. Carr*

Library of Congress Catalog Card Number: 91-90191

Dedication

To my four families:

My own family -
Captain Frank ("Mick") O'Beirne, Jr., USN (Ret.)
Michael
Heather

My parents:
General and Mrs. T. W. Parker

My parents-in-law:
Vice Admiral and Mrs. Frank O'Beirne

The Military Family:
all of you who have served, do serve,
and will serve as members of the
Armed Forces and your families

Other Books Written and/or Published by Author

Making a Home In the Navy: Ideas to Grow On
(1980; revised 1985)

Charting Your Life in the United States Coast Guard
(COMDTINST PO1750.4 -- 1983)

Class of 1959 Smith College: 25th Reunion
(1984)

*Let's Go Fly a Kite! Activities for Kids in
N.E. Florida and S.E. Georgia*
(1985)

*Choosing the Right Plants
for SE Georgia and NE Florida*
(1986)

Articles in this collection have appeared previously in:

Camden County Tribune
Charting Your Life in the United States Coast Guard
Dolphin
Family
Florida Times-Union
G/C/T
Ladycom
Let's Go Fly a Kite! Activities for Kids in N.E. Florida and
    S.E. Georgia
Making a Home in the Navy: Ideas to Grow On
Naval Institute Proceedings
Savannah News-Press
Wifeline

Introduction

Have you had a kindness shown?
Pass it on.

Hold thy lighted lamp on high,
Be a star in someone's sky.

From Stanzas 1 and 4
Pass It On
Henry Burton (1840-1930)

Pass It On! The time-honored philosophy of sharing in a domino fashion instead of expecting a direct reciprocation is one of the strongest traditions in the military lifestyle. Kindnesses given are not only given to the individuals in need (new neighbors, sailors stranded in an airport after the last shuttle to their new base, or a young bride in tears in the bank), but also to the long line of military families that stretches from our frontier Army and Revolutionary Era Navy into the unforeseeable future. (The linking of one's past, present, and future is another theme you will find over and over again in military families' lives.)

Throughout this book you will hear the phrase or the concept from sponsors, researchers, husbands, wives, and children willing to share their perspectives and experiences in the hope that readers of these collected magazine articles would be enabled to <u>cope,</u> even to <u>thrive</u> in our lifestyle.

Over the recent holiday season, my husband and I found how pervasive the tradition is. We went to a potluck dinner sponsored by our lake residents' association. It is a group that we don't know very well yet, but I knew the host and hostess were a retired Navy couple.

When I told the wives about my work on this book, they asked what I had chosen for the title. When I said, *Pass It On*, it was as if the room were transformed and memories flooded in. One wife, in particular, said that that very evening was the anniversary of her arrival in New London, Connecticut, many years ago. A week before Christmas, she and her two little girls got off the train at the station and found themselves knee deep in snow. After a memorable taxi ride, they were able to get the keys to their empty set of quarters and "moved in." Her husband was at sea and their car was en route. They had what they had carried in their suitcases. Neighbors soon knocked on their door and loaned them assorted chairs and mattresses until their own furniture arrived after Christmas, and they brought food galore. She remembers it to this day as a delightful period of reading with her children, watching the snow continue to fall, and knowing that her neighbors cared. She has "passed on" the tradition many times over.

Others in the room talked of their military experiences (previously unknown to me), and by the end of the evening, we were a far tighter group of folks than our choice of housing would have occasioned. Intensity of shared experiences and friendships is another theme you will find throughout this book.

As an Army daughter, a Navy wife and mother, and a teacher, I have been even more inclined to share "lessons learned" than most. As I became increasingly aware that my experiences were not unique to me, and that voice needed to be given regarding the dearth of support services for military families in the late 1960's and 1970's, I began to research and write. Eventually, I was able to teach military family policy and research at very senior levels to empower members of all Services to *make a difference*.

I've been fortunate over the last 15 years to be associated with publications whose primary audience is wives of officers and enlisted personnel. I've always felt as if I could picture you, the readers, and was comfortable sharing some of my own experiences so that you would say, "Oh, she does that/feels that, too! *Pass It On!*

Throughout my career in journalism and in military family policy and programs, I have been privileged to know an incredible collection of people who care as deeply as I do and have as strong a sense of "passing it on" at levels from neighborhoods to nations. They believe in supporting military families and helping us to be happy, healthy families -- to be all that we can be in spite of (and sometimes, because of) the challenges that come with our lifestyle: mission, relocation, and unaccompanied tours.

The concept of coping with our lifestyle is much in vogue, but I would like to go one step further, and urge thriving in our lifestyle. To thrive, according to *The Random House Dictionary of the English*

Introduction iii

Language (1987) is "to prosper; to be fortunate or successful; to grow or develop vigorously; to flourish." This raises our expectations and ennobles our life's work.

<u>Why</u> *Pass It On?* A June 1990 article from the Navy News Service quoted the Chief of Naval Personnel, Vice Admiral Mike Boorda, stressing "the need for an informed Navy, from the top down, to keep fleet sailors aware of current issues that affect them, their families, and their futures -- getting it from their closest source, their supervisory personnel.......'It's important to pass the news on, and make sure that everyone understands the message.'" His motivation was not only out of concern for the individual sailor, but also for the good of the Service. Two years ago the average cost to recruit and train one soldier across the Services was $22,000. And most Services will admit that it takes three new soldiers, sailors, airmen, marines, or coast guardsmen to replace one who has left the Service (to replace him or her numerically, not in terms of experience). So <u>readiness</u> and <u>retention</u> are additional themes you will find in this book.

(According to *Defense '90*, there are currently 2,100,000 active duty members, 1, 670,000 Guard and Reserve, and 1, 065,000 civilian employees that are part of the Department of Defense and the Coast Guard in 1990. Add approximately 3 million family members for these 4,835,000 members, plus approximately 3 million retirees and their families, and you know the magnitude of our military population.)

A 21-year member of the Navy Wives Club of America has another reason for working so hard to keep her local chapter afloat. "Even when the numbers of members are small and the amount of work is great, I continue so that it will be there for others like it was for me.... to *Pass It On!*."

As I was readying this collection of articles for publication, our country mobilized and entered the conflict with Iraq over Kuwait. The newspapers have been full of photographs and articles about members of the National Guard and Reserves who are experiencing the call up that they and the nation as a whole, hoped would never occur. On the whole, their families are ill-prepared to cope with their prolonged absence. They are, in a very real way, where active duty families were 25 years ago -- so this is an opportunity to *Pass It On!* (News media have noted, with some acrimony, that mobilized Reservists were going to have a hard time making it financially on military pay --- *pass that on!*)

The articles in this book range from 1969 to the present. Over this span, the progress for military families has often seemed unbearably slow, because <u>we are living it</u>. But it has been, historically, a period of

Introduction

remarkable positive change. One of the reasons that I have left the articles in their original state was so that you can see where changes have occurred and where we still need to work.

You will note that most of the references were to <u>wives</u> -- partially because of the demographics at the time, the fact that I wrote mostly for magazines for wives, and because we had not become sensitized to using the word "spouse." For those of you who are members of dual military couples, single parents, or civilian male spouses, please don't mistake period language for current insensitivity, and please adapt the information to suit your needs.

This book is not meant to be a compendium of all of the issues that face military families, but rather a collection that, for the most part, is timeless in its message: *that it is not only possible to thrive in the military lifestyle, but highly likely.*

No formal, official approval of this book is claimed. The opinions and ideas expressed herein are those of the author.

The illustrations are primarily the work of Helen M. Carr, a former member of the Navy herself, who is now a graphic artist with her own portable home-based business. Married to STGCS(SW) John D. Carr, she is the proud mother of ten year old Justin.

Additionally, there are illustrations drawn for Department of Defense publications by Jack Arthur and SSGT Lynne Strawn, U. S. Army.

My gift to researchers and inquisitive military family readers is the kind of index I always want to find in a book. You will find the names of people who have shared their insights, the names of researchers and publications, and you will find references to <u>concepts</u> as well as actual words used throughout the book. *Pass It On!*

Kathleen Parker O'Beirne
February 1, 1991
Mystic, Connecticut

Contents

Section I: Moving — 1
1. The Seven Emotional Stages of Moving — 3
2. On the Move Again — 10
3. Traveling Tips for Military Families — 13
4. Sponsors: Making the Difference — 17

Section II: Deployments and Unaccompanied Tours — 25
5. Those Who Wait — 27
6. Sailors Wives <u>Should</u> Have More Fun! — 42
7. Key Wives' Recipe for Success — 45
8. Keeping Love Alive — 51
9. When Dad is Away at Christmas — 57
10. Reunion Strategies — 63
11. Shore Duty: Great Expectations — 65

Section III: Financial and Housing Matters — 71
12. Family Money Matter$ — 73
13. The Ins & Outs of Credit Cards — 81
14. Military Spouse Rights & Benefits — 85
15. Pits & Palaces: Military Housing — 94
16. Overseas Living Information Service — 101
17. Home, Sweet Trailer? — 103

Section IV: Family Support Services — 115
18. Military Safety Nets — 117
19. Teenage Military Brides — 123
20. 10 Myths About Spouse Abuse — 132
21. Eating and Exercise Disorders — 140
22. Breast Cancer — 151
23. The USA Still Needs the USO — 161

Section V: Coping With Our Lifestyle — 167
24. Our Five Families — 169
25. Isolation Matrix: A Tool for Discovery — 174
26. Getting Organized — 184
27. Be All You Can Be! — 194
28. Sources of Pleasure — 201
29. Taking Stock: Freedoms — 211
30. Coping With Burnout — 217
31. A Recipe for Friendship — 221
32. Friendship and Dragonflies' Eyes — 225
33. All Kinds of Time — 231
34. Thanatos: Military Wives Deal with Death — 237
35. Caring for Aging Parents — 240

Section VI: Potential Roles for Spouses — 247
- 36 Roles of the Military Wife — 249
- 37 Military Spouse Roles of the '90's — 255
- 38 Creative Innovation — 265
- 39 Leadership — 272
- 40 Lifescaping: The Art of Balanced Growth — 279
- 41 Blueprint for Wives' Clubs — 287
- 42 Practical Protocol — 290

Section VII: Portable Careers and Education — 295
- 43 Portable Careers — 297
- 44 Banking Your Skills — 301
- 45 Home-Based Businesses — 307
- 46 The Real Costs of Working — 314
- 47 Internships: Hands-On Experience — 325
- 48 Back to School — 332
- 49 Educational Options for Military Wives — 341
- 50 Earning Your Degree — 346

Section VIII: Women in the Military — 353
- 51 The Changing Roles of Military Women — 355

Section IX: Parenting — 367
- 52 Parenting Ph.D.'s — 369
- 53 Baby Costs — 375
- 54 Happy Endings: Maze of Military Adoptions — 382
- 55 ABC's of Toy Buying — 393
- 56 Parenting, Military Style — 400
- 57 The Value of Photographs — 407
- 58 An IOU from Dad — 410
- 59 Child Care: 1990's Board Game — 415
- 60 Alone After School — 423

Section X: Children's Educational Needs — 431
- 61 A Kid's Eye View of the Military — 433
- 62 New Kids in School — 439
- 63 Parents: Partners in Education — 443
- 64 Challenging Children — 451
- 65 Precious Play — 455
- 66 Summer Fun — 461
- 67 Summer Job Strategies for Teens — 465
- 68 Hints for the College-Bound — 471
- 69 Television Viewing — 479

Glossary of Acronyms — 488
Index — 490
About the Author and Illustrator — 509

Section I

Moving

1

The Seven Emotional Stages of Moving

My reaction to a recent *Washington Post* headline -- "Average American Moves 12 Times in Lifetime" -- was that someone must not be doing her share. When I was 32, I added up the moves I'd made as an Army daughter and Navy wife and found they totalled 24, not counting a few temporary shifts! Here I am, another move and several years later. Am I any wiser? Does it get any easier? No! It hurts every time.

• A young Army wife, who has moved six times in the eight years she's been married, talks of the crying she did when she moved in as a young bride and the crying she does now as she moves away.

• Another Army wife, with 19 moves in 18 years, speaks of her "grieving period," the six months following a move when she sorely misses friends at the last post.

• A Navy wife remembers the last three moves, with less than two weeks' notice each time, and the resulting financial losses.

• A senior Air Force wife says her agony comes watching her furniture being loaded onto yet another van.

As I listened to many military wives talk about their moving experiences, I noticed a basic pattern of seven stages accompanying each move: Orders, Move, Househunting, Making It Home, Finding-Discovering, Self-Discovery, and the Turning Point: Recognition, at which time the wife finally feels at home in her new community. The passages of adjustment vary from person to person and move to move, but recognizing the pattern and knowing that others share it may lessen our own problems.

4   Moving

Orders

The Orders set the pattern in motion. We feel excited telling our friends where we are going, and are curious about the new area. We sometimes feel relieved to end some obligations that would be hard to sever graciously if we were to remain. I was having difficulty convincing my environmental organization in Connecticut that five years as president was enough. Orders to Washington made my argument convincing!

We also sense the loss of our position in our community. Many wives are torn between appreciating every last minute in the old community and wishing they could hurry and move so that the tension of loss would be over. I can remember bursting into tears after church on our last Sunday; how I wished we could get in the car and be gone. Some women withdraw from community commitments wben they sense orders are due in order to lessen the hurt of the actual departure.

Moving

Because the work of Moving household belongings is physically exhausting, a loss of five pounds is common at this point. The sheer busyness of all of the details of packing can help to keep emotions hidden, but can also provoke emotion. Watching the packers non-chalantly pack a household of treasures accentuates how impersonal this move is to others. The shutting of the van door closes a portion of your life, too -- moments now forever gone. If the family has been unhappy in this spot, leaving may be a relief. I practically carried boxes to speed our departure from Charleston (S.C.), but wandered around our empty Mystic (Conn.) house trying to make a mental scrapbook of Christmases and beloved gardens.

Househunting

The third stage, that of Househunting, can continue the emotional "high" of departure and the physical exhaustion of the move. Women frequently enjoy househunting as long as it doesn't take too long or make too great a drain on finances -- then desperation can set in. Many exper- ience sleepless nights going over and over the pluses and minuses of each possible dwelling.

When the choice is made, they spend more nights mentally arranging the furniture. Such planning is both an artistic and physical necessity -- the movers will set that buffet down only once! My worst goof this last move was forgetting to plan places for the rugs. I knew in which room I wanted one, but how far under the piano? "Think, Lady! We're not moving it again!"

Making It Home

Stage four, Making It Home, continues to be a physically exhausting time. Such intensity of effort rarely surfaces again, unless one's mother is coming to visit. The spot decisions and the obvious progress that takes place each day give a feeling of true accomplishment. The first full course dinner served on one's own plates with all the necessary knives and forks is indeed an occasion to celebrate.

Almost unnoticed at this point is the daily solitude. Dad has probably gone to work and the kids to school. (If you have pre-schoolers, forget the solitude stage!) The phone doesn't ring. I remember how I had looked forward to absolute quiet, relieved to have left the incessantly ringing phone in Connecticut. Well, I got my silence. If the phone rang, it was my husband, my mother-in-law, my sister-in-law, or a wrong number. And with relatives nearby, I had more possibilities for outside contact than most newcomers have as they run up the basement stairs in eager anticiptation of contact with the outside world.

If this settling-in stage includes the immediate need of a job for the wife, it can be a very chaotic time emotionally. Delaying the job hunting until at least the basics are settled may represent financial loss, but that will be less than the emotional drain on an unsettled family. Any woman will be a more impressive applicant when she can find her job records and recommendations, an unwrinkled outfit, and her self-assurance. She will also have a little time to assess the new community's job market.

Finding/Discovering

We now begin the Finding Period, during which the local map and yellow pages are our constant companions. We find the commissary and learn the layout. The local stores, where none of the salespeople know us, are a whole new world. We locate the Scout troop, the Little League, the dentist, the church, and the piano teacher. This is a period of constant search and evaluation. We are testing schools, services, neighbors, and new acquaintances; they, in turn, are testing us. For the family, this is a time of intense dependence on each other because we haven't made new friends yet. We feel isolated as individuals and as a family.

If the wife decides to work, she will have the challenge of convincing prospective employers of her specific skills. Letters of recommendation and school records give material evidence of her worth. Once she finds a job, learning the new routine and meeting other employees may keep her on edge for many weeks. Some women may have to take a job below a previous position and go through the frustration of working back up. It is one of the many not-so-hidden costs in a move.

6   Moving

The Finding Period is co-existent with the Discovery Period: the discovery that all of the appliances in the new house were waiting to serve notice of their (a) idiosyncratic personalities, or (b) their immediate demise. Each military wife could write a volume on her discoveries -- family treasures, all of them -- a year later when they've become history! One of our now-favorite classics was the demise of the antiquated piping in our new-old Mystic house five days after we'd moved in and two days after my husband left on submarine patrol. My letters describing the event and my $750 bill didn't reach him; meanwhile, he sent me the Charleston phone rebate check of $3.96, with the note, "live it up, kid!"

This stage of finding and discovering takes a wife anywhere from a month to a year. We all adapt at our own pace, and even if we appear to be settled superficially, we know how much further we have to go.

Self-Discovery

During the Self-Discovery Period, it is the wife's turn, after settling her husband, her children, and her house, to make long-term decisions for herself. What will her commitments be? Will she try something new; will she continue to do the same kind of volunteer or paid work? There may still be plenty to keep her busy at home, but is busyness fulfilling? Is it the same as happiness?

New acquaintances will have been made at this point, but true friendships require long cultivation. Finding companions for bowling or garage sale jaunts takes a while. We need a variety of friends, but often need to be urged by new acquaintances to join them. One young Army wife said she felt too unsure of herself to go anywhere the first time she was asked. But she added that she certainly hoped she'd be asked again.

During the Self-Discovery Period, a wife may find that others suggest subtly, or not so subtly, what she "ought to do." In the Washington, D.C area there is an insidiously persistent variation in the form of, "Are you working?" Perhaps employment is common here due both to the opportunities resulting from the women's movement and to the financial stress of living in the area. (Other areas are certainly not exempt!)

Those who enjoy volunteer work may not face this period of internal questioning. For those who find the job of creating an attractive home sufficient fulfillment, a move can often be an enjoyable opportunity for decorating. But for a woman who seeks commitments outside the home to fit specific long-range goals, this self-discovery period can be very difficult. With each move, a goal-oriented woman must readjust to her environment. Further education may require transfer to a different college or university. A job she enjoyed at the "old home" may not be available at the new one. Recognizing this period for what it is may be half the battle. While she takes the time to plan her life, she may need courage to decline peripheral commitments and to accept the fact that she is going through a period of self-doubt and sometimes loneliness.

Turning Point: Recognition

The final stage in this pattern that is repeated with each move is the Turning Point: Recognition. A major claim to fame will be being recognized as "Michael's-Mom." I felt I'd been accepted when my son's friends showed up on the way to school with a turtle they'd found and hoped we had a box. The fact that I was still in my bathrobe didn't faze them a bit (nor did it faze me -- an indicator that I was out of my self-conscious/newcomer phase).

More important recognition will take the form of being appreciated as a friend or valued as a person of talents (rather than a hoarder of boxes!). One young Army wife found that she experienced the turning point when her husband was assigned as sponsor for a new family. She excitedly wrote three pages of hints and bought two days' worth of groceries for them, because their sponsors had done the same and said, "Pass it on."

This pattern of *Orders, Move, Househunting, Making It Home, Finding/Discovering, Self-Discovery,* and *Recognition* will repeat itself move after move. When I asked wives from all Services which moves had been easier and which had been harder, the responses were consistent from the youngest wives of enlisted men to wives of senior officers. Over and over they said that no move is "simple" or exactly like another. Some moves bring additional changes, such as the change to foreign duty, shore duty, or separations. In any case, family members are at different stages and ages with each move. Older wives felt that moves had been relatively easy until their children were in late elementary school. They said that once the mechanics of the packing had been mastered, emotional baggage was relatively light. However, the early years brought more moves due to training required for the husband. Once the children were old enough to make good friends, leaving was much harder. An uprooted teenager may find separation from friends disastrous.

By the time children have left home, most parents find they can move their household goods more easily. However, Skip Brown (Mrs. George S. Brown), wife of the Chairman of the Joint Chiefs of Staff, said that instead of finding life easier once the children had left the nest, she has found that the frequency and abruptness of moves have increased as her husband has become more senior. So the middle years of a serviceman's career may tend to be more stable geographically than the early or later years.

8   Moving

Officially, the military can help ease the trauma of moving by providing sufficient time and funds when transferring personnel is necessary. Secretary of Defense Harold Brown agreed that a policy of assigning people to several tours in one geographic area is economical for the government. It would also be economical for families, both financially and emotionally, and should be widely applied.

Whenever a permanent change of station occurs, orders should be received early enough to allow legal notice to landlords, to sell homes, and to arrange for other myriad details. No one should be in the position of one Naval officer who lost $1,500 on each of his last three moves, excluding the loss he took on the rushed sale of his homes, because he was given less than two weeks' notice each time.

Families renting an apartment or house must have time to "give notice" to avoid losing security deposits that might have paid utility and rental deposits in the new area. All Service families should remember to insist on the "military clause" in rental contracts that allows a lease to be broken early, with proper notice -- usually 30 days.

Moving-related allowances should be increased. Current funds rarely, if ever, cover the true costs of a move.

Sponsors should be matched with incoming families so that those in similar family situations can advise one another. Bachelors or single women would likewise appreciate information from other unmarried personnel.

These official accommodations could lessen the frequency of moves and improve the support for those that are necessary, thereby making the military life a more attractive career in these days of all-volunteer services.

Suggested Reading

The following books may be of interest as you prepare for, or recover from, another move.

<u>On Moving as a National Problem</u>
A Nation of Strangers by Vance Packard (David McKay Co.)
The Moving American by George Pierson (Knopf)
Corporate Wives --Corporate Casualties by Robert Seidenberg, M.D. (Amacom)

The Seven Emotional Stages of Moving

On Moving in Practical Terms
Help Your Family Make a Better Move by Helen Giammettei and Katherine Slaughter (Doubleday). Written by two wives, it is especially good on preparing for the physical move.
How to Live Cheap But Good by Martin Poriss (American Heritage Press). An outstanding paperback on searching for an apartment, cleaning it, and furnishing it -- "for nothing."
How to Survive as a Corporate Wife by Norma Upson (Doubleday). Contains a fine "Two-Week Plan for Easier Moving" for details of packing.
The Family Guide to Successful Moving by Carl Warmington (YMCA Association Press). Very good on checklists for the physical move and specific organizations for help and service in the new community.

Originally appeared as "The Seven Stages of Moving" in Ladycom, *September 1977.*
Later adapted in Making a Home in the Navy: Ideas to Grow On *(1980) and* Charting Your Life in the United States Coast Guard *(1983).*

2

On the Move Again

St. Marys, Georgia -- Margie and Al Johnson are moving again, their 12th move in 15 years. As soon as school is out in June, the Johnsons will be leaving the Naval Submarine Base in Kings Bay, Ga., for a three year stay in the Philippines. The end of the school year typically marks the opening of moving season for many Americans. But for a Navy family, moving is a recurring part of life. The Johnsons describe their move with a mixture of pleasure and panic

"I tend to have the wanderlust in me -- an excitement about the unknown," Mrs. Johnson said. "Moving helps you remember that your health and family is so important."

CDR Johnson, public works officer, has managed a stay of five years at Kings Bay by linking two tours in a row. For the past five years, Mrs. Johnson has been the base librarian. She must leave six months short of reaching tenure in the Civil Service.

Where?

Their children, Rachel (11) and Benjamin (10), are reacting to the move in different ways. Rachel suspected the move was coming. When her parents announced that the family was moving to an island, Rachel said, "Hawaii?" "Over more," said their dad, as he got out the globe and pointed to the Philippines.

Rather than hold farewell parties, the children will be holding celebrations in honor of their friendships. Rachel will have a slumber party, while Benjamin will take his buddies to a baseball game and then a pizza parlor.

Telling their grandparents was more difficult, because the family will be halfway around the world from them. Though CDR Johnson has served overseas, the family has never gone along. Mrs. Johnson did her graduate work during those unaccompanied tours.

When?

To ease the departure for the grandparents, Mrs. Johnson and the children will spend the summer in Wisconsin with her parents. Housing will be unavailable that soon, the monsoon season will be in full force, and the family has made a tradition of visiting grandparents and cousins in the summer.

Research

The Johnsons have learned that research and planning are key skills for a move. The officer that CDR Johnson is relieving in the Philippines has offered advice about living arrangements, schools, climate, and the job. He even sent CDR Johnson a typical month's calendar to hint at the tempo of the job. The Johnsons have checked the base newspaper and a base newsletter for recreation, travel, and television.

What to Take?

Their second car has been shipped. They won't ship much furniture, but they are including their piano, which CDR Johnson calls his "therapy." Each child will pack a footlocker for advance shipment. They have chosen personal items. Rachel has filled her trunk with stuffed animals and sticker books. Benjamin has included his fan, footballs, a breakdancing book, and his remote control toy van.

Severing the Ties

They are severing their ties in St. Marys. CDR Johnson notified his church that it will need a new organist after his four and a half years of service. Mrs. Johnson has notified the base and her acquaintances at the Historical Society Commission. Mrs. Johnson has no idea what job she will have in the Philippines. Most jobs for which she is qualified are held by local nationalists there. Rachel is writing a book for her teacher in the middle school gifted program called *Moving Again..* She is on Chapter Five now.

The family members seem to be treasuring their past, savoring the present, and anticipating the future.

12 Moving

A Checklist for Moving

It helps to have a checklist when moving, says LCDR Cara Curtin, director of the Navy Family Services Center, Naval Submarine Base Kings Bay, Georgia. She has moved six times in her 15-year career. She and her Navy husband had four hours' notice to leave Iran with only their passports and ID cards in February 1979.

Her checklist for moving, in no particular order:

- Finish current projects
- Collect all family, medical, dental and school records.
- Fill out change of address cards for your mail.
- Arrange for your pet's move.
- Clean your closets and drawers.
- Decide what to do with items the movers won't pack, such as aerosols, flammables, and refrigerator items.
- Stop local services, collect deposits or refunds.
- Decide what clothes to take.
- Pack a basic tool kit for easy repairs.

Originally appeared as "Navy family on the move again," Florida Times-Union, May 14, 1985.

3

Traveling Tips
for Military Families

Every military family's dream is that our summer will enrich our children and draw our family even closer together. The reality is often a drain on our finances and squabbling in the back seat. A little advance planning will help to bring reality closer to the your dream. The trick is to think of all contingencies, involve the children in the preparation as much as possible, and be prepared to fill up the kids' travel time with as many car activities as you can. With this check list, you should go a long way towards making your vacation a joyful one for all members of your family.

Ahead of Time

Anticipating the trip can be half of the fun. Depending on the ages of your children, they can be involved in:

- Selecting the sites to visit.

- Ordering maps from Exxon's Touring Service (1251 Ave. of the Americas, NY, NY 10020), Mobile Travel Routing Service (P.O. Box 25 Versailles, KY 40383), and Chambers of Commerce en route.

- Highlighting the route on their own copy of the map. You can photocopy a map, cut it to easy car size, and staple it together.

- Researching areas to visit in the library (history, geography, geology, wildlife). Consider a thematic trip with a focus for the whole family (or one per child) such as wildflowers, rocks, or new animals.

- Making their list of clothes and supplies to take along and packing their own suitcase.

14 Moving

- Pack a roll of large plastic bags for garbage, laundry, rain coats, seats on damp ground, and wet towels and bathing suits.

- Make up a tote bag and treasure box (an old lunch box is perfect because it is a hard surface to write on). Be sure to include water-based coloring pens or crayons (pencil & pens are too sharp for little ones in a moving vehicle); snub-nosed scissors; glue-stick (can glue pictures to cardboard and make puzzles); 3x5 cards (for flash cards, collections, and their own card games). They can punch holes in the cards and connect them with a ring to make a small scrapbook or baby's picture book; a spiral sketch or lined pad for journal, small game pads (pre-printed mazes, scrambled words); deck of cards, small games (e.g. cribbage); small plastic bags for collections; rubber bands/twisties; puppet or soft doll/animal (for solo or joint play); magnifier, compass, and jackknife (for those old enough to whittle, not in the car). Be sure to keep the treasure box out of the sun.

- Get nature guidebooks in paperback (or from the library) to identify birds, flowers, rocks, shells, snakes, and insects. *Audubon* and *Peterson's Field Guides* are tops. Other books to take along (or purchase en route): fairy tales -- everyone in the car hears on his or her own level -- particularly good after lunch/pre-nap; high quality coloring books on nature, history of sites (Dover Books are superb); Scout badge books -- to complete requirements or simply to get ideas for activities; workbooks -- games, math, puzzles, mazes; *Anti--Coloring Books* -- they require imagination; a good drawing book -- the Ed Emberley series can get any kid creating wonderful whimsey.

- Don't forget snacks: include cups and thermos for juices, plus a jug of plain water; raisins and apples travel well.

Enroute with the Clan

- Put a suitcase between two kids in the back seat to separate them and to provide a game/writing surface.

- Pack a pillow per kid -- allows snoozing.

- Get sunglasses for children to reduce their irritability due to squinting.

- Wear layered clothing to remove/add as weather changes.

- Take frequent big-muscle breaks, and eat lunch where the kids can explore the area. Have a ball and jump rope handy. Picnic lunches save money and allow more flexibility of timing.

- Consider driving an hour before breakfast to give an added break. Try a picnic breakfast, too.
- Set car rules early. Everyone should be buckled up, or, if young, in a car restraint -- always. No sudden noise (it alarms the driver). Everything stays inside of the car (arms and trash).
- Have quiet time for everyone. After lunch is a good time.

Activities in the Car

- Depending on the age of your children, try some Mental Math -- silent computations.
- Compute -- miles per gallon, miles per hour, distance to next town.
- Navigator & Accountant (for mileage, meal costs, tolls) -- increase length of time and difficulty according to age.
- Word wealth -- choose the name of a town, state, or new tree in the area and make as many words from its letters as you can.
- Juxtaposition -- look for odds or opposites next to each other, such as a new car by an old bar, a guide in historic garb plus tennis shoes.
- Mime Treasure Box -- pretend to open a box and take out a wondrous object; by motions and facial expressions only, indicate what it is and pass it on to the next person (who must show that he knows what it is by miming before he puts it away and takes out his own item).
- Progressive Story -- one person starts and weaves the beginning, stopping after two minutes or at a climax; the next person must continue.
- Sing -- share your heritage of children's classics and folk songs.
- Chart things to see -- for a sense of history, draw a time-line across the top of a piece of paper: old-----new. Add dates if desired. Could include everything from an arrowhead or fossil to a baby bird or space model.
- What If? -- Write up a variety of tricky questions. Let children draw and/or tell their solution.

Activities at Destination

- Locate local guide books for seeing sights with children (in museum store, bookstore or Chamber of Commerce). These may trigger some unusual hands-on experiences that will be long remembered because they are appropriate for their age/interest: working museums, markets, farms, county fairs, factories.
- Let children use basic camera and keep record of photos taken so they can label later. Ration film so they will be selective.
- Read local newspaper for activities, points of view.
- Try a variety of modes of transportation: trolley, barge, steam railroad, bicycle, pedal boats.

16   Moving

- Choose restaurants which demonstrate (crepery, Oriental stir-fry) or have view of people, boats.
- Living Then/Here -- get kids to imagine their daily life if they lived at the site visited.
- Determine total spending money per child. Let them calculate their daily portion, but allow them to spend as they choose within the limit.
- Fund the purchase of four postcards per day per child: two to keep and two to send to friends and relatives.

Overseas Travel

- Add language books to your collection.
- The AAA is one of two agencies which issue international driver's licenses. It also has reciprocal arrangements with foreign auto clubs for assistance and information.

Travel with Babies

- Carry a set of portable bed railings. Push the bed against a wall, and use suitcases where railings leave gaps (pillows are a smothering hazard for small babies). Carry waterproof pad for bed.
- Carry one or two nightlights.
- Carry two military belts to use in restaurants if high chairs don't have restraints.
- Sit in back with child periodically.
- Play the same developmental games you would at home.
- Take frequent exercise breaks to lessen your toddler's frustration in the car seat.

Keep a balance of quiet and active time, of physical and mental activity, and group and solo time. The three most important things to take along are free and take up no space: patience, imagination, and a sense of humor. With these fully operable and shared with our children, we will have an enjoyable journey together.

Orginally appeared as "Traveling Tips for Military Families," Family Summer Living '84 and Let's Go Fly a Kite! Activities of Kids in NE Florida & SE Georgia (Kings Bay Officers' Wives' Club, 1985).

4

Sponsors: Making the Difference

Relocating your family is stressful. There's no doubt about that. From the first-timer to the seasoned military officer's family, everyone feels the pressures of getting settled at a new location.

That's the main reason military-sponsor programs are so vital. But as *Family* examined the current state of sponsorships, we sensed a lack of enthusiasm the programs need to be successful worldwide. As a result, sponsor programs have become the major weak link in our military family support programs.

And yet, these are the programs most envied by corporate civilians. While senior civilians may be given fancy relocation packages (including house-hunting trips, employment assistance for the "trailing spouse," and computerized choices of schools and neighborhoods), few corporations offer the personal family-to-family welcome that military sponsors can when they are at their best.

In order to describe some all-star sponsors, *Family* asked you, our readers, to tell us about your terrific sponsors or your own winning techniques. We were delighted to receive responses from all over the world, all Services and ranks, and from singles and families alike. Your responses have reminded us again that military people and their families are indeed special. Here's what you said:

Sherry Chestnut (Schofield Barracks, Hawaii/Army): "When we moved to Hawaii three years ago, we had no sponsor. Since this was my husband's first duty station, it was hard. Neither of us had been away from home before, which made us feel in a way unwelcome here. We had no car for a long time, so we walked three-quarters of a mile up a hill to a grocery and spent $100 on three to four bags of groceries. What a waste, when at the commissary we would have tripled the bags for that cost, but we had no way to get there.

"Since then we've helped a few other families that came here with the same circumstances. We weren't officially their sponsor, but we acted as one. I feel a sponsor should be able to help newcomers find suitable dwellings within their pay range. Also, have an insight as to where cheap, secondhand furniture in good shape can be found. If the family has no vehicle, help them find one and be available if they need a ride somewhere until they get one. Also, let them know about the area in which they live; what's available to them, areas to avoid and places to see. The sponsor needs to make sure the wife gets into groups to make friends so she feels more comfortable with the new home area."

Cherry Harmond-Early (Germany/Army): "My husband and I thoroughly enjoyed our first tour of duty in Germany, even though he was an E-4 at the time. We were initially assigned a sponsor of like rank, but when a minor crisis prevented his fulfilling his duty to us, First Sergeant Duard Wright (E-8) and his wife Caroline voluntarily stepped in and took over. When we expressed a desire (via correspondence) to travel concurrently, he suggested that we send him some money and a limited power-of-attorney so that he could secure economy housing for us. Although we were somewhat apprehensive about giving such authority to a total stranger, he proved to be more than worthy of our trust.

"Sgt. Wright greeted us at the airport, armed with a thermos of hot coffee to cheer us during the two-hour ride to our destination. After serving us breakfast, he took us to see our economy quarters -- small, but very charming and quite reasonable for a junior enlisted family. (It was to be our home for seven months, until government quarters were available.) The rest of our first day included a trip to the commissary and dinner.

"The Wrights' kindness did not end there. They provided us with transportation until we were able to purchase a car, and had us over for holiday meals. Because one's *initial* impressions are the longest lasting, I remember that *first* kindness most vividly of all. And it means even more to me now, in light of our second tour of Germany, which unfortunately started off negatively, largely because we had no sponsor at all. Yes, we're seasoned oldtimers now, and my husband's a senior enlisted (E-7), but we still would have appreciated a helping hand..."

Jeanne Guiness (Quantico, VA/Marine Corps): "In the summer of 1982, my husband graduated from the Marine Security Guard School at

Quantico, and was to become the commander of the Marine Detachment at the U.S. Embassy in Katmandu, Nepal. He would be working for the Department of State. At that time there was no program to prepare spouses or families for this particular program, so we felt pretty much on our own. It was very comforting to see some American faces at the arrival gate after 36 hours of travel through six countries.

"One of the Marines introduced us to a lady with a welcoming smile - Lee Lacy, the community liaison officer from the American Embassy. She suggested that we go directly to our new house and get settled in."

Much to their surprise, the Guineses discovered they were to live in a house behind two red gates, inhabited by a housekeeper and guard-gardener, and stocked with four to five days' worth of groceries -- all of which Lee had arranged.

"Before she left she invited us to her home for dinner the following Sunday, and said she would be checking on us to see if we needed anything. That was our first experience with a sponsor program of any kind. My experience with Lee taught me how important it is to take this responsibility seriously. It's important to realize that you can make such a big difference in someone's life. Good sponsorship can make the difference between a really good tour and a very disappointing one."

Inconsistency in Programs

Because sponsor programs tend to be the responsibility of units, and can be highly dependent upon the enthusiasm (or lack thereof) of the commanding officer and the senior enlisted personnel, they are very uneven. Generally, there is an awareness that provisions need to be made for those headed overseas, but even those programs have been spotty.

Orientations for military personnel are mandatory at all installations, and most offer informational programs for family members even if that translates to attending portions of the military orientation. However, they are often too little too late (and often are poorly advertised).

Researchers now know that the first two weeks in a new location are critical. If a new military member and spouse are not welcomed and supported during this highly vulnerable period, as well as during the second most vulnerable period (the post-orders period at the old location when the need for information is very great), the transition will be painful and the adaptation to the new environments (work and living) will be prolonged and counterproductive. Readiness and retention of the military member will be negatively affected.

Winning Tips from Winning Sponsors

Not all sponsors are for those headed overseas or for families. Our readers provided us with the following examples.

WT3 Ann Marie Chirinko (Naval Station, Rota, Spain/Navy): "In January 1984, after having been stationed at Rota for a little over a year, I was assigned the task of sponsoring a young woman coming from Keflavik, Iceland -- an E-3 like myself. I was so excited...I sent the perfunctory 'welcome aboard' package from the Family Service Center and a lengthy, informative letter. But I wanted something to make her feel right at home from her first day at work...so I decided upon a snapshot of everybody in my division, in some sort of casual pose, in uniform or civilian clothes. I had photos of people buying lunch at the mobile canteen, peeking over a *Stars & Stripes*, and sitting on the hood of a pickup truck. On the back of each shot I wrote the name and rank of the subject.

We worked together for almost two years, and the real reward of being her sponsor came during a division Christmas party when she told me not only did she treasure those photographs during all of her PCS confusion, but that she hoped to be picked to be a sponsor someday so she could do exactly the same for another anxious and worried sailor!" (**Pass it On!**)

Becky Juett Miller (Belleville, IL/Army): "In 1976, I served as a sponsor for a single female officer like myself, voluntarily. I wrote at least twice and met her personally upon arrival. My husband and I have been assigned sponsors who did nothing more than call. I think you need to assist with phone numbers, realtors, and other pertinent information such as churches in the area, schools, etc."

Marge Holt (Charleston AFB, SC/Air Force): "I grew up in a military family (Army, officer) and married an Air Force airman basic. That makes almost 47 years of service-related memories, experiences and opinions....Whenever my husband told me to be a sponsor, I wrote a letter to the wife/husband saying what the shopping and schools/colleges were like. I also included a Sunday paper from the local area (English language, if overseas), and a brief rundown on what was available locally and on base for children and adults (library, drama and hobby clubs, NCO and officers' clubs).

"I made a 'cheat sheet' of often-called numbers (hospital, billeting, taxi, etc.), a 'how-to' list (how to call off base, how to say, 'I need a doctor'), and a list of a support group of men/women in the unit with babysitters, car pools, translators, etc. Then, if possible, I got to the billeting room ahead of their arrival and put bread, peanut butter and soft drinks in the room. I left comic and coloring books on the kids' beds and $10 in local currency in an envelope in the drawer....I am proud to say as we near the end of our military career, that I still get letters from families I welcomed with a huge sign and a warm hug at the Frankfurt, Germany, international airport from 1974 - 84."

On the Receiving End

Pamela Dornsife (Germany/Army 0-5 spouse): "Becky and Ralph Civjan (LTC O-5) should be nominated "Sponsor of the Year." After meeting us at the airport, they helped us find a hotel. They drove us around and showed us where important things to know were located -- the PX, commissary, work, hospital and clinics and stores. They showed us how to use the local bus system, and they offered babysitting services while we took driver's license course and testing, and on many other 'in-processing' occasions. They offered to take us many places until our car arrived."

Kim Stephens (Warner Robins AFB, GA/Air Force): "Our family has had excellent sponsors twice...the same family both times! My husband's squadron is small, so many of us cross paths several times. When we moved to Clark AFB, Philippines, we sent letters requesting regulations concerning pets. Staff Sergeant David Boone (E-6) sent us paperwork for tax exempt forms and pet regulations that aided us in getting our 80-pound labrador through the Manila airport where he met us in a vehicle large enough for us and the dog. We then spent the next two weeks in the Boones' house off base waiting for our house to be available, and my husband rode to work with David every day.

"The second move around, to Georgia, my husband stayed with the Boones on his househunting trip. Later, the Boones kept our *two labradors* in their single wide trailer (along with their three children and a dog) while we spent six days in the TLQ (temporary living quarters). As I was six months pregnant, Kathy Boone made me an OB appointment and accompanied me on my initial visit, as well as babysat my two-year-old as needed while we settled into this new base."

Sandra Stutz (Ft. Monmouth, NJ/Army): "Back in November of 1975, my husband was selected to attend the Indian Defense Systems Staff College in Wellington, South India. We had three weeks to pack for an entire year. We received only one letter from the previous year's student with the advice: 'Bring things to make yourselves comfortable.'"

The Stutzes followed that advice, taking paintings, clocks, china, and silver, etc., but were very uncomfortable with so many things once they saw that other families were not so fortunate. When political strife threatened them with evacuation, they really wished they had brought fewer things.

Gunnery Sergeant Virgil L. Davis, III (Panama/Marine Corps E-7) sent many good ideas for sponsors, including the advice, "The lead-off sentence I always use is, 'I have volunteered to be your sponsor.' This sets the receivers' viewpoint that someone who they do not know has already taken an interest in their well-being." If time permits, he suggests writing (or calling Autovon) and asking specific questions on the size/desires of the family. He also tells them what to expect at the airport and where he will meet them -- and to count on dinner at his house the first evening.

Marsha Boyette (Ft. Sill, OK/Army Reserve) and her husband David have sponsored 13 foreign students at the Field Artillery Training Center in their year and a half with the Allied Liaison Division, including officers and enlisted personnel from Zimbabwe, Israel and the People's Republic of China. They have found it an 'enriching and rewarding experience,' and also an opportunity to pay back the kindnesses shown to David when he was in the Army in Japan. A Japanese family "adopted" him and frequently invited him to their home on weekends.

Kelly Ann Wheeler (Misawa AB, Japan/Air Force O-3 spouse): "Our sponsors, Captain Larry and Kathy Wells, made our PCS to our first overseas assignment a snap! They wrote and called us several times in the months preceding our move, made our reservations at billeting, and let us know we could use one of their cars until we were able to buy our own. When we arrived at the MAC terminal, they had brought the entire squadron to welcome us....Within the next two days, we were moved into our new home, our furniture was delivered and unpacked, and I slept in my own bed the third night at our new base!

"If every sponsor did *only* a few things that ours did, I really believe there would be people trying to go overseas more often and more coming back with wonderful friendships and stories. They gave us a wonderful experience that I hope one day to pass on to others with my husband and I join the sponsor program." **(Pass it On!)**

Tackling Problems with Today's Sponsor Programs

Delegates to the October 1988 Army Family Action Plan Conference voted relocation assistance/sponsorship *the number one problem* for the Army Family today. At the November 1988 tenth anniversary conference of the first Navy Family Awareness Conference, relocation assistance and sponsor programs were among the major issues surfaced. As a result, three key Army and Navy leaders have shared their Service's initiatives with *Family*.

Sponsors: Making the Difference

Lieutenant General Allen K. Ono, U.S. Army Deputy Chief of Staff for Personnel, and Shauna Whitworth, Chief, Army Family Liaison Office, offered their views on how to improve the current delivery of sponsor services. General Ono emphasized four basic points:

- "We need to make sure that *all* incoming personnel have a sponsor *whether they think they need one or not.*" Spouses need to know that military members can request a sponsor very easily by filling out a simple request form, so 'they didn't give me a sponsor,' is not always a valid excuse. Relocating military members can and should request a sponsor.

- "The sponsor should communicate with the incoming member ahead of the move."

- "We need to provide sponsors with training so that they know what to do. Ideally, the training is done at the base level." Whitworth noted that Army Community Services usually trains at the unit level upon the unit commander's request.

- "We need to put some responsibility on the *losing commander*. As a part of the process of caring for the soldier, ask if he has a sponsor. If not, then the losing commander can get in touch with the receiving commander and comment on the quality soldier he is receiving, and 'by the way, he needs a sponsor.'"

- When asked, "What's in it for the losing commander?" Gen. Ono saw the readiness payoff. If "waning soldiers" can get the information they need about their new locations in a timely fashion, they and their families have a sense of control. They can make decisions, and the soldiers can be productive members of their losing commands until moving time.

Gen. Ono indicated that sponsorship will be a core program discussed in commanders' and NCO training throughout the Army. He believes that sponsorship should be part of the training given at pivotal points for commanders, sergeants, majors, and first sergeants. They need to know that healthy sponsorship programs bring faster integration into the unit because of the sense that the receiving unit "cares."

Pinpoint assignments are part of the key to this idea. They are "extraordinarily difficult" for junior enlisted members because of the deferments and deletions in orders. However, Whitworth and Ono pointed out that the soldier headed overseas will head to a receiving unit, and within 24 to 48 hours will know specifically where he/she is headed. "The units do a good job of welcoming soldiers." For example, the "S-Bus" (sponsor-bus) picks up all soldiers and families who come through the

24   Moving

Frankfurt/Rheinmein, Germany, airport and delivers them to their areas. The families arrive after their soldier has had a chance to acclimate to the area.

"Air Force regulations require that a sponsor be named after notification of your new assignment. The sponsor is expected, at the minimum, to write you concerning the base, the unit's mission, and your job. Also, your sponsor is expected to meet you on arrival and help you in-process....If you do not hear from your sponsor within 60 days of your reporting date, contact your local Director of Personnel INTRO Program Manager. Upon arrival, if you are unable to contact your sponsor, the 24-hour arrival point in the Base Billeting Office will assist you in contacting someone from your organization." The *Base Welcome Aboard Book* at Nellis AFB (Las Vegas, NV) uses standard language and follows it with the local contact phone number.

The Navy Overseas Duty Support Program has a unique program: OTIS, the Overseas Transfer Information Service. You may contact them via their Autovon line (224-8392/93) or their toll-free number 1-800-327-8197. Their number is put on all orders for enlisted personnel headed overseas. They provide information by pamphlet and by phone that is generic and area-specific.

Gerry Carlon, Branch Head, Overseas Duty Support Program (Navy Family Support Program), is responsible for writing the policy for the sponsor program. She cited the Navy Sponsor Program (OPNAVINST 1704.3 of March 1982) as a comprehensive program guide with sample sponsor letters, "welcome aboard " packets and sponsor evaluation forms. Sponsors are mandatory for overseas assignments, and are encouraged for CONUS assignments via the Sponsor Request Form NAVPERS 1330.2). She feels that the policy is very complete. The key now is to ensure that all unit commanders and all personnel who are transferring are using the sponsor program fully.

*****Family* wishes to thank the following Army and Navy spouses and military member who brainstormed the pluses and minuses of sponsors one evening at the Ft. Myer, VA, USO: Dale Jovero, Janis Penning, Christie King, Cheryl Frischhorn, Tammy Cavanaugh, and Master Sergeant and Mrs. Francesco Martinez. They helped us target good models to share.

Originally appeared as "All -Star Sponsors," <u>Family</u>, March 1989.

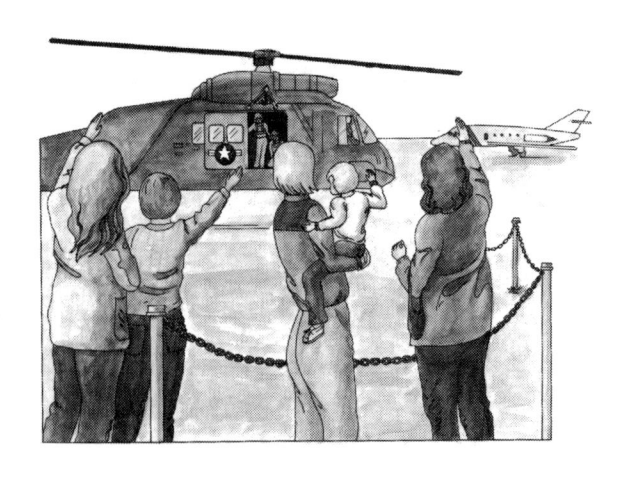

Section II

Deployments and Unaccompanied Tours

5

Those Who Wait

*Author's Note: This was written originally in 1969 as a research paper for a sociology course that I took primarily to learn more about communities -- especially about our submarine community in Groton-New London, Connecticut. I received the enthusiastic assistance of the wives whose husbands served with mine aboard the U.S.S. PATRICK HENRY (SSBN 599) (Blue Crew), who eagerly shared the results with their families and Navy neighbors -- it was the earliest research on submarine families readily available to and understandable by those living the lifestyle. This version is the revision made in 1975.

Background

The Groton-New London area has approximately 5,000 Navy wives who husbands are currently assigned to sea duty aboard submarines. Norfolk, VA, Charleston, SC, San Diego, CA, and Honolulu, HI are also areas out of which large numbers of submarines operate. The husbands who are attached to the poseidon submarines, which carry the fleet ballistic missiles (hence, the FBM's), spend seven months of the year deployed from the area, in a fixed schedule of three months home, three and a half months away. Those stationed aboard nuclear-attack submarines are away six to nine months of the year, on short and long operations. An average tour of duty is almost three years; and often two tours of duty at sea, or more, occur before one period of shore duty.

This paper deals with the situation in which the officer and enlisted submariner's wife finds herself during operations which take her husband away for two months or more. This is not to deny that a separation of less than two months presents problems to her, but they will probably be less intense due to the shorter time span.

The destination of the submarine usually is not made public, for reasons of security, so frequently the wife has only a vague idea where her husband is when he is away. This vagueness and its resulting uneasiness was demonstrated by the reactions of hundreds of wives to the loss of the U.S.S. THRESHER. When the sub was first reported missing, the general location was given, but the name of the sub was not. Navy wives in this area verged on mass hysteria; rumor is one of the most prevalent problems with which the chaplains and captains' wives must cope. This problem is taking on new dimensions now that the FBM's are sometimes making port calls during the patrol cycle, unannounced before departure. On any old Monday morning, a wife may get a long distance phone call from her husband. Though husbands should discourage thoughts of sabotage, collision, or illness, rumors to this effect do have a way of getting started. More on handling this situation later.

Family Communications

Communication by letter is dependent upon whether or not the sub goes into port or can pass its mail on to surface ships. Therefore, two-way correspondence can be highly irregular or non-existent. For example, when the poseidon submarine really submerges for its over-60 day patrol, the men may no longer communicate with their families; and the wives are allowed five familygrams of 20 words each, which the Navy radios to the fleet. It is a challenge to send news that is morale-building, non-coded, personal, and readable! Many wives think that only their husband sees their message. This is far from true as the message must be checked by the opposite crew; it must be transmitted, and the ship's radioman must receive it and let the captain read it before the husband finally receives it. It is recommended that all wives be made aware of this quasi-public nature of their messages so that they will not be embarrassed.

Now that the draft has ended and the Navy is a truly volunteer force, it is hoped that those joining the Navy, and further volunteering for the submarine service, will understand that separation will be part of the nature of their commitment. If the husband can share his enthusiasm for his duty, both ashore and at sea, the wife will perhaps see his sea duty as less of a painful absence. Many wives have seen patrols as one more aggravation against the Navy as a large, impersonal force that takes their husband away, instead of a very personal commitment to the defense of one's country and freedom.

Geographic Distance

In addition to being separated from her husband, the wife may also live at a relatively great distance from other Navy wives in general, or from "wives on the boat" -- one's husband's boat or ship becomes hers, too, at least in terminology. Though there certainly are nearby areas in Groton and Gales Ferry which become almost totally "Navy" through individual purchase or rental, these are sometimes financially out of reach for enlisted families. Navy housing is available, but the waiting list is long; so most of the very young couples find themselves either accepting unpleasant housing nearby that is within their means, or else living at quite a distance. Many buy mobile homes because they are their own. (A study of housing and its effects could be a volume in itself.)

There is, also, an element of choice in being so far away. In 1969, two chaplains for Flotilla II, CDR Edwin S. Jones and LT John W. Pegnam, saw a definite attempt on the part of some husbands to keep their wife geographically separate from other "wives on the boat." Some men fear the gossip that will be spread about their activities while they are away (the FBM's spend a month "inport" in Scotland, Spain, Guam, or Charleston before submerging). For some who do engage in extra-curricular activities, this fear is justified. Others simply choose to be separate from all things Navy, and think this can be accomplished by geographic distance. This alienation of one's wife from couples on the boat is frequently carried to such an extreme by enlisted men, that at the crew departure, the wife has not met anyone connected with the boat. This is less likely to occur in the wardroom because the officers form a smaller and more social group.

Geographic separation from one's husband and other Navy wives frequently results in an exodus to "Mother's" when the ship leaves. Wives without jobs or school-aged children often go home for extended periods of time when their husband leaves. This, of course, can be only a temporary solution at best. I firmly recommend only short visits to the family to "break up" the patrol cycle. Staying with her family for long periods of time, the wife tends to slip back into her role as dependent daughter, instead of growing and maturing as a self-sufficient wife. Also, the family and friends "back home" tend to feel sorry for the Navy wife whose husband has "left her;" I think it's bad to hear too much misguided sympathy.

Finances

When a moderately low pay scale is added to the fact of separation, difficulties often arise. For enlisted personnel, the subsistence allowance is not paid while the men eat aboard the sub. A compensation of $30.00 a month is added when a husband is away for more than a month to help pay for repairs that the man would have been able to do himself. Ironically, this is usually paid in a lump sum <u>after</u> the husband's return. The option of taking advance pay prior to patrol often poses major problems in budgeting throughout the patrol. There is the advantage of having funds more readily available in times of crisis, and of earning interest in a savings account, but the husband and wife should try to assess their money-handling ability before taking advance pay.

Not infrequently, the husband on his departure does several things which affect his wife's financial status. He often takes a lump sum with him to pay for his expenses and entertainment while away. This leaves her account a little low until the next pay day. Also, he frequently indicates that he would like her to save a certain amount while he is away, usually more than they save while he is home. The implication is that she should stay at home and not spend money. This often takes on monumental proportions psychologically, and the wife feels guilty about getting out and leaving the children with a babysitter, when it may well be the best thing for her, the children, and, in the long run, their marriage. Caging a wife, economically or otherwise, may have dire results.

Dysfunctional Marital Patterns

The Flotilla II chaplains also emphasized the fact that more than a few husbands leave their wives in real doubt as to whether they are loved as individuals or as sex mates. Their wives tend to put up with their domineering antics or perpetual teen-age behavior, knowing they will soon go on patrol. This is not a majority, but a large enough segment to be worthy of comment. In a civilian environment, these marriages would probably dissolve; but the patrol or operation cycle lends itself to failure to really solve the problem.

Emotional Cycle of Deployment

The actual departure of the husband brings about a pattern of behavior that most submariners' wives experience to a greater or lesser degree. This pattern was studied by two psychiatrists at the Submarine Base in 1968 - 1969: Dr. Richard A. Isay and Dr. Chester A. Pearlman. Each wife, depending on her age, her educational and family background, copes with the departure and arrival of her husband in her own way. Dr. Isay and Dr. Pearlman found that there seems to be a sequence of emotional stages through which she passes; and for each woman the stages will vary in length and intensity.

These four stages are: "protest against acceptance of the separation, despair, detachment (repression of the feelings of loss), and reunion."

The first reaction to the departure usually comes within the last week or two before the long separation; and the wife feels tense and wonders "Why does he really have to go?" This is usually kept to herself because it is part of the Navy tradition that one doesn't verbalize publicly something as selfish and unpatriotic as this. At Wives' Night, the official gathering of wives (and husbands) about a week before deployment on an FBM, the captain reiterates the fact that the nuclear Navy is "America's first line of defense," the poseidon subs her "foremost weapon." One feels guilty to have wanted to keep him home or to wish someone else's husband would go instead.

Such ignoble thoughts and the guilt resulting from them contribute to the arrival of the second stage, a tearful period during which the wife feels "I'll never live through three and a half months without him." This phase often includes difficulty in sleeping, which is due not only to depression, but is frequently due to the process of getting used to the noises in one's home at night that one doesn't hear when the husband's home and fills the role of protector. (Quite interestingly, this sleep disturbance reoccurs just prior to the man's return when the wife is again in the process of adjusting her role.)

The third stage, that of detachment, is the level on which the wife will live until the arrival turmoil, which is external as well as internal, begins. Some find that they almost adjust to the third stage within the week before separation, and find themselves wishing the husband gone so that their suspension between stages would be over.

At the end of the operation cycle, another sequence occurs. Those who adjust before the husband's return claim that they get two honeymoons a year courtesy of the FBM cycle. Those who find that their adjustment overlaps the actual return, admit that after several days of getting-to-know each other again, which is a tense period, they settle into a more relaxed relationship. The first several weeks home is the "R & R" (rest and recreation) period on the FBM's; during this time the husband may take leave or simply report in once every three days, so he is physically in the house the whole day, or a major portion of it.

Needless to say, the six-and-one-half month cycle that includes a three-and-one-half month patrol, when he is completely away, and the "R & R" period when he is almost completely at home, and two months of normal work days (coupled with training-away time), requires a wife's flexibility! (And, I should say here, each husband suffers a variety of stresses and changes, and he, too, must be a remarkably adjustable individual.)

The adjustment to separation and return has been oversimplified as the adjustment between the woman's role as dependent wife and independent woman or mother. Though this dichotomy does exist, it would be erroneous to believe that the change is from clinging vine to oak tree and back again. It would also be fallacious to suggest that a Navy wife "gets used to it," and, therefore, feels the separation less with experience. As Dr. Pearlman found, in agreement with all wives to whom I've spoken: "No matter how often the experience has been repeated, each separation is a psychological crisis. After successful adaptation, patients often showed little overt evidence of this crisis, but closer observation revealed the characteristic emotional reaction under a defensive covering." Though each woman, through experience, finds a way to make her own adjustment, it is still required with each departure and arrival. Many are able to work through the adjustment prior to the actual deployment and return, instead of afterwards, but the estimated average period of reaction overt or otherwise, to each is three to four weeks; therefore, on FBM's the "separation - reunion sequence involves about six to eight weeks of emotional turmoil every six and a half months." (Pearlman)

The new plan to allow some subs to make unannounced mid-patrol port calls means that wives who have reached the third stage, that of detachment, may all of a sudden receive a long distance phone call from their husband. This is likely to cause them to go through some of the adjustment phases again, which is unsettling. However, these mid-patrol port calls have been exceedingly successful for the men, so that would make some of the distress at home "worthwhile."

Submarine Spouse Profile

When the men leave for patrol or operations, they leave behind a young woman (the average age of the wives aboard an FBM falls somewhere between 21 and 25), who, in addition to having the experiences that all young wives have in common (such as problems connected with social, emotional, and marital maturity, and perhaps motherhood), has probably moved geographically within the last two years. She is probably distant from her family. She probably lives at some distance from wives on the boat. She may not know more than one or two of them, and only superficially at that. If she has children, she must be mother and father for an extended period of time, with no relief. The responsibility of making all of the decisions is a challenge. One can understand how mechanical difficulties, illness, and unforeseen expenses can seem overwhelming under such circumstances. The Navy Wife's Law can be stated thus: within one hour after the ship's departure, either the car, washing machine, or number two child will need repair!

Official Support Systems

There are certain "repairmen" provided by the Navy. Medical care is provided for the wife and children. Crisis help as well as financial help and budget planning are provided by Navy Relief. Legal assistance is offered by the Navy. The legal officer helps the wife most in the areas of consumer complaints, wills, powers of attorney, and real estate contracts.

The four chaplains assigned to the Submarine Base assist in the areas of religious counseling, personal and family counseling, and welfare and morale of families during duty hours. There is always a duty chaplain whose phone number is available through the Submarine Base Duty Officer. There is also one chaplain assigned to the hospital. The chaplains' role seems to be predominantly crisis oriented, as opposed to preventive medicine, due to the gross understaffing. (Ordinarily there should be one chaplain for every 1200 men -- and obviously the four come nowhere near meeting that quota.)

The chaplains have an almost overwhelming number of people for whom they are responsible in the areas of personal counseling. They are not the ones most likely to be aware of births, deaths in the family, or any other crises that affect the man's family while he is away, as they are no longer responsible for forwarding emergency messages to the fleet (these now go through Sub Group Two or the squadron). Although it is extremely difficult to delineate their function precisely, they serve as a "sounding board," a conscience, a buddy with whom one can and should be honest if sincerely seeking help. They know who in the Navy or in the community could best help when a wife is hospitalized and her children need care. They frequently handle the same type of emotional problems that the base psychiatrists handle.

The medical care is free and generally good. However, a large number of wives have experienced long waits, impolite corpsmen, and busy, impersonal doctors. One could write a separate study on the resulting myth of the Navy doctors promulgated by those who have watched officers' wives, especially those with husbands along, be put ahead of their turn, and by those who have been told that their abdominal pains are figments of their imagination due to their husband's absence (and have ended up in a civilian hospital days later with surgery required). Improvements in politeness and concern for the patient are number one on the list for a majority of wives. As the number of military doctors continues to decrease, we can expect an increase in waiting lines, in difficulties in obtaining appointments, and in preventive medicine in general. Emergency care and care for the service man or woman will have to come first.

The Navy Relief Society is a voluntary organization which provides financial aid in time of need, layettes for needy Navy families, and a nurse who helps in a myriad of situations. An example of Navy Relief's aid in an emergency situation is the $100.00 given outright to victims of fire, plus clothing and utensils, if needed.

Informal Support Systems

All of these Navy departments can help the wife at the time of crisis; but preventive medicine is also needed, and this is "extra-Navy," in that the wives of a particular crew form a natural, though usually unorganized group. At its best, this group can provide the sense of belonging in a new community that is so desperately needed by many wives. Because of the built-in hierarchy in the military, which also exists among the wives, there is almost a matriarchal structure to this group. Most of the captains' and Chiefs of the Boat's wives fall in the age range of 34 - 42, though, and dislike being thought of as mothers! Nevertheless, their experience level is comparable. One is a part of the boat group automatically, though certainly if a wife feels no desire or need to participate, involvement is not required. The leadership should be shared. The captain's and executive officer's wives, along with the Chief of the Boat's wife, should function as the organizers, and then the natural leaders among the women should be encouraged to help.

On an FBM, the largest submarine, there are approximately 13 officers and 124 members of the crew; this usually averages out to about 85 wives. On the nuclear attack submarines, the average number of wives will be about 60. The wardroom wives, i.e. the officers' wives, often function socially weekly or bi-monthly when the men are away. The group is small enough for one or two wives to hostess easily; and it is an unusual boat on which this is not done fairly frequently. However, the larger number of crew wives requires planning and communication, plus a belief on the part of the wives of the captain and executive officer that getting the enlisted wives together is worth the effort. Many have made efforts in this direction in the form of a crew-wardroom dinner just before the return of the men. This, of course, is two and a half months too late on the FBM's.

Suggestions

I would like to offer a number of suggestions that we have found valuable in the past seven years on several FBM's. When my husband first arrived as the new executive officer, there existed a classic state of anomie. Few wives knew each other among the crew; as usual, there had been a turnover in almost one third of the officers and crew, so new people were added to a non-functioning group. I, as a new executive officer's wife, in the absence of the captain's wife who had not yet moved to the area, experienced "initiation by fire." There was no contact with outgoing wives, so we had to operate from crisis to crisis until all wives on the boat finally got together five weeks after deployment. With the help of many individuals in the next six months, we got together as a whole frequently, took a long hard look at the small crises that we could prevent or soften by acting as a large buddy system, and formulated a plan of action that we hope will be continuous on our own submarines, and hope will serve as a valuable guide to others. (In the five years since this paper was first written in 1969, my husband has served a second tour as executive officer, and a three year tour as captain. I have utilized the following plan and found it highly flexible and effective.)

Many small things can be done to make newcomers, almost one third of our number each patrol, feel at ease. Even before the men leave, the captain's wife, executive officer's wife, and Chief of the Boat's wife work on such things as the phone tree and Wives' Night. The phone tree is our means of spreading news and invitations rapidly. We have carefully organized our list on a geographical basis so that crew wives call others who live near them. This provides opportunities for them to ride to functions together, share information on babysitters which are hard to find in a new area, and to perhaps aid the buddy system. First names are put on the list to erase the quasi-anonymity of "Mrs. Adams," plus a phone number. I usually ask all of the chief's wives to serve as callers, if they wish, and then add other natural leaders as we need to fill in the list. Five or six names are about enough to call on a regular basis. A few long distance calls (collect) for emergency or arrival information only could also be given to each caller.

Wives are mailed invitations and called for Wives' Night, an evening shortly before deployment at which the captain answers questions that the women (or men) may have. Slides of the ship are shown, as well as some of the wives' activities. Seeing the eating and sleeping areas of a submarine that they may never physically see (because it operates out of Scotland, Spain, Guam, or Charleston) is very reassuring to wives. It provides mental images to fill in thoughts while husbands are away. For new wives, the chance to meet others and see samples of their functions is valuable in making the adjustment to the separation easier, and to encourage their participation when the first dessert or picnic comes.

Wives are called for Wives' Night for three reasons: to check out the accuracy of the phone tree; to make personal contact before the husbands leave; and to be sure they have received the invitation. Much to our dismay, we have discovered that husbands are irresponsible about carrying home the invitation, and that some actually destroy the official invitation mailed by the captain before their wife has a chance to see it. This is part of the attempt to keep her separate from the Navy.

We try to mail the invitations to the first dessert so that they will reach the wife the day after the husband's departure. This gives her something to look forward to during the first week; it has proven to be a great morale boost to be given a week to adjust, and to know that at the end of that week there will be an opportunity to meet new and old friends, and to plan projects and activities for the duration of the patrol.

At the first gathering all are encouraged to get to know several people as well as possible. Each time, one wife makes up a party game which requires each woman to write in the names of wives who expect a baby, can't drive, wear mini-skirts, know how to make suki yaki, sew, paint, etc. This may seem foolish to those unaware of the real trauma many people go through when they have to meet a roomful of new people, and their husband is not there to help. The game also opens up opportunities to help others, learn from others, or to spot potential problem areas -- the youngest wife, usually 16 or 17, will face the additional problems of being under legal age. We always ask who the youngest is, who's a nurse, a teacher -- potential helpers.

The wives of the Captain (CO), Executive Officer (XO), and Chief of the Boat (COB) share the chance to meet the new wives and to "exude" a balance of confidence and concern. The COB's wife usually leads a discussion on what those gathered would like to plan for the patrol: picnics with and without children, cultural expeditions, pot luck dinners, and "how-to" demonstrations.

The captain's and XO's wives talk <u>briefly</u> about the emotional experience that we have in common due to the patrol cycle and offer suggestions that we have found valuable for coping with the sense of loss. Knowing that one's feelings are shared by others, and that one is not "abnormal" helps a great deal. Projects that produce some recognizable accomplishments at the end of the three months help to lessen the sense that the months of separation have been both long and wasted. We talk about both "inner-directed" and "outer-directed" activities: there has to be a balance. For real maturity and capacity to be alone, one cannot simply busy oneself endless in external activities.

We recommend keeping a journal so that a wife can share her activities and thoughts every few days, "have a conversation," albeit one-sided, with her husband that she can send to him when he surfaces. This helps his reunion , adjustment, and helps her think of him frequently, which alleviates the tendency half way through the patrol to have dreams in which his face fades or she cannot remember what he looks like.

Our chief recommendations are the buddy system and involvement in the local civilian community. Ties to the boat and one's neighborhood fill two needs. Another Navy wife, preferably one whose husband is on the same patrol cycle, is the best possible "buddy." Each woman needs to have one or two friends with whom she can "let down her hair," with whom she can share interests, and whom she can use as a sounding board.

The ideal choice is a friend whose husband is on the same boat because his schedule (chronological and emotional) will be exactly the same. No one who is not a Navy wife, including one's family, will have the same frame of reference and understanding. This includes a second sense of when she needs to share a meal -- dinner time is the hardest time for most Navy wives because, in addition to what civilians recognize as "meal preparation-and-five-o'clock-havoc," there is the heightened sense of loss of a father and/or husband. Many wives find that communal activities ease the three worst periods: mealtimes, Saturday nights, and Sundays. A real friend provides one with help when needed, and an opportunity to be needed in return.

In addition to a "patrol-buddy," each individual needs to find some ties to the community which are continuous, not subject to patrol schedules. For some this is a job. For others it is involvement in church activities, a bowling league, an art course, civic organizations, college clubs, scouts, musical groups, the Navy Wives' Club, gray lady work at the hospital, or Navy Relief work. There is a definite need for an on-going activity, as well as the sense of belonging that results.

One further suggestion is to get to know one's neighbors. It is both frightening and sad to find how few know a single family well who lives nearby. A great majority of our wives come from tiny-to-small home towns where they "knew everyone." Loss of a husband and community at the same time can be extremely distressing; hence, many go home, never learn to cope, and agitate until their husbands leave the Navy or get divorced.

Our "preventive medicine" has not solved all problems; but the dimensions of troubles are smaller and less emotional, on the whole. Two fires in one patrol were handled with great generosity and concern by all of the wives. In fact, the contributions of food, clothing, and household items were so great in one case that much was donated to Navy Relief. External crises and emotional problems of a mild nature are handled well because the wives as a group feel needed, and can identify with the situation. Problems of a deep emotional or moral nature are not within our frame of awareness or ability. The chaplains and psychiatrists have the training and official position needed to cope with these.

Training and Support Needed

Knowing to whom one should turn is not easy. In the past, due to personalities, policies, and lack of organized concern, the wives of each individual boat had to function as well as they could without trained direction. As a result of discussion during the course of researching this paper six years ago, I urged the beginning of a "seminar" by the base psychiatrist, Dr. Pearlman, in which problems such as those covered here were discussed. The plan was that eventually this seminar, of three - four one hour sessions, would be offered to (and, hopefully, accepted by) all wives of captains (CO's) and executive officers (XO's) at the beginning of their husband's command. They, in turn, could share the results with their Chief of the Boat's wife, and could work out within each trio an overall plan of activities, and the degree to which each wished to be involved. It would be hoped that when orders would come for any one of the trio to leave, that the replacement would attend the seminar, and the trio would again evaluate and plan. (The seminar continued for a number of months, and our attendance record was fabulous -- our only problem was getting the original 13 wives to turn over their slot to someone else!) Wives cannot be ordered to participate; however, awareness of the overall situation and the need for their cooperation often will move those normally reluctant to become involved.

I do think it's important to say at this point that the CO, XO, and COB's wives <u>don't have to take on these responsibilities</u>. Sometimes the men and wives on submarines take this leadership for granted, as something owed. I think it must be very clear that these wives give of themselves, their energies, time, and emotions because they choose to do so. And perhaps, those who do not choose to play an active role could honestly discuss this and "clear the air" so that others who are willing to help will know where they stand.

Because many of the submarines are submerged for long periods, each man needs to feel confident that his wife will be happy and cared for in an emergency. Otherwise he will not function at his best, and could be a potential danger to the ship. This concern for one's husband's safety, plus a moderate concern for others in general, should be sufficient impetus to enlist the aid of most wives whose husband's job puts them in a position of potential responsibility. Often the more senior wives, of both officers and chiefs, have gained a wide circle of friends in the Navy and community through past tours of duty, and tend to forget how alone they were "in the beginning."

In May, 1975, the Navy Relief Society sponsored a CO-XO-COB's wives' "First Aid Course," which brought together for a morning representatives from many of the Navy support services. If repeated every three months or so, with the exception of the summer months, it will be a valuable service. It would give information to those new to their potential responsibilities, plus providing an opportunity for sharing techniques and ideas that have been successful for "experienced" wives. What became apparent in the first session was that in the economic crush, the Navy has had to deplete the support services. There are fewer chaplains, still two psychiatrists (but there will be a void of six weeks between loss and replacement), and there is relatively little awareness of the on-going wife problems. In an all-volunteer Service, such an awareness is crucial.

Separation and frequent moves have recently become a way of life no longer unique to military families. Books such as Vance Packard's *Nation of Strangers*, George W. Pierson's *The Moving American*, and Robert Seidenberg's discussion of corporate wives' problems in *Corporate Wives - Corporate Casualties?* deal with the stresses common to a large segment of the American population. Knowing that some of the strains we experience as Navy wives would also be a part of our life if our husband were an executive with Dupont, Westinghouse, Lever Brothers, or IBM helps to put our lifestyle in a somewhat more accurate frame of reference. There is a list of further reading along this line at the end of this paper.

The suggestions made through this paper for easing the separation difficulties may appear obvious or optimistic, depending on the reader's awareness of the Navy wife's situation. However, they are neither. They take into account the increasing individualism and anonymity in the average American's life, and the intensified transience and separations of the Navy family. That many of our Navy wives do succeed in leading mature lives of fulfillment and commitment with their husband away half of the year or more, plus a move every two or three years, is remarkable. That they should often be viewed by the civilian community as different at best, and unreliable and inferior at worst, is unfortunate for both the misunderstood wives, and the shortsighted community.

* * * * * * * * * * * * * * *

Bibliography

1. "COMSUBFLOT TWO Instruction 1750.1C, Flotilla Chaplain's Organization and Functions, " September 6, 1968, pp. 5.
2. Gabower, G. Behaviour Problems of Children in Navy Officers' Families: as related to social conditions of Navy family life. Ph.D. dissertation for Doctor of Social Work. The Catholic University of America Press, Washington, D.C., 1959. pp. 263.
3. "Friendship , Service are Aims of Thames Navy Wives' Club." Dolphin, Vol. XIX, No. 24 (April 18, 1969), p.3.
4. Isay, Richard A., M.D. "The Submariners' Wives Syndrome." Read at 124th Annual Meeting of the American Psychiatric Association, Boston, Mass., May 13-17, 1968, pp. 8.
5. Jones, Edwin S., CDR, CHC, USN and LT John W. Pegnam, CHC, USN, Submarine Flotilla II Chaplains, New London, Conn. Interview, March 13, 1969.

40 Deployment and Unaccompanied Tours

6. Lengyel, Elizabeth. "Long Separations are the Major Problem." New London DAY, November 5, 1969, p. 1.
7. MacIntosh, Houston, M.D. "Separation Problems in Military Wives," American Journal of Psychiatry, 125: 260-65, August 1968.
8. Navy Relief Society Training Guide, Navy Relief Society, Washington, D.C., 1963. pp. 33-40.
9. Pearlman, Chester A., Jr., LCDR, MC, USNR. Abstract of "Separation Reactions of Married Women." To be read at the 125th Annual Meeting of the American Psychiatric Association, Bal Harbour, Fla., May 7, 1969. pp. 12.
10. Questionnaire sent by the author to 68 wives whose husbands were aboard the USS PATRICK HENRY (SSBN 599) (Blue crew). April, 1969. 38 replies.
11. Welcome Aboard: Submarine Base on-the Thames: 1968 Unofficial Guide. Boone Publications, Inc., Lubbock, Texas, 1968. pp. 10, 15, 21, 22, 24.
12. Personal experience of the author in 21 years as an Army daughter, and 16 years as a Navy wife -- particularly these last 7 years as wife of the executive officer of the USS PATRICK HENRY (Blue crew), USS VON STEUBEN (Blue crew) and wife of the captain of the USS G. W. CARVER (Gold crew).

Materials/resources for further research: (*these became available between the publication of my original paper in 1969 and the revision above published in 1975)

Bey, Douglas R., M.D. and Jean Lange. "Waiting Wives: Women Under Stress." American Journal of Psychiatry, 131:3, March 1974, pp. 283-6 (focused on wives of servicemen in Vietnam).

Bermudes, Rev. Robert W. "A Ministry to the Repeatedly Grief-Stricken" The Journal of Pastoral Care, Vol. XXVII, December 1973, No. 4, pp. 218-28 (Groton minister interviewed wives of deploying submariners as well as others, such as long distance truck drivers).

Ebbert, Jean. Welcome Aboard: an Informal Guide for the Naval Officer's Wife, 7th ed. Naval Institute Press, Annapolis, Md., 1974.

Ladycom, a magazine for military wives distributed through the commissaries; also available by subscription. (*Now known as Military Lifestyle.)

McDermott, T. J., CDR, CHC, USN. "Counseling in the FBM Program, Submarine Flotilla Six," July 1972.

Navy Wifeline Guideline Series available from The Navy Wifeline Association, Building 172, Washington Navy Yard, Washington, D.C. 20374. "The Bluejacket's Mate," "Naval Social Customs," "Launching an Enlisted Wives' Club," "Sea Legs,"

and "Guidelines for the Wives of Commanding and Executive Officers" -- the last is the most to the point for our study.
Packard, Vance. A Nation of Strangers. David McKay Co., Inc., New York, 1972.
Pierson, George W. The Moving American. Knopf, New York, 1972.
Seidenberg, Robert, M.D. Corporate Wives -- Corporate Casualties? Amacom, New York, 1973.
Stone, Bonnie. "The Time Alone," Marriage and Family Living. Reprint in Dolphin, February 7, 1975. (She interviewed psychiatrist Thomas G. Gutheil, M.D., Assistant Clinical Director, Mass. Mental Health Center, who had been at Submarine Base New London previously.)
"What Every FBM Wife Should Know About her Programmed Man," Navy Times, January 10, 1973. (Article by Radioman First Class Bruce L. Callahan).

****

1991

This piece is interesting from several perspectives: how desperate we were to learn about our lifestyle, how little material there was, and how much more we knew and had been published in the six years between 1969 and 1975.

As we look back from 1991, we must remember that the Services did not begin to have their family awareness conferences until 1978 (Navy) and 1980 (Army and Air Force). While there had been sporadic attempts at family support services by both official and quasi-official agencies, there was nothing of the calibre of the family service-support centers with most/all of the family agencies under one roof. We have come a long way! Many of the roles played by overloaded chaplains and psychiatrists in 1969-75 are shared today with the family service/support centers. Ombudsmen share the leadership role with the CO, XO, and COB's wives. Along with support services have come improved policies and regulations that are family-friendly. To the Services' credit, they have recognized the changing demographics of Service members and their motivations for joining and remaining in an all-volunteer force.

Originally appeared as "Those Who Wait," class research paper for Sociology 258: The Modern Community, Connecticut College, May 1, 1969. Revised, July 10, 1975.
Later appeared as "Waiting Wives," Naval Institute Proceedings, September 1976, pp. 29-37.
Was incorporated into the deployment sections of two Services' official family handbooks: Making a Home in the Navy, 1980, and Charting Your Life in the United States Coast Guard, 1983.

Sailors' Wives <u>Should</u> Have More Fun!

Your husband is attached to a ship, submarine, or air squadron, and you are about to wave goodbye for awhile. You will have responsibilities, but will you have fun? Fun should be a high priority; martyrdom should not. Why not liven up the separation by getting to know other wives literally in the same boat. They experience an emotional rhythm similar to yours -- the same turmoil at departure and arrival, and the same day-to-day existence in between. Having special occasions to look forward to breaks up separations into manageable units of time.

The following ideas are based on my own experiences as the wife of a submariner. You can get these projects started with the cooperation of an eager group of wives -- and the help of such agencies as Special Services, clubs, and the chaplains' office. Here, then are some thoughts for wives during that next deployment.

Potluck: With the popular potluck, no one person has too much to do, and you can sample a wide range of exotic foods that the kids would never agree to eat! Variations:
- *international night* (add films)
- *progressive potluck* (progressing to a new home with each course)
- *recipe night* (your husband's favorite recipe plus a photo of him next to the dish. This is effective near the end of the cruise when wives are making emotional preparations for the return. The photo helps us to see each other as a part of a pair.)
- *potluck-plus-guest-speaker* (invite a chaplain and his wife for dinner and discussion; a nutritionist, nurse, or home decorator)
- *backyard barbecue* (once we all cooked lobsters, sharing a dad's expertise and courage!).

Sailors' Wives Should Have More Fun! 43

Mystery Auction: One hilarious activity we looked forward to during patrols was the mystery auction. Each wife brought a wrapped item (except those of high value which were viewable) to be auctioned *cheaply*. Money went to the Wives' Fund.

Anniversaries Celebration: An anniversaries celebration, to which wedding albums are brought, is a special sharing of wives' past. Our relationships with ship wives are frequently one-dimensional, the present only.

Halfway Night: Most submariners celebrate being halfway through patrol, so we wives decided to celebrate, too! Halfway night evolved into a potluck plus inventive skits, "Initiation" of new wives, and election of Ms. Halfway (the lady who contributed the most to the camaraderie of the wives each patrol). Our cheeks often ached from laughing so hard. We finally filmed these extravaganzas so our husbands could see a portion of our creativity!

Mail Night: Mail night is a joyous night for FBM submarine wives. The husbands have not been able to receive mail for two months, so the wives accumulate all the letters they have written and place them in one mail bag. A decorative mail bag may be created and used patrol after patrol by adding another symbolic sub, heart, etc. This final night is also the occasion for presenting pins to those leaving who have been frequent participants in the group. (The Wives' Fund on our sub paid for a disc pin with the boat's seal on the front and the wife's name on the back -- a treasure to wear proudly and remember good times.)

Banner Night would be the equivalent for ships returning to home port. Wives can be very creative with a sheet, materials scraps, and lots of errant stitches!

Children's Activities: So far, the activities mentioned have been mom's chance to get out and be with contemporaries. Activities including children are also necessary. We like other people to know our children because they are an important part of our lives. There is also a real need on the youngsters' part to feel a tie to ship people whom they see often in happy situations. Try picnics, with playgrounds for toddlers plus a ball field or volleyball court for older children. In the summer, we had a standing agreement to meet at the beach on Sunday afternoons -- casual company for moms and children (and wives without children) on the longest day of the week. For winter swimming, rent a room or two at a motel, and the pool privileges are yours. Charge per person, and any extra dollars can go into the Wives' Fund. Ice skating or sledding enlivens dreary winter days with sports that wives might be leery of doing alone. Skates are available at Recreation Services. When the circus comes to town, grab your kids, donuts, and juice, and go watch the elephants raise the tents -- for free.

Holidays: Christmas and other holidays loom especially lonesome when husbands are away. Thanksgiving is a day for sharing a large turkey, with each family bringing something from their tradition. Christmas activities should be a mix -- something for the children, a craft-sharing time, and perhaps a glamorous evening for the ladies. A children's party is traditional on most ships, with Santa giving out the gift each mom has wrapped for her child. Santa suits can be reserved through Recreation Services. A wreathmaking session teaches a new skill with trimmings contributed by all. A gift-exchange can be accompanied by a cookies exchange or candlelit potluck. One version that warms up a group is to have each wife bring a wrapped gift; numbers are then passed out, and in order, each wife may either take a gift from under the tree or may take the gift that anyone else has previously selected -- and then the giftless person may do the same until it "deadends" by someone taking a gift from the tree. Then the next number starts the whole process all over again. Enticingly wrapped items will keep the evening moving!

Sheer frivolity is not my message. When a group coalesces by having fun together, that "community" then is capable of taking on the next level, the supportive sharing of all phases of Navy living. Having fun, feeling at ease with others, smiling, looking special - these are important to our whole well-being. Over the last eight years, our ships' wives found their civilian friends and neighbors envying our variety of social activities and wealth of friendships. We wives enjoyed the opportunities to cultivate talents and friends, and our husbands found that they came home to wives who, while not fond of separations, know how to make the best of them.

Originally appeared as Those Who Wait *(1969 & 1975), and then as "While the Husband's Away..." in* Wifeline *(Fall 1976). Portions later used in* Making a Home in the Navy: Ideas to Grow On *(1980) and* Charting Your Life in the United States Coast Guard *(1983).*

__Ingredients:__
*Deploying air or sea units
Enlisted wives
Staff NCO wives
Officers' wives
A pinch of each of the following:`
Navy Relief, Family Services Center,
American Red Cross, Special Services,
Medical and Dental representatives, and
any other family support services on base.*

Key Wives' Recipe for Success

Determine number to be fed and how hungry they are. Obtain funds for rest of the process. Explain recipe to husbands and wives, and seek volunteer wives. Mix together, in equal proportions, Enlisted, Staff NCO, and Officers' wives from same unit. Bake this mix for 40 hours under the careful eye of a professional. When almost ready, season with information from military support services.

Product: well-informed, caring wives who are willing and equipped to serve as the unit's command-support link to 10 - 20 families each.

- *I went into this program reluctantly, and I've gotten more out of it than I could have imagined.*
- *This is the kind of training everyone ought to have.*
- *Some of the wives are leery of the program at first -- they are stunned that someone from the squadron has actually called.*
- *Our training broke down so many of the barriers between wives ...we're close...it's a tremendous feeling.*
- *If I help just one lady......*
- *A lot of listening. I have listened for two hours at one whack!*

So spoke Sandra Murray and Barbara Hite, who husbands are gunnery sergeants at Cherry Point Marine Corps Air Station. They are Key Wives whose enthusiasm for Cherry Point's brand new project is obvious in their conversation.

The Second Marine Aircraft Wing at Cherry Point, North Carolina, has recently designed a highly successful Family Readiness Program for deploying squadrons. Recognizing the need to help families prepare for, and be supported during their scheduled six-month separations, or during emergency deployments, the Second Aircraft Wing has launched a project every bit as exciting and effective as a new cargo plane or a fighter.

The Key Wives Program consists of three parts: the selection of wives of officers, staff NCO's, and enlisted men who have shown an interest in serving; their training in skills necessary to be effective in source of support; and a structured relationship with the command.

Each squadron will eventually have a cadre of wives who have agreed to be the key contact for ten to twenty families each. (Many readers will recognize this portion of the organization as similar to the telephone call-tree used by air units and ships when husbands are deployed.) However, it is a vastly improved concept because of the training given to wives, their formal support by, and access to, the commanding officer of the unit.

A program of this magnitude does not simply rise out of thin air. More than a year ago, the Commanding General of the Second Marine Aircraft Wing, Major General Keith A. Smith, and his wife Shirley commissioned a survey to assess the attitudes of wives towards their role in the Marine Corps. The survey, which a group of wives helped write, was mailed to the wives of the commanding and executive officers (CO's and XO's) of all wings and station units, along with an invitation to attend a follow-up seminar.

At the seminar they broke into seven groups of 15 wives to discuss the contents of the survey, the role of Marine wives, and needed improvement to the Marine family environment. In the group summaries that resulted, it was clear that the fact that the commanding general had initiated the survey and seminar was greatly appreciated. One wife wrote, "By including me in your survey as a Marine wife, you've made me feel welcome." Respect for the wives' input in the beginning stage was in itself a very positive step.

As a result of the CO-XO wives' seminar, the Key Wives Steering Committee was formed. It consisted of a Marine major (the Staff Secretary of the Wing), five Marine wives, and a Program Development Specialist who was to serve as the committee advisor. This steering committee had three tasks: to assess the results of the survey and seminar, lay out the basic concept for the Key Wives organization, and design training for the pilot program.

Selecting the first group for the pilot course was not hard. Marine Aircraft Group (MAG)-32 had shown great interest on the command and spouse level; two squadrons were selected. Letters sent to each family included the Family Readiness Survey and an invitation to an evening meeting for Marines and their spouses at which the Key Wives concept would be outlined. The steering committee was wise to include husbands in this presentation, just as they had briefed the CO's and XO's on the program, so that any questions or reservations they might have could be answered openly.

The Family Readiness Survey demonstrated coping skills already used, some areas needing improvement, and the overwhelming support of the concept of a Key Wives group in each squadron. According to the survey, most of the senior NCO and officers' wives planned to remain in the area during the upcoming deployment, and more than half of the enlisted wives planned to do so.

Problem areas that showed up included the lack of a welcoming contact when families moved to the area, and the continuing lack of a closeness to other families in the unit. A very high percentage wanted closer ties to others in the squadron, and indicated that they felt their attitude toward the Marine Corps would improve if they could learn how to handle the stress of military life better. That response solidified the organizers' belief that there was need and a desire for their program.

As a further help in focusing the training materials, the survey asked the MAG-32 wives to rate the problem most often faced by military wives that they had come in contact with. Their response was:

#1 financial problems
#2 husband's pressure from work affects family unit.
#3 discipline problems with children
#4 divorce, separation, or marital problems
#5 emotional problems
#6 alcohol/drug abuse; husband/wife unfaithful
#7 child/wife abuse

Interestingly enough, when the program planners offered sessions on finances, listed as the number one difficulty, the wives in the first group to go through the training always opted for more time on self-esteem and interpersonal communication skills instead. The impression given was that as they gained skills in other areas, financial problems ceased to be a primary focus; they could handle that basic area more efficiently.

With needs focused, the planners felt confident to begin training the first group. The 33 members of the first class were selected from all three grades (enlisted, staff NCO/E-6/9, and officer). The reasons for this even distribution were twofold: the wives themselves believed that the talent for leadership is spread randomly throughout the unit (in others words, not by rank or age); and, as Sandra Murray pointed out after her first few months as a Key Wife, "We have found it best to match Key Wives and their contacts by their husband's grade because they can listen better. But, Key Wives mix well with each other."

Major David G. Buell, the Staff Secretary of the Wing who served on the steering committee, chuckled as he described the first group. We had expected to lose up to half of the group through the 4-hours course, but *nobody* dropped out." Everyone was known by first names-only plus an adjective to help trigger their memory -- such as "Glorious Gloria" -- so that they all knew each other as equals and felt increasingly comfortable as they went through a variety of exercises as pairs or small groups. Only weeks later did they discover "who" some of their members were (such as Shirley Smith and Barbara Smith, the two Wing generals' wives), "and by then it didn't matter."

Training focused on self-esteem (learning to value their own strengths and talents, and helping others to do the same), listening techniques, stress management, and problem-solving skills. The wives also received information about how each of the various support services on the air squadron can be helpful to Marine families.

In order to keep them up to date on services provided, there is a monthly Commanders' conference for all Key Wives. In addition, each unit's Key Wives get together once a month to share the kinds of problems they are hearing, to share success stories, and to relay new resources they have found.

The bond formed between a unit's Key Wives is similar to that experienced by their husbands when they "give their all" for their mission. When questioned about the possibility of burnout from such a commitment, Janet Flatley explained the concept of stepping aside after one year and letting someone else have the opportunity. Having served as the main contact for the wives in her husband's deployment squadron this last year, she admitted that the energies and emotions expended could be great -- but the rewards were worth it. She quoted one unit wife who had told her, "This is the first place I've been anywhere in the Marine Corps where I haven't been dumped when my husband left."

This sense of belonging comes from the Key Wives' regular calls to their contact wives. They call to talk about meetings or social events coming up, and they offer their assistance if a need should arise. "We do not solve their problems," Janet accented. "We help *them* solve their problem."

Often this is nothing more than helping them to know which service on the station can assist them. "The most vulnerable wife is the one who lives out in a trailer park and her husband takes the car to work. He doesn't bring home the station newspaper or the squadron news, and she never goes to squadron or wives' gathering. Many times he prefers it that way." A Key Wife would open up the lines of communication by her personal call and make the isolated wife part of the unit family.

As Captain Mark Thoman remarked,"The bottom line is that people resent being helped. They want to be enabled to help themselves, and they want the opportunity to make a personal contribution" (versus a command-pressured obligation).

Personal contribution came up in discussions with others as well. Mrs. Flatley stressed that the success of the program is due, in great part, to its being a "grass-roots effort...much more effective than operating from the top down. Each wife's input really makes a difference in the final program." The flexibility for tailoring the course and the structure of each unit's Wives will continue to be a part of the plan to insure meeting the unique needs of each group.

The Key Wives meet with the squadron commanding officer to see that his needs are met and that theirs are heard as well. The decision to operate at the squadron level was General Smith's. He and his wife Shirley have worked with various sized groups, and have found that "the squadron is big enough (usually 250 - 400 men) to provide support, and yet small enough to know faces and individuals."

The Smiths' commitment to the Key Wives program is evident on both the official and personal levels. The fact that many of Shirley's fellow classmates did not know who she was is an indicator of her leadership style. She is comfortable and approachable, but behind the scenes is a determined fighter for the program which she and her husband feel can make a major difference in Marines' readiness and retention: when men know that their families have a good support system to rely on in their absence, they can concentrate on the job at hand. When wives make friends in the squadron, which Key Wives say is the biggest benefit they personally reap from their service, their happiness affects their husbands' decision to remain in the Marine Corps.

When her husband attended conferences at Marine headquarters in Washington, Shirley would drive up with him and use the time to lobby for the minimal funding ($5,000) necessary to hire a professional trainer to write and provide the first two training courses. (On the surveys, wives had indicated that they preferred professional training, and the Smiths believe that by institutionalizing the training, they will provide continuity in the units so that family support does not rely simply on current personalities.) Four sessions have been completed now, and the next step is to train Marine wives as professional trainers so that they can help to speed up and spread the availability of the program. As Major Buell says, "Our main problem right now is that we cannot give the training fast enough." With 53 squadrons in the Wing, and the capability of training only two squadrons at a time, the process would be painfully slow without Marine wife trainers.

The Smiths have discovered two interesting phenomena at Cherry Point: "There is a great pool of potential volunteers out there waiting to be asked, and the graduates of the Key Wives' course are more willing to volunteer greater amounts of service after their training than before."

A sample of the wives' enthusiasm for the program is found in the fund-raising done by squadron wives. They pitched in with bake sales to raise enough money to cover child care fees for junior enlisted wives who wanted to be Key Wives but found the cost a significant barrier to their attendance. The Smiths then lobbied for sufficient funds for child care for succeeding sessions.

A second example of the calibre of volunteer commitment to arise out of the program is the development of the *Cherry Point Resource Book* (a compilation of official support services, community facilities, emergency procedures, personal affairs, and pre-deployment preparations). Six wives, under the leadership of Jo Nettleingham and Peggy Brown, prepared the resource book patterned on a similar project at Naval Air Station Oceana about six years ago. Using a 3-ring notebook, they have ensured easy updating of the information which will be invaluable for Key Wives to have at their fingertips. Just as they borrowed a good idea from Oceana, the Key Wives are hoping that their program will spread through the Marine Corps and other Services.

Major M.D. Ashworth, the CO of H&MS-32, summed up his evaluation by saying, "The Family Readiness Program .... was long overdue. The heartfelt response that my wife and I have personally received from numerous dependent wives tells me that it's not only worthwhile, but indeed an invaluable leadership tool for the Commander... The fact that this program is working for over 300 married couples in a squadron of over 700 Marines indicates that it can easily work in smaller units."

In the dictionary, *key* is defined as: of crucial importance; an instrument designed to open a lock; new or vital information; to lock together with pins, bolts; to furnish an arch with a keystone; to coordinate; to bring into harmony. Key Wives fulfill all of the above.

Originally appeared as "Key Wives' Recipe for Success," Family, *February 1983.*

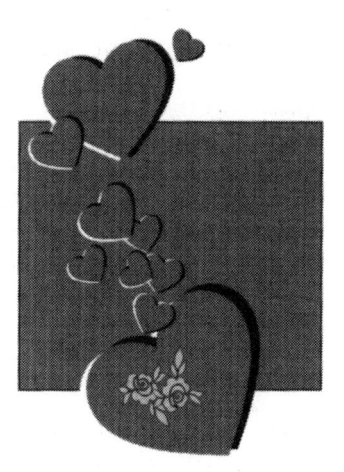

8

Keeping Love Alive

"Your husband's a submariner? That's an ideal marriage -- he'll be away half the time!" Such was the response I got from a British admiral's wife when visiting my parents during my husband's second patrol. She saw the schedule of three and a half months away and three months home as the best of all worlds. "It's delicious to miss him and yet be free to do your own work, and then delicious for him to come home again."

I didn't see it that way. Although I was teaching high school full time, still there were significant blocks of hours that grading papers, chaperoning dances, and mowing the lawn didn't fill. Even though I was growing daily in self-sufficiency, I missed my husband a great deal.

Somehow, I suspect, the *ideal* lies somewhere between her seemingly cavalier assessment of the ideal marriage and my desire to have my husband home more than he was away. One thing is certain: military couples are not as likely to take each other for granted as those who are together all of the time. There are the built-in emotions of departure and return, so we are not lulled by predictable daily routines and are more likely to share special times when we are together.

A couple who live in one place most of their lives with little traveling connected with their livelihood may find that they settle into a calm, sometimes boring, acceptance of each other. Our mobile lifestyle, combined with separated duty, keeps us from slipping into any such comfortable rut.

That doesn't mean we don't have to work to keep love alive in our marriages. Being separated for long periods of time from our spouses is difficult; it is a situation that demands our creativity. In honor of Valentine's Day, we will take a look at the myriad of ways military spouses have responded to the challenge of keeping romance alive in the face of long absences. *Family* readers from Jacksonville and Mayport, Florida, who experience long destroyer and carrier deployments, from Kings Bay Georgia, who experience submarine patrols, from West Point, New York, who are academy trustees' wives, and from the all-Service area around Fort Myer, Virginia, have sent us their hints on keeping romance alive in their marriages.

Pre-Departure

Pre-departure can be a difficult time when wives and husbands feel the tension mounting as the final day draws near. Physical weariness is a major component as those leaving and those staying try to get all of the preparations done. Guilt and anger are also present -- guilt over leaving one's family and guilt over being so unpatriotic as to wish one's spouse didn't have to go. Anger comes from the same sources.

In order to combat this unpleasant period, Donna and Lance Jasitt, who are both Naval officers, share their preparations for Lance's deployment. "We tried to anticipate anything that might go wrong and take preventive measures (i.e., have the car checked out, make any house repairs, etc.). Since he was going to WESTPAC, we agreed for him to take the 35mm camera and get me an inexpensive one to take photos at home. We purchased several boxes of stationery and stamps (affixed to the envelopes to ensure they did not get stuck together), as well as a cassette player for his use."

Clara White, a Navy wife and Executive Director of the Mayport Auxiliary of the Navy Relief Society, used her pre-deployment time creatively. "Before one Med run, I spent a month combing stores, home, and the office for tiny things to wrap and send with him. (Submariners don't have much storage space!) I made a list of each item and then dated it so that I would be able to sit down with the list and 'share' the event even though I wasn't there. The things were a reminder of home for him, sometimes touching and sometimes silly. They ranged from 'dirty' fortune cookies to a model of his motorcycle. Each one carried a special message. My favorite was the Playboy jigsaw puzzle. Before I wrapped it up, I created my own 'glitch.' I removed several puzzle pieces from the container and wrapped them up separately dated for a week later. It was a good morale boost for the crew because after the first few were opened, the crew would follow him around to see what craziness I had come up with next!

"It served a better purpose for me because instead of brooding about the departure, I went into it with a positive attitude. Our parting was not a time of sorrow or guilt because he was 'deserting' the family."

Departure

There is usually a tearful period that occurs right before his departure and extends for some time after he is gone. Thoughts like "How will I ever live through these next few months without him?" are common. It is a good time for whoever is leaving (it's not always the husband these days!) to be especially attentive. A rose brought home, or a bottle of perfume with the instructions, "Wear this daily to remind you how special you are to me," can go a long way towards making us feel loved.

After your spouse has left, you usually go into a state of relative calm and confidence in handling day-to-day living. Sometimes it seems more comfortable not to think about your absent spouse very much. But our readers recommend setting aside a routine for doing so, either at dinner time or after the children go to bed in the evening. Those away need to find an equally quiet time to write or send tapes.

Most people have found that tapes and letters are more effective than phone calls, if the mails are reliable, because a phone call can jerk the one at home out of a calm state with no emotional preparation The exception would be pre-agreed dates to call, especially on birthdays, anniversaries, or other special days.

Joan Sears, a Navy wife of 18 1/2 years, shares two ideas that worked well for her husband's overseas cruises on aircraft carriers. "A love letter recorded on a cassette tape can be very special. You can catch that dreamy mood, hum a little tune, whisper a little secret in his ear, make up a poem, or even shed a tear. Tell him your secret fantasy, or shout, 'I love you!' When he sends his tape to you, I'll bet you could pretend he was almost there next to you.

"Another way to personalize you long-distance romance is by sending little messages with his favorite food. Once I baked a large batch of brownies. Then on separate pieces of paper, I wrote a different personal message, and carefully wrapped one with each brownie. My husband parceled out his brownies as long as possible, enjoying each little surprise message during his own private moments. He said that the anticipation was very exciting."

One Kings Bay wife used to send a jar filled with M & M's, "approximately one for every day that we were apart. A small label instructed him to eat *only* one every day. Another time I made up a coupon book for him. Every coupon was something that we both like to do together. Some coupons were for a walk on the beach or for his choice of restaurants. Some were romantic blanks that he was to fill in!"

This same inventive wife shared another hint. "When I was cleaning out the cabinet the other day, I found an old bottle of 'Sunshine Pills.' One time I bought some empty capsules from the pharmacist and wrote *little* happy thoughts to put inside. I made a label for 'Sunshine Pills' (because my husband calls me Sunshine), with the instructions to take one when you're down to brighten your day.'"

For those whose husbands will have few mail deliveries, a Coast Guard wife shares her technique for getting her husband to think of her daily on his polar cruises. As she packs his duffle bag, she rolls "juicy comments" in each pair of socks and underwear. She claims that he unrolls each piece carefully so that bunk mates don't find them lying around or add to the laundry squad's day!

When Gail McGlothin's husband was on a mine sweeper, she used a roll of adding machine paper. With a red marker, she wrote message and drew cartoon and hearts from one end to the other, then re-rolled it, and had a compact object to mail. Her husband said he could have papered his entire office with it -- not large on a mine sweeper!

Wives whose husbands are on nuclear submarines cannot send or receive mail from them during patrols, so their five "familygrams" (like telegrams) sent by the Navy have to carry a wealth of caring. Janet Pachkoski used to send "our special little 'I want you' phrase, taken from a very private joke years ago While the message was cleared for release by the executive officer, no one could understand why 'think it will rain?' would make my husband so excited and anxious to get the old 'bucket of bolts' to the pier."

Janet also told the story of her husband being away about two months on a six month UNITAS cruise when he found their youngest child's red sock in some of his stored clothes. He put it up on the bulletin board in his office -- a little touch of home. I'm sure that you creative souls out there can see some opportunities in that one!

Husbands Can Plan, Too

Husbands can plan ahead, too. In fact, submariners have to. Barbara Sears sent us "a romantic, special idea from a fellow commanding officer's wife. As half-way night approached, the wives received engraved invitations to dinner at a local restaurant. They were given a choice of entrees and had to RSVP. The had cocktails upon their arrival -- *everything* had been paid for prior to their deployment. The men had even sent a floral centerpiece." As Barbara says, "What a nice way of letting the wives know they were being thought of."

Again, those who cannot rely on the mails could consider leaving a present with a friend or neighbor to deliver. Janet Pachkoski remembers one deployment. "I was really having the blues when my birthday approached -- no letter, no phone call. I checked the mail -- nothing. Later the kids found a package wedged in the door mail slot. Inside was a cassette tape -- one side of music I'd enjoy and the other thoughts about 'us.' I still have that tape and when he';s gone I play it, smile, and cry."

Husbands can also leave little messages and little gifts scattered in strategic spots around the house -- sort of like an on-going Easter egg hunt.

Sending Gifts

On his WESTPAC cruise, Lance Jasitt sent a variety of things to Donna at home, including picture post cards from ports of call, small inexpensive gifts that could be sent in padded envelopes or in cards, "pictures of where he was and what he was doing. He sent flowers through the Navy Exchange on our anniversary, and sent copies of the ship's newspaper so that I knew what was going on in his day-to-day work life and gave me a chance to put faces to names of people he had talked about."

One unsuspecting beau was watched by his friends when he went out to buy his sweetheart a valentine. As soon as he left, they swooped in and bought up all the rest of the identical cards. The young lady received a dozen cards exactly alike, with all sorts of funny remarks from his buddies!

Pictures

Pictures were mentioned by a number of our readers. They help combat that mid-cruise panic when you can't picture you spouse in your mind -- a very common occurrence.

An Army general's wife wrote, "When Ted left me with three babies under the age of three and a half to go to Iceland in August, 1941, he said he didn't want any pictures -- no room on his desk. I sent them anyhow. A returning officer told me he kept them displayed for everyone to see. I did the same for the next two years (in Europe) -- and he sent me some of him. It really helped."

One final hint for husbands away: one enterprising young man bought some uniform pajamas. With the aid of a permanent marker, he wrote,"I love you" in every language he could find and drew cartoons fore and aft. His true love has enjoyed those pajamas for years!

Return

As the return finally draws nigh, plans can be made for trips, nights out, or weekends away together soon after arrival. The anticipation is half of the fun, so communicate about these plans at some length. Tell him what you will be wearing so that he can spot you on the pier and picture you in advance. Most husbands prefer that you wear one of their favorite outfits rather than a new one for this occasion.

A U.S.S. SARATOGA wife wrote of a tradition that she finds works. "it started a year ago when my husband was away in January. January is always a depressing month with having to stay indoors and having post-Christmas blues. So I had a lingerie party, and invited not only my friends in the military, but civilian wives as well. Everyone enjoyed trying on dainty lingerie and outrageously funny things.It was a huge success not only enjoyed by us gals, but eventually by our husbands as well. Never once has my husband complained about how much I spent!"

One word of caution: avoid over-programming the first few days home. Your returnee will be physically exhausted in most cases, and you may be, too, if you follow the frantic housecleaning dance most build in to keep the last few days from dragging by. Don't expect too much from each other right away. Then, with the emotions and expectations lowered just a little, perhaps your reunion will be more rewarding.

Journalist First Class John Redo from Naval Air Station Jacksonville sums it up when he writes, "My wife and I have been married for 16 years, and for 16 years we have been each other's 'best friend.' Moments of passion may come and go -- but true friendships will last forever -- with or without periods of separation."

Originally appeared as "Keeping Love Alive," <u>Family</u>, *February 1985.*

When Dad is Away at Christmas

Last Christmas, as I was singing the *Messiah* with our church choir, I found myself wondering where the next Christmas would find our family. Orders were anticipated, but the destination was unknown. Both of our children were high school seniors, with their college acceptances still in limbo.

The wave of uncertainty faded quickly. Later, when I mused upon why it had been so fleeting, I realized that I knew that wherever we might be, I would be singing the *Messiah*, making Hermit Cake, and hanging our quilted tree.

Tradition was the source of my calm, as I suspect it is for many military families. While all of us have our own family rituals, we probably have many in common. Because traditions can be important coping skills in times of stress, such as a recent move or a father's *(parent's)* absence at holiday time, I would like to share some of our favorites and those of friends.

Our family traditions took shape as our children grew old enough to participate in the joy of Christmas. Their reaching nursery school age coincided with the beginning of a seven year cycle of submarine duty for my husband Mick in Groton-New London, Connecticut. Because of the nature of the three-and-a-half month patrols, which alternated with three months at home, Mick was away five of the seven Christmases, and managed to bring his crew home a day before Christmas for one of the two home years. Needless to say, I became the "tradition-carrier."

The children's plans for their dad's Christmas had to begin before he left. Because he could take only what we could squeeze into his Christmas shoebox, we had to think small. I bought small games or craft kits, funny cards, and favorite candy whenever I saw them, and I hoarded them for his treasure box.

IOU Coupons

The children used a small spiral notepad to draw pictures of what they would provide when their dad returned and asked them to make good on their IOU coupons. They offered to do jobs, to help give him things that they thought he would like. *Breakfast in bed* was a popular offering (which usually was cereal in the early years). Michael promised him *a pair of cowboy boots* and *a puppy* when those were big items on his own list. These were carefully and lovingly illustrated, and gave the children the opportunity to tie the present (a dad about to leave) with the future (over and beyond the period of separation).

Students at Mary Morrisson Elementary School in Groton, Conn., have recently drawn what they would like to give their dads this Christmas. The sixth graders in Mrs. Virginia Effman's class and the first graders in Mrs. Gail Munn's class would like to share some of their coupons with *Family* readers.

The school is close to a Navy housing area, so many of the children know the disappointment of having their dad away at Christmas. Talking about it in class can be a very helpful way to vent some of the emotions that accompany the loss. Researchers across the country have found that about one third of the students whose fathers are away do act out in class, or withdraw, or do work of a lower level than usual. Hopefully, small projects like this will be helpful in avoiding such problems.

Types of IOU Promises

The Mary Morrisson students' drawings tend to fall in several categories. A favorite is offering to *rake the yard* or *mow the lawn*, two tasks they associate with their fathers and being grown up. They obviously would look forward to sharing the work with dad when he returns. Variations on the theme of being together include *playing in the snow, a game in sports, washing the car, cleaning the house* (complete with a drawing of the vacuum cleaner), and *going to the base with you.*

Another popular coupon motif is a favorite meal -- again to be *shared!* One features steak, salad, baked potatoes, and fudge. Another menu includes *roast beef, mashed potatoes, corn on the cob, carrots in butter sauce, and broccoli -- all of your favorites!* Being precise is good for children. They focus specifically and should be aided in producing the goods when father returns. Vague offers of "a gift" are not as helpful for the giver or the recipient.

A third important category promises is love: *a big hug* and *3,000 kisses*. The illustration for the 3,000 kisses shows the father waving from the ship on the horizon, while his son on the pier has a cartoon bubble from his heart showing hearts reaching out toward his dad. What a treasure for a dad at sea!

A fourth group drew things they would make or buy: *a snowman with a bird and hat on top, a cowboy, a clown costume, cookies,* and *a gingerbread man and a rainbow.*

Departing Parent's Preparations

The cowboy and clown remind me that dads (*parents*) need to do some preparations before they leave, too. (Submariners cannot mail anything once they leave port, so thinking ahead is critical.) Ideally, they could make or buy some special item for each child and write out the gift card for him or her. There were times when this was not feasible for my husband, so he wrote out cards with special messages that I could attach to gifts that I bought after he left. Mike and Heather cherished those notes in his own inimitable script, and would often try to mimic the wild slants of his letters.

Holiday Decorations

Another experience unique to military families is the length of time the Christmas tree is up. I can remember driving through Navy housing in October and seeing trees already up -- as well as in February. My husband usually left before Halloween, missed Thanksgiving, Christmas, and New Year's. If he was home on Halloween, he missed Valentine's Day. As a result, we adopted the habit of leaving up a large quilted tree that he and I had made for a party the year Mike was born.

We had a live tree that needed to go outside to be planted after a very short stint inside, so the cloth tree was put in the living room to keep the spirit.

We sewed rick-rack swags and little felt candles on the tree. All of the rest of the decorations are pinned on each year. Friends who know our tradition have given us lovely little ornaments, so that decorating that three is as emotional an event for me as writing Christmas cards. The tree used to remain up until Mick came home from patrol and could share it with us.

Recently some Navy dads talked about what they had cherished when they were at sea at Christmas. One took his own little artificial tree and decorations -- though he was on a distinctly larger ship than a submarine! But all military units have a tree and wives can send decorations. One wardroom wives' group made photo balls by slicing styrofoam balls flat on one side and attaching a picture of their family. Not only would a father see his own family, but he had the sense of being part of a large ship's family.

Family Holiday Traditions

Knowing what traditions are being followed at home also gives Dad a sense of belonging ...even at a distance. If he can know that certain kinds of cookies or cakes are being baked (and maybe sent), and favorite items are used as the centerpiece, he can at least imagine himself there, and that helps.

As soon as our children were old enough to stand up on kitchen stools, they put on aprons and helped me make cookies. (I quickly learned to lay a shower curtain on the floor to catch all the stray sprinkles!) Spritz cookies are a favorite because kids can turn the handle and produce a forest of Christmas trees. (One year they made blue butterflies! When I protested that no one would eat blue cookies, they proved me wrong -- they were the first to go at our local science center party!) As they became more adept, we mixed red and white dough and produced candy canes and wreaths using the tube star disc -- and these continue to be popular at parties.

Another cookie project was to roll out sugar cookies for which we used a wide array of cutters. We tried to add at least one new one a year, so we now have a whole village of houses and a church, a whale and a duck to symbolize favorite creatures in our community, as well as the traditional angel, Santa and bell. These cookies were decorated with great care and artistic pleasure, and were given to our mailman, teachers, and Santa. (*For Christmas 1990, Mick, now retired, made me a submarine cookie cutter! The tradition goes on!!)*

The cookie-making process was spread out over many days because their attention span and my sense of humor were of short duration. The time we spent together, though, was very important to us. I usually took the phone off the hook and the mailman would peek in the windows of the door to our basement steps, where the cookies were stored, and comment on our progress.

Through some quirk of fate, we, whose father was not usually home, ended up giving the neighborhood Christmas party all of the years we were in Mystic. One year when Mick was home, we invited 50 of the neighbors and their children to come with instruments and song books to make music. The next year we added a taffy pull in the basement to the agenda, which delighted my parents as much as "the kids." Ever thereafter, the children in the neighborhood would start asking when the party would be -- even if Thanksgiving had barely turned the corner. We continue the tradition now in Arlington, Virginia, with dad at home.

Our centerpiece was usually made of greens from our bushes plus several of our small musical instruments. One year we used the children's small drums. Other years the table has featured a wooden dancing man (an Appalachian percussion toy), bells, a melodica, and most recently, an old fiddle, hand-carved by an O'Beirne family ancestor (a nice connection with the past). I have learned that a brightly colored sheet makes a fine tablecloth -- one that I don't have to worry about with punch and children.

Another tradition at our house is wrapping the presents in the attic. It is not a glamorous spot, but there is a sense of magic about a place high above the rest of the house. With a table and chairs, a soft light, and a radio, we seem to be in our own special world. All of the wrappings are left out, and the kids wrap their presents for us, enjoying their secrecy. They also help me wrap all of the presents for cousins and grandparents so that they have a sense of belonging to our larger extended family.

Santa

I took the children and Santa to my parents' house in Albany one Christmas and got snowed in. The kids had an absolute ball, but I was a wreck wondering if we could get home in time to meet the ship. Thereafter, my parents came to us. They did not have deadlines to meet; my dad could help me with house repairs that had piled up in Mick's absence, and I counted on my mother's sewing expertise when working on draperies and bedspreads. And Santa knew where to find us.

As the children grew old enough to write their own letters to Santa, we took them down to our little West Mystic Post Office. The postmaster and postmistress meticulously wrote a reply to each child. They also served as an invaluable source of information to parents when the children were able to write their own words alone and seal the letters before we could see the request! (*Years later, when our children were in college, the postmistress was retiring and sought to return all of the letters she had saved over the years to each family. We had moved a number of times in the years in between. She saw my name on an article in <u>Family</u>, so sent them via the magazine! What treasures to read -- I hadn't realized the kids' desire for Legos, so for their stocking that year, I bought them each a small set for their stocking and enclosed it with their letters to Santa.)

On Christmas Eve after church, one small package could be opened. The children would have tested each package under the tree to see which one met their private criteria for being opened on Christmas Eve.

Santa would be left a glass of wine, some of the special cookies that each child had made, and a note thanking him and wishing him a safe journey. The postmaster and mistress used to kid me about showing up for the wine that the kids had promised!

Other families have a traditional visit from Santa on Christmas Eve. One friend of ours told us of hearing bells on Christmas Eve and then a knock on the door. When her parents opened it -- there was Santa. In he came, with his "Ho, Ho, Ho,' giving little bags of apples, nuts, candies, and one little toy to each child. He stayed long enough to have some cookies and then left. Years later her parents admitted they had *absolutely no idea who he was* and they were just as astonished as the kids!

Christmas Day dinner traditionally brought my parents and our adopted family of special friends who needed to enjoy the children as much as I needed adult company. To this day, with Mick on shore duty, we still feel the need to have a multi-generational celebration.

This tie with people of all ages functions much as our other traditions do. It is part of the glue that holds us together, wherever we may happen to be at Christmas. Our traditions link us with the past and, through our children, to the future.

May you have a joyous holiday season.

****

When this article was originally written, we did not have as many female members deploying and going on unaccompanied duty as we do today. Obviously, mothers going away at the holiday season need to be remembered and need to make special preparations for their family in advance of their departure, just as dads do.

**Illustration by Justin Carr, age 10 -- son of our illustrator, Helen Carr.*

Originally appeared as "When Dad is Away at Christmas," Family, November 1983.

10

Reunion Strategies

Surprising as it may seem, researchers have found that families have more emotional challenges when a deployed military member returns than when he or she leaves. Our natural inclination is to believe that the going away part must be the hardest. Perhaps that myth is a major contributor to the problem. Our expectations are that delight and perfect harmony will be the only dynamics -- and something akin to fictional honeymoons. The reality is that it takes work, patience, and careful pacing to make room for the changed spouse, parent, and/or "child" when he or she comes home.

Reunion is stage four in the deployment cycle *(see page 31)*. Many wives experience an almost incredible emotional and physical frenzy, getting every inch of the house and themselves ready for their husband's arrival. He arrives exhausted from the final days at sea, eager to be home. His first few days of unwinding bring long conversations, which are attempts to catch up. He also spends lots of time sleeping. During this unwinding process, there is bound to be some friction; after being so totally separated and then being totally together, each needs a little time alone to sort out the whole process. The husband, especially, has been surrounded by people the entire time, and may feel more of a need for solitude than his wife, who may have had more than enough solitude. Being aware of each other's needs is crucial at this point.

There is some evidence that longer deployments with irregular communications between couples make the reunion-adjustment period harder and longer. It really is common sense that more has to be shared before things return to a **new normal** -- there's no going back!

- A good way to discuss the return-reunion cycle is to use the short play (text or video tape) "Coming Home -- Again." The script is free from the Navy Family Support Program (OP-156/N-66), Department of the Navy, Washington, D.C. 20350.

Dad's (or mom's) return is an especially intense time for children. They must vie with him for mom's attention, and they may have idealized him in his absence. His return brings a very human, and often very tired man who may need sleep and quiet time -- not the constant presence of energetic, adoring children. One father remembers having his eyelid opened by his three-year-old daughter saying, "Are you in there, Dad?"

- Older children suffer some of the same reunion friction that their mother experiences. Judgment of growth, whether physical or emotional, takes place. Consciously or unconsciously, dad evaluates his children. He can't help feeling astonished and slightly uneasy about how rapidly they change and how little time he has had with them recently.

- When teenagers are responsible and helpful in a parent's absence, they carve out a new niche for themselves in the family structure. When dad (or mom) returns, the tendency is to "go back to normal." But a new normal has to be negotiated. New partnerships need to be formed based on respect for growing capabilities and responsibilities.

- "Easing back into their lives requires the tact of a diplomat and the patience of Job! In my heart, I want to be right where we were when I left; but I know (and my wife keeps reminding me!) that I need to be approachable and let them find me in my workshop or my favorite chair." This father of five knows that children can withdraw from dad. They can be angry with him for "deserting" them, and can decide not to depend on him anymore so that his repeated departures won't continue to be a source of pain. Parents need to talk with their children about loving others (family or friends). They need to admit their own feelings, and help a child understand the need to love one another despite temporary absences.

Some dads make a point of doing something special with each child separately after they return.

- "Fishing with my daughter early one morning soon after returning gives us a brand new start with each other."

- "My son and I always go camping overnight when I get back. His mother isn't too big on camping, so it's our time together.

Time together and a sense of special valuing of one's family time are noticed by neighbors in our civilian communities. One of our most treasured memories is an experience we had soon after my husband returned from sea. We had taken the kids for an early morning walk down to the river. One of the local merchants came over and told us he couldn't resist saying that he knew we were a military family. We kidded him and said we knew it was my husband's haircut that was the giveaway. And he said, "Nope! In all the years I've lived here, I've noticed that military parents take more time to enjoy their kids." Maybe our deployments and separations help us value each other more.

Originally in Charting Your Life in the U. S. Coast Guard *(1983)*

11

Shore Duty: Great Expectations

When I heard Gertrude Stein's poem, "*Storyette H. M.,*"* sung as a duet at Kennedy Center recently, I chuckled with the rest of the audience at the wife's final "I am content." I suspect, however, that my reason was different from most who understood the wife's contentment as acquiescence...being fulfilled through her husband's emotion. My reaction was that it was a delightful rendering of what a Navy wife may come to accept as her angle of vision concerning sea duty separations. She may learn to be content both because her husband is pleased with his job, and because she has found that separations can give her time to pursue her own development as an individual. *(Read Chapter 5 for this evolution.)*

A companion poem needs to be written about the adjustment from sea duty to shore duty. Many husbands and wives, having adjusted unwittingly to the cycle of sea separations, find that the first year of shore duty does not bring the unequivocal contentment they had so eagerly anticipated. My husband and I were amused after realizing that the friction that appeared three months after we had moved to Washington, D.C. had surfaced, almost to the day, that his last submarine was going to sea. Seven consecutive years on FBM submarines had given us an unconscious rhythm of living that once recognized, could be changed. Couples in other Services and recent retirees may find many parallels to the experiences related by Navy people "coming ashore."

---

* *Gertrude Stein's poem was one of six tn Leonard Bernstein's "Songfest," which premiered at the Kennedy Center on October 11, 1977. The poem follows the internal-external dialogue between a husband and wife as he is leaving. Phrases appear like "going off alone to have a good time," " he came in all glowing," but the one remaining at home "was not glowing." Then there is the sequence of content and not content, with both finally being "content."*

When I visited Great Lakes Naval Station as Navy Wife of the Year in 1974, wives whose experiences with separations made them sympathetic to my views on the need for ship wives' cohesion, felt that an even greater problem of adjustment came when they and their husbands "came ashore" after several sea duty tours. That this was not unique to wives of enlisted personnel became apparent at the annual submarine officers' cocktail party in the Washington area. One recent submarine commanding officer (CO) suggested that my next topic should be the emotional adjustment from submarine CO to duty in the Pentagon. My husband and I had noticed that the parking lot was totally filled when we arrived on the dot of 7:30. Though military people are known for their promptness, this was obviously more than etiquette. We discovered how eager the submariners and their wives were to be with people like themselves, many of whom they had known before; even those who were unknowns, but had shared our way of life, were easily met and conversations flowed.

Shore Duty vs. Sea Duty

Both the ex-CO and the wives had put their finger on a common pattern: the nature of the husband's job had changed, and the fact of his continuous presence in the family necessitated a not-so-subtle shift in the marital structure. Frequently the husbands, whether enlisted or officer, had felt that their work aboard ship had been visibly productive. The end product was that the ship did operate at sea and fulfill its mission. Shore duty billets often brought less immediately assessable progress. For the man who had been a division chief or had commanded a ship, duties had been clear cut, frequently immediate in their nature, and rarely political.

Though I know that I am grossly over-simplifying when I say that shore billets tend to be the opposite, it is fair to say that paperwork, long-range problems and planning, and political vs. military decisions are more characteristic of the shore jobs. (At this point I must qualify what I mean by "shore duty:" there are schools with student and teaching billets, construction duty, sea-going staffs, and Washington, with many variations in between. For my purposes here, I specifically do not include schools, and I do recognize that Washington is extreme shore duty with its attendant long and often unpredictable hours and expensive living.) Shore billets do have in common the unlikelihood of immediate satisfaction with a completed task and the difficulty in measuring one's own impact.

The size of many shore duty staffs may contribute to a sense of quasi-anonymity. A man may have felt very a part of a sea-going division, crew, or wardroom. That happens less often ashore unless staffs work at socializing and see a worthwhile reason to do so. There is a tendency to have a greater separation between work life and one's off-hours' existence.

The clearer distinction between work and "play" is felt by the wife and children. If working hours are not too extreme, there may be more time for family activities, and a greater dependence on one another for socializing than there had been in a close-knit sea unit period. This can be felt as a fine opportunity to enjoy one's own family, or it can be oppressive; this depends on all members' ability to shift gears. The couple may have come from a ship social unit which had been almost stifling in its cohesion, and may see shore duty as a relief from this. But after a few months of this void (a get-together once every six months is not unusual for Washington staff), then it may seem pretty lonely. The civilian community may not be the source of instantaneous friendships for the couple as a duo; it is a good time to learn to build relationships slowly but firmly. Retirement will bring the same challenge.

Marital Dynamics

Both the husband and the wife may have consciously or unconsciously put up with the other's irritating idiosyncracies knowing that sea duty would soon bring relief. The wife may have looked forward to sea duty, and the departure of her troublesome spouse, just as much as a man may have seen the cruise as an escape from a nagging wife, financial difficulties, obnoxious children, or the responsibilities of being head of the household. Shore duty, with the husband's continued presence in the household, brings the necessity for renegotiation of each spouse's rights and responsibilities. Even in what would be considered well-adjusted Navy homes, the wife needs to learn to relinquish the absolutism she has enjoyed or been burdened with in her husband's absence. (I would have to admit that I rather enjoyed selecting and buying our current house, and found that I needed reminding when my husband came home that he would like to be part of the decisions on carpeting and kitchen remodeling.)

By the same token, the husband must learn to reassume his fair share of responsibilities that his wife has found she can do when he is away, but which should be part of his obligations. When the separation-home cycle has been short, though repeated continuously, such as the FBM submarine pattern of three and one half months away and three months home, some responsibilities have not been exchanged because continuity was more desirable than the upheaval that perfectly balanced accountability would have brought. Examples of this might be the family checkbook and child discipline. A mature answer: share these.

Shore duty brings the friction of balancing out previously unbalanced responsibilities. It may also bring friction in the domain of personal freedom. I'll never forget how furious my husband was when he came home early from the ship a day or two after his return from an FBM patrol, and found that I had not left a note saying where I was. In retrospect, I know that he was concerned about my safety. But at the time, I felt that I, who had managed the whole household in his absence, and had gone out and come home for months without anyone's concerned eye, had been disciplined like a child. During sea duty operations, both the husband and wife are accountable essentially to themselves alone, or at least not to each other on a daily basis. Accountability, in terms of emotions, finances, and physical location, then, is one of the major areas of adjustment to shore duty.

Ages and Stages

The pattern of assignment to sea and shore duty is not an absolute by any means; but a rough sequence for a Naval officer starts with a short period of school/training after entering the Navy, which is followed by fairly prolonged sea duty, perhaps as much as six to eight years. The first shore duty billet of any duration often comes as a man approaches 28 - 30. This is followed by sea duty again, culminating in a second shore duty assignment as one approaches 40.

If the assignment to short duty coincides with one of the "predictable crises of adult life" `a la Gail Sheehy's *Passages (1976)*, then the military couple gets a double or triple dose: a change in duty (and maybe location) plus a personal disequilibrium shared by most other adults of their age. Ironically, two fairly common periods of shore duty assignment in the submarine service fall at transitional times in a man's personal development. The first shore duty often comes as a young submarine officer has completed his division officer's tour. This may be an advantageous shift if it comes when he is on the verge of leaving his outwardly adventurous twenties which have been spent in training and at sea. The move ashore may coincide with the normal personal shift toward a settling-down, both in terms of career and geography. A young family may be part of this picture; his wife may be naturally family-oriented at this point, too.

The second shore duty billet, however, may fall at the end of his tour as a commanding officer, at approximately age 40. This is the prime period for the midlife crisis described by Gail Sheehy as filled with "a sense of stagnation, disequilibrium and depression." She notes that the inner moves to new stages of development will come regardless of outer events; but many people tend to notice the event, such as a move or shift in jobs, and see it as the cause of their inner discontent instead of a coincidental occurrence.

The midlife crisis is a period of re-examination of one's career and personal goals: the validity of the original goals themselves plus how far one has come toward being successful in attaining them. Intense introspection is rarely comfortable because we tend to judge ourselves mercilessly. In the husband's case, he may not see shore duty as productive career-wise, though most of his seniors would argue the point from their own experience.

The wife will do a bit of flailing herself, assessing her own personal accomplishments. The women's liberation movement has added fuel to this normal fire, so many wives belittle their family and volunteer accomplishments and think in terms of employment. A shift to shore duty and the geographic move which usually accompanies it may be a boon in releasing her from previous commitments, to allow her to seek employment without strings in the new community. Or the move may come just after she has spread her wings and disrupt her budding career. The main point here is not to confuse the inner events with the outer move. It is a great temptation. On close, honest inspection, the man or woman will probably find that the seeds of discontent were ripe before the move; the move simply provided fertile ground. Our lives are constantly changing shape, even if we were to remain in one job and one place.

Achieving Contentment

To achieve contentment at work and at home in a shore duty assignment brings challenges in the balance of dependence and independence in the family unit -- a challenge due to one's own personal age and development, and a challenge in the social life of the couple, where the close-knit ship unit no longer provides much of the sense of belonging that many of us need. The shift ashore frequently brings a financial adjustment to lower pay, due to the loss of sea/hazardous duty pay. If a geographic move is involved, that added cost is a further aggravation.

In his doctoral dissertation on the adjustment of recent Army retirees and their wives, Ronald J. Platte* cited a number of problem areas that can be compared with the shore duty frictions. Like the shore duty adjustments, these retirement adaptations surface in the first year or so. Platte describes the "role confusion" experienced by both the husband and wife. He notes that this is greater where the man perceives his new job as less than his previous assignment. In the case of the active duty man, his perception of his new job is the key. Those at sea often belittle the "armchair admirals" and the "paper shovers," and that serves to diminish his view of his new assignment, whether in reality this is true or not. Platte also sees "adjustment to a new and more intense pattern of family interaction" as a trouble spot in the retiree's transition to his civilian status.

*Platte, Ronald J., "The Second Career: Perceived Social Mobility and Adjustment Among Recent Army Retirees and Wives of Retirees," Ch. 18 in <u>Families in the Military System,</u> edited by McCubbin, Dahl, and Hunter, Sage Publications (Beverly Hills, 1976), pp. 258-287.

70 Deployment and Unaccompanied Tours

"Integration into a permanent community after a life of transiency" is a third adjustment noted by Platte. In the shift from the sea duty separation cycle to shore duty, husbands often experience difficulty in involvement in the civilian/permanent community. While they are on sea duty, many excuse their non-participation in church/Scout/civic activities as impossible due to geographic and time constraints. However, when shore duty presents the opportunity to become involved, many have not learned how as young adults, and are either intimidated by the prospect, or must admit that their own personal desire to avoid such involvement is a matter of choice instead of necessity.

There are steps that can be taken to lessen the impact of the shift from sea to shore duty. Recognizing the pattern for what it is worth is half of the battle.

Knowing that family friction and even slight depression is not abnormal, that it is indeed to be expected, may diminish the emotional expenditure and, therefore, free the individual to use his or her energies more creatively. Understanding this shore duty syndrome will allow acceptance of oneself as a normal human being and recognition of an opportunity to experience personal growth. Staffs could make an attempt to provide more cohesion for their people. The husband and wife should use this time to learn how to be involved rewardingly in their community, in their nuclear and extended families, and in fulfilling hobbies. Retirement is not the time to begin; it will be still harder then.

One final suggestion would be that the Services make staff jobs more personally and career satisfying -- quite a challenge for the bureaus of personnel! The Secretary of the Navy's directive to the current selection board for admirals stresses the value of shore duty, a step in the right direction. Because retention is a prime concern for all Services, retention of men ready to give their best whether in the field, at sea, or ashore, understanding of the shore duty syndrome is valuable in terms of economy and quality of production.

For the military family, contentment is not a once-achieved and, therefore, settled state. In addition to the age changes that confront us all, civilian and military alike, the military husband and wife must add their own verses, none simple, full of counterpoint, to Gertrude Stein's charming poem.

MS for "Shore Duty: Great Expectations," written in November 1977. Later adapted for use in <u>Making a Home in the Navy: Ideas to Grow On</u> (1980) and <u>Charting Your Life in the United States Coast Guard</u> (1983).

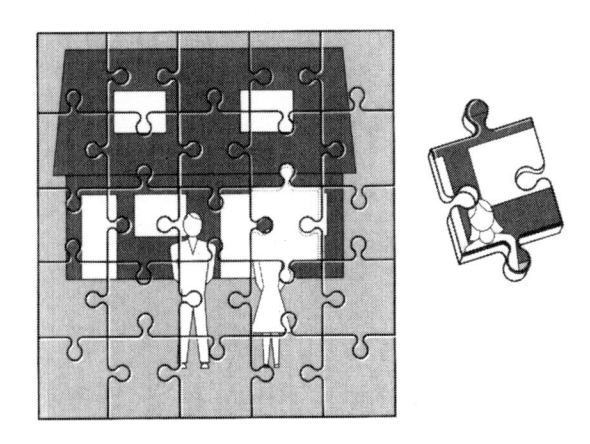

Section III

Financial and Housing Matters

12

Family Money Matter$

How do other military families spend and save their paychecks? Some people seem to have "money sense," and other earning the same amount seem to live from paycheck to paycheck.

We've been raised not to discuss our finances in public. In fact, many families make the mistake of not talking about money matters in front of their children, much less letting them see the decision-making process as they grow older. The result is that it's often hard to have a "ball park" figure on what might be an appropriate amount to spend for food, housing, transportation, and clothing.

Family is pleased that three military families have agreed to share their approaches to making ends meet. You may find that one of the three systems appeals to you. Ideally, the money management method you choose will give you structure and flexibility. Budgeting should be a tool, not a straitjacket.

Army Family:
The Terrys

Sergeant Duane L. Terry (E-5) and his wife Cassandra live in quarters at Fort McClellan, Alabama. She worked at Army Community Services as a temporary-hire secretary/computer operator until February. She has been a full-time homemaker since then. Their two children are Stephanie, age 7, and Duane Jr., age 5.

The Terrys kept track of their expenditures for a seven-month period: last December through June. Their monthly, average was:

Housing and utilities covered by housing allowance	$ 316.00
Savings (monthly allotment to savings account)	100.00
Life insurance (monthly allotment)	75.00
Groceries (flexible biweekly is $85-100)	200.00
Clothing (socks, underwear, etc. - all other clothing in layaway 3 months before school)	40.00
Car insurance	9.35
Transportation	36.00
Telephone	40.00
Cable television	40.00
Orthodontist (to end in August 1987)	60.00
Son's preschool	100.00
TOTAL	$1016.35

In June, when their preschool payments ended for the school year, they bought a washer and dryer, on which the monthly payments run $81.

In February, when their income tax rebate came for $800, they deposited $350 into their savings accounts. They used the rest to take a weekend vacation to Florida and to pay all other outstanding bills.

Cassandra explained their low car insurance by stating that they have liability coverage only on their "old" car --- a 1977 Ford LTD "in mint condition that's all paid for."

Hints from Cassandra Terry

Cassandra Terry has provided hints that help her family make ends meet:

• Keep a savings account away from where you reside. People often have an account in their State of Record.
• Make an allotment for your savings account; whatever amount you can afford without hurting your budget. Slowly increase it, if possible. If you never have the money in your hand, you can never miss it.
• Try not to use your savings account money except in cases of emergency. The Terry actually have three savings accounts and no checking account. One is their "use only in emergency account" in their home state. The second in their home state is a "dip-from account" used

for vacations, appliances, etc. The third savings account is with the local credit union at Fort McClellan, where they may draw free checks or use the automatic teller machine (ATM). "The advantage is that we have to leave $25 in that account; we can't ever overdraw on the automatic teller, so that eliminates impulse buying."
• Try to minimize charge accounts. Let one major credit card serve all purposes so that there will be one monthly bill coming in, not several.
• Try to pay cash for household necessities, major appliances, furniture, etc.
• Everywhere you go, there is a military exchange where you can use a layaway plan. For example, in September each year, I layaway everything for Christmas. This alleviates the problem of running into debt right after Christmas. Therefore, our Christmas money can be used for our own enjoyment, and we have the advantage of no last-minute rushing.
• Whenever possible, try to get the due dates for your bills scheduled after your pay periods to avoid late charges.
• Many military families do not use the services the military has to offer, such as free counseling and financial planning at the Army Community Service and legal assistance. All of this is free and administered by trained professionals. Check around on post and find out what our military community is all about.

At the ages of 28 and 27, Duane and Cassandra have a firm hand on the present and an eye to the future. Duane leaves for Korea this month for an unaccompanied tour. Cassandra will return to their home area in Jacksonville, Florida, for the duration, where they will buy a house and she will make use of the extensive Navy medical, commissary, and exchange facilities to stay within their budget.

Navy Family:
The McGlothins

Senior Chief Hospital Corpsman (HMCS) Hubert J. McGlothin and his wife Gail volunteered for *Family's* project before he made E-8. Our focus was to be on E-5 through E-7, because most families are looking for ways to make ends meet in that pay category. However, Gail, in her role as a USO Branch Director at Naval Submarine Base Kings Bay, Georgia, had so many good hints that we agreed to pass along her system that has worked for the Navy wives with whom she has shared it.

Gail and "Hub" are 36 and 41 years old, with three children: Mika (15), April (11), and Jake (7). They had three back-to-back tours at Kings Bay, for seven years, arriving with the first contingent at this new base when housing was non-existent in a price range for enlisted personnel. After scouting the community, they settled on a double-wide mobile home in one of the few "decent" parks. Their experience with selling it as

76   Financial and Housing Matters

they moved to New Orleans has convinced them to rent for the time being -- until they are ready to buy property for retirement. As USO Branch Director for NSB Kings Bay, she eloquently argued for affordable off-base housing units before audiences of hundreds of real estate investors, developers, and government officials.

As a result of having to budget their own income carefully, Gail offered workshops to military families on her tried and true system. It would be fun to know how many families scattered worldwide buy a spiral notebook in December, thanks to Gail McGlothin. She now keeps not only her household accounts straight, but those of The Volunteer Center of the Greater New Orleans Area, of which she is now the director.

Sample Budget	Amount Spent	Total
Monthly income		$1000
Car payment	-$150	850
Rent	- 250	600
Charge card	- 75	525
Electricity	- 60	465
Telephone	- 15	450
Savings	- 100	350
Food	- 200	150
Gasoline	- 60	90
Clothing	- 25	65
Spending cash	- 25	20
Car tag	- 12	8
New checks	- 4	4

Leave balance in checking account!

Hints from Gail McGlothin

"The first thing I do at the end of December is to buy a spiral bound notebook (70 sheets) and write the year on the front. This is off-limits for anyone to grab as scratch paper!

"The first page has **Savings** written across the top. Then I list everything I need to save for that year: vacation, Christmas, tires, car down payment, insurance payments, etc.

"This is a good time to look at a calendar and do some planning for the whole year. Add up your items and divide by the number of paydays so you know how much you need to save each payday. If the sum is unrealistic, then perhaps a different type of vacation and making

Christmas gifts throughout the year are alternatives. But of the things that are not optional, it's better to be a little short for three months than having to use an entire check for tires and ending up at Navy Relief.

"I tape a small card-size, full-year calendar (free at some card stores) on the inside cover for easy reference.

"I write the names, addresses, and account numbers of all of my bills on one of the back pages for easy reference (if I lose an envelope, move, or if I am making out a credit application).

"I have one page labeled **Goals**. These are personal goals, but having them in the book keeps me aware of the things I want to achieve.

"I keep one page for a list of **Donations**. Those two dollar raffle tickets add up, plus I don't have to go back through a year's worth of checks to find them at tax time. (* *Nor do you have to look far to check if a charity is sending you a second request right after you have given -- a very common practice!*)

"I head one page **Christmas Gifts**. Here I write all of the people to whom I must give gifts and some ideas. I also keep a wish list so I have a ready reply when people ask what we would like.

"To determine what will be spent during the month, I total our monthly take-home income and subtract our expenses. I make notes on the top of the page of the next month as I think of things that are going to come up then. Don't forget **Birthdays,** some **Spending Money** for each person, **Lunch Money, Babysitting Costs**, etc. The tighter the money, the more detailed the budget should be. **Postage, Birthday Cards,** and **Car Tags** all add up fast!

"When I start subtracting, the absolutes are first, such as **Rent, Car Payments, Credit Card Payments, Utility Bill,** and **Savings.** You know the amount that has to be paid. Then come **Food** and **Gasoline** for the month. Both are necessities, but the belt can be tightened if need be on these two items. Go grocery shopping once a week and do not go between trips. If you run out of bread, don't eat sandwiches.

"If the gas money is going to run out, don't drive the car. Walk, take the bus or carpool with friends. The next category includes such things as clothes, shoes, auto upkeep items, etc. In the final category are things like charitable donation, entertainment, craft supplies, and personal spending money."

Financial and Housing Matters

Air Force Family: The Ouimettes

Technical Sergeant Rodney A. Ouimette (E-6) and his wife Susan have undergone a major transition in their lives this year. After serving eleven and a half years in the Air Force, with her last assignment in the White House in the President's Emergency Operations Center, TSGT Susan Ouimette left the Air Force. The reason: she was pregnant with their second child due in August. Their first child is their seven-year-old daughter Kimberly.

Monthly Income:

Take-home pay	$3259.46

Deductions:

FICA (Social Security)	187.60
FITW (Federal Income Tax Withheld)	279.58
SGLI (Serviceman's Group Life Insurance	8.00
USSH (U. S. Soldier's Home)	1.00

Allotments:

Bond	12.50
Life Insurance	68.15

Average Monthly Expenses:

	Jan-Mar (owned home)	Apr - June (rented apt.)
Housing	$1200	$640
Utilities	150	30
Phone	30	30
Food	100	100
Transportation*	100	100
Gas/car upkeep	100	100
Child care*	100	100
School & bus	110	110
Clothing	50	50
Misc.	100	100
Entertainment	100	100
Household repairs	100	
TOTAL	$2640	$1860

Rodney, who has worked in Air Force Personnel in the Pentagon for the past three years, described their decision this way: "Last January, knowing Sue was pregnant and was going to get out of the Air Force to take care of the children, and knowing that we will be moving to Geilenkirchen, Germany, next June, we put our house up for sale. We closed on the house in April and moved into an apartment so we could be settled before the child was born.

By not waiting until the last minute before moving overseas, we had time to get the best price. The profits from the house (in Alexandria, Va.) went into the savings account. Since we moved into the apartment, we have put at least $1,000- to $1,500 per month in savings to get us used to one paycheck."

* These expenses were reduced or eliminated when Sue separated from the Air Force (or when summer break came for school expenses.)

Hints from Susan Ouimette

"We don't have any formula way to manage our money We just know what we have and stay within that amount. We have Sure Pay into our checking account and take it from there. Whatever is left over at the end of the month is either put in savings, used for extra purchases, or used for yearly expenses such as car insurance.

"After I went on terminal leave this summer, we no longer had to pay day care expenses (over $300 in the summer) and saved on my transportation to work and lunch money. This allowed us extra money for baby items, summer entertainment and savings.

"We are both Catholic and chose to put Kimberly in a Catholic school for the discipline and good religious foundation. She wears a uniform, so we don't have to keep buying her school clothes. We bought several uniforms last year and they will last through this year as well.

"We don't normally charge things unless we expect to pay them off at the end of the month when the bill comes. We use our charge cards more for the convenience and to keep a good credit rating. We normally like to build an extra cushion in the checking account if we know there is a big purchase we want."

Rodney and Sue, at ages 36 and 31, have a philosophy that drive their financial decisions: owning high-cost items such as a new car or a huge stereo set doesn't constitute success. Being in control ("Sue is the manager," says Rodney) allows them to put their money on the important things (such as Kimberly's schooling) and live comfortably.

Financial and Housing Matters

It Makes Cents

Each family has a different way of handling money and each has moved or will move within a three-year span (the McGlothins last year, the Terrys this year, and the Ouimettes next year) -- right on the average for military families. And all three families can tell you that budgeting your money is never easy; it's something you must work at. But if you work diligently at it, you'll find that those pennies you scrimped and saved for start adding up, and make it all worthwhile.

****

Family received an unusually large "Letters to the Editor" response on this article. Most were complimentary and pleased with the hands-on budgets. But some were irate, saying that the budget quoted from the Terrys was unreasonably low, and others, including a home economics teacher in a high cost of living area, outraged at Gail McGlothin's methodology -- "if you run out of bread, you don't eat sandwiches." But the magazine stuck behind our contributors, feeling that they live the lifestyle of the E-5/8 and know whereof they speak (unlike our letter writers) --- and that when one runs out of basics and has to do without, it's less likely to happen again in the near future. "Borrowing" from another account is a dangerous precedent in the precarious world of budgets.

In the years since this article first appeared, we have experienced vast and rapid increases in gas, heating fuels, and, as a result, practically every other item in our budgets. Without a strong grasp on one's finances, there is no way to survive such unexpected and unrecompensed rises in costs. The best we can do as military families is to know how to budget, and do the bulk of our shopping at our military commissaries and exchanges (where savings are required to be a minimum of 20% and state sales taxes are not levied).

Originally appeared as "Family Money Matter$" in Family, *October 1987.*

13

The Ins & Outs of Credit and Debit Cards

Now that military exchanges accept credit cards, it's important to know how to use credit wisely. 1986 brought the welcome change to Army, Navy, Air Force, and Marine Corps exchanges: major credit cards became acceptable for most large purchases. That meant that it was easier to shop when prices are low instead of only when cash was/is available. With the opportunity for credit comes the need to understand the variety of options available to consumers.

Types of Credit Cards

There are three general types of credit cards:

1) Retail credit cards are issued by specific stores and oil companies. The customer either pays the bill in full once a month without interest charges or pays a minimum monthly amount plus significant finance charges on the unpaid balance.

2) Bank/Savings and Loan credit cards, such as MasterCard or Visa, may be used at numerous participating retail stores, restaurants, service stations, airlines, and now, exchanges. Some issuers also allow you to borrow money through a "cash advance" (actually a loan) which must be paid back with interest. Just like retail credit cards, there is a monthly finance charge on any unpaid balance. There may also be an annual fee and/or service charge.

3) Travel and entertainment cards, such as American Express, Diner's Club, and Carte Blanche, come with an annual fee and your monthly bill must be paid in full each month. Check cashing privileges and accident insurance come with some of these cards.

Choosing and Being Chosen

Before deciding which card (or cards) will suit your needs, research the following:

- Annual fee -- this can range from nothing up to $250.
- Credit limit -- you may have to start fairly low and build up as your credit history accumulates.
- Availability of emergency cash and personal check cashing -- automatic teller machines make this attractive to travelers.
- Effective annual percentage rate of interest -- how much is it and when do the finance charges begin?

"Banks and credit unions set their own standards concerning credit card customers," said Martin Handel, Comptroller of the Army and Air Force Exchange Service (AAFES). "They all have their own scoring formulas for screening applicants. This means a poor credit risk at one bank could be a prime candidate for credit at another."

Before issuing credit cards, institutions look at the applicant's income level, employment record, financial obligations, credit history and length of time spent living in the community. But each institution weighs these factors differently. "A bank that's looking for credit card business may have a lower income level requirement than one that isn't," Handel explained. "And a credit union that deals with a lot of military customers may not see frequent moves as a negative factor."

Some banks and credit unions have "starter programs" for young people applying for their first cards, Handel said. Under these plans, institutions issue younger applicants cards with lower limits than cards issued to more established customers.

But just because an institution accepts you, that doesn't mean you should accept them. Each institution sets its own terms for credit card service. Many charge interest on the unpaid balance from the prior month, with interest rates ranging from 14 to 24 percent annually. Some charge a flat annual fee ranging from $15 to $40. Others charge a fee plus interest on the unpaid balance. Still others charge a percent of the purchase cost when the card is used. So be sure to read the credit contract carefully. If you do not understand it completely, see your base/post legal officer before signing it.

Advantages and Disadvantages of Credit Cards

Women should establish credit in their own name, if their income level meets the requirements. If not, married women may request that credit accounts report the history in both of their names (e.g. Frank and Imogene Smith). Military widows have had painful experiences trying to obtain credit in their own name when all previous credit history was their husband's alone.

Credit cards provide some significant advantages if used wisely. For example, you usually have 30 days to pay once your account is billed. if you pay your bill in full toward the end of that period, you essentially have had an interest-free loan. Because individual companies vary in their efficiency in submitting their individual charges to your account, you often have the equivalent of a two-month or longer loan.

Credit cards can also be a shield against goods or services that are defective, don't measure up to the claims made for them or are not what you ordered. The federal Fair Credit Billing Act gives you the right to refuse to pay for goods or services that are defective or were not delivered.

If you have a complaint that your bill is not correct or you never received the item being billed for, then (1) notify your credit card company in writing within 60 days after you get the bill, (2) give your name and account number, and (3) explain how much the error is and why you think there's an error.

When the company gets your letter, it must investigate your claim and cannot bill you for the item until its investigation is complete.

If you have a complaint about poor quality goods or services you received, then you should: (1) notify the merchant in writing and give him a chance to correct the problem (keep a copy of the letter) and (2) if that doesn't work, notify the credit card company and ask to have the item charge reversed. (However, in this situation, the item must have cost $50 or more, and sale musty have taken place in your home state or within 100 miles of where you live.) Because of this protection, there are times when you may be wiser to use your credit card for a purchase instead of cash or a check.

Credit cards enable you to make purchases by phone. You save a great deal of time by not having to send a check and wait for it to clear before your tickets or merchandise can be sent. And hotel reservations can be guaranteed beyond the usual check-in time.

Your receipts provide good records for insurance and tax purposes.

Finally, you can take advantage of sales or purchase an item in short supply without having to have the cash in hand or keep too large a portion of your money in a non- or low-interest checking account.

Disadvantages to credit cards usually cluster around their immoderate use. You might decide that your own rule of thumb would be not to charge more than you can pay in full when billed.

Debit Cards: Advantages and Disadvantages

There are other kinds of cards, called debit cards, that allow you to withdraw only the amount that you have in an account. An automated teller machine card is a debit card. You can obtain other name brand bank cards, such as Visa or MasterCard, that function the same way. The advantage of these cards is that you don't have to carry a lot of cash and you can't spend more than you have in the account.

However, you don't have the Truth in Lending Act protection given for credit card purchases and you must be a superb record keeper of all of your withdrawals and the current balance in your account. Otherwise, it's easy to get low in the account and be left without access to funds.

Also, if someone uses your debit card without your authorization, you could lose up to a maximum of $500 of funds withdrawn illegally. Your only protection is to report your loss within two days after you discover it. Then your maximum responsibility is $50 per card, the same maximum you have on a credit card. If you fail to report an unauthorized transfer that appears on your bank statement within 60 days after the statement is mailed to you, you risk *unlimited loss* on withdrawals. This includes all of the money in your account, plus whatever credit line the bank has extended.

Protecting Your Cards

If you do use credit cards, be sure to protect them. Keep your cards in a case separate from your wallet. In your home file, keep a record of your card numbers, their expiration dates, their credit limits, and the phone number of each company so you can report any loss quickly. Sign new cards right away and cut up your old ones. If you receive unrequested cards, cut them up. Keep all of your receipts and be sure to check them against your bill. (The credit card companies can make mistakes -- charging you twice for an item, for example.) Then save only the receipts you need for tax or insurance purposes, as thieves can use these to obtain your number and signature. (You should ask for all of the carbons when you charge an item for the same reason.)

Originally appeared as "The Ins & Outs of Credit Cards," Family, April 1986, and was later adapted by American Forces Information Service for their PressPack.

14

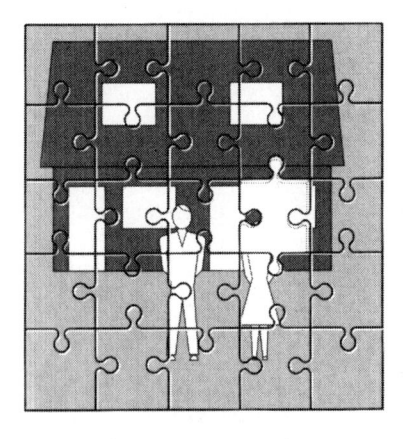

Military Spouse Rights and Benefits

*Because the specifics of your benefits change constantly, it is important that you check with your post/base experts to know the current provisions. Sources of information will be your finance and legal offices, family service/support center, Health Benefits Advisor, and Retired Affairs Office.

On the day that you became a military spouse, you also received a puzzle of benefits. If you feel like some of the pieces are missing in your understanding of the system, you are not alone. There are about 1,160,000 spouses of active duty members, and the number of widows and spouses of retirees is even greater ..... very few of us understand the whole puzzle.

Not only are you faced with partial directions (the total would be cumbersome to carry, much less read), but the puzzle itself changes periodically, due to new laws and policy. *Family* believes that you need a basic outline, with sources of further information for putting together the difficult portions.

Although there are increasing numbers of husbands of military women, most military spouses are wives. In order to make putting together the puzzle as easy as possible, we will assume that you are a wife. For those who need to translate, please do so).

Definitions of Rights and Benefits

Definitions of *rights* and *benefits* are hard to find. In fact, the military often mixes the two. However, a "pure" approach is:

Right: a provision to which one is entitled by statute or regulation.
Benefit: a provision for which one is eligible by "grace," by "space-availability."

Constitutional Rights

A military spouse retains all of her constitutional rights, except in some overseas situations. You may vote (in fact, you are encouraged to do so), participate in political activity (though military members and civil service employees are banned from political activity by the Hatch Act), and may write to your congressman/woman or senator. You may join organizations of your choice, though common sense should be exercised.

You retain your freedom of speech. However, there may be circumstances when disclosure of information about your husband's work or whereabouts may be harmful to the mission in which he is involved, or may jeopardize your own safety and that of others. Military commanders are caught in the bind of how much wives should know of their husband's work for morale purposes versus the potential damage that such information might do in the hands of the wrong people.

When you live in military housing or drive your car on base/post, you are subject to the regulations that go with the privilege. There has been a fair amount of discussion recently about the military member's control of and responsibility for the behavior of his wife and children. This is required by regulation in those arenas where he is your sponsor (in government housing and military facilities, and presence on base/post).

Cautions for those Overseas

When military families go overseas, the military member retains the protection of the U. S. government, while family members, depending on the Status of Forces Agreement (SOFA) with each country, may come under local laws. Therefore, there are instances in which an abused wife or child has less legal protection than she or he would have in the U. S.

Some of the other instances of loss of due process of law, as we know it in the United States, are related to car accidents and possession of illegal drugs. Knowledge of these discrepancies is very important. Families need to attend the briefings for newcomers in foreign assignments to make sure you understand where the "holes" are in your safety net.

Some additional losses overseas include your right to work. Depending on the Status of Forces Agreement, a military spouse may not be allowed to be employed by host country nationals. You may also find that American credit card companies cancel your credit once you accompany your husband on an overseas assignment (and have an overseas address -- you can combat this by using a reliable stateside address from which your mail can be forwarded).

Military Spouse Rights and Benefits

If you accompany your husband overseas on an unaccompanied tour of duty, you are not "command sponsored." As such, you give up your eligibility for numerous support services that are provided for "command-sponsored" family members.

Domicile and Tax Rights

Military spouses have numerous special rights not held by our civilian peers. For example, we have the right to choose our legal residence. In years past, a military wife was usually considered a resident of the same state as her military husband. This is not necessarily true today. Some wives elect to maintain a different state as their legal residence because of an attractive tax structure or college tuition rates. To be sure that you have a firm claim on which to base your legal residence, check with your base/post Legal Officer.

The state in which you currently live (versus your legal residence) generally may tax you only on your own income earned in-state, and tax property that you hold in your name. (For this reason, many military families maintain the car in the military member's name only unless they are living in their state of legal residence because the military member is protected by the Soldiers' and Sailors' Civil Relief Act.) You may obtain your driver's license from your state of legal residence (or from the state in which you live), Ideally, you will have two out of the following three that match: your car registration state, your driver's license state, and the state in which you are living/driving. If all of this is confusing, ask your Legal Officer about your specific situation.

Commissary and Exchange Shopping

With an appropriate family member's ID card, you have the right to shop in military commissaries and exchanges for items for use by your own family or for bona fide gifts. Your average savings on identical purchases in civilian stores ranges between 20 and 25 percent and does not include state sales taxes.

Spouse Hiring Priority

As a military spouse, you are given preference over other civilians when you apply for a non-appropriated fund job (NAF), thanks to Executive Order 12568, signed by President Reagan October 2, 1986. Whether you are overseas or stateside, your Civilian Personnel Office (CPO) on base/post will have a listing of all local NAF vacancies, usually with the exchange, child care, and recreation services.*Regulations have improved in this domain -- check carefully with your Civilian Personnel Office.*

The Army makes it easy to transfer your NAF employment to your new post. Army Regulation 215.3 permits "non-competitive reinstatement" (that means preference in hiring) to any NAF activity within six months after leaving your old duty station, without a break-in-service notation on your record.

The Department of Defense (DoD) gives hiring preference in the United States to spouses of active duty military members for positions at all grade levels. You may apply for "direct hire" positions (no requisite for prior civil service) or for merit promotion positions (and then you must have appropriate civil service experience) at your sponsor's new duty station. (The spouse preference.legislation was designed to help spouses forced to relocate due to the military member's reassignment. You may use your preference only once per duty station, and you lose use of preference once you accept *any civil service position* at the new duty station.)

"Spouse preference points" are lower than veterans' points and points for handicapping conditions, RIF's (reduction in force), etc. "Spouse preference points" work to your benefit if you are among the "best qualified" when rated against the requirements of the position - a rating performed (based on information provided in your SF-171 application) prior to the granting of interviews for the vacant position.

For spouses overseas seeking federal positions, preference is granted at all civil service levels. Upon their return Stateside, spouses who have held civil service positions overseas are granted hiring preference and entered into the Priority Placement Program (PPP).

Each of the Services handles priority placement for spouses slightly differently, so you should check with your current CPO. For example, for moves within the U.S., the Department of Army (DA) requires that you provide a copy of your military spouse's permanent change of station (PCS) orders, and gives you seven working days after arrival at the new station to register for DA jobs in the commuting area.

Spouse Benefits

The spouse employment counseling you may find at your base/post falls in the category of benefits, because it is a service for which you are eligible if it is available. The House Armed Services Committee has directed the Department of Defense to establish spouse employment assistance centers "at as many installations as possible, and to fill currently vacant positions related to such family member employment programs as a matter of high priority" (report on the 1987 Defense Authorization Bill).

In July 1986, the DoD issued guidelines that officially allow family members living in government quarters to conduct home businesses. You must submit a written request to the commanding officer of your installation. Some of the stipulations may include using a post office box number when advertising your business, not selling to subordinates, and meeting local licensing and insurance requirements.

Education Benefits

Educational opportunities on base/post are related benefits. You may take college courses and a variety of educational tests (for credit, college admission, etc.) on a space-available, paying basis. Army spouses may attend Headstart classes (a combination language and culture course) on a space-available basis. For further details on educational programs, including scholarships and grants for military spouses and education benefits for widows, check with your base/post Education Center.

Medical and Dental Benefits

By law, military medical facilities are only required to care for active duty military members. Spouses are eligible for medical care and very basic dental services (cleaning, X-rays, and simple fillings), on a space-available basis. The result is that you may experience very complete care at one military facility at a given point in time, and very limited care at another. To compensate, military families may use CHAMPUS (Civilian Health and Medical Program of the Uniformed Services) after obtaining a non-availability statement for the care being sought. Your Health Benefits Advisor (HBA) at your local military medical facility will provide information and assistance on the process.

CHAMPUS is not free; there are annual charges per person or per family, and you must pay a percentage (20 - 25%) of your "allowable charges" (plus any amount in excess of the "allowable charges"). Because the regulations change constantly, your safest route is to talk over your options with your HBA before seeking any non-emergency civilian medical care.

Eight former U. S. Public Health Service hospitals and two clinics serve as Uniformed Services Treatment Facilities available to you. They are located in Baltimore, MD; Boston, MA; Nassau Bay, TX; Seattle, WA; Staten Island, NY; Galveston, Houston, and Portland, ME; and Cleveland, OH. Your HBA can provide detailed information.

The Services are testing satellite contract operations in cities with large military populations. Their services are limited to outpatient care. Check your HBA for your area.

CHAMPUS Prime, a plan presented to Congress by DoD in November 1986, will be tested in 1988 in six states (Hawaii, California, Georgia, Florida, North Carolina and South Carolina). Family members of active duty military and retirees under age 65 will be eligible to sign up for a minimum of one year. They must agree to seek all civilian medical care from specified doctors and hospitals; in exchange, all of their inpatient and outpatient care, except for small office visit fees, will be covered.

For further information, you may obtain the *CHAMPUS Handbook* from your HBA.

Survivor Benefits

Nobody likes to think about the possibility of being a widow, but it is important for you and your husband to discuss the provisions that are available if he should die on active duty or after retirement. For specific information and counseling, you should go to your husband's career counselor or your family service/support center. (For Navy families, a limited number of copies are available of *Navy Rights and Benefits: Survivor Benefits* from the March 1986 issue of *All Hands*, Dept. of the Navy, NMPC-05, PAO, Washington, DC 20370.)

In addition to a number of allowances for burial, grave markers, and the death gratuity (usually available within 24 hours after the active duty member's death), an "active duty widow" may be eligible for Dependence and Indemnity Compensation (DIC) payments from the Veterans Administration. You may collect 90 days of BAQ and VHA housing allowances. If you are living in government quarters, you may remain for 90 days, or collect proportional BAQ and VHA allowances if you leave sooner.

A Casualty Assistance Calls Officer (CACO) will be assigned to assist you through the official maze. He or she will help you with the forms for insurance ($50,000 under the Serviceman's Group Life Insurance -- SGLI -- unless your husband has elected less coverage), a new ID card, movement of household goods, and application for social security benefits.

Retirees

For those of you whose husbands are about to retire, a new requirement went into effect March 1986. If your husband wishes to elect less than the maximum coverage under the Survivor Benefit Plan (SBP) at retirement, you must sign an agreement with his decision. There can be good financial reasons for such a decision, but this requirement is a protection for you -- so that there are no surprises.

Each Service has a mutual aid organization (which military members may join based on rate/years of service) that provides "death benefits" and assists widows in filing for government benefits:

- Army Mutual Aid, which serves Army and Air Force members -- Bldg. 468, Ft. Myer, VA 22211
- Navy Mutual Aid, which serves the Navy, Marine Corps, Coast Guard, Public Health Service, and NOAA -- Arlington Annex, Room G-070, Washington, DC 20370

Unremarried widows of active duty military and retirees usually continue to be eligible for commissary, exchange, theater, and club privileges, as well as medical care on a space-available basis. Your CPO can help you understand the job preference benefits available to widows. The Veterans Administration will give you information on your eligibility for a GI Bill home loan and educational assistance.

The 99th Congress extended survivor benefits to cover: a widow who remarries at or after age 55; dependent children of retirement- eligible members who die on active duty, if there is no surviving spouse or if the surviving spouse subsequently dies; and incapacitated dependent children who are incapable of supporting themselves (full coverage).

Ex-Spouse Benefits

The Uniformed Services Former Spouses' Protection Act, P.L. 97-252, enacted in September 1982, has been amended and clarified each year since then. For example, an amendment to the 1987 Defense Authorization Bill, P.L. 99-661, effective November 14, 1986, enables the courts to award Survivor Benefit Plan (SBP) coverage to a former spouse. If you are a beneficiary of SBP and remarry before age 55 (used to be 60), you lose SBP.

EX-POSE (Ex-Partners of Servicemen/Women for Equality) emphasizes that:

- You must be married for a minimum of ten years (and be divorced for two years) before you can share your ex-spouse's Social Security benefits when you both turn 62.
- You are eligible for an ID card with full medical, commissary, and exchange privileges if your ex-spouse served at least 20 years of active duty and your marriage lasted for 20 years of the active duty period. If your 20-year marriage covered only 15 years of the 20-year active duty period, then you will be eligible for only two years of medical care (at the

end of which you will have the opportunity to enroll in a DoD-established group health plan).

• Your Legal Officer can provide information on former spouse rights and benefits. However, as you initiate divorce proceedings, EX-POSE recommends that you seek a non-military lawyer who is trained in divorce law in the state in which you will seek the judgment.

For the specific wording of the current ex-spouse legislation and complete coverage of benefits to which a former spouse may be entitled, *Family* recommends *A Guide for Military Wives Facing Separation or Divorce* (3rd ed., 1986), by EX-POSE, P. O. Box 11191, Alexandria, VA 22312 -- $3.50 for non-members, and $2.75 for members.

Another resource is the 1985 *Guide to Divorce and Military Retirement Pay -- Under the Former Spouses' Protection Act* ($8.95 ppd. from SMS Productions, 3332 Mather Field Road, Suite 210, Rancho Cordova, CA 95670). This guide offers information on a state by state basis.

Additional Spouse Benefits

A myriad of official and unofficial support services are available to military spouses, such as:

• Family Service/Support Center or Army Community Service Center (for personal, marital, and budget counseling, information and referral on a wide range of needs, and healthy family workshops).

• Chaplains (for weddings, baptisms, and other religious rites, counseling, marriage and spiritual enrichment groups).

• Legal Assistance Program (for counseling, legal documents such as a will and power of attorney).

• Your ID card may authorize you as a patron of the base/post theater and recreation services (such as a swimming pool, bowling alley, gymnasium, hobby shop, Officers'/NCO/and Enlisted Clubs, etc.).

• Alcohol and drug abuse treatment programs are open to spouses on a space-available basis. These include general awareness courses, non-residential screening and counseling, and residential rehabilitation. If space is not available, you are eligible for CHAMPUS benefits for rehabilitation (check with your HBA).

• Organizations such as the American Red Cross, the Armed Services YMCA, and the USO provide services and programs for military spouses.

Military Spouse Rights and Benefits 93

- The Navy Wifeline Association provides materials and answers questions from sea service spouses (Washington Navy Yard, Bldg. 172, Washington, DC 20374).

- The National Military Family Association educates the Services, Congress, and military families themselves about their benefits and deficits (6000 Stevenson Ave., Suite 304, Alexandria, VA 22304).

- The emergency aid associations for each Service (Army Emergency Relief, Navy and Marine Corps Relief Society, and Air Force Aid Society) can provide assistance (usually with the permission of the military member).

- Officers' wives' clubs and enlisted wives' clubs are social and service oriented organizations on each post/base. Navy Wives Clubs of America is open to all wives of Navy, Marine Corps, and Coast Guard enlisted personnel. Chapters are worldwide; for your local chapter, check with your installation family service/support center.

- Ombudsmen (spouses who serve as official links between Navy family members and the command) provide two-way communication on ship arrival schedules, complaints, and support referral.

****

Family wishes to thank the following organizations for their help in assembling this article: All Hands (Department of the Navy, Internal Relations Print Media Division), EX-POSE, National Military Family Association, U. S. Army Community and Family Support Center, and Women's Equity Action League (2 Fact Sheets available, $3 each, Project on Women and the Military, 1250 I Street, N.W., Suite 305, Washington, DC 20005).

****

**Since this article was written in 1987, the Delta Dental Plan for military families has greatly enhanced the dental care benefits for active duty families. If you have not enrolled, talk to your HBA. Military family organizations and, indeed, HBA's themselves, highly recommend that military families take out supplemental health insurance to cover the costs that can strap families using CHAMPUS.

Originally appeared as "Putting It All Together: Solving the Puzzle of Military Spouse Rights and Benefits," Family, March 1987.

Pits & Palaces: Military Housing

Keep the address of every place you have lived for security references and government employment forms. When I read advice like that, I must confess that I sometimes have trouble with the street numbers or names; but if modern technology could photograph what I visualize, there would be a most amazing collection!

I was born at West Point and returned to converted bachelor quarters with an improvised bar in the bathroom (due to the era and size of the quarters). My folks lived in a progression of civilian houses and military quarters than ran the gamut from a duplex in Minneapolis, to "roach heaven" in Paris, Texas, to a mini-chateau in Paris, France (pits to palaces!) Some historic Army quarters and modest-sized family owned housing came in between. As a Navy wife who has been a mortgage contributor and house painter, I have seen fewer pits and no palaces. Nevertheless, we all could regale our civilian counterparts with places we have lived.

To any military family, our housing history is of great importance because as we move to a new area, *where* we are going to live is our first consideration. Recently,, each of the four Services has put time, energy, and money into improving the housing situation for military families. So, we at *Family* thought it was about time for a status report.

Each of the services varies in its provisions of military housing, and the overseas situation differs from the stateside situation. In order to get a current status report, I talked with senior housing officials in the Army, Navy (which includes the Marine Corps projects), and the Coast Guard.

Roughly 33% of those eligible in the Coast Guard are in military housing, 34% of eligible Navy families, and 44% of eligible Army families are in government housing. Two qualifiers need to be stated here, though. In the Department of Defense, one becomes *eligible* after attaining the rank of E-4 plus two years of service. That means that someone who marries right out of boot camp cannot expect to be in government housing for almost two years, except in unusual circumstances. One of those unusual circumstances might be the availability of substandard units. This term generally is used for quarters that are in good condition but do not meet the square footage requirements for a given rank. Ineligibles and eligibles waiting for permanent housing may live in these units and pay no more than 75% of their Basic Allowance for Quarters (BAQ).

The second qualifier is location. Captain Brian J. O'Connell, the Assistant Commander for Family Housing in the Navy, explains: "We range from 100% in government housing (in Adak, Alaska and Guantanamo Bay, Cuba) to almost none (in Washington, D.C.)."

Flexible Options

The reason this varies so greatly is that the Services are allowed to construct, lease, or buy housing only when the housing available in the civilian community does not meet the needs of the military. An annual survey is taken to determine needs and availability. By the very nature of the requirement to show need, and then request funding for construction, purchase, or lease, there is a built-in gap.

That gap is narrowing in some instances, however, when a Service can have the flexibility to purchase already-built homes that meet its standards and price requirements. An example is the Navy's purchase of 132 units in the San Diego area.

"We were able to buy these units in three different locations. We got our price and got them earlier than if we had had to construct them. They are very attractive units, and they are dispersed throughout the community," explained Captain O'Connell, who cites this purchase as a mutual benefit to military families and the civilian community because the depressed housing market had left developers with unsold units. The community had requested that the Navy not build another large enclave in the area, feeling that the isolation that occurs is not good for the civilian community or the military residents. The Navy has ended up with 132 of the 290 units it needed, and the units are "literally community level housing with pools and recreation areas."

The idea of community level housing was echoed by Master Chief Petty Officer of the Navy Billy C. Sanders. "In the future our plan is to build communities, not just a bunch of houses. A community center with an area for teens, ball diamonds, basketball and tennis courts will be part of the whole plan."

Discussion of the future led to the projects to be funded under the Jobs and Recession Relief Act. This Congressional funding is for *stateside* military housing repairs and improvements. Captain O'Connell and his counterpart from the policy branch, Commander Thomas J. McGinty, Head, Housing Branch - Housing Division (OP-157), stressed that these Congressional dollars were not a windfall, but were an accelerated funding of projects already planned.

The Navy and Marine Corps share about $33 million in funds from the Relief Act. The Navy's three big maintenance and repair projects generally will be "whole house repairs." Captain O'Connell said that the plan is to work on a group of houses as they become vacant. The maintenance and repair work is "to sustain the life of existing units and must be begun by September 30th this year. We have a backlog of half a billion dollars' work of this type, so this money is a help."

About half of their funds will go to improvements on thirteen Marine stations, many of which involve upgrading kitchens. As Commander McGinty explained, upgrading the kitchens in some of the older quarters costs more than was paid to build the quarters in the first place.

Historic/Vintage Quarters

Vintage quarters came up for discussion in all three interviews. The Navy's oldest quarters are listed on the National Register of Historic Places (1724 at Portsmouth, New Hampshire) and their newest are 400 units for junior enlisted personnel in New London, Connecticut. The Army has about the same spread with quarters built on the East Coast in the early nineteenth century, followed by forts in the Midwest; their newest are at Ft. Stewart, Georgia. The average age of Army quarters is 26 years old. The Coast Guard counts historic lighthouses from 1797 and World War II housing in its inventory, plus brand new colonials in isolated areas.

Maintenance and Repair vs. Improvements

The Navy has put its emphasis on maintenance and repair while the Marine Corps has spent its Job Act funds on improvements. The Army, which received about $73 million, as did the Air Force, has focused on a mix of the two: "essential projects that will improve livability and decrease maintenance costs," said Colonel Everett L. Tucker, Jr., Chief of the Army Housing Management Division in the office of the Assistant Chief of Engineers. He described the Army projects which have been chosen to spread the funding throughout the country and to take care of the most critical needs. Most will involve the repair of roofs, kitchens, bathrooms, exterior siding, and some painting.

Homeowner Approach

Although each post has the discretion to determine what needs doing most, Colonel Tucker said that the Army is doing much the same as a homeowner would to achieve a "reasonable lifestyle. If this were my house and my money, would I make this investment? We are looking at quarters as if we were the owner and deciding which projects will improve their external atmosphere (the aesthetics) and will decrease the maintenance and energy costs. Our first priority is to fix what we've got, and the second is to bring them up to reasonable standards."

He gave the example of old kitchen and bathroom fixtures that still hold water, but are unsightly and have corroded piping. "*Appearance, sanitation,* and *inadequacy* are the three factors in our decisions."

Spouse Input Being Sought

When improvements are being made, such as increasing inadequate counter and cupboard space in older kitchens, the local commands are encouraged to ask for the assistance of wives living in the quarters. Colonel Tucker said this cooperation is a direct outgrowth of the Army Family Symposium last fall. He admitted that the symposium discussions echoed what his wife had said for years: "*Who* designed this kitchen?!" Now the Army is beginning to tap into the vast reservoir of "free" expertise.

Captain O'Connell mentioned the Navy's self-help programs in which occupants do some of the maintenance tasks they would do if they were homeowners. "An increasing fraction is willing. It reduces maintenance costs, helps to keep damage down, and teaches the residents how to do the basic repairs."

Energy Savings Help Contain Overall Costs

Since 1975, quarters residents have saved 17% per unit on utilities. Captain O'Connell attributed that sizable reduction to the Navy's investment in more energy efficient insulation and windows, but mostly to the occupants' awareness and cooperation. That is a considerable saving in the Navy's total housing budget ($700 million for Fiscal Year 1984 -- starting this September -- for 72,000 family units. This covers new construction as well as operations and maintenance, and comes out to be roughly $10,000 per family unit.)

Military Housing Overseas

All of the projects above have been within the United States. When I asked for long-range needs, the Army and Navy housing officers talked of the need to upgrade existing quarters overseas and to construct new ones. Political issues are obviously a factor in this arena, but the Services are aware of the need. After publicity last summer by General Frederick J. Kroesen, Commander in Chief, U. S. Army Europe and Seventh Army, on the lengthy wait for, and condition of, Army family housing in USAREUR, Congress voted $30 million in supplemental funding. It was used to do such basic repairs as lighting and ventilation for laundry rooms in housing complexes.

Colonel Tucker noted that two other factors have helped to ease the dissatisfaction with housing in Europe. A film has been produced to show to families with orders to USAREUR. It shows what the conditions are as realistically as possible so that families will be well informed about their upcoming move. Knowing what is ahead and how to prepare has made the transition easier for those headed overseas.

Also, the Housing Referral Offices are trying to give more personal assistance to those who must live on the economy. "Junior enlisted, E-4's and 5's who are overseas for the first time are receiving more help in their housing search. Providing someone who speaks the language and Army transportation are two ways the Housing Referral Office can help."

Colonel Tucker is very optimistic about the long range Army family housing situation. The decision to turn over responsibility for budget requests to each individual Service, instead of their all being funded through the Office of the Secretary of Defense, has allowed the Army to increase its commitment to housing starting this September. By 1990, the Army hopes to take care of the living quarters shortage.

Housing Referral Assistance

Technology is also helping families know what to expect at their new duty station. HOMES is a computer system now operational at Ft. Bragg, North Carolina, that allows an in-coming soldier to get an instant position on the housing waiting list and a forecast of when a unit will be available. Colonel Tucker hopes to see HOMES in place throughout the Army in 1984. He sees the instant information as a retention issue: it can lessen frustrations and eliminate inaccurate information. It will also be cost effective in that repairs can be planned during a unit's vacant period and speed up its being ready for the next family.

The Navy urges its members with orders to call the Housing Office at the new station to determine first hand what the situation is. If quarters are unavailable or the wait will be long, they can talk to the Housing Referral Office about sales or rentals in the civilian community. They can use the Autovon phone lines for calling the Housing Office and their sponsor. All Services urge greater use of the Sponsor Program to get personal assistance in the move.

"Customer satisfaction" is a phrase these senior housing officials mention over and over. As a result of the Army Family Symposium, Colonel Tucker added new sections in the courses given to career housing personnel. "People are people. We're trying to improve the number of good days, to remove as many irritants as possible." One example he cited was standardization of the check-in and check-out requirements "so that people will know what to expect."

Captain O'Connell echoed the need to help housing employees "know how important their interface with military families is." All agreed that when service people report in to the Housing Office at their new duty station, they are tired and often scared. (WHERE will I house my family?) Working with people in a stressful situation day after day calls for calm competence; the Army and Navy training centers for housing personnel are emphasizing this skill.

Variable Housing Allowance

The final question put to our senior housing officials and the Master Chief Petty Officer of the Navy concerned the impact of the Variable Housing Allowance (VHA). All felt that the *concept* is great: an allowance updated annually to fill the gap between one's BAQ (Basic Allowance for Quarters) and the *real* rent or homeowner's cost. As Master Chief Sanders pointed out, however, when Congress puts a percentage cap on it, then the gap is not filled. The allowance does not do what it was designed to do. "Right now, due to the cap, we are 15% behind. Navy families based in expensive urban areas are finding that their VHA does not really cover their costs. We are going to have to keep an eye on whether VHA can do the job or whether we will have to build more units."

VHA has made a noticeable difference to some military families, however. Colonel Tucker noted the fact that "VHA has opened up areas to our people that are adequate and affordable. It *can* be a vicious cycle because it also tends to establish that rent level. It has reduced the Army's requirement to build houses as we only build when there is insufficient affordable, adequate housing in the civilian community."

In some areas, social workers are noticing a decrease in spouse and child abuse. They attribute it to the VHA and the decrease in financial stress.

Two of the Navy representatives made an interesting plea for providing Navy housing for families when the men are at sea. Commander McGinty said that his wife's first reaction to his new job was, "Oh, now maybe you can get all the families with men at sea in housing." Master Chief Sanders saw the issue in terms of security. He said that the men felt that their families would be safer, and maintenance would be provided in quarters. "The housing lists still show a preference for Navy housing. There is very little fall-off with VHA except for senior enlisted and senior officers who want to get equity in a home."

The services are making some very important starts on housing improvements. But in the final analysis, once they have made them sanitary, safe, and energy efficient, *we* have to add the final improvement: we have to add the elements of *caring* and *community* that can change them from "just a bunch of houses."

Originally appeared as "Pits and Palaces: Military Housing Status Report," in <u>Family</u>, August 1983.

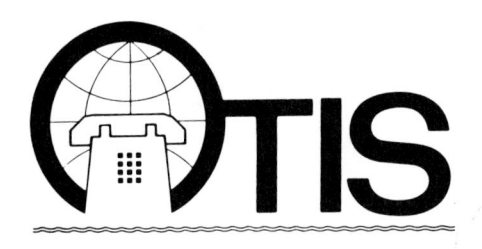

Overseas Living Information Service

OTIS does *not* want to be the Navy's best kept secret. If you are headed overseas, to Adak, Augsburg, Keflavik, Subic Bay, or any of the myriad of other exciting but unknown places to which the Navy sends its people, you have a wonderful resource at your fingertips. The Overseas Transfer Information Service (OTIS) has been established to help you make as smooth a move as possible.

Petty Officer First Class Samuel C. Salyer is the director of this innovative service which maintains up-to-date information on each of the 81 different countries to which Navy personnel move. He urges you to call OTIS *as soon as you receive orders* because "we can tell you where to start, the things that have to be done first in the limited time you have before going overseas -- especially if you are on short orders."

OTIS maintains a list of recent returnees from each station who are willing to share their impressions. OTIS also can send you a "Culturgram" on the country to which you are headed -- a four page synopsis of customs and courtesies, the lifestyle, government, and climate, plus suggested reading for in-depth information. The Personnel Office on each base has the OTIS information sheets on all overseas bases that cover such topics as: area entry approval, climate, hotels, housing (military and civilian), and a variety of other topics.

Books on moving overseas are also available in limited supply. *Good-bye, House* is sent to families with young children. *The USO Directory* of their facilities overseas is very helpful to singles and families. *Survival Kit for Overseas Living* is a basic primer for Americans living and working abroad. You may request these, as well as the super "Overseas Checklist" designed by OTIS, by calling collect: **(703) 694-8392 or 8393** between 8 a.m. and 4:30 p.m. EDT.

You may also write: **OTIS**
Navy Department (NMPC-62G)
Washington, D.C. 20370

Final words of wisdom are that military families would be wise to maintain an official copy of the birth certificate for *each* member of the family. (We tend to remember the kids and forget us adults.) You will need it to obtain a passport, and fast orders could catch you without the necessary papers to travel together.

OTIS recommends that as soon as you get orders overseas:

1) Go down to the Personnel Office and fill out the housing application to speed your position on the housing list.

2) Get your Dependent Entry Approval Message sent out.

3) Request a sponsor. (Even though a sponsor is mandatory, the actual assignment sometimes falls through the cracks.) They're *your* orders, so double check.

OTIS can do some referral on spouse employment possibilities (via the State Department Skills Bank and DODDS Schools). "We are not the final authority on Navy policy; however, we have access to the people who are," says Petty Officer Salyer. "We are a link for the folks who don't know what to do. If we can save people a little bit of money and give some peace of mind during their transition overseas, then it's all worthwhile."

Originally appeared as "Heading Overseas? Call Otis for Help," in
<u>Family</u>, *August 1983.*

17

Home, Sweet Trailer?

One out of every five new homes in the United States is a mobile home, and in areas of rapid growth, such as those around military bases with new units assigned, the proportion is even greater: more than half of the new housing permits are for mobile homes. Because housing costs are the largest single monthly budget item for most military personnel, mobile home living has become a considered option for thousands of military families.

Because such a decision is a complex issue, *Family* has been investigating the pros and cons, the facts and fiction, for the last nine months. On-site tours and interviews were conducted in civilian and military mobile home areas in Connecticut, Florida, Georgia, and Virginia. Interviews with bankers, fire and police officials, urban planners, county social workers, military housing and household goods transportation officers, mobile home salesmen and mobile home occupants have added information and misinformation. All have provided pieces of this difficult puzzle.

After careful evaluation, *Family* urges you to turn the usual decision-making process around. Most prospective mobile home (MH) renters or owners look at the MH unit first. It is easy to make an isolated, emotional decision this way, to lose the perspective of the desirability of MHs in general and your future location in specific.

Instead, start with an overview. Your time and lodging costs will be wise investments in your final decision. When you are given information as a prospective buyer or renter, be sure to clarify that you are receiving facts related to the *specific* unit or lot you are considering -- not *generalized* information that could be true (or false) about other units or locations. There are nine steps to avoid potential problems.

104   Financial and Housing Matters

#1:   Visit your base/post Housing Office.

Determine the availability of on-base/post mobile home spaces. What is the waiting list? The cost?

If you buy your own MH and install it on base, can you sell it on site when you leave to a military buyer, or must it be removed?

What are the average monthly utility costs for MHs in the area? Air conditioning in some areas averages $200+ a month, even after owners have applied reflective paint to the roof.

If base/post MH spaces are not available, ask if any civilian MH dealers, parks, or communities have been blacklisted by the Housing Office.

Use the Housing Office to see which MH parks and communities are listed -- that means that the owners have granted the Housing Office the right to inspect their facility -- a good protection for you. Prices are listed.

#2:   Check with your state Office of Consumer Affairs.

Their address is in your phone book in the blue section under State. Their information on dealers and parks will be invaluable to you. Some publish a handy guide with information on your rights and resource agencies, such as "The Mobile Home Lot Renter's Handbook for Prince William County, VA."

#3:   Visit the MH parks.

Before you even talk to dealers, look at what is offered. Value your first impressions -- keep notes, as the parks will blur in your mind. Is it neat? Are the roads paved?

Do the MHs seem well-spaced? The range of units visited by *Family* ran from four per acre (and all long-ways to the street) to a park that required only a minimum of five feet separation (and the units were all at odd angles to one another)! Remember that the American Planning Association (APA) recommends a maximum of seven, preferably six per gross acre. Think of the fire and privacy issues. In the crowded park, neighbors' children could be heard running inside their own MH from the living room of another with the windows closed and the air-conditioning running!

Is each MH on a concrete pad? Is there a concrete patio-entrance area? Are there common recreation areas and laundry facilities? Is there a mixture of MHs and small camper-size units? Are the MHs skirted? This is attractive and usually helps insulate pipes, but it is an added cost.

Is the park in the prevailing wind pattern of a major industry that spews out a corrosive? Your MH can deteriorate rapidly in these locations.

#4:   Talk to potential neighbors.

What pluses do they see in their MH unit and park? (This starts your conversation off on a positive foot and builds confidence.) What minuses?

Who owns the park? *Family* found many instances of local mayors or fire chiefs owning the parks -- often those in the worst condition. Occupants have little leverage to get improvements made if the owners "run the town." However, if you are already in such a situation, your base/post Housing Office and Legal Officer can give you some clout.

#5:   Talk to the community or park owners.

What is the lot cost? Does that cover trash collection? Are you assessed for services or utilities beyond the lot fee? What is the average monthly cost of water? Is there a security deposit? Sometimes it is the equivalent of two months' rent.

#6:   Talk to fire department officials.

Ask about the frequency and severity of fires in the MHs in the area. How far is the fire department from the MH parks you have looked at? Are there fire hydrants nearby, or does the fire department have to bring pumpers? Is it a volunteer fire department, or is there a full-time staff?

Fire continues to be the number one hazard for MHs. Fire officials in St. Marys (GA) warn against the use of *any* kerosene heater. (Underwriters have removed their approval from all varieties at this time.) People often use gasoline instead of kerosene, which turns the heaters into fire bombs. Electric heaters that don't shut off automatically when tipped over are another hazard.

A 12' x 70' MH with a wood paneling interior can burn down to the frame in 10 - 15 minutes. Kingsland (GA) Fire Chief Peebles says, "If we don't get to a trailer in the first five minutes, then it usually is a total loss." He does agree that he is seeing fewer fires now due to the new codes. "Most fires are in the older units." The "flash-over" that occurs in the ceiling spaces spreads the fire and smoke rapidly. MH dwellers frequently succumb to smoke inhalation before they can push out escape windows.

In the older MH units aluminum wiring was common. As the paneling was installed (often stapled), the wiring behind was broken. Most states now ban aluminum wiring in new models.

Overloading circuits is one of the worst problems, according to Chief Peebles. "The microwave, television, and radios are often put on one circuit." If there is an electric fire, shut the power off at the *outside breaker* to slow down the fire.

Check to see if your area is tornado or hurricane prone. Tie-downs are required to meet insurance requirements. Use of heavy cable anchored in concrete footings can lessen damage, but even so, MHs are more vulnerable than conventional homes in severe storms. Of last year's tornado victims, 45 percent were MH occupants.

#7:   **Talk to the police department.**

Is there a high level of crime in local MH parks? Burglary and family violence tend to be high in such areas. One county social worker interviewed said, "We know all of the trailer parks around. Each one has at least one 'famous' (or infamous) street or section."

#8:   **Talk to finance sources, if you are considering purchase.**

VA loans on MHs have dropped recently to their lowest point in more than two years: 14 percent for an MH without a lot, 13 1/2 percent on the combination of an MH and lot. The VA loan rate for a conventional home is 11 1/2 percent. One banker interviewed indicated that MH loans are not popular with banks because the home is movable and it *depreciates* in value. (The IRS puts MHs in the 10-Year Property Class for depreciation.)

Financing is available through FHA and VA and conventional loans; 15 years is common for single-wides, and 20 years for some double-wides. If you buy your MH with a VA loan, think carefully about allowing your buyer to assume your VA loan. You can't obtain another VA loan until your MH loan is paid off by your buyer, and if he defaults, the foreclosure goes on *your* record as the original mortgage holder.

Ask about ease of resale. Be aware that most MH owners feel lucky to be able to sell their MH for the assumption of their original loan. In other words, you usually don't make any money at sale time. You do have the income tax benefit on the mortgage interest, but you will have to weigh your monthly mortgage and utility bills plus set up costs against rental of a conventional apartment or house.

#9: Check with your city/county tax agency.

What fees and permits are required (zoning, electricity, sewage)? Remember the other costs above and beyond your MH unit: steps and concrete blocks, insurance, site rental or purchase, and property tax.

#10: Check with your base/post Household Goods Transportation Office.

Would you want to move your MH if you were to purchase one? Mrs. Grace Vickroy, the Personal Property Officer at NSB Kings Bay (GA), told *Family*, "Every time a Navy man comes into our office wanting to move an MH, we kind of shudder. There are just more problems than positives." Marlene Stewart, a shipment clerk at Kings Bay, and an Air Force wife for 24 years, echoed Mrs. Vickroy's concerns. "Excess costs are collected from military members on almost all MH moves. Really heavy furniture has to be moved out of your MH before the move because of the weight of the structure. The new well-built ones are especially heavy.

"The military does not pay to move any outside equipment such as fences, blocks, steps, or a utility shed. Long distance moves are very hard on MHs -- the wear and tear is great. Some states will not allow 80' trailers (and some even 70') to pass through on their highways, nor to be set up. Therefore, they have to be re-routed, which is expensive. The military pays purely on a rank and miles equation." Her personal reaction was, "I would discourage a military family from buying a mobile home."

Questions for Dealers

If purchase (or rental) of an MH still seems like a good idea to you, look at dealers and units with the following questions.

How long has a specific dealer been doing business in the area, and what is his or her reputation? You can ask your local Chamber of Commerce, the Office of Consumer Affairs, and local banks. MH dealerships come and go with considerable speed. Who will back up a service warranty if your dealer leaves town in a hurry?

Is your dealer guaranteeing you a space in the MH park of your choice? Some parks and dealers are linked. When you get ready to sell, can you sell it yourself, or must you go through the park owner if the MH is to remain on your space? Get it in writing!

What is the fire retardation level? Check the certificate. Are there smoke detectors near the bedrooms? Is formaldehyde an ingredient in the insulation? The fumes generated by this substance, even when the new MH is not on fire, have caused occupants to be terribly sick -- to the extent that they have had to leave, rent an apartment and wait for legal action for reimbursement of their investment.

Are appliances included? If so, are they quality brands, or would you be better off buying your own?

Are furniture and carpeting included? If so, what is the quality? Often these items are of very low quality, and when you explore taking the unit minus these, the dealer will take very little off the sales price.

Look at the layout very carefully. Many floorplans have bedrooms at the two ends. Children are separated from their parents -- a cause for concern in case of fire. Is there enough storage space?

A dealer will tend to urge you to buy an MH right off the lot with the pitch that you know what you are getting and you can have it right away. Remember that he or she has invested in that unit and wants to get the money out of it as soon as possible. Are you willing to compromise and go with fewer options?

Options you might want if they fit your budget:

• Sheetrock paneling (gypsum dry wall) -- it doesn't burn as rapidly as the wood paneling and can be a light color, which increases your sense of space.

• Storm windows and doors, double insulation and a heat pump. They really pay for themselves in savings on your utility bills.

• A 30-gallon hot water heater. The standard 20 gallon heater is not enough for children's baths and dishes.

• A ceiling fan to disperse heat and air conditioning.

• Cathedral ceilings -- they give a real sense of height.

• A covered entry. You could add this as part of your entry steps -- or at least add a piece of rain gutter above the door.

Before signing a lease or purchase contract, take it to your base/post Legal Office. The Veterans Administration has taken legal action against MH dealers who inflated sales lot prices with appliances and furnishing that were not delivered. Your legal office can alert you to potential discrepancies.

Also before signing, have a firm agreement with the park in which you will locate. Know the regulations, fees, and provisions.

MH owners recommend using a careful check-list prior to accepting a unit -- and refuse to accept it until all things are right. They tell of toilet tank tops not fitting and not being able to get one in the succeeding four years!

Mobile Home Spaces on Military Installations

MH spaces on military installations offer the advantages of rental rates lower than those in the civilian community, shorter commuting distances, and nearby fire and police protection. The Department of Defense has requested funds for the 1986 housing budget to build more than 300 MH spaces. Additionally, each Service is handling the provision of MH sites differently. The Army has conducted an opinion survey which indicates the amount of interest in MH living if on-post spaces were to be available.

According to Jerome Kidd, Acting Chief of the Army Management Division (Office of Assistant Chief of Engineers), "The Army leadership is looking for all sorts of innovative ways to solve the housing deficit. Major commands have been requested to apply some dollars to fix up their existing MH parks."

Richard Hibbert, of the Naval Facilities Engineering Command, explained the Navy's situation. "The Navy created 1400 MH spaces between 1971 - 74, but now lets each base decide whether to ask for any more sites. There are waiting lists at most bases, so you cannot count on moving right in. The costs for a double move are prohibitive.

"In urban areas, like San Francisco and San Diego, where lands costs the most, we are torn about putting such expensive land to temporary use (i.e. MH spaces). And yet, people need low cost options there the most."

Under the Model Installation program, the Department of Defense has given 16 - 18 bases from all of the Services the option to do what they can to meet the needs of military members and build morale as quickly as possible. Among the innovations being considered are MH exchange programs and leasing land on base to a civilian contractor for the construction of MH spaces.

Your decision to rent or buy an MH narrow to the basic questions of *availability* and *affordability* of other housing options, and *safety*. *Family's* general assessment is that where other housing is available, MHs generally are not attractive options from the standpoints of finances,

Financial and Housing Matters

safety, and general environment. Where military sites are available, safe spacing is provided, and your intent is to sell on departure, then a fairly new model MH is worth your consideration.

Definition:

Manufactured Housing: Technically all factory-built units that can be moved to a site come under this definition, but in common usage, this term refers to those units that are attached to permanent foundations. Often requirements are that they be "ground set" and their siding and roofing materials and design are similar to conventional "stick-built" or "site-built" homes.

ARMY MOBILE HOME SPACES
as of July 1985

Location	Spaces
Fort Rucker, AL	46
Yuma Proving Ground, AZ	8
Camp Roberts, CA	24
Fort Irwin, CA	50
Rocky Mt. Arsenal, CO	4
Dover Armament R&D, DE	5
Hunter AR Airfield, GA	23
Fort Stewart & HQ 24 Inf., GA	45
Stewart Subpost, GA	7
Fort Benjamin Harrison, IN	100
Fort Polk, LA	398
Fort Devens, MA	30
Aberdeen Proving Ground, MD	44
Fort George G. Meade, MD	33
Fort Dix, NJ	22
Fort Monmouth, NJ	24
Fort Wadsworth, NY	9
Fort Indiantown Gap, PA	33
Fort Eustis, VA	32
Fort A.P. Hill, VA	10
Fort Pickett Army Gar., VA	12
Pedricktown, VA	5
Fort McCoy, WI	16
TOTAL	980

For Fiscal Year 1986, the Army has tentative plans to add 334 more spaces.

Mobile Homes (MH): one form of manufactured housing built on a chassis. They are transportable units that sit on temporary supports and can, at least in theory, be moved to another location. The construction of these units is governed by the Department of Housing and Urban Development (HUD) Codes.

NAVY MOBILE HOME SPACES
as of September 1984

Location	Spaces
NAVACAD Annapolis, MD	16
NTC Bainbridge, MD	68
NAS Brunswick, ME	20
NAS Cecil Field, FL	32
NWC Charleston, SC	60
NAS Chase Field, TX	20
MSGA Chesapeake, VA	59
NWC China Lake, CA	22
NAS Corpus Christi, TX	28
NWS Earle, NJ	8
NRC Forest Park, IL	11
NAS Glenview, IL	65
PWC Great Lakes, IL	156
NCBC Gulfport, MS	25
NOS Indian Head, MD	52
NAS Jacksonville, FL	36
NRS Jim Creek OSO, WA	2
NAS Key West, FL	42
AIRENGCEN Lakehurst, NJ	54
NS Mayport, FL	50
NAS Memphis, TN	50
NAS Miramar, CA	108
NSB New London, CT	105
NS New York, NY	24
NETC Newport, RI	40
NAS Oceana, VA	96
PWC Pensacola, FL	52
NSY Philadelphia, PA	36
NCBC Port Hueneme, CA	20
ASTRO GRB Rosemont, MN	6
NAVADMINU Scotia, NY	7
NSG Thurmont, MD	18
NWS Yorktown, VA	40
TOTAL	1,418

Make sure your dealer can produce the HUD certificate. Many dealers prefer the term "manufactured housing" to mobile home or trailer because less stigma is attached, and in some cases, community zoning permits their placement in residential areas not open to mobile homes (MH). But unscrupulous dealers can give prospective clients information about "manufactured housing" that is not true of MHs.

Definitions:

Mobile Home Community: An MH development with special facilities for common use by the occupants (e.g., recreational buildings, laundries, and open spaces).

Mobile Home Park: A parcel of land under single ownership on which two or more MHs are occupied as residences.

Mobile Home Subdivision: Lots which are sold for residential MHs.

Maximum Density Limitations: According to the APA (American Planning Association) study, "Regulating Mobile Homes" (1981), they propose that the *maximum density* in MH areas "not exceed seven units per gross acre for detached single-family dwellings' -- i.e., 6,223 square feet. "Gross acreage" is all the area within property boundaries, including common open space, streets, management and community buildings, as well as MHs.

*Definitions taken from "Regulating Mobile Homes," American Planning Association.

MARINE CORPS MOBILE HOME SPACES

Location	Spaces
MCLB Albany, GA	20
MCLB Barstow, CA (inactive)	17
MCAS Beaufort, SC	120
MCB Lejeune, NC	112
MCAS Camp Pendleton, CA (includes MCAS El Toro, CA)	..148
MCAS Cherry Point, NC	76
MCRD Parris Island, SC	100
MCDEC Quantico, VA (outdated)	31
TOTAL	624

There are tentative plans to add 300 new spaces in Fiscal Year 1987, including 100 more at Camp Pendleton and 75 at Camp Lejeune.

AIR FORCE MOBILE HOME SPACES

Location	Spaces
Eielson AFB, AK	84
Robins AFB, GA	100
Wright-Patterson AFB, OH	80
Biancur Field, FL	9
Edwards AFB, CA	164
Eglin AFB, FL	227
Hanscom AFB, MA	84
Chanute AFB, IL	100
Keesler AFB, MS	51
Laughlin AFB, TX	54
Lowry AFB, CO	220
Vance AFB, OK	12
Andrews AFB, MD	212
Charleston AFB, SC	75
McGuire AFB, NJ	176
Scott AFB, IL	105
Travis AFB, CA	50
Beale AFB, CA	192
Grand Forks AFB, ND	9
Griffiss AFB, NY	50
K.I. Sawyer AFB, MI	199
Malmstrom AFB, MT	64
Minot AFB, ND	164
Pease AFB, NH	50
Vandenberg AFB, CA	172
Peterson AFB, CO	50
Avon Park AFR, FL	10
Cannon AFB, NM	63
Davis Monthan AFB, AZ	125
England AFB, LA	48
Ft. Fisher AFS, NC	12
Gila Bend AFAF, AZ	31
Holloman AFB, NM	78
Indian Springs AFAF, NV	23
Langley AFB, VA	28
MacDill AFB, FL	100
Makah AFS, WA	22
Moody AFB, GA	49
Myrtle Beach AFB, SC	65
Nellis AFB, NV	100
Seymour Johnson AFB, NC	45
TOTAL	3,552

114   Financial and Housing Matters

For further information, call the toll-free Navy Information tape:

1-800-367-6289 (in VA 1-800-572-4052). Ask for tape #203: "Mobile Home Purchases and Location."

Communities wishing to publish their own handbooks may contact: Office of Consumer Affairs, Prince William County, 15960 Cardinal Dr., Woodbridge, VA 22191. Theirs is a good prototype.

****

FOLLOW THAT STORY

In the September 1985 issue of *Family*, I wrote an article on the pros and cons of trailer ownership. After *Family* went to press, there was a hurricane in the Southeastern United States that brought tragedy to military mobile home owners. Hurricane Elena hit over the Labor Day weekend, doing more than $1 billion of damage, including destroying one mobile home park in Pascagoula, MS in which many USS SIMON LAKE families were located. More than 250 mobile homes were demolished -- only 12 were left standing.

As the submarine tender had only recently left Naval Submarine Base Kings Bay, Georgia, the USO there coordinated the relief effort, collecting canned food and clothing for crew families and delivering it to them.

I urge that mobile home owners take seriously my recommendation that you find out if the area in which you propose to live is tornado or hurricane country.

****

Readers should be aware that the charts listing the mobile home spaces by Service were accurate in 1985. At that time, there was no Department of Defense-wide list of mobile home spaces on military installations and I went to great effort to compile one. You should check your own installation for accuracy of the figures given above.

Appeared originally as "Home, Sweet Trailer?" in <u>Family</u>, September 1985 and as "Follow that Story,", in <u>Family</u>, December 1985.

Section IV

Family Support Services

Military Safety Nets

Military families are a lot like tight rope walkers. As long as everything is in balance and under control, they can be top performers. They learn to check their equipment, determine that their wire is appropriately connected, and know their own capabilities at any given point in time. But seasoned performers as well as novices need safety nets, that is, programs to help cope with our unique, mobile, and highly stressful lifestyle.

Lately we have been seeing improvements in programs and policies that impact on military families. Many attribute this betterment to the heightened public and military awareness following the suicide of 13-year-old Danny Holley in August, 1984. Certainly, some of the holes in the system received attention as a result, but many of the improvements had been started at grass roots levels well before then.

In fact, over the last seven years, all of the Services have worked at improving their safety nets for military members and their families. Since the Navy Family Awareness Conference in 1978, followed closely by the Army and Air Force symposia, each of the Services has consolidated and enhanced its support systems. Improved information and referrals, plus additional in-house short term counseling, have been made available at practically all major installations.

Family Service/Support Centers

Although called by different names, the Navy and Marine Corps Family Service Centers, the Air Force Family Support Centers, and Army Community Services provide the first layer of safety nets. While they offer crisis assistance, they prefer to offer long range educational workshops to help individuals develop the skills necessary to thrive on challenge. Workshops on financial planning, job skills, and better parenting now abound at most installations. However, those who have developed these programs have been greatly disappointed by the turnout.

Survey Needs and Scheduling for Success

For example, at the Naval Submarine Base Kings Bay, GA, the variety of workshops provided by the Family Service Center (FSC) over the last couple of years has resembled a candy store -- everything any body could possibly want. But only two or three participants were showing up per offering. In order to determine how the FSC and other service-providers on base, such as Recreation Services and the chaplains, could better meet the needs of singles and families, the local chapter of the Navy Wives Club of America conducted a survey. They made copies available all over the base, and went door-to-door to contact everybody in base housing.

The results have helped the FSC and others tailor their topics to meet the interests expressed, and to schedule them on base (where they can be reached easily) at suitable times. For example, they found that many workshops had been scheduled to start before the kindergarten bus picked up children in housing, which made it impossible for military wives to attend. So child care is now often provided by hiring a sitter specifically for each session; the provision of a sitter has been a key to attendance.

For the military member, a good case has to be made that the entire family benefits from participation in the programs offered. There are many husbands who want to keep their wives "separate from" the military. Some reason that they can "keep them caged and pure," and others fear that they might learn their true pay scale or duty schedule.

Partnership and Responsibilities of Military Families

Awareness of services offered is a two-way street. Not only should program providers do their best to get the word out, but in the final analysis, military family members have a responsibility. We must play an active role in our own development, our own on-going training for our lifestyle by taking advantage of the information and courses the Services provide.

General John A. Wickham, Jr., Chief of Staff of the U. S. Army, has talked of the "partnership" that the Army has with its families. That is another way of expressing the two-sided responsibilities. The Army has tackled its role of providing a safety net with vigor. Under the Army Family Action Plan, a number of innovative programs have been initiated to improve military family life.

Army Innovations

One recent one that has helped a great deal with frequent moves is the security deposit waiver/reduction programs at Fort Bragg, NC; Fort Belvoir, VA; Fort Campbell, KY; Fort Hood, TX; Fort Polk, LA; Fort Richardson, AK; Fort Jackson, SC; and the 200 cities in Georgia served by Atlanta Gas and Light Company. Military families used to be required to pay a high utility deposit before service would be provided. Under this program, this has been eliminated altogether or greatly reduced in a variety of ways. For example, in lieu of a deposit, the Atlanta firm will accept a letter from one's last gas or electric company stating that a good payment record has been maintained. For those at Fort Benning, Fort Stewart, Moody AFB, and Warner-Robins AFB (GA), this can be a great savings.

Direct-Deposit and Sure-Pay

Two other innovative programs established by the Services to aid members and their families financially are direct-deposit (given different names by each Service) and the use of credit cards in the exchanges. While some may argue that the direct-deposit of pay forces a service member to establish a banking account (and, therefore, may not be a desirable plan), the Services argue that their programs ensure that monies will be available on payday wherever the member goes. Members *should* be able to write checks for rent, purchase of food in the commissary, or cash (up to $100 maximum per day through the exchange cashier). The "catch" may be the acceptability of a check written on an out-of-town account by a member in transit or at a new duty station for a civilian landlord or merchant.

Lt. Col. George Sumrall of the Army Compensation Office feels that the benefits of the Army's "Sure-Pay" system outweigh any difficulties. "Sure-Pay" remains an option for those who joined the Army before September 30, 1985. For those joining after that date, it is mandatory. An Army survey found that 81 percent of active duty soldiers worldwide have access to a "free" checking account (no minimum balance required) at their home post. When moving on Permanent Change of Station (OCS) orders, soldiers can draw a Treasury check or Traveler's checks (free of charge) for PCS costs. If they choose to close out a previous bank account, they can convert the money to Traveler's checks as well, if they worry about their old bank's check being unacceptable or put on "hold" in their new location.

Lt. Col. Sumrall sees "Sure-Pay" as a great advantage in the event of emergency mobilization of a unit. The money would go, as usual, to the soldier's bank account, not to the field with the unit. He also encourages military members to use allotments for a specified amount per month to his/her spouse for basic household expenses, car purchase, life insurance, and savings. A potential "hole" for the spouse continues to exist if the soldier does not have pay sent to a joint account (or does not give his/her spouse Power of Attorney) -- the Army does not require soldiers to do either.

Credit Cards in Exchanges

During 1986, all of the Services began accepting major credit cards in exchanges in the continental United States and overseas. For those who can make wise use of the credit extended, this allows tax-free purchases of big items at the good prices offered by the Service exchange systems.

Social, Emotional, and Cultural Support Programs

Along with financial safety net provisions, the Services and civilian care providers are developing programs to serve military families on social, emotional, and cultural levels. The Air Force Family Support Center in Yokota, Japan, offers classes for Japanese- and Korean-born spouses taught in their native languages and English and Japanese for the English-speaking, plus an assortment of culture-awareness seminars, walking tours and restaurant ventures to introduce singles and families to their new environment.

In Baumholder, Frankfurt, and Hanau, Germany, the USO has opened Women's Centers in easily accessible locations. Based on the premise that women need a place where they can find help, information, support, and relaxation, the centers' programs address the needs of all women -- enlisted or officers' wives, soldiers, or civilians -- and in an environment where children are also welcome.

Elke Dresdow, a USO program manager, points out in the *USO News* that these centers are particularly important for young mothers who need a place to meet new friends like themselves. One very basic service provided is a place to nurse their babies instead of having to use restroom facilities at the military shopping center.

Fort Stewart Spouse Center

Spouse Centers can be valuable at Stateside posts or bases as well. Fort Stewart, GA, is located about 45 minutes from Savannah, outside the small community of Hinesville. The Spouse Center, formed in April 1984, is visible from the front gate of the post. When *Family* visited the center last year, Pat Fellman, the director, explained that it had been modeled on Reynolds House at Fort Hood, TX. However, Reynolds House has a paid staff, while Pat and all of her workers are volunteers.

Military Safety Nets   121

As an Army wife for 18 years, with five children ages 10 - 23, Pat had been mayor for her post housing area. When the Quality of Life Coordinator, Pat Sharp, gave her the materials on Reynolds House, she immediately saw the possibilities for Fort Stewart.

The programs include one structured offering per day. Because wives often bring in handiwork to work on while there, impromptu lessons occur in knitting, crocheting, etc. Unit coffees are also held at the center. Other centers on post are so full with regularly scheduled meetings that the Spouse Center serves an important function. Now that the Teen Center has moved to a new facility, it is available in the evenings for this purpose, as well as during the day.

Pat makes the point that the center is a comfortable spot for wives to be -- both physically and socially. "You would be surprised at the number of men who don't want their wives in a club, and a club is an expensive place for wives' groups to meet because they can't bring their own food." Unit coffees bring in about 20 wives per meeting, and the Center serves approximately 600 women per month. Army Community Services (ACS) funds the center as a part of its Outreach and Relocation program. "Because the *place* existed, the only major costs have been coffee, cookies, and punch," says Pat.

Some of the workshops do require more funding, and ACS or the chaplain sponsors these. "But by and large, "we have no trouble getting volunteer instructors. Everyone who walks through the door wants to help. We're big on crafts (over 100 people showed up for wreath-making!), informational sessions (such as CPR, child abuse and molestation -- a puppet show sponsored by the Family Advocacy Program, and classes by Cooperative Extension agents), and Jazzercise three times a week."

The center is a place for a wife to wait if she rides in from one of the many surrounding trailer parks with her husband for a medical appointment or for shopping at the exchange or commissary. Most young wives cannot find employment in the rural area around the post, and their husbands are in the field five to seven months a year. The Spouse Center is a place to be.

Support Staffing Problems

What are the holes or weak spots in our safety nets? The ratio of mental health providers (psychologists, social workers, etc.) to active duty military members varies widely by Service. In the Army, the ratio is 1:1200. The Air Force ratio is 1:2400. The Navy and Marine Corps have

1:8900. If you add family members to these active duty numbers, you can begin to appreciate the magnitude of the problem.

Manpower is the biggest hole in our safety nets today. As volunteers who ran many of the helping organizations in years past have moved into the full-time paid workforce, their loss has been felt deeply. Many organizations do not have even one salaried employee to provide continuity of service to clients or support for volunteer efforts. Of the 3,000 chapters of the American Red Cross across the United States, over half are run entirely by volunteers. Not even a salaried secretary keeps the office on an even keel.

Rear Admiral Ralph H. Carnahan, USN (Ret.), Vice President of Navy Relief Society, told *Family* last year that 20 of the 51 auxiliaries are run totally by volunteers. Only 31 locations have salaried directors. On 95 of the larger ships in the Atlantic and Pacific, shipboard offices, staffed by active duty personnel, serve crew members. The result is that where no permanent director exists, volunteers cope, with phone contact to the nearest auxiliary or headquarters, with crisis services only. Little prevention work gets done. Therefore, the crisis cycle never ends.

There is a great need for more permanent paid support jobs to augment those in volunteer positions. The Spouse Center at Fort Stewart makes a superb contribution to Army families through its developmental and educational programs because the Quality of Life Coordinator and the ACS Volunteer Chairman, with Command support, provide the ongoing official support necessary. Other care-providing organizations need to learn from the success of this model.

Originally appeared as "Military Safety Nets," in Family, *June 1986.*

19

Teenage Military Brides:
It Isn't Easy Being Young!

"Whatever you do, don't call my parents. They won't come!" said a teenage submarine wife worried about who would care for her children after emergency surgery. (Her husband was on patrol.) She was right; her parents wouldn't come. "She married against our wishes. It's her problem."

Today's military has more married young people than ever before. "Exact numbers are hard to come by," says Shauna Whitworth, Research Director of the Military Family Resource Center (MFRC). "The most recent figures (September 1982) show 20,909 adolescent military personnel who are married. Adolescents are those 19 and under, and those married represent one percent of the total uniformed personnel. However, the number of teenage military wives is probably considerably higher than this because there is a 2.4 year discrepancy between the ages of American husbands and wives. We can presume at least this many other teens could be married to older personnel."

Military Marketing puts these numbers in a new light: 11.4 % of the wives of active duty military are teenagers. They usually are married to junior enlisted personnel whose pay scales were designed for single members. Separation from their husband for short or long periods of time is almost guaranteed. The early years for a service member are often the most mobile, with training in various locations and the the first major assignment, which usually requires sea duty for the Navy or field duty for other Services.

Military housing is not available to those in rates E-1 to E-4 with under two years' service (except in rare instances). These young people usually must rent in marginal areas -- marginal in quality and safety, and

124   Family Support Services

often at some distance from the base or post. The husband usually requires the car to get to work daily so his wife is left in the trailer park or apartment area, unable to use military facilities such as the clinic, commissary, or family service center. Many do not have a phone and few get a local newspaper daily.

Success Stories

As *Family* interviewed young wives and those who provide services to military families, looking for characteristics of this age group and programs designed to assist them, isolation was the loudest common denominator. The negative seem to outweigh the positives until one talks with a Pattie Brown, Beth Carey, or Jan McDaniel.

This trio was busy planning some upcoming activities at the USO Outreach Center at Bellevue Navy Housing (Washington, D.C.) when I popped in on my way to visit the Time Out program. Pattie, who was the USO Volunteer of the Month in March, has just turned 20, is expecting her second child, and was enjoying her hour and a half time out from her year old daughter. Married to a 20-year-old member of the Navy Ceremonial Guard, she admitted, "I still have $60 phone bills; it's my first time away from home." (She had lived at home during her husband's boot camp.) "Most of the men in the Guard are real young, 18 - 20, though the range is 17 - 25. One young wife, who's 16, has gone home to finish high school. She found it hard to do here."

Beth Carey married at 18 and went to Korea with her Navy husband at the age of 20. "You have to grow up fast, but I think I was well prepared for the experience. I wanted to travel. I had dated West Point cadets -- I was a country girl." Even with this positive outlook, she remembers her own huge phone bills. "There is a tendency to call Mom when you haven't made new friends yet."

Jan McDaniel, the Center Manager of USO Outreach, was celebrating her tenth wedding anniversary when we talked -- at age 27. As she thought about the occupants of the 400 units at Bellevue, she commented: "It has become a closely-knit community. People know their neighbors -- especially in the summer! Everybody's outside...kids, barbecuing. You live so close you have to know your neighbors!" Most who live at Bellevue are Marine and Navy E-5's and below. The housing is classified as substandard, meaning it does not meet the space requirements for those more senior, so many junior enlisted rate housing in this area where most families are hard pressed to find affordable rentals. "The young people are more active in our community than the older women. They're more willing to go meet their neighbors, make friends, and bring their two children to our meetings. They're more willing to help. The majority of my volunteers are very young. I think they're lonely. Some young Marine wives go home when their husbands in the Drum and Bugle Corps go on trips."

Child Development Programs

But more are staying and becoming involved in community programs which allow them to help their neighbors while learning and making friends themselves. One such pilot project is High Scope, which is supported by the Naval District Washington Family Service Center at Anacostia Naval Station. The Deputy Director, Dorothy Benford, is enthusiastic about the quality of the two weeks of training in child development that the volunteers receive from the Ypsilanti (MI) program. After their training, the volunteers become Home Visitors, each assigned to up to three families. They share with the parents what they have learned about a child's needs at certain ages, and become a friendly resource for parents who are often far away from their own families. Their first group of volunteers trained last November and began their home visits in March. By October, Mrs. Benford hopes to train a second group of volunteers and to extend their services to Bolling Air Force Base next door.

Other military communities have participated in the High Scope program, and have found that some of their original parents, who had been "at risk" due to age, finances, or emotional stress when first assigned a Home Visitor, have become volunteers themselves. They know how much they were helped, and now want to reciprocate. (**Pass It On!**)

The Bellevue High Scope volunteers, however, have added their own dimension to the program. Eager to share what they have already learned with a larger number than they can serve as Home Visitors, they have started a weekly program for children ages six months to five years. Called Time Out, it is designed to give mothers an hour and a half of their own on Wednesday mornings -- absolutely free. They serve single military parents as well as couples.

Valerie Shusko, a Marine wife from Bellevue, has served as the coordinator. The program is offered in eight-week sections. Parents signed up through the Family Service Center. "We started Time Out because we were really sorry to see our training end. I had the job of recruiting the volunteers. Four of us are neighbors. Some were new to the community, so this was their way of meeting people. All of us have become very close friends. We want to recruit more volunteers so that we can serve more people." The volunteers are not far from teenage themselves. They understand well the stresses special to young couples and have enjoyed the opportunity to learn how to parent their own children more effectively.

Welcome, Baby Programs

A similar program that draws on military wives to assist young mothers far from home is Welcome, Baby. Betty Jones, the Program Director of the Navy Family Service Center at Charleston (SC), describes it as "a formal program to do what many captains' and chiefs' wives did informally when our Service was smaller." Volunteers at the Charleston Naval Hospital make contact with mothers age 21 and under the day after their baby is born. They also see all mothers of a first baby, all wives with a husband deployed when the baby arrives, and all teenage wives and dependents who have given birth.

"The teenage military wife needs the most emotional support," says Betty. "She is isolated from her own family and usually doesn't know Navy life well yet. Our volunteer visits her for a half hour or more, lets her know she is there as a friend for support, gives her information on referral services, and talks about any concerns she might have. We work a lot with the Navy Relief Visiting Nurse, who also tries to see all first time mothers in the hospital to talk feeding and bathing procedures.

"The volunteer then calls two days after the new mother goes home and two weeks later. Although the volunteer sees her only at the hospital, making no home visits, she does give her phone number to the mother. We follow up for a year by sending "Amanda the Panda" pamphlets on the baby's developmental stages. Half of our volunteers are officers' wives and half enlisted wives. Several are former recipients of this care." (**Pass It On!**)

The Welcome, Baby program spread to Portsmouth Naval Hospital this spring. *The average age of the mothers of the 400 babies born there per month is 19!*

Additional Mothering Workshops

Because the response in Charleston has been so favorable, a brand new offering has been added: the Mothering Workshop. The participants bring their children and discuss parenting skills in eight weekly sessions.

Employment Assistance

Although many teenage wives feel that becoming a mother makes them an adult, in their own eyes and those of their parents and the community, others choose to seek adulthood through employment. Each of the Services now offers some spouse employment assistance through family service centers ("family support centers" in the Air Force and Army Community Services in the Army). Betty Jones in Charleston related that 85 wives had shown up for the three day workshop on employment in February. At the Air Force Military Spouse Skills and Resource Center, Bolling AFB, Washington, D.C., where spouses of all ages are assisted in their search for employment, Kim Reynolds commented: "usually the very young wives are harder to place because they have no work history. But wives of E-5's and under automatically qualify for Pell Grant assistance if they take a full time undergraduate college program. Our office would help them find part-time work if they wanted to supplement their income while studying."

Programs Specifically Targeted for Teenage Wives

While these programs have not been targeted specifically for teenage wives, they have served primarily this age group. At the U.S. Army Field Station in Augsburg, Germany, the first Junior Enlisted Spouse's Workshop (E-1 through E-4) was given in April 1983. Coordinated by Chaplain Max D. Sullivan and funded by the Officers' Wives' Club, the free workshop included three days of training in decision-making and leadership skills, the chance to make friends, and an opportunity to organize an on-going group to meet their needs. All this plus free child care, transportation, and a final banquet with their husbands!

Most who attended were age 16 - 19, and often were not command-sponsored. Harriet Howe, Director of Special Projects at MFRC, described the results. "Many desperately needed to be hooked into the military system. They were especially isolated overseas. For the first group, the organizers found 20 though unit rosters. Folks had to go out and pick them up to bring them to the seminar. By the end of three days, it was amazing how far they had come; all actively hooked into the system and have continued their affiliation."

How to find these young wives in order to make them aware of the many services available to them is the number one problem. One way is the informal approach. Shauna Whitworth, at MFRC, remembers her days as an Armed Services YMCA worker on a major Marine Corps station. (She wrote her master's thesis on families of Marine E-1 -- E-3's.) She urges those of us who are even the slightest bit older to be aware and to be open to talking to young wives and their children. "Teen wives are very anxious to do their job of mothering well. I haven't met an adolescent parent who doesn't want to be a good parent. They're eager to learn. They observe the world carefully -- and observe others -- so all of you are modeling for them. When they see you in the commissary or at the clinic, they're watching to see what you buy, how you treat your children."

She also urges teenage wives to "talk to people in commissary lines. Older people will react well to questions about food. Talk to other people where you live. Get more than one friend so that you are not left alone when one friend receives orders and moves. There are lots of lonely people your age."

Shauna also reminds young couples that almost every community near military installations has helping groups above and beyond the family service centers. Churches, YMCAs, USO centers, and American Red Cross chapters have courses and services to help them. "Often the connecting links are missing, so you must reach out."

Finding Young Couples and Serving Them

A number of programs are trying to forge those links. Many involve going door-to-door in military housing or an area off base where many junior enlisted couples live. At Bellevue Navy Housing, volunteers go door-to-door delivering flyers on programs sponsored by the USO and the FSC. Many are offered in the evening so that husbands can attend as well as their wives (babysitting is provided). The topics range from budgeting, eating right on a budget (complete with a cooking demonstration by an Air Force nutritionist), basic insurance, a three-part marital series: Spouse Communication, Conflict-Management in Marriage, and Decision-Making, and a three-part parenting series: The Developing Child, Tools for Talking with Your Children, and Disciplining Your Child (What Works!). Kathy Lunsford, the Anacostia FSC Program Coordinator, says these family life evenings are open to all military service families.

Their three-part series on assertiveness and building self-esteem is also a favorite of Bobbie Brenton's, the Housing Outreach Coordinator at the Norfolk Navy Family Services Center (FSC). "We call ours, 'How to Make the Navy Work for You' and 'TEAM: To Enrich and Appreciate Myself.' These workshops help wives feel confident enough to go out and get things done for themselves. We also help young wives learn how to make friends. After living in their own hometown for 18 years, knowing everyone, it's hard to start in a new area."

Bobbie is an enthusiastic admirer of teenage military wives: "I love them! They're young, spirited, and willing to accept change. I like to work with them because we can set a tone and pattern with them that will be positive."

She is working in two housing areas to ensure that each new resident will be greeted by one neighbor who knows her way around, and will be invited to at least one coffee. The idea is to increase her likelihood of making good friends because she will have more to choose from.

Jon Parry, the Senior Social Worker at the Norfolk FSC, emphasizes the need to reach out and find young wives where they live. "We don't see many; they must come voluntarily. The Red Cross sees them only in their health and welfare referral checks. These occur because they have trouble maintaining contact with their husbands at sea. Often they are not skilled at words -- expressing intimacy in writing to keep relationships alive."

Jon finds this age group the least likely to use formal services. They tend to be crisis clients. He used to be a community worker in East Ocean View, "a nesting area for the young military...many one bedroom apartments with landlords who aren't selective. Many seemed not really connected to anyone. They often had had short courtships and were married two to three weeks before the ship deployed."

The Wives' Club of the LPH GUADALCANAL, a helicopter carrier, has tried to reach the young wives of their crew by holding their meetings at the Armed Service YMCA in East Ocean View. They hope that by being close, they can reach those who usually would not participate.

Training and Information Opportunities

Jon's description of many teenage couples as "impulsive versus experienced in planning," is echoed by Kay Standish, Executive Director of the D.C. Auxiliary of Navy Relief. She urges young couples to take advantage of all of the budget planning sessions provided by Navy Relief, ACS, and the family service centers.

Dr. Ann O'Keefe, Head of the Navy Family Support Program, urges young wives to get all of the free training and assistance they can. The Ombudsman, Navy Relief, Red Cross, or hotline training courses are a great way to learn what services are available. She thinks a young husband should be counseled by his seniors on the value of such opportunities to learn and to meet appropriate friends. The tendency to "cage" one's young wife, to keep her separate from his military life, is not a protection in the long run.

They Will Pass It On!

These young military wives need to feel a part of the larger military family community, to be drawn in and supported in the transition from adolescence to adulthood. And who knows, ten years from now, those of you who are teenage wives today will be the "seasoned" wives who will be sharing your memories and lessons learned, with other younger wives.

Legal Problems of Minor Spouses

Commander Steven E. Wright, Head, Legal Assistance Policy, Office of the Judge Advocate General of the Navy, shared with *Family* some of the general legal problems a "minor spouse' might encounter. (Generally "minor" refers to under 18, but some states still have 21 as the legal age for entering into contracts.) If you have a legal problem, consult your legal assistance officer or the nearest Office of Consumer Affairs.

Wills and Contracts

Drafting a will -- most states require one to be "18 or lawfully married."

Basic contract law -- in most states contracts signed by minors cannot be enforced against them unless the minors lied about their age, or the thing purchased was a "necessity" -- such as food, clothing, shelter, or tools of a trade. Cmdr. Wright ways, "That means if a minor wife buys a dress on time, she can be held to that contract; but on non-necessities, the onus is on the seller to determine the age of a buyer on contract.

"In order to disaffirm a purchase on contract, you must do so in writing and return the merchandise in good shape."

Because protective laws do exist to help those under 18, Cmdr. Wright suggests: "If you are a minor, as you approach legal age, you may want to take a hard look at your financial commitments to see if there are any you should disaffirm."

Preventive Actions

Cmdr. Wright much prefers a preventive mode of action and gives six suggestions:

1) "Learn to budget."

2) "Learn to recognize some legal warning signals, such as change of your status in any way (injury, citizenship, marriage, parenthood, and property ownership). Before you buy insurance, talk with your legal assistance officer for a non-biased view.

If anything abnormal occurs, are there legal ramifications? (e.g. storm damage). Should you have or extend a power of attorney? A limited power of attorney is safer for the individual granted it, and more likely to be honored for the individual receiving it. Powers of attorney do not have to be honored. Before an unaccompanied or deployed tour, go in to the bank or credit union to check what will be their preferred form and what will be honored.

3) "Bills -- when you receive them don't ignore them! Negotiate a partial payment if you cannot pay the total.

4) "Keep good records to minimize your risks, and report all loss or damage promptly. (Keep receipts for bills, tax records for at least three years -- up to six is even better, furniture and appliance purchase records, photos of your belongings, and the inventory of your last move. The last two should be in you safety deposit box, along with you marriage and birth certificates and insurance policies.)

5) "List payment due dates on your calendar.

6) "Read all contracts carefully before signing. Ask questions if you don't understand. On car repair agreements, check the boxes that require that you be called if more is required than the estimate, and draw a big **XX** on the sheet below the agreed-upon repairs so that none can be added after you sign your name and leave."

If you have a legal problem, consult your installation legal assistance officer or the nearest Office of Consumer Affairs. Check the location through your city or county government. Lists of locations plus helpful consumer hints are available in a free publication: *Consumers' Resource Handbook,* Consumer Information Service, Pueblo, CO 81009.

Originally appeared as "Teenage Military Brides," in Family, *June 1984.*

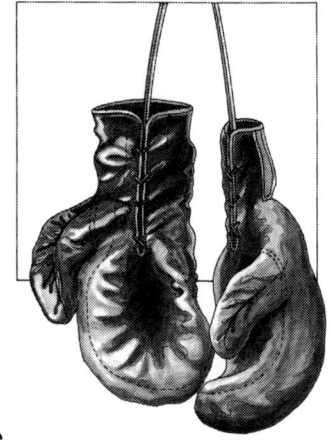

10 Myths About Spouse Abuse

She had lived with his violence for years. The final blow came one night when he pushed her down the stairs. Her foot caught in the railing as she fell. He went back to bed. Their teenaged children found her and called the ambulance. After the surgery, she will never walk normally again......
He was promoted (in spite of the abuse), and his Service moved him out of the area quickly. Now, finally, she is in divorce proceedings.

After his duty overseas in World War II, he married a young European girl, brought her to the U.S., and then the beatings started. After thirty years of marriage, all of the nerves in her shoulders and back have been injured, and she needs medical care two to three times a week.

A sailor did not report to work on time. Investigation by his superiors determined that he had been struck by his wife with a metal frying pan while asleep.

****

These three actual cases can help us explore the facts and fiction about spouse abuse -- a subject that is so distasteful that it has been swept under the rug for years. The first two come from the files of EX-P.O.S.E. Ex-Partners of Servicemen (Women) for Equality. Based in the Northern Virginia area, this organization has provided information and assistance to spouses, as well as lobbying in Congress for improved legal and medical benefits for former military spouses.

The third incident was shared by a Navy Ombudsman.

Myth #1: Officers do not abuse their wives.

A film produced by the University of Wisconsin Department of Preventive Medicine, "Domestic Violence," says that "wife abuse cuts across socio-economic, racial, and educational lines." A recent article by Dr. Joyce Brothers cited the finding by an attorney who handles many battered women's cases: "Doctors, lawyers, and policemen (not necessarily in that order) are the chief wife-beaters." Dr. Brothers then added, "I believe that military men and professional athletes, who use force in their jobs, also tend to use force when dealing with their mates and their children." Abuse occurs in all age categories as well, including retirees.

Those who work in the field of military family violence suspect that in years past only a small percentage of the cases have been reported because of the fear that the military member will be automatically discharged. That brings us to myth number two.

Myth #2: A spouse abuser is a bad Soldier, Sailor, or Marine.

At a workshop last summer at Naval Air Station Jacksonville, FL, the regional medical officer gave the profile of average abusers: "E-4 to E-6, and most have a 4.0 rating."

In order to help the workshop participants understand how that could possibly be true, Dr. Peter Neidig, Ph.D. of Behavioral Science Associates in Beaufort, SC, and his associate Barbara Collins asked us to list the characteristics of the ideal Soldier, Sailor, or Marine. You will see our responses in the block below. We then were to pair those characteristics with the ideal husband or father. The role conflict is immediately clear.

Ideal Soldier-Sailor-Marine	Ideal Husband-Father
Responsible -- duty first	Family first -- at home a lot
Decisive	Tolerant
Gives or takes orders	Requests or compromises
Obedient	Independent of spouse (or at least inter-dependent)
Neat	Not neat to an extreme
Proud-professional (can become a workaholic)	Sensitive
Macho, unemotional	Shows emotion
Respect (automatic)	Subjective as well as objective
	Earned respect -- use judgment

Clearly there are facets of the military way of life that build in the dichotomy of appropriate behavior on the job and at home. Dr. Neidig has been working with Marine Drill Instructors (D.I.s) at Parris Island, SC, for the last three years. He and Mrs. Collins, a Marine wife with an emergency room nursing background, have determined that these men's "level of marital conflict becomes increasingly severe during the two year tour as a D.I."

As D.I.s, they are expected to "model an almost super-human level of dedication, endurance, and performance." They are expected to be "objective, impersonal, and decisive...to demand perfection and to be constantly alert to shortcomings among recruits and to point them out in no uncertain terms."

Dr. Neidig comments on the contrast between their D.I. role and their role of husband and father as "striking, and the consequences of confusing the two, severe." If they use the same hypercritical standards appropriate for recruits on their spouse and children, then home is no longer a haven for any of them. Cleanliness of the household, promptness of meals, behavior of children all become tasks to be evaluated. If a wife doesn't perform these with the same vigor he applies to his job, she is seen as lazy at best, and unsupportive of his career at worst. Instead of being the supportive partner that each of them needs in an assignment of high stress, they become competitive -- who worked harder today?

Coping Strategies

Dr. Neidig and Mrs. Collins, in their workshops for Ombudsmen, Family Advocacy representatives, members of the commands, and counselors in the Navy family support system in the Jacksonville area, shared ways that military families can help to separate their work life and their family life.

• Their first suggestion was that the military member **change clothes** upon arrival at home. This is both a symbolic act and a physically separate act. They emphasized that *the first 15 minutes are critical.* Many of us learned long ago that our best strategy was to save any big issue until after dinner -- until our husbands and we had time to settle into a calm after the five o'clock "horrors" with children.

• They also urge that couples associate with a **wider group** of friends than just military peers. The D.I.s tended to cling to each other in off duty time, with the sense that no one else would understand them as well as other D.I.s. But there needs to be a balance. Friends made through hobbies, sports, neighborhood, and church give a broader dimension to our lives. We need both our work associates and our other friends.

- Another coping technique for families in high stress assignments is the **recognition that the tour of duty is limited** to two or three years' duration. There will be an end. Many readers are no doubt saying to yourselves, "My husband isn't a Drill Instructor, but his job is equally stressful." Deployments, separated duty, and temporary assignments all bring stress returns. Recognizing them for what they are, times of role reversals, is half the battle of coping with the stress they bring.

Myth #3: The abused spouse probably deserves it.

Dr. Neidig has discovered a lot of "free-floating anger" among military personnel in high stress assignments. When people feel powerless to change the system, or are in the position of receiving orders, being controlled by others all day long, they may lash out at others. Spouses, children, and pets have been the undeserving targets of festered rage that they have not *caused*, but they may have *triggered*.

In 1979, Lenore Walker first identified the three-phase violence cycle with which most therapists agree today.

- Phase One is the *tension-building* phase, which may last anywhere from an hour to many months. Dr. Neidig and his associate, Dale H. Friedman, teach their clients how to identify the cues that their spouse is getting angry, so that they can take corrective action at this point.

- Phase Two is the *explosion*, the violent episode. Neidig and Friedman have found that a "common occurrence just before the violence is for one party, usually the man, to withdraw by refusing to communicate further. In many cases, husbands report that they cannot keep up with their wives, who seem to think and speak faster and generally seem to have the advantage in any verbal conflict. His retreat, then, is often out of frustration. He may signal that he is about to 'lose it' and demand that his wife 'back off.' She, in turn, experiences this withdrawal as a sign that he doesn't care or is not taking her concerns seriously, and this misunderstanding is likely to increase her efforts to break through to him by moving closer, speaking more loudly, or physically preventing him from leaving. The conflict escalates through this pattern of circular feedback as each partner misunderstands the intentions and behavior of the other."

Neidig and Friedman accentuate that the escalation process is a *two-way street*. If the husband and wife can learn to recognize their own and each other's *signals and triggers*, and learn new communication skills and behaviors, they can nip potential violence in the bud.

- Phase Three is *remorse*. Promises never to repeat the violence and a genuine sense of guilt may lull the couple into believing that all will be well with them. The abused spouse often gains the upper hand during this phase, and may not see the warning signs that the three-phase cycle is starting again.

Myth #4: Repetition of violence is unlikely.

Statistics refute this myth. Without counseling, couples who experience one episode of spouse violence will experience two more within a year's time. Neidig and Friedman have found that violence not only increases in frequency, if not treated, but escalates in severity.

They distinguish two types of violence. *Expressive violence* is "primarily an expression of emotion (anger, jealousy)" and it occurs in a situation of "mutual combat." They have worked with over 200 Marine couples and have found that 90 percent fall in this category. With treatment, 80 percent have remained violence-free for up to three years (the length of their study.)

Instrumental violence is used "primarily as an instrument to achieve a goal," and is "unilateral -- the victim and perpetrator roles are fixed." Instrumental violence is seen as a "deliberate effort to punish or control, with low provocation, and relatively sudden and rapid progression to violence." There is no remorse.

The first two cases at the beginning of this article are prime examples of instrumental violence, and if more details were known, the third might be a response to it. With expressive violence, the possibility for accidental injury is high. "With instrumental violence, there is the potential for violent retaliation, homicide, or suicide." Dr. Neidig fortunately finds "hard-core battering *very rare* in the military."

Myth #5: People who have grown up in abusive household will take all steps necessary to avoid violent behaviors as adults.

A child who has the misfortune to grow up in an abusive family is 600 times as likely to be abusive as an adult than a child from a non-abusive family. This has to do with failure to learn appropriate coping skills and shades of emotion. "Often the Marines I see have only two emotions: *okay* and *rage*," says Dr. Neidig.

Adults who experienced or witnessed abuse as children need to recognize that they are in a high risk category, and should avail themselves of the marriage enrichment, communication skills, and parenting workshops given through their base/post chapel and family service centers.

Myth #6: Husbands are the only spouse abusers.

A survey taken in 1981, by Straus, Gelles, and Steinmetz for their book, *Behind Closed Doors: Violence in the American Family*, found that more women abused their husbands than the reverse! One out of every 26 American wives is beaten by her husband. One out of every 22 husbands is beaten by his wife.

One of the reasons that most people perceive husbands as the major abusers is that women do sustain 90 percent of the serious physical injuries. Men's physical superiority means that once the violence cycle is started, regardless of who initiates it, women are going to fare worse than their mates.

Myth #7: Women's Liberation and working wives have caused more spouse abuse by raising the level of competition and frustration experienced by their husbands.

Dr. Neidig is quick to say that he finds that the more *equal* spouses are, the less likelihood there is of abuse. A working wife has some financial independence and has a circle of friends from whom she has emotional and social support. A far more likely wife to be abused is a wife who is isolated in her home with few outside contacts.

Some wives whose cultural heritage promotes subservience to their husbands are also in a higher risk group than their "liberated" peers. American servicemen have often married women overseas whose culture and separation from their family would guarantee a high level of dependence on their husband, because that met a very real personal need for control. In order to retain that control in the United States, some restrict their wives from mingling with American wives in their neighborhood or military unit.

Myth #8: Alcohol or drug abuse causes spouse abuse.

Dr. Neidig's retort to this myth is, "People don't beat their spouses because they were drinking; rather, they drink in order to beat their spouses....Alcohol can serve to excuse spouse abuse by relieving people of full responsibility for their behavior."

Full responsibility for one's behavior is the cornerstone to the treatment program designed by Dr. Neidig and Dale Friedman. They differentiate carefully between *causing* and *enabling*. Others may provoke, childhood experiences may predispose, and drugs may uninhibit, but in the final analysis, one must own one's actions.

Abuse of alcohol and other drugs plays a part in 60 percent to 80 percent of wife-battering and child abuse cases nationally. In the military population seen by Dr. Neidig over the last three years, he has found that alcohol played no role in one third of the cases. In another third, alcohol was involved to a limited degree, and definitely involved in the final third.

Myth #9: An abuser will be discharged from the military automatically.

The policy of the Services is to examine case by case, and to try rehabilitation before deciding to discharge an individual. The military member abuser will be ordered into counseling; the spouse is usually encouraged to attend as well. Retention depends upon their remaining violence-free.

Ideally, an abused spouse will go to the family service center on the base or post. If she or he goes before the violence mounts to the point where emergency medical treatment is required, the counselor can maintain confidentiality of the file (to the extent that the husband or wife will not know of the visit, if that is desired). All of the Services have a vast array of support resources designed to help abusive families cope with the stresses inherent in military life.

Myth #10: Abused spouse shelters will try to break up your marriage.

Shelters provide a safe time-out during which spouses may begin to participate in desperately needed counseling. While the best choice for some is divorce, Dr. Neidig says that the literature shows that 70 - 80 percent of the women who go to shelters do eventually return to the marriage.

The bottom line is that the Services today are aware that a dysfunctional marriage impacts on the long term performance of a military member. It is in their best interest to help the Soldier, Sailor, or Marine learn how to function appropriately -- not only because it is morally right to do so, but because retention of highly trained personnel is desirable. Abuse will not be tolerated, swept under the rug. Assistance will be given to enable the couple to become healthy members of the military family.

Resources:

EX-P.O.S.E., P. O. Box 11191, Alexandria, VA 22312

Dr. Peter H. Neidig, Behavioral Science Associates, Inc., P. O. Box 1485, Beaufort, SC 29901-1485

To order his book, *Spouse Abuse: A Treatment Program for Couples.* by Neidig and Friedman, send $14.95 ppd. to:
Research Press Co., 2612 Mattis Ave., Champaign, IL 61821

Originally appeared as "10 Myths about Spouse Abuse" in Family, *March 1985.*

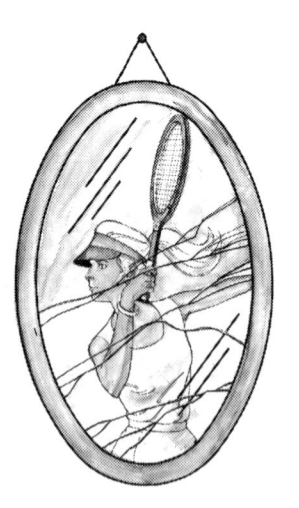

21

Eating and Exercise Disorders: Control out of Control

*Mirror, mirror on the wall.......*People with eating and exercise disorders have a love-hate relationship with mirrors. They no longer believe what they see reflected. Distortions, of their own making, squeeze them in or bloat them out -- like the images we used to laugh at when we went to the circus fun house.

But eating and exercise disorders are deadly serious. They are life-threatening at their worst, and life-shortening in any case. The four major variations, anorexia (starvation), bulimia (binge-purge), overeating, and overexercising, are examples of control that gets out of control.

While each of the variations has some unique facets, we will deal first with factors they have in common. They are not a new phenomenon, but we have seen a frightening rise in their prevalence in the last fifteen years, with anorexia and bulimia rising to epidemic proportions. Long known as modes of rebelling against external controls, these disorders have flourished in a society that puts heavy emphasis on the consumption of food, exercise, and the slender feminine figure as the ideal.

The recent flood of women into the workforce has contributed further to the prevalence of eating disorders as they struggle not only with the historical issue of body-as-sex-object, but now with the body-as-career-success issue as well.

Military families share these factors with society at large, but have some added triggers above and beyond the norm: mobility, fishbowl existence, significant control as a desired trait, and husband/father absence. These cumulative factors place military families at risk.

Eating disorders usually afflict daughters and wives, rarely sons. When sons are involved, they generally are athletes striving to maintain an unrealistic weight limit, or they are sensitive souls who take a passive route to express their need for control instead of other active, undesirable expressions of rebellion. And it is rebellion -- usually against a family member whose attempts to control are invasive.

Teenage daughters, with their latent sexuality, are troublesome not only to themselves, but also their parents. The fairy tale of Sleeping Beauty reminds us of the competition felt by the wicked Queen and her desire to place the young beauty in limbo. She accomplishes this with an apple, a symbol of forbidden Knowledge that ties her to Eve. She is to be awakened only by a handsome prince. In real life, however, the prince may not come in time, or if he does, he may be repulsed by what he finds.

But, you say, the wicked Queen *caused* Sleeping Beauty's condition in the fairy tale. And so she does in real life, though the young daughter plays a role as well. (It is not uncommon for the Mother-Queen to have an eating or exercise imbalance herself and to be seeking a sense of control at least over those weaker than she is -- as she struggles with the King who is controlling, powerful, and one whom it is inappropriate to oppose in public.)

Let's look at some real life examples. By and large these are not people with disorders caused by genetic hormonal imbalances. Rather, they are afflicted with emotional disorders that are demonstrated through eating and/or exercise abnormalities. *Do you know any of these people -- these people who are crying out for help?*

Anna the Anorexic Daughter

Anna is usually the second or third child in the family who has a low sense of self-esteem. She sees herself as heavier than those around her, homely, unintelligent, and unlikable. She often has parents who are so focused on their own careers or concerns that she is starved for attention and love. Not given to open confrontation, this dutiful daughter instead may become the care-giver in her family. In a military family, she may find frequent moving painful, and may find her mother's dependence on her in her father's absence overwhelming.

As she seeks to establish control through "perfection," she simultaneously limits her own food intake while often taking over the responsibility for much of the food preparation in her family. She works obsessively hard at her schoolwork. Her achievements are prized by her parents.

She withdraws from social connections, needing a great deal of time for her increasingly demanding regimens. Beyond health food fetishes, schoolwork, and often exercise, she establishes secret patterns which she _must follow._ As she becomes increasingly and appallingly thin, she becomes equally aggressive in protecting her modus operandi.

While she initially starts controlling herself so that she _won't eat_, eventually she _can't eat_. Her physical starvation is a poignant indicator of her emotional starvation. Rather than lashing out, cutting family ties, and seeking emotional support elsewhere, she is reactive and dependent on her family. Events that are common triggers for potential anorexics are normal developments such as going off to college or moving ahead in a career decision, when separation from her parents is threatened. As her weight loss becomes extreme, she loses her menstrual period, becomes constipated, her hair thins, and her skin becomes dry and flaky (eventually covered by a downy hair to keep her warm). She becomes short of temper. Change of routine becomes unbearable as she becomes disoriented easily. Vitamin and mineral deficiencies diminish her intellectual functions. Her control has gone out of control.

Annas make up three percent of the female college population (or one in every 250). They come from all socio-economic backgrounds and are most prevalent in the age range of 13 - 22 (though girls as young as eleven and women as old as 60 may become anorexic). Their mortality rate is 10 - 15 percent.

Alta the Anorexic Older Wife

Alta turns to anorexia as her children, who have been her primary source of comfort and achievement, leave her household. She has focused all of her attention on her children and husband and seems incapable of thinking or talking about her own needs. She's the mother she wishes she had had. She has done everything for everyone else so that she has been needed. She keeps busy so that no one can accuse her of selfishness -- an accusation she heard as a child. She avoids conflicts with others, even when they hurt her -- because she fears the fault is hers and fears abandonment. She is not used to being dependent on others. .If her husband does not provide the emotional support she needs, she may believe that she will be loved if she is thinner.

Betty the Bulimic Daughter

Betty, usually the firstborn in her military family, is keenly aware of the expectations of her parents. She often senses their disappointment that she is not a son. (Ancient military tribes killed their infant daughters, keeping only sons -- an interesting heritage!)

In our current period of great social change, in which able daughters often select their fathers as role models instead of their mothers, Betty runs head-long into military lifestyle "voices."

"If you eat that, you'll gain weight --- you won't be attractive."

I would really like that food.....you never let me have or do what I would like to.

"You have such a nice slim waist, but those hips......If you would exercise every day like I do..."

I hate my body.

"If you wore this instead of that, you would look thinner."

I like this....it hides my body. It's what the other kids wear.

"Your friends are not special like you are. You should make other friends. Your friends are embarrassing to your father and me."

I like my friends. They accept me for what I am.

"Who are you, young lady, to talk back to your father and me? You are rebellious, proud, thoughtless...."

I may be rebellious and proud, but I am thought-full -- struggling to find what I think is right, what I value, what I can do that is my own.

"Whatever you are is a result of this family that you have been brought up in....and don't you ever forget it!"

I certainly am -- but in ways you little understand.

"What you need is discipline."

You want discipline, I'll show you discipline! I will ensure that <u>I control</u> and <u>I will shut you out completely.</u> **********

And the result of these external and internal "voices" may be an eating and/or exercise disorder. Other results, which are not perceived as damaging by the parent, but researchers know have long term negative effects, are that the daughter will cave in and present a false self. She will seem to be the dutiful daughter putting her energies into her studies, but for her *whole self*, healing still remains to be done. En route, the finally outwardly rebellious daughter may choose an inappropriate marriage partner, experience divorce, etc.

Betty does not necessarily start out to find control through a combination of binge and purge. She often simply starts dieting (like one out of three girls ages 11 - 18, according to a 1988 study at the University of Michigan School of Public Health. Half of them do it to please their mother.) She may become bulimic by self-discovery or through friends. The reported rate of incidence is wide ranging. Some studies show as low as 1.3 % of college girls and 0.1% of college boys (University of Pennsylvania in Philadelphia, 1987). Others say one in five college age girls show symptoms of bulimia.

Less usual in military families, but important to note, is that chaotic families may also produce bulimics.

Betty is caught between needing food (and the soothing sense of well-being that it represents) and maintaining the "ideal" weight. Racing from one end of the seesaw to the other (from craving food to hyper-control of her weight), she is a polar personality.

Binging and purging become frequent routines, as do the uses of laxatives and diuretics. Like her anorexic counterpart, she loses critical vitamins and minerals, so she can experience physical, emotional, and intellectual imbalances.

A bulimic is harder to identify than an anorexic. She may simply look slender to the casual observer. Suspicions arise when she consumes an inordinate amount of food, often sweets, and yet does not gain weight. If she disappears during or after a meal with regularity, she may give herself away. Her dentist may be the first to recognize the telltale symptoms of tooth enamel breakdown and gum recession. The stomach acids that accompany vomiting eat away the calcium on her teeth and burn the lining of her esophagus (making her a prime candidate for cancer or rupture of the esophagus, which can be fatal). She sees herself as clever -- she "has it all".....food and figure. But she is *fragile.* What starts out as control, as she sees it, becomes a craving -- a pattern out of control.

Becky the Reckless Daughter

An extreme form of Betty's bulimia is Becky's profligacy in a variety of domains. She not only gorges on food, but carries her obsessive sampling into drugs, alcohol, and sex. Then she fasts. Becky courts disaster. She is often the product of a highly ordered family in which conformity is prized. Not allowed to disagree, to develop critical thought in a healthy way in adolescence, she reacts in extreme ways. Knowing that she can't ever "measure up," she adopts the opposite behavior pattern. In school she is an underachiever. While aggressive, she, too, is reactive, rebelling against a controlling environment.

Viola the Victim of Family Violence

Sexually abused daughters may become anorexic. Viola, a victim of incest, finds her extreme thinness abhorrent to her abusive father and she is left alone. Unable to seek protection from him and still needing the "support" that her family constitutes, she finds anorexia a solution. From a safe position, she gains control in her chaotic world and accuses her father by her mere physical appearance.

Patty the Exercise Perfectionist

A relatively new popular obsession, over-exercising has been prevalent in certain fields of pursuit for a long time. Gymnasts, dancers, and marathon runners have sought control over their bodies through exercise, sometimes coupled with an eating disorder.

Today, their passionate search for the perfect body has broadened to many "mere mortals." The popularity of spas, gyms, aerobics classes, and jogging is proof of many Americans' search for physical fitness. Pursued to an extreme, exercise may result in many of the symptoms of eating disorders.

Researchers at the Universities of Wisconsin and Indiana this year reported that "athletes start the semester with more energy and in better mental health than the other students, but by the end of the term, they're actually worse off." Mood tests (covering tension, anger, depression, fatigue, confusion, and vigor) showed that athletes started off eight percent better than non-athletes, but ended up 19 percent below their non-athletic peers -- quite a mood swing over one semester.

Other researchers at the University of Arizona and the University of Massachusetts at Boston have drawn the parallel between male "addicted athletes" and female anorexics. Common to both is that they are unusually introverted, come from achievement-oriented families, and are extremely demanding of themselves. A sort of "exercise-withdrawal" has been noted when running addicts are unable to run for a period of time. Depression, lack of energy, loss of interest in eating, diminished self-esteem, and insomnia are the symptoms. Many will continue to run even while injured, and focus their lives on exercise -- often ignoring their families and careers.

Patty, the young exercise perfectionist, has heard voices criticizing her figure. Seeking control and achievement, she works out beyond sensible limits. (Particularly vulnerable are those who lead aerobics classes! Seeking to be role models, they over-extend themselves while diminishing their food intake. There's no camouflage in their workout suits and they become hypercritical observers in the omnipresent mirror.)

Over-exercise often results in irregular or non-existent menstrual periods. While it may be a relief to be free of the monthly inconvenience, the long-term effect can be sterility. Military spouses have told *Family* that they were saved from the dangerous direction that their exercise regimens were leading by observant military doctors. Following their doctors' advice to reduce their exercise and make a modest weight gain, these young women in their late twenties and early thirties were able to conceive and bear their much-wanted children.

In addition to the risk of sterility, irregular or non-existent menstrual periods also cause permanent bone loss. Studies reported early in 1990 indicated that women athletes without periods were unlikely to regain the lost bone density, even if their periods returned. Not only was their bone density equivalent to that of 60 year old women (though their average age was 25), but they were at risk for stress fractures. Osteoporosis is an additional risk as they grow older.

Pietra the Overeating Daughter

Pietra, the female Peter Pan, has moved too often. She finds its very hard to make friends, and even harder to leave the few she is comfortable with and clings to. Her parents see moving as part of their military lifestyle and are annoyed by her "childish" resistance.

Her father may be absent frequently on field exercises or deployments, so that she is not getting his key support as she grows into her increasingly adult body. (Or he may be physically present, but emotionally absent.)

Food becomes a soothing outlet. Her bloated body gets her parents' attention, albeit usually negative attention. She is reactive and dependent.

In much the same way that an anorexic signals her discomfort with her family and lifestyle, an overeater rebels in a "safe" way. Her dad may be a perfect example of the "lean and mean" military man with everything under control. She (and her mother) may be embarrassing statements that he isn't in total control.

Sadie the Overeating Spouse

Sadie slid slowly into her overeating. As a young military spouse stationed away from her own family, she finds that her husband's assignments take him away more than she can cope with. She gains more weight than she should with their first child and doesn't lose it before she is pregnant again.

She and her husband are feeling financial stress. She usually doesn't work outside of her home. She is surrounded by children and other wives whose sense of self-esteem is low.

Food, which brings both a sense of comfort and discomfort, occupies her thoughts much of the time. Mealtimes loom especially large when her husband is away. In periods of stress, she copes by treating herself to foods she "loves" (usually unbalanced in terms of important nutrients).

When he is about to return, she may suffer pangs of remorse (that she has failed to lose weight and, therefore, is out of control) or pangs of anxiety over rushed intimacy (so if she's unattractive, maybe he'll leave her alone). Sadie is a sad, lonesome person crying out for support from her husband, family, and friends.

Sadie's Older Sister

After too many moves and the increasing awareness that she competes unfavorably with the real apple of her husband's eye (Ms. Mission), Sadie's older sister may become an overeater. Previously slender and seeming to cope well with the lifestyle, she gains weight suddenly.

The gain is usually coupled with a major life event. Accelerated promotions, visibility, relocations, and absence may give a husband a heightened sense of achievement, but his wife may become intensely aware that people court her only for access to him. Coupled with mid-life, this sense of tandem worth may drive her to send a signal that she needs loving and valuing.

Anna, Alta, Betty, Becky, Viola, Patty, Pietra, Sadie, and her older sister are all amalgams of people known to *Family*. Military family counselors have remarked on their prevalence in military families in general, and in high stress environments in particular.

As a rule of thumb, the more trapped that military daughters and wives feel, the more likely they are to seek an inappropriate solution through an eating and/or exercise disorder. Examples of trapping environments are small unit assignments overseas or stateside where families live and work in "fishbowls." Over-identification with the lifestyle and failure to establish one's own sense of worth independent of one's parents or spouse is also a trap.

Research

There has been very little documentation of eating disorders in military families. Records, if kept, generally are not collected and clumped as eating disorders.

However, the existence of conditions which are symptomatic has been documented. For example, Dennis Orthner, in his 1988 study of Air Force sons and daughters, compared them to their civilian peers. He found that Air Force (AF) sons, if they "bought into" the lifestyle, had the greatest sense of self-esteem of any of the four groups (AF sons, civilian sons, civilian daughters, and AF daughters). In fact, the macho environment attracted AF sons to join the military at twice the rate of their civilian male counterparts.

However, in terms of self-esteem, a sense of personal worth, the AF daughters showed a distant fourth. Not only were they at the bottom of the heap, they were significantly depressed. Almost one third of the AF daughters studied had depression sufficiently severe to warrant professional help.

The youth studied were a mixture geographically and socio-economically, so their sample was seen as a fair assessment. Although similar data does not exist for the other Services, one can learn from the warning signals.

Recent research by Carol Gilligan, of Harvard University, and her fellow researchers working with girls and boys in a variety of locations (near Boston and Cleveland), have identified a disconcerting pattern of development of girls from ages eleven to twelve. Prior to this age, girls seem to "hear their own voices," to be keenly aware of their abilities and values and to act on them. By the time they are twelve, most have "gone underground." Pressured to behave like "nice girls," they put their energies into their schoolwork and avoid listening to or speaking in their own voices -- unless they feel very secure with the researchers.

When Ms. Gilligan and her cohorts presented their work at a conference in Cleveland this past March, the reaction from the audience was "What can we do?" Most were teachers in schools for girls and were eager to make good use of Ms. Gilligan's findings. The "answers" were to be good role models and to value the "rebels" -- the girls who don't give up their voices, thoughts, and values.

Resources

Military families are fortunate in that we do have several sources of support on most installations: the medical center (with its team of professionals including medical doctors, psychiatrists, and nutritionists), the family service/support center (with its counselors, information and referral services, and extensive programs for healthy families and families in stress), and the physical fitness center.

At the Naval Submarine Base New London, CT, *Family* talked with Katy Henn, the Health and Fitness Educator. By professional training in the field and life experience (her husband, Lieutenant Commander Terence Henn, is a nuclear submariner), Katy is well aware of the potentials for eating and exercise disorders in the community that she serves. She is a certified health and physical fitness instructor with course work in both physical fitness and basic nutrition.

She indicated that she tends to see more wives with overeating disorders than other types of problems, though she has seen bulimics (especially those who abuse laxatives in an effort to lose weight). She sees depression over the responsibilities wives experience during deployments as a major factor. "They hear the message that the wife's job is to relieve her husband of responsibilities so that he can concentrate on his job. She should solve problems, be independent, keep her worries to herself. She is not patriotic if she burdens him."

She also sees that it is hard for wives with small children to get away and exercise for themselves. Time and childcare costs are factors.

Katy sees several helpful solutions. One is to make "drop-in" childcare more readily available. A second is that wives should find a variety of support groups or interest groups. Not only is it desirable to be part of a unit or command spouse group, but also a church or hobby group will add to their sense of self worth and connectedness to other people.

In order to find time for oneself, Katy suggests finding a neighborhood group of friends, and maybe swap child care time so that each mother gets some free time for herself. She also sees the need for more *informal* nutrition classes -- not just Weight Watchers. For example, a class for pregnant women -- to get information before a weight problem starts. She also sees the need for self-image classes. (As a brand new mother at the age of 30, she is especially aware of the challenges pregnancy brings in terms of nutrition and fitness.)

There are also two good books (available in many libraries) for further reading about eating disorders: *Treating and Overcoming Anorexia Nervosa*, by Steven Levenkron (Charles Scribner's Sons, New York, 1982) and *Hunger Strike: The Anorectic's Struggle as a Metaphor for Our Age*, by Susie Orbach (W. W. Norton, New York, 1986).

A paperback designed to help teenagers find a healthy balance in their lives is *Perfectionism: What's Bad About Being Too Good* by Miriam Adderholdt-Elliott, Ph.D. (Available for $8.95 from Free Spirit Publishing, 123 N. Third St., Suite 716, Minneapolis, MN 55401). It should be required reading for parents as well!

Military families, even more than our civilian counterparts, need to help family members find two key components in our lives: care and control. We traditionally have accentuated the personal control factor, without perhaps understanding the many arenas in which military family members sense little or no control (over orders, promotions, and departures). Finding ways in which we as adults and ways in which our children can establish appropriate controls in our lives _within a caring environment_ is critical to our physical and emotional health.

Learning to accentuate the positive, to compliment ourselves and our children for our successes day by day, instead of being our own drill instructors would be a very positive beginning. While our leaders are saying that "people are our most important resource," we often haven't believed it yet -- let's start right within our own families.

Originally appeared as "Eating and Exercise Disorders," in _Family_, August 1990.

Breast Cancer:
One Out of Every Nine....

"Two weeks after my second baby was born, I felt a lump in my right breast. At my six-week postpartum examination, the doctor thought that it felt like a cyst and said, "Let's wait until six months and check it then.' At six months it felt the same, but the doctor referred me to a surgeon.'just to see what he thinks ' The surgeon also thought it was a cyst, but referred me to Bethesda Naval Hospital to have it taken out.

"At Bethesda, they found not only a benign cyst, but a tiny fibrous mass underneath -- so I hadn't even felt the cancer! They had removed a four centimeter square area -- one centimeter of cancer.

"After consulting with surgeons and radiologists, I decided to choose lumpectomy followed by radiation. The following week they did a lumpectomy and took out 26 lymph nodes."

"One week later, the surgeon called to tell me that not only did they find more cancer in the tissue that was removed, but that five lymph nodes were also found to be cancerous.

"The next week they did a modified radical mastectomy. A few weeks later I started chemotherapy for six months. Compared to others, I was really lucky. I didn't lose any hair and threw up only once."

"At the end of March this year, I had reconstructive surgery. Dr. Michael P. Vincent performed a TRAM-flap procedure. Part of my abdominal muscle, fat, and skin was used to create a new breast."

Brenda Urda had just turned 29 when her cancer was diagnosed. Now 30, she is the wife of Lt. Cmdr. Ted Urda, stationed at Naval Air Station Patuxent River, Maryland, and the mother of a four and a half year old and a two year old.

She did not have to go through the surgery alone. Thanks to a remarkable support group in the Washington, D. C. area to which she was referred by the surgical ward at Bethesda, she was able to talk with military wives who had experienced the same decisions she was having to make in such rapid order.

She called the hotline number she was given for My Image After Breast Cancer. Rosemary Locke, another Navy wife and co-founder of My Image, was her contact. In thinking back on the help she was given, Brenda says, "The best thing they've done for me is to take a lot of the fear out of the situation by having more information. I'm a nurse, so I had an advantage as far as medical background, but I hadn't dealt with oncology. At each stage, I talked with someone who had gone through the specific operation or procedure I was going to have. She told me <u>details</u> of what to expect -- the procedure, the atmosphere of the room, what she had felt, and how she had reacted -- it really helped.

"I want people my age to recognize that it can happen to you. You may think you're too young.....but you're not! Do your monthly breast exams and <u>don't ignore</u> any symptoms that you may have. Be persistent and get appropriate treatment."

Brenda and her husband are transferring to the Washington area in November, and she plans to do volunteer work with My Image then. "I've helped one young wife already -- by describing chemotherapy. And other young wives in the squadron who have found lumps have called me. They want to talk with someone who has experienced the fear."

Brenda Urda is proof that My Image After Breast Cancer is a support group whose services are critical, and whose clients become committed volunteers reaching out to others.

Origins

My Image exists because a Navy surgical nurse at Bethesda, Lt. Cmdr. Artis Goulart, and plastic surgeon Cmdr. Michael Vincent took the initiative to bring together about 15 women who had had a positive reaction to reconstructive surgery. "It was May 1986," says Rosemary Locke. "I was surprised -- I was the second or third oldest person in the room! I was 47 when I had my surgery. There were four women there who had had breast cancer under the age of 30. "We are working with many young women diagnosed because of lumps before the recommended baseline mammogram at age 35 or 40. It is especially frightening when diagnosis comes associated with pregnancy. Treatment can still occur. Problems occur when pregnancy masks lumps -- it's very important for pregnant and nursing mothers to do self-examinations and not be complacent if the doctor diagnoses a lump as 'pregnancy-related.'"

Breast Cancer on Rise

The incidence of breast cancer is increasing at an astonishing rate. In just the year since *Family* first talked with Rosemary (after a chance meeting in the Fort Myer, Virginia commissary and the query, "What have you been up to?"), the United States rate has gone from one out of every ten women to <u>one out of every nine</u> of us will have breast cancer at some point in our life. Bonnie Campbell, Rosemary's co-founder of My Image, notes that the rate was one in twenty-five in the World War II years. (Part of this is due to a greater awareness and a higher detection rate, but the other factors are puzzling.)

Historically, the age group of women most vulnerable to breast cancer has been those 50 and older. A recent report in *Ladies Home Journal* indicated that scientists are unsure why breast cancer in young women is rising, but suggested several triggers: women are waiting longer before having their first child (and therefore, experiencing the monthly bombardment of estrogen), a high fat diet (especially in adolescence), stress, and lack of preventive care.

As Rosemary points out, current research is very confusing. "A National Cancer Institute (NCI) researcher cited one study that found that in the pre-menopausal group, thin women are more at risk; yet in the post-menopausal group, those who are overweight. Previous studies suggested that alcohol may increase risk, as may estrogen-replacement therapy or the birth control pill. When you are diagnosed, you are plagued by the question, 'What could I have done to prevent this?'"

Support Group

"What <u>*could I have done*</u>?" has become "What <u>*can I do?*</u>" Rosemary Locke has become a determined and effective advocate since that day in 1986, when she met her co-founder-to-be, Bonnie Campbell. Both are admirals' wives (Rear Admiral Walter M. Locke, U. S. Navy (Retired) and Rear Admiral Arlington F. Campbell). Both have remarkable organizational and research skills, and both have been careful caretakers of their bodies. Both are conscious of their diets and exercise regularly. Bonnie had none of the risk factors usually associated with breast cancer. "No family history. I had my babies when I was supposed to and breast fed," says Bonnie. However, Rosemary's Irish grandmother and great grandmother both died of pre-menopausal breast cancer, though she didn't know that at the time of her diagnosis. (A number of *Family's* contacts have mentioned that some ethnic and generational groups were amazingly quiet/secretive about their disease.)

"When you find out that you have cancer, it surprises you....violates you....makes you angry." Bonnie's words were echoed in Rosemary's description that a great deal of anger comes with breast cancer. "You have the sense that your body has <u>betrayed you.</u> This is especially true for women who have taken good care of their body.

"I had almost decided not to go to the meeting. I had had immediate reconstruction after a double mastectomy and had had great care with the Navy. I was doing well, but I was curious.

"At that meeting were women, all strangers, who were saying the things I felt but hadn't voiced. They understood.

"After the third meeting, we felt we needed to change the focus from ourselves (post-breast cancer) to pre-surgery -- to work with early intervention." Rosemary cites the advice of the former Walter Reed Army Hospital commanding general who told them that "*intervention is key within the first 72 hours* after diagnosis -- when they're still in shock. A bonding develops."

"The first question is, "How long since your surgery?' They're looking for a role model and they're looking for hope. We can provide support -- to listen to fears (emotional) and we can provide printed information (intellectual)."

Rosemary remembers her own experience vividly. She went through the trauma essentially alone. A few days before her mastectomy and reconstructive surgery, she met someone in a social situation who had not elected reconstruction, who imposed her value system on Rosemary. "I had no one else to talk to about implants -- to ask very personal questions. Even if you know others who have had breast cancer, you may not feel comfortable approaching them and they may not have the knowledge and personality to make them appropriate role models. This shouldn't be just accidental."

"Bonnie and I were tasked at an early meeting to put a program together." Rosemary had served as president of the National Military Family Association (1979-80), and then as their head of government relations (1981-82). Bonnie, a nurse, was a personal friend of Rear Admiral Richard Schaffer, then the Commanding Officer of the National Naval Medical Center (Bethesda).

As seasoned Navy wives, they knew that they would need to develop a well thought out program to present to RADM Schaffer and key department heads at the hospital. With Rosemary's newly acquired computer skills and equipment, they put together a very professional briefing packet that made a difference. "We convinced the chain of command that peer support could help patients facing treatment."

They succeeded where others might have failed because, as Rosemary says, "the right people were willing to listen and approve.". (Rosemary credits her husband with "extreme support -- he purchased the equipment I needed, like a laser printer and copier, and helps proofread our materials.")

"Thanks to the Bethesda staff, we jointly put together a program that is unlike anything else going on -- even in the civilian sector," says Rosemary proudly. "A pharmaceutical firm doing a national directory indicated our uniqueness when talking with our hotline director."

Spreading Out

After a number of meetings with hospital administrators and surgeons to ensure compliance with the hospitals' mission, My Image has won the support of not only Bethesda Naval Hospital, but Walter Reed Army Hospital and Malcolm Grow United States Air Force Medical Center as well. Rear Admiral H. James T. Sears, former Commander Naval Medical Command, has gone on record supporting the work of My Image. In his June 1989 letter to the command, he wrote about their history and service and said, "This extremely beneficial group has the support of myself and the Surgeon General." Rear Admiral Donald Hagen, the current commanding officer of Bethesda Naval Hospital, is the head of the My Image advisory board.

Posters and brochures are available in key clinics and the surgical staff tell newly diagnosed breast cancer patients about My Image. "If they would like to talk to one of the trained volunteers, they fill out a request form."

Rosemary explains how the connection then works. "A trained volunteer calls the patient, usually the same day, and offers compassion, understanding, and a listening ear. She answers questions dealing with treatment options, provides the newest printed material from the National Cancer Institute and other approved sources, and gives tips for the hospital stay.

"Although the volunteers can't give medical advice or opinions, they can encourage patients to explore treatment options and participate in the treatment decision-making process. After surgery a volunteer, usually the same one, visits the patient, and provides encouragement, support and practical advice. The volunteer also tells the patient about the support group's on-going activities and encourages her participation."

What makes My Image exceptional is their pre-surgery contact. Most patients who utilize national hotlines and agencies call post-surgery. "It takes a highly motivated woman to make a call pre-surgery. Your treatment decisions can make a difference in follow-up options. "If you have a mastectomy *after a lumpectomy and radiation*, reconstruction is made more difficult. Also, you have to be in relatively good health to have reconstructive surgery. Remember, it's an elective procedure," explains Rosemary.

To ensure that My Image can connect a newly diagnosed patient with an appropriate volunteer/role model, the support group has taken great precautions to build their credibility and their expertise. Volunteers are matched to hotline callers by type of breast cancer, the treatment options, and their age......after volunteers have taken training offered by the organization.

Rosemary and Bonnie decided that My Image should affiliate with Y-ME National Breast Cancer Information and Support Program, located in Chicago, after they attended the organization's national conference and observed their toll-free hotline. Both women recognized that My Image needed help in training volunteers. Y-ME could provide comprehensive training, using the National Cancer Institute's *Breast Cancer Digest* and other up-to-date articles on detection and treatment, as well as sessions to enhance listening skills. All volunteers are tested and certified. Four My Image members are now credentialed Y-ME trainers, led by Capt. Cherry Hatten, U. S. Navy (Retired).

Hotline

At times, Rosemary has coordinated the My Image hotline. Bonnie Campbell, her co-founder, has been in Charleston, South Carolina for a two year tour (and started a My Image group there), but has just returned to the Washington area and will serve as co-director. Recently, another Navy wife, Gina Plummer, has served as the full time hotline coordinator.

Gina, another nurse, is married to Capt. Galen Plummer. She does all of the initial screening and response to calls (1339 in 1989 alone!), listening carefully to try to select the right volunteer match for the newly diagnosed caller. She selects from 34 trained volunteers, who range in age from their mid-30's to 79, with a disproportionately high number of nurses (both retired military nurses and spouses). In some cases, a patient will talk with several volunteers, depending on her issues and decisions to be made.

Breast Cancer

Gina admits that her hotline work requires a full time commitment, between the phone calls, the hospital visits, and the seminars. "I didn't volunteer to be a cancer patient, but there's something wonderful out of something awful. We don't want someone to go through breast cancer alone if we can help her."

She joined My Image two years ago. She had had her surgery three and a half years ago at Tripler Army Hospital in Hawaii. "The hospital was wonderful, but there was no support group there -- so I looked forward to joining and working with the group when we moved to Washington. Tripler had the team concept, where all the information in the hospital is made available to you. Comprehensive teams are also in place at Bethesda and Walter Reed in the D. C. area that include the surgeon, pathologist, oncologist, radiologist, and plastic surgeon-- they're ahead of most civilian hospitals. The team sees you before surgery. Each member evaluates from his specialty and then they make a group recommendation."

On the day she talked with *Family*, she had had six hours of counseling -- six patients. "I had a call from a young wife today. She said, 'I just had a biopsy today. I have cancer and I'm going crazy! I have two small kids.'

"My response to her was, 'You feel victimized.' 'Right!' You let her get her rage and screaming sense out. Then you give her information and help her know her rights -- like the fact that she can check out her records and slides of her mammogram and take them for a second opinion." (Just the vocabulary alone is a whole new world for patients. Making decisions on complex situations in crisis with words you don't understand can be overwhelming.)

On-Going Support

"Our volunteers give one-on-one support as long as it's needed," explains Gina, but then, when they're ready, they are encouraged to join the monthly open-door meetings. They find friends in the whole pool of women and receive up-to-date information on current cancer research. Guest speakers are featured from the medical community. Patient advocacy news is shared with the group and questions are welcomed.

Questions can be very personal at times. Joan Bacon, the wife of Vice Admiral Roger F. Bacon, Assistant Chief of Naval Operations (Undersea Warfare), tells how important it was to her as a nurse, who had seen some of the old radical procedures, to have a My Image volunteer say, "Would you like to see what it looks like?" Joan says, "The surgery really is remarkable. It certainly smoothed over my fears. They were

158 Family Support Services

there when I needed them most -- even at the point when I knew I needed a biopsy." Contrary to the claims of some that they're just as they were before their breast cancer, she comments, "They're dynamic women going about their business in an *even more dynamic way than before*."

Anne Torma, wife of Brig. Gen. Michael J. Torma, the new command surgeon for the Strategic Air Command at Offutt Air Force Base, Nebraska, first learned about My Image by reading a notice in the *Washington Post.* when they were new in the Washington area. She had had her surgery prior to the move at Scott Air Force Base in Illinois. Her husband, a physician, went to the My Image meeting with her. He was serving on the Air Force Surgeon General's staff at the time, so was interested personally and professionally. They both found My Image very supportive and were pleased that the volunteers "don't try to make you unhappy with your physician -- just provide the questions to ask for further information." She then took the volunteer training and "found it a valuable way to reach out."

Reaching out has been the motivation for all of these women. "Our motto is "No woman must face breast cancer alone." Understanding your options is so important. This was the most difficult thing in my life to gear myself to go through," says Rosemary.

"Breast cancer tends to strike when women have never felt better and often, with children on their way out of the nest, have the freedom to launch themselves. Then a physician tells you, when you feel okay, that you need major surgery. You don't understand the options and don't know how to assess them. You fear that your choice will make a difference of life or death. By and large, that isn't true, in a choice between mastectomy and lumpectomy."

"Your emotions range from fear of death and disfigurement to not being willing to deal with the treatment -- surgery and chemotherapy. "I entered the program on a high -- I had caught it early. Now, having worked with women for three and a half years who are living and dying, I have come to respect breast cancer as a very deadly disease. A person really has to pursue an evaluation. Some doctors have very subtle, and not so subtle, ways of letting you know that they're the professional and you should not question their recommendation."

Although the beginning members all had reconstructive surgery, which was quite new when they started four years ago, My Image encompasses volunteers who represent a wide range of treatment options. "We became sensitive to the total range of treatment, including that of pre-cancerous conditions which require careful monitoring. One particularly difficult cancer is 'lobular in situ.' It usually doesn't show up on a mammogram until it has become invasive. Then the treatment ranges from 'do nothing and watch' to 'take both breasts,' explains Rosemary. "Volunteers from the civilian community have joined and enriched the My Image program, providing a more stable pool in the highly mobile military community."

Summing up, Rosemary notes that "Bonnie, Gina, and I see our work as a special calling -- an opportunity given that we chose to accept. You have to be willing to drop everything else in your life and give quality time to someone who is hurting. While you are vulnerable to someone else's pain, you are privileged to be there." (Five of the 34 My Image volunteers have had recurrent cancer in the last two years alone. The group is now dealing with how to cope the second time around.)

What Can You Do For You?
Early detection is the key.

This is not a time for modesty nor for wishful thinking ("If I don't think about it, it won't happen to me!") A National Institutes of Health statement makes your risk clear: "In the 1990's, more than 1.5 million women will be newly diagnosed with this disease; nearly 30 percent of these women will ultimately die from breast cancer."

1) All women over 18 should practice monthly breast self-examination. Booklets provided by the gynecology department of your hospital or the local chapter of the American Cancer Society will show you how. Make it easy to remember. Make it something you do five days after your period (if you are pre-menopausal) or (post-menopausal) on the first of each month (just like paying bills!)

2) Have an annual pap smear and breast examination by a physician. Pick your birthday as an easy reminder that your check up is due. Your installation medical center is the place to start. If the wait is too long, check public health options in your area or get a statement of non-availability from your military hospital and use CHAMPUS.

3) Have a baseline mammogram at age 35. Between ages 41 - 49, have a mammogram every 1 - 2 years. From age 50 - on, have an annual mammogram. This schedule is for women without symptoms (lumps, breast pain, discharge, skin thickening, or dimpling). For those of you in a high risk category (personal or family history of breast cancer, childless, or first child after age thirty), your doctor may recommend an earlier baseline and greater frequency. Breast density (a measure of tissue vs. fat determined by a mammogram) is a newly discovered indicator of high risk (c.f. *Ladies Home Journal* - July 1989). Those with a density level of 65 % or more have four times the risk than those with five % or less.

160   Family Support Services

4)   Consider making a charitable contribution to an association fighting breast cancer. For those of you in the Washington, D. C. area, you can designate funds through the Combined Federal Campaign. The number for My Image is #2199.

Resources   (clip and save in your home medical file.....for yourself or a friend)

My Image - For those of you who live in the Washington, D.C. area, contact the hotline at (703) 237-1797. The Charleston, South Carolina affiliate, coordinated by Gay Coon, may be reached at (803) 556-8340.

Y-Me (the national organization with which My Image is affiliated) operates a toll-free hotline: 1-800-221-2141 (9 - 5 weekdays). Or you may use their 24-hour live hotline service (not toll-free) seven days a week: (708) 799-8228.

American Cancer Society - your local chapter will have information on sources of inexpensive or no-cost mammograms and may offer a program, "Look Good...Feel Better," for those who have experienced chemotherapy or radiation treatments   Professional cosmetologists and donated brand name products are part of this esteem and skill building service.
    The society also has a national program that has been in place since the early 1950's for both pre- and post-surgery patients called "Reach to Recovery." Arden Leach, the wife of Capt. Robert Leach, U. S. Navy (Retired) in Mystic, Connecticut , is the coordinator for the New London County unit of "Reach to Recovery." "We have 14 volunteers and see 5 - 6 people a month, ages 20 - 80's. We would like to see more people pre-operatively -- coming to us because they know about our service or because they have been referred by a friend, a nurse, or a doctor." All of our volunteers are trained and certified and have to be at least one year out of surgery or treatment themselves. Our aims are to give practical advice and to be role models of those who have survived and triumphed over the disease." Arden, herself, had surgery 14 years ago at the age of 46, and today continues to be a vibrant, red-headed community activist who looks at least ten years younger than she is.

National Cancer Institute - for informational booklets. Call 1-800-4-CANCER nationwide (or 808-524-1234 on Oahu) to reach a counselor who will identify booklets you need, or request by mail from Officer of Cancer Communication, National Cancer Institute, Bethesda, MD 20892.

Note: The symbol for My Image is a butterfly; hence our ullustration. Oiginally appeared as "Helping Ouselves," in <u>Family</u>, October 1990.

23

The USA Still Needs the USO

> *We face a new world now because of their sacrifice, and it is their continued sacrifice that will preserve this new world. They ask so little from us. They ask for our appreciation. They ask for the means to do their job. And they ask for our support for themselves and their families.*
>
> General Colin L. Powell
> Chairman of the Joint Chiefs of Staff
> USO Christmas Gala - 1989

In this time of rapid global political and military reassessment, the USO still has a critical role to play for military members and their families. Reduction in forces is expected to produce a smaller more mobile force. Mobility means moving military units or individuals on short notice (often on unaccompanied duty) and it means moving families -- back from overseas, among widespread Stateside posts and bases, and, in some cases, out into the civilian community as they separate from the armed forces.

Serving people on the move is one of the things USO does best. No longer just a celebrity tour or coffee-and-doughnuts organization, the USO continues to serve our nearly five million military men and women and their families. In 1989, they made more than 4.1 million visits to USO's 156 locations worldwide. Here's what they found.

USO Airport Centers

At 39 locations, USO offers assistance with travel connections, room to store luggage, advice on things to do as well as things to avoid, and comfortable lounge chairs in which to catch one's breath or take a nap. Many have nurseries for small children in an attempt to give military folks a spot that feels as close to home as an airport can.

Family Support Services

Some of the airport facilities are open around the clock, staffed by volunteers who know how tired, frightened, or inexperienced new recruits, families headed for their first overseas tour, or military members on emergency leave can be. The USO sign is a warm beacon. It means a place where they will be helped, a place where they belong.

During last year's military operation in Panama, the *Philadelphia* and *Charleston (SC) USO Airport Centers* worked 24 hours a day to ensure that military members could get where they needed to be.

USO Fleet Operations

Sailors, Marines, and their families find USO fleet centers and mobile port operations at 36 points worldwide to help them enjoy local sights and eliminate problems they might encounter when visiting foreign countries. Military spouses following the fleet - "seagulls" -can learn the latest information on the ship's schedule at the USO -- an important communications link for those at sea and those awaiting their arrival.

During the holiday season, USO fleet centers operate day and night, making arrangements to connect military members with their own families or providing a home away from home with local families.

Working closely with host country civilians, these fleet centers plan community activities through which military members can bridge the cultural gap. One especially poignant connection was featured on TV's "Today" show in 1987. The whole country wiped a tear with a sailor as he bid farewell to a young boy he had come to love when he and his fellow shipmates visited an orphanage in Toulon, France. Neither boy nor sailor will ever be the same!

USO Fleet Center Israel arranges big brother days. Local children who have cancer tour visiting ships with their Sailor hosts. Also, volunteers make chicken soup (home!) for 1400 visiting Sailors and Marines.

USO centers in cities like San Francisco, Jacksonville, FL, and New York City provide special fleet programs for our own military personnel and offer cultural orientations for allied foreign military visitors.

USO Intercultural Programs

The USO encourages community linkages that help military families feel at home in their new cultures -- in the United States and overseas.

For 20 years, *USO Korea* has helped Korean brides of U. S. servicemen prepare for their move to their new home in the United States, sharing everything from language and shopping skills to insights on American home life and traditions.

"Wie Gehts" (how's it going?), a two-day orientation at *USO Baumholder*, Germany, teaches military spouses how to get around on the economy with confidence, and provides information on military community support programs. Most USO's in Germany have similar offerings to help speed up feeling at home in a new country.

Bringing home to others is an annual function of the *USO of Mannheim*, Germany. American soldiers treat residents in a German nursing home to an American Christmas party, decorating the home together and sharing the hundreds of Christmas cards made for the patients by a third grade class in West Virginia.

USO Holiday Programs

The USO knows that the hardest time for military members to be away from home is the holiday season, so they have provided some creative solutions.

Last year, *USO Rome*, with help from AT&T, served a traditional Thanksgiving dinner to more than 250 military personnel and their famílies stationed at Stuttgart and Frankfurt (Germany), Rota (Spain), and four Italian bases -- that's how far folks will come for a taste of home! (And 10 free phone calls to the U. S. as door prizes!!)

USO Rome serves as the official representative of the U. S. military to the Vatican for Papal audiences. Last Christmas they had 2500 tickets for services at St. Peter's, one quarter of the seating in the basilica.

USO Seoul, Korea, visits the demilitarized zone (DMZ) at Christmas, taking cookies, gifts, and carollers -- almost like home.

USO Camp Foster, Okinawa, Japan, sponsors a Christmas gift shop for more than 2,000 children. The elves -- Marine volunteers -- often reach into their own pockets for those who don't have quite enough money.

USO Atlanta 's "Holiday Exodus Program" enables thousands of military members and families to exit or arrive for the holidays through the airport USO center (open 24 hours a day).

USO Keflavik, Iceland, in conjunction with the USO of Northern Ohio, sponsors Santa at the North Pole. Military children may write Santa -- c/o USO Keflavik, NAS Keflavik, FPO New York 09571.

USO Family Programs

The USO creates programs to fill voids where military family support programs and recreation services are not able to meet all of the needs of families. With innovative programs, family member volunteers, and a nonofficial, homey atmosphere, the USO can be especially effective with those often missed by the traditional official services.

USO Long Beach has started "Warmline," providing a touch of home for military latchkey children.

USO Hampton Roads, Virginia -- the first Stateside USO to be located in a shopping mall -- serves more than 25,000 military members and their families. In addition to the Hampton Mall facility, the USO also conducts a mobile outreach program for junior enlisted families in the area.

Women's resource centers at *USO Strassburg* and *USO Neubrucke*, Germany, provide a place where women can find help, information, and support. In an environment where children are welcome, the centers address the needs of all women -- enlisted or officers' wives, soldiers, or military civilians.

The Emergency Housing Program, co-sponsored by the *USO of Metropolitan Washington, D.C.* and the Apartment and Office Building Association of Washington, provides up to 60 days of housing in furnished, donated apartments for junior enlisted members and their families who have a lack of financial means and/or a medical crisis. This pilot program has been expanded to *USO San Diego*.

The Budweiser/USO Scholarship Program, sponsored by Anheuser-Busch, Inc., provides 25 scholarships of $1,000 each to outstanding military youth and spouses. For consideration in 1991, applicants may obtain forms at their installation family support center or by writing: USO Scholarship Program, USO World Headquarters, 601 Indiana Ave., N.W., Washington, D.C. 20004. The deadline is March 1st.

USO World Headquarters coordinated the offer by former President and Mrs. Reagan to fill their plane with military family members when they flew to Japan last year. Family members from 35 states were enabled to visit their service members on unaccompanied tours in Japan. "Whenever we have traveled abroad, Nancy and I have been deeply impressed by the wonderful people who wear our country's uniform. They sacrifice so much on our behalf, especially being separated from their loved ones. We knew immediately what to do with the extra seats on the airplane."

USO Community Service

Local USO's link military and civilian communities by sponsoring projects that facilitate their interaction and good will.

USO Jacksonville's Mayport facility forms teams of military and civilian volunteers to fix up senior citizens' homes.

USO of Metropolitan New York entertains 13,000 patients at Veterans Administration Medical Centers in New York, New Jersey, and Connecticut.

USO Camp Schwab, Okinawa, brings Marines together with local school children and orphans several times a year for "Friendship Day."

USO Corpus Christi, Texas, sponsors "Adopt-a-Service-Person," to allow military and civilians to share similar interests and foster better understanding.

USO Celebrity Tours and Tickets

Glamorous shows in far-flung places and tickets to Broadway shows and baseball games continue USO's heritage of entertainment. Funded by corporate sponsors and provided logistical support by the Department of Defense, troupes of celebrities go where they are needed most to make it clear that the USA appreciates our men and women in uniform.

In the Philippines, Miss USA (sponsored by Procter & Gamble) visited military members who were restricted to the base due to terrorist activities. She also toured in Europe and the Mediterranean (Pan Am).

Lee Greenwood (with help from AT&T) visited Panama during tense times to share his always stirring message, "I Love the USA."

This year, John Denver went to the DMZ, Randy Travis (AT&T) to Egypt, Turkey, Spain, and Italy. Bob Hope went to Paris. The Dallas Cowboys Cheerleaders wowed the troops in Turkey and Spain. Ricky Skaggs(AT&T and Northwest Airlines) took his wonderful sound of home to Okinawa, the Philippines, and Diego Garcia.

166 Family Support Services

Charlie Daniels went to Cuba, Pearl Bailey to England and the Persian Gulf (Pan Am and AT&T), and NFL players went to the Pacific (Northwest). And just like the boy and sailor in Toulon, the performers and the military audiences know that something special has happened in their lives that they will always remember. The US has been kept in the USA by the USO.

The future? .... Reduction of the defense budget will place greater demands on non-government funded agencies that provide services to military members and their families. The USO, vital and committed, will expand its role to meet their needs....to let them know that we at home appreciate their commitment around the world to keep us free at home.

Articles on the USO have appeared in Family *in August 1981 and November 1988. This version was commissioned for the USO 50th Anniversary magazine,* Almost Home, *Winter 1990-91.*

Section V

Coping With Our Lifestyle

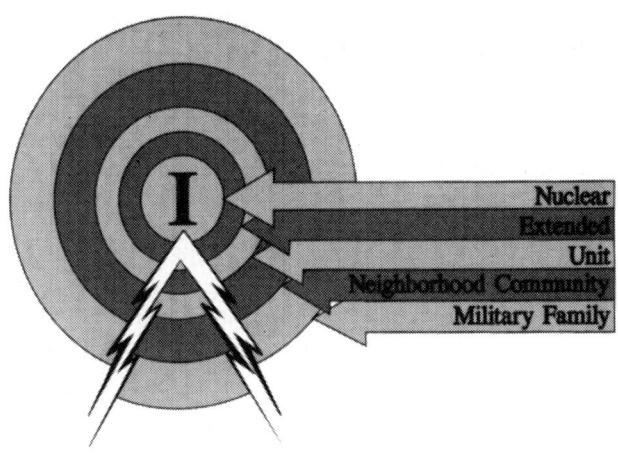

Our Five Families

There is a saying in corporation circles that a corporation wife relates to her husband's company through him and he relates to the community through her. The parallel to military families is immediately apparent. But is this traditional model the ideal?

Each of us, whether married or single, has the potential of belonging to five families -- or communities, if you will.

1. *Our Nuclear Family* is that to which we belong as a spouse, and perhaps as a parent. It is our smallest family. (For singles, this includes your parents and brothers and sisters.)

2. *Our Extended Family,* in my definition, has two parts: that of our relatives (such as aunts, uncles, cousins, grandparents, and perhaps grandchildren) who may or may not live close by -- probably not; and our network of *very* close friends from previous duty stations, or our hometown -- or our adopted hometown -- who have known us awhile and constitute a tie with our past.

3. *Our Military Unit Family* -- made up of the military personnel in the specific unit to which our husband (or wife) is assigned and their families. For example, the sailors assigned to my husband's submarine, and their wives and children, thought of themselves as the Carver Family -- the U.S.S. GEORGE WASHINGTON CARVER family.

4. *Our Neighborhood Family* -- again two parts: our immediate geographic neighbors whom we should know well enough to depend on for emergency support; and our friends in the whole community in which we live, whether on base/post or off.

5. *Our Overall Military Family* which includes official and unofficial support. This family ranges from the medical facilities level to the immediate rapport we feel when we meet someone new who simply says, "I am an Air Force wife". We share a common bond instantly.

When at least four of these five families are operating well, we as military families tend to feel secure. We can deal with difficulties with relative ease and can indeed say that our lives are *challenging and pleasant*. We can do something about that -- especially on the unit and neighborhood family levels to create ties that bind us to both our unit and neighborhood families. Our ties may be purely social, or may grow in depth to include ties of service, a sharing of our time, talents, concerns, and joys.

Unit Family

When I helped research materials for the <u>Navy Leader's Family Manual</u>, an interesting connection between retention and mission excellence became obvious. Winners of the Golden Anchor Award, an award based on retention, shared one thing in common -- the senior officers and enlisted men all showed concern for, and gave support to, the crews' families. Not surprisingly, many Golden Anchor units also won Battle Efficiency E's -- retention and expertise are logical results for crews that have closed the gap between mission and family.

It is important that a man can share what he does with his family -- they can appreciate his tasks and challenges when they see the complicated equipment he works with, and can visualize where he sleeps and eats when he is away from them. His kids can tell their friends what their dad *does*, instead of being at a loss to describe his work, as many of my high school students have been.

Ideally, he will share his fellow workers with his family, too. A sense of belonging to one huge, often multi-generational family comes when we all share in unit picnics, Christmas parties, outings for the children, and gatherings for unit adults. Then, when emergencies occur, we know each other well enough to help. During unit exercises, the families can share information and can share the emotional rhythms that are part of any mission. Some of my civilian friends have envied the very close friendships that resulted from unit families, and our husbands can focus more clearly on their mission knowing that the families left behind will truly take care of each other.

We as spouses can help our husbands establish the climate of family concern in the unit, and we can initiate, with our husbands, a variety of activities that help us to play and grow together as one specific unit family. (To show how completely that can work, take our ship's Santa, who called the base beauty parlor to set up an appointment to have his beard trimmed. The manager, who was sure she was being conned, asked what ship he was attached to, and he said, "The CARVER -- you know, Mrs. O'Beirne's ship!"

Pearl Buck has seen a trend toward companion-type marriage in highly mobile couples -- marriages that can isolate a husband or wife from the additional support of friends that were traditional in years past. Our unit family is the natural extension of a military couple -- the work schedules and the challenges being shared experiences.

Neighborhood and Community Family

Because our rhythms and responsibilities in relation to the unit family fluctuate, and because our membership is by chance -- by assignment instead of by choice -- we also need on-going ties to our local community -- be it a military or civilian neighborhood, or perhaps a combination of both. Our geographical neighbors are also "by chance" acquaintances; whether or not we progress to the level of friendship is our choice. But we ought to know one or two geographic neighbors well enough to depend on them for emergency assistance. Without that much security, we can be truly isolated in our community.

I continue to be appalled at how many Army and Navy wives tell me that they don't know *any* of their neighbors in their civilian apartment complexes. It's dangerous -- and I urge each one of you to insure that you play that role for those who live near you. I was amazed when ship's wives would call me at night during patrol to say they heard sounds outside or that someone was peeping in their window -- I lived twenty minutes away, yet constituted their only tie.

Sometimes this isolation was the result of a husband wanting to keep his wife from the other Navy wives and neighbors because he believed that would protect her from what he perceived as inappropriate ties. Our husbands need to share their wisdom on that point with others in their unit and neighborhood. An isolated wife is a disaster waiting to happen.

Beyond security needs, we need on-going involvement in our community that allows us to share our interests and abilities, and to expand them in the process. Whether this is through a job, a church, a bowling league, a service organization such as the American Red Cross or Girl Scouts, or through a combination of the above, *we need to live in and through the community in which we find ourselves.*

Husbands and Singles Connecting to their Community

Wives have been the traditional glue to the community, but husbands and single service members should explore this domain as well. As human beings mature, we feel a need to simply give of ourselves and to be valued for our offering.

One prime example of young soldiers, male and female, enjoying their gift to their post family was last year's family Halloween party at Fort Myer, VA. The USO Outreach Center advertised in the barracks for monsters and Spook House leaders, and found itself overwhelmed by the soldiers' enthusiasm. Now they have formed an on-going planning group for other USO activities and feel a real part of their post community, not just inhabitants.

Wives' Clubs can certainly serve as catalysts and clearinghouses for community connections as they change their roles to meet today's military family needs.

Multi-Ethnic Families

One thing that we all can do where we work as employees or volunteers is to build a climate in which people of many different ages and backgrounds will feel welcome to participate (much like the climate in our ideal unit family). For example, one of my volunteer jobs this year in my civilian community is the Arlington Public Schools' Advisory Council on Instruction. One of my tasks is to find 340 volunteers to serve on our 17 advisory committees, ranging from subject areas like English and Science, to fields such as School Lunch and the Gifted and Talented programs. I have cast a wide net to find the traditional volunteers (mothers), but also grandparents whose children have long ago left the system, singles who are new in the area and are looking for a way to make friends and work in interest area, fathers (and we get *many*), and high school students who are more aware than anyone of the day-to-day situation in their schools. Sadly, few so far have been military connected; if more were visible, perhaps there would be less perception of us as parasites.

Our Lifetime Composite

The roles that each of us will play in a lifetime will be many, and they will vary according to our own age, stage, personality and goals, the assignment our husband may have, and where we live. Our lifetime composite, the braiding of the various strands of our life, will be the important measure. Each of us should strive for our own *creative balance* - balance of time for ourselves, our family, and our military and civilian communities. One important ingredient in our roles, however, is *choice*. I insist for myself on the right to choose the commitment I make. I believe that the *quality* of my work is greater as a result, and probably the *quantity* -- and I believe that the exercise of this freedom by each of us will result in meeting the important needs of our community.

Two questions that we can ask of ourselves, whether we are a military member or a spouse, are:

- Has my living *here now* made a positive difference in my life?

- Has my living *here now* made a positive difference to "my unit" and my community?

Each person who chooses to serve his or her dual communities can make a difference. Marilyn Ferguson, the author of <u>The Aquarian Conspiracy</u>, urged spouses at the Army Family Symposium in 1980 to be people of good will working for positive change in their communities. We need to be such a group. We need to strive for the maximum use of the many talents that belong to our military families. When we share at our highest level of ability, then we will bridge the gap between the military and its families, and the gap between the military and the civilian community. Isolation will be banished as we become active members of our five families.

Originally appeared as "Our Five Families" in <u>Family</u>, November 1982 and <u>Charting Your Life in the United States Coast Guard</u> (1983).

Isolation Matrix: A Tool for Discovery

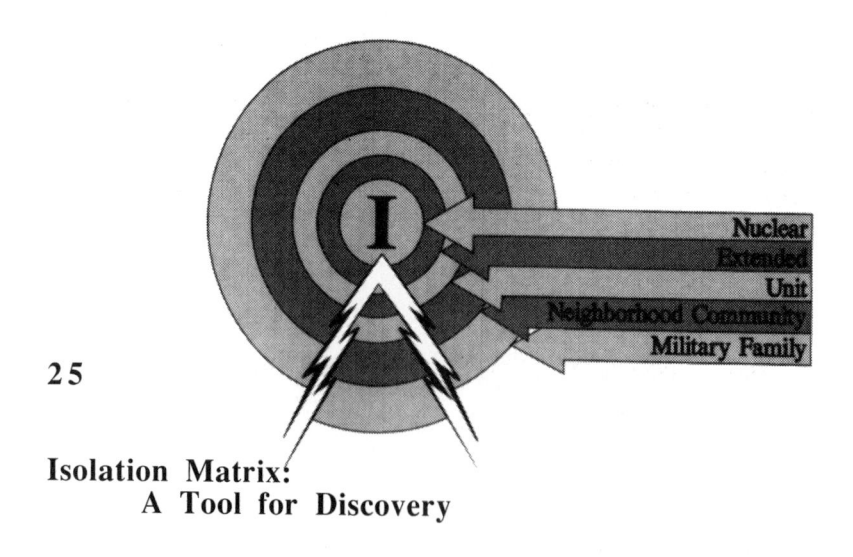

"Natty Bumpo didn't have a wife!" The officers in "Military Family Studies," Elective 246 at the Industrial College of the Armed Forces (ICAF) in Washington, D.C., reacted to this insight with laughter and then some pensive expressions. They remembered the hero of James Fenimore Cooper's *Leatherstocking Tales* and other such heroes of American literature who had peopled their boyhood reading. They were isolated men, loners, explorers. The women were not complex characters. They were cardboard creatures named for virtues like Honor and Chastity, even though prototypes for heroines abounded in remarkable frontier women.

Today's Natty Bumpos, in the persons of American military personnel, do have spouses who share their potential for heroic stature. Opportunities for meeting challenges above and beyond the commonplace do exist for military family members. Their awareness of the noble dimensions that are possible in their lives can be an important coping skill. Knowledge of their strengths and weaknesses enables military families and their care providers to deal with the omnipresent challenge: isolation.

Our Five Families

Recognition of the positive, as well as the negative aspects of isolation can be aided by the following matrix. The five families of which military family members may be a part are:

Nuclear Family -- one's spouse and children, if married; or one's parents and siblings, if single.

Extended Family -- one's relatives (who may or may not live close by) and, for a military family, the network of very close friends from one's hometown and from previous duty stations.

Military Unit Family -- the personnel in the specific unit to which one is attached, and their families.

Neighborhood Family -- immediate neighbors plus friends in the community in which one lives, on or off base/post.

Service Family -- the overall Army, Navy, Air Force, Marine Corps, or Coast Guard which provides official and unofficial support services to military families.

When an individual has support from four or five of these families, he or she can function well. With only three, he or she experiences stress. Fewer supports place him "at risk." *See Chapter 24 for a full explanation of this concept.*

Types of Isolation

The vertical axis includes four major *types of isolation* (that are due to the military setting vs. personality disorders):

Geographic Isolation -- physical separation

Social Isolation -- at the level of acquaintants, surface recognition

Emotional Isolation -- at the level of deep friendships, lasting ties, recognition of one's abilities and thoughts

Cultural Isolation -- a catch-all category which includes:

> *ethnic isolation* -- foreign-born spouses; living overseas or in a new section of our own country
>
> *aesthetic isolation* -- lack of quality visual and performing arts, education, and intellectual endeavors
>
> *spiritual-philosophical* -- lack of pursuits of a religious and/or ethical nature

Uses of the Matrix

The Isolation Matrix can be used by a wide variety of participants. The officers and spouses who are students in my ICAF course have found

176   Coping With Our Lifestyle

that discussion of the matrix allows them to share insights that would be too personal in other contexts, and it accentuates the complexity of the military family lifestyle.

- An individual may fill in his or her own profile, spotting strengths and weaknesses.

- A military unit group, such as the Key Wives in the Marine Corps Air Station Cherry Point Family Readiness Program, can work up a generalized profile which will enable them to pinpoint ways in which they can provide support. They will also find areas which the Service Family or one of the other five families could serve best.

- Service providers, such as family service/support centers (FSC), could do likewise.

Examples of Isolation

Some of the examples of isolation that have been suggested by ICAF students and Key Wives may trigger your own thoughts. The symbols (+), (-), and (+/-) indicate the evaluation they placed on each experience. Some "cures" are added.

Geographic:

- Husband deployed or TDY; physically absent (-), but if communication is possible (+/-).
- Lack of phone, newspapers for junior enlisted families (-).
- Living at a distance from extended family:
  - (-) if family is supportive;
  - (+) if one joined the military to escape bad situation at home;
  - (+) if one learns independence

- Living at a distance from other unit families (-).
- Lack of sponsor (-).
- Deployed units leave families behind (-). Cures: visit or tour similar ship; use videotapes or films to show activities at home or aboard ship.
- Ghetto of military housing overseas (+/-).

- Lack of transportation from base or trailer park to town (-).
- Fishbowl existence when living on post -- no privacy (-).

- Loss of vistas of one's youth; lack of natural ties with the earth (-). Cures: annual visits "home;" canoeing, hiking, gardening wherever one lives.

Social:

- "Caging" of wife, association with neighbors or unit wives forbidden (-).
- Very young children, especially if no $ for child care (-).
- Lack of skills in making friends, especially true of those who grew up in a small town (-).
- Cabin fever, often climatically induced (-).
- Difference of lifestyles (between member and extended family, unit families, or neighborhood families) (-/+). Comment: military families often outgrow a provincial background, come to value differences.

- Strident separation of officer and enlisted families (-).
- Failure by Commanding Officer (CO) to initiate whole-unit activities which would help families identify with the workplace, mission, and each other (-).
- Isolation of very senior and very junior personnel unless seniors initiate and assist (-).

- Unit family is by chance, not by choice (-).
- If unit is large, anonymity may result (-).
- Military families seen as lower class by locals (-).
- Social isolation of wife when husband is deployed (-).

- Increase in number of working wives leaves less time for socializing outside of family unit (-/+).
- Sense of immediate common bond with other military families (+).

Emotional:

- Companionate marriage style strengthens a couple, but may isolate them from natural support groups (+/-).
- Reliance on nuclear family due to frequent moves (+/-).
- Some military personnel of the lone hero variety exclude spouses and children from their world (-).

- Differentiate between creative solitude (+) and loneliness (-).
- Lack of continuity in location, hours of duty, roles, etc. requires great emotional flexibility. An individual may grow to this challenge (+), or may decide not to invest in order to avoid hurt upon separation (-).

- Lack of family or close friends nearby to validate individual (-).
- Loss of unconditional love of grandparents and cousins due to distance (-).

- Development of intense friendships with unit families due to common experience (+).
- Lack of knowledge of normal emotional rhythms common to given military assignments (e.g. submarine wives' syndrome) (-).
- Failure by unit commanding officer (CO) to value family's role in readiness and retention (-).
- Refusal by some to be more than sociable (i.e. will not risk vulnerability, admission of hardships because it might hurt career) (-).

- Failure to know immediate neighbors (-).
- Strong ties to past unit or location may preclude investment at new post/base (-).

- Lack of frequent contact with other military families (-).
- Lower rank families feel like outsiders in the military community (-).
- Co-location of military family support services (+).

Cultural:

- Reliance on television families as "knowns" wherever one moves vs. active cultivation of new friends (-).
- Continuation of one's own traditions and artistic pursuits as link with past and future (+).

- Double culture shock for foreign-born spouses to U.S. military community (-/+).
- Culture shock of living overseas and re-entry (-/+).

- Loss of common class ethics or behavior, sense of being different from others (teens, whether spouses or children, feel this intensely) (-/+).

- Difference in cultural background (racial, ethnic, or educational) of neighbors or military unit families (-/+).
- Change in living conditions from that of one's past (rural or urban; density of housing, climate, location) (-/+).

- Lack of representation for military families on governing bodies (e.g. School Boards) (-).
- Lack of cultural opportunities for participation or attendance (-).
- Lack of understanding of military family traditions (-).

- Lack of religious faith (-).
- Non-valuing of military profession by others (-).

The Next Step

The predominance of negative factors is common to a first listing. Problem areas are more rapidly identified than positives or "cures." The next step in the use of the matrix is to focus on a specific area, looking for positives that were overlooked in the first general delineation, and looking for support services and "cures."

For example, at pre-deployment briefings one might hear a wife say, "Deployments give me time to really concentrate on my job or to pursue some long-term projects." A husband might admit that he enjoys his time at sea, and though he misses his family, he does not experience the daily friction between his two commitments. A wife might recognize that her self-sufficiency grows when she is responsible for finances, repairs, and child-rearing. Both might see that the deployment is a growth opportunity for all members of the family, an experience that their civilian counterparts probably do not have.

Making It Your Own

Where negatives remain, the task is to think of preventives or cures. One of the most productive exercises for pre-deployment briefings is to brainstorm ways to keep the person leaving emotionally present, even if physically absent. This problem-solving can take place on all levels, from the personal family level to the military unit and Service levels. Although many suggestions that have grown out of such meetings could be shared here, part of the value is the ownership generated by coming up with solutions tailored to the needs of one's own family, unit, or command.

Military families can live lives with heroic dimensions. They *explore* new domains, both geographic and emotional. They are often *alone*. Their terrain is full of peaks and pits with very few plateaus. The military lifestyle offers the opposing possibilities of greater success or greater failure than are common to most of their civilian peers.

The environment most conducive to human development is one sufficiently changeable to pose constant challenges, but not so severe as to prevent successful response. Use of the Isolation Matrix will help families and their care providers meet the requirements for Arnold Toynbee's ideal environment.

Originally appeared as "Isolation Matrix: A Tool for Discovery," as a presentation at the Ninth Biennial Psychology in the DoD Symposium, April 19, 1984, U. S. Air Force Academy, Colorado Springs, CO.

Kinds of Isolation	Nuclear Family	Extended Family
Geographic		
Social		
Emotional		
Cultural		

Isolation Matrix

Military Unit Family	Neighborhood Community	Family	Service Family

Kinds of Isolation	Nuclear Family	Extended Family
Geographic	husband TDY/patrol lack of phone, newspapers lack of $ -- distance from base	separated from relatives (+/-) joined military as escape from family situation
Social	"caging" of wife age of children affects socializing lack of friend-making skills teen wives - age barriers	difference of mil. lifestyle from home--lack of understanding mil. families outgrow provincial
Emotional	"companionate marriage" (+/-) mil. men as lone hero types lack of continuity in location/hours requires great flexibility	use of family traditions (+)
Cultural	appropriate in some cultures for wife to remain home TV "families" (-) continue traditions (+) (religious/aesthetic)	foreign-born not accepted by spouse's family double culture shock to U.S. & military

Isolation Matrix

Military Unit Family	Neighborhood Community Family	Service Family
distance from unit families deployed units leave families behind + = seagulling + = active wives' group	lack of transportation to town from trailer parks distance from base & other mil. families with whom to carpool/socialize (+/-) ghetto of mil. housing overseas unsavory housing areas in U.S.	provide transportation to FSC/ACS provide secure transporation for kids to school
frequent separation of officer/enlisted isolation of jr. & sr. -- unless srs. initiate failure of CO to establish unit bond	mil. families seen as lower class by locals odd woman out when husband is deployed -- seen as threat in civ. & mil. groups weather affects socializing	USO Outreach Centers--get neighbors to meet/interact meet with peers service-wide (CO's & XO's wives)
lack of close friends to share unit rhythms ignorance of normal deployment emotions refusal to be vulnerable	minus a few close friends lack of frequent contact with wives via clubs or job strong ties on last post preclude making new friends	recognition of high use of med. facilities at beg. & end of deployment FSC's/ACS's will help focus assistance (+) jrs. feel outside
opportunity to know others from foreign cultures (+ but threatening) maybe few with same values, education	sense of being different: foreign-born wives; fams. overseas; fams. in U.S. but in area different from past; lack of representation on School Boards, etc.	no understanding of mil. traditions no longer a homogeneous past for Services

26

Getting Organized

Here's a step-by-step plan to help military families organize their homes and their lives -- and get more enjoyment out of them.

Successful military families -- find them and find their keys to survival. That was my task for the Navy Family Program handbook for Navy families. What I found were people who were methodical in the organization of their household records and finances so that they had time and energy left over to enjoy their family, friends, and community. They exercised what I would call *organized flexibility*: structured habits which they were able to vary when circumstances made changes desirable or necessary. Theirs was a *secure* as opposed to *haphazard a*pproach to living. Creative variations, instead of chaos, and humor seemed to be major ingredients in their lifestyle.

As a former Girl Scout leader, I was struck by the similarity of the badgework and our task at hand. Girl Scouts today have added a series called "Challenges" that lead to the equivalent of the boys' Eagle Scout award. A Challenge itself is preceded by a set of requisites that are logical steps in preparation for the known or surprise Challenge. Military families certainly are challenged by expected and unexpected events, so let's see what the requisites would be for our challenge:

THE CHALLENGE OF ORGANIZED FLEXIBILITY

Purpose: To achieve an organized approach to our daily and overall family life so that we can minimize the financial and emotional stresses and maximize the enjoyment of our unique lifestyle.

Requirements: Make use of at least one suggestion from each category below. Check off as accomplished.

1. Tools and Places

[ ] Establish a working place for the family record keeper(s) away from busy family centers -- even a niche in a large closet will do.

[ ] The file cabinet should be nearby. Two small colorful file cabinets topped by a door combine for an efficient, inexpensive work space. (Until you buy a metal filing cabinet, you can use large accordion envelopes or a sturdy box with a cover.)

[ ] Basic necessities:
A. File folders and/or large envelopes -- recycle envelopes from your mail.
B. 3x5 card file for addresses of friends and repairmen.
C. Address stamps or labels to use for mail and book/music ownership. (I add my husband's office/ship address to the labels and use them on commissary checks and laundry slips.)
D. Notebook for listing household expenses and purchases.
E. Stapler to fasten receipts into notebook. (Tape dries out.)
F. Carbon paper for copies of business/complaint letters or multiple copies of letters to relatives. (Carbon paper is cheaper and closer than photocopying.)

[ ] Establish a family information center (the back door in the kitchen will serve nicely) with a *large* bulletin board, calendar, and phone. The calendar should have very large spaces so that everyone can record his activities for a given day. The calendar should have a flat finish so that pencils can be used (and changes erased).

[ ] Messages should either be attached to the bulletin board or placed at the person's place at the dinner table so he will be sure to see them.

[ ] Keep a good local map plus the Yellow Pages in your car.

[ ] Use the same format/tools/desk everywhere you move.

2. Daily Organization of the Household

[ ] Read the master calendar each morning *before the family leaves the house!*

[ ] On the bulletin board attach:
A. Children's school schedules, teachers, and lock combinations.

B. List of books each person has out of the library (calendar carries notation of due dates).

C. 5x7 envelope to hold tickets to plays, plus information you'll need (invitations, team/course schedules)

D. News of free and interesting activities in the community.

E. Rules for babysitters.

[ ] Tape emergency and work phone numbers to call.

[ ] Establish one chair or shelf for all letters to be mailed, library books to be returned, dry cleaning, etc.

[ ] Discuss plans for the next day at dinner time. (I put notes to myself at my place at the table because I *know* I will eat, and it is a good time to catch everyone for a joint planning session.)

[ ] Carry a mini-calendar and notebook for notes to yourself and others.

[ ] Keep a first aid kit and book in each car at home. Train family members in their use. (See *Sources* list.)

[ ] Record more than social dates and babysitting on the calendar. Write dates when major bills must be paid, birthday cards sent, and the lawn fertilized. Save your calendar as a reference.

[ ] Determine your own priorities for uses of your time instead of allowing others to do so. Try to maintain control of your schedule set according to your family's values, and turn down conflicts. (For example, we have established dinner together as a weekday "absolute," and rarely make exceptions.)

3. Household Finances

[ ] At the family information center, keep a running list of items needed at the commissary, exchange, etc.

[ ] Before shopping, check a master list such as the *Family Magazine* "Family Shopping List" to trigger thoughts about necessities not already listed.

[ ] Make your own rough route through the commissary, buying damaged items and heavy necessities first, and the rest of your list second. (Studies show that people who shop an *entire* supermarket spend more than twice as much money as those who shop at selected areas only!)

Getting Organized

[ ] Be flexible enough financially to buy bargains when you see them.

[ ] Maintain enough food on hand to provide for surprise guests or emergencies such as sickness or snow.

[ ] Buy food in quantity for economy, but package for your freezer according to your family size. This is especially crucial for a wife alone during deployment; you will eat more reasonably and nutritiously.

[ ] Determine your set costs for the month: rent or mortgage, normal utility and phone costs, and any debt payments. Don't forget to plan for big items like taxes and insurance. What you have left over is your "disposable incomes" for food, clothing, recreation, and savings.

[ ] Set up an allotment in the wife's name that will cover these basic monthly costs. This will guarantee enough funds to operate the household in spite of a deployment or separated duty.

[ ] Work out your taxes together so that each of you will know how in the other's absence. (Remember that your family service/support center probably has VITA volunteers -- Volunteer Income Tax Assistance -- to help you with any questions.)

[ ] When you buy an appliance or item that requires replaceable parts, get a good supply (e.g. buy a lot of bags and a few belts for your vacuum cleaner, extra liners for your child's thermos, and plenty of staples for your stapler). Our mobility and manufacturers' planned obsolescence work against us!

[ ] Some military families choose to buy major appliances from national firms that have outlets and repair centers throughout the U.S. and good mail order catalogs. (These catalogs also are handy for comparative shopping.)

[ ] Buy when you see:
A. Items for your children's car "treasure boxes" for your next move or vacation.
B. Items for dad's or mom's deployment "treasure box" (little puzzles and cards to open while away).

C. Christmas stocking stuffers (but keep a list of what you have on hand so that you don't forget!)..Christmas paper, too, so you have it on hand for early mailing or dad's/mom's deployment.

D. Inexpensive birthday gifts for your kids' friends -- they always forget to tell you about tomorrow's party!

[ ] Barter or swap services and items -- everything from kids' ice skates and winter jackets to piano lessons in exchange for babysitting, haircuts in exchange for skirt hemming.

4. Records

[ ] On your calendar, write in birthdays and the dates on which all major bills fall due (car, household goods or homeowner's insurance, local state, and federal taxes). Transfer these at New Year's as one of your resolutions! Read your calendar at the beginning of each day and month.

[ ] Maintain a spiral notebook that contains the following information:
   A. *Utilities bills* -- Water/refuse, electric, gas, and oil/fuel. Maintain running charts on use and cost to help you conserve and estimate costs. Staple bills to sheet facing chart.
   B. *Repairs* -- Star (*) those that will be tax deductible for homeowners. Maintain chart on date/item/place purchased/ and cost. Staple in receipts.
   C. *Major purchases* -- Keep same information as above and enter any movable items such as furniture of appliances on the inventory you keep in your safety deposit box.
   D. *Paint colors* -- Date, name, number, place purchased, and items/rooms painted (list same on cans).

[ ] Maintain separate file folders for:
   A. Car insurance and car repairs.
   B. Life insurance (information only; policy itself should go in your safety deposit box).
   C. Household goods or homeowner's insurance (policy in bank).
   D. House ownership or rental information (current and pertinent past records).
   E. Bank accounts (separate folder for each account).
   F. Taxes (one folder for each year for state, local, and federal taxes. Slip in all receipts, cancelled checks, or notes to remind yourself of volunteer time, mileage, contributions, etc. Keep photocopy of final forms filed.)
   G. Loan, credit card, and charge accounts -- though current bills should be in your desk file.
   H. Stocks and bonds accounts -- some prefer a small ledger.
   I. Husband's employment records -- all orders, awards.
   J. Wife's employment records.
   K. Social security (for children, too).
   L. Legal papers -- *copies* of wills, power of attorney, birth certificates (*originals* should be in safety deposit box).

Getting Organized 189

M. Family letters, photos to save -- especially information from parents on names of their neighbors, doctor, lawyer, and bank.

N. Inventory of safety deposit box contents -- some keep the key here.

O. Warranties and instructions for appliances -- receipts can be attached to the warranties or kept in the household notebook.

P. Medical/dental file for each member of the family -- make a copy of *all* medical records for this file before returning your official record to the hospital to guarantee you one complete set. Keep shot record and school dental insurance papers here.

Q. School file for each child (and adult!) -- includes report cards, honors, camp records, newspaper clippings.

R A list of addresses where you have lived -- often required for government clearance/employment.

S. Change of address -- keep all cards/forms that come with your magazines, stocks, etc. Keep a running list of these for transfer times.

T. Moving papers -- maintain inventories of the last two moves.

U. Car games -- that can fit in a file.

V Maps -- for towns where you have lived.

W Phone book -- for hometown or town where you own a home -- for list of friends, repairmen.

X Local bargain outlets and local sightseeing ideas.

Y. Decorating and house design ideas.

Z Education -- booklists for children and adult reading; ideas on college financing.

[ ] Maintain a desk top file or box for bills and letters that need current attention.

[ ] Retain in your safety deposit box:
A. Birth and baptism records.
B. Citizenship papers.
C. Marriage certificate
D. Wills
E. Powers of Attorney
F. Deeds
G. Titles to automobiles
H. Household inventory (small notebook listing items, date purchased, price, plus photos of expensive items and whole rooms and closets to help for insurance claims.) People who have served overseas *emphasize* the importance of leaving heirlooms with relatives, and putting special family photos and duplicates of important papers in a stateside box.
I. Bonds and stock certificates.

Coping With Our Lifestyle

[ ] *Don't Panic* has a good "Family Data Bank" form. Both spouses should know where all family records are kept. Advise your parents and older children of your pertinent data and its location as well.

[ ] Vote regularly and pay state taxes in order to maintain your home state residency.

[ ] Wives, use your college vocational offices as a free job referral and employment record center.

5. Deployment or Separated Duty Planning

[ ] If you have maintained the previously mentioned records jointly, then your preparations at this point will be much simplified.

[ ] Preventive maintenance by a departing spouse can save a great deal of emotional stress and unnecessary expense. Focus on the car(s), major appliances, and apparent plumbing/electrical problems.

[ ] Departing member show your spouse and older children how to do basic maintenance and repairs on all of the above, and leave written instructions for them.

[ ] List preferred repair people for auto and household emergencies.

[ ] Organize the workbench and tools so that all members of the family (kids, too) can find tools for minor repairs.

[ ] Keep your check off list of "things to do before deployment" in a file folder, and add things you missed. Next time you won't have to start from scratch!

6. Mobile Decorating

[ ] Choose 3 basic colors to use throughout your household. This provides visual unity and makes interchanging of rugs and furniture possible after each move.

[ ] To lessen physical and mental chaos after each move, purchase your own storage pieces so that you can put books, sewing, and desk items in the same location regardless of where you live.

[ ] When buying drapery material, buy enough extra to add on or make valences at your next spot. Use pleater tape to make width of drapes easily adjustable.

Getting Organized 191

[ ] Put sample of all furniture and drapery materials, plus wall colors, in a see-through plastic bag to carry when you shop.

7. Frequent Moves

[ ] Start one notebook in which you will keep all information relating to the move. Add a "lessons learned" section!

[ ] A book on moving hints would be a good lifetime investment. Keep notes in the margins.

[ ] Make a list of all people to notify of your move. Keep this list for next time in your change of address file.

[ ] Keep a record in your notebook of all costs of the move and star (*) those that will be tax deductible.

[ ] Maintain a folder on ideas for moving.

[ ] The Armed Forces Hostess Association can provide you with all kinds of information about the new area you are moving to. (Room 1A-736, The Pentagon, Washington, DC 20310)

[ ] Hand-carry copies of your medical, dental, and school records for immediate availability (even though the school must send an official record later).

[ ] Try to avoid accumulating things. Many people discover items as they move in that they haven't seen or used for years. How about a moving-in yard sale?!

8. Travel

[ ] Maintain separate file folders on past, present, and future trips. Save lists of items to take, things to do before leaving, and lessons learned to trigger thoughts for your next trip. List motels used (to locate lost items or to use again).

[ ] *Don't Panic* has a good list of emergency equipment you should carry in your car. Empty milk cartons make good flares.

[ ] Use military lodges or motels that offer reduced military rates. (See Sources list.)

9. Children in Military Families

[ ] Give your children responsibilities for the daily operation of your households for their competency and sense of worth.

[ ] Teach them how to find and use basic tools so they can repair their possessions and minor household items.

[ ] Maintain family traditions to give continuity in spite of mobility (Holidays, Sunday afternoon family time). Be flexible enough to add new ideas from new communities.

[ ] Provide a bulletin board each for all of your children to display their treasures; it functions as a visible scrapbook by reminding them of friends, interests, and their own accomplishments.

[ ] Teach your children the lifetime skills of organization. By 5th or 6th grade, provide them with a 3x5 card file for their friends' addresses, a file or folder for their special school papers, an address stamp or labels of their own for mail, books, and "business cards" (for odd jobs and paper route). By junior high age, they can use a basic ledger and check your monthly bank statement. These skills show up on state competency tests!

[ ] Allow each child one foot locker for treasures; he must sort out all of his own collections to remain within the limit.

[ ] Keep your kids ID and medical cards in your wallet because both are required for emergency medical treatment. Perhaps at age 13, they can keep their own ID.

10. Ties with Far-Flung Family and Friends

[ ] Correspondence is your lifeline to family, friends, and spouse during deployment or unaccompanied tours. Write "deep letters" regularly to keep these relationships alive.

[ ] Use carbon paper for multiple copies of a letter and add a special note on each. Both sets of grandparents or sisters will hear from you more often this way.

[ ] Send photos often to family and your deployed spouse.

[ ] Birthdays are important occasions for your extended families and friends. let your children be part of cards to grandparents, and jog grandparents' memories of upcoming birthdays in your house.

CHALLENGE FOR THE MILITARY SPOUSE: Accomplish the above requisites as a family *and work* outside your home as a volunteer and/or salaried employee, while maintaining your sense of humor at least two-thirds of the time!

Obviously, much of what is discussed above would be desirable for many families; but the security of being prepared and the lessening of unnecessary confusion is crucial to military families whose lifestyles require a great deal of adaptability. Arnold Toynbee sums up our situation perfectly: *The environment most conducive to human development is one sufficiently changeable to pose constant challenges but not so severe as to prevent successful response.* Order gives us a sense of control in the midst of the changes posed by our age and military occupation. Methodical though flexible living is the key to our survival and success.

****

Sources of Further Information: *(*Those out of print may still be found in your local library and they still have worthwhile information.)*

1. <u>Bonnie's Household Organizer</u> by Bonnie Runyan McCullough (New York, St. Martin's Press, 1980) -- filled with practical advice/charts.
2. *Keeping Family-Household Records: What to Discard* can be ordered free from the Consumer Information Center, Pueblo, CO 81009 (#623H).
3. <u>Don't Panic!</u> by Ruth Winter (Golden Press, 1975) -- handy guide for the whole family, but is especially reassuring for the wife. It includes first aid, appliance care, and a family date chart.
4. Irene Cumming Kleeberg has written the best book I know of for moving hints: <u>The Moving Book</u> (Butterick, 1978).
5. <u>Military Travel Guide</u> (P. O. Box 9654, Washington, DC 20016) -- lists military lodging and civilian hotels/motels that offer military rates. Also contains a good checklist to take when traveling.
6. <u>Temporary Military Lodging</u> (from Military Living, P.O. Box 2347, Falls Church, VA 22042) gives military lodging world-wide.
7. <u>Better Times: The Indispensable Guide to Beating Hard Times</u> (Dolphin Books, 1975) -- has great tips for saving on housing, food, clothing, energy, credit, health, and travel. It also contains good charts on nutrition, meat, appliance wattage, etc.
8. Mike and Marilyn Ferguson's classic: <u>Champagne Living on a Beer Budget</u> (C. P. Putnam's Sons, 1968) -- this offers the "sport, gamesmanship, craft, and art of economizing."

Originally appeared as "Getting Organized" in <u>Family</u>, March 1981.

Be All You Can Be!
Optimal Health for All of You...

    I awoke one morning recently, aware that I had been dreaming -- dreaming of an encounter with women who were saying,"Are we so *awful* that we need all of these programs on physical fitness, nutrition, parenting, dress-for-success, and color-me-beautiful?" I dreamed that I was the program chairman for a military wives' group and had just presented my plans for the year. I could hear myself saying, "No, no, it's because you have shown such interest in these areas and concern for your health that I thought you would enjoy them."

    Their mumbles and doubtful glances convinced me that I needed to explain further. I remembered an experience that I had had in a factory outlet about an hour away from our base. When I had finally found the fabric of my dreams and was excitedly carrying it to the sales clerk, she turned to me and my fellow bargain hunters and said,"you're military wives, aren't you?" We weren't sure if we should be pleased by her identification, but agreed that she had us pegged.

    "Oh, I can always tell. There's something about you all...you don't look alike, but there's something *healthy* and *happy* about you." We were relieved, and rather deeply moved, that such a delightful reputation had been established by our cohorts over the years.

    My imaginary wives' club began nodding their heads and telling their versions of similar encounters wherever they had lived. "My children's school principal asked if the military taught us how to move because the kids had adapted so well." "The cashiers at the commissary have commented on how friendly people are while they wait in line, how they share ideas on foods they see in each other's baskets, and how they seem to be balancing their budgets and menus in creative ways."

Research Shows Military Families Healthy

Statistics show that military members and their families are generally healthier than their civilian peers. But we still have room for improvement. As families, we have counted ourselves successful if we *prevented* illnesses and if we have maintained a pleasing physical appearance and a healthy attitude.

The Department of Defense (DoD), on the other hand, has measured its successes by illnesses cured, substance abusers returned to active duty, and weight lost. In the past, DoD has focused on *curing* the crisis instead of *preventing* it. Although cures are easier to measure than preventives (and, therefore, budget), wiser directions are now being sought. *Wellness* will now be the emphasis.

Wellness Approach

Dr. John H. Johns, a retired Army brigadier general, has been appointed Deputy Assistant Secretary of Defense for Health Promotion. Shortly after a tour of military installations in Europe, he shared with *Family* some of the reasons for this new approach.

"When we took a look at the ten leading causes of death in the U.S., we found that perhaps as much as 50 percent of the mortality is due to unhealthy lifestyles; 20 percent to environmental hazards; 20 percent to innate biological conditions; and only 10 percent to inadequate health care."

When those statistics were added to the mushrooming costs for health care in this country over the last 20 years, it became clear that DoD could effect an important savings in dollars and in individuals' quality of life and productivity if the emphasis were to be *prevention* vs. *treatment*.

As Dr. Johns explained, "We can continue to work on improving working and living conditions to reduce environmental hazards, but the major breakthough will come in the area of lifestyles. Many kinds of cancer, cardiovascular diseases, child and spouse abuse, and liver diseases can be traced to lifestyles."

Focus on the Positive More Effective

The catch is, however, that "most isolated efforts to change specific behaviors such as weight control and exercise habits, are not as successful as a strategy which focuses on the promotion of a more general healthy outlook." In other words, when we accentuate the positive, we are more likely to make a long term change than when we dwell on what we couldn't do. And we are more likely to make a permanent positive change when we have the support of the people around us. Much of the interest in years past has been on physical fitness. Dr. Johns plans to enlarge the idea of wellness to include *four* areas: our physical, mental, social, and spiritual well-being.

Four Areas of Well-Being

Our physical health is more than an absence of disease. it includes fitness (the ability to meet the demands of the environment) and performance (the ability to accomplish our tasks).

Our mental health includes our coping skills and our basic attitude about our ability to control our lives.

Our social health can be measured by our ties to loved ones, friends, and members of our military and civilian communities; our sense of belonging has a great deal to do with our state of overall health.

Our spiritual health, according to Dr. Johns, is not necessarily religious in nature. Our commitment to a "cause or group whose goals transcend the individual" brings us well-being on a higher level than the first three. Being part of something bigger than we are whose purpose is noble can give our lives deeper dimensions than if we simply exist from day to day. When our social environment supports the same values we hold, we are more likely to follow what we know is best for us.

Grass Roots Effort

Dr. Johns explained that the DoD health promotion program is not going to be a master plan imposed from Washington. "The key will be reaching military families at the grass roots level, getting them to determine their own needs, set their own goals, and buy into it. It needs to be *of the people, by the people, and for the people.* We need to have the sense of community, as something we belong to, not just a workplace."

General John A. Wickham, Jr., Chief of Staff of the Army, stated the same theme in *White Paper 1983: The Army Family.* "In promoting family wellness, we must find ways to transfer the skills, experiences, attitudes, and ethical strengths of the many healthy Army families....The strength of a community lies in the contributions and talents of its members. If the right elements are together in the right environment, the end product is often greater than what would otherwise be expected from the elements functioning independently."

Dr. Johns is excited by the multi-generational aspect of those who can be involved at the base or post level. The Retired Officers' Association has already pledged to work with the wellness program on the national and local levels. Dr. Johns sees uniformed members as important volunteers, as well as spouses and teenagers. Our teenagers have a great deal that they can share and we need to help them feel useful in their community.

Moderation is the Key

Health promotion has often been characterized by extremists in the past. Dr. Johns emphasizes that moderation is the key to his philosophy. "I am not a fitness fanatic. I don't run when I hurt. I believe in moderate but regular physical exercise."

Fitness is a family affair. His wife Barbara, besides running a household of three youngsters, walks 50 miles a month "at a fast clip." Cammie, now a college freshman, competed in her local Junior Miss competition last year, a program which requires a high level of scholastic competence, talent, and physical fitness. Bobby, 13, and Barbie, 12, play superb soccer on local teams with national standings.

Dr. Johns leaves us with a final thought -- parents are the role models for our children. If we really want to ask the mirror who is the fairest of them all, we must look at ourselves as the answer for our children.

There are those of you who will shout, "Unfair! No more guilt trips for parents, please!" But no amount of wishing it away will change the impact that we have, for good or ill, on those closest to us. With that in mind, let us take a look at a variety of little changes we can make, that when added together will radically improve our sense of well-being.

THE FOUR YOU'S

Your Physical Health:

Exercise:

- Choose a regular exercise program that suits your own needs. Laurence E. Morehouse, Ph.D., in his book *Total Fitness,* has five requisites in his plan: standing (two hours a day), twisting, lifting, a brief burst of motion to get the heart rate up, and sufficient activity to burn 300 calories a day. Start slowly and increase your expectations moderately but regularly.

198   Coping With Our Lifestyle

- Walk upstairs rather than taking the elevator. Walk up or down an escalator.

- Get off your bus one stop early and walk home, or park your car at the far end of the parking lot.

- Do your own housework and yard care. (Most of us don't have a choice!)

- Walk with your spouse after dinner. It will improve your physique and your communications!

- Walk, run, or bicycle with a friend after the kids go to school in the morning.

Nutrition:

- Consider a fairly firm policy that the family eats dinner together. This insures a full balanced meal vs. catch-as-one-can meals for everyone going in separate directions. The continuity and security that the pleasant family dinner represents can lessen the stress factors for children and parents. Get your community activities to arrange their schedules around the dinner hour.

- Make breakfast a requisite in your household. School children and adults need nourishment for their morning tasks.

- Remember your four basic food groups: fruits and vegetables; breads and cereals; milk and dairy products; meat, fish, and eggs.

- Think *color* in each meal as an easy reminder of the balance needed. If you have a dark green, a red, a dark brown, and a yellow-orange, you not only have an appetizing meal but are likely to have included critical basics.

- Think *variety*. Try something new two to three times a week. Your family will learn to be flexible in their tastes (a lifetime skill) and will probably find that their vitamin and mineral requirements are met.

- Buy vegetables and fruits in season. Wash them well to remove coatings used to make them marketable.

- Use as little salt and sugar in your cooking as possible. Let your family add a moderate amount of salt at the table, if desired. They really will receive enough salt and sugar in pre-prepared foods to meet their daily needs.

- East at fast food restaurants less. Pack your own lunch. Use the money saved for other kinds of entertainment.

- Give the children a cookie and milk or a fruit snack after school to pick up their energy.

- The commissary will be featuring many useful handouts on nutrition which will add to your resources.

Health Care:

- Mark ideal dates for annual physicals and dental check-ups for all members of the family on the calendar when you switch over at New Year's. Moms are the people least likely to get the annual preventive care we need. Keep your gynecological checks and immunization card up to date. If you feel the need for a more complete check-up, request it at your gynecological exam. Your doctor can direct further blood and urine analysis, plus any specific follow up on complaints.

- By participating in annual checks, your children will see wellness as the norm. Those who go to the doctor or dentist only for emergencies form a very negative impression of care-givers.

Your Mental Health

- A friend is good for your health. We all need someone who knows us well enough to share our peaks and our pits. Women tend to share more with other women, while our husbands tend to turn to us first (they can be too vulnerable career-wise to share with their peers).

- Cultivate your sense of humor. It is your Number One coping skill. When you can distance yourself enough from a problem to laugh at it (or yourself) you are in good shape. Help your children appreciate the fun and value of kidding.

- Remember that one person, *you*, can make a great difference in the lives of the people around you. That can be a positive or negative difference. Your conviction that you count and can accomplish good is probably your single greatest strength for a lifetime.

- Take advantage of the many mini-courses offered on parenting and other family-related subjects. Dr. Hamilton McCubbin, who has done a lot of work with POW/MIA and Army families, has collaborated on a major study, *Families: What Makes Them Work* (Sage Publications). He suggests that we build our repertoire of coping skills so that we are prepared for that riskiest of all stages: families with adolescents. Even those coping well in this stage are considered "families at risk!" His recipe for varied structure and flexibility, plus communications with our family members throughout our family cycle, is most helpful.

- Another helpful basic book for families is *The Well Child Book* by Mike Samuels, M.D. and his wife Nancy (a 1982 paperback by Summit Books). One especially interesting section for military families is the stress scale for preschool, elementary, and junior high age children.

Your Social Health:

- Find people who share your values. It is hard to maintain your standards when all around you seem to march to a different drummer. Seek them where similar hobbies, education, or religious affiliations will help them congregate.

- Get to know your neighbors and members of your military unit well. You all belong to these natural groups and can provide a great deal of valuable support for one another.

Your Spiritual Health:

- Find a cause or belief bigger than you are to which you can devote your energies and talents. In this day of "me-first" and occupationalism vs. commitment to a profession you need to find something that can make your striving worthwhile.

Originally appeared as "Be All You Can Be," in <u>Family</u>, February 1984.

Sources of Pleasure

Do you remember the fun you used to have when you went to a penny candy store with a dime in your hot little hand? And the anguish? How could you choose just ten, and the right ten, from such a mouth-watering array?

I had to re-live the experience with my own two children a number of years ago when an old cider mill in our village added a penny candy counter. The first few times, the kids took *forever* to decide, having had little opportunity to test the flavors. By the third of fourth visit, though, they both knew that although it was fun to try a few new ones, chocolate and licorice were their favorites, caramels were a close third, and most of the marshmallow-centered candies were not worth their money.

When we moved to Washington with all of its marvelous museums, concerts, and mini-courses for adults and children, I often found myself saying that we lived in a candy store. There were so many opportunities and we wanted to taste them all. Our calendar looked as if we had twenty children instead of two, and twenty-four waking hours in a day.

My husband would say that it still looks that way, but I would have to disagree. I have slowly moved to the point where I know that chocolate and licorice are my favorites, and that I have only a dime.

Choice

Choosing the uses of one's time has become part of the modern woman's goals. Her freedom to do so is terribly important in terms of the satisfaction she feels and the product she produces. The product may be her own growth or that of her children; it may be volunteer or salaried work; it may be a creative project, etc.

However, *choosing* may not be all it has been cracked up to be. If we choose, then we are responsible for our choices. I have heard more than one woman say in exasperation, "Just tell me what you want me to do, and I'll do it. It's easier than having to figure it out for myself, and I can blame you if it doesn't work out!" And even when we do choose, we find that our decisions will not last forever.

Strategies for Choosing

In order to help me set my own priorities several years ago, I adapted a little exercise that I had been given in a training session for Girl Scout leaders. We were asked to list things that we enjoyed doing; Later we were told to code the things we enjoyed doing alone and those we enjoyed sharing.

My version had to be more sophisticated because I needed a way to help me decide whether I would work full or part-time, whether I wanted to be salaried or a volunteer, and most of all, what combination of challenges and working conditions would give me the greatest source of pleasure. My *Pleasure Profile* was the result, and I would like to share it with you.

Charts

Start with the first chart entitled **Sources of Pleasure** (page 203). Put a piece of paper over the columns on the right so that they will not distract you during your first task. In the big section called *Sources of Pleasure,* you are to list at least 20 sources of pleasure (in the sense of enjoyment or fulfillment). I found that I listed "big" things first, such as teaching, singing, gardening (even weeding!), and exploring the woods. As I added to the list, some of the "smaller," but very important sources began to surface. I found myself writing things like "sending and receiving Christmas cards" (a time of remembering good friends and the parts of our lives that we have shared), "taking evening walks with my husband," and "waking my children in the morning" (those few precious moments when they are truly peaceful!).

You may find that you will keep adding to your list over the course of several days. Mine bears clumps of additions that I make each time I share this with others, be they military wives or my eleventh graders in summer school English.

Step #2 is to uncover the columns on the right. In the first one, check the activities that you like to do alone. The second column is for those sources of pleasure that you enjoy doing with others. You may overlap in these two columns.

SOURCES OF PLEASURE	alone	with others	top 5	requires a block of time	can be spur of the moment	have done in last 6 months	hope to do at next duty station
1.							
2.							
3.							
4.							
5.							
6.							
7.							
8.							
9.							
10.							
11.							
12.							
13.							
14.							
15.							
16.							
17.							
18.							
19.							
20.							

In the third column, darken in the square to show which are your <u>top five</u> sources of pleasure. You do not have to number them; simply identify them. Ideally, you will include these in your long-range goal planning. Even in the short-range, you will need to fulfill at least three of these five to feel happy in the deepest sense of the word. When two or fewer are part of your life, you will experience stress.

In the fourth and fifth columns, you should determine if each activity can be done on the spur of the moment or if it requires a block of time. If blocks of time are needed, you will need to build them into your life.

Those of us who have our husbands away for an extended period of time on deployment, TDY, or unaccompanied tour, know that we can target that time for special long-term projects. In fact, many wives of nuclear submariners get into the habit of having every other three months "to themselves," and often do not realize how they have internalized the rhythm until they confront shore duty and omnipresence! (The same is true for retirement.) Then, new ways of carving out the necessary blocks of time have to be found.

The last two columns will help you focus on how recently you've done what you've really wanted to do and how to make room for these sources of pleasure in the future. There is no reason that you have to wait until the next duty station. Make your own time line. My summer school students have learned to say "next fall" or "next year," whatever they feel will be their most logical time for change.

Needs and Goals

Now that you have a fairly precise sense of what gives you pleasure, it is time to work on the second chart: **Needs and Goals** (pages 206 and 207). You will probably want to expand the chart considerably, but our illustration shows the outline.) The *Needs* section gives you an opportunity to analyze your needs in both specific and general, short-range and long-range terms. For example, under the <u>Financial</u> section, I have included the need to send two children to college a year from now as short-range need. My long-range need is for sufficient financial security to be free from worry about having the basics of food, shelter, and medical care. I have also assessed my general desire for enough funds to live comfortably, but not extravagantly. A Honda suits me just fine, but I do need a car.

<u>Practical</u> is a kind of catch-all heading that includes space. For example, while I really would like to have a small room of my own for my work space in the long-range, I am willing to settle for a corner in a room infrequently used by my family for the present. Flexible blocks of

time that are not committed to other activities are necessary for my research and writing. I cannot chart these out ahead of time, because my writing seems to occur when I am ready subconsciously, rather than by a structured calendar. So, short- and long-range, I must leave time for *me*.

You may have practical changes you feel necessary or desirable in your living conditions. Perhaps privacy within the household or within the neighborhood is needed. Perhaps you have repair projects in mind.

Under the Physical section, list needs that relate to your own personal physical needs. You might include exercise, diet, sleep, and relaxation. You might also include an assessment of when you have the most or least energy.

The Emotional section may run the gamut from needing quiet time away from children, to needing one or two very close friends with whom to share your deepest disappointments and joys. Part of my emotional section is a need for a meaningful attachment to the community in which I live. I need to feel that my living *here now* has made some kind of difference to the people around me -- as well as to me.

Your Intellectual needs may sound like an awesome category, but some suggestions in this area include: Do I feel a need to further my education? Formally or informally? Do I need to read regularly? You could include cultural needs here -- the need to express yourself via music, dance, or art; or the need to appreciate others' expressions.

Spiritual needs include your religious, philosophical, or ethical beliefs -- or holes. Many military wives and children have acknowledged their need to know that God is with them wherever they happen to go. The need for family standards and traditions as a foundation for mobile families is mentioned frequently by those who cope well with our lifestyle.

Progression Repeatedly in Mobile Lifestyle

You probably have noticed that this list of needs progresses from the most immediate needs experienced by a young couple to the most complex. Interestingly enough, it is also the progression we experience each time we move. We have to start all over again at the shelter level, work though our emotional attachments to our new community, and finally find the time and opportunity to provide for our intellectual and spiritual needs.

How do we avoid going all the way back to *Start* in all areas each time we move? I think that a set of goals for the long-range gives us an

NEEDS:
Financial—
short range:
long-range:
Practical—
short-range:
long-range:
Physical—
short range:
long-range:
Emotional—
short-range:
long-range:
Intellectual—
short-range:
long-range:
Spiritual—
short-range:
long-range:

overview on which we can focus as we make short term decisions. <u>Without this, we are playing a game called *My Life* with unknown rules, unknown objectives, and unmarked spaces!</u>

Goals for Your Life Game

    The internal rules for your game plan should come from your sources of pleasure and needs; the external rules come from society at large and spiritual/ethical codes. The objective are yours to choose. I would

GOALS FOR MYSELF:
Financial— short range
long-range:
Practical— short-range:
long-range:
Physical— short range
long-range:
Emotional— short-range:
long-range:
Intellectual— short-range:
long-range:
Spiritual— short-range:
long-range:

compare your game objectives to your long-term goals. Your short-term goals will be beginning strategies for reaching your long-range goals.

In each of the categories in which you have assessed your needs, you now have the difficult task of determining how best to satisfy the short-range and long-range goals. For example, in the short-range financially, I choose not to work full time while my children are still in high school. However, I do want to do enough teaching and writing to build their first-year-of-college fund, and to keep my credentials updated. Long-range, I would hope to work full time, or nearly that, once they are in college. That goal is a mix of a financial need/goal and my emotional and intellectual needs/goals. I want to keep my skills and experience at a level where I could be self-supporting, if I ever should have to be. (That is different from saying that I *want* to be self-supporting!) You will probably find that your goals are hybrids, too.

Motivation

Why go through this excruciating exercise? There are a variety of good reasons. A study of college students found that those who had definite career plans by the mid-tenth grade were far more likely to be successful than their peers who had no target to aim for. Even if they later changed their targets, they had determined the amount of education they would need and had learned the necessary skills of decision-making and commitment. They could draw upon their past successes for the courage to make changes as they saw best while their unfocused peers felt the frustration of chaos.

Another good reason to go through this mental-emotional exercise is that an increasingly popular technique with interviewers today is to ask job applicants, "What are your long-range goals?" There are obviously some that are none of their business! You may want to be prepared, though, with a crisp response, explaining those that you choose to share.

Military spouses who choose not to be salaried employees will feel more comfortable about their priorities when faced by the sometimes-not-so-subtle pressures from other women to measure their worth in dollars.

Those being pressured to "volunteer" in an activity that really does not match their sources of pleasure list can be fortified to say "No," graciously, but firmly. My current response is that a given commitment suggested by others "does not fit my creative balance that I have worked so hard to achieve."

Things I've Done Recently Chart

This brings you to you final chart: *Things I've Done Recently*. With this chart you can explore what volunteer activities and employment you have been involved in for the last year or two. (You may expand the time frame, if you wish, to get a fuller picture.) List everything you can think of from church choir, to children's sermons, to required courses taken to update teaching credentials, to wives' club activities, and recent salaried employment.

THINGS I'VE DONE RECENTLY	By choice	By pressure (outer)	Evaluation (+ or −)

After listing your collection (and you will be amazed by how much you have done in a year or two!), use the columns at the right. Did you become involved due to inner pressure ("I ought") or outer pressure ("You ought")? You may find you have some overlapping here. *Pure choice* is a rare occurrence.

The evaluation section gives you the opportunity to say that each involvement was a plus (+) or a minus (-). You may find you have some mixtures (+/-) because we often learn valuable lessons, gain important experience, or meet special people in activities that are mixed blessings.

One of the things I discovered was that my choices did not lead me unfailingly to pluses. I did have one job I had to resign from in order to meet my source of pleasure requirement. A handsome salary did not compensate for incompetent leadership and unsettled work space. Even so, it was not a total minus because it helped me learn some important lessons about my own requirements for salaried or volunteer commitments.

Another discovery was that some activities that I felt I had been pushed into by others have been sources of real pleasure for me. I did not know that the choir presidency in my church would lead me to do publicity for our concerts. I have discovered that I really enjoy working with graphics, and my children have added their talents in drawing and calligraphy to make joint products.

When I refused to work as an in-school volunteer for the PTA (because I am a teacher by profession and felt the conflict would be unproductive), I was coerced to serve instead on the county expository writing panel. That opened up a whole new area of involvement for me -- at the policy level of education. As a result, I have served on advisory committees in Arlington, VA, for the last six years, sometimes two a year, and my daughter now serves as a student representative as well.

Your profile will help you determine where your choices can be made and what directions they should take. It will probably indicate, as mine has, that even some non-choices have brought us pleasure. Achieving the unique balance best for each of us will be aided by re-drawing our *Pleasure Profile* throughout our life's ages and stages. We still have only a dime, but our tastes may change after awhile, if we agree to try a few of the new varieties suggested by others. They may become some of our choices, along with chocolate and licorice!

Originally appeared as "Sources of Pleasure" in <u>Family</u>, September 1982. The charts are from <u>Family</u>.

29

Taking Stock: Freedoms

This is a good time of year to take stock of our lives....of where we've been....and where we're headed. After the holidays have come and gone, and decorations have been packed away for another year, we find ourselves saying things like, "I wonder if we'll be able to have a live Christmas tree next year," and asking questions like, "Will we be moving again this year?"

Now is the perfect time to measure our pluses -- and minuses. Time to relish those parts of our lives that we enjoy, and to set goals for things we'd like to change.

`While it's easy to dwell on the barriers in our way, it's far more productive to remember the freedoms we have -- *the freedom from.... and the freedom to...*These are the positives we need to recognize and invest time in, year after year.

Past, Present, and Future

I know that I will be moving this year. You may suspect the same will be true for you. How should we approach this? I will miss many of the friends and experiences I have enjoyed in Arlington, VA. I will miss the house that we have lived in off and on for ten years, and the views I have grown to love. I will miss my church choir and the remarkable music we've sung over the years (and even the Thursday night choir practices when nothing seemed to go right). I could dwell on what I will *miss*.

But it is far healthier for me to *savor the here and now*, to enjoy every minute that I am with friends and neighbors, that I'm walking my dog in my neighborhood -- and know I've made every minute count.

Now, how to *look ahead*?? Two and a half years ago, when we were getting ready to move from the Naval Submarine Base Kings Bay, GA, I received a brochure from Wesleyan University, my graduate school, offering a wonderful week-long course for writers. My husband saw me poring over the material, as I had done for at least the three preceding years (and had always found a family conflict to prevent me from attending -- a move, children coming home from college or going off to summer employment).

"Why don't you go this year?" His recognition of my yearning and his willingness to dog-sit removed some of my mental obstacles. I was sure I could get the new house sufficiently unpacked and sorted in two weeks so that he could camp out, and our two college-aged children would have gone off to their separate summer locations.

Why Not?!

Why go? became *why not?* And the freedom to invest in continuing education in my field became a wonderfully exciting experience. Often during the week at the university, I stopped to think about my personal freedoms that enabled me to be there and to be productive.

Physical Freedom

My physical well-being allowed me to walk the campus freely and swim during lunch breaks to clear my mind from information overload. I felt safe on campus, to walk where I needed to go, even by myself.

In fact, I had overcome a long standing fear of driving distances, especially in unknown terrain. My writing and consulting business had forced me to rent cars in unfamiliar airports, pick up a map of the area, and get moving -- not easy, but necessary.

I had other means of physical freedom that week that helped me assess my daily routine in a new way. I was in a dormitory room by myself. My total maintenance responsibilities were to make my bed -- if I chose. I could read as late as I wanted or get up early to study my assignments further. My learning came first....household cleaning commitments haven't had the same urgency since!

Social Freedom

The students were men and women of all ages -- from young newspaper reporters, to middle-aged fiction writers, and some senior poets. I found that I was able to make friends of all ages -- our work was what mattered, not our years. That freedom from "generation gap-itis" (or rank or social status, for that matter) enables us to value people for their ideas and abilities -- a very great social and intellectual freedom.

Emotional Freedom

I had emotional freedom because of my husband's encouragement, but also because of the "lone wolf" in me. I like people and need them for replenishment. But I also need time alone, time that I don't feel guilty about taking away from others' needs (a rarity for today's professional-wife-mother).

This ability to function socially and emotionally in the absence of one's mate is a trait often found in military couples who have experienced a fair amount of temporary duty and deployment or unaccompanied tours. Our inclination is to view these separate times as total negatives. But our competence as individuals can grow during these periods, even when we would much prefer to have our spouse at home. My husband's submarine patrols were trying in many ways, but I must admit that I was able to plan major projects to complete during his absence -- projects that gave me a sense of pleasure in my own growth and the opportunity to focus, without excuse, on my own accomplishments. This can be very difficult when a husband's career and mission become all-consuming.

So, as this new year arrives with a new family move, I know I can make the very best of what lies ahead by concentrating on my freedoms. You can, too!

Chart Your Freedoms

On our **Freedom Chart** (page 216 - enlarge it as you need to), start with your physical freedoms. List those aspects you enjoy. (I have listed "freedom from ill health and handicapping conditions." Other than five pounds I don't want and the increasing need to wear reading glasses, I am healthy. Also, in this category, I have listed "freedom from fear." With some basic caution and good sense, I can walk or drive anywhere I want to go. When my husband is away, I have a big dog for company and protection. I am free from physical fear, and therefore, can concentrate on other issues.

The Inhibitors

Under the column labeled Inhibitors, list the obstacles in our lives that prevent you from doing certain things. For example, many military families find that financial worries keep them from pursuing educational and cultural activities. For this reason, you might include "financial inhibitors" under this column.

Need To's

The third column, **Need To's**, is reserved for projecting ways to overcome the **Inhibitors**. For instance, here is where you can list ways to save and/or make money to overcome financial obstacles.

On my chart, "physical space" falls under the **Freedoms**. Over the years, I have carved out some awfully strange work spots: my sewing desk in a big closet, my typewriter in front of the tool shelves in the basement, and my cascade of papers on a hall tilt-top desk. Today, however, I have work space of my own. The freedom to spread out my writing projects on a desk that visitors will not see in my basement is sheer luxury. (This overlaps with intellectual freedom and freedom of time.

Time of Your Own

I have to qualify freedom of time. I work full time for the Department of Defense, but my time at home is "free" to focus on my own projects and shared time with my husband. My daily child-rearing responsibilities have ended, now that our two children have graduated from college. They need our love and support, but they are not at home for long periods of time. Time overlaps with social and emotional freedoms.

Social Freedoms

You can list a variety of freedoms under the social category:

- freedom to enjoy neighbors, acquaintances, and friends from a wide variety of geographic and ethnic backgrounds;
- freedom from social constraints that may have plagued you as you grew up;
- freedom to make friends of many age groups; freedom to make friends in your civilian community as well as you military unit;
- and freedom to entertain in the way you feel most comfortable.

Emotional Freedoms

You may find that emotional freedom overlaps with some other categories. For example, many young couples feel that geographic distance from their families is beneficial, especially in the first few years of marriage when feeling adult and working through the emotional complexity of marriage are exciting, but challenging tasks.

That same geographic distance from family may be helpful when our spouse is away on deployment or unaccompanied tour. We can "go home" to visit, but return to lead our own increasingly self-sufficient life, coping with all sorts of experiences that enable us to grow at a rate far greater than those who live in the same town year after year with few unknowns.

If your parents are in good health and are financially self-sufficient, you have an emotional and financial freedom that enables you to focus on your own needs. There may come a time when you will not have this freedom.

Cultural Freedoms

Cultural freedom covers several aspects, including your freedom to live in a foreign country and absorb the positive you cherish while assessing the negatives. Your measure of your own country and upbringing will be forever changed by such an experience. When you return to the United States, few (except other military families) will ever really understand. You have had the freedom to be a citizen of the world.

Cultural freedom can also overlap social freedom. You may be more democratic in your evaluation of people of other cultures than many Americans, and you may be far more adventurous in your tastes -- in food, art, and home furnishings.

Intellectual Freedoms

If you have lived overseas or in parts of the country other than where you grew up, you may have gained a new perspective on many of the "absolutes" you learned at home or in school. You may be freer to question due to your exposure to other approaches than you would have been in your original environment. As a result, you may feel you can make a difference in your own family, in your neighborhood, and in your community. You may feel free to set goals for yourself that would never have occurred to you in other settings. You may be free to dream.

As a woman, you may find your whole way of life significantly freer than that of your high school classmates. Reunions can be opportunities to measure what you are and what you might have been!

You're on your own in the **philosophical** and **spiritual freedom** categories. Figure out what is best for you, and pursue it.

Becoming........

Freedoms -- not easy! But what a glorious feeling when you have focused on them and pondered how to move forward.

Coping With Our Lifestyle

Freedom Chart

Types of Freedoms	Freedom To	Inhibitors	Need To's
Physical			
Social			
Emotional			
Intellectual			
Aesthetic Cultural			
Philosophical Spiritual			

*Draw yourself a larger version of this chart to hold all of your freedoms.

Last spring, my niece called one evening and said, "Aunt Kathleen, my high school psychology teacher gave us an awful assignment today. We have to interview someone who is over 50 and ask some very personal questions. You're the only one I know who's almost 50 that I'd dare to ask!"

She then proceeded to ask me to assess how I would evaluate my physical, social, emotional, and intellectual health when I was 20, 30, 40, and now 50. It was a snap -- because of my week at Wesleyan and quiet times thereafter. (Can you imagine her surprise when I had answers ready?!) You may want to be prepared -- some day your niece may call!

Originally appeared as "Taking Stock" in Family, January 1989. The chart is from Family.

Coping With Burnout

New Year's Resolution #1 for 1984:
Take care of and make time for myself.

Sounds selfish? No......self-preservation! It was nine years ago, in 1974, that I first made that resolution for myself. I had just been through a holiday season without compare. My submariner husband was, as usual, at sea on his 18th cruise in 15 years of marriage. The wives of his crew were telephoning for company or crises so often that in order to eat dinner, my two elementary schoolers and I had to take the phone off the hook (**pre-answering device days!*).

My church choir had decided to schedule rehearsals at 5:00 p.m. instead of our usual 7:30 hour, heedless of my cries of dinner hour for youngsters and impossible for babysitters. Who was I? --- except the Chairman of the Music Committee, the lady who had teamed with the organist to raise the funds for and select the new rehearsal piano, a Scout leader, and the ever-present sponsor of the Junior Choir who fed the cherubs at rehearsal, calmed the director, and designed (and sewed half of) the new surplices. Who was I to complain?

And so it went through practically every relationship in my life at the time. Mothers failed to show up to collect their Brownies after Scouts. One of my oldest and closest friends reneged on her offer of Christmas dinner; a single teacher friend needed to stay and recuperate from an accident over the holidays; and yet another dear Navy friend needed to stay with me for a week while settling on housing for an upcoming move -- with two small children to be taken care of.

I had had it! You may wonder why I didn't have the courage to shout STOP! I had no energy left. I was, in today's terms, "burned out!" It was not a topic talked about at the time. Those who experienced it did so alone, guiltily. We did not share and learn from our experience, except on an individual basis.

I retreated to gardening, hiking in the woods, reading, playing the piano for hours, and writing poetry......sources of comfort on which I could always rely. Until I could carry on a conversation with friends instead of breaking down into incoherent sobbing after one or two minutes, I took the phone off the hook. I needed private, un-interrupted time for <u>me</u>, and sensitive neighbors turned out to be available when I sought them out. In time, I was able to emerge with a new sense of commitment to my own integrity as my number one priority -- without protecting it, I would have nothing left to serve my family or others.

Research on Burnout

In the ensuing years, I have seen articles on depression and have recognized the affliction that gripped me so mysteriously and so totally that Christmas. I have also learned that holiday times are the hardest times of the year, mostly because we have such memories of jubilant seasons past and such expectations for those present and future.

Since then, I have talked with those studying crises that afflict submariners' wives and others who experience many consecutive years of husband absence and responsibility. What at first was diagnosed as mid-life crisis is now seen as "burnout," coming too soon for the later normal developmental phase.

The stress which causes burnout is <u>cumulative.</u> It does not just go away after each patrol or deployment is completed. The impact shows up in women in their early thirties and, interestingly enough, tends to afflict the super-copers and the doers the most!

Teachers' experiences with burnout have been much-written about. I have asked ministers and social workers, who are also in caring professions, about their experiences. Some reply that their strength comes from God, so they do not suffer any lack of motivation and energy. Others respond, "You bet!" They mention annual retreats as absolutely necessary for their sanity and their renewal of faith.

Retreat

Retreat -- that is really what I did. I focused on my little family and some creative projects that would give me a sense of accomplishments, areas that I could control. I dropped most of my external commitments and planned on a trip to visit my parents in their new home in Tucson. It would be a new place to visit -- new sights to see, new flora and fauna -- and I would be cared for. But I would not be going until I felt I had regained a healthy perspective on what I owed to whom and why.

Loss

I lost something of myself that winter. I have never given as freely of my talents and concerns again. But I learned a very valuable, if sad, lesson: that no one else can or will be as concerned for my welfare as I must be -- welfare in the sense of wellness, wholeness. In order to protect myself, I had to fence off portions that I had gladly, if unwisely, shared.

I have had occasion to think of this again recently after reading Carol Gilligan's *In a Different Voice*, a book that will provide many hours of thoughtful reverie for months to come. She carefully explores the different routes that men and women take to so-called maturity, and speaks eloquently of the need to value the feminine mode as much as we have the male. In her discussion of women's tendency to see ourselves against a network of relationships, she comments on the need to protect ourselves from total absorption by these relationships. It is a shame that that lesson is often learned under duress.

Coping with Depression

In later years I have read a good deal on mild depression, and have found that I intuitively did what therapists would recommend as self-help activities:

1) Focus on your special hobbies, interest, or strengths.

2) Do some physical activity (like jogging, bicycling, swimming, or gardening your heart out).

3) Talk with someone you trust.

4) Find a change of location or involvements (i.e., go on a vacation; eliminate most old commitments and maybe try only one new one).

5) Work through the soul-searching period knowing that you will emerge as one who has become more honest with yourself than perhaps ever before.

6) Write out some guidelines to follow and post them where you (and important others) will see them often.

Sabbaticals

Colleges and wise public school systems build in sabbaticals to give their faculty renewal time; perhaps the military should take a serious look at providing the same relief from prolonged sea duty or overseas tours. Meanwhile, spouses who are often the presumed providers of numerous humanitarian services to their military and civilian communities are unlikely to see a structured relief. We will have to build it on our own.

Maybe being forewarned is being forewise. If I could give my now college-aged daughter and son a special gift, it would be a less painful route to caring for themselves as carefully as they care for others -- an ideal balance, hard to maintain. To you who are a little older than they, may I share a mite of experience that may enable you to redistribute your priorities for the New Year? Your fortune cookie says, "She who is a careful cook will not burn the center, and will share the recipe." *Pass It On!*

Originally appeared as "Coping with Burnout," in Family, *December 1983.*

> **Friendship**
>
> *By Kathleen O'Beirne*
>
> 1 cup Common Interests
> ½ cup Uncommon Interests
> 2 Tbs. Loving Care
> ½ cup Tribulation
> *(may substitute Stress or Sorrow)*
> generous pinches of: Levity, Humility, Vulnerability, Capability to Listen, Proximity, Energy, (Physical & Emotional) and Honesty
> ¼ cup Time *(add more than called for)*
> Sift together Common Interests and Uncommon Interests. Cream together Loving Care and Tribulation. Mix dry and wet ingredients in one bowl; add remaining ingredients to taste. Pour batter into a well-greased pan. Bake for 3 hours, starting at 250° and gradually increasing to 350°. Let cool thoroughly before removing from pan. Serves 2.

A Recipe for Friendship

A friendship reminds me of the complicated fruitcake that I make only once a year, at Christmas time, to share with special neighbors, family and friends. Each year I wonder if I am going to invest the time necessary for this remarkable concoction......and then I always do. I would miss it terribly.

As more of us are spending increasing amounts of time away from home, in salaried or volunteer work, we find that we are having to pare down some of our activities and expectations. We simply cannot do all of the things that a full-time homemaker can. Each of us makes her own choices, or simply eliminates by omission.

Sin of Omission

One of the omissions, usually not a premeditated decision, is diminished time with friends. One friend with whom I worked for awhile alerted me to this phenomenon. She and a special friend joined the downtown YWCA with the plan that they would swim several times a week at lunch and have time together. It was a good plan; but the nature of their jobs precluded guaranteed lunch hours, so it had been months since they had seen each other. My friend said she was simply going to have to make seeing friends a <u>calendar item.</u>

Several springs ago, a young major who had worked a great deal with military families and was about to return to troop duty, opened another facet of the phenomenon for discussion. He worried that as more women headed into the work force, that they would lose that something special that he had always envied -- women's enjoyment of and openness with each other. He saw it as one of our greatest strengths. Men, he felt, rarely could be as open, as vulnerable, with each other. "In a military situation, everyone is either your superior, your subordinate, or your competition. I can't risk sharing my deepest concerns with anyone except my wife." He wondered if women, too, will find that the competition in the marketplace will overtake our propensity for networking. (*He died in the terrorist attack on U. S. Marines in Beirut in 1984.)

Companionate Marriage

Another issue lies hidden in his remarks -- dependence on one's spouse as one's only friend. There are dangers in overloading the marital relationship. In years past, men and women each had their own sets of friends, in addition to their friendships held in common.

Two factors that tend to be destructive of military wives' friendships today are *mobility* and *decreased discretionary time*. We usually use "discretionary" in relation to income, but I think time can be even more valuable. A capital F *Friendship* is much like the recipe at the beginning of this article. While it requires a variety of ingredients, its most important requisite is time. It must start slowly at a low temperature, and progress through higher heat over a long period.

It is a "from scratch" recipe, not a jiffy mix or fast food item. While there are short cut versions like acquaintances, they never have quite the flavor of the slowly cooked, well-seasoned *Friendship*.

Need for Reflection in Others' Eyes

Several years ago at a symposium sponsored by the Association of Foreign Service Women, Dr. Sidney Werkman spoke of women's needs for a few of these *Friendships*. So much of most women's lives are spent in enabling others to grow, in making connections in our communities so that beneficial activities or services are provided, that we do not have portable, visible credentials. Often what we value most about ourselves can only be attested to by others -- important others. While I know that we all should be sufficiently self-contained to be able to provide our own sense of self-esteem, I think most of us need to see ourselves reflected in others' eyes periodically or we could drown in anonymity at the beginning of each move.

I have a very special friend who has made it a point to visit me wherever I move, within the first several months. She says it is so that she can visualize where I am when I write to her, but I suspect the sharing goes deeper than that.

I know her parents, and she mine. We share our concern for them as they grow older, and her mother feels somewhat comforted by the fact that

I will be her daughter's friend into the unknown years ahead. What we do for each other is to tie together all of our tenses: our past, our present, and our future.

She also brings much needed skills, having wallpapered at least one room in each of my last two houses. Whenever I see those rooms, I think of her.

Laughter

Levity is the final ingredient that I sprinkle generously into my friendship batter. When writing the handbook for Navy families, *Making a Home in the Navy: Ideas to Grow On*, I did a "quick and dirty" chart of all of the characteristics of every military wife I could think of. A sense of humor showed up as the primary characteristic for those who coped well with our way of life. The ability to see the ridiculous in what otherwise might be overwhelming, the distancing of a situation from what is most deeply oneself, is a critical skill. Sharing that with a friend helps to keep life's crises in a healthy perspective -- and besides, it's fun!

Please add your own variations to my *Friendship* recipe and *Pass It On!*

****

Study on Work and Friends

These impressions have been confirmed by a 1983 book entitled *Lifeprints: Today's Women*, by G. Baruch, R. Barnett, and C. Rivers. The book explores the two components of women's sense of well-being. The researchers found that the component of <u>pleasure</u> was dependent upon the relationships formed by women: with their spouse, children, and friends. Married homemakers tended to score high on this component. However, only those women who worked had high scores on the <u>mastery-control</u> component.

The study(*) makes clear that self-esteem comes from personal, not vicarious, achievement. Interestingly enough, the highest scorers on the two scales were those who are married, have children, and who work outside the home.

The Need for Balance

The authors present the need for a balance in our lives between the extremes of "workaholic" and "lovaholic." Women in the past have tended toward the latter. Today's new career women risk over commitment to their work, just like their male peers. However, when looking for balance, the authors remind us that it might require the long view, rather than the short view of any given moment in time.

There are worrisome points in this study for military wives. Each scale, <u>Mastery</u> and <u>Pleasure</u>, has components that are easily disrupted by our lifestyle. Under the <u>Mastery</u> scale, one finds self-esteem (confidence, competence, and pride), the absence of anxiety or depression, and the sense of control over one's life (the sense of being able to shape one's life vs. feeling helplessly carried along).

Often military spouses, and sometimes the members themselves, do not have any sense of control over orders to new duty stations. When couples do exercise control by opting for geographic bachelorhood for an assignment (she stays and he goes), retention of the military member of the marriage often suffers.

The fact that achievement needs to be one's own, not vicarious, means that military spouses need to find arenas of success that are not based on their husbands' or children's accomplishments. With the mobility rate of military families, this is quite a challenge.

In order not to overload one's family as a source of pleasure, deep friendships need to be cultivated and maintained. Military spouses need to be ingenious in ways to support these special connections over time. Visits, phone calls, or letters of sufficient length and depth are critical to balancing this end of the <u>mastery-pleasure scale.</u>

One of the pluses of our lifestyle is that the periodic unaccompanied tours or deployments do function as times for us to work on our <u>mastery and pleasure scales</u>. We have the time and opportunity to become adept at self-sufficiency in a myriad of ways, and to reach out to other military wives, neighbors, and friends at work as social support systems (which we might not do if our husbands were home meeting most of our adult companion needs). We get the chance at growth on the <u>mastery scale</u> that recent divorcees experience, without the permanent loss of our spouse.

* *The study referred to was funded by the National Science Foundation, the National Institute of Health, and Time, Inc. in conjunction with the Wellesley College Center for Research on Women.*

Originally appeared as "A Recipe for Friendship" in <u>Family</u>, February 1986. Later adapted in the <u>Camden County Tribune</u>, June 12, 1986 and the <u>Dolphin</u>, February 21, 1991.

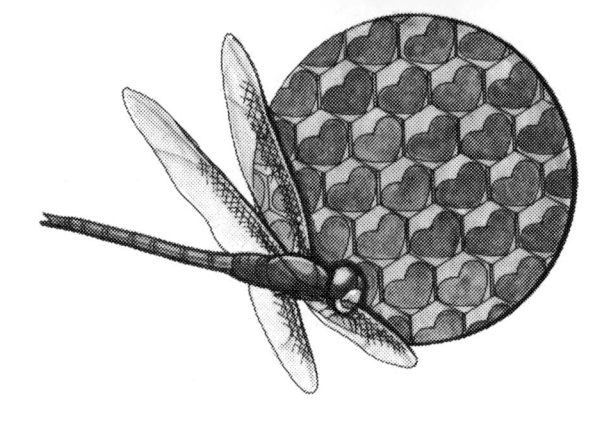

Friendship and Dragonflies' Eyes

What do friends and dragonflies' eyes have in common? Dragonflies' eyes see the same object 24 times, like a multi-faceted prism. Friends enable us to see ourselves many times over as well -- each holding a slightly different mirror to our eyes.

As military spouses, we know that moving can play havoc with our friendships. Friendship takes awhile to mature, and in the interim after a move, we must rely more heavily than usual on our immediate family for our view of ourselves.

As Georgia O'Keefe, the American painter who looked so intensely at flowers, commented, "...nobody sees a flower -- really -- it is so small -- we haven't time -- and to see takes time, like to have a friend takes time." It takes time both to *make* a friend and to *keep* a friend. Friendship is one of the soundest investments of time that you will ever make.

Your Wildflower Meadow of Friends

As you think of the people you consider friends (both past and current), you will probably notice that they are a disparate collection. Imagine inviting them all to the same party. Which ones would connect with others? We tend to make friends all along our personality spectrum, so two friends at opposite ends of our interest might not understand each other at all.

But it is just in this "wild" collection that we thrive. They allow us to explore a variety of aspects that make us richer human beings. As military spouses, we can adapt more readily to new places and new situations if we consciously broaden our interests.

Friends also allow us to cherish ourselves. Many of us were not brought up believing that this was okay, in fact, good for our mental health. If criticism, given in the name of "bringing you up right," was the staple in your family diet, you may have wondered if you were being self-indulgent when you relished the support, compliments, and genuine pleasure in your presence voiced by friends. It was almost too good to be true -- or to be "appropriate."

Friends are Good for your Health

Researchers are finding that people who have friends actually are healthier than those who don't. They are not sure of the reasons, but suspect that friendships either provide a sense of well-being or encourage people to take good care of themselves -- because others value them. How often do we say or write, "Take care..."?

Friends can stretch us, challenge us to grow and then provide the nurturing environment we need to have it come to pass. Through conversations, through interest in our ideas and well-being, they enable us to risk growth and challenge.

Friends Provide Strength

If, for example, you are thinking of applying for a job, friends can tell you your strengths and maybe warn you in a constructive way of some potential pitfalls. By role-playing, sharing what they know, and just plain rooting for you, they give you the courage to try and the sense that failure to get the job would not be the end of the world. You are still a valued person, and they will be there -- no matter what.

"No matter what" is a phrase we hear often about friends. Ralph Waldo Emerson phrased it a different way when he wrote in *Friendship:* "My friend gives me entertainment without requiring me to stoop, or to lisp, or to mask myself." He wrote of the luxury of being *oneself*, without all of the levels of "dissimulation, courtesy, and second thought" with which we usually protect (or mask) ourselves in the presence of others. We can share our deepest thoughts and concerns, not the shallow, guarded observations or brief glimmers of ourselves that we save for acquaintances. In short, we can be ourselves.

Friends Keep Things in Perspective

Friends provide a reality check. When we experience something unsettling that seems "out of sync" with the ways we have thought of ourselves, we can share our confusion and concern, knowing that friends will provide those mirrors we need to assess our experiences accurately.

For example, if your boss or co-worker launches a particularly unpleasant personal attack, you could wander around for days, weeks, or longer wondering what you had done to deserve the treatment. A natural inclination among women is to believe that we deserved it somehow. You might feel unable to share the experience at work, but a friend can provide the distance and the safe haven to analyze, to test the reality. Several friends are even better.

As women are moving into the domains of work and leadership that used to be reserved for men, we are finding that we have less and less "disposable time," and yet a greater and greater need for friendships. Ideally, we should seek out friends where we live (our neighborhood), where we play, and where we work. (Overheard in my office was a classic remark made by two friends who knew each other only through their aerobics class: "I've never seen you 'dressed' before!")

Friends in Your Unit

Military spouses need the added connection of friends in our military community and in the unit to which our military sponsors are attached. The unit connection is especially important if the unit deploys, goes into the field for training, or has TDY or unaccompanied duty. There are emotional rhythms that are shared by your group of unit families for each deployment or separation. Friends in other groups may know these rhythms rationally, but they are not experiencing them with you.

Those of us with husbands in the Submarine Force, for example, know that there are certain stages of wishing he wouldn't go, anger, fear, handling it, and then anticipating reunion, that we go through with each patrol or deployment. When people in different stages are mixed for an evening, there are certain awkwardnesses and a decision not to share what we're really feeling.

On the other hand, when you are with those in your own unit group, there is a willingness to "let your hair down," knowing that your vulnerability will be respected, that you are not an oddball, but indeed your emotional portrait is mirrored by those around you.

Overwhelming Breadth

Army wives at Fort Benning, GA, asked me to come last fall to share my presentation on multi-gifted women. I was amazed to see more than 100 eager faces awaiting me. Their questions helped me understand their interest. Many commented on the fact that they had learned to adapt to frequent moves by becoming involved in a wide variety of activities. They tended to do whatever was needed or interesting in each locale, and ended up with knowledge of an amazing breadth.

The Fort Benning wives found that that breadth was sometimes overwhelming to those who hadn't been exposed to their mobile lifestyle: either their own parents, old friends they grew up with, or those in their civilian communities. This is another good reason to have friends in your military community -- to share common experiences, test reality, and appreciate each other for what you are and what you are becoming.

You are *becoming* with friends -- in all senses of the word. You are growing and you are attractive in friends' dragonflies' eyes.

* *

Finding New Friends

There are lots of places you go where new friends can be made. Below are just a few spots to help you find them. Look for friends in:

- Places where you work, worship, or spend your leisure time -- at the golf course, tennis court, bowling alley, or swimming pool.

- Organizations whose goals/activities match your interests:
    - Girl Scouts (as leader, first aid volunteer)
    - Business and Professional Women's Association (a new military spouse version of this organization has started in San Diego, Honolulu, the Washington, D.C. area, and New London, CT)
    - League of Women Voters
    - College alumni/alumnae club or AAUW (American Association of University Women)
    - Navy Wives Clubs of America
    - American Red Cross, USO, and the Armed Services YMCA
    - Army Community Services
    - Navy, Marine Corps, and Coast Guard Family Service Centers
    - Air Force Family Support Centers
    - The Services' emergency aid societies
    - Ethnic clubs such as the Philippine-American and the German-American clubs

- Children-related activities:

    - nursery school or day care
    - your neighborhood playground
    - soccer and other teams
    - dance and music lessons

Friendship and Dragonflies' Eyes

- Military unit support groups and wives' clubs.
- School -- if you take adult education or college courses.
- Craft or hobby shop classes.
- Even in the waiting room at the hospital or in line at the commissary!

****

Striking Up a Conversation

There is an art to giving people enough information (a "hook") about you to enable them to pursue a conversation with you. Here are some pointers on how to do this.

- When you are new to a place or an organization, use your newness to say, "I'm hoping that I will enjoy it here as much as I enjoyed _____ (last place or organization).

- Wear something that is a conversation opener. (I have a brass pin with an unusual stone that I made when my Girl Scout troop worked on their rock and mineral and jewelry badges. It never fails to get noticed and I can share my Girl Scout experiences as a "hook.")

   In the commissary line, notice somebody's purchase and ask her how she or he serves it.

- In a waiting room (dental, medical, or airport), carry an interesting book (*Future Shock, Color Me Beautiful,* or a new decorating or diet book).

- If you've gone to a big meeting/group where you are afraid to meet people, think in advance of one or two topics you'd really like to know more about. Sometimes this is used as a "mixer" for conference groups. (Two years ago at the big Department of Defense Volunteer Management Training, I decided to look for someone who knew a lot about what to wear/pack for a conference. People were fascinated with my question, offered a few suggestions, and on I went. Through the conference, and actually two years later, I've had people come up and say, "Did you ever find somebody really good at wardrobe planning?" They had a hook!)

- Make yourself approachable. Instead of sitting inside waiting for someone to knock on your door, walk your dog, wash your car, mow your lawn, or plant a few flowers -- be where people can stop by to chat.

- Make it a point to make a little small talk with the *same* commissary cashier, the librarian, the mail carrier (don't laugh -- he or she *knows* your neighborhood), the bowling alley attendant, and your minister or chaplain. You lose your anonymity and have a sense of fitting in.

- Listen to the small pieces of information that new acquaintances give you -- they are adding to the sketchy portrait you have seen so far. Like Georgia O'Keefe's flowers, they take awhile.

****

Finding Old Friends: The Military Locator Services

Air Force:	U. S. Air Force, AFMPC/D003, Randolph AFB, TX 78150
Army:	U. S. Army, HQDA-DAAG-PSR, Alexandria, VA 22331
Coast Guard:	U. S. Coast Guard, HQ USCC (6-P5-1), Washington, DC 20593
Marine Corps:	U. S. Marine Corps, HQ (MSRB-13), Washington, DC 20380
Navy:	U. S. Navy, NMPC-641E, Washington, DC 20380

In order to find a "lost" military member and spouse, write a letter to your friend and put it in a sealed envelope. Put your friend's full name and last-known rank in the center of the envelope. Put your return address in the upper left-hand corner of that envelope. Proper postage is also required on the envelope.

Put this envelope inside a second envelope and all identifying information about the friend you have -- service record, Social Security number (if you know it), birth date/year, schools attended, etc., and mail it to the appropriate address above.

Originally appeared as "Through Your Friends' Eyes" in <u>Family</u>, *February 1989.*

All Kinds of Time

    Returning from my daily walk this evening, I noticed that the sky was a lovely peach above the stands of pine, live oak, and bay trees. Bats were swooping after insects, and sea birds were silhouetted as they plummeted in daredevil dives -- their foghorn cries coming as they pulled up, pressing the air from their lungs.

    My hands were full of fossils found along the dirt road. Scallops and clams, mostly, from the Pleistocene Era -- one million years old. They would be treasured specimens to add to my Christmas shell wreath. They came from dredge material scooped from the bottom of the bay to make room for the new submarines coming to our base four years from now.

    The very new and the very old have a special partnership here in the marshes of Georgia. A brand new Naval base is being constructed from scratch in the land of alligators, shrimp, fox squirrels, bobcats, and armadillos. Perhaps the armadillos are the most curious of our creatures -- prehistoric with no known predators, and yet Whiskers, my black Labrador, has a wonderful time chasing them.

    Time is a frequent topic of conversation here. Newcomers wonder how long it will take them to feel at home. The nearest cities are one hour's drive away.

    And yet, in another sense, time has stood still in our little nearby towns. If one insists on living on a paved road, realtors often close their files and say, "We have nothing to show you." The Teeny Weeny Gro. (grocery) makes me chuckle every time I drive into town. When I told the mayor's wife I need to go "downtown," she nearly fell apart laughing when she discovered I meant St. Marys, not Jacksonville, Florida.

Everything moves slowly here -- due to distance and climate. Those of us who refuse to slow our pace or expectations are often hot and bothered -- but we are getting more company all of the time.

Archaeological and Architectural Time

Time confronts us in so many intriguing dimensions. Construction halts when bones or pottery are found. Indian remains from 1500 B.C., their teeth ground by the sand in the shellfish, are identified and catalogued by the base anthropologist. Sharks' teeth from the Pleistocene Era are mounted on our base plaques, and camels' teeth are not uncommon finds.

Navy wives have participated in archaeological digs on base (two plantation sites) and just across from the base gates at the ruins of a mid-1800s sugar and starch "factory." Clad in heavy duty boots (so their machetes won't slice their toes) and bug repellant, these intrepid souls have sifted layer after layer for clues to plantation life that was productive 150 years ago.

Ground was broken for the commissary last year, and within a year's time, a modern facility was constructed. Modern inside. Its exterior repeats the architectural motifs found throughout the base: the arches, seamed roofs, and various designs in the brick work -- as old as Savannah and as new as today.

The Orange Hall Committee and the Historic District Commission in St. Marys work hard to preserve the survivors of the Greek Revival and Victorian periods. Now that our county is doubling its population in a short span, there is a need to protect portions of the town as it has been for well over a century. A sense of the past will be an important heritage to pass on to newcomers and the oldtimers alike.

Moving Time

Newcomers are arriving in moving vans, watching their possessions being moved into new quarters. Friends are leaving after two-or three-year tours. Their last weeks here take on new meaning. When a neighbor and I emerged from the piney woods with white button pipeworts yesterday, the neighborhood weaver looks at them intently. "I could soak those and weave them into my baskets. No one in Pascagoula, MS, would have those to work with! Where did you find those?" An excursion to collect the long-stemmed buttons was added to her list of things to do before departure.

Time functions so differently for those coming new and waiting *forever* to feel settled and at home. Those leaving either cherish every last moment that rushes by far too quickly, now that it's valued, or they wish time would fly so they can be gone and "done with this move."

Our local radio news editor, Rhonda Trull at WLKC 93 in St. Marys, summed up our varying reactions to time as she interviewed our Officers' Wives' Club president. She grew up an hour inland from St. Marys "in a very similar environment where dads worked hard at the mill and came home too tired to play with their kids. They probably always meant to do something with us, but before they knew it, we were grown up and gone." She has observed her Air Force brother with interest as he prepared to go on a two-year unaccompanied tour. "The last few months, weeks, and days became time for intense involvement with his family. Your values are based on supply and demand -- the less time you have, the more you value it."

Her observation of military families having a sense of needing to use time together or to use time *fully* is one I have heard over and over from civilian observers in the North and South. They see us as models -- people who value their family time, because deployments and separations are common experiences. We, as opposed to civilian families, have much more clearly designated time together and time apart.

Time Management

Today's emphasis on time management teaches us how to jam as much activity into a given day or week as possible. (See section at the end of this chapter.) Time management is not new. Benjamin Franklin wrote about his plan in his autobiography. He knew that reading, which is thoughtful time, would need to occur before the rush of his business day, so he arose at 4:00 a.m. every day.

On a daily basis, time plans can be efficient. What they tend to lack is an awareness of the other kinds of time that are important to our well-being: *personal time, pensive/philosophical time, social time, physical time, and emotional time.*

Emotional Time

The classic example of emotional time is the final scene in Thornton Wilder's play, *Our Town*. Emily has asked to relive a day in her life. She is advised to choose the least important day in her life because it will be "important enough." After seeing her 12th birthday as she never saw it while alive, she flees back to the Stage Manager and says, "I didn't realize. So all that was going on and we never noticed....Oh, earth, you're too wonderful for anybody to realize you. Do any human beings ever realize life while they live it -- every, every minute?"

Physical Time

Physical time has become a national concern because it is a key to good physical and mental health. Lieutenant Barbara Ford, a Navy dentist at NAS Jacksonville, makes sure that she has a full schedule of tennis and surf planing. They allow an exuberance that she needs after "inflicting pain" day in and day out.

Social Time

Social time is often seen as frivolous by workaholics -- male and female. But our lives are enriched by those with whom we associate, so we need to invest ourselves socially on a regular basis. Working mothers who attempt to juggle all of their various roles will admit that they feel the loss of time just to be with people they like, with whom they can share little and big thoughts.

Personal Time and Pensive/Philosophical Time

My definition of personal time is maintenance time -- of body, wardrobe, and soul. Somehow everybody else' mending gets done before mine. Women, in particular, have been raised to believe that time spent on ourselves is the height of selfishness. But failure to maintain ourselves physically, emotionally, socially, and intellectually is just plain bad business. Any manager who doesn't see that equipment is kept in top notch condition and that thought is given to innovative ways to improve or add to the product, is not going to be successful over the long haul.

Sometimes we can combine maintenance time with pensive and philosophical time......"maintenance" in the sense of gardening or painting windows and bookshelves. I have found that I can get double my hours' worth if I use my mind while my hands are busy performing work that is important and enjoyable, but does not need 100 % of my attention. Last year as we left our Virginia house, I painted window mullions with a pencil and paper on the step ladder so that I didn't have to get down from the ladder every time I had an idea for an article.

Later, a special friend, who was to move the same day we were, stopped by. We talked about our hopes for ourselves and our children -- as the window sills got a silky coat. The windows got done in no time and looked terrific!

Productive Time

Productive time must be protected, whether we work inside and/or outside of our homes. Each of us senses when we are most alert, early in the day or at the end when everything has finally quieted down. Knowing our own best time for productive work leads to strategies to protect it.

I am a morning person, so I work from 7:30 until noon, with the phone off the hook, if necessary, to prevent intrusion on critical time. I leave afternoons for errands, phone calls, and bed making (except on the day the exterminator comes -- one must maintain one's image!)

While my precise research must be done in the morning, evening time can be used for reading that I will want to mull on as I go to sleep. I keep a scratch pad near the bed and often write nearly unintelligible notes during the night. They form an outline to work on the next morning.

As a consultant, I work only six hours a day, and "never" on Friday. You laugh, but when I explain the logic to employers that I am creative, and paying me for more hours would be a waste of money, I get no arguments. I keep Fridays for bassoon lessons (for my daughter), the commissary, and a hair appointment when necessary -- cultural and maintenance time.

As we strive to juggle our day-in-and-day-out schedule, it is easy to get lost in the minutiae. What is vastly more important is the sense of the whole of our lives. Recognizing that the specific age at which we might be, the ages of our children and parents, our specific military assignment, and our spouse's commitments make our combination different at various points in our lives, helps us have a balanced perspective.

Ellen Goodman wrote a column for *The Boston Globe* on New Year's Day 1983, entitled "Gentler Resolutions." She noted that we tend to make resolutions to pursue discipline, rarely to pursue pleasure. Her suggestion: that we look over our lives for the good moments, and then decide how to look for happy potential in the future. Good advice! Happy New Year!

****

Time Management Techniques

Definitions: Efficient means using the least amount of time necessary to produce a given product. *Effective* may or may not include *efficient*. It has the overtone of a job well done using a variety of scales of measurement, instead of time alone.

Schedules and Plans:

Most plans will tell you that you are wasting time if you don't block off segments for specific tasks and hold to them. I believe in time-saving devices, but I believe in sufficient flexibility to pick up and run with an exciting option. A good book with schedules is: *The Superwoman Syndrome,* by Marjorie Hansen Shaevitz (Warner Books, 1984).

Prioritizing:

Many time managers will tell you to *list* and *do* the "big bear" tasks that all of us have a tendency to put off. I believe in listing such tasks or topics and doing the basic research on them. But then allow time to mull over what the best, most creative answer might be. Use time management as a *tool*, a *means* to a desired end, not the *end itself.* Agnes De Mille said, "The one thing I could not learn in college was to think creatively on schedule." Creativity actually requires a disciplined beginning, started far enough ahead of a deadline, so that the subconscious artistic process has time to work out an effective solution.

Calendars:

Time management specialists insist that you carry your calendar with you everywhere you go. I choose not to. It gives me the leeway to "consult my calendar" and make more considered responses, instead of being nailed on the spot for a commitment.

Perfection:

If you wait to produce a book or give a party until everything is perfect, it probably will never come to pass. There are times when it is important to produce a less-than-perfect product which you can revise at a later date or move on to something else that needs doing. Simply do the best you can at this point in time.

Dr. Hamilton McCubbin and Dr. David Olson in their book *Families: What Makes Them Work?* (Sage Publications, 1983), put to rest the myth that "well-functioning families are efficient and effective. The data clearly indicate that in the context of modern America, families are faced with the stressor of incomplete tasks." Does that sound like anyone you know?

The assumption each of us has made is that *others do manage.* But McCubbin and Olson, in their study of over 1,000 healthy families, found evidence that task finishers must be few in number, if they exist at all -- and that finishing all of the tasks we set for ourselves, or that we have culled from a rosy and probably distorted ideal, is not requisite to having a well-functioning family .... or life.

Originally appeared as "All Kinds of Time" in <u>Family</u>, *December 1985.*

Thanatos: Military Wives Deal With Death

"*Thanatos* is the Greek word for death. The Greeks saw death as a door to immortality, so we decided it was a good name for our group." Chaplain Ed Olander (U. S. Navy) was describing the origins of the group formed to assist the Beirut widows living in the area around Camp Lejeune, North Carolina.

Within about three weeks after the October 23, 1983 bombing, Chaplain Olander recognized the need to provide on-going support for the 48 widows with local addresses. His letters and announcement in the base newspaper brought one wife to the first session, seven to the second. Word of mouth has brought a total of 24 at one time or another, with eight to 20 regulars.

One of his greatest sources of information and support has been Kathy Nelson, whose first husband was killed in Vietnam. "She called about two weeks after the group started and offered to help. She was an answer to prayers." The widows see her as a survivor. "She looks normal; there's hope. Often she says, 'You may not believe this...' or 'You may not want to face this, but...'"

Facing the seemingly endless stages of grief and adjustment has been the group's task. When *Family* visited the group last spring, it was the first time the group was ready to share their story with the press. They could see how far they had come, but they were still very vulnerable -- and will be for some time to come. For that reason, *Family* agreed to protect their anonymity and respects the remarkable courage with which they are meeting one of life's most difficult tasks -- the sudden death of their husbands. They feel that sharing what they have learned about the value of a group such as theirs is a gift they can give to military families.

Most of the participants in the group are wives of Marines and Sailors killed in Beirut. Some are mothers and some are wives whose husbands died in Grenada, air incidents, or experienced sudden death due to non-military causes. They are generally under the age of 30 and have at least one child to care for.

They talked of the time right after Christmas 1983 as being the worst. Their energies had been focused on the funerals and the holidays up to that point, and then the reality of their loss began to really sink in.

Reactions from Others

They shared their anger at the insensitivity of others -- especially those checking their ID cards and questioning whether they rated medical or commissary privileges. "They simply don't read KIA (killed in action) or dec. (deceased) with any understanding. I cried the first few times; now I deal with them with anger."

Others seem to send the message: "Aren't you better yet?" The group members now find that they can manage a pretty brave front for the world at large, knowing that they have a place to come to weekly where others do understand, and where they can let their hair down and cry, if necessary.

They have found that men seem generally uncomfortable around them, probably because they don't know how they will act and whether or not they can contain their own emotions. And yet, military widows need information and advice from their husbands' peers. Chaplain Olander and Chaplain Dan Wheeler (who was himself a casualty in Beirut) have been invaluable in providing the male perspective and in being sources of assistance on military benefits.

Casualty Assistance

Although a Casualty Assistance Calls Officer (CACO) was assigned to each widow, many of the CACO's lacked information the women needed. For example, while most understood that the Commanding General at Camp Lejeune had agreed to allow the Beirut widows to remain in military housing up to one year, a few were not informed. Some wives who left the area right away to stay temporarily with relatives missed this information, so, therefore, made decisions they might not have made so hastily.

Those who knew of the one year reprieve have had time to "get our heads together and to finish the school year. There have been so many decisions to make, so many papers to fill out. It was not necessarily good to go home."

Sense of Humor

Humor has been one of the wives' best resources. While they admit that it was a "pretty black humor" for awhile, these women have a capacity for deep joy -- as well as deep sorrow. They, too, are survivors, like Kathy Nelson, whom they admire.

They know that there is a lot of healing yet to occur. Kathy has warned them that the second year will be worse than the first, and they wonder how that can be.

They are struggling through the legal and financial paperwork, and wonder if there will ever be an end to it. Many have been left with no insurance beyond the Serviceman's Group Life Insurance (SGLI) policy -- the basic amount provided by all of the Services. However, the Beirut Relief Fund, started by the Officers' Wives' Club and coordinated by the Family Service Center at Camp Lejeune, has been invaluable in bridging the financial gaps so far. The coffers now total over $200,000.

As some of the members of the group are slowly making decisions to leave the area, those who remain have determined to keep the group active -- for their own needs and for those who love loved ones in incidents in the years ahead. *(Pass It On!)*

For readers interested in establishing a similar group in your own area, you may contact Chaplain Ed Olander at the Family Service Center, Camp Lejeune, NC 28542. *(*Seven years have passed since Family visited. I recommend that you simply address any inquiry to the Family Service Center.)*

Originally appeared as "Thanatos," in Family, March 1985.

Caring for Aging Parents

We got a call saying that Mom was in the hospital. She had fallen and broken her hip, and she was probably going to have to be in a wheelchair for the rest of her life. She was going to be in the hospital for about ten days, and after that we had to have a place for her to go.

LexaLynn Hooper's recounting of her short notice for big decisions sounds like what most of us have feared in those quiet dark moments when we allow ourselves to ponder the what if's in our lives.

Counselors in military family support programs -- especially those overseas where distance from family makes concerns of this nature loom large -- report an increasing number of military families who seek information or assistance as they attempt to provide appropriate support for their own parents.

This past Christmas, three of the 12 spouse employment assistance coordinators in the Washington, D.C. area called to say they would not be able to come to our potluck gala with spouses because of the illness, death, or other care-giving required for their parents. A small sample? Yes, but it began to hit home.

The Navy Family Support Conference in Norfolk last November (1988) focused on the year 2000. Demographics projected an increase in non-children dependents (i.e. parents). Military families have the same concerns as our civilian peers -- but they are exacerbated by our frequent moves and deployments or unaccompanied tours. Because you may have to make decisions quickly (most parent-care decisions are precipitated by a crisis of some sort), *Family* has talked to four military spouses who have four totally different options for your consideration.

In LexaLynn Hooper's case, her friends told her to hold off making any decisions about her mother until they were absolutely necessary. However, it might be wise to spend some time now thinking, discussing, and researching your possible options, so that you will be prepared to make realistic decisions later.

LexaLynn Hooper and Her Mother

LexaLynn first spoke with *Family* last summer. At that time, she and her husband, Brigadier General Lynn C. Hooper, were very happy with the living arrangements that her mother had settled on. Four years ago they both had visited Roseburg, OR, where LexaLynn grew up as an only child. Her stepfather had been hospitalized with terminal cancer, and they did not want her mother living alone; she had her own physical problems. She was significantly handicapped with multiple sclerosis and rheumatoid arthritis, and, therefore, depended on a wheelchair, cane, or walker at any given time. She didn't drive, and her house was situated on a hill with plenty of steps. This left her quite isolated.

They visited foster homes -- in-home care facilities with one's own bedroom and a common living room and dining room. Usually several other elderly people lived there as well, but "you are at the whim of the family you live with." The costs ran $800-$1,000 per month, not including medication.

They looked at nursing homes, which were terribly expensive. The lowest was $1,695 a month, and that was for a two-to-a-room accommodation with three meals a day in a dining room. And she would have had to give up her own furniture.

They settled on a retirement residence, part of a chain, with a monthly rent that goes up periodically, but is reasonable. The renter retains all of his or her own estate. One does not have to invest one's life's savings and give up the flexibility to leave. The approximate cost was $1,300 a month, including medication. She was able to have her own living room, bedroom bath, and patio. More importantly, she could keep some of her own furniture and get three hot, well-balanced meals in a beautiful dining room each day. About 90 people lived there and a manager or assistant manager was on duty at all times, in case of emergency care needs.

Emphasis on <u>Living</u>

Most important of all, LexaLynn said that the people there saw themselves as "living" vs. those in the nursing homes who were "dying." Recreational and social programs were provided, as was a chapel. The residents served as a large extended family for each other. They went out to dinner together and relished the time when LexaLynn would come to stay with her mother -- usually twice a year for seven days each time.

During her twice yearly visits, LexaLynn would take her mother shopping (she saved up quite a list), and would go visit her own high school friends. She never considered taking her mother away from her hometown because her mother knew her doctor and had friends with whom "she had the freedom to grow old gracefully, at her own pace, privately."

Key Helpers

However, last November the call came with news of her mother's broken hip and hospitalization. LexaLynn flew out to Oregon from the Washington, D.C. area, and knew that she had a week to learn about all of the post-hospital options. Two people were key to her making wise decisions: the <u>social worker at the hospital</u> and the <u>Senior Services representative</u>. ("In Oregon, one joins Senior Services. They keep a file and know your needs.")

Her first search was for an appropriate nursing home that could provide therapy during her mother's recuperative period. Her mother had a very negative reaction to LexaLynn's first choice, based on what friends from her residence advised. But, she and her mother were able to agree on a second choice and LexaLynn felt relieved that the <u>ombudsman</u> there would check on her mother regularly.

Her next chore was to sell all of her mother's furniture, keeping only the treasured movables, and cleaning out the apartment. She helped her mother turn her finances over to a retired banker, now a <u>financial adviser</u> who provides bill-paying services for an hourly rate. He also sold her mother's car. LexaLynn did all the things that she will not be able to attend to from a distance. The fact that her husband would soon have extended temporary duty periods overseas (and LexaLynn planned to accompany him) added to her mother's concern for getting all of the loose ends tied up.

The final decision was where her mother should go when she had recuperated sufficiently to leave the nursing home. LexaLynn found that they were rushing into the decision out of their need to feel that everything was in place, and LexaLynn felt she was taking control before it was necessary. Deciding that it was better to let her mother make as many decisions as she was capable of, she talked with the Senior Services representative and worked out an arrangement so that she would be a constant contact and support system.

Finally, LexaLynn boarded the plane and headed home, feeling assured that all would go well. (She also discovered that you can extend a non-refundable airline ticket on the basis of a medical emergency. Once her mother was ready for a foster care home, Senior Services found it for her. Foster care homes are private homes that are equipped for ambulatory, non-ambulatory, and/or bedridden patients. The State supervises and certifies them. In Oregon, once a person is in a nursing home or foster care home, he or she is not to be removed if the finances run out. The State picks up the financial responsibility, not the family. In LexaLynn's mother's case, she pays $1,100 a month vs. the $1,695 fee for the nursing home.

At the age of 69, LexaLynn's mother has progressed to a walker, and uses her wheelchair only on her bad days when her MS flares up. She and her daughter value independence and self-sufficiency highly, and they are comfortable with their solution. They will now take the future one step at a time.

Joyce Kersh and Her Mother

Joyce and her husband, Rear Admiral John M. Kersh, have settled on a different solution. Joyce's mother came to live with them permanently a year ago. "She had often come to visit for several months in the winter when we lived in warm climates like Monterey and Key West," Joyce said, "but she didn't stay long in Scotland!"

As a very senior citizen, she did not have the health to continue to live in her own home in Pennsylvania, or the interest to live in a retirement community. "She is bright, sharp, and organizes her own taxes." Other than a dizzy spell that landed her in the hospital, she was physically self-sufficient until she fell and broke her hip a year and a half ago. "She broke it 'just right' so that a hip replacement was required, enabling her to be up walking with a walker two days later," Joyce said. "As a result of the hospital time, she met fine medical specialists who have continued to be her physicians."

New House Layout Required

The fall, however, intensified the Kershes' search for a house for the three of them with a bedroom and full bath on the main floor, and easy access from the garage. They spent a year and a half looking before finding a house -- much farther away from RADM Kersh's office than anticipated, and far enough from their original home in northern Virginia that Joyce now has to establish all new shopping patterns. "It really has been like moving to a totally new area."

The only modifications they have made to the house are the addition of a special space heater for her mother's room (so that she can be as warm as she likes) and some attractive teak rails from a boat yard to make nice narrow handrails along the hall from her room into the kitchen (so that she can cook when she wants to and keep them well supplied with cookies!). They also had the step from the garage into the house widened so that she can negotiate it with her walker.

Today their only major difficulty is finding a social outlet with her own peers. But they enjoy her company. "She's wonderful to have around, very positive, as helpful as her mobility and strength allow," smiles Joyce, and almost always in a good mood."

My Grandmothers

Compatible personalities are certainly critical for live-in arrangements. My Aunt Kay (Katherine Peterson) cared for my Grandma Parker for 25 years, until she died at the age of 89. As a young Navy wife during World War II, Kay lived at home the first few years because Uncle Pete was at sea. When he was assigned to San Diego in 1943, she moved out there from Minneapolis with their first child, and Grandma went with her. Unable to manage financially on her own, she became Uncle Pete's dependent, and was entitled to medical care, travel on orders, and was considered when housing was assigned. My dad, an Army officer, sent monthly financial assistance as his way of helping out. Kay says, "I would do it again. She was easy to live with, not demanding or interfering, and the kids (all eight of them) adored her."

As my parents moved around the world, my mother's mother was cared for by Mom's three sisters who remained in the Minneapolis area. At any given time, at least one sister (a nurse) and her husband lived in Grandma Hill's house, sometimes two. Thus, she was able to remain in her own home until my aunt died. At that point, she moved to the Methodist Home, which combined residential and medical facilities. My parents' role was financial support and visits when possible.

Marylee Seesholtz and Her Mother

Marylee, wife of Rear Admiral J. Richard Seesholtz, U. S. N. (Ret.), was fortunate in having one of her brothers near her mother. After her father died, her mother was left with the responsibility of selling three farms in Pennsylvania. One of Marylee's brothers decided to build a new house in the area and provided her mother the option of living with them in her own wing. "It was wonderful for about two years. She had her own living room, bedroom, bath, and kitchen. But then she got sick."

After an operation for cancer, she was put in a nursing home while undergoing chemotherapy. Marylee drove up to visit her every week. She found the drive from Virginia (where her husband was still on active duty) to Pennsylvania tiring and the quality of care discouraging, so she gave her mother the choice to come live with her, if she would not feel isolated from the rest of the family and her lifetime friends.

Marylee is a nurse, as was her mother. "She was a special person. We got along so well together. I had watched her care for others all of her life and felt I should care for her now." Marylee provided all of the extensive care that she required, believing that she should be in a loving home environment.

"I wouldn't recommend it for everyone. In the last hours as Mother lapsed into a coma, I considered hospital care a few times, but Mother's attending physician encouraged me to let her remain as comfortable as possible. The role reversal, caring, and nurturing, were very special."

Close Enough for Independence

The mother of an Army wife friend of mine made an interesting choice recently. After being widowed and moving from the family home in New England into a nearby townhouse for a couple of years, she decided that she wanted to be closer to her eldest daughter in Virginia, "but not in her hair." So mother and daughter looked at options and selected a condo in a senior citizens' residence. She purchased the condo and may sell it when she so wishes. There are a number of support services, such as a recreation director who arranges trips to the theater and symphony, and a driver who is available for excursions of all sorts.

She is a good 45-minute drive away from her daughter -- a distance that became "too far" when surgery was called for last spring and two round trips were daily fare during her recuperative period. Nevertheless, the independence and yet proximity seem to be a healthy mix.

Senior Housing Options

Congregate & Group Housing Apartments: Some are privately financed and others are publicly assisted. Where low-income facilities exist, application is made through the local Housing Authority.

Accessory Apartments: This is an independent living unit with its own outside entrance, kitchen, and bath. These may be especially desirable for younger families who want their older relative(s) near, or for older residents of large houses with space that could be converted.

Retirement & Life Care Communities: Many retirement communities offer single family dwellings, rental apartments, condominiums, and cooperatives, sold or rented in the usual manner.

Some offer only the basic services such as police and fire protection. Others offer transportation, home-delivered meals, and some in-home services. (Inquire about additional fees.)

- "Life care communities" require an initial payment (ranging from $15,000 -- $175,000+) plus a monthly fee ($150 -- $2,000+) for services such as maintenance, housekeeping, meals, and other personal care services.

- "Graduated Care" arrangements permit residents to move from their own apartment into a nursing home unit, if needed. Caution: States vary widely on their regulation of such facilities. Be sure to visit the facility, check on the financial solvency of the organization, and consult an attorney before entering into contract with a "graduated care" facility.

Shared Housing & Home Matching Programs: There are three primary benefits to this option: financial benefits from pooled resources to pay rent and utilities, etc., shared responsibilities for maintenance, and social interaction. Family agencies will help match individuals.

Echo Housing and Mobile Homes: "Grannie flats" are usually small living units in the back or side yards of a single family home. Mobile homes, where permitted, can serve the same purpose.

Resource

Family recommends an outstanding book for your reading: *How to Care for Your Parents: A Handbook for Adult Children*, by Nora Jean Levin (Storm King Press, P. O. Box 3566, Washington, DC 20007; $6.95 ppd.). A former "Nader's Raider," Levin has used her remarkable research skills to provide a sensitive guide to a sensitive subject. She has lived it, and she understands when her readers have dealt with all they can handle.

While all of the people who have been generous enough to share their stories with *Family* have been wives of senior officers, their concern and their solutions know no rank and no age. Their parents' ages have a range of 23 years, and if you add in my Grandma Parker who lived with my Aunt Kay after one and a half years of marriage, we are all in the zone of concern.

Originally appeared as "Caring for Aging Parents" in Family*, May 1989.*

Section VI

Potential Roles for Spouses

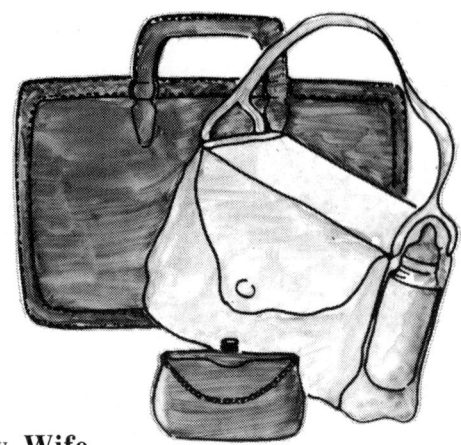

Roles of The Military Wife

"I need *answers!*" declared a military wife recently at a workshop at Fort McNair, in Washington, D.C. A working mother with school-age children, she is increasingly typical of military wives today who wonder how to juggle their time and energies at different points in their lives.

The recognition of "predictable crises" in our adult years has added to our understanding of the many roles women have had to fill. Our chronological age has a great effect on major concerns in our lives, and these concerns, at some ages, may be in direct conflict with what others expect of us. For example, just at the point where our children no longer need us every moment, and we have an urge to do something that interests us deeply, our husband's job may put us in the position where others expect us to volunteer our time for a project that does not interest us at all.

The women's liberation movement has increased our options, but as a result, women sometimes feel overly pressured to achieve. We must have the courage to decide for ourselves *what* we choose and *why*. The knowledge that we do have *choices*, and that others agonize over them just as we do, may help to lessen the sense of isolation that many military wives experience.

To reach that level of honest self-examination, it often helps to talk about the stages we are passing through with others who share similar problems, goals, and challenges. Getting something off one's chest with a friend or confidante can be very, very comforting, and it may provide the necessary support for a plan of action. But it might not necessarily provide a means of developing that plan. To accomplish that, workshops with structured discussion can be really effective.

Workshop to Share the Frustrations and Choices

Recently, I had the opportunity to develop the workshop for about 50 wives of students at the Industrial College of the Armed Forces (ICAF) at Fort McNair. ICAF graduates go to new duty stations at the end of the one-year course. Their wives, who voluntarily signed up for the three-hour Saturday morning session, were very much concerned about what their responsibilities would be at their husbands' next assignments. Many expressed a need to think through their expectations and, therefore, wanted to discuss the trends in society and in military life that are affecting them.

As an introduction, we talked about some of the changes and stresses that are part of today's family experiences. *Companionate marriage* is one of those changes. It is a marriage in which the husband and wife are not only romantic partners, but also are "best friends." In years past, wives had their women friends with whom to share their ups and downs; their husbands shared business and political discussions with other men. Now, perhaps because of the increased mobility of Americans (close friendships take a longer time to develop) and wives' higher levels of education, husbands depend on their mates more than ever to fill the role of companion. Women need to have close friends, as Navy wives are keenly aware during deployment cycles, so this narrowing of the traditional friendships to the marriage partnership alone may be cutting women off from important sources of support. We also reviewed general mid-life conflicts and typical conditions within the military community which have increased pressures on wives, especially command wives.

After about 45 minutes of "stage setting" remarks, the ICAF wives broke into small groups -- five women in each. Workshop registrants had been handed colored slips of paper as they entered -- one color for each branch of Service; to form a quintet for discussion, all they had to do was to make sure that the women in their group were holding different-colored slips of paper! We hoped that by keeping the groups small, and separating people from the same Service, that each woman would feel free to express herself candidly. Organizers of some other workshops I have attended have decided that a range of ages as well as Services would be desirable in small-group discussion so the composition of groups had been pre-arranged. Whatever method you choose, should you decide to organize a workshop for wives in your area, keep in mind that it would be wise to ensure that wives of one command are split up.

Factors That Affect Role Choice

In order to help sort out our ideas on the potential roles for military wives, I asked that each group focus on the following set of factors and discuss how they might affect a wife's role choice:

Roles of the Military Wife   251

1) her age
2) the ages of her children and her husband
3) geographical locations (urban vs. rural; overseas; on-post vs. off-post)
4) her own personality and desire for personal development
5) the changing of a wife's role, and varying combinations of all of her roles.

Role Models are Hard to Find!

In order to help the workshop participants analyze the influence of these factors on their lives, they were given a chart of six military wife "prototypes" to discuss. Coming up with these models was not easy. It is difficult to find a set of roles that examines a wife's choices on the basis of her own personality, need, and desires (most studies with which I am familiar evaluate wives' roles from the perspective of what their husbands' company or organization or their family requires of them as spouses and mothers, not on the basis of their own goals).

The source that helped me refine these six models for the ICAF workshop was *Ministers' Wives*, by William Douglas, a study of 6,000 clergymen's wives. Their lives parallel those of military wives in many ways. I have adapted his five models to six, and I have cast the role models in a military setting. They are presented here in alphabetical order, moving form the most involved with the military community to the least involved. *There is no judgment implied as to which is "best."*

The order in which each role model is presented is:

- **1** *her personality/motivation*
- **2** *her family/community involvement priorities*
- **3** *her role choice*
- **4** *activities: Service-related; her own*
- **5** *friendships*

A. AUDREY: Organizer - Leader

- **1** is work-achievement oriented; motivated internally, emotionally
- **2** sees service to others 1st, family 2nd
- **3** sees her role as co-worker with her husband; therefore, is not jealous of her husband's responsibilities to the Service
- **4** believes wives should be given training for their special leadership responsibilities which are more than those of most civilian wives; helps conduct leadership training; is president of the wives' club, chairman of volunteers for Navy Relief, ACS, etc., or ombudsman for her husband's unit; counsels wives with problems; is often

252 Potential Roles for Spouses

equally involved in her civilian community; time for a personal hobby is consumed by other activities
- 5 closest friends are other military or civilian wives of her age, and friends from school or college days; has many acquaintances

B. BETTY: Participant-by-Design

- 1 likes involvement; prefers being a helper instead of a leader
- 2 sees her family 1st, military and civilian activities 2nd
- 3 feels any leadership on her part would infringe on her husband's role; finds his irregular work schedule frustrating
- 4 is moderately involved in military and civilian community activities; attends wives' club, volunteers for Red Cross; sometimes informally counsels wives who have sought her advice; enjoys decorating and other home arts/crafts
- 5 her closest friends are family; she has many acquaintances in the military and civilian communities

C. CAROL: Participant-by-Personality

- 1 motivated by a desire to contribute through useful work; often a military daughter; tends to feel unsure of herself in social and leadership positions
- 2 rates service to others 1st, family 2nd
- 3 understands her husband's commitment to the Service
- 4 believes it is important for her to be a member of the wives' club; enjoys volunteering for the Red Cross or Thrift Shop; does not do counseling; enjoys the homemaking arts
- 5 feels unable to have close friends in the unit because of the need to avoid favoritism, but has many acquaintances

D. DIANA: Comfortable Individual

- 1 feels free to be herself; is confident in her abilities
- 2 places her family 1st, community 2nd
- 3 sees herself as no different from civilian wives; has a high opinion of the military, but is bothered by the unit's demand on her husband's time (interferes with his attention to his family)
- 4 chooses activities in the military and civilian communities in which she sees real worth, such as being an officer in a women's group, a Scout leader, or church committee chairman; has creative hobbies
- 5 has close friends of all ages from the activities in which she participates

E. ELIZA: Defiant Individual

- **1** resents the demands made on her by others, with few reciprocal supports
- **2** her family comes 1st at the moment (because her husband expects her to carry most of the load to free him for his work; she wants more companionship from her husband)
- **3-4** finds fulfillment in individual pursuits that are neither home nor military community-oriented
- **5** her friends rarely are military wives; instead they are those she works with and parents of her children's friends

F. FAY: Non-Participant by Design

- **1** is not defiant, is simply separate
- **2** focuses on her own interests; usually has no children
- **3** sees total separation between her lifestyle and military community; sees her husband's military service as his job
- **4** recognizes no need to participate in any military or civilian service organizations
- **5** has acquaintances, but no close friends

Group Reactions

After the discussion period, we re-grouped to share ideas. A woman from each group summarized their analysis of the effects of age, duty station, motivation, etc., on their lives as military wives., and brought out new aspects that they felt had had an impact -- finances being the main one! By looking carefully at the six role models, most saw that they had moved from one role to another at different points in their lives, and expected to continue being ever-changing combinations of the models in years to come. I think that they felt a certain relief in being told, "it's O.K. to choose what you want to do or be," but felt puzzled about how it would all work out if *every* military wife were to do so.

I'm not going to go into all of the comments recorded at the ICAF workshop in this article, because this really isn't an article about that workshop - it's an article about a *workshop format* that will enable you to create your own environment for fruitful discussion. The conclusions of *your workshop* are the conclusions that will be important to *you*.

Some women, like the wife who said she was looking for answers -- will be disappointed that no ready-made solutions are offered in this workshop format. What is more important is that each woman learns that she does have choices, and while making those choices is not easier than simply conforming to the expectations of others, it certainly is more fulfilling.

Our workshop was far too short, according to the participants, who wouldn't leave their groups even to grab a cup of coffee! In planning the session, we had wondered if working women would be willing to sacrifice more than just Saturday morning. The response was a resounding *yes!* So, I'll pass along to *Ladycom* readers a couple of the alternatives that were suggested: either a day-long session, breaking into the same discussion groups twice during the day, and mixing during a brown-bag lunch, or a series of two or more mornings, at least a week apart.

Those women who do accept leadership positions in the military community would be wise to recognize and encourage the enthusiasms that result from wives choosing to participate. It will be a challenge to break the old "thou shalt" habit, but the end result will be worth it. A workshop would be a good place to start.

For Your Bookshelf

A Nation of Strangers by Vance Packard (New York: David McKay Co., Inc., 1972).

The Moving American by George W. Pierson (New York: Alfred A. Knopf, 1972).

Corporate Wives -- Corporate Casualties? by Robert Seidenberg, M.D. (New York: Amacom, 1973).

The Executive's Wife by Ninki Hart Burger (New York: The Macmillan Co., 1968).

Ministers' Wives by William Douglas (New York: Harper and Row, Publishers, 1965). This book is out of print; try your library, or ask your chaplain or clergyman if he or she can lend it to you.)

Guidelines for the Wives of Commanding and Executive Officers, Navy Wifeline Guideline Series. Available free of charge from the Navy Wifeline Association, Building 172, Washington Navy Yard, Washington, DC 20374.

Originally appeared as "Roles of the Military Wife," in Family, *September 1980.*

Military Spouse Roles for the '90's

The "Princess and the Pea" is a parable for our times. You remember that the Queen Mother insisted on testing the candidates for her son's bride-to-be by a great many questions. And the final test of royalty was sensitivity -- the pea under layers and layers of mattresses.

You may have seen the modern version, "Once Upon a Mattress," which starred Carol Burnett. She arrives, having just swum the moat and climbed the walls of the castle, to apply for the job of princess. Removing her boots (and all of the frogs therein), she announces that her name is Winifred, "but call me Fred." The Prince is smitten immediately.

Our version opens with the Queen and King talking about the need to find the right wife for their son -- the heir to the kingdom. The King (a four-star general-admiral) is busy with kingdom business, so he tasks his wife with the mission. The Queen has been a remarkable consort for her husband, hosting tasteful parties, raising their only son, and having a sense that times are changing; her son will need a very special wife to help him govern wisely.

As she begins to make up the announcement of the princess competition, she allows her son to have his input (and, indeed, he will have veto power). But she turns to other wise women (*you*) in the kingdom to describe the ideal characteristics so that the qualities and abilities sought would be plain for all to see.

Coast Guard Spouses

Spouses at the Third Annual Coast Guard Wives' Convocation in Arlington, VA, last September gathered from duty stations around the country. Wise women of the kingdom that they are, they brainstormed the following qualities as requisites for the Princess:

adaptability
plenty of self-esteem
desire to grow and learn
patience
decisive abilities
sexy
self-reliance
fix-it/do-it-yourself capabilities
appreciation/adoration of spouse:
  no matter what!
understanding
nutritionist/cateress
physically fit/has stamina
motivator
independent
realist

flexibility
sense of humor
organizational ability
nurturing attitude
optimism
communication skills
honesty and sincerity
budget stretcher/financial wizard
crisis manager
nurser
can handle isolation
chauffeur, navigator
activist
compassionate
wardrobe consultant

CO--XO Wives in Norfolk

A pretty long list, you say. But spouses at the CO-- X0 Wives Training in Norfolk, VA, in the fall of 1987, added more desirable qualities and talents:

non-judgmental
adjustable
spontaneous
a planner
sense of humor (their number
  one requirement)
punctual
good listener
responsible
loyal
insightful
creative
a role model
religious
sensitive
assertive

thrifty
her own person vs. a shadow
a good mother
empathizer
somewhat organized
intelligent
good communicator
good-natured
caring
professional
compassionate and passionate!
self-starter
leads by example
unselfish
innovative
and wise enough to use all of these
  traits!

CO-XO Wives in Charleston

Other groups, including CO-XO Wives in Charleston, SC, who gathered the year after, have repeatedly described the ideal applicant for Princess in the same incredible terms. They kept the spirit of the fairy tale with such characteristics as:

flexible as a willow bough,
  but not as limp
wise as Solomon
a lady of many talents
self-pacing.....can take a day off,
  read a book, no telephone
resourceful
has a genuine affection for people

patience of Job's wife
as faithful as Ruth
gracious as a Queen
Julia Child's clone -- the
  Hasty Gourmet
intelligent -- not necessarily
  book smarts, but common sense

I had a few personal favorites to add if they left them out, such as:

balances family and community
chooses her role
seeks out others' needs
is tenacious

is divinely discontent -- has a
  compulsion to improve
praises others
touches others/ shows support

Applicants are Interviewed

Finally the advertisement, in all of its lengthy scroll, has been posted on every tree and door in the kingdom, and the day of the competition has arrived. The Queen is pleasantly surprised by the amount of interest shown, as the number of eligible young folks has been rapidly dwindling in the kingdom, and the stipend for the Prince, while regular, is not extravagant.

Each of the applicants must step forward and state her philosophy of life. Each has been given a name based on her quest.

Princess Sequester states, "My father believes a princess should remain aloof from the rabble to preclude contamination. I will have no profile, no involvement in the affairs of the kingdom."

Princess Bequester announces, "My father will bestow a fortune on me so that I will bring riches to my household. This will enable the Prince to support me in the fashion to which I am accustomed. My mother has taught me the *rules* by which I must live -- I will be guided by protocol, etiquette, and the way things have always been done before."

258   Potential Roles for Spouses

Princess Requester stipulates, "I am familiar with all prerequisites needed for the wife of the Prince. I will ensure that all those who serve in the kingdom know who I am and what I deserve."

Princess Noquester meekly steps to the stand and says, "I do not seek anything at all. Whatever comes will be."

Princess Peaquester (Pea stands for problem-seeker, perceptive pioneer) draws the analogy to a clam. "It is better to have felt the sand and been distressed, than never to have sand at all." She obviously has a sense of humor, is sensitive, and capable of producing a pearl.

The Prince knows immediately that he has found the love of his life, and his mother the Queen nods her approval, as do the wise women of the kingdom. The King is a little puzzled, and privately awed by the strength and commitment of his future daughter-in-law. He senses that she could run the kingdom, if the times should ever require or permit it. Deep inside he feels both a sadness he can't explain and an envy he is equally hard-pressed to admit.

The Prince and the Princess are married amidst great jubilation, and they live......

Parables are powerful because they are part of our collective unconscious. The groups that have worked with this parable for our times have seen the parallel immediately, and have chuckled through the serious assignment to describe the idea military spouse for the decade ahead.

Stages of Leadership

I have used this exercise in conjunction with my "*Leadership Strategies for Women*," a process for understanding the stages in which individuals or groups find themselves, and the strategies necessary to work productively with them.

- **Stage I** is the chaotic newcomer.
- **Stage II** is the rule lover.
- **Stage III** is the rebel. Military spouses have spent much of the last decade in Stage III, breaking loose from the ask-no-questions, follow-traditions, rank-has-its-privileges Stage II.
  As we look back on the 1980's, we see a decade in which military family issues were dealt with seriously because military spouses became effective adversaries, and, eventually, effective advocates -- Stage II and Stage IV.
- **Stage IV** -- it doesn't take participants long to discover that they've described a Stage IV leader in our Princess.

The Last Decade

The Navy Family Awareness Conference in 1978 was the first massive conference on family and spouse issues. The Army and Air Force followed quickly, but with very different configurations. The Army Family Symposia of the early 1980's originated with spouses. The Air Force held its first conference on families in 1980, for military personnel only. By 1981, the decision had been made to include family members as well -- including dual-career couples and single-parent families.

Problems were identified and necessary actions were stipulated. Formal support programs at the headquarters and installations levels were initiated, some at the instigation of Congress and others by commitment from the Services.

Heading into the 1990's

A new decade finds military spouses with legislation governing rights and benefits and installation-level support services that include developmental and crisis counseling unparalleled in most corporations today.

Most military spouses are employed, part-time or full time, to supplement the income of their military member and to pursue their own achievement. As such, they mirror their civilian counterparts and have revolutionized the military family. The word *revolution* is stronger than most military spouses would prefer, so perhaps *evolution* -- gradual, but significant change -- is more appropriate.

As John Adams recognized during our Revolution, revolutions and evolutions take place in the hearts and minds of people, not just on battlefields and in legislatures. The decade of the '80's has been remarkable in terms of changes in perspective *by* military spouses and *for* military spouses and families.

It culminated symbolically in the directive issued by the Secretary of Defense in the spring of 1988, stating that spouses shall not be pressured to volunteer in order to obtain favorable considerations or assignments for their military sponsor. Many senior military members wondered privately if the "good old days" of volunteers would be gone forever, and some senior military spouses worried that their sacrifices might not now be perceived as worthless. Had the rules to the game changed mid-season?

The Air Force, the Service receiving the most noticeable bad press on the issue, assembled a Blue Ribbon panel which, after prolonged and careful study of the whole issue, determined that Air Force spouses would like to continue to volunteer -- but they would like their commitments to be indeed *voluntary* and *meaningful* . In other words, less of the formal "face time" and more of the "meeting the needs of the community" and "meeting my needs" kind of work.

Volunteers as Ombudsmen

Another major change in the '80's was the growth of volunteers as ombudsmen -- military spouses who are appointed by commanding officers to serve as official liaisons between the commands and their families. The Navy established their program in 1970, as a result of one of Admiral Elmo Zumwalt's famous "Z-Grams." Today Navy spouses, mostly wives of enlisted personnel, receive structured training for their highly responsible position, including annual Ombudsman University training and monthly seminars on issues of interest. More than 4,200 spouses serve in this capacity worldwide. The other Services, including the Coast Guard, are adopting the concept as appropriate.

Ombudsmen form a trained cadre who serve as connecting links for deployed commands and advocates for family issues. They have, to a great degree, replaced or supplemented the traditional spouse support structure (the commanding officer's spouses and spouses of the executive officer and senior enlisted member). The fact that we now say "spouse," illustrates a move forward in sensitivity.

Support for Volunteers

Yet another major breakthrough in the '80's was the recognition that volunteers and volunteer managers need support -- both financial and training. The Department of Defense (DoD) Office of Family Policy noted the need for training on a worldwide scale, and in 1986, joined with VOLUNTEER - The National Center, to piggyback its annual conference with a military add-on. Since then, the number of attendees from installations as far away as Guam, Alaska, Panama, and the Netherlands has grown substantially. With each succeeding year, more spouses are selected as presenters for the DoD track -- a recognition that we are both professional and experts on our lifestyle.

Rank Friction

One issue that surfaced during the 1988 conference in San Francisco was "rank friction:" the fact that spouses still wear, or conversely, stereotype each other according to their sponsor's rank. Kathleen McCleskey, an Army wife, met the issue head-on at the 1989 conference in New Orleans. She and a talented group of spouses put together a skit that focused on an officer's wife and an enlisted spouse being interviewed for volunteer positions at a military relief agency. The interviewer held stereotypical expectations of each spouse's qualifications and, therefore, placed them inappropriately. The aside remarks were wonderful/. The conference attendees had no difficulty in assessing the scenario. An unplanned bonus was that the real spouse of an enlisted Navy member who acted in the skit, rushed out to don her white suit and silk blouse for her own presentation in the following session -- a very thoughtful talk titled, "Take Care of Yourself" -- a topic she had proposed after attending the conference a year before.

Commands are sending both paid staff members (such as directors of family support centers and volunteer coordinators) as well as volunteers themselves (under invitational orders). One group that is growing by leaps and bounds is the National Guard family support group volunteers. Members have recognized the need to become "smart" in a hurry. They are about a decade behind the active-duty sector in terms of family awareness and support.

For further information on the conference, contact VOLUNTEER - The National Center, 1111 N. 19th St., Suite 500, Arlington, VA 22209. The conference is usually the third week in June.

Research on Spouses

Military spouses and their traditional organizations are being studied with great interest by the Services. The Air Force Morale, Welfare and Recreation Division has done a survey of spouses, but a formal report was not available at press time.

The Army Family Liaison Office conducted a survey of wives' clubs in 1989, and discovered that one of the ongoing problems is communications. Many clubs continue to rely on getting their mail through an officers' club or NCO club, and the pass-on rate is slow or never. One absolute necessity in this domain is that each wives' club establish a post office box number for perpetuity!

Even with a return rate of 36 percent, the survey established that the responding clubs gross about $2 million annually. They give away 92% of their gross revenues, retaining only 8% for operating costs. One long-range plan that Shauna Whitworth, director of the Family Liaison Office, has voiced is that clubs could pool a certain percentage of their annual monies raised, and within five to ten years, be out of the annual pressure to raise funds. Through investment, the monies would provide the ongoing funds for local donations, and clubs could focus on activities that members feel are most important.

One point that needs stressing is that clubs should invest in themselves and their leadership -- seriously consider budgeting for training for their officers. Giving away all of the monies raised may not be the most fiscally clever thing to do. By exposing the incoming board to the wide variety of training available, a club may reap benefits beyond the traditional scope.

The Future

Military Spouse Day, the second Friday in May, is an opportunity for each installation to plan noteworthy programming that will meet the needs of spouses in the region. Use it.

Military spouses are experiencing the same "accretion of duties" (a wonderful Civil Service term that is used for justification of a promotion) that their civilian counterparts are noting. The big difference is that we have the added factors of mobility and deployment. One of the interesting resulting trends is the tendency of military members to become "geographic bachelors." The Services generally view this phenomenon with alarm, because the track record is that families can sustain one such tour, but the second brings either a divorce or a departure from the service. Without the support of a resident family, a military member may not be as "ready" to tour a second time.

We will continue to see an increase of dual military career couples/families and single parents in the decade ahead. Both bring their own specific need for support.

The 1990's will be a time in which we will become more comfortable with the diversity of choices military spouses will make over the course of their military-connected lifespan. The three keys in my forecast are: *comfort, diversity,* and *choices.*

Comfort -- It is always tough to be on the cutting edge of social change, but we have seen more than a decade of effective spouse advocacy for family support programs and solutions to the ongoing issues of child care and spouse employment. The first half of the decade ahead will continue to be "uncomfortable," but a great opportunity to strive.

Diversity -- We will see a great breadth of choices for spouses, a variety of age groups, educational backgrounds, cultural and ethnic heritage (some of which do not value volunteerism or leaving the household), and a variety of financial needs. We will need to enlist more non-traditional volunteers (including the young spouses and active-duty members) and be more adept at finding ways for employed spouses to participate in their military and civilian communities.

Choices -- Traditional spouse activities will need to provide potential members with choices in programming and activities. While the social interaction will continue to be important for welcoming new families to the area and new spouses to the military lifestyle, there will be an increased demand for special interest groups such as the Military Spouse Business and Professional Network/Association and the local chapters focused on military benefits sponsored by the National Military Family Association (NMFA). For example, wives in the Officers' Wives' Club at Loring AFB, ME, established an issues group affiliated with NMFA that would study one benefit or area of concern each month. The wife of the commander of the Strategic Air Command learned of their initiative, recognized its positive impact, and has urged its adoption by wives' clubs throughout the command. (That is a sample of courage to create at the installation level and savvy supportive leadership at the command level.)

Because of conferences, communication, and organizations, the '90's will bring greater worldwide linkages for military spouses. Our own mobility will be enhanced by communications technology for a cohesion and power that we have never experienced before. Two of the key players will be:

The National Military Family Association
6000 Stevenson Ave., Suite 304
Alexandria, VA 22304
(703) 823-NMFA

Military Spouse Business & Professional Association
7300 Whitson Drive
Springfield, VA 22153
(As of 1991, the association has sister organizations in San Diego, Long Beach, Hawaii, Sigonella (Italy), and New London, CT.)

A Hunger for Information

All of the Services have noted a hunger for information on the part of military spouses -- across age and rank-related lines. Participation in training for the wives of new admirals and generals, for example, has grown from about 50% to almost 90%. And the breadth sought has increased as well. The CAPSTONE course, originally one or two days at the end of husbands' six weeks, has grown to a jam-packed week, and the wives choose to attend, in spite of being employed outside of their homes.

This hunger for information does challenge the Services to fund spouse information and training opportunities. While there has been nearly across-the-board support for symposia and seminars at the installation level, or for spouses whose sponsors have been selected for various levels of responsibility, there rarely is any *financial support* built in. Money continues to be a significant problem for trainers. The Services would be wise to designate funds.

On-Going Issues

Issues that need support by the Services are:

• a continued pay level that will enable members and their families to remain in the Military Family;

• a valuing of true volunteerism and the services rendered (by both spouses and military members);

• spouse employment support services to enable spouses to find appropriate employment promptly; and

• child care -- both for employed spouses and for volunteers.

We have come a long way! A group of Navy ombudsmen at the Submarine Base, New London, CT, summed up their assessment of what has made the difference: respect. They now have a greater respect for themselves than they have ever had before, and a sense of self-worth is a powerful motivator. Additionally, they receive respect from their husbands and the families they serve, who are amazed by what they know about their community and services available. And, finally, the commanding officer, who may originally appoint them because he is required to have an ombudsman, grows to respect them as they provide crisis and preventive support to crew families. Their caring and increasingly expert approach increases readiness and retention of the unit for a minimal cost to the Navy, and, in return, gives them skills for a lifetime and respect ...the way of the future.

Originally appeared as "Military Spouses: Roles for the '90s" in Family, January 1990.

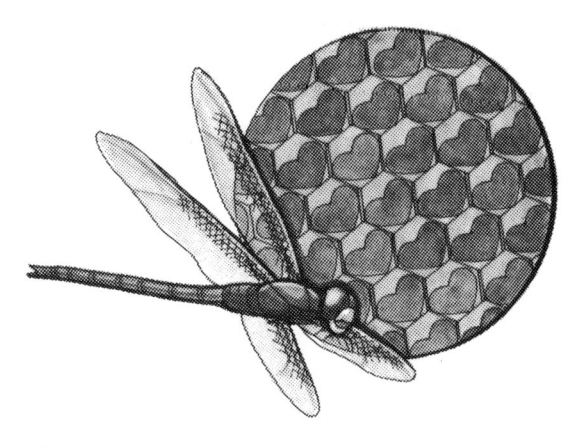

Creative Innovation

That's been tried before, and it didn't work.
Impossible!
What if.......
You've got to be kidding!
How about.......
They'll never agree to that.
We can't really make a difference.

Does this sound familiar? How many wives' groups, big and small, have the real desire to make some changes, to be catalysts in their military communities, and are met with the enthusiasm-killers above!

I recently had the experience of being a group facilitator at the Army Family Symposium in Washington. It was a landmark gathering of 300 able women who represented commands and wives' clubs from the continental U.S. and abroad. They came eager to identify common problems and to begin finding solutions. When the all-too-short conference ended after two intense days, I felt a joy at having seen so many bright, concerned women ready to tackle monumental tasks. These women *could* go back to their individual military communities and serve as catalysts for healthy, exciting growth and change...but I had the sinking feeling that without some tools to help them, they would find more discouragement than even their enthusiasm could counteract.

Scopes for Innovation

In order to talk tools, I need first to talk about a favorite toy. Do you remember that joy of joys....a kaleidoscope? As a child, I was fascinated by the variety of patterns a kaleidoscope could produce, and often wanted to share an especially intriguing combination -- but as I passed the scope to a friend, it would jiggle ever so slightly, and my chosen pattern would be gone. Beautiful, fragile, and, I discovered, of limited variety -- limited by the number of colored pieces of glass.

Several years ago, I discovered a *teleidoscope*, a scope through which the viewer looks at the world around her, and patterns are formed by the rippled surface of the lens. This offers more potential variety in patterns, but even so, the variety is finite, limited by the specific lens.

What we as innovative catalysts need is a new toy (or tool) that combines these two. It would allow us to look at the world around us through a scope to which new pieces of glass could be added. We would be able to see infinite patterns from which to choose the ideal. For want of a better name, let's call this an *ideascope*. The world viewed would change continuously as would the fragments in the scope. Each of us is just such a toy, adding our many experiences and visions as we look at our family, our community, and our world.

Creative Innovation Process

Creative problem-solving is a relatively new technique being taught at the university level to executives, and being taught by some outstanding teachers in elementary schools. It is a process that all of us could use in our daily lives, as well as on the higher level of finding solutions for community problems. Because "problem-solving" has a negative sound to it, and I want the process to be used as a highly positive approach, let's call our version *creative innovation* -- innovation being an introduction of something new, different, but not necessarily better; creative adds the idea of imaginative production.

There are seven basic steps in our process which can be followed by an individual or a group:

1. **Target** the general area of concern or interest.

2. **Gather** information -- either formally or informally.

3. **Focus** on one specific segment of the general area with which you want to work.

4. **Brainstorm** ideas -- come up with at least 20 ideas, the wilder the better at this stage, because you want ideas to bounce off each other, and lead to others. *Do not* stop to evaluate these ideas now. Sometimes people leap through the early parts of the brainstorming without realizing that they are creating (and rejecting) ideas. Write them all down for now.

Creative Innovation 267

5. **Evaluate** your ideas. In later samples I will show you how to set up a chart to weight complex ideas; simpler ones can be viewed without such a formal process.

6. **Plan** how you would put your chosen idea into action. Try to foresee all necessary steps and any potential difficulties. That way you are able to answer potential difficulties and doubts of others, and to cope with setbacks.

7. **Get Moving!** Put your plan into effect. Keep an eye on when and if additional changes may be necessary to keep it effective.

Sample Process on Topic of Housing

As I worked with two groups at the Army Family Symposium, I found that the participants were quite capable of targeting general problem areas (Step 1). Information gathering was informal because of our time constraints, so we moved quickly to Step 3. In the general area of housing, for example, we could see a number of segments that could be handled separately: quarters (their condition, availability); rentals (cost, condition, availability, distance, safety); purchase (cost, sale, absentee landlording); and many more.

For the sake of showing how the brainstorming works, let's target *rentals for young couples*. This particular segment is one that a young couple could brainstorm for themselves or a concerned group could take on for the community at large. Specific question: What are some alternatives to the standard one-bedroom rental apartment? Step 4 is to brainstorm at least 20 ideas. *Do not judge any suggestion now.* Just keep generating additional ideas. Please write in the margin as the ideas below trigger your own ideas.

1 An efficiency unit in a private home.
2 Room in exchange for work (household help or child care.)
3 Housesitting while families vacation or Navy wives follow the ship.
4 Vacation house or condominium -- out of season.
5 Tent (avoid evaluating now!)
6 Mobile home.
7 Resident manager of apartment complex -- get apartment free.
8 Caretaker-guide of historic home -- apartment plus $.
9 Caretaker apartment of museum, science center.
10 Boarding House -- long term arrangement.
11 Apartment or rooms in on-base quarters for specified service (household, yard)
12 Live-in teacher or foster parents -- spouse job.
13 Store security -- apartment overhead, especially in older buildings.

Potential Roles for Spouses

14 Motel or hotel manager -- spouse.
15 Blue-Gold rental for non-overlapping tour (such as on two-crew submarine).
16 Church apartment in return for maintenance, security, clerical work.
17 Fire department apartment -- for # of duty nights in return.
18 Live-in elderly care -- spouse job.
19 Private school -- security, maintenance.
20 Private club -- apartment in return for security.

This brainstorming section is really the most critical step. Depending on the complexity of your challenge, you will need a short or long period of time to come up with the required minimum of 20 suggestions. I find myself thinking of possibilities when I least expect them, and rush to jot them down. (I stop vacuuming to write or hurry though a bath ....or, horror of horrors, jot notes after going to bed, and a grouchy voice says, "For heaven's sake, turn on the light so you can read it in the morning!") Your mind keeps working on the challenge and allows association to produce remarkable results.

Serendipity

Serendipity is one such result. It is the seemingly coincidental coming together of events or ideas that produces a new idea. Some see this as almost magical. Others recognize that the brain's continuous unconscious attention to the problem has provided fertile ground for a variety of seeds from other sources to grow, producing a hearty new species. Inventors know serendipity. Conference planners find *the right speakers* "by coincidence;" and researchers read material they've read before with a new eye.....serendipity. Use it and enjoy it!

Step 5 brings evaluation of the ideas you have brainstormed. Examine them informally, if the problem is a simple one, or more formally if it is complex. Let's go back to our housing possibilities. There may be some that can be eliminated immediately due to personal inclinations or community possibilities. The others could be put on a chart and weighted on a scale of 3 - 0; for super (or not inhibiting), 3; good, 2' fair, 1; and awful, 0 -- or other such terms! On the chart that follows, (-) not applicable.

A sample chart for a young soldier and his nurse-trained wife might look like this. The categories across the top are those priorities across the top are those priorities or values against which each idea can be measure. Make sure that a slot is left for the basic appeal of the idea; sometimes an idea (or a would-be beau!) can be a very appropriate choice intellectually, but emotionally has no appeal whatsoever! Eliminate any choices with zero appeal.

Creative Innovation Chart

	allows independence	spouse has appropriate training	career enhancing for spouse, free time	allows free time for service member	community has possibility	financially attractive	we like the idea	TOTAL
1. efficiency unit in private home	3	(-)	2	3	2	1	2	13
2. room in exchange for work	1	(-)	0	1	3	1	1	7
7. resident manager of apartment complex	0	2	1	1	2	3	3	13
11. boarding house—long term	3	(-)	3	3	1	1	1	12
13. live-in foster parents	0	3	3	0	3	3	3	15
18. live-in elderly care—spouse	0	3	3	3	3	3	2	17
14. job store security—apt. overhead.	2	(-)	3	1	2	2	2	11

Our young couple finds that two choices are close: live-in elderly care and live-in foster parents. Step 6 brings them to a plan of action. Obviously they must seek out such possibilities, interview for the specific choices available, and, on the basis of positions offered, make a choice. If they are offered more than one position, they need to return to an evaluative chart to assess the pros and cons of each possibility. Let's say that they decide on elderly live-in as being the most career-enhancing for her, the least restrictive of his free time, and the most pleasant living conditions.

Step 7 is accepting the job-plus-live-in arrangement, and assessing periodically its continued appropriateness for their financial, personal, and career needs.

Community Policy Decisions

If you were dealing with housing alternatives as a policy-level community service, your chart would have to deal with the number of community offerings, acceptability of the ideas by military members and civilians, etc. If your decision includes making the young couples aware of housing alternatives, your plan of action would need to include groups you could contact for information on units or jobs available (such as the local Chamber of Commerce, local business organizations, employment agencies, or referral services) and ways to publicize the information. Who would be the best support service to coordinate all of this? The military housing office? The Navy Relief or ACS. The AUSA (Association of the U. S. Army), local Navy League, USO, or YMCA? You find evaluation necessary here again; and then, when a final choice is made, put your plan into action with some built-in, ongoing evaluation so that its success can be monitored, and corrections can be made as necessary.

Second Sample Process: Furniture for Young Couples

Because the brainstorming technique is the first key to your success, I want to give another illustration, again from the area of housing. One of the groups at the Army Family Symposium indicated that furniture seemed to be a target area of concern for young couples. It was felt that if they could provide their own basic necessities, they could save money by renting an unfurnished apartment; money saved could be invested in possessions or savings. So we brainstormed how furniture could be provided or obtained reasonably. In spite of the "That-will-never-work" refrain from a few, enthusiastic participants pursued ideas starting with "aloha kits" of basics to borrow from Navy Relief, ACS, or Air Force Family Services, use of military thrift shops, garage sales, and secondhand shops. Another suggestion was a special course in basic furniture construction at the post hobby shop. These were early suggestions, and were more or less what one would expect. As we worked our way toward 20 ideas (and there was not enough time to get that far), the quality of ideas improved greatly. One sample: one wife put together the desired goal of teaching young people how to finish or re-finish furniture with another goal -- that of the military taking care of its own. She suggested that a unit could take in and re-do used furniture, just as the Marines have refurbished toys at Christmas.

One interesting technique to be learned from this last suggestion is that of borrowing from an already successful program. When you're ready to make up your plan of action, look around for healthy programs in your community; can you borrow ideas or piggy-back? Avoid repeating an idea that has failed; instead, build on success so that the "halo effect" can help you get that important start.

Putting the Process to Work

Can we do this? We, whose education stressed "the right answer?" instead of imaginative answers? *We*, who have lived within a system that has not encouraged our participation at policy-making levels? You bet! Without realizing it, we go through the basic steps of problem-solving almost daily; while the challenges are often small we do much of it "in our head," we often cope with choices much more complex than are normal fare for our civilian counterparts.

We need to refine the brainstorming step, pursuing it longer rather than opting for a less imaginative early solution; and we do need to feel confident in our abilities to tackle broader military community tasks and policies. At a time when each Service is realizing that families are a major key to retention, and have agreed to open more areas to our input, we would be foolish not to take the opportunity and use the best tools.

Not the Same as "Decision-Making"

You may hear your husband say, "Oh, that's nothing new. That's just "decision-making" with a new name!" That's where he'll be wrong and you can demonstrate some one-upsmanship. The decision-making process that executives have used in the past is heavy on systems analysis, but very light on the free-wheeling brainstorming, the exercise of imaginative sound-boarding that is our source of ideas. Our decisions can only be as good as our ideas. This combination of imagination and evaluation uses both sides of our brain -- the creative right side that has been neglected by schools and organizations, and the logic and memory of the left side.

The scientific-engineering background of military leaders, combined with the pervasive opinion that wives have no role in military community leadership and policy, have not been conducive to our exercising our abilities in these areas. The climate is changing, and we need to prepare ourselves with the tools necessary to meet the challenge.

At the Army Family Symposium, Marilyn Ferguson, author of *The Aquarian Conspiracy*, showed us how we are part of the conspiracy...the joining together of men and women of good will, working toward a better future. She agreed that new ideas often are not welcome at first and can be resisted; but by focusing on what works well, we can precipitate real breakthroughs. Our first breakthrough must come from confidence in our own abilities to contribute to our society on a new level. Her theme song was, "It's in every one of us to be wise."

Originally appeared as "Creative Innovation" in Family, May 1981. The chart is from Family.

39

Leadership

Only half of our struggle is to convince men that women can be fine leaders. The other half is convincing ourselves.

"A *wife* writing about leadership?" a senior Naval officer asked incredulously. "That seems mighty presumptuous! Why don't they just go back to their wives' clubs and Navy Relief and leave leadership to us?"

Military wives have been leaders in our military and civilian communities for many years. Our modes of operation have usually been learned from our predecessors or have been the result of instinct. It is hard to share one's instincts with others, and we may no longer want to copy the styles of our predecessors.

Impact of Societal and Military Changes

Two major societal changes have contributed to the need to take a fresh look at the variety and effectiveness of leadership styles and behaviors. The women's liberation movement has released many military wives from a wide range of "expected duties;" they now feel a freedom to *choose* what their commitment will be.

At the same time, the various branches of our armed forces have recognized the value of military families in relation to retention. In an effort to provide a climate attractive to families, the various branches are providing new opportunities for wives to play active roles in *policy decisions affecting families.* The loss of services provided by wives as volunteers (willing and unwilling) has had a major impact on provisions for military families. The 1978 Navy Family Awareness Conference first dealt with the problem, and the Navy Family Program grew out of the conference recommendations, to which wives made significant contributions.

An even more significant role was played by Army wives who arranged their own Army Family Symposium last fall, with the support of the Association of the United States Army. They will conduct a second symposium this fall, and Air Force wives will hold their first national conference this year. With such fine opportunities to play actives roles on the national and local levels, we want to find the most effectives ways to participate.

At the Army Family Symposium last fall, I was delighted by the obvious talents exercised by the 300 delegates in their task of pinpointing problem areas. I was dismayed, however, by their lack of experience in problem-solving and effective leadership.

Types of Leaders and Leadership Styles

There are *two types of leaders* who may use a variety of *leadership styles*. The first is the status leader, the person who by a position of power or by appointment automatically assumes the leadership of a group. The second is what I call a natural leader; she is one who emerges, over a long or sometimes short period of time, as the real or functional leader of a group.

These two types of leaders may choose any one of four styles of leadership. The sequence from the most hierarchical to the least controlled is: the autocratic (clearly one-person rule); the paternalistic or maternalistic (in which the leader pretends to be listening to the group's wishes, but really is aiming at her predetermined goals); the democratic (in which the leader enables all members to participate and reach a consensus); and laissez-faire (which is really no leadership, just chaos).

In years past there were theories about the *personality traits* of leaders. There were so many exceptions to each theory that most people today feel that the effectiveness of any given leader depends on the people being led and the situation. The people being led today are more likely to be true volunteers than they were several years ago. When wives believed that they held the same rank as their husbands, the senior wife automatically became the status leader. She may or may not have enjoyed the responsibility. Depending on her behavior, she may or may not have received willing cooperation from "her junior wives." Hierarchical leadership could be *efficient*, if not *effective*. Many military wives copied the pattern they saw their husbands using.

Enabling Status Leaders

However, sensitive status leaders learned that another style of leadership was possible. They could initiate the first get-togethers of the group, could provide the planning and the climate to get things started, and then could allow the natural leaders to emerge and carry on the functions of the group. Wives' clubs in which the senior wives served as sponsors only are samples of this form. Elected leaders eventually could come from the total membership. In this leadership style, the status leader has a key role to play in helping the group to form for its early meetings and to provide the atmosphere and the support needed for the group to function democratically. (Examples of this situation are specific unit or ship's wives' groups, or post/base-wide wives' clubs.) It is possible that the status leader might emerge as the natural leader of the group. She should not feel that her status either precludes or demands her functioning as the leader.

The natural leader is one whom the group has selected, formally or informally. Skills in communication, organization, and enabling members to contribute their best to the task at hand are her major assets. She recognizes that a decision that is truly that of the group will bring the members' commitment to action. While getting group consensus is rarely an efficient process, its effectiveness is worth the emotional time and energy. A natural leader will rely on group consensus for all major decisions; however, the group may give her the responsibility for day to day "housekeeping chores," such as notices of upcoming meetings, press releases, and representation of the group at public or command meetings.

Factors that Affect Group Effectiveness

Any leader needs to recognize two factors that affect the functioning of a group. One factor is the pattern of a maturing group, and the other is the types of participants often found in groups.

Whether a leader is a status or a natural leader, she needs to know that a normal group grows through four stages in its process of maturing. Time and the intensity of the need to solve a problem affect the rate of growth. In the *first stage*, the group usually has some commitment to the task at hand (especially in a volunteer group where the choice to participate has been made freely). If the group is meeting once only for a very short-term project, perhaps the task will be the major concern for the leader and not much effort will be expended on the social-emotional needs of the members.

However, most groups find working on a superficial level is unrewarding and move to the *second stage*. Members still feel ill at ease and vulnerable; their concern with themselves blocks effective group effort. In the *second stage*, time needs to be spent on getting to know each other on social, emotional, and intellectual levels so that a real sharing of talents and concerns can take place. The leadership needs to help the group determine its goal as well, so stage two is a highly charged period in group growth.

Stage two can be a danger zone. Most people who have studied group dynamics have noticed a dip in a group's progress at this point. The vying for leadership and the surfacing of the ulterior motives of some group members can cause friction and disillusionment. At this point the classic types of group members, of both the bothersome and the "double-minus" varieties, can threaten group success. (More on these types shortly.)

Most groups come out of this dip stronger than before because they have chosen a leader, talked through their differences, and have committed themselves to their group task instead of their own individual priorities. Knowing that this is a normal set-back that usually produces greater group cohesion may help leaders work with their groups more confidently.

Stage three brings real growth on the task level. Group members fulfill their problem-solving quite well without much prodding from the leader, but she may need to continue efforts to build their social-emotional cohesion. *Stage four* is that of the mature group, which requires much less active support for task or social cohesion from the leader.

In a very simplified way, this progression of the group mirrors the progression of a parent-child relationship. Stage one is mostly concentrated on tasks (achievement of basic skills). Stage two is the period when a child questions his parents, tries "no" regularly, and is not altogether lovable. Stage three is a period of relative progress emotionally and on tasks, but there is dependence on the parent leader for support. (The teen years are a reversion to the dip!) In stage four, a mature person can function basically on his or her own with only occasional support from parents. Our aim with a group, as with a child, is a happy, productive unit that can accomplish not only the original task, but can accept other challenges as need be.

Group Participant Types

While the make-up of each group is unique (and that is part of the fun), group members should be aware that there are certain stereotypes who may populate their committees. No one group will be blessed or cursed with all of these, but recognition of them and strategies to accent their positive offering while diminishing their negative effects are part of a skillful leader's techniques.

Potential Roles for Spouses

PARTICIPANT TYPES		
(+) PLUS	**(-) MINUS**	**(--) DOUBLE MINUS**
1. Initiator/Contributor 2. Information Provider 3. Explainer 4. Conceptualizer (has an overview & sees the ramifications of planned action) 5. Constructive Conflictor 6. Expediter (gets things done) 7. Summarizer (synthesizes ideas of group so it can move on) 8. Action-Lover (keeps group from bogging down) 9. Devil's Advocate (when taken as a posture to help group know what arguments are against their plans) 10. Special-Interest Lobbyist (can assure a balanced approach) 11. Silent type (who listens & when she does contribute, is worth listening to) 12. Peacemaker 13. Positive Risk-Taker (pioneer mentality) 14. Cooperative Followers	1. Clown (may make light of too much & block progress) 2. Sympathy Seeker (wants help for own problem only) 3. Recognition Seeker (leader must help her focus on group instead of self) 4. Conflict-Avoider (willing to compromise anything to avoid unpleasantness) 5. Summarizer (can block progress if action is flowing & he stops to sum up) 6. Action-Lover (may urge action before sufficient preparation completed) 7. Detail-Lover (sometimes valuable, but can insist on details when group is still in the total picture stage) 8. Special-Interest Lobbyist — limited vision. 9. Rules/Regulation-Lover (can block free flow of ideas, but can be of value, too) 10. Pressed to Talk (uses up valuable time) 11. Endless Studier 12. Opinion Provider (usually facts are more valuable) 13. Middle-Roader 14. Change-Resister (*all* change) 15. Slow-Learner (needs constant explanation) 16. Easily-Distracted (and often inattentive — requires repetition of point just made) 17. Issue-or-Goal-Changer (mid-stream wants to change focus)	1. Power Seeker 2. Know-it-All 3. Mrs. It-Can't-Be-Done 4. Mrs. It's Been-Done-Before-and-it-Didn't-Work-Then 5. Nay-Sayer (will block anything and everything) 6. Conflict-Causer (for sake of blocking action; get rid of this one) 7. Silent-Resister (who then sabotages group decision outside of group; get rid of this one) 8. Devil's Advocate (blocks action) 9. Special-Interest Lobbyist (can block action) 10. Issue-or-Goal-Changer (of the extreme variety)

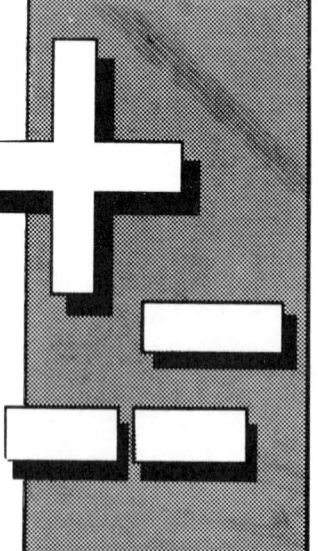

**There is a fourth category: the zero (neither + nor -). Into this category fall the Silent-non-Participants and the Sheep.

**Suggested activity: try role playing; each member in the group draws a stereotype or the leader's role to portray. Use a familiar problem (such as plans for the next fund-raising event).

Meeting Strategies

A leader not only has to think about the interactions of group members, but also needs to think about the setting of meetings.

- Are refreshments desirable?
- Would a break at a strategic time allow for physical revival, as well as valuable informal interaction, so that the rest of the formal meeting would be more productive?
- Can seating be circular so that everyone can see each other (or U-shaped so that an easel or blackboard can be used to focus members' thoughts?)
- Should the duty of recorder/secretary be spread around so that one person is not prevented from playing an active role at every meeting?
- Should members be seated strategically? Sometimes leaders elect to put people who are troublesome to their left so that they are physically blocked from over-participation. (A right-handed person tends to talk more with the people on her right or across the table from her with whom eye contact hence signalling, is easy.)

Behavior Strategies

A leader also must think about how her leadership style and behavior affect not only the members of her group, but also others with whom she comes in contact as the representative of her group. As we move from working with other women only into the fields still dominated by men, we need to determine what our priorities are and how many battles we want to fight at once. I would suggest that we research well the attitudes of those with whom we must interact, and then choose our strategy carefully.

Let me give you two examples. A study of reactions to female ministers has shown that as long as they are careful to choose nurturing topics and approaches (though not "motherly"), reactions of male and female parishioners are positive. When they choose topics that are challenging in the threatening sense, some men react with an almost child-like temper tantrum, and the women in the congregation are unsure of what to expect. We are in a transition stage nationally, and certain populations are less far along than others in accepting women as leaders. The military and small towns may be prime examples of this.

The second example I would offer comes from my personal experience in a civilian environmental-historic preservation group. By maintaining my role as a firm but not abrasive spokesman for our cause, I precluded the opposition from dragging the fight down to their level. The tantrums by both men and women on the opposing side puzzled me at the time, and certainly reduced their credibility. Win or lose, we need to maintain a stature of which we can be proud. Let's keep the advantage that being "a lady" gives us.

Because women are often perceived as illogical and emotional, we need to accentuate our thorough research of background information and make sure our presentations ar factual and logical. Though we score well on diagnosing problems, we lack experience in decision-making. Our practice in creative problem-solving techniques should remedy this deficit.

At a recent symposium on the role of Foreign Service wives, I noticed the reaction to a self--proclaimed "radical feminist" whose abrasive behavior hurt her cause. Her policy position was injured by her choice to fight two battles at the same time: policy and behavior. I recognize the need to take seemingly radical positions policy-wise in order to allow room for compromise and moderate progress; but we must assess the sensitivities of the power holders and choose our approach carefully. We need to keep our eye on our group's overall goal and avoid wasting energy on such lesser concerns as terminology (chairpersons vs. chairman) and apparel (we can wear a pink dress when a charcoal suit would announce another battle; we can wear red or bright colors when we want attention or remembrance at a public hearing or conference).

A lot to think of? You bet! You won't be able to remember it all and use it naturally at once; but knowing the theory is a fine foundation for the exercise of natural instincts and abilities. Women actually test higher than men on innate abilities. While we score equally in a majority of the abilities tested, and men continue to excel in the two areas of physical strength and structural visualization, women are superior in six areas. These range from finger dexterity, accounting skills, and observation, to the flow of ideas, word association, and abstract visualization (an aptitude helpful in banking, management, writing, and politics!).

Today we are still in a position where women, given a choice of a male or female leader, will choose the male because his style of leadership (usually autocratic) is a known -- not necessarily *the ideal*, but *known*.. We may not have had as much experience as men, and our style may be different from theirs; but tests prove that we have the raw materials and our style, which tends to be that of the natural leader in a democratic process, is the style that corporations are now trying to teach their managers. It has been proven to be the most effective in the long haul. I vote for the long haul! Let us bring what is our unique strength to our goal of creating a humane environment for families.

Originally appeared as "Leadership" in Family, *September 1981. The chart is from* Family.

Lifescaping:
The Art of Balanced Growth
(A New Approach to Volunteerism)

Mary, Mary, quite contrary,
How does your garden grow?
With silver bells, and cockle shells,
And pretty maids all in a row.

There was a time when ideal gardens (and maids) were "all in a row." Military wives' roles were prescribed. The landscape rules were precise: one needed two clumps of Grey Lady work, one patch of decorating-the-officers'-club, a variety of contributions-to-the-annual-bazaar, and scattered luncheons and teas for the company wives. The end product was the perfect career scheme -- it couldn't fail. But it did fail, and those who had labored dutifully felt cheated. They had followed the blueprint!

This plan was replaced by one-crop farming and grey-flannel suits -- for women as well as men. One Ivy League woman recalls a recent reunion: "There we were, ten years out of college, successful career women by all standards, financial and otherwise. But, we had a common sense of dissatisfaction, of something being missing from our lives. At our class dinner, our dean really put her finger on the root of our sense of loss. She pointed out that while we'd been busy doing for ourselves, we certainly hadn't done much for anyone else!"

Modern "Gardeners"

What is the philosophy for the modern gardener, the *truly liberated woman*? Just as environmentalists have been sensitive to the variety and balance found in nature, thoughtful women are seeking their own design with nature. We choose perennials and evergreens that give stability and reliability to our landscape, but also want to try some annuals or ornamentals -- showy short-termers that add color and drama to our scheme. Each plan is unique, reflecting the personality of the gardener, as well as her age and the climate in which she lives.

Part of our climate today is the increase in salaried options for women. Many of us have felt the need or desire to work for pay. As we put our energies into paid jobs, many of the offerings in our communities that we grew up taking for granted have diminished or disappeared entirely. Some had outlived their usefulness, but the loss of others will make a difference in our lives and those of our children. For example, as a Girl Scout leader, I counted on being able to secure instruction in child care, lifesaving, and first aid for my troops from the American Red Cross. I was surprised to discover that all of these depended on volunteer instructors. I ended up having to teach the "Tending Our Tots" course myself, and felt blessed to find an Air Force wife nurse who gave one session. Our canoeing and water safety courses were in jeopardy until a retired Marine and his daughter came to our aid. The first aid course was arranged through a past Scout leader who had to leave her bank job early to come to our meetings. We were *lucky*. With persistence and the generosity of these four people, we were able to provide, as few troops can these days. But today there are fewer women willing to give their time and energy to help other women's daughters grow in self-sufficiency and service to others.

We all can find similar examples in other community services. At a time when budget cuts are making any "frills" unlikely in our schools, parents find that they have little time and energy to help in the schools or provide out-of-school activities for their own children. The military hospitals and support organizations, such as Navy Relief and Army Community Services, feel the same loss in volunteer help just when expectations of services have escalated.

Choosing Your Creative Balance

In this climate, how do we as gardeners choose our *lifescape*? I will argue for what Eliot Richardson has called a "creative balance" -- a creative balance between salaried and volunteer time, between time for others and time for ourselves, between long-term and short-term commitments, between reasons for volunteering and types of tasks. I see this balance as continuously varying. Just as a garden needs weeding and pruning, so will our commitments.

My major concern is that we *choose* what we do instead of drifting into or being pressured into activities that do not fit our plan (like a gardener who allows the ivy from a neighbor's yard to invade her azaleas, feeling too embarrassed to cut it off at the fence line). I believe that if *everyone does find his or her creative balance, then the important, truly necessary community services will thrive.* The cosmic balance between giving and receiving will be achieved.

Salaried and volunteer time -- As we seek our balance between salaried and volunteer time, we should keep our life-view in mind. There will be years when we give more time to salaried work, and others when volunteer activities fit our need for flexible commitments. Volunteer activities can sometimes provide a greater challenge to our intellect or managerial talents than available salaried positions. Many of us who have been teachers find that our profession is less portable than it used to be, but service on school boards, educational advisory committees, or the PTA uses our past experiences, helps us grow professionally, and certainly gives us room for impact on community schools.

Time allotted for others and time reserved for ourselves -- As we seek our balance between time allotted for others and time reserved for ourselves, we need to be aware that all of us need an oasis. We need quiet time for renewing our physical, emotional, and spiritual energies. Unlike the mythical Superwoman, we get squirrely, irritable, and less than effective when over-programmed. My favorite example of the fruit of haste is my son's elaborate drawing on a T-shirt of his then-hero Superman. Drawing in indelible ink, as unerasable as our activities, he rushed to complete the letters under his figure -- SUPERMAM! Embarrassed and frustrated, he had to pass the shirt on to his sister! Deep down inside, we know when we need to slow down and stand firm against others seeking to fill our hours.

Long-term and short-term commitments -- Our balance between long-term and short-term allows us to grow perennials and short-blooming annuals. Constants allow us to grow in favorite areas of interest. For example, I have sung in either church choirs or community choruses since I was fourteen. Singing is a creative outlet for me, and perhaps (?!) of some service. I have worked in education almost every year since college, either as a teacher, researcher, volunteer lecturer, or advisory committee member. I have been allowed to grow and serve my community in spite of a number of moves in the process.

However, short-term activities can be fun, too. Teaching Sunday School, playing the church organ as a substitute, leading nature walks to make people aware of the value of open space, giving sporadic children's sermons -- all of these have been useful to others and have spiced up my life. As military spouses, we may find that the short-term commitments fit our transient lifestyle, but I urge some constants that can give us a sense of completeness when we survey our *lifescape*.

282   Potential Roles for Spouses

<u>Simple vs Complex Tasks</u> -- Short-termers are usually relatively simple activities; we need complexity, too. Volunteers in under-staffed organizations often find that their opportunities are more varied and interesting than a specific salaried occupation could offer. A Boy Scout leader or a wives' club newsletter editor will certainly be limited only by time in the variety of talents that can be explored and shared.

<u>Military and civilian community commitments</u> -- When balancing our commitments, we should consider our two worlds. Ties to each community bring special rewards. Helping our military family is "taking care of our own." We share stresses and pleasures unique to our way of living. Involvement in our civilian community, whether paid or volunteer, gives us geographical and social roots. It also prepares us for the day when our mates become civilians. One friend who is deeply involved in rewriting a handbook for military wives has been counseled to find a new outlet immediately, so that her transition upon her husband's imminent retirement will be a positive one instead of an experience of loss for her... the old eggs-in-one-basket syndrome.

Volunteers' Motivations

Our reasons for volunteering are as varied as the offerings in a seed catalog. Some are <u>inner-directed</u> such as:

- *it's fun;*
- *it's where the action is;*
- *it's a way to make new friends and be with others like me;*
- *it's a way to know my new community;*
- *it's a chance to learn new skills;*
- *they need me, and I need to be needed;*
- *it's a way to repay what others have done for me;*
- *it's a good cause;*
- *it brings me power and influence;*
- *it gives me a sense of achievement.*

Duty, obligation to a friend who has asked my help, and the fact that others see it as having status are <u>other-directed</u> reasons for volunteering. Most of us will probably have a mix of these, but being a "volunteer" means being uncoerced. in the long run, I think the most satisfying commitments are the ones we choose for ourselves.

Cumulative Value of Choices

When we do choose, the ideal choices would be dual in nature; they would allow us to grow and we would be serving real needs of others. It would not be unusual for one person to have several reasons for her varied commitments. One general's wife serves as a volunteer in her child's school testing eyes two days a year. She helps a good cause and has the opportunity to size up the teaching skills of the teachers in the grades ahead. One Navy wife has served on the historic district committee of her town in order to meet people like herself, preserve the heritage of her new hometown, and, in the process, protect the value of her own home. Being seen and valued by a potential employer can be a valid reason for volunteering. Navy wives have found themselves joining the Mystic Seaport staff after a stint as volunteers; school principals keep their eye on skillful volunteers when they have positions to fill. One Navy chief's wife serves as a town counselor, an elected position of real power in her community -- power not only for herself, but power in advocacy for other military families. If I sound proud of her, it is because she was a high school student of mine! She balances her commitments by also being highly supportive of wives on her husband's submarine which he serves as Chief of the Boat.

Volunteerism Cuts Across Rank Stereotypes

Often thought to be the sole domain (and responsibility) of officers' wives, voluntary organizations have been increasingly successful in attracting the spouses of NCO's and junior enlisted personnel as well. Navy Relief finds that often their most competent and empathetic interviewers and budget counselors are those who have experienced first hand what brings their clients to seek help. Having "been there" and coped makes them highly credible. The only "trouble" Navy Relief experiences is that their trained volunteers are so attractive to local businesses that it is hard to keep them as long as they would like.

Volunteer Options

That brings me to the kinds of volunteer opportunities that exist. Some certainly offer very basic tasks that need to be done; but one would not want to make a career of these. I include preparing mailouts and wrapping Christmas packages in this category -- okay for short-term commitments. If the group working with you is fun, then the time is enjoyably spent.

Other levels of volunteering provide the opportunity for on-the-job training which might lead to a salaried position, or which simply provides invaluable information and experience. The Navy Relief training course falls into this last category, with reactions from wives such as, "I've been a Navy wife for 19 years and didn't know half this stuff about rights and benefits." The American Red Cross courses not only give practical information, but some are worth continuing education college credits. Army Community Services have gotten their course in volunteer administration accredited, as have the Girl Scouts (for attendance at Nationwide Learning Opportunities). On-the-job training which can lead to a salaried position can be found in the dental-assistant arrangement in some military clinics. One Navy wife who participated in this program in New London, CT, later put her husband through law school with the skills learned. The coordinator of volunteer services at the Norfolk Navy Family Services Center is an example of those who have become salaried volunteer coordinators, using skills they gained through experience and training.

(*As the military offers more formal support programs, I would caution that there is the potential for the abuse of military spouses who volunteer their time and are not considered when salaried positions are created.)

Some organizations are experimenting with an alternating pay/volunteer arrangement under which a person is paid for several hours' work and then gives equal free time. The organization benefits by getting twice as much work for a reasonable investment, and the volunteer can quote a higher hourly rate on her salary history for future (or current) job applications. Some organizations offer free babysitting while volunteers give specified amounts of time (e.g. Navy Relief, American Red Cross) and some cover basic transportation and insurance costs for volunteers. Some may find that they can attract those who cannot afford the "luxury" of volunteering if they experiment with pay/volunteer contributions. Post or base thrift shops are good examples of valuable services that could be staffed out of profits and could produce a triple benefit: provision of inexpensive clothing and furniture, an opportunity for spouses to supplement their family income, and an opportunity for more to enjoy the emotional profits of volunteering.

Advocates

Another type of volunteer is the advocate, one who is not necessarily attached to an already-existing organization, but must start her own group of fellow activists. She works for a cause in which she believes deeply, has the challenge of finding her support where she can, doing her research, and presenting her arguments to the sources of power. While it is not a "secure" position, and is sometimes costly in terms of energy and funds, its rewards come in the joy of working with equally committed supporters, and in the form of open spaces for one's town, a highway of lessened impact, or the establishment of family support services for military families. The Army wives who stuck out their necks and worked so hard to offer the first Army Family Symposium, which led to the establishment of the Army Family Liaison Office, are outstanding examples of volunteer advocates.

Considerations before Volunteering

1. Before contacting agencies or the Voluntary Action Center near you, think about, and perhaps write down:

- my skills, training;
- things I *like to do*;
- the level of work I'd like to do;
- do I prefer individualized work, group work, or supervised work?
- what kind of support would I want from a staff?
- how many hours could I give?
- on what schedule?
- do I have a transportation limitation?
- am I willing to volunteer in my "professional" field, or do I want to do something different?
- what are my reasons and goals for volunteering?

2. After offers of placement have been made by an organization:

- take time to think about the offer;
- visit the agency and meet the people you would work with;
- leave a "gracious exit" in case the agency and people do not fit what you had in mind;
- do the agency standards fit with yours/
- stipulate a Letter of Agreement -- your image as a thorough, professional volunteer will be enhanced.

The "just a volunteer" posture should be erased from your thoughts and theirs! You can drive a harder bargain than if you are job hunting because you are offering a great deal -- your time and skills for free.

Records to Keep

As volunteers, we should keep careful records in our own work log of the kinds of tasks we perform, the responsibilities involved, the specific accomplishments, awards, and training received, and the hours worked. Names of supervisors and addresses should be included, as should newspaper articles and photographs about our work. For tax records, unreimbursed mileage/parking/transportation and other costs such as uniforms and postage should be recorded. Considerate organizations will offer letters of commendation or recommendation. Some volunteers have discovered that it is wise to ask for such a letter twice a year; this keeps contributions they have made fresh in everyone's mind, and provides an opportunity to assess a possible move to a new opportunity within (or outside of) the organization.

Bill of Rights for a Volunteer

A Long-Term Volunteer Has the Right to:

1. *Careful screening* prior to the placement of oneself and of those working with the Volunteer.
   a. The Volunteer has the right to be protected from inappropriate work mates, especially if the organization serves children (e.g. Girl Scouts owe their Scouts and leaders the careful selection of leaders for suitability, and speedy removal of faulty selections).
   b. Placement in accordance with the Volunteer's skills, talents, and interests. Voluntary Action Centers serve as a link between would-be volunteers and organizations; they do the preliminary screening, but the final screening/selection must be done by the organization to be served and the individual choosing to serve.
2. An annual *Letter of Agreement* which would include:
   a. the Volunteer's job description (which should be "enabling" vs. "restrictive: in nature) and should include the name of the specific staff support person with whom the Volunteer will work;
   b. the training to be given'
   c. space and materials and any enabling funds to be provided by the organization (for babysitting, transportation, insurance, meals, and lodging when traveling for the organization);
   d. length of service being covered by the agreement (six months or one year is long enough before renegotiating this agreement);
   e. chance for advancement -- if the Volunteer wants to be considered for salaried positions or advanced volunteer positions as they become available, this should be included in the Letter of Agreement.
3. *Annual written evaluation* of the Volunteer's contributions by the staff, with a letter of commendation/recommendation when appropriate
4. *A relationship of working with*, not for the organization staff.
5. *A gracious exit* if the Volunteer or the organization finds the placement erroneous.
6. *Representation* on the policy board of the organization. There should be a built-in avenue for sharing suggestions and concerns with the decision-makers.
7. *Regular and effective communications* from and to the organization.
8. *High regard* by the salaried staff for the Volunteer's *given time.*
9. Above all, the individual Volunteer should feel that his/her having been there has made a positive difference.

Originally appeared as "Lifescaping: The Art of Balanced Growth" in Family, October 1981.

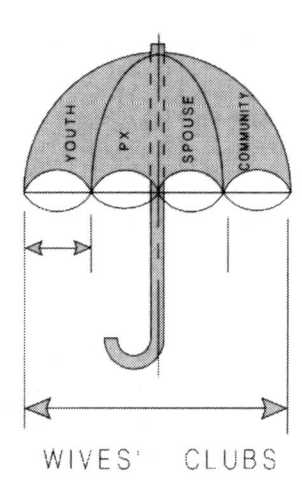

Blueprint for Wives' Clubs

Most wives' clubs have seen their membership drop radically over recent years. Many have attributed this decrease to the increase in the number of military wives who are employed full or part-time. Employment may be one of the reasons for the decline in club membership, but it is not the only, nor the most important reason.

Most clubs have failed to meet the needs and interests of their potential membership. For example, the number of wives who regularly attended our one submarine crew wives' activities on a weekly or bi-weekly basis a few years ago was twice as large as the entire roll of the Navy Wives Club of America in New London, CT. Our membership potential was 90 wives of officers, chiefs, and enlisted men versus the 8,000 wives in the area; but we were meeting the very basic social, emotional, and eventually, cultural/intellectual needs of our group. The involvement of most of the wives in the planning and preparation stages ensured that we continued to do so.

Needs Assessment

As clubs search for ways to involve and serve their potential members, I would suggest a philosophical base and a model for an ideal club. We have heard the words "needs assessment" used in the realms of business and education; wives' clubs should adopt this approach for determining what potential members see as necessary or desirable. They should do the same at the end of each year to know where they have been, how well they have functioned, and where they want to go next year.

Abraham Maslow's *Hierarchy of Needs* would provide a useful approach when making up an assessment. His theory is that we all need to satisfy our basic needs for food, housing, health, and safety (both physical and emotional) before we can move onto the next levels of seeking affection, group affiliation, self-esteem, and esteem from others. The highest levels include our desire to develop as individuals as far as we can -- intellectually, aesthetically, and philosophically. If a club is aiming its programming at the art museum level when potential members need help with economical decorating and shopping ideas, then it is failing to provide appropriately. By the same token, a club which starts on the basic need levels will find that it can gradually raise the level of its programs as members cope with the basics and grow toward upper level requirements for intellectual and cultural stimuli. An example of programs meeting the needs and interest of members was the offering of "I'm OK -- You're OK" at the New London Submarine Officers' Wives' Club several years ago. Members were encouraged to bring chiefs' wives as guests and we had the largest attendance in memory -- because the topic dealt with a real need. Submarine wives often find themselves playing the role of counselor during deployments; we needed ideas on how to cope ourselves and how to help others.

Program Strategies

Because most wives' clubs are likely to have a membership mixture, involvement by as many people as possible is desirable -- for their sense of belonging and contributing, as well as insurance of appropriate offerings. In years past, some clubs thought they were accomplishing this by assigning each command one month's program responsibilities. However, unless there is an overall plan for the year's key programs, the result is a casserole with uncoordinated ingredients. I think there could be ample room for creative flexibility within a master plan based on the needs and interest survey. The time of meetings could be flexible, too.

In addition to the traditional monthly programming, I would suggest an organization model that provides a way for our increasingly concerned wives to play an active role in policy decisions that affect the quality of life on our various military installations. The officers' wives' club, the chiefs' or NCO wives' club, and the enlisted wives' clubs are *command sponsored*. As such, they can provide the "legal" channel for wives to have a participatory or advocacy role in base/post-level decisions.

A wives' club could function much like a civilian civic association or a county advisory council. For example, in Arlington, VA, the school board, which is comparable to the base/post commanding officer, has established a two-tier advisory system. The Advisory Council on Instruction is the volunteer umbrella citizen group that receives and passes on (with comment) reports from the volunteer advisory committees (such as the advisory committees on math, science, English, gifted and talented, special education, school lunch program, maintenance, etc.). These committees are either tasked by the school board with areas that need study, or the committees themselves choose their own areas for oversight and evaluation. Each committee writes an annual report to the school board, and may initiate action any time that an issue requires attention.

The umbrella Advisory Council on Instruction acts as an intermediary, listening, evaluating, but sending on the committees' reports en toto. I see that as an ideal role for the various wives' clubs -- to serve as a channel, officially sanctioned, for wives to make their assessments and suggestions known. An advisory capacity is thereby granted to each committee with a specific area of interest, without putting members in an adversarial, quasi-combatant role, which is distasteful to many military wives and husbands. An individual club might structure itself with the following advisory committees: Youth Activities, Exchange-Commissary, Foreign-Born Spouse Assistance, Community Relations, and Inter-Wives' Clubs Activities.

Wives today are saying that our efforts and time must *count* --- we are vulnerable, as are our husbands, when we choose to play an active role in wives' activities. The Powers-That-Be are bemoaning the loss of "the old volunteers." Their major concern should be how to utilize these wives' intellect and social service commitments to provide an opportunity for growth for all -- wives, families, and the military Services. Wives' clubs could assess the needs, sanction the committees as needed (avoid standing committees that lose immediacy and validity), and work with other wives' clubs on base/post where there are common concerns. The Army Wives' Club of the Greater Washington Area established a committee last year to plan the First Army Family Symposium. It was a great success, and was followed by a second this fall, planned by new committee members. They are meeting a national need, are training delegates to serve their own posts well, and are growing themselves in the process.

My emphasis on providing opportunities to work on projects that concern members does not mean that I think the social aspect is not important. Is is a requisite for productive group activity. Club leaders should include ways to encourage wives to get to know each other well in every meeting. Working and playing together are much more effective than minor conversations over tea and name tags. When wives' clubs assess the needs and interests of their potential members, create organizational units that allow for programming and service that match expressed needs, and provide meaningful social interaction, then they will be viable contributors to our military communities.

Originally appeared as "Blueprint for Wives' Clubs" in Family, November 1981.

Practical Protocol:
A Guide to Military Etiquette

If you're a new military bride this month, you may have already heard your first bugle call and wondered what to do. Welcome to the world of military etiquette!

"Seasoned military wives" can still remember their own first trips on post or base, confused and overwhelmed by the do's and don'ts of military social protocol. Some were given a huge etiquette book as a wedding gift -- a rite of passage of sorts -- to read and follow religiously. Others were left to figure out the proper procedures on their own.

Family would like to share the comfortable approach to etiquette and protocol that many senior military wives have adopted these days. There has been such a resurgence of interest in the field that wives' clubs are sponsoring speakers and publishing booklets on the topic.

Randy Gracey and Brenda Hall

Randy Gracey (wife of the former Commandant of the Coast Guard, Admiral James S. Gracey) and her partner, Brenda Hall (wife of Rear Admiral Henby Bell, USCG [Ret.]) give day-long training sessions during graduation week for students in the Coast Guard Officers' Candidate School at Yorktown, VA. They focus on the students taking part in formal graduation week activities and reporting to their first duty station.

Mrs. Gracey believes the intense interest in protocol and etiquette that she sees these days is due to the fact that many young people have grown up during a period when families have not stressed dinner table manners, meals together, or other niceties that may have received more attention when both parents were not employed outside of the home. "These young people, who didn't see formal dinner parties at home, are now entering the military (and the corporate world), and are ill at ease. Many are high achievers, want to be upwardly mobile, and have a sense that they could have 'egg on their face' without realizing it. Therefore, we help them gain self-assurance and poise by knowing the drill."

Glynda Rich: Teaching the Finer Points

Glynda Rich (wife of Rear Admiral Roger Rich, Jr.) was nudged into her current work as a newsletter columnist and workshop speaker when a senior Navy wife was concerned about the lack of awareness of younger wives regarding responses to invitations. "Someone needs to be teaching the fine points." She looked around the room and said, "Glynda, you're the one." Mrs. Rich recalls that she was "born to a Southern mother who believed that etiquette was a part of everyday life." She started with little talks, and now does two-hour presentations across the country. Even though she has moved to Washington, D.C. (*and later the Philippines), she continues to write her column, "Notes from the Gentle Reminder," for the San Diego Naval Officers' Wives' Club's *NOW News*.

Mrs. Rich attributes today's interest in etiquette to the swing away from the "me generation," which did its own thing, to a generation that respects some of the niceties and values that protocol and etiquette demonstrate. "My emphasis is not so much on the details -- there are books on that -- but on helping women feel that they are okay, that they can make mistakes, and be themselves."

Good Reading

She recommends two books. *Emily Post's Etiquette -- A Guide to Modern Manners*, by Elizabeth L. Post (14th edition -- 1984, Harper & Row, $18.95) -- check your library or exchange for this one. References to the military lifestyle are sprinkled through this comprehensive book. *Protocol: The Complete Handbook of Diplomatic, Official and Social Usage*, by Mary Jane McCaffree and Pauline Innis (1985, $21 including shipping), is used extensively by the State Department. Write to Devon Publishing Co., 2700 Virginia Ave., N.W., Washington, DC 20037.

Another good resource is *Social Customs and Traditions of the Navy*, an 18-page booklet free of charge from the Navy Wifeline Association, Bldg. 172, Washington Navy Yard, Washington, DC 20374-0001.

The Once Over...Lightly, by Army wife Bibs Reynard, is in its second version and seventh printing -- a testimony to its timely contents. Send $3 for a copy to Lite Lines, P.O. Box 10003, Arlington VA 22210.

Defining Social Terms

According to Webster's New Collegiate Dictionary, *etiquette* is defined as "the forms required by good breeding, social conventions or prescribed by authority, to be observed in social or official life." *Protocol* is "a rule prescribing the etiquette in ceremonies of state; the code prescribing deference to rank...as in diplomatic exchange and ceremonies."

My own years as an Army daughter and a Navy wife have brought me to the same perspective shared by Randy Gracey and Glynda Rich -- that etiquette and protocol are *tools* that help us enjoy a comfortably gracious lifestyle. With these in mind, let's take a closer look at some of the social customs observed in today's military world.

Flags, Parades, and Other Ceremonies

As a new civilian or military member out of uniform, you stand at attention or put your hand over your heart for a variety of flag ceremonies. In the morning or at dusk, you hear the bugle calls for raising ("colors") and lowering ("retreat") the flag. If you are outside, stop, turn and face the direction of the flag, and stand at attention or cross you heart. (Military members in uniform salute.) If you are in your car, pull over to the side of the road, stop, and wait until the call is complete before proceeding.

If you are seated at a parade, you will stand as the American flag approaches the left edge of your vision. Stand at attention (or cross your heart) until the flag passes beyond your right field of vision. Then be seated. If in doubt about when to stand and sit, watch the senior military member for your cue.

Party Invitations

When writing invitations for your parties, our experts agree that you should feel free to be imaginative for informal occasions. Those of you with artistic or poetic talents are encouraged to be creative -- just make sure that you give the basics: what, when, where, who is hosting, dress, and response expected.

You may use *R.S.V.P.*, plus your telephone number, if you want all of your guests to reply whether or not they plan to attend. *Respondez, sil vous plait* translates to "reply, if you please." Mrs. Gracey suggests that guests call their hostess before putting the invitation away. It is too easy to forget and leave her wondering if she should set a place at the table for you. (As hostess, you may write "R.S.V.P. by June 20th," so that you are free to call those from whom you have not heard by the given date. "I was afraid that you might not have received your invitation....")

Mrs. Gracey advises another way to invite people for a small party: call each of your invitees and determine whether they will be able to attend your planned event. Then send an invitation on which you have written "To remind you" at the top, and enclose a map if your house is hard to find.

While "Regrets Only" has become popular for large buffets and cocktail parties, and popular with hostesses who are frequently away from their home phone, both Mrs. Rich and Mrs. Gracey have horror stories to tell about guests who don't respond and don't come...and there you are with all of that food!

The Dress Code

When you receive an invitation and are unsure about the appropriate dress, ask your hostess. It is not a breach of etiquette to do so -- far worse would be to arrive "out of uniform."

Formal -- White Tie means full evening dress for military members and floor-length evening dress for women.

Formal -- Black Tie means full evening dress for military members (but may be the white mess jacket in season for those who have this uniform), and floor-length or short evening dress of women.

Civilian Informal or *Informal* means the dress uniform for military members or a dark business suit, and a short cocktail dress or dressy suit for women.

Casual usually means sports jackets for men and a variety of short or long dresses, or blouse and skirt combinations for women. Ask your hostess what she plans to wear.

Setting the Table

If you are giving a sit-down dinner, there are some carefully defined rules to setting your table. Napkins may be placed to the far left of the silverware, or may be set on the dinner plates (helpful if space is tight). If the napkin is folded into a rectangular form, it should have the folds facing the edge of the table and right toward the glassware. The theory is that a guest picks up the napkin in his left hand, slides his right hand under the left corner, and lays out the napkin in his lap without ever raising it to table level. (You will find variations on this.)

Silverware is set so that guests work from the outside-in. On the far left, you would place the salad fork, then the dinner fork, and closest to the plate, the dessert fork. From the far right working toward the plate, place the soup spoon, the dessert spoon, a teaspoon for coffee, and the dinner knife, with the blade facing the plate. If you use a butter knife, you

294   Potential Roles for Spouses

may place it diagonally across the butter plate or horizontally above the top of the dinner plate with the blade facing the plate. Set out only those utensils necessary for your menus. (You will find variations on this arrangement if you are giving a very formal dinner.)

The salad plate is placed at the left of the forks (and napkin when placed to the side). The butter plate is directly above the forks. The water goblet is directly above the dinner knife, and the smaller wine glass is slightly to the right and closer to the spoons. The dessert plate and coffee or tea cup are brought in for the final course.

Seating and Serving Your Dinner Guests

If you must seat guests formally, you should look up the protocol for seating guests of honor and tables of eight or ten (ten being the arrangement that works best for alternate seating of men and women).

Most of us don't have hired help to serve at dinner parties, but children can very helpful and feel very grown up. Bartering your services with friends is another solution. For an informal dinner, you may serve and clear the dishes. Use this simple rule: "Serve from the left, remove from the right. Another popular solution today is to serve the soup and/or salad and dessert, but have guests serve themselves the main course buffet-style.

Thank You's

After a delightful evening in someone else's home, you should call or write the hostess to let her know how much you appreciated her efforts. A note is easy because you do not have to find the hostess at home.

In this brief overview, we have given you a start on gracious but comfortable entertaining and etiquette. The most important thing is to try your best, learn in the process, and above all, enjoy the opportunity to share your home, your cooking, and your desire to let others know you and each other better. The two keys to success are *observation* (watch what others do and learn from them) and *hands-on experience.* Many wives' clubs have programs featuring ideas for entertaining or table-setting competitions. The final luncheon of the year can be a potluck and the hostess can leave all of the table setting, centerpieces, and serving to club members. It's an easy way to learn and have fun doing it.
****

If you'd like to our expert for more tips, write to: Mrs. James S. Gracey, 1411 S. 21st Street, Arlington, VA 22202.

Originally appeared as "Practical Protocol" in <u>Family</u>, June, 1988.

Section VII

Portable Careers and Education

43

Portable Careers

Turtles and hermit crabs have more in common with military spouses than you may imagine. Turtles carry their houses with them. As they grow larger, they simply expand their same shell, which also protects them in time of danger. Their pace may be slow, but as Aesop's fable tells us, they reach their goal in the end.

The hermit crab, on the other hand, travels from shell to shell, choosing a bigger one as he grows, or simply when another suits his fancy. Because he can travel without the burden of a shell, he can move quite rapidly; and, because he can fit in many of the empty shells on the beach, he can wear a variety of outward guises. However, he is vulnerable in moments when he is "between shells."

As more and more spouses enter the workforce out of necessity and/or choice, our means of making our jobs and careers portable follow the options of the turtle and the hermit crab. Some spouses choose arenas of activity that they literally carry with them -- artists, writers, consultants, and craftspeople fall in this category. Their market is wide enough in scope that their livelihood is not place-specific. Others rely on being able to "plug into" each new local community, much like the hermit crab. Teachers, secretaries, nurses, and bookkeepers are some traditional examples of this mode of employment.

Research on Spouse Employment

Statistics on the number of wives who are working today vary widely depending on the source of information and the locale. Nationwide, about 55% of married women are counted in the labor force, according to a recent *Washington Post* editorial. A more startling figure is that 90% of all American women are employed at some point in our lives.

298   Portable Careers and Education

The Rand Report, released in March 1982, gives an overview of military spouses working in 1979. The percentages varied only slightly by services, with the overall running about 40 % for spouses of enlisted personnel, plus about 3% seeking employment. Officers' spouses showed 50% labor force participation, plus almost 5 1/2 % seeking employment. In terms of the number of weeks worked per year, the percentages were very similar for spouses of enlisted and officer personnel working 1-26 weeks. Beyond the half-year mark, more spouses of enlisted personnel were employed, and they also contributed a greater proportion of the total family income than did officers' wives.

However, that data is now three years old, and the consensus of many working in the employment counseling field is that a far greater number of military wives are employed today. Current Navy figures, for example, list 59% of all Navy spouses worldwide participating in full or part-time employment; 70% of those living in the Washington, D.C. area are employed. In any geographical location, the cost of living, the number of employment possibilities, and the perceived need to be involved in military family social or volunteer activities are factors in the decisions to commit time and energy to a paid job career.

Job vs. Career

For our purposes, a *job* is a specific position held at a given point in time. a *career* carries the idea of a plan for employment that will stretch over a period of time and may include a variety of specific jobs. Many see a career as the sum total of one's life work, the amalgam of experiences in one particular field, or, increasingly, in several widely differing arenas.

Air Force Spouse Initiator: Nancy Hamilton

Nancy Greer Hamilton, the director of the Military Spouse Skills and Resource Center at Bolling AFB in Washington, D.C., finds that placement is very rapid for certain occupations in the region. She lists bankers, bookkeepers, interior decorators, temporary or permanent office staff of any sort (data and word processors, in particular), freelance writers, artists, nurses, medical or dental technicians, social workers (master's degree), photographers, dog trainers, caterers, and personnel specialists as all in demand. Other portable careers that Nancy sees are investment advisor, cosmetologist, physical fitness expert, the tourist industry (including travel agents, hotel managers, and clerk positions), pre-school teachers and child care aides, part-time teacher on the college level (especially in continuing education and business courses), marketing specialists, piano and voice teachers, and cottage industries. Listed as a "really hot skill" is fund-raising. In Civil Service, she recommends the clerk-typist, accounting and finance, contracting, and personnel classifications.

The Bureau of Labor Statistics has recently projected job categories with the most openings through the 1980's. As you might imagine, the top three fields are computers, health, and engineering. However, many other jobs look strong as well: secretaries and stenographers, retail sales workers, custodians, cashiers, nurses and aides, orderlies, truck drivers, food service workers, office clerks, waiters and waitresses,teachers (elementary school), kitchen helpers, accountants and auditors, trades helpers, auto mechanics, blue-collar worker supervisors, typists, licensed practical nurses, carpenters, and bookkeepers. Add to that list the current dearth of high school science and mathematics teachers, electronics technicians, and the current explosion of condominiums and apartment complexes which need managers. Many of these fields are non-traditional for women, but one thing that military wives have learned is flexibility.

Finding Your Niche

When looking for the job that might fit your skills, think of services that fill the needs of a predominantly military clientele. An example would be an emergency child care service for children with mild sicknesses who cannot go to their regular day care center or school. Dual career parents are willing to pay higher rates for such care.

Another service would be the daily check on a house or apartment when the owners are away or have ben transferred before being able to sell or rent it. One enterprising military wife with a real estate license in two states formed a relocation service, using her own expertise plus that of other military wives with specialties in areas such as educational placement. An Air Force wife runs nationwide speakers' bureau, no matter where she moves. An Army wife, who is a consultant in the education and relocation fields, takes her business with her when her husband moves, but keeps all of her contacts alive wherever she lives.

Multiplicity of Careers

In *Future Shock*, Alvin Toffler predicted that it would not be unusual for each of us to have five different occupations in a lifetime and that the straight-forward career progression would become a rarity. Military wives have been forerunners in this area. Hit by the triple whammy of economic necessity, the opportunities opened by the women's liberation movement, and the rapid swings in career options due to technology and age changes in the population, military wives also experience frequent dislocation. Our mobility may be a curse or a blessing, and the irony is that it is awfully hard to know which it will be in the long haul.

Many military spouses, in looking back over the myriad of places they have lived, the things they have done and seen, feel that their life's tapestry is richer for its variety and its lack of pre-planned pattern. Others envy the regularity and predictability of their civilian sister's career patterns.

It takes courage to live our lifestyle under any circumstances. In *Future Shock*, Toffler referred to one psychologist's concept of the Modular Family. Because corporation people have had to become so mobile, the suggestion was made to match up the mobile executive with a new family in each new location He could "plug into" a family-community matched to his previous family situation. While it might be an efficient idea, it is not very appealing to most of us. But the concept of modular job career may be the answer for many of us.

In Chapter 44, *Family* examines the skill bank/job referral centers that are beginning to open on various military stations in order to help spouses "plug into" local employment. *Family* will also begin a series of articles on jobs and careers that military wives have found rewarding and portable. Their hints, as well as their role as models of success, may help us determine if we are turtles or hermit crabs or some wonderful evolutionary creature yet unknown.

*Nancy Greer Hamilton went on to serve as the Director, Employment Resource Center, Marine Corps Headquarters, and initiated systems to measure the impact of spouse employment on Marine Corps families' income, wrote a handbook on resumes for retiring and separating Marines (and spouses), and played a leadership role in the formation of the Joint Employment Management System (JEMS) for all Services in the Washington, D.C. area.

Originally appeared as "Portable Careers" in <u>Family</u>, December 1982.

44

Banking Your Skills: Wave of the Future

In your two days here at Great Lakes, we've arranged for you to speak to Navy wives, the Girl Scout Council, the Women's Auxiliary of the VFW, Fort Sheridan Army wives' clubs, and the Chamber of Commerce.

As Navy Wife of the year in 1974, I felt relatively comfortable talking with military wives and Navy leaders at the Naval Training Center, but I certainly wondered what I could say to the local Chamber of Commerce. Did I dare tell them how important it was to the civilian community itself that the military families assigned to the station be allowed, indeed encouraged, to be part of their community for the duration of their stay? Did I dare say that the most meaningful gesture to military couples would be a willingness on their part to hire military spouses?

I decided it was a golden opportunity to build understanding, and risky or not, I should chance it. I remembered my own experiences with job hunting and the tales of others who had had to camouflage their husband's career on applications, and launched into my spiel on why hiring military wives was just plain good business. At the end of the talk, I was swamped by men handing me their business cards saying, "I need a secretary...a salesperson...a bookkeeper." I asked them to write the jobs open on the back of their cards, and I would relay the information to....to whom? The local Navy Relief office graciously agreed to serve as a contact point for job openings.

That was eight years ago, and it was much too fragile an arrangement. Today the volume of military spouses wanting to work requires improved strategies. Having a skill bank and employment referral center on post has become a very important issue among military families.

Job Bank Prototype

Fortunately, we have some good forerunners to learn from. Foreign Service wives formalized their request for a centralized skills bank in March 1977. In their report, *The Concerns of Foreign Service Spouses and Families*, the Association of American Foreign Service Women recommended the formation of the Family Liaison Office (FLO) in Washington. The Spouses' Skills/Talent Bank was to be part of the FLO. Career counseling, information about the local job market, and referral for employment while at overseas posts were seen as key functions. Research already completed by spouses and a questionnaire asking educational and occupational experience (paid and volunteer) gave the necessary proof of the need for such a service.

Volunteers did the groundwork, but eventually a coordinator was hired to assure continuity. Susan McClintock, a Foreign Service Wife, volunteered her services for two years and then served as the first coordinator for two years. Part of the wives' recommendation was that Foreign Service wives be hired for all FLO positions, and that their terms be two years only, to insure sharing the opportunity to build one's resume with as many wives as possible.

The same philosophy operates in the overseas part-time/intermittent/ temporary service positions (PITS) for which Foreign Service spouses may be hired for a maximum of one year. If there is no other qualified person available, the same wife may be re-hired after a three month break in service. Sonya Sandman, the current Career Counselor at the Department of State FLO, stresses that this format helps as many as possible to gain two years' service in appropriated fun positions so that they can qualify for Civil Service career-conditional status when they return to the U.S.

After four years' operation of the skills/talent bank, there is a new trend toward decentralization. While the original hope had been to facilitate the hiring of spouses before they headed overseas (and some of this does still occur as personal services contracts with the large government agencies and corporations that hire from the U.S.), the maintenance of up-to-date resumes in Washington has proved difficult. Current procedures have the wife hand-carry her employment records and check in with the Community Liaison Office (CLO) coordinator when she arrives at post. The CLO maintains the job requests from American businesses with foreign offices, and knows what openings there are in mission appointments. The FLO and CLO's are not placement agencies, but they can advise and refer wives to companies who have hired Foreign Service wives already, and they do keep job announcements.

Career Counseling

Another service of the Washington FLO office is to join with the Overseas Briefing Center in offering a four-day career counseling seminar twice a year. Wives are given tips on skills assessment, writing their resume, the job search, and interview techniques. Monthly career network meetings are held at the FLO office for wives who are new to the D.C. area and are interested in the job market. Career change counseling is also an important provision for those who have never been employed or have been away from their field for some time.

The Department of State Career Counselor also maintains resource materials. In addition to her notebook of local job announcements, Sonya Sandman has individual country files, including directories on businesses and organizations operating overseas, as well as work regulations.

Nationwide Transferability of Skills as Goal

Military spouses, knowing of the Department of State model, began to seek a comparable format for the armed forces. An early pioneer was Maureen Nutting, a Coast Guard wife, whose plan for helping career-oriented military wives made her a semi-finalist in the coveted White House Fellowship competition in 1979. Her plan was wide in scope, calling for nationwide transferability of educational, union, and Civil Service credits, as well as a DoD-wide skills/job bank.

The 1980 Army Family Symposium produced six major recommendations, including the establishment of job centers, a worldwide skill bank system, and career planning programs for family members. The 1980 Air Force Conference on Families also recognized the need to "help spouses and family members who desire or need to work and whose careers or educational goals are disrupted by Air Force moves." The skill/bank system would be quite costly and requires a great deal of effort, both nationally and at the grass roots. The Army has yet to fulfill that recommendation of the 1980 Army Family Symposium.

Bolling AFB Making a Start

In the interim, several job centers and skill banks have cropped up around the country which, hopefully, will be linked to provide optimum help for the mobile military spouse. In July 1981, the Air Force created the Military Spouse Skills Resource Center at Bolling AFB as a prototype and hired an Air Force wife as director, Nancy Greer Hamilton. Nancy has an office in the headquarters building and has an airman secretary. Her mandate is to serve the 15,000 active duty spouses in the area, plus AF retirees and their spouses. Part of her provisions are workshops for spouses. At one recent series, which included three sessions on interests and assessment, resume and cover letters, and interviewing skills, there were over 1000 people!

While some clients are looking for help in determining their long-range goals, most want a job immediately. As a one-woman office with 30 new jobs listed a day, and about as many deleted, and 200 people in her files currently looking for jobs, she needs help. (She is willing to train volunteer interns who would commit to five days a week, six hours a day, for six months. "They would learn all they'd need to know to work in or run a military or civilian employment agency." A portable career, folks!)

Nancy has assisted other Services as they have begun to set up their own versions to meet the needs of their populations. The Navy Family Service Center at the Anacostia Naval Station in Washington, D.C. is in the beginning stages and is learning from Nancy's expertise.

Ft. Belvoir Education and Employment Resource Center

Army wives, with Nancy's help, have initiated a program of even wider scope. As they pooled their interests, talents, and visions, they determined the need to broaden their offering from an employment referral service to include volunteer and educational opportunities. Under the leadership of Lynne Armstrong, Army wives have researched, planned, and have now opened the Education and Employment Resource Center (EERC) at Ft. Belvoir, VA.

Serendipity seems to have been at work at Ft. Belvoir. There had been an awareness of the need for a job referral center ever since the 1980 Army Family Symposium. The Ft. Belvoir Family Advocacy Council (now the Family Forum) listed it in their concerns in April 1981. The Officers Wives' Club, under Lea Ann Walker's presidency, considered taking it on as a project last year. Then, just as the Army Community Services (ACS) officer, Major David O'Donnell, was wondering how he was going to get things moving, in walked Lynne Armstrong with her belief in the need to provide vocational counseling for military spouses. Shortly thereafter, Pam Otteson expressed her desire to provide a resource library of educational opportunities on post and in the Northern Virginia community, and Lea Ann Walker offered her services as publicity chairman. The EERC was on its way.

Lynne and Lea Ann have kept careful track of how their 700 and 125 hours were spent prior to the center's opening on September 20th, and Lynne plans on pulling that information all together so that others can duplicate their successes and avoid their errors.

The scope of their offerings includes: weekly workshops on a variety of topics; on-going training of counselors to increase their skills as they work on a one-to-one basis with clients; the educational opportunities resource library; information on jobs and volunteer options available in the community; and assistance to clients in identifying and/or developing their own marketable skills. Lynne emphasizes that they teach a spouse *how to search for a job*, rather than acting as a placement agency, because then he or she will know how to do it again when necessary. Services are targeted for spouses of active duty personnel and retirees, as well as teen-aged dependents. A summer-hire program for teens will be initiated this next summer. Courses in typing, shorthand, and word processing will be arranged for spouses wishing to learn these skills.

Volunteers Staff the Center

Lynne feels that their origin as a volunteer committee will be important to the on-going commitment by volunteers to work in the center. Those who serve as EERC counselors have received three days of training from Wendy Wise, an Air Force wife. They have been required to make a one year commitment to give a minimum of three hours a week in return for their initial training, plus on-going in-service training. Gloria Leonard, a counselor who already works full time, will counsel at the noon hour and one evening a week. Such flexibility will greatly enhance the services of the center.

Those who volunteer as receptionists also receive training in the skills necessary for meeting clients and for recording all key information on job openings -- that is harder to do than one might imagine.

The third group of volunteers is vital to the job referral portion of the center. They are the employment resources specialists who job it is to sell the program to the business community via visits and phone calls. Under the leadership of Wilett Bunton, they will do on-going research on area employers and job openings. Lynne will serve as the volunteer director for the first month. Because the director needs to be full time to coordinate volunteer efforts, the ACS officer is seeking authorization for the position to be an appropriated fund position. (**It was so designated and Lynne Armstrong was hired as the first director.*)

The Future

Nancy Hamilton longs for the day when the Air Force, Army, and Navy Centers, plus the Department of State's Skills Bank, can network via a computer. Their fragmented resources could be greatly enhanced by such a tool, and it might be the step toward the DoD-wide service envisioned by Maureen Nutting in her White House Fellowship proposal.

Meanwhile, the directors are sharing as much as they can within the limitations of their time, staff and mission requirements. Lynne Armstrong, at Ft. Belvoir, has also reached out to the civilian community for assistance. The Fairfax County Volunteer Action Center, with eight different offices, will help those interested in volunteering in the civilian community find an appropriate placement, and will do workshops at EERC. The Northern Virginia State Employment Commission has agreed to give EERC volunteers training and access to their computer job bank if they agree to volunteer one full day a week.

Lynne is a pioneer. She and Nancy Hamilton, Sonya Sandman, and Maureen Nutting may not look like their forerunners in covered wagons, but they have been exploring unknowns and have had the courage to blaze trails for the rest of us to follow.

****

When this article appeared in December 1982, it was accompanied by a second article, "How to Set up a Job Bank," which gave hands-on details and sample client information and job information cards developed by Nancy Greer Hamilton. This became a popular resource as installations around the world sought to duplicate her system. Nancy later became director of the 18 Marine Corps Employment Resource Centers and acquired the software to link them all together to serve relocating families.

In the years since this article, each of the Services has made great strides toward spouse employment assistance programs at most installations. In geographical regions where joint-Service cooperation is feasible (San Diego, Hawaii, Washington, D.C., and Hampton Roads, VA), there have been a variety of linkages tested. One of the most promising, the telephone job bank sponsored by the Department of Defense Office of Family Policy and Support in the Hampton Roads area, may be incorporated in the Congressionally-mandated relocation services.

A great deal of work still remains to be done to convince civilian employers that military spouses are desirable employees. We must accentuate our flexibility, our breadth of experience which may bring fresh ideas, our spontaneous bond with other military families (that is especially effective in sales, teaching, and counseling positions), and the fact that our spouse's assignments are longer than before and are likely to keep us in the region for two - three years. (The national average for length of stay in a job by civilians is two years -- we are more likely to stay put in a job once we find it than our civilian peers, because we know that we will be into the job search mode again when orders come, and why cause any more dislocation than necessary!)

Originally appeared as "Banking Your Job Skills, the Wave of the Future?" in Family*, December 1982.*

Home-Based Businesses

Looking for added income?

Looking for flexible hours?

Want to be your own boss?

Want to be at home with your children?

Want to carry your business with you when you move?

All of the above are reasons for starting your own home-based business. Often called "a cottage industry" or self-employment, your own business can be the source of pride, a sense of control in an otherwise chaotic lifestyle, and a source of income.

Over the years, I have written a number of articles for *Family* featuring military spouses who own their own businesses -- as the sole workers in their enterprise, or as the directors of a staff:
 a puppeteer in *Portable Career: Ventriloquist-Puppeteer*
 a weaver in *Mopsy Phillips: A Compulsive Creative*
 an interior designer in *Decorating by Design*
 two military wives in the health care arena in *Military Wives Manage
  a Multimillion Dollar Business While On the Move*
 a military daughter in the closet organization business in *Closet
  Wizardry*
 the owner of a craft consignment shop in *Christmas Crafts*
 a trail-blazing chef in *Wilderness Cook*
 three military protocol experts in *Practical Protocol*
 a needlepoint artist in *Portable Stitchery*, and
 a wives' club that published a book in *Publishing Possibilities*

Surge of Interest in Home-Based Businesses

The *1985 Department of Defense Survey of Military Spouses* showed that less than 4.5% of officers' spouses and 2.5% of the spouses of enlisted personnel were self-employed. In the past three years, there has been a significant increase in the number of military spouses who own their own home-based businesses for several reasons:

1. the Department of Defense and all of the Services have published regulations that *permit and support* military family members' quarters-based businesses;
2. the Services have established support and training for home day care providers;
3. the surge of women in the civilian sector into their own businesses has swept military spouses along with the tide; and
4. the Services are beginning to provide good training through their family member employment assistance centers for would-be entrepreneurs.

The brief summary below comes from the Department of Defense pamphlet *Home-Based Business in Military Housing*, available from your installation family service/support center employment assistance program.

Full Support Where It Counts

It's clear that the armed forces support the idea of cottage industries. They've each established guidelines for starting up a business in quarters:

Army—"The Department of Defense has directed that we foster and encourage the use of family quarters for certain limited commercial activities...such as handicrafts, child care and sale of products to be conducted by occupants of government quarters."

Navy—"To increase the employment opportunities for military spouses, private commercial enterprises are permitted in military family housing..."

Air Force—"It is Air Force policy to promote and encourage limited commercial activities which may be properly carried out from military family quarters. Commercial activities are defined as business enterprises conducted for profit by family member(s) assigned to the dwelling unit."

Marines—"ALMAR 115/87 provides for family members to conduct home enterprises from government quarters. Concerns such as child care, dressmaking, tax preparation, etc., are allowed as long as a number of provisions are followed and permission is obtained from the base commander."

For more information on your branch's rules and regulations for home enterprises, contact your installation administrative office; they'll point you in the right direction. •

The regulations established relatively recently by the Services have had limited publicity. Installation commanders have the final say on implementation, and most Stateside have been supportive. The implementation of the Army guidance has been somewhat more difficult in Europe, due to Status of Forces Agreements and other host country laws. You should check with your installation administrative office to know where the point of contact is for your base/post. In some cases, such as the Air Force, the Housing Officer enforces the regulations. In other instances, separate offices control "solicitation;" and even though your proposed business might not include direct sales, you would need to be cleared through this office.

The Department of Defense supports quarters-based business (spouses may have home-based businesses in rented or owned housing simply by meeting local license and lease requirements) because spouse employment and satisfaction with the military lifestyle are closely intertwined and directly affect retention of the military member.

Day Care -- Another Plus

Another plus for the Department of Defense is licensed home day care in quarters. This allows spouses who wish to remain at home with their own children to earn an income and provide flexible-hour care for up to six children per household. It is significantly cheaper for the Services to provide the training and supervision necessary for certified home day care than to build child care centers, and military members with unusual or extended hours can be better served by home child care providers. To find out how to become certified, check with the child development services coordinator at your installation.

Family Service/Support Centers Assist

Military family service or support centers provide workshops on home-based businesses through their family member employment assistance programs. *Family* attended such a workshop at the EERC (Education and Employment Resource Center) at Ft. Belvoir, VA. Linda Graziano, an Army wife, researched and collected material on the field and presented her workshop the first time as a volunteer. It was so well received that she has been hired as a home-based consultant to repeat her workshop at Ft. Myer, the EERC, George Mason University, and the Fairfax Re-entry Center.

The Birth of a Home-Based Business

Lynda Helton, the wife of a Navy Seabee (E-6), attended Linda's workshop at Ft. Belvoir to learn how to proceed with her business in quarters on the post. She had gone to the post housing office and had experienced some confusion over what the regulation permits. At the time she was considering offering sewing lessons for children after school. But she also had significant experience in art (caricatures, portraits, and calligraphy) and her husband has helped her with banners, posters, and signs.

As she mulled her possibilities and began to think of a business name that would encompass the areas she might grow into (and in which her husband might join her), she decided on "Crowning Touch Designs." Because she is a "scatter-talent," she had the problem of focusing on one area in which to start. With her husband's nudging and support, she decided not to start with the sewing, but instead to plunge into the love-of-her-life, her art work.

As *Family* went to press, Lynda had obtained all of the necessary licenses and had participated as a vendor in the Italian Festival in Alexandria, VA. She had obtained her business license from her county and her vendor's license (sales tax) from the city of Alexandria. She had noted the festival in the calendar of events and had applied to sell her caricatures. (Her experience as a teenager drawing caricatures ten hours a day for six days a week at Six Flags Over Mid-America in St. Louis prepared her well!) Her first day's earning of $100 paid all of her start-up costs, including her canopy, costume, and supplies. "From here on out it will be sheer profit!"

Taxes

Lynda must now file an estimated federal income tax form for each quarter of the year so that she keeps pace with her earnings. She must also check her state regulations -- some states do not tax earnings under a basic minimum. She will need to keep accurate records of her expenses and receipts. This can be a very simple ledger in which she records monies received (source and date) in one section, and monies expended (for what/to whom and date) in another.

She can call her local Internal Revenue Service number and ask for the following publications:

334 -- *Tax Guide for Small Business*
505 -- *Tax Withholding and Estimated Tax*
533 -- *Self-Employment Tax*
535 -- *Business Expenses*
552 -- *Recordkeeping Requirements and a List of Tax Publications*
583 -- *Information for Business Taxpayers -- Business Taxes and Identification*
587 -- *Business Use of Your Home*

While all of this paperwork could seem overwhelming, Lynda knows that she has made the right choice. She is 31 years old, has four children at home (the oldest is ten), and has a creative drive and a financial need to satisfy. She did offer one piece of advice to those who might follow her into the world of business: "Make sure that you have gotten yourselves well-organized at home." She used her local library to find books on time management for homemakers and felt far more professional once she had her own household under control.

Her targets this fall include making contacts with caterers (who do parties and might want a caricaturist or who do weddings and might need a calligrapher), party organizers for companies and retirements, and families in her neighborhood who would like their children to have group art lessons after school

Getting Started

Information on starting your own business can be found in your library. An example of a detailed "how-to" is *The Complete Guide to Self-Publishing* by Tom and Marilyn Ross, for those of you who have considered freelance writing or self-publishing as a portable career. You may order a copy from Writer's Digest Books, 9933 Alliance Road, Cincinnati, OH 45242 ($19.95 plus $2 shipping and handling).

The Cooperative Extension System, located in every county in the United States, offers workshops and materials on home-based businesses, sometimes in cooperation with the employment program at your base or post. (Look in the blue pages of your phone book under State.)

The Small Business Administration has inexpensive seminars and materials on many detailed aspects of owning your own business. Many community colleges and adult education programs schedule mini-courses in the evening to assist you in determining your market and setting up your business.

Learning from Others

You can also learn from other military spouses who have blazed the trail before you. The Military Spouse Business and Professional Association, a new organization for spouses who are interested in the career development (via employment and volunteer work) was the vision of Kaye Cook, Head, Navy Spouse Employment Assistance Program. Monthly meetings are held in the Washington, D.C. area to enable participants to meet military spouses in the same or other lines of work and to hear presentations on common areas of interest. Their goal: that chapters will spring up around every military installation and be connected

312 Portable Careers and Education

with the military spouse employment assistance programs. Job/skill/mentor banks would then be possible. (You may contact the association at 7300 Whitson Drive, Springfield, VA 22153.)

Two other formal networks exist: the chapters of Business and Professional Women and the National Alliance of Homebased Businesswomen (for information on NAHB, write to: P.O. Box 306, Midland Park, NJ 07432).

Leslie's Lace

An informal network helped *Family* find a number of military spouses who own their own businesses. Army wives sent us to Leslie Bloxham who owns Uncle Sam's Lace. After touring the Jacquard Lace Factory with the wives' group from Ft. Rucker, AL, Leslie realized that she could design military and university seals to be reproduced in lace. her mail-order business includes sales to military museums, wives' clubs (for fundraisers), and direct sales. One of her most popular samplers is "Home is where the Army sends you." Her lace panels ($5 plus postage) are designed to fit standard 11x14-inch frames sold in military exchanges. For information on her collection, write: Uncle Sam's Lace, P. O. Box 13112 Huntsville, AL 35802.

Barbara's Catering

Leslie sent *Family* to Barbara Racinowski, an Army wife in San Antonio, who has carried a catering business with her as she has moved. "When catering out of my home, I have never advertised, but relied on word of mouth," Barbara says. She stresses that organization and making ahead are the keys to her business. She has just added a video on setting tables with flair and ease. The setting demonstrated include a wine and cheese table, luncheon, informal dinner, and buffet tables. "I hope it will help the young military wife (no matter what rank her husband may be) realize that one does not need expensive or matching china, crystal and silver in order to entertain." At $19.95 plus $2.50 for shipping/handling, the video will be a resource for wives' groups, individuals and training sessions at the company, battalion, and brigade levels. For further information on her catering business or the video, write to 8019 Copper Trail, San Antonio, TX 78244. (*This was a 1988 address.*)

Jane's Smocking Business

The same network connected *Family* with Jane McPherson, another Army wife who began her business ten years ago in Charleston, SC, as a smocking retail business plus classes. She and her Navy wife partner eventually published a book on smocking, and Jane bought her partner out in 1985. Her husband is now on his third overseas tour -- in Mainz, Germany -- but with her sister's help, Jane maintains her mail-order business out of Atlanta. A key factor: when military spouses move overseas, a stateside address is critical for tax and mail purposes. She has expanded the business to include "Little Labels," a variety of woven labels to sew into homemade items, and "Laughing Stock," a line of notepads with 80 different sayings. One of her most popular is "Home is where the Army sends you!" Wives' clubs around the world purchase her military-related notepads at wholesale and use them as fundraisers. She also markets to gift shops. Twice a year she flies back to the United States for the big trade shows to market her products, and stays a week to lay business strategies with her sister/partner and distributors for their products. "Our phone bill is enormous!" If you would like to reach Jane, write to: Jane McPherson, 459 Blanton Rd., N.W., Atlanta, GA 30342.

Linda's Baby Patterns

Linda Storm, another Army wife, can sympathize with the difficulties of running a creative business from overseas. *Family* featured Linda and her nursery-related patterns in our article *"Baby Costs" (April 1987)*. She started her business when she was living in New Mexico seven years ago. When her husband received orders to Germany, she shipped her files and inventory to her parents in Ohio. "They are both retired and agreed to fill orders and maintain the day-to-day records plus give my business a permanent address -- people go through magazines and order three and four years later!" She kept the files and marketing information and continued to design, write, and promote the products from Europe.

Linda shares the hint that getting publicity in Europe is not very difficult. Each community has its local paper, and the *Stars and Stripes* is very receptive to human interest stories. Armed Forces Network television has a Gasthaus segment at 7:50 p.m. weekdays, which is an interview show. She also mentioned that writers can attend the Frankfurt Book Fair (in September) which draws publishers from all over the world. Crafters can participate in the International Handcraft and Textile Show held in Cologne in April, as well as link with the numerous boutiques in Stuttgart, Heidelberg, Mannheim, Darmstadt, and Hanau, which allow consignment of craft items. "Craft shows and bazaars are drawing good crowds and provide nice incomes to crafters."

Linda Storm with her line of "Grow-With-Me" and "Nurseries and More," may be reached at: Babies by Storm, 786 Westchester Park Drive, Springfield, OH 45504.

Originally appeared as "Cottage Industries" in Family, September 1988. The chart is from Family.

The Real Costs of Working

To work or not to work, that is the question! Actually, all military spouses work at home, so the proper question is to be or not to be employed outside of the home?

It is a question shared by our civilian peers, but we have two additional factors that cause us to make the decision more often than they do: our mobility and the nature of our military spouses' work. Mission requirements bring deployments and erratic hours -- not experienced as often in civilian households. In order to bring some order to our often chaotic decision-making, *Family* interviewed spouses from three Services and three geographic areas. All underscored the need for flexibility based on the ages and stages of family members and on the opportunities at a given.duty station.

The Boswells

LT Day Boswell, U. S. Coast Guard, and her husband, Walter W. Boswell, Jr. ("Chip"), have made a decision that many would think unusual (and that some would envy). Chip stays home with the children, C.J. (nine years old) and Genny (two years old). Although they have moved to the New London, Connecticut area recently, this is not a new arrangement for them. Day, who is the Public Affairs Officer at the U. S. Coast Guard Academy, has sixteen years of service. They met when they were both active duty enlisted members. After five years, Chip left the service to pursue a two year chef's training certificate using his G. I. Bill. He also took care of C.J. when his schedule permitted, both to cut down on child care expenses and to enjoy his son. Upon completing his training, he worked for as many as three caterers at once in the Washington, D. C. area, sandwiched around child care.

When Day received orders to Fort Benjamin Harrison, Indiana, they re-evaluated his situation. Based on the relatively low cost of housing in the area and the equally low pay rates, Chip decided to return to school -- this time to Purdue University, to pursue a degree in horticulture. (This is part of their long-term goal that they will own and run an inn a la Newhart upon her retirement from the Coast Guard. They have studied such enterprises, and have come to the conclusion that her marketing skills and his culinary talents will not be enough to maintain a year round income. Adding a pick-your-own berry farm would do so.) He completed three years of his degree (and won the honor of Horticulture Student of the Year), while caring for their new baby, before their move to Connecticut last fall.

Having sold their house in Indianapolis, they wanted to reinvest in Connecticut. This time they hit a high cost of living area. They hired a real estate broker to look for the best possible option for them. (A broker works for the buyer, whereas an agent works for the seller.) They found a "handy-man's special," a 125 year old Victorian in the City of Groton.

"I wasn't a handyman, but I'm getting to be!" In the first ten days before their furniture arrived, they tackled sheetrocking the walls and ceiling of the master bedroom, painting all of the walls and woodwork in their four bedroom house, and refinishing all of the wood floors. When their broker visited several weeks later, he felt they had already added between $20 - 25,000 to the resale value of the house.

When *Family* visited at the five month point, $5,000 worth of materials and a great deal of "sweat equity" had upped the value by $50,000 -- "not a bad 'income' by any measure," bragged a proud Chip, as he and C.J. made a batch of fresh pasta in the spacious kitchen. He has found that it's hard to get big projects, such as laying ceramic tile in the kitchen, done during the day when he must keep an eye on their two year old, so he usually waits until evening or the weekend when Day can relieve him of child care.

Now 32 and 33 years old, they expect a three to five year tour in the area. Once the bulk of the renovation is done and the gardens are in, Chip may reassess his current commitments. He may return to college to finish his degree and may freelance as a chef. But one thing he and Day know for sure -- it has been important to them that their children have one parent at home as much as possible during their early years. As Chip says, "I've been doing this Mr. Mom thing since before the movie! I know a number of dads who really would like to do what I do -- it's not easy yet in our society."

Air Force Spouses in Tucson

Sheila Crump, Director of the Family Support Center at Davis-Monthan Air Force Base in Tucson, Arizona, and Steven Rountree, a social services assistant who coordinates employment assistance at the center, helped *Family* talk with Air Force spouses who have made a variety of decisions. The first group of three have decided to volunteer at the center. While they had some reasons in common, they also had unique situations.

Jacie Crawford, the wife of Sergeant John Crawford (E-4) has contributed over 1,000 hours to Family Services in the last two years. As the 25 year old mother of two children ages three and six and a half, she volunteers three days a week. The Family Support Center pays her child care costs ($1.50 an hour for the first child and $.50 more for the second). Davis-Monthan (known as D-M) is her first Air Force Base.

She grew up in Wichita, Kansas, so this is her first time away from family. She stayed at home her first year in the area and says she didn't know "anyone or anything. I felt sorry for myself and worried that I was becoming depressed. I made a decision to get out and do something with my life. I'm basically a shy person, and people can't believe the change in me. Because of the work I do with Family Services, I know more about what the Air Force provides to families than my husband does, and he is amazed " She is now going to Pima Community College as well, having obtained a grant through the college.

Kazue Pfeffer, the wife of Staff Sergeant Leslie Pfeffer (E-5) echoed Jacie's comment that the free child care attracted her to volunteering for the center. At 32, Kasue has two children ages one and three. Before marriage, she completed her bachelor's degree in English literature in Japan.. At their first duty station, Kadena Air Force Base, Japan, she found it easy to get a job because she was multi-lingual. She stopped working when her children were born.

When they moved to Tucson, she found the idea of working "scary." She wondered if she could qualify -- her language skills and her gap in employment worried her. But she made a new year's resolution to do something for herself. By volunteering three days a week at the center, doing some typing, filing, and mailing, and learning a new kind of computer, she has built her self-confidence and has had the opportunity to think about what she would really like to do. She will keep her eye on the jobs listed with the employment assistance office, hoping to find something that will enable her to contribute to the cost of the new house they have bought.

Pamela Barthell, the wife of Captain Joe Barthell (O-3), knows that they will move to Aviano, Italy shortly. Even before the orders came, however, she had quit her job because she was dissatisfied, not fulfilled. Once she and her husband had gotten financial obligations out of the way, she felt free to do something she cared about -- to support the networking of Air Force families. Volunteering two or three days a week, depending on the center's need, she is using her associate's degree in computer programming to assist the center put spouses' job skills into the relocation job/skill bank. At age 38, with no children, she is free to focus on finishing her bachelor's degree (half a year to go) and committing herself to supporting the Air Force Family. Service to others has become her priority

The second group of spouses \were four who are *in the workforce by choice or by necessity.* Judith Cormier, wife of Staff Sergeant Larry J. Cormier (E-5) and Esther Guerra, wife of Airman Nicolas G. Guerra, IV (E-2) work out of necessity. At the beginning and end of their husbands' careers, they must supplement the family income.

Judith Cormier (age 36) and her husband, currently live on base. But he will retire after 20 years' service this June, which will necessitate a move into the civilian community with attendant costs, and they have significant medical bills that have accumulated due to their oldest son's prolonged cancer treatments. "When he was undergoing chemotherapy, I couldn't work outside the home, so I worked a home party plan." Now she serves as a receptionist for an employment agency. She admits a personal need to be "out in the world doing something."

Esther Guerra (age 19) and her husband have a 15-month old baby and find it hard to make ends meet. Because base housing is not provided until one reaches the rank of E-4, they must live off-base in an apartment. "We have to budget all of our money. My husband heard about the employment assistance program in classes soon after we got here. I did some babysitting, but it wasn't enough money. We have a truck without air-conditioning. With a baby, a truck is difficult and we know we will need air-conditioning for summer in Tucson, so we are saving to buy a car."

Esther has long-term goals to become a certified public accountant. She had accounting/bookkeeping training in high school, including a work-for-credit job, so she is pleased to have found a job with Alpha Graphics as a key punch operator entering bookkeeping data at $5.00 an hour, which should increase to $6.75 an hour at the end of her first month. She is getting experience in her chosen career field, and after six months, will receive the additional benefit of being reimbursed for schooling.

Child care on base will cost her $46.00 a week, but there is a four - six month waiting list. Meanwhile, a woman close to their apartment takes care of their son for approximately $45.00 a week. She economizes by brown-bagging for lunch frequently, and she carpools to work with another Air Force spouse (and their husbands carpool as well). Her husband has a four year tour at D - M, but supervisors have indicated that they like to keep the people they've trained, so a 6 - 8 year tour is possible. So she can make long-term decisions and commitments.

Judy Salinas, the wife of Technical Sergeant Joseph B. Salinas (E-6), went to a one-year business school at the age of 29, and has worked one year as an administrative assistant for a security firm. "With no one at home needing my care any longer (she has a 15 year old daughter), and the need to pay off my student loan, I now work outside of the home." Previously, she and her husband felt that there was no financial need for her to work. "The cost of child care was so great ...if you could find someone you could trust and who had the same values. I was protective. So I babysat for other military families. Now we have gotten used to the two incomes."

Candice Merkle, Program Coordinator, Family Support Center, was the fourth employed spouse to share her decision-making process. The wife of Lieutenant Colonel Raymond P. Merkle (O-5) and the 36 year old mother of an adopted two and a half year old Korean boy, Candice has gotten a job wherever they have been stationed. With a master's degree in psychology (earned with her GI Bill benefits from prior service in the Air Force as a missile technician), she has worked for the Civil Service in family advocacy overseas and in the private sector stateside. She works to fulfill her own personal goals.

When they moved to Tucson, there were no appropriate Civil Service jobs available, so she took a job as a counselor in the local prison. When the program coordinator position opened at the center, she returned to federal service, because she wants to build seniority ("I've been at the bottom of the totem pole so often") and she wants to keep open the option of working overseas after her husband's retirement.

Child care was a major issue for her when they came to Tucson. "Centers were charging $80.00 a week for toddler care and I wasn't happy with the quality. He is in home care now. I like the family and the cost is $45.00 a week."

Army Spouses at Fort Myer

Seven Army wives and one Navy wife gathered at the USO center at Tencza Terrace, Fort Myer, Virginia to discuss the real costs of working with *Family*. **Dale Jovero**, wife of a Navy chief (E-9), **Tammy Cavanaugh**, wife of Sergeant Larry Cavanaugh (E-5), **Cheryl Frischkorn**, wife of Staff Sergeant Kenneth Frischkorn (E-6), **Teri Goldhammer**, wife of Sergeant Gordon Goldhammer (E-6), and **Shari Grimes**, wife of Specialist 4 Robert L. Grimes (E-4), all work for the USO on a full or part time basis. With the exception of Dale, who must drive some distance to work, all live and work in walking distance on post. Tammy and Teri work in the outreach center at Tencza Terrace, so may have their children with them on the four days of the week that they are at the center. The fifth day may take them out of the building for staff meetings. Cheryl and Shari work in the USO office at post headquarters.

Dorita Babino, wife of Sergeant First Class Lucius Babino (E-7) worked as a "temporary casual clerk" for the Post Office during the past holiday season on the 10:30 p.m. - 7:00 a.m. shift (when her husband could take care of their five and ten year olds). She is mulling the desirability of continuing some kind of employment, but is concerned about the high cost of child care (the post child care center takes children only through age five, so she would have to use the county extended day program for her older child, and the fee, based on her salary and her husband's, would be $65.00 a month. The possibility that her husband will be sent on a one year unaccompanied tour to Saudi Arabia inclines her to remain at home so that she can chauffeur her children to sports activities and not be concerned about the reliability of child care on top of "single parenting."

Tonya Blain, wife of Staff Sergeant Greg Blain (E-6), has been a babysitter and now works part time (Sundays) at the post chapel. When her youngest child goes into first grade next fall, she expects to get a full time job

Suzanne Lewis expects to join her husband, Sergeant First Class Benjamin C. Lewis (E-7) in Japan this summer. She has held full time positions as a supervisory security guard, but stopped work when he left ahead of the family for Japan, because her long and irregular hours made child care very difficult.

Conclusions

With the help of all of these military spouses, who freely shared their experiences in order to help the rest of us make wise decisions, *Family* has designed the following charts to help you clarify your motivations for seeking employment outside of the home or choosing to remain at home.

We first became interested in exploring this topic upon hearing of a young Army couple at Fort Huachuca, Arizona, whose story was told in hearings on military child care before the House Armed Services Committee. With two children in the post child care center, the couple found that they were $5.00 a week *in the hole* after adding in only the wife's transportation to her job! Their plea was to decrease the sliding scale at the child care center and/or not base it on their joint income. *Family's* concern is that they made their decision on her employment without determining all of the facts.

My Motivation for Seeking Employment Outside of the Home

[ ] **Financial** - The amount you earn matters to you. If you need money for basic necessities, check this box. For example, Esther and her husband have a hard time making ends meet on an E-2's pay.

[ ] **Social** - Adult company can be an important plus if you are new to an area or if your military spouse is deployed for long periods. This is the acquaintance level.

[ ] **Emotional** - Friendships in your workplace provide support. Pamela in Tucson felt that the people she knew in her workplace were shallow, primarily focused on financial success, whereas those she met at the Family Support Center were "solid, caring people."

[ ] **Self-Esteem** - Your work brings you a sense of pride and achievement. Kazue in Tucson found that her volunteer commitment brought her confidence and skills on a new computer system.

[ ] **Intellectual** - Your work is challenging and provides opportunities to grow mentally. It is career-enhancing. Candice in Tucson has always sought employment in her field of counseling to continue her experience and her general upward mobility (which at times has seemed downward or horizontal!). Jacie talked of her decision to go to college because of the stimulus of her volunteer job. Esther will hope that advancements bring her to this level in her chosen field of accounting.

[ ] **Philosophical** - Your work has aspects of a mission or a crusade, something you feel very deeply about. Pamela, in saying that she expects to continue to volunteer n the family support arena once she moves, is expressing this level of commitment. She has found a cause that gives her a deep sense of worth beyond herself. (One side benefit she noted was a significant loss of weight "without really trying, because I am focused on my real priority.")

Reasons for Choosing to Remain at Home or Hidden Costs of Working Outside Home

*This time, a check mark in the box can be a reason to remain at home.

[ ]   **Financial** - Sometimes you actually go in the hole. (Our third chart will help you determine this.)

[ ]   **Physical** - Our military spouses noted that sometimes employment outside of the home brings less regular exercise, weariness, less sleep, bad eating habits, and negative stress. Will your spouse/family share household tasks, or will you add a job on top of your current load?

[ ]   **Social** - Will you have less time for wives' clubs, church groups? Less opportunity to be with people of your choice?

[ ]   **Emotional** - Less time for family? Friends? Will you be missing out on your child's development? Guilt? Will you be/are you irritable, short-tempered?

[ ]   **Self-Esteem** - If under-employed (i.e. your skill level is far higher than job calls for), will you be frustrated? Embarrassed?

[ ]   **Intellectual** - If under-employed, will you have less time to read or pursue creative, growth-enhancing interests?

[ ]   **Philosophical** - Does the job mesh with or further your overall sense of what you should/could do with your life?

True Rewards or Costs of Employment

Income

Your gross income	+$_____
Child Care Credit	+$_____
Earned Income Tax Credit	+$_____
Total Gross Income	+$_____

(* See explanation on pages 322 - 24 to compute each of the categories.)

Outgo

Social Security withheld (FICA)	-$_____
Federal Income Tax	-$_____
State Income Tax	-$_____
Life Insurance	-$_____
Health Insurance	-$_____
Child Care	-$_____
Transportation	-$_____
House Care	-$_____
Meals at Work	-$_____
Family Meals	-$_____
Work Clothing	
Purchases	-$_____
Cleaning	-$_____
Personal Care	-$_____
Professional Growth	-$_____
Personal Spending/Pocket Money	-$_____
Conscience Spending	-$_____
Total Outgo	-$_____
Total Net Income or Outgo	+/-$_____

Your Gross Income - Compute your annual salary (<u>before any deductions</u>) as other computations will be based on that figure. (52 x your weekly salary, 26 x your bi-weekly salary, or 12 x monthly salary.) **Dependent Care Credit** - For children under the age of 13 (or aged dependents), you may qualify for this credit if you work full-or part-time

The Real Costs of Working 323

(or are a full-time student) and incur care costs for time at work. Amounts are figured on a sliding scale based on your joint income, with a minimum credit (for those earning $28,001 and over) of $480 for a single child or $960 for two or more dependents. For a joint income of $18,001 - 20,000, the credits are $600 and $1200. (Check IRS rules.)

Earned Income Tax Credit - If you have one or more dependent children and have a total family adjusted gross income (includes basic and special pay plus basic allowances for quarters and subsistence) of less than $19,340, you may be eligible for this credit for low-income householders. You may earn the maximum $910 credit with an income of less than $10,500. Above that the credit tapers off.

Total Gross Income - This figure is the addition of the three sources of income above.

Social Security - For 1989, the FICA withholding rate was 7.51 % on earnings up to $48,000. Your employer can tell you the annual figure or you can do a quick computation.

Federal Income Tax - The percentage due will be based on your total family income, not just your spousal income. In 1989, if you filed jointly, you paid 15% on taxable income under $30, 950, and 28% on income over that amount (but less than $74,8750). If you filed as "Married filing separately," you paid 15% on taxable income under $15,475, and 28% on income over that amount (but less than $37,425). (Check IRS rules.) For those of you whose military spouse has a taxable income of $40,000 or more, you are into the 28% bracket on your first penny earned. A conservative estimate for this category is that you will see no more than 65% of your income -- and that's before state taxes!

State Income Tax - Regardless of your military spouse's state of record/domicile, you will pay income tax in the state in which you work and earn money. He/she likewise is liable for local state income taxes on moonlighting income.

Life Insurance and Health Insurance - Life insurance is usually a voluntary expenditure, but some employers require that you contribute to a group health plan. This may duplicate your military benefits.

Child Care - Include all child care costs here (even the extra hours you need for shopping, etc.) so that you get an accurate picture of your costs (vs. amount you can deduct under Dependent Care Credit).

Transportation - If you know the cost of public transit, enter it here multiplied by daily roundtrips. Otherwise, calculate miles and multiply by the IRS figure of $.24 a mile. Add parking costs, if appropriate.

House Care - If you hire someone to clean your house or yard (tasks that you performed prior to employment), add the costs here.

Meals at Work - A "hidden cost" frequently mentioned; while some attempt to brown bag as often as possible, meals out are added costs.

Family Meals - Experts estimate that when both parents work outside the home, more meals are eaten out and there is a tendency to buy more highly processed (translate "more expensive") groceries for meals in a hurry. Judy in Tucson said that their family of three tried to go three months without eating out, because their fast food costs had gotten so high. But they discovered that members of the family then ate less well-balanced diets, scrimping by with soup and sandwiches too often, so went back to meals out and figured it a cost of their lifestyle.

Work Clothing - Most had to add significantly to their wardrobes to have appropriate clothing for their workplace (including hosiery, shoes, purses, and dress-slacks in addition to suits or separates). Dry cleaning was a big hidden cost, with many fabrics that can't have home care.

Personal Care - Hair care, cosmetics, and physical fitness costs

Professional Growth - Courses, training, books, magazines, and newsletters may be hidden costs in this domain.

Personal Spending/Pocket Money - One shouldn't travel around without emergency funds of some sort in his/her wallet -- and somehow it gets spent on miscellaneous items.

Conscience Spending - The little gifts for your children/spouse when you travel or "to make up" for your time away.

Total Outgo - Add all of the above items and subtract them from your **Total Gross Income** to determine your **Total Net Income (or Outgo)**.

This has been a great deal of work for you, but it will serve as a firm basis for determining whether your anticipated (or actual) gross income/outgo meets your financial needs. This is especially important if your primary motivation for seeking employment is financial. If you find yourself going in the hole (often because of child care costs), you might want to look into volunteer opportunities that pay your child care expenses, or you might want to look into a home-based business. As our panels of military spouses indicated, each change in lifestyle (getting married, having a child), each change in duty station, and each change in our military spouse's mission requirements may cause us to reassess our previous decision on staying at home or seeking employment outside of our home.

One "seasoned" Navy wife, who has been employed over the years, has been involved in significant work as a volunteer, and is the mother of seven children who are now either graduated from or still in college (as is she, working on her Ph.D.), offers experienced advice: *You can have it all ....just not all at once!* Military life isn't easy! But many military spouses feel that they have emerged from our challenging lifestyle with an overall amalgam far richer than that of our civilian peers, and it has been hard won -- not taken for granted.

Originally appeared as "Why Some Military Spouses Work" in <u>Family</u>, *May 1990.*

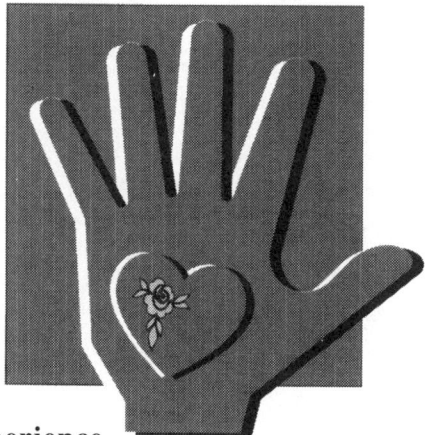

47

Internships: Hands-On Experience

Are you looking for summer or short-term employment?

Are you entering the job market for the first time, or returning after a period of years?

Do you, like many military spouses, have lots of different kinds of employment instead of a career pattern?

Do you have a high school or college student wondering what career to choose?

If so, an internship may be the best possible investment of time, energy, and interest that you or you high schooler can make at this point. An internship is usually defined as a short-term opportunity to gain on-the-job experience under the supervision of a mentor. Additional benefits may include college credit and/or pay.

Being an intern or an apprentice was very common in the Colonial period; it was often the only route to many occupations. Today's version usually occurs when an organization and a would-be intern meet each other's needs: the need for additional staff and the intern's needs to get hands-on experience above entry level work.

Such a confluence of needs occurred in my office last year. In addition to my work for *Family* as Associate Editor, I was teaching "Military Family Studies and had a contract to revise my book, *Making a Home in the Navy: Ideas to Grow On*, for the Navy Family Support Program. An additional book on plantings that do well in southeast Georgia for my garden club was awaiting my volunteer attention. I needed help!

So did Heidi Smith, a 20-year old Navy daughter who had completed her freshman year at the University of Maryland in Munich. When her dad was ordered to Naval Submarine Base Kings Bay, GA, arriving in mid-fall, she was not enrolled in a college program. In the spring, she took several courses offered on base by a nearby junior college, but had no sense of direction. She was drifting in and out of a variety of waitress, housecleaning, and child care jobs.

I met her when she and her mother worked on the research stages of a book I was coordinating for the Officers' Wives" Club. She seemed to thrive in the company of adult learners and enjoyed the research and writing tasks. In the fall of 1985, she and I worked out a contract for learning which stipulated the opportunities and training that I would provide as well as the duties that she would perform. The term of our contract was "indefinite," but we agreed to a minimum of 20 hours a week on a flexible schedule. Her modest stipend of $100 a month was supplemented by the college credits she would earn.

College Credits

With the help of the Valdosta State College representative on base, we negotiated a precedent-setting arrangement: Heidi would take my "Military Family Studies" course (five credits at $170) and would receive ten credits for her work as my intern (at $340). She had not yet taken a course on campus, but the President and the Dean of the School of Communications waived the requirement that a student be a second-semester junior or a senior for internship credits after my presentation to the faculty on the educational needs of military families.

Their flexibility allowed Heidi to avail herself of a once-in-a-lifetime opportunity. Helping the verification process for the Navy handbook, she learned word processing, sources of information on the base (such as the Public Affairs Office, Librarian, Legal Officer, and the Family Service Center), and how to set up files on a narrow, complex topic.

No small part of her work was the record keeping required for a small business. Heidi maintained my ledger on travel costs, postage, supplies, and phone calls, and worked with me at tax time. She also had to file her own tax return and document her financial status for her student loan.

At the same time, she wrote her own newspaper articles, publishing a total of six different pieces in local military and civilian newspapers and *Family*. The Navy journalists and photographer with our base newspaper showed her layout techniques and taught her to develop her own black and white photos. Navy and civilian printers shared their craft, and she worked with the editor of a local weekly paper on stories that she submitted.

Internship: Hands-On Experience

Her journal was a daily record of lessons learned. This was necessary for documenting hours and tasks for college credits, but also helped her remember the hints (and errors) that would make each new project easier and better. Some lessons were related to her formal tasks; others included choice of clothing for interviews at college and presentations (she accompanied me on a number, criss-crossing the state), and stress management skills (how to prioritize and how to "hang in there").

For her project in "Military Family Studies," she researched current newsletters produced by the almost-70 Navy Family Service Centers worldwide. Finding common problems, she took an issue and redid it completely to demonstrate more effective use of graphics, layout, and tone. Her product has been distributed by the Navy Family Support Program to all of the centers -- great feedback on the quality of her work!

Heidi's Big Project

Her final project, the culmination of all of the things that she had been learning, was *Choosing the Right Plants for SE Georgia and NE Florida*. Working from the manuscript by a St. Marys garden club member, and illustration by two local artists, Heidi formatted the entire book on the computer and delivered a camera-ready copy to the printer. She had worked with club members on colors of ink, textures of paper, binding, and proofreading. She consulted the typesetter for title font choices and layout, and then worked with the printer through the entire printing and binding process. When the book emerged in May 1986, she felt as if she had given birth! The book is now in its second printing.

When Heidi took her portfolio to Valdosta for final review by the Dean of Communications, she went with confidence in her learning and her products. She enrolled as a full time junior in the School of Communications this past fall, validating the experiment Valdosta had accommodated. In her case, the internship helped her focus on a potential major, gave her work experience in a professional field, and gave her a portfolio of flyers, articles, and a book. Although she did a lot of nitty-gritty work, she also had separate, specific projects of her own. She had a contract and a built-in evaluation process to credential her credits.

Heather Interns with the Camden County Tribune and USO

Internships were not new to our family when I made the contract with Heidi. Both of our two children had had a variety of internship opportunities, with and without pay. For example, our daughter Heather, who is a college senior, sandwiched her first short internship into two weeks between the end of her junior year and the start of her job at the National Music Camp in Interlochen, MI. On her first day at the *Camden*

County Tribune, she was handed a camera and told to cover the unsanitary conditions at the county animal shelter. She made the next day's deadline and had the excitement of a front-page story that stirred up significant public interest. In her remaining weeks, she wrote four more stories, typeset many of the pages, and got to know a variety of role models. As she starts her job search for her "real job" after graduation, those articles in her portfolio will be valuable.

Her big internship was in the Celebrity Entertainment Division of the USO World Headquarters in Washington, D.C. Having completed her first three years at Smith College in two years (due to advanced placement credits from high school), she wanted to take a year away before returning for her senior year with her classmates. She talked with Abbie Beller, Program Director for USO World Headquarters, who had just said goodbye to Bobbie Bott, a Marine Corps wife who had worked as a USO intern for the four months her husband was assigned to the area.

After assessing Heather's interests and abilities, Ms. Beller decided to place her in the entertainment section where staff was needed badly. As a 19-year-old, Heather coordinated talent, press, publicity, and logistics for overseas tours. her own specific project was to organize the Germany tour of the L.A. Rams' Cheerleaders from start to finish. She designed their jacket and poster, and wrote the script for the radio spot announcement. Later she went to the audio studio to coordinate the music and voice-over. Press packages were designed and distributed, and she wrote correspondence for a variety of tours. The most glamorous part of her internship was going to Dallas to help with the 45th Anniversary Gala.

So, for the cost of room and board in a friend's home, she spent a semester exploring a potential career field. As she prepares her resume and starts her job search, she knows that though she received no pay, she made a wise investment in her future.

Michael Explores Architecture Through Internships

Our son Michael initiated his first internship the summer after he graduated from high school. He had felt for some time that he wanted to be an architect, and had attended the summer career exploration program in architecture, landscape architecture, and urban planning at Harvard University the preceding summer. (That program is for anyone, high school senior -- on, who wants hands-on experience in the three fields. College students and people as old as his parents (!) were there.)

Although he had lined up some part-time work for the summer selling sporting goods and lifeguarding, he wanted to work in architecture. With three high school courses in mechanical drawing and architecture, he was able to "sell himself" to the Arlington County Planning Commission as an unpaid intern. He was assigned a mentor, who in turn, assigned him two specific projects: to design a new park sign and to design a small urban park near a new subway stop. He went to "work" every Monday all summer, dressed for an office environment. He learned how to take the subway, make his way in an adult bureaucracy, and present his designs to the committees that made the final decisions. He saw how plans were made for the county, and was able to soundboard with planners on designs in the works. he had been wait-listed at the college of his choice, Rhode Island School of Design (RISD); soon after they heard of his internship, he was accepted.

His second internship fulfilled the requirements of his sophomore year RISD Wintersession. He negotiated a six-week internship with the architectural firm, John Tuten & Associates, in Brunswick, GA. Though the internship was to fulfill six credits, he was pleasantly surprised to be offered minimum wage (raised after his first week of work). Mike had interviewed with Mr. Tuten the previous summer as he sought employment after our move in mid-summer. He felt that he had learned more in his one hour's interview than any classroom experience he had had that far. The architect's enthusiasm and innovative approaches really appealed to him. So, when he could offer himself as an intern, the firm was a natural. Located in an historic building that had been renovated, the firm worked on domestic, commercial, and government buildings. The following summer, Mr. Tuten offered him as much work as he wanted. As Brunswick was a one hour drive each way from Kings Bay, Mike chose to work three days a week (and fish the other two!)

This past summer, Mike had yet another experience with interning. He won a Yankee Magazine Internship. These internships, in conjunction with the National Trust for Historic Preservation, employ college students in non-profit historic preservation projects. A stipend of $2,500 is paid for 12 weeks' work. Students who are residents of, or attend college in the six New England states are eligible. (For information, contact National Trust for Historic Preservation, 45 School Street, Boston, MA 02108.) The National Trust makes the applicants' files available to agencies or communities involved in preservation work so that a match of skills and needs can be made. Mike was hired for a National Park Service project in Lowell, MA. As the only intern, he was the youngest of five on a team making measured drawings of some of the nineteenth century textile mills for the Historic American Buildings Survey -- Historic American Engineering Records. He thoroughly enjoyed climbing through the old mills, encountering the resident pigeons who would take flight through the long factory rooms where young farm girls had worked long hours among the looms. The notation on his resume will only hint at the many things learned over the summer before his senior year.

Resources for Information

- Your base/post Civilian Personnel Office and Family Service/Support Center Spouse Employment Assistance Program.
- Your high school or college career/vocational office.
- Your local Chamber of Commerce and Business and Professional Women's organization
- Trade and professional associations (get names and addresses of those in your field of interest via directories in your library).
- Your library -- look for books such as: *Internships*, ed. by Lisa S. Hulse (compiled annually). Available by mail for $14.94 plus $2 shipping from Writer's Digest Books, 9933 Alliance Road, Cincinnati, OH 45242. This book lists 35,000 internships by career fields and geographic areas (including suggestions for international internships).

Adapt Concept for Adult Internships

Although all of these examples have been college students, most military spouses can adapt the concept for their own purposes. Under *Resources* (above) and *Where to Look for Internships* (page 331), you will find places to look for existing internships. But remember that you can also initiate one in a business or organization in which you are interested. Non-profit organizations are always under-staffed and count on volunteers to "flesh out" their core staff. With a contract stipulating the opportunities, training, and supervision you will receive, the duties you will perform, and the evaluation process, you will not be "just a volunteer."

****

1991: Interning and mentoring continue to go on in our household.
• *Heather found that her work sophomore year in college as an intern instructor for behaviorally disadvantaged high school seniors was the key to her first job after college -- her prospective employer was impressed by her commitment.*
• *Michael, now an architect in Boston, continues to intern one day every two weeks with an outstanding specialist in his specific area of interest in architecture. He has been able to negotiate working longer days for nine days so that he can be free on the tenth to learn "from the master."*
• *At the Department of Defense Office of Family Policy, I was able to use the talents of a Navy wife one summer when she offered to serve as an intern to research, write, layout, and publish a brochure on home-based businesses in military housing. She had the joy of a first print run of 100,000 copies and we were able to get important material to military families sooner than our staff could have accomplished the project.*

Where to Look for Internships

Your base or post Civilian Personnel Office (CPO) will know of all of the internships available in your geographic area. Unlike many college intern programs, the government internships are fast promotion programs that pay well.

C. Rick Hastings, Chief, Recruitment and Placement Branch of the CPO at Ft. Myer, VA, explained the Army's program to FAMILY. (Each of the Services has a comparable program.) For Fiscal Year 1987, the Army has slots for 3,719 interns in 22 career programs worldwide. The entry level is GS-5 or 7, with the target rating GS-9 or 11, depending on the particular career program. The minimum acceleration time is 24 months for a GS-5 to 9, or 36 months for GS-5 to 11. The rule of thumb is 12 months per grade; the rating series skips at two-grade intervals.

Mr. Hastings says that the majority of intern positions worldwide are in the CPO administration, comptroller and automated data processing programs. Those also happen to be fields that have wide transfer opportunities.

Intern programs allow the Army to "grow our own specialists with skills not found in the local job market in order to meet future staffing needs. By the end of August or early September each year, we receive the final allocation of intern positions for which we can begin to recruit. However, recruitment may occur throughout the year if interns are transferred, so you should go in to your CPO *at any time of the year*."

Requirements for the GS-5 entry level are a bachelor's degree or three years of general administrative or technical work (i.e., nonclerical in nature). There are some exceptions to these requirements in occupations such as the accountant and auditor programs, which have specific education requirements. "Sometimes we have people come in who have absolutely no previous background in the given career field, but strong credentials," explains Hastings. "The recruiter looks for a self-starter with a lot of initiative, good communication skills and one who is doing personal development on his or her own. I was an intern, so I am a believer!" He came in as a GS-5, and five years later was a GM-13.

"The interns range in age from their twenties to forties, and are a representative sample of race, sex and national origin. In our area, competition is stiff—600 applications for eight slots in 1984—but the success rate is at least 99 percent. I don't think we've ever had anyone leave the program due to adverse situations—only due to transfer or the decision to move into another career program. The intent is that the individual will be placed at the local level, but if the spouse is transferred, the Department of the Army and the CPO work to place the intern at the new duty station because we see it as an investment in our worldwide needs. For this reason it is ideal to get into your own service-related program."

The *Federal Junior Fellowship Program,* coordinated by the U.S. Office of Personnel Management, is for graduating high school seniors who have a demonstrable need for earnings from summer work in order to continue in school. Both public and private school students are eligible. Obtain information and forms from your school vocational office.

The *Department of State Student Intern Programs* are designed to offer highly qualified college junior, senior and graduate students an opportunity to gain firsthand knowledge of the foreign affairs process. Two programs are offered: paid summer internships and unpaid work-study year-round internships. A few are with embassies and consulates overseas, but most are in Washington, DC.

The deadline for summer programs is November 1st. Those interested in a fall or spring work-study should apply six months prior to that time. Most of these positions require a security clearance, which can take four to six months, so send for information *early* from: Recruitment Div., Dept. of State, Box 9317, Rosslyn Station, Arlington, VA 22209.

The *Washington Center* serves over 600 colleges and universities, offering students an opportunity to work, live and learn in the nation's capital. The center matches students, who are second-semester sophomores and above, with sponsors from over 800 agencies. Each student has two to four options from which to choose. For further information, write or call The Washington Center, 514 Tenth Street, N.W., Suite 600, Washington, DC 20004 (202) 289-8680.

—*Kathleen O'Beirne*

Originally appeared as "Hands-On Experience" in Family, *May 1987. The chart is from* Family.

Back to School

When I grow up, I'm never going to school anymore! Have you ever heard this in your house? Do you remember saying it with relish? Join the crowd -- the crowd that is returning to take college courses and other forms of adult education in droves.

We can expect to have five different careers in our lifetime, and our lifetime will be longer than ever before. Alvin Toffler in *Future Shock*, set the scenario for the variety in our employment; and Dr. Sharon Lord, at the Second Army Family Symposium, urged wives to think in terms of living until age 80 or 140. "Don't stop starting so soon!"

As a result of predictions like these, numerous communities with shrinking school populations are finding that there are more people enrolled in their adult offerings than in their entire K -- 12 program. Ft. Hood recently provided an opportunity for spouses to obtain their GED diploma (high school equivalency), and was overwhelmed by the response. College campuses have been invaded by many who are no longer teenagers. They often are enrolled for the first time, or are returning to college after time out for raising a family or earning a living. They have returned to hone rusty skills or to pursue additional areas of interest for their own pleasure or for increased employability.

Sharon Given

Sharon Given and Pam Roach are two wives who are part of this campus migration. Their experiences and hints may be helpful for those of you who are considering such a step. Those of you who have already made the commitment may recognize yourselves in their motivation and challenges.

Sharon is enrolled in the Northern Virginia Community College program that leads to an associate degree in business or office management. Two years ago she had returned to a full time church secretarial job after becoming, what she laughingly calls, "Miss Volunteer Lady of the Year." At 35, she organized her household (two pre-teenaged children and husband Jim who works for the Naval Sea Systems Command), headed the local PTA, and was involved in many church-related activities. She took the church secretary position when it opened because she had noticed that she was the only woman in her neighborhood during the day. She was literally isolated in her own home with no friends to visit casually; they had all returned to work.

Sharon had worked as a secretary for the government both before and after her marriage. As a high school senior in West Virginia, she had planned to go to college and become a teacher. After one summer semester she was interviewed by a Civil Service recruiter who could offer her a better salary than her favorite high school business teacher was earning. She came to Washington, D.C.

Her return to full-time secretarial work for a year nudged her into assessing some long-range plans for herself. She felt the need to move toward a position of more responsibility and creativity, using skills she already had.

In the library she picked up information about local colleges, and decided to look further into Northern Virginia Community College because one campus was about four miles away from home and the price was right. She could take a course there for credit for less than she could take a no-credit course through her county adult education program! After talking with a counselor, she found that requirements other than a high school diploma were waived for the over-30 student.

She took only one course the first quarter which she highly recommends to others starting back for the first time. Now she takes two each quarter ("one fun course like psychology and one hard course like accounting"), and takes the summer off to have fun with her family.

Pam Roach

Pam began her back-to-college work at the community college, also. As a secretary during the day, she had accumulated college credits by attending the University of Pennsylvania in the evening before marrying her Navy lawyer husband. Thereafter, three children plus moves overseas and within the United States, and involvement in church and community activities kept her busy. The move to the Washington area four years ago, however, brought the opportunity to begin her school while her youngest was in nursery school. Her family's reaction was."You don't need college." That coupled with the fact that she had "always known that I did not love school" meant that "I went back with great trepidation."

She found that she could transfer 21 credits. She took CLEP exams (College-Level Examination Program) in French and biology, and was able to earn credit for her French that way. Because she wanted to move ahead quickly on her associate degree in general studies, she did take two courses per quarter. The campus was close and her children were not requiring a great deal of time after-school chauffeuring at the time.

After graduating with honors, she looked carefully at majors offered by all of the bachelor's degree-granting institutions in the area. She leaned toward anthropology and religion, so selected GWU (George Washington University). Her decision to take only one course her first semester there proved a wise one. Transportation was more difficult and time-consuming than before, and so was the pace and level of the course She paid $60 for one-on-one testing and counseling to help her focus more clearly on her potential major and to know her strengths and weaknesses.

Now after several semesters there, she feels more at ease with the campus, the professors, and her two course load. Her daughter, Elizabeth, who is a high school junior, joined her last summer and this semester to take math courses not available in her high school. Pam is pleased to share "her college," but is reminded that part of her impetus to finish college herself is to be able to finance the years ahead for her children.

Motivations

While increased employability is certainly a factor for many who go to college after starting their families, they talk of other motivations as well: to serve as a "role model" for their children, to "keep up" with their husband who has had more education than they have; to maintain teaching credentials (6 credits every 5 years in most states); and last, but not least by far, to have the opportunity to continue growing. Motivation is very important when the going gets rough every now and then, so the more reasons we have the better. One reason that we know intuitively now is backed by educators: *the single factor most able to predict a child's achievement in school is the level of his mother's education.* The old rule of thumb used to be the father's occupation, but mother's impact is felt again!

Adult Achievement Levels are High

That is kind of a burden, isn't it? Something to cheer us up is that most adult students achieve at a high level. This can be attributed to our determination to prove our capabilities to ourselves and our families; but additional contributors are the fact that we usually carry a smaller load of classes than the regular full time student and have the increased experience of living a few more years. One other point in our favor is that educators have discovered that our *verbal abilities continue to grow, if we exercise them, until at least age 65*, when a plateau may be reached. Our mathematical abilities do peak sooner, in our early thirties; but again, there is no appreciable decline if we use them regularly.

Study Skills

Study skills do seem to be the area of greatest weakness, either due to dormancy or never having been developed in high school. Having taught summer school to eleventh graders the last couple of summers, and college English before that, I feel confident in sharing my tried and true hints for studying and taking exams. Having taken several courses myself in the last year and a half, I also have a few memories of tossing in bed, being irritable with my children and husband, and a few fleeting signs of nausea to remind me that one never gets over "examinitis!" BUT....there is little that is as exhilarating as doing well on a big paper or test.

How to Find Time to Study

This is the hardest problem. It requires a decision on your part that you rate having blocks of time to study. A half hour snatched here or there will not be as productive as less time spent concentrating on the work at hand. While some find they can read basic assignments on the bus to work or during lunch, most agree that any work requiring analysis or composition needs a block of time, be it two evenings a week, or during the time your children are at school. I have never forgotten part of my college dean's final message pre-graduation: "Read. Read two hours a day. Get a babysitter, if necessary" While I chuckled at the time, I did hire a babysitter while I finished my final course for a master's degree with two little people underfoot. I listed it under *Sanity*, not *Extravagance*!

Another strategem that works for some is to get up earlier than the rest of the family; or try the other end of the day, if you are a night owl. One Army wife talks of her hours "snatched in the middle of the night; and I know I wasn't the only one....you should have seen how many other lights were on on our street!"

Where to Study

Obviously, if you are snatching hours post-midnight or pre-dawn, you cannot be studying in the bedroom unless you spouse is at sea -- which is, by the way, a super time to take courses. Bonnie Stewart, a

Navy wife, has just completed her MBA (Master's in Business Administration) in marketing by going full time during her husband's eight month WestPac cruise.

Where, then, do you study? You rate a place of your own that is quiet, that has space for your texts, dictionary, and materials -- materials not to be "borrowed" by your progeny or spouse! I have used the guest bedroom (pre-children), a large closet, a room of my own (glorious!), and now a corner in the basement workroom. When I talked with my eleventh grade students last summer, I found that a quiet, reliable place to study was a key problem. The dining room table with the distractions of family members and the TV just did not qualify as ideal.

Sharon Given says that she is an evening person, so she often studies in the bedroom with a small high intensity light. She needs quiet time for concentrating, so has a policy of not accepting phone calls during study time. Her family serves as super message-takers to insure her block of time.

Pam Roach studies in a variety of places, but tries to do much of it during the day while her children are in school. Sometimes she gets up at 4:00 or 5:00 a.m. In the evening, the old girls (16 and 13) have studies or activities of their own, and young Ashley (8) is kept out of her hair as much as possible by his dad. She does make the point that at GWU, some courses take an enormous amount of research time, both at the university library and the Library of Congress. She passes along the hint that courses with one or two texts are easier to handle than those with lots of extra reading from reserve library texts. "It's a struggle to be there when they're available." She says she tries hard to pace her work, aiming to get papers done a week before they are due to lessen stress. "Time management is critical."

How To Study

Many of our high school students never have been taught how to study, a great disservice to them, so please share these hints with those in your house who could use them:

1. Start the assignment when it is made. Not only do you avoid the last minute fear of failure to complete it, but you allow your brain to work for you. Both consciously and unconsciously, it will make connections with information you have learned or experienced before, and those links will enhance your learning enormously. Because we older students have had more experience than the regular college-aged students, we tend to have a far richer composite at the end of an assignment.

2. Read your assignment prior to the lecture on the material covered. Your lecture notes and class discussion will be much more profitable if you have. Underline important sections and write in the margins. Your marginalia, plus notes in a notebook or references listed on the inside covers, will be invaluable at exam time.

3. Learning styles vary. If the material is complex, you may find that making some kind of chart will help you sort it out visually. In a course I took on curriculum development, one chapter on various philosophies and their key ideas had me thoroughly confused. I had been assigned the task of presenting that chapter orally to the class, so I opted for a chart that I could give to each member. The professor was so impressed that he asked to be allowed to share it the next time he taught the course; so don't be afraid to admit your confusion and try a visual technique.

4 Find a "buddy" in the class to share notes for sessions missed and to "soundboard" with before or after class. In the most recent course I took, I heard students kibbitzing with each other before class on points they had found confusing. If they were still unsatisfied, they questioned the professor at the beginning of class, which paid off on very difficult exams.

5 Research papers should be started early because you will be amazed how class lectures tie in and trigger thoughts for your project. If you wait until later, you miss many of these connections which would have enriched your learning and the quality of your paper. Another reason for starting early is that the early bird gets the resources. If several of you are writing on similar topics, you may find the materials you need already checked out. Try your local community and military libraries as well.

Additional Study Hints

Pam Roach took a short "How to Study" course at her community college, and found that the counseling office at GWU had sheets on study hints. She adds a few of her own: "Go over your notes soon after class to fill in what you wrote hurriedly while you still remember. If the lecture covers material in the text, mark coordinating pages in the margin." She often writes key phrases on 3x5 cards to trigger her thoughts as she approaches exams.

Sharon Given really marks up her texts using yellow underliner and making notes. She finds it more efficient than outlining the chapters as she originally tried to do.

Both accent the need for good lecture notes. These are usually the primary source of exam questions. The instructor feels he has labored to share his vast wealth of knowledge, so you had better get it down. Your instructor will be speaking from an outline, and you should end up with something resembling one when he is done. Take down key phrases as opposed to complete sentences.

How to Study for an Exam

Both Pam and Sharon stress the need to give yourself plenty of time.

1   Determine the material to be covered. The best source is your instructor. "Force" him to be specific about *what* is to be included.

2   Also ask him to tell the class *what kind* of exam it will be: Essay? Multiple choice? Fill-in-the-blanks? A mixture of these? It makes a big difference in the way you study whether you are expected to be able to give short answers and definitions or an essay that requires you to substantiate your answer with examples

3   Study all of your notes. I underline important parts in red pencil and add additional notes in the margin. If the material is vast, outline or chart.

4   Re-familiarize yourself with the texts, reading underlined sections and notes and noticing pertinent quotes.

5   Pose questions for yourself. Determine the major themes and practice giving responses. A handy way to do this is to make flashcards out of 3x5 cards with key questions on one side and major points on the other.

6   Do all of this prior to going to bed at a normal time. Your brain will synthesize the material while you sleep, and in the morning you will be delighted by your increasing control of the information.

As Sharon says, though, "I'm always frustrated when I go into a test. I never feel totally prepared." Amen!

How to Take an Exam

1   Put your name on it right away!

2   Read the whole exam before starting to write. Make sure your instructor has indicated if there are limitations on time. Some give only the class period; others allows more leeway. Allot the proper percentage of time depending on each question's value and its difficulty for you.

3   Do the easy sections first. Always leave extra space after writing answers so that you can add more later.

4   Brainstorm ideas for the points you want to make in the margin of the exam or inside the cover of the exam booklet. That way, while you are working on one answer, your mind may be working on another at a different level of consciousness. When an idea pops into your head, write it in your brainstorm section so you won't forget it.

5   Order those brainstormed ideas so that the answer is logical and cohesive. For an essay question, use complete sentences.

6   Lightly mark in the margin questions you want to return to later.

7   When you are completely done, reread your entire exam. Correct and add as necessary. My experience in giving and taking exams has been that the most outstanding exams are among the last to be turned in.

8   Sharon adds the warning that you may experience a "block out" on your first exam. She advises, "Sit calmly, and hope and pray that you get your senses back!" She attributes it to nerves more than a lack of sleep, so feels that knowing some kind of relaxation process would be handy.

Juggling Family and Studies

Both Pam and Sharon urged me to be honest and say that stress is part of being a student at any point in your life, but really a noticeable factor when one has a husband and children with their own needs and expectations. Juggling your time, energy, and interests is a real challenge. Sharon, in listing her pros and cons, said., "You *must* have a very understanding husband and children." Heidi, her sixth grader, commented that her mom does get "irritable" at times, and Chris felt he and his dad have to help a little more at home; but all admitted being pretty proud of their Dean's List Mom.

Sharon admits to feeling "torn in many different directions and being a bit envious of those who have only school responsibilities. When you attend school, it's not thought of as being employed. You just have to go several hours a day, so you still have plenty of time to do a little more volunteer work. There's no awareness of the time needed for homework, research, or transportation. It would have been easier to go the college route right out of high school, but I am getting so much more out my courses now than I would have then."

To help you get more out of your courses and plan the most appropriate schedule for you, both women highly recommend using the counseling services available at your school. The Director of Counseling for Continuing Education at George Washington University is Mary Guertin, an Army wife and a continuing student herself -- now a dissertation away from her Ph.D. in human development and counseling. For students who are returning after a long break or entering for the first time, she recommends taking the course "Developing New Horizons," which includes a series of six tests (aptitude, vocational interest, and personality testing) to get a good profile of the student, speakers in vocational fields in which each class of students shows interest, job analysis, job search, and interview skills. She feels the group experience is particularly nice, providing support and networking for the students. Her office helps students take CLEP exams to test out of basic review courses.

Most of us are geared to thinking school in the fall. If you want to begin in the fall, you need to do your research *now*. Many schools are on a quarter or trimester plan and begin as early as August. As you get that first scent that is unmistakably *School*, and panic comes in waves, remember that there are lots of us out here to cheer you on. We know that dry mouth and light-(empty?)-headed feeling, but we also know the triumph that comes in a variety of ways: from a professor's compliments on a paper well done to students in our classes saying, "I wish my mom was like you."

Some Ideas for Financing Adult Education

1 The Navy Relief Society initiated its Guaranteed Student Loan Program in March 1981 -- No interest is charged on a maximum of $2,500 a year up to 4 years for Navy and Marine Corps spouses. Check your Service emergency relief organization for similar provisions.

2 Various military wives' clubs offer scholarships to spouses. (*In 1990, the Budweiser-USO Scholarship program made its first awards to military spouses for $1,000 each. March 1 deadline each year. Write to USO World Headquarters, Scholarship Program for further information: 601 Indiana Ave., N.W., Washington, D.C. 20004)*

3 Community colleges can be very reasonable (e.g. Northern Virginia Community College charges are $10.75 per credit or $128.00 a quarter for residents; about three times that for non-residents.)(*1982 figures!)*

4 Resident-rate tuition is granted to dependents of military personnel for all or most college institutions in all but three states in the nation. Check with your installation education center for details for your state.

5 A number of universities, such as GWU and Stanford, offer free tuition to employees and their dependents. If you serve as an instructor or secretary, you and your children can attend free of charge.

Originally appeared as "Back to School" in Family, *May 1982.*

Educational Options for Military Wives

For many military spouses, the thought of going to college is beyond their wildest dreams. Constant moving makes it hard to finish in the same place they begin. The length of time required to complete an Associate's Degree or a Bachelor's Degree seems overwhelming, as does the cost. Fear is also a very real factor. Can they keep up?

Now a number of practical programs exist that are designed to help highly mobile learners such as military wives turn their life experiences and credits collected through a number of sources into a degree.

The Company You'd Keep

Those of you who elect to return to college or go to college for the first time will find that you have the company of your own age group. Recent statistics show that 52.1% of college students are women; over one-third of all college students today are over 25 years of age; and over 29 % attend part-time. Colleges know that the typical full-time student under the age of 21 is an increasing rarity, so they are tailoring their offerings to attract older, non-traditional students.

At a recent conference of the Council on Military Education in Georgia, educators discussed how increased education helps military families cope with their challenging lifestyle. Skills that are important include research and analysis, communication (both oral and written, as well as reading comprehension), and sufficient experience with evaluation not to be intimidated by failure.

The variety of roles military spouses play in their own families, plus the variety of jobs and/or volunteer commitments they may have, require great flexibility -- flexibility that is based on confidence in competence. And education can give that to a person.

Bachelor of General Studies Program

Navy wives Sandy Adler and Lillian Bohannon have just completed their Bachelor of General Studies (BGS) at the University of Connecticut (Avery Point Branch) in Groton, CT. This degree program is not unique to UCONN; it is offered by an increasing number of other colleges and universities. The BGS program is for college juniors and seniors. It requires an associate's degree or 60 semester credit hours. Those with fewer credits can build on what they have and apply to this program when ready. it is individualized and interdisciplinary in nature, and may be pursued on a part-time basis.

Sandy Adler returned to college at the age of 43. She had gone to junior college right out of high school and completed her associate's degree at that time. Then she married. As her four children became high school and college age, she returned herself. "I had no career motive, but most Navy wives I knew had college degrees. I wanted a program that would let me take things I *wanted* to study -- like history and English -- and stay away from science and math."

Sandy carried three courses her first semester, and was working part-time until "I decided the job had to go!" Although at first she had a hard time keeping her mind from drifting to neglected household tasks, she soon found that setting hours aside to study helped her be more organized. "I found I *enjoyed studying and learning*, and was much more interested in everything." Sandy grinned as she thought of the fun she has now reading historical novels because she knows more of the background. "We sought the why's. It was so thought-provoking." She was delighted that her classes were small. "The personal touch was so important to me. I wouldn't dream of going into class unprepared - I knew I'd be called on."

Although Sandy talks of "staying away from math and science," she did have to fulfill the distribution requirements in three categories. However, she found there was flexibility. She could take a psychology course in lieu of a math course, for example. Her final course, the BGS Summary Project, helped tie her various areas of study together. She, Lillian Bohannon, and another student designed a textbook anthology for their project. Each worked separately on her area of interest and expertise, and met weekly to discuss their progress.

Lillian Bohannon returned to college at age 50. "My reason was selfish -- I did it for *me*. All of my life I had been hanging everybody else's stuff on the refrigerator. It was my turn! I had had three years of

Educational Options for Military Wives

college before marriage, and had been a *fair* student. I started with only one course because I was so terrified. When I got an A as my first mark in 25 years, I though, "the sky's the limit!" I screamed, bragged, and showed the whole family!"

From then on, she took three courses per semester, one summer course, and went to Connecticut College for a course. She had not gone back with the intent of getting a degree, and did not sign up for the BGS degree until after seven or eight courses. She simply took things she liked, such as a short story class, some history, and creative writing. Wining the UCONN short story competition further convinced her of her abilities.

Both women feel that their music and art appreciation courses expanded their lives. Lillian found herself "more sensitive to things -- everything is just better now, whether or not I ever use it commercially." She is toying with going on for her master's degree, "just because I enjoyed it so much."

Mohegan Community College Prior Learning Program

In another program, Mohegan Community College in Norwich, CT, has joined forces with the Navy Family Service Center at Naval Submarine Base New London to offer the Assessment of Prior Learning program. This one-semester four-credit course gives students a chance to earn college credits for learning gained through life-work experience.

Barbara Gager, the Educational Services Specialist at the Family Service Center, is an eager sponsor of this course, having earned her own associate's degree with 68 credits gained through the program. In order to make it as convenient and inexpensive as possible for military family members, the Mohegan Community College instructor comes to the FSC for the two evening classes per week. Her salary is funded by the FSC.

The Assessment of Prior Learning course teaches students how to write up their experience for credit. The five steps in the credentialling process are:

1   researching in college catalogs to find courses of study that parallel the student's experience;

2   obtaining a specific course outline from an accredited college or university;

3   describing experiences/learning that meet the course requirements in a prescribed written format;

4   obtaining supporting letters from employers, volunteer supervisors, or other authorities in a position to testify to the student's performance;

5   submitting the documentation portfolio to the college credentialling committee for assessment of credits to be awarded.

Needless to say, keeping good records of your employment and volunteer experiences is valuable. Keep dates, names of supervisors, recommendations written, and your own log of work done.

Barbara Gager is justifiably proud of the three-year track record of students in the FSC-Mohegan program. For example, 75% of the fall 1983 class (9 out of 12) graduated with their associate's degree in the spring of 1984. The 11 students in the fall of 1984 class earned between 7 -- 99 credit hours, with the average being 30 hours. The flexibility of the program was particularly important to one class member, Ronald Banister, who had to go to sea in the middle of the course. His wife, Linda, taped the classes and took notes so that he could complete the course at sea.

Cost is always the bottom line. Those who take the Mohegan-FSC course receive the four credits for the basic course *plus* all of the credits awarded on the basis of their credentialling portfolio at *absolutely no cost*. Their only fee, if they have enough credits to obtain their associate's degree, is a $35 graduation fee! The Family Service Center contract with Mohegan pays all of the rest.

Alternative Degree and Credentialling Programs

The Mohegan credentialling program is not unique. More than half of U.S. colleges and universities will give credit for non-traditional, experiential learning. To obtain information on such opportunities near you, write to: The Council for the Advancement of Experiential Learning, American City Building, Suite 212, Columbia, MD 21044. Ask for their *Directory: Opportunities for Prior Learning Credit.*

Both of the programs described above provide classroom experience. Students have the support of others in their programs as well as that of an instructor. On the other hand, programs that are totally test, computer, or mail-oriented provide for flexibility of pacing and geographic mobility. Which you choose depends on your temperament and circumstances.

Correspondence Schools: These usually offer technical or business degrees for jobs such as medical or dental assistants, bookkeepers, computer programmers, etc. If you have never finished high school, it is also possible to get your diploma through the mail. To find out which

Educational Options for Military Wives

programs are offered by accredited organizations, consult the *National Home Study Council Directory of Home Study Schools* or *The Encyclopedia of Second Careers* by Gene Hawes. Both of these should be available in your post/base library and Education Office.

Continuing Education programs: Many colleges and universities offer courses at night or on weekends to meet the needs of working adults.

Regents College Degrees: (University of the State of New York, Cultural Education Center, Albany, NY 12230): These degrees combine the credentialling of previous credits earned plus testing for credit. Associate's and bachelor's degrees in the liberal arts, business, and nursing are available through this accredited program. It was designed to meet the needs of on-the-move-military personnel and parents who choose to stay at home with their children.

CLEP: Remember that your Education Office may offer to test military family members through the DANTES (credit- by-examination) Program.

Television Courses: More than 400 institutions in 40 states are offering at least one of the Annenberg Corp. for Public Broadcasting courses from the Annenberg School of Communications at the University of Pennsylvania. In order to get credit, students must read a textbook and study guide and pass a final examination.

To those of you thinking about continuing your education, try a single course in which you have great interest to whet your appetite and renew your confidence. Consider it an investment in your sense of well-being. Your employment options will be enhanced, and your repertoire of skills for living our challenging lifestyle will be enlarged. You may well join the ranks of lifetime learners. As Lillian Bohannon says, "The sky's the limit!"

Adapted from "Educational Options for Military Wives" in Family, August 1985.

Earning Your Degree

Have you dreamed of having a college degree, but the thought of spending the equivalent of four academic years in a classroom seems overwhelming? You may be surprised to learn that there are faster, less expensive means to your desired end. *If you have the will, there's a way!*

Marine Corps wife Susan Washburn shared her will and her way with participants at last year's Department of Defense Volunteer Management Training in San Francisco. She was on the program by popular demand; participants in the preceding year's training had heard her comment that she had earned much of her bachelor's and master's degrees by getting credit for her volunteer and paid work experience. Susan agreed to share her information with *Family* readers because, as former Deputy Director of the Family Service Center at Marine Corps Air Station (MCAS) Cherry Point, NC, she knows how valuable it will be to those of you wondering how you can become a college graduate yourself, and to those who counsel military family members.

Susan Washburn

Susan graduated from Watertown High School, Watertown, NY, in 1969, and attended one year of community college. Prior to her marriage in 1971, she attended six months of business college to prepare to work while her husband completed college. "In 1972, my husband was commissioned. For the next ten years, we moved from coast to coast and overseas." Duty stations included Pensacola, FL; Quantico, VA; El Toro, CA; Jacksonville, NC, and Iwakuni, Japan.

"Our three children were born between 1974 and 1977. That kept me busy the next few years! Meanwhile, my husband completed a master' degree and left me far behind in the academic race.

"From 1982 - 84, we were stationed at the Naval Base, Keflavik, Iceland. In such a remote area, opportunities for things to do were somewhat scarce. Fortunately, employment and educational opportunities were readily available aboard the base. I was selected as the program coordinator for the Family Service Center. Working with professionals who had not only college but post-graduate degrees made me want to complete my education and have that all-important college degree. I enrolled in classes with the base education office and began what would be a four-year quest.

Credits Through Testing

"I discovered that few military installations have compatible college programs, and because of the varied schedules, limited credit transfer policies and availability of courses, it would be virtually impossible to complete a traditional college program in my chosen field."

While stationed in Iceland, Susan completed eight traditional classes and attended several military schools as a part of her job, but she was not enrolled in a specific degree program.

"When we returned to the United States in 1984, I was again fortunate in the job jungle and went to work for Richard Milburn High School for Adults at Marine Corps Base Quantico, VA. My office was located in the Education Center, and this provided me with a great deal of information and inspiration for non-traditional education programs. The base education officer, Kathryn Cranford, was extremely helpful in finding independent study programs, CLEP (College Level Examination Program) testing programs, and experiential learning opportunities."

The base education office usually administers CLEP. "This program allows students who have gained specific knowledge through self-study, continuing education, or experiential learning to be tested to receive credit, if their learning equates to a college-level curriculum."

General testing is available in English, math, the sciences, and history." There are also CLEP and DANTES (Defense Activity for Non-Traditional Education -- for military members only) tests available in specific subject areas ranging from languages to psychology. A nominal fee is charged and there is no penalty for failing to receive a high enough score on the tests. They can be retaken.

Awarding of credit is determined by the institution or college. Additionally, colleges offer their own tests on subjects. "I was able to 'CLEP out' of mathematics and the humanities, which added 12 semester hours to my growing credit bank.

External Degree-Granting Program

It was at this point that I needed to apply these credits to a specific program. *You have to get a degree from somewhere!*. I had already accumulated more college-level credits than most graduates, but I did not have a college willing to award a degree. After researching several programs that offer *external degrees*, I chose Regents College from the University of the State of New York (Regents/SUNY).

"While there are many similar programs available on military installations worldwide, I chose Regents College because of their proven track record with military personnel, my natural affiliation with New York state, and because the costs, requirements, and time limits were reasonable and attainable for me.

"You enroll in the program and send transcripts from any schools you have attended. Military personnel are also able to send documentation for credit of military training that is accredited through the American Council on Education Guide.

"Regents accepted my community college credits, my business school courses, and all of the college classes that I had taken up to that time. There was some duplication in my courses and I could not receive duplicate credit. I was assigned an advisor who helped me determine what courses I needed to complete my degree in liberal studies with a concentration in sociology, approved course selections, and kept me apprised of my status. I still needed upper-level science, history, and psychology. It was the fall of 1986, and I still had 19 hours to go! That was when I really had to get creative!

"We were stationed at MCAS Cherry Point, and the education programs at the undergraduate level were limited. The nearest university was 90 minutes away, did not offer the courses I needed, and for an out-of-state resident were too expensive to be practical. As a traditional university, they were not willing to accept transfer credits and they were on a regular semester schedule of day classes, which precluded my attendance. I was able to take two classes on base through their extension program, but I was still short 13 semester hours.

Independent Study and Experiential Learning Programs

Susan began to look for independent study programs and learned of the Lifelong Learning Program offered by Ohio University in Athens, OH. "From the beginning, I was very impressed with their program. They have a toll-free number for information and assistance, and I was able to get fast answers, which was important to me by this time. They have a

Earning Your Degree 349

variety of options available, from independent study to testing and credit for experiential learning. I opted for credit for experiential learning because I felt my work experience had provided me with a great deal of knowledge and education. To complete this process, I enrolled in a portfolio development class. This class itself carried credit and guided me through the process of documenting my learning experiences.

Documentation became my battle cry! I had to produce certificates of training, letters of reference from people qualified to assess my level of knowledge in a particular subject area, and even get brochures, job descriptions, and photographs to illustrate my learning experiences. Working closely with an adviser, I completed the course and applied to receive credit *for three other subjects* by submitting lengthy, detailed proof of my ability or knowledge in a specific subject area." These subjects were chosen from the college catalog. Her portfolio for each was evaluated by the college professor who taught that course on campus.

Perseverance Pays Off!

Her final transcript of credits was forwarded to Regents College and Susan graduated in May 1986. "Having a college degree has certainly opened the doors for employment, but more important is the feeling of accomplishment from completing the program. The lifestyle of military wives is a challenging one indeed, and we often focus on the difficulties of a mobile existence. In my case, these things were turned into real opportunities for education and employment. Few of our civilian counterparts would have had the same opportunity for travel and education, nor the requirement to develop management skills to meet the challenges of such a demanding lifestyle."

Susan is currently the marketing officer for Morale, Welfare and Recreation at MCAS Cherry Point. Her husband, Lieutenant Colonel Gary E. Washburn, is now stationed at nearby Camp Lejeune. Susan is starting a second master' degree in human resource management with Golden Gate University, which has a program on base. She may test out of courses that are pre-requisites for advanced courses. It sounds as if she's off and running again!

Nancy Weisensee

Navy wife Nancy Weisensee has also earned college credits for volunteer work. She and her husband, Captain William J. Weisensee, have both completed their bachelor's degrees through Southern Illinois University (SIU) on base at the Naval Submarine Base New London, CT. She now serves as the assistant coordinator for SIU's local Department of Vocational Education Studies.

She and the program coordinator, Richard N. Cilley, Ed.D., are enthusiastic about their required internship program through which students earn five or ten credits. Called Independent Study, the volunteer internship allows students to put their classroom learning to practical use. They must put in 200 hours for five credits, or 400 hours for ten credits, and may spread it out over two to three trimesters.

Flexibility of SIU Program

While most of the 60 - 65 students enrolled in the SIU program each year are military members, spouses are welcome. The internships, most of which are done in the evening or on weekends, must be flexible to accommodate work schedules. Nancy's internship enabled her to give individualized support and attention to students in the two-week remedial program for Submarine School students. In the evening, she reinforced what the educational specialist taught during the day: basic skills such as reading and spelling. Nancy periodically sat in on the daytime coursework so that she could monitor the night study sessions productively. The remedial program enables the Navy to keep many of the sailors who would have failed otherwise.

Nancy's degree is in vocational education studies, with a specialty in education, training, and development. She would like to teach basic English and reading skills. Nancy started the SIU program two years ago to build on her associate's degree. She could complete SIU's 36-hour program in a year, or, as Dr. Cilley says, "whatever you need to finish. There's no time limit, which is great for those who move." Nancy is proud to complete her degree at the age of 49.

Types of Internships

Dr. Cilley records the internships that previous students have held so that current students may contact the employers and agencies that have provided productive opportunities in the community. Six or seven students per term teach evening courses in GED preparation, English as a second language, and adult basic education at area high schools and the Navy community center. One student designed a job fair for the base. Another designed a one-day training on insurance for Navy career counselors, the Family Service Center staff, and community counselors.

The rest of the SIU classes are offered every other weekend for a trimester. SIU works around sea time to make its offering as flexible as possible for military family members. Dr. Cilley works with students to tap financial aid resources. The internship costs the same as regular course hours: $121 per credit hour. (*1989 figure*) (SIU has extensions at 16 military installations -- check your education center.)

Karen Crowley

Karen Crowley, the installation volunteer coordinator at Ft. Benning, GA, provides continuing education credits (CEU's) for the training she sponsors. Through an arrangement with Columbus College, and previously with Georgia State University's on-post division, she gives no-cost CEU's. Karen wrote a grant proposal which allowed her to offer volunteer management training at Columbus College. Volunteer coordinators interested in her concept may contact her office at (404) 545-5602 or Autovon 784-4811.)

Additionally, the Family Member Employment Assistance Program grants CEU's for its typing program and job search strategies classes. While CEU's do not count formally toward a degree, they do count as verifiable training and meet the requirements for certain certificates. They also carry significant weight toward selection for Civil Service positions. Karen cites the example that when a GS-9 position opened for director of leadership seminars, the spouse who got the job could prove her training in the field. CEU's also provide the kind of *documentation* that Susan Washburn talked about for your portfolio-for-credit.

Fannie Harris

Fannie Harris, Director, Family Support Center, Bolling AFB, Washington, D.C., has initiated a volunteer intern program at her center. Since the fall of 1989, students at a local university may earn up to five credits toward their undergraduate social work degree. They interview family members at the center to identify basic family life problems and they offer workshops. "Their experiences are congruent with those required by the university catalog," Fannie explained. "For example, we provide supervisors with the credentials required for accreditation of their work."

Other Programs

The Marine Corps Family Service Center at Twentynine Palms, CA, offers volunteer internships for post-master's degree students who are working toward licensing as Marriage, Family and Child Counselors (MFCC). Dr. Steven Morgan, deputy director of the center, says that their current intern initiated her internship with them. She needs 3,000 supervised hours prior to being allowed to take the certifying examination. In an isolated area, their program meets the needs of individual students as well as increasing support services available to military family members.

At Puget Sound Naval Shipyard in Bremerton, WA, Marlene Reifenberger offers vocational counseling. As the Spouse Employment Assistance Program coordinator, she helps spouses determine if they are good candidates for prior learning credits (like Susan Washburn's) or challenge tests, and then refers them to specific colleges. "One takes a challenge test for about $100. If you pass, you receive full credit for the subject matter. If you fail, your test fee goes toward the cost of taking the course for credit," she says. In addition to local community colleges, Marlene recommends City University. While it is not part of the Navy shipyard campus program it does have extensions all over the world offering two-year, four-year, and master's degree programs.

Marlene suggests that spouses seeking prior learning credits obtain a copy of the "I Can" lists developed by the Educational Testing Service (Princeton, NJ 08541). The lists help volunteers and homemakers to translate their experience to work (and portfolio experience). Your installation employment assistance coordinator may have copies.

Resources

• Council for Adult and Experiential Learning, 10840 Little Patuxent Parkway, Suite 203, Columbia, MD 21044; (301) 997-3535. The council can provide information on opportunities near you.

• Ohio University's Portfolio Development Program, Adult Learning Services, Office Of Lifelong Learning, Tupper Hall 309, Ohio University, Athens, OH 45701-2979; (614) 594-6569.

• Regents College Degrees, Cultural Education Center, Albany, NY 12230; (518) 474-3703.

Many colleges have come a long way from rigid requirements to accrue 120(+) credit hours in formal classroom courses for a bachelor's degree. In so doing, they have combined the best aspects of standards of excellence, apprenticeships (like reading for the bar for would-be lawyers), and classroom instruction. They recognize that "education" is both broader and deeper than sitting in a classroom. Piecing together your own special amalgam from past experiences and present formal courses may require more self-discipline than simply signed up for already-offered courses, but where there's a will, there's a way.

Family wishes to thank VOLUNTEER-The National Center for its materials and sponsorship of annual conferences that include the Department of Defense Management Training (1111 North 19th Street, Suite 500, Arlington, VA 22209).

Originally appeared as "You, Too, Can Have a Degree" in Family, August 1989.

Section VIII

Women in the Military

The Changing Roles of Military Women

The day has not yet arrived when men and women have equal opportunities of jobs and promotions in the military. The big stumbling block, of course, is whether or not women will be allowed in combat situations. But both men and women have come a long way in working together in the military.

A first class Air Force cadet who reported on the status of women at the Air Force Academy last March (1984), summed up the progress: "When women first came, everyone figured they were getting leadership positions and high grades as tokens. Now that they've been here for eight years, we *know* that they have *earned* them."

The relatively rapid progress of women in the military actually has been built on the slow successes of those before them. In order to take a realistic look at the status of women in the military, charts have been prepared for your easy reference and comparison. The charts were compiled from a variety of sources. While the most current figures available were used, they vary as to month of release.

The Three Stages of Women's Integration in the Services

Stage One was comprised of the formal and informal military service by women from the Revolutionary War through World War I, including the formation of the Army and Navy Nurse Corps. Stage Two combined the World War II and Korean War periods, which saw a vast influx of women in the military during periods of conflict. The WAC, WAVES, Marine Corps Women's Reserve, and eventually, the WAF were formed at this time.

WOMEN'S HISTORY IN THE MILITARY

1775-83: Women served the Revolutionary Army as laundresses, cooks, nurses, and combatants (artillery especially).

1861-65: Women served the Confederate and Union armies as spies, couriers, scouts, guides, nurses, and soldiers.

1901: Army Nurse Corps formed.

1908: Navy Nurse Corps formed.

1917: Navy enrolled women other than nurses to free men stationed ashore for sea duty.

1918: First woman enlisted in the Marine Corps.

WW II: Army and Navy nurses rose to 67,000.

1942: Women's Army Auxiliary Corps (WAC) established.

Women Accepted for Voluntary Emergency Service in the Navy (WAVES) established - Reserves.

Marine Corps Women's Reserve authorized by Congress.

Coast Guard Women's Reserve (SPARs) established.

1944: Congress modified previous restriction on sea or overseas duty for women—voluntary shore duty permitted in certain U.S. territories.

1945: More than 100,000 WACS.

1946: About 9,000 WACS.

1947: Army Reserve opened to members of the Army Nurse Corps and Women's Medical Specialist Corps.

1948: Women's Armed Forces Integration Act allowed all prior service women to join the reserves, but 2% ceiling on female strength imposed.

1950: Reserves opened to non-prior service personnel, but women limited to 10% of officer and 2% of enlisted force.

1951: Defense Advisory Committee on Women in the Services (DACOWITS) established by Secretary of Defense.

Korean War: Women reservists from all Services recalled to active duty.

1952: Of the 48,700 women on active duty, only nurses served in Korea; other specialties stationed in Japan, Okinawa, and the Philippines.

1967: The 1950 limitation on women's participation in the Reserves lifted, as well as the 1948 ceiling for active duty women. Women allowed appointment to flag and general officer rank.

1970s: The acronyms WAVES (1973), WAF (1976), and WAC (1978) were eliminated; Women Marines Director position eliminated (1977). Women in the military were to be mainstreamed.

1972: First women enrolled in the NROTC program with full scholarships.

1973: Formation of the Committee on Women in the NATO Forces.

First Naval Officer Candidate School coed class.

Six women first to earn wings and be designated Naval Aviators.

1976: First women admitted to the military academies.

First Navy woman line officer appointed to rank of Rear Admiral.

Navy Manpower R&D Program study (by Grace & Steiner) showed 36% of Navy wives sampled would discourage their husbands from re-enlisting if the law were changed to permit Navy women to serve at sea.

The Changing Roles of Military Women   357

1977:	*Secretary of Defense ordered Services to examine ways to increase the utilization of women.*
1978:	*Navy began assigning women crew members to auxiliary ships.*
	First woman promoted to Major General in the Army.
1979:	*The Air Force and Marine Corps promoted women to general officer rank.*
1980:	*Census reported women are 4% of all veterans and 1.2% of all American women.*
1984:	*Navy assigned first woman Executive Officer aboard ship.*
	A woman was first in her class at the U.S. Naval Academy.
	Department of Defense Task Force on Equity for Women established.
	203,310 women serving in the Armed Forces as officers and enlisted personnel (9.5% of the active duty force). For the first time since World War II, more than 200,000 women make up 10.8% of the total Reserve components.
1985:	*First female Marine selected to general officer rank by a board of her peers.*
	Rep. Mary Rose Oakar (D - Ohio) introduced a resolution to establish a memorial in honor of women who have served in the Armed Forces.

Stage Three began in 1967, when the previous limitations on women's participation in the Reserves and on active duty were removed. The mainstreaming of women in the military became a reality in the 1970's as the WAVES, WAF, Women in the Marines, and WAC ceased to exist as separate entities.

Stage Three is basically an all-volunteer military phenomenon. The number of women in the Services continues to increase. Due to the overall increase of military members, however, the total percentage of women in the Services remains about ten percent. The recruiting bulge under President Carter has slowed under President Reagan's administration, as the Services reassess their utilization of women.

Issues of Concern

The issues that concern women in the military run the gamut from recruitment policies to opportunities for advancement. *Family* has sought a balanced perspective from current research, and from interviews with lobbyists and female military personnel -- on and off the record.

Inequity of recruiting standards for men and women can bee seen clearly when one considers the charts of the Services. The higher scores and/or levels of education required for women enlistees in the Army, Navy, and Marine Corps build in an imbalance of abilities. Not only are the women's mental categories higher than those of their male peers, but they can even be higher than those of their non-commissioned officers.

WOMEN IN THE ARMY

Active Duty:
Approx. 9,500 officers, 66,100 enlisted (10.05%).

Duty:
More than 96% of officer specialties are open to women. Enlisted women may serve in 302 of 351 military occupation specialties (86%).

Women are excluded from jobs which might be routinely engaged in combat.

Some of the areas open include: air-traffic control, computer repair, aviation, military intelligence, equipment maintenance & operation, communications and law enforcement.

Enlisted Recruitment Goals:
At close of Fiscal Year (FY)85 - 67,000 (10.2%).
At close of FY87—70,000
Previous projections had been as high as 87,000.

Recruitment Policies:
See below for explanation of tests and categories.

Army not recruiting any Mental Category IV females, but does accept Mental Category IV males who are high school graduates, and who score 16 on the AFQT.

Since 1981, Army requires *all* women to have high school diploma to enlist, but only 65% of male enlistees must have diploma.

Army currently prohibits enlistment of women with General Educational Development (GED) certificates.

Army Reserve:
Oct. '84 - more than 83,000 women (17%).

Army National Guard:
Oct. '84 - 23,700 women

RECRUITMENT TESTS AND TERMS

AFQT:
The Armed Forces Qualification Test, used by all Services to determine eligibility for enlistment, measures basic verbal and quantitative abilities.

Mental Category:
Determined by score on AFQT. Services actively recruit those in Mental Categories I, II, and III. Congress has limited Category IV enlistees to 20%. No Category V accepted.

Mental Category	AFQT Range
I	93-100
II	65-92
IIIA	50-64
IIIB	31-49
IV	16-30
V	0-15

GED Test:
The General Education Test determines if a person can be issued a high school equivalency diploma or certificate. State requirements for passing vary widely.

Family is grateful to "WEAL Facts" (Jan. 1985) for much of the above information.

Personnel who took the ASVAB test in the 1977-1980 period were given a mis-normed test, according to Carolyn Becraft, Director, Women and the Military Project (Women's Equity Action League). "So when the Services thought that they were getting people in Mental Categories II and IIIA, they were really getting the lower Categories IIIB and IV. This means that the non-coms of this period are often not as bright as the recruit pool, which right now is running 95% high school graduates. The Army saw the problem about a year or so ago. It has always been a problem for women."

WOMEN IN THE NAVY

Active Duty:
  6,640 officers (9.3%), 42,258 enlisted (8.6%).

Duty:
  Women officers serve in all officer communities except submarine and special warfare. Enlisted women are in 82 of 99 ratings.

  Women excluded from permanent assignment to aircraft or vessels which would serve combat roles, but may be assigned for up to 180 days if units are not expected to have combat missions during that time.

  Some of the assignments now open for temporary duty (with permission of fleet commanders) are helicopter pilot, explosive ordnance disposal units, oilers, and mobile logistics vessels. Other assignments open include repair ships, research vessels, salvage ships, and fleet tugs.

  FY87 goal is to have 31% of 46,500 enlisted women in non-traditional ratings.

Recruitment Goals:
  At close of FY85 - 44,300 enlisted (8.9%).
  At close of FY '87 or '88 - 7,200 officers, 46,500 enlisted.

Recruitment Policies:
  All new female recruits must be high school graduates.
  New recruits with a GED and non-graduate non-prior service male recruits need an AFQT score of 49 or better.

Women Aboard Ships:
  FY83 - 170 officers and 2,623 enlisted aboard 30 ships.
  FY84 - 180 officers and 4,187 enlisted aboard ships.
  FY85 - target 200 officers on 46 ships and 5,125 enlisted on 44 ships.

Navy Reserve:
  Women officers are nearly 6% and enlisted over 10% of total force.

Right now the male scores are higher than they have been in a long time. But it is doubtful that they will remain there as the male applicant pool diminishes over the next few years due to demographics; the group of soon-to-be 18-year-old men is simply smaller than it used to be.

The basic philosophical approach to life differs between the men and women who enter the military. Studies done after the entry of women into the Corps of Cadets at the U. S. Military Academy showed that the young men tended to come with a conservative perspective. The women, who were breaking traditions by joining the military, were much more liberal in their outlook.

Harassment has diminished since the early pilot programs. The Services have worked hard to eradicate it completely. With the women *Family* interviewed, the issue surfaced only rarely and off the record. Most incidents seem to be related to promotional rituals. The women interviewed feel they can rise above the daily slights and get on with the work they want to do.

WOMEN IN THE AIR FORCE

Active Duty:
10,800 officers, 55,335 enlisted (11.38%).

Duty:
Women officers are assigned to all career fields, with combat exclusion and facility limitations being only constraints.

Enlisted women are assigned to all but 5 skill areas.

Women excluded from combatant aircraft and jobs with high risk of capture or injury in wartime.

Some of the assignments now open to women officers are communications, medical, maintenance, engineering, intelligence, and science.

Enlisted women may serve in positions such as AWACS and KC-10 aerial tanker aircrews, munitions, vehicle maintenance, and fuels management.

Security police opened to women Jan. 1985.

Recruitment Goals:
At close of FY85 - 58,500 enlisted (11.9%).

At close of FY87 - enlisted at 19% to meet goal of 1985 Defense Authorization Act.

Recruitment Policies:
Male and female GED holders need an AFQT score of 50 or better.

Male and female high school graduates need an AFQT score of 21 or better.

Non-high school graduates need an AFQT score of 65 or better.

Air Force Reserve:
Oct. '84 - almost 14,000 women (20%). 86% of all career fields open to women.

Air National Guard:
Oct. '84 - 10,000 women, 94% of all career fields open to women.

Uniforms continue to be an irritant for women, both in terms of appropriate design for small figures, and in obtaining necessary items. Where there are relatively few female officers stationed, the exchange doesn't always stock an adequate supply. However, it is possible to mail order necessary items from the central uniform support center.

Assignment to the same geographic location as one's spouse is a cause of great concern to dual career military couples. Most of those interviewed have had good luck with co-location so far, but recognize that as they become more senior, there will be fewer places that can offer a career-enhancing position for each of them. Most say that at that point, they will have to alternate assignments to benefit one and then the other.

Military women married to civilian husbands find that relocation of their husband's careers gets harder as they get older. In some cases, the choice is that the husband will remain behind while the wife becomes the "geographic bachelor." Major Suzanne Awalt (USAF) laughed when she heard her marriage described as "bi-coastal." She felt that her new job with the Military Family Resource Center in the Washington, D.C. area was "too good to miss." Her husband has remained in northern California. "We are fortunate that we have no children and our finances are strong enough to afford monthly meetings."

Leadership styles most conducive to high productivity by military women have been studied by Captain Doris R. Vail, USN. As part of her doctoral research for George Washington University (1978), supported in part by the National Defense University, Capt. Vail found that "a more individualized supervisory style tending toward the paternalistic" was most effective when supervising the younger men and women of the Navy." She found the style that was most effective for the young women was equally effective for the men, in terms of performance and retention. The strictly authoritarian giver-of-orders is no longer seen as the ideal leader.

Policies that deny women *equal opportunity for advancement* center around the combat exclusions in all of the Services. Although many specialties have been opened up to allow women entry into a number of non-traditional fields and sea duty, the most career-enhancing slots are still protected by their combat-likely nature. The Navy has recently expanded opportunities for a few women who will be given *temporary assignments* of up to 180 days as helicopter pilots and explosive ordnance disposal officers on ships not expected to have combat missions during their stay. According to WEAL's Fact Sheet of January 1985, "the assignment is still subject to the discretion of the ship's commander who can refuse to allow women aboard."

A recent three-year study by the Marine Corps found that women are not being assigned to many occupational fields and specialties *already* open to them. So now, Headquarters Marine Corps will attempt to manage female careers so that they are spread more appropriately throughout the various non-combatant occupational fields. The same study urges the assignment of women to the Fleet marine Force to the extent possible, because promotion boards weight this duty heavily, and because this allows women to carry a fair share of the overseas assignments -- i.e., it relieves the pressures on men.

The day when complete integration of women in the military, taken for granted by both men and women, is not as far away as many may believe. In the civilian world, corporate executives are fathers of daughters whose capabilities are clear to them. Although they may feel threatened if their wives now seek equity, men are increasingly becoming advocates and mentors for women of their daughters' generation. Also, the number of military daughters who are joining the military is making that choice an acceptable career move. The big question that hangs over policy makers' heads is the combat what-if? Given our demographics (fewer young men in the population) and our still-undermanned Reserves, our military leaders may no longer have the luxury of protecting women from combat roles. Soon, their exclusionary stance may be unrealistic. *They owe women the training that will enable them to be full partners in the service of their country.*

Women in the Navy: Kings Bay

In order to get a better idea of what the lives of military women are like, *Family* interviewed eight women stationed at the Naval Submarine Base Kings Bay. They represent quite a cross-section of women in the Navy. They include rates and ranks of E-5 through O-4. They run the gamut from single to married; some have children. Some of those married have military husbands, others, civilian. The one thing that seems to unify these women is that they are all achievement oriented -- in fact, early promotion shows up with regularity among this group.

Storekeeper Chief Patricia Rogers

Storekeeper Chief Patricia Rogers (E-7) has been in broken service in the Navy for 14 years. (She got out for 15 months at one point.) Married to a Navy chief, she is currently the supervisor of one of the largest and most modern warehouses in the navy. While supervising 17 civilian and military personnel, she also serves as a command duty officer.

She joined the Navy to get away from home. (She was the eldest of nine children.) "I wanted to get off on my own, earn my own living. I was tired of going to school, but I wanted security. I grew up around the Navy -- our house was right next to the air station in Los Alamitos, CA, and two uncles and grandfathers had been in the Navy."

Patricia has had two shipboard assignments during which she fulfilled a childhood dream of visiting the Vatican and Pompeii. She is the only woman chief on base now. "I was able to make chief only because sea duty billets opened up to women that enabled selection." She hopes that "male chauvinism will just go away. Women are out to prove that we can do it, so we work twice as hard. The women I've worked with have been *good workers*. I feel as if I have to prove myself 500 times a day, whereas my male counterpart doesn't." But that can "be an advantage. By doing well, we can perhaps prove ourselves more capable in stressful situations than our male counterparts."

She and her husband met on the *U.S.S. DIXON*. In their three years of marriage, they were separated during the first ten months. Although a couple may not serve together on the same ship, they now have been co-located in the same geographic area.

LCDR Kay Campbell

Lieutenant Commander Kay Campbell (O-4) is now the commanding officer at the Military Entrance Processing Station in Knoxville, TN, which processes recruits for all of the Services. She was previously director of the Navy Family Service Center at Kings Bay, as well as senior watch officer (responsible for the training of the command duty officers and officers of the day). As a Naval ROTC Instructor at Texas A&M University, she taught Naval Engineering. In her summers away from her ROTC billet, she taught Naval Orientation and Naval Science at the Officers' Candidate School at Newport, RI.

Kay joined the Navy after teaching health and physical education in a Florida middle school. Her dad had called her "Sarge," because she was always directing the kids on the block. Her parents and her peers were against her joining the Navy, but she found the equal pay, challenges, and travel enticing. Continuing education has been important. Kay has earned three master's degrees, two of them through night and weekend courses. GI Bill monies have been helpful.

In the service for 12 years, Kay has consciously chosen assignments for their challenge and visibility and has tried to make sure that she has not received "female-only" types of duty. She pursued the designation as senior watch officer. "It was a lot of work, but I learned a lot and my work was visible." Of her current assignment, she ways, "It's considered a small command, but it's all mine!"

Married five years ago to a retired Marine, she has personally enjoyed the mobility the military offers, but now I have someone else to be concerned with." She has had to move on less than 30 days' notice and is now having to be a "geographic bachelor." Her husband needed six more months for tenure in the Civil Service, so he and their dog remain in Georgia, at least temporarily.

LT Barbara Ford

Barbara Ford is a lieutenant in the Dental Corps (O-3) with two years in the service. She serves on the Family Advocacy Committee, audits the gold and precious metals recovery, was the Preventive Dentistry Officer for a year, serves on the Officers' Club Advisory Committee, and is a Duty Dental Officer.

She joined the Navy after two years of civilian practice with a large practice in a small town in North Carolina. As a single women, she had no commitments and wanted to travel. Her dad was an Army officer, and she was accepted by the Air Force, "but I like the coasts!"

One of the great pluses she has experienced is the quantity of continuing education, particularly, specialized dental training. At Kings Bay there are no specialists, so she has had the freedom to practice the full range of her training. Other pluses include the people she has met in the military, the supportive work environment, and the non-discriminatory pay.

Tennis and plane boarding consume her off-duty hours. She sees them as an important way to keep herself relaxed. "You have to be relaxed to be able to deal with others' hurts daily. It can be emotionally draining. So you have to take time away for exercise and technical training. I pay a lot of attention to my career. It's my whole support system. It gives me a lot of satisfaction to be a professional. I have to work at it every day."

LCDR Debra Roberts

Debra Roberts is a lieutenant commander Medical Corps (O-4). She is currently a general practitioner and teaching officer at the Kings Bay Medical Clinic. Married to an ex-Navy doctor, Debra entered the Navy to pay for her medical training. She won a Uniformed Services Health Profession Scholarship which paid for her tuition, books, and fees, plus a $400 a month living allowance. During her year of internship in San Diego, she was paid as a lieutenant (O-3), which was double the pay of her civilian peers. "I was 22 when I joined, and was still having to get every penny from my dad. He could have put me through medical school, but I wanted to earn my own way, have freedom and responsibility."

Prior to coming to Kings Bay, she served on a destroyer with nine women officers; toward the end of her assignment, the female complement was close to 100. "It helps to have a large number of women at the same station."

She has found travel to be a plus in her five years on active duty. She has seen every corner of the U.S. "The scary part is not being stationed near my husband. His specialty (undersea medicine) limited the number of places he could go, but I could go many places."

Another plus has been "more time to practice. I don't have to worry about administrative duties like paying employees, etc. When the base was still quite small, I really had almost a family practice, but we're losing intimacy now -- the chance to really see a patient."

Debra is leaving the Navy this summer to gain flexibility in her working schedule. She is the new mother of an infant daughter, and feels she would like to practice only two to three days a week for this next year as her husband begins his residency. In a year or two, she will return to training herself -- a three year residency in family practice. "The Navy gave me hands-on experience between my internship and my residency. Many in the civilian world go straight through. The Navy gave me time to grow up."

Chief Journalist Theresa Laws

With 14 years in the navy, Chief Journalist Theresa Laws (E-7) is now an instructor at the Defense Information School at Fort Benjamin Harrison, IN. Previously, she was the first woman to make chief petty officer at NSB Kings Bay, where she was assistant public affairs officer (PAO). She has served as the PAO for Naval Communications Area Master Station Western Pacific in Guam, Assistant PAO at Naval Air Station Cecil Field, FL, and Assistant PAO at Naval Station Guam (where she was selected as Sailor of the Year 1976).

Married to a civilian, she has 10-year-old twins and a 7-year-old daughter, with whom she enjoys sharing camping, fishing, and bicycling. Theresa's assignments to some isolated duty stations have made it hard, at times, for her husband to work in his field. They have had to be flexible about his employment, househunting, and schooling for the children.

Electrician's Mate First Class Nongyow Willett

EM1 Nongyow Willett is the senior electrician (E-6) on YTB 789 - TOMAHAWK. She is responsible for all electrical gear aboard the harbor tugboat, which moves submarines as they enter or leave port or the dry dock, or change piers. As one of three tugs, the boat is busy night and day. Hours are long....65 -- 105 hours a week. During a move, *all hands* work the deck. At five feet and 100 pounds, Nongyow lifts ropes that are 7 lbs. per foot *when dry* (and they're rarely dry!). "During freezing weather, the decks were icy and the ropes had icicles!" she exclaimed.

Born in Thailand, she moved to the United States at age 17, having had one year of college in Bangkok. Accounting had been her major. "I joined the Navy to get a job. My step-father was in the Army. He knew that going to school in the Navy would be valuable. I wanted to be on my own, take care of myself." She thinks all young people should be in the Navy for four years -- to learn discipline. With six years in the service, she has been promoted rapidly. "My mom is so proud." Her specialty is a sea-going rating. Its normal rotation is 4 1/2 years at sea to 2 1/2 ashore.

Navy policy stipulates that when both spouses have sea-going ratings, one must be on shore duty (which her tugboat assignment is), and one on sea duty. Her sea duty was the shipyard at Pearl Harbor (overseas assignments count as sea duty for women). She and her Navy EM1 husband have now been co-located geographically, but they do worry about the next set of orders. She sees financial discrimination against dual career enlisted personnel. On shore duty, she draws BAQ (housing allowance) and COMRATS (food allowance). On sea duty, he is allowed neither, and yet he lives and eats at home.

LT Donna Jasitt

Lieutenant Donna Jasitt (O-3) is the director of the Counseling and Assistance Center (CAAC) at Kings Bay, which provides screening, counseling, and education on substance abuse. Human Goals, an equal opportunity program, is also part of the center' work. With six years in the Navy, Donna previously was oceanographic watch officer in Antigua, West Indies, and Pearl Harbor. As watch officer, she had to memorize vast quantities of technical data, and stand long watches with little sleep. At Pearl harbor, she was in charge of 8 officers and 55-60 enlisted personnel.

She joined the Navy to get away from home, for a sense of adventure, freedom, and self-sufficiency. Since then, she's developed "a strong sense of my abilities and the importance of my job -- the power and the responsibilities. I had the ability to launch an aircraft as an ensign by picking up the phone!" She expected to be able to go to sea,"but so few go each year that my chances were slim. Women at sea have to be at the top of the totem pole, but the lowest male graduate of various schools gets to go."

Donna feels she has had to "fight for salutes. There are many chiefs and enlisted out there who don't want to salute a female ensign or lieutenant junior grade (O-1 and O-2). When you go to a new command, you have to prove yourself, your watch-standing capabilities, etc. Women don't have a lot of medals. The presumption is that you've come from a cushy administrative job."

Master at Arms Second Class Linda Junker

MA2 Linda Junker (E-5), with three years in the Navy, is a dog handler for one of the Navy's "drug dogs." Totally responsible for the physical needs and training of her black labrador, she has also been trained in criminal investigation, finger-printing, and some military law courses. Together with her dog, she does inspections all over the base and aboard ships in port when requested. Linda joined the Navy because it offered job security, health benefits (which are especially important to her as a single mother with three daughters), and because of the opportunities offered "to go as far as you can go." Her sea/shore rotation is 3 years at sea/3 ashore. Her first assignment was aboard the U.S.S. SIMON LAKE, a submarine tender. "The shipboard duty was rugged for a single parent. I stood duty every five days. I usually tried to find another single parent and we'd switch off watching each other's kids. She expects future overseas shore duty for her sea duty obligations, as the big animals don't go to sea.

Originally appeared as "Salute to Women in the Military" in Family, May 1985. Charts are from Family. Later appeared in Savannah News-Press, October 20, 1985 and Camden County Tribune, October 24, 1985.

Section IX

Parenting

Parenting Ph.D.'s

The license plate on a van near our local elementary school caught my eye: PHD -- MOM. It could be an accurate statement of her two roles, or of his and her roles, or that she feels as if she has her Ph.D. in Childrearing.

There is no mail order diploma for this Ph.D., no short track. New parents often find their new role wearying, frustrating, and sometimes, terribly worrisome. But that's not the whole truth. There is also excitement, enjoyment, education, and an excuse to do all of the things you'd feel foolish doing without a child in tow! So let's look at your new role of parenting with the same kind of research you use when getting an advanced degree by looking at the physical, social, emotional, cultural, and spiritual role adjustments that go along with parenthood.

Physical Adjustments

Your first major adjustment to a newborn is that you no longer control time, pace, and schedule. Being awake at varying hours of the day and night for feeding, and conversely, being able to sleep only in small segments, turns your life topsy-turvy. Military members who have experienced standing watch may have gained some ideal coping skills for this challenge! Parents who rotate the baby watch not only give respite to each other, but share the opportunity to bond with their child.

Another physical adjustment is the amount of carrying you do -- both of the baby and all of the gear that goes with a newborn or a toddler. A study by the Montreal Children's Research Institute has found that babies who are carried for at least three hours a day are more content and fuss less by six weeks. (When you add up feeding time alone at that age, you have almost fulfilled your three-hour quotient.) Gently rocking your baby, either as you stand or sit in a chair, results in faster weight gain, sharper vision and hearing, and earlier regular sleeping.

Learning how to fold up, carry, pack, unpack and set up the carrier seat, stroller, playpen, and the omnipresent diaper bag, calls on latent mechanical abilities and unused muscles as well as all of your planning techniques. This is an area in which military members often shine -- they've had lots of practice with equipment and campaign strategies!

You find that you need to slow your pace, build in lots of time to do even the simplest tasks. And yet, as your infant is ready, you can make small excursions. You will see your world in a whole new way -- partly because you have time to really look around as you sit in the yard with your baby, and partly because obstacles seem to loom for every previously simple outing.

Navy Lieutenant Donna Jasitt (see Chapter 51) and her husband, Lieutenant Lance P. Jasitt, are the proud (and sometimes exhausted) parents of toddler Ian, who accompanies them to craft fairs and shrimp festivals in southeast Georgia. Donna says, "We do have to go slower, pre-plan and give segments of time for him to play, to walk around on a blanket on the grass." She and Lance find that they can switch play time duty while the other looks at the fair.

You will experience your five senses again in a way that you have rarely felt them since your own childhood because they are now issues of safety and stimulation for your baby. The sun's heat, the shrillness of sirens, the smell of sauerkraut, the softness of a diaper or a sleeper seam all take on new meaning. Respond to those that endanger your infant and enjoy the "simple pleasures" that get lost in our efficient lifestyles.

One final item under physical adjustments is the use of constraints, such as play pens, when it is in the best interests of your child and you. Two issues are at stake here: setting limits and providing the secure environment for self-entertainment. When your toddler is ready to understand rules about what he or she may investigate and what is off limits, then the playpen may become a punishment instead of a safe place.

Social Adjustments

Lance and Donna Jasitt as fortunate that they are surrounded by other young military couples trying to balance career and child. When Donna was pregnant, she had the comfort of a military doctor and dentist on base who were new mothers, plus the support of other military wives and service members. She has a real sense of being part of the Navy Family. At parties, she is encouraged to bring Ian along -- others enjoy seeing him and peeking in on him in a back bedroom. One major social adjustment is learning that other families enjoy being a part of your support system. For simple afternoons or evenings out, a baby can be an acceptable guest. But be sure your infant is welcome before arriving at the door!

A very important social time for your baby is mealtime. Pediatricians recommend that you feed your infant ahead of time, but then let her stay with you as you eat and talk with others. You are sharing warmth, affection, the sense of being part of a family, plus the cadences of speech.

Of course, mealtime will be only one of the many times in the day when you talk to your baby. A recent study by Dr. Earl S. Schaefer of the University of North Carolina found that infants who had been stimulated and praised showed significant gains as early as four months. (The study followed children through the third grade. The parents of over 80% of the children who had to repeat a grade had talked to them less than average.)

Emotional Adjustments

In the early days after you have first brought your baby home, you are not only physically weary, but after showing off your baby to relatives and friends, you realize with a lump in your throat that you are really responsible for the life of another. Although this is an awesome, frightening feeling, be grateful for your own depth of care and concern. Your own emotional growth has just experienced a quantum jump (you're well on your way to your Ph.D.).

As you read about when a mother can return to work full or part-time (this is for those who have a choice, versus those whose maternity leave is dictated by policies beyond negotiation), you usually see material on the age at which a baby can distinguish and remember his parents (about the four-month point, according to Dr. T. Berry Brazelton, Associate Professor of Pediatrics at Harvard Medical School). But part of the decision is also the surprise that many new mothers experience over their own unexpectedly deep love for their child. Pre-baby, it seems easy to talk of scheduled return to work; the post-baby reality has unexpected emotional levels.

This results from the process known as *bonding*, the establishment of close emotional ties. Brenda Mitchell, the Child Development Counselor at the Family Service Center, Naval Air Station Jacksonville, FL, often sees children who are failing to thrive because of a lack of bonding. Through individual family counseling and parent education groups, she helps parents understand the process of holding and talking to their babies. "They weren't parented and so don't know how," says Brenda. "A baby takes a lot of time and is demanding. A baby *takes* a lot, but *doesn't give* a lot at first." She finds that parents who feel uncertain of their parenting skills enjoy being with other parents. The parenting groups offered by many organizations not only give new parents information they need to feel confident in their new roles, but also relieve the social and emotional isolation they experience. Babysitting is often provided, but in any case, babies are welcome members. This is helpful when family budgets have already been stretched to the limit by the baby's arrival.

Cultural and Educational Adjustments: Dad's Roles

It is especially helpful when both parents can attend classes in parenting together (doing joint research for your Ph.D.'s). Your common base of information makes adjustments easier. parents may discover that they have differing notions about childrearing based on their own upbringing. This is a good time to begin to design your joint ideals, based on what you have admired in others, plus current research and information shared in class.

For example, many military fathers wonder what their approach should be with the noisy, fragile newcomer in their house. Dr. Brazelton's findings about a father's nurturing would encourage any hesitant dad. While mothers tend to have a low-key, gentle interaction with their baby, fathers are more playful -- poking, tickling, and making exaggerated noises and faces. The result is that even a three-week-old child, upon hearing his father's voice, will hunch his shoulders, elongate his face, and arch his eyebrows -- all indicators that he expects excitement.

Dr. Brazelton also says that when a man is involved with his child, there is an increase in the child's IQ, "the child is more likely to have a sense of humor, to develop a sort of inner excitement, to believe in himself or herself, and to be more motivated to learn. And these things are probably more critical to a person' future than anything else."

The shift between roles played at work and at home can be especially dramatic for military members. Dr. Peter Neidig found in his work with Marine Drill Instructors at Parris Island, SC, (see Chapter 20) that changing out of uniform when they got home helped them differentiate between their military environment (where the giving and taking of orders predominates) and their home (where a more democratic, supportive approach is desirable).

Educational adjustments for parents center around the amount of information they seek out to make them feel more competent. Just as they are processing an enormous amount of information and learning new skills, their baby is going through the period of greatest physical and intellectual development in his or her lifetime. (See the Resources chart on page 374 for some fine books that detail the normal stages of development to help you understand what you can do to assist.)

William J. Bennett, Secretary of the U.S. Department of Education, has written of the "simple" things that parents can do. "Parents are their children's first and most influential teachers. What parents do to help their children learn is more important to academic success than how well-off the family is." But he reports the disturbing evidence "that many parents are doing much less than they might. For example, American mothers on average spend less than half an hour a day talking, explaining, or reading with their children. Fathers spend less than 15 minutes. The best way for parents to help their children become better readers is to *read to them* -- even when they are very young. Children benefit most from reading aloud when they discuss stories, learn to identify letters and words, and talk about the meaning of words." Given Secretary Bennett's observations, part of parents' adjustments is the need to see ourselves constantly as teachers. Your child is learning all of the time, not just when you are consciously teaching. Your behavior, your approach to life, is perpetual instruction, whether you recognize it or not.

Spiritual Adjustments

Brenda Mitchell, the NAS Jacksonville Child Development Counselor, says, "I'm not seeing many young parents with strong commitments of any kind -- moral, spiritual. It's frightening." The military lifestyle has some real challenges for young couples -- some positive and some negative. Without a code of ethics, a sense of commitment to something beyond oneself, we can be like rudderless boats in our ever-changing seas of people and places. Failure to develop on the ethical-spiritual level is being less than we can be.

Once you become a parent, you are no longer responsible only for yourself -- physically, socially, emotionally, intellectually, morally, or spiritually. Your greatest gift to your child will be the sharing of your faith. In the final analysis, he or she must make it his or her own. It will be a coping skill, a heritage, and a chance to be a fully developed human being. Churches in your civilian community and your base/post chapel are family-oriented organizations. Most provide child care during services so that you can have the quiet meditative moments you need to replenish your strength for the weeks ahead. Once you have made, or begun to make, all the adjustments necessary to raise a child, you have gone a long way towards doing the coursework in your degree in parenting. But if you are still having trouble, don't feel uncomfortable about discussing your problems with friends, family, or even a therapist. Having a baby is hard work!

RESOURCES

To find parenting classes for couples or single parents, check with your post Army Community Services or base Family Service/Support Center, your post/base chapel, the USO, YMCA, American Red Cross and County Extension Service. For example, over 600 parents participated in last year's annual Baby and Toddler Fair in Frankfurt, Germany. Babysitting was provided while parents attended workshops and broused through the new and used baby clothing, toys and maternity items.

Your post/base or community library may have these books:

Brazelton, J. Terry, M.D., *On Becoming a Family: The Growth of Attachment* (1981) and *Toddlers and Parents* (1976).

Pulaski, Mary Ann, Ph.D., *Understanding Piaget* (1980). She covers birth to 3 years, with two sections for each period: intellectual development and appropriate toys and games. Her Appendix A is an especially helpful outline of cognitive development.

Sparling, Joseph and Isabelle Lewis, *Learningames for the First Three Years* (1984). These are simple things that often require nothing beyond energy, imagination and items you have on hand.

Spock, Benjamin, M.D., *Raising Children in a Difficult Time* (1985). His work, while controversial with some who see his stance as too permissive, is a classic with valuable information.

Striker, Susan, *Please Touch* (1986). She shows how to help children's creativity. She produces the "Anti-Coloring Books."

White, Burton L., Ph.D., *The Frist Three Years of Life* (1975 and rev. ed. 1985) and *A Parent's Guide to the First Three Years* (1980). The first book provides a very detailed look at a child's development. The second has a good section on toy selection.

Single copies of the following booklets are all **free**:

"Your Baby's First Year - The ABC's of Infant Care." Obtain this plus other free materials from your Army Community Services Center or Family Service/Support Center.

"Caring About Kids" booklets: "The Importance of Play" (ADM 81-969), "Learning While Growing: Cognitive Development" (ADM 81-1017), and "Stimulating Baby Senses" (ADM 77-481). Request from Public Inquiries, National Institute of Mental Health, 5600 Fishers Lane, Rockville, MD 20857.

"What Works: Research About Teaching and Learning," by William J. Bennett, Secretary, U.S. Department of Education (1986). Obtain from Information Services, Office of Educational Research and Improvement, U.S. Dept. of Education, 1200 19th St., N.W., Washington, DC 20208-1826. •

Originally appeared as "Parenting Ph.D.'s" in Family, *February 1987. Chart is from* Family.

53

Baby Costs

Have you ever wondered what it costs to have your first baby these days? While most of us never would make our decision to have a baby on purely financial grounds, it is helpful to know a ballpark figure (*1987 figure*) and learn ways to get the most for our money.

Family asked Navy Lieutenant Donna W. Jasitt and her husband, LT Lance P. Jasitt, to keep a careful account of their expenses for furniture, equipment, and clothing as they prepared for their firstborn. Donna, being a meticulous soul, went several steps further, keeping wear and use records on all major items for Ian's first year, and has shared some lessons learned as well.

Military Maternity Uniforms and Civilian Maternity Wear

Donna's first research in the field focused on the uniform costs, leave policies, and childcare needs for active duty mothers-to-be. In a paper for a course in "Military Family Studies" at Jacksonville University (FL), she found that the average officer spent $105 on maternity uniforms, and the average enlisted woman spent $69. Enlisted women are entitled to a one-time maternity allowance which covered this minimum investment, if only one season is involved and if one did not add the costs of necessary underwear. Her recommendation was that maternity uniforms be treated as "special uniforms" which are *issued at no cost to the member* for special duty, such as flight suits and jackets for aviators are issued.

She found that in 1985, a very basic collection of civilian maternity clothing ran $384: two gowns, six underpants, two bras, a slip, six pair of hosiery, two jeans, a pair of slacks, four tops, three dresses, and two pair of larger shoes.

Furniture and Decorations

She tackled the challenge of choosing baby furniture, equipment, and clothing with equal vigor. With research, imagination, and many hours with paint brushes or sewing needles in hand, Donna provided a delightful environment for the arrival of young Ian.

FURNITURE

car seat (catalog)	$ 49.00
high chair (exchange)	28.00
cradle	gift
bed (used)	50.00
mattress (exchange)	40.00
chest of drawers (used)	10.00
corner shelf (to hang above chest)	50.00
book shelf (homemade)	10.00
carry seat (used)	3.00
bath tub (used)	1.00
rattan toy chest	12.00
rattan diaper chest	10.00
safety gate	11.50
stroller	gift
walker	21.00
swing	27.00
	$322.50

DECORATIONS

picture	$10.00
soft sculpture train	8.00
soft sculpture soldier	15.00
clock (used)	7.00
picture and hooked balloon	gifts
windsock	4.00
night light	gift
	$44.00

This obviously is a category in which personal taste matters, but you should be aware that bright colors are more pleasing to your baby than the pastels that parents often choose. You can economize greatly here. One source of colorful, waterproof designs that can be used on changing tables, cut out for "decals" on chest of drawers or used as pieces for a mobile is self-adhesive plastic. Your exchange and commissary carry the solid colors and grids, and your exchange may have the alphabet pattern. One roll of wallpaper (or a valence roll) will provide you with lots of options, as will sheets.

"We converted a large utility closet near our bedroom into the nursery," said Donna. "We were able to find a lot of the pieces second hand, but did buy the car seat through a catalog. I would recommend looking at it before buying. Ours did not give enough support for a very young child. It really needs to have four to six positions for growth and comfort and to fit your car's contour."

All states now require that you use a car restraint ("car seat"). To obtain one reasonably or free of charge, check with your base/post family services. They will know if they, the local Red Cross chapter, or state human resources department loans them.

Buying Used Furniture and Equipment

Buying used items can be economical and safe. However, as with your purchase of new items, you need to make sure that they meet safety guidelines, such as the maximum distance for crib slats (2 3/8 inches apart) and the maximum size of mesh for cribs and playpens (1/4 inch holes). The U. S. Consumer Product Safety Commission warns that nursery products that are more than ten years old are generally more dangerous than new products. You may call or write the Commission (see *Resources* at end of chapter) for an evaluation of a specific product or copies of their free pamphlets.

When looking for new baby equipment, don't forget your post/base exchange and its mail-order catalog. Unfinished furniture can allow your creativity to blossom. For used items, watch the classified section of your military and civilian newspapers, garage sales, post/base thrift shops, and church rummage sales.

When and If to Use Specific Equipment

Donna's comments on the swing and walker: "We thought we would use the swing more earlier, but found it most useful at eight to nine months when he could watch us as we worked in the yard. You can use a swing up to a weight of 25 pounds. We bought the walker when Ian was about seven months old. He could be more mobile without the fear of falling down." Make sure that use of the walker does not limit the baby's crawling time. Crawling is a developmental skill necessary for all sorts of coordination later including the hand-eye skills necessary for reading.

Another major item that many parents purchase is a playpen (some new versions are called "play yards"). There is a controversy on the value of this item, but Dr. Burton L. White, the Director and Principal Investigator of Harvard University's famed Pre-School Project, sees it as a safe place to put a baby (ages 5 - 15 months) for short periods of time. Others suggest using it even earlier to accustom the baby to seeing it as a play environment versus a prison.

You do not have to purchase all of these items before or just after your baby's birth. For example, you don't need a high chair until your baby is ready for solid foods. You can do very nicely without a changing table (using the crib or the floor to diaper and clothe your baby). You may find that an inexpensive canvas bag is more useful than a bulky, and sometimes expensive, diaper bag.

LINENS AND TOWELS

hooded towels	gifts
washcloths (4 gifts and 4 purchased)	$ 2.00
bumper pads (homemade)	5.00
sheets (homemade)	20.00
quilts (2)	gifts
crocheted blankets (3)	gifts
everyday blanket	gift
blankets	16.00
mattress pads (2)	10.00
	$53.00

"Ian kept poking his toes through the holes in the crocheted blankets," explained Donna. "The open weave was not good. I made the crib sheets because bright colored solids were not available. We'll probably use the hooded towels until he is two-and-a-half or three years old. They are so soft and comforting."

DIAPERS

1-3 months	
9 cases at $8	$ 72.00
4-6 months	
12 cases at $8	96.00
7-9 months	
12 cases at $8	96.00
10-12 months	
8 cases at $17.95	143.60
	$407.60

"All diapers were disposable and bought by the case. Day care on base changes diapers every hour on the hour, so he went through eight a day there, plus more at home." Donna noticed that she made a considerable savings by shopping in the commissary for diapers instead of civilian stores or the base exchange. The Family Service Center at Naval Station Orlando (FL) lists four dozen cloth diapers in a baby's birth-to-four-month "wardrobe."

FOOD

Formula

1-3 months	
9 cases at $9.93	$ 89.37
4-6 months	
12 cases at $10.50	126.00
7-9 months	
12 cases at $10.50	126.00
10-12 months	
84 cans at $.95	79.80
	$421.17

Juice

3-6 months	
4 pkgs. at $1.24	4.96
7-9 months	
12 gals. at $1.39	16.68
10-12 months	
24 gals. at $1.39	33.36
	$ 55.00

Cereal

4-6 months	
4½ boxes at $.62	2.83
7-9 months	
7 boxes at $.59	4.13
10-12 months	
18 boxes at $.59	10.62
	$ 17.58

Baby Food

4-5 months	
60 jars at $.34	20.40
6-7 months	
90 jars at $.27	24.30
8-9 months	
120 jars at $.27	32.40
10-12 months	
135 jars at $.27	36.45
	$113.55

Graham Crackers

3 boxes at $1.19	$ 3.57
	$607.30

"The first four months we bought items at our local supermarket, because the commissary wasn't finished," explained Donna. "We switched to the base commissary as soon as it was completed. At the 11-month point we started introducing regular food. Believe it or not, it takes *more* planning.

SPECIAL CONTAINERS

infant feeders (3)	$ 9.00
nurser kit	10.00
glass bottles	4.80
plastic bottles	5.70
drink straws	1.90
plastic bowl w/suction cup	1.50
two-handled cup	2.95
knife, fork and spoon	gift
	$36.80

"The infant feeders work on a suction principle, so once started, the food goes *into* the child, not *on* him. The glass bottles were a bad purchase; I could only use them at home, since day care required plastic bottles. A bottle with a straw device (purchased separated), which allowed vertical flow, was used when Ian was sitting in his high chair or stroller. This allowed him the freedom to look around normally, rather than hold his head in a tilted position. The suction cup on the bowl didn't work well on a plastic or metal high chair tray."

CLOTHES

bibs (4)	$ 10.00
bibs (6)	gifts
socks	25.00
shoes ("tennis")	17.00
shoes (2 pair)	gifts
clothing (including 2 sweaters, 4 outfits, 2 caps, hat, 7 sleepers, 3 two-piece infant sets, 2 short one-piece outfits, christening outfit and two short jumpers) estimated value: $125	gifts
clothing (including: 14 sleepers, 8 short one-piece infant outfits, 8 two-piece sets, 8 overalls/pants, sweater, jacket, 6 shorts outfits, 5 tops, and 7 other assorted outfits)	299.25
	$351.25

Donna's "wear charts" helped her see what items had worked well. She found that those with growth features, such as double snaps, buttons that could be moved, or two pieces, had good records and were good investments. She found some items at a swap meet, and now buys ahead on sale for "grow-into" items. A few of her clothing hints:

- "Sleepers with feet (for warmth) are not available in two pieces until well beyond the infant stage. The drawstring gown sleepers didn't work very well because Ian kicked too much.
- "The long and wide bibs are much more effective than the small ones. I used paper towels as bibs when he was very little.
- "Diaper shirts were great for around the house when he didn't need to be in a nice outfit.
- "Two summer short sets were too cool for the air-conditioned day care center, so could only be used on weekends.
- "A cheap layette set 'with everything you need' fell apart the first time I washed it -- too sleazy and not worth repair.

380   Parenting

- "Two overalls with heavy grommets (3-month and 6-month sizes) were not practical for an infant sleeping most of the time -- the grommets hurt him when sleeping on his tummy.
- "Tennis shoes are ideal because they have good arch support and the gripper treads prevent slipping. I use the lace-up variety because he can get out of the velcro too easily."

Toys

Ian received quite a variety of toys as gifts, and his parents invested in several soft animals, soft blocks, a musical mobile ($18), ring stand, a car ride toy, books ($25), and a large bear ($40). The total, including gifts, was estimated to be $215.50. "His primary Christmas gift was a two-foot tall bear with eyebrows and a soulful look on his face," says Donna. "Because the bear was about his size, he talked to it like it was another baby. At ten months, he would crawl over to the bear, pull to a standing position, and lean against the bear. I have caught him kissing the bear on the forehead. I would not be surprised if the bear kisses Ian, too!"

Donna made a play corner for him in the den. "It has a mirror on the wall at Ian's height and various toys in the vicinity. He talks to his reflection, plays pat-a-cake, and kisses the little boy he sees."

Many of the toys were bought "used." Lance and Donna have supplemented his supply with "found items" such as a block or a ball in an empty milk carton -- wonderful for shaking. Plastic bowls can "nest," and all toddlers know the joys of pots and pans.

Because both Donna and Lance are active duty personnel, they have significant child care costs. They do get a tax credit for child care expenses that is tied to their tax bracket. However, the maximum that may be claimed in any tax bracket is $2400 (for a tax credit of $720) or double that for two or more children.

CHILD CARE	
12-Month Period	
base day care center	$1285.00
private day care at $80 a week	960.00
baby sitters at $2.50/hr plus base day care center some evenings	77.00
alternate day care (baby sick)	45.00
two friends duty childcare	no charge
(usually $20-$30 for a 24-hour period when her husband or she could not provide care)	80.00
Total	$2447.00

If we add up the first year costs for a pair of parents and a healthy baby, *excluding child care and maternity clothes, the total is $2081.90.* This figure is lower than it would have been if the Jasitts had not been able to use the commissary and exchange. Hopefully, with their help, you've learned a few ways to save money on your "baby costs."

RESOURCES

- Check with Army Community Services or Air Force, Navy or Marine Family Service/Support Center for classes for new parents. Also, your local American Red Cross, USO and YMCA/YWCA.
- For evaluation of a product before you buy or for free pamphlets, call the Consumer Product Safety Commission toll-free: (800) 638-2772 from anywhere in the U.S. (including Alaska, Hawaii and the Virgin Islands). If you are overseas, write to: Office of Communication, Consumer Product Safety Commission, 5401 West Bard Avenue, Bethesda, MD 20207.
- Two paperback handbooks with detailed information on specific baby equipment are: *Consumer Guide's Baby Equipment Buying Guide* (Signet Books, 1985, $3.95) and *The Childwise Catalog* (The Consumer Federation of America, 1424 16th St., N.W., Washington, DC 20036, $7.95).
- "Tips for Your Baby's Safety" is free, with a self-addressed, stamped, business-size envelope, from the Juvenile Products Manufacturers Association, 66 East Main St., Moorestown, NJ 08057.
- Look in your library for *A Parent's Guide to the First Three Years* by Dr. Burton L. White (Prentice Hall, Inc., 1980).

—*Kathleen O'Beirne*

Originally appeared as "Baby Costs" in <u>Family</u>, April 1987. Charts are from <u>Family</u>.

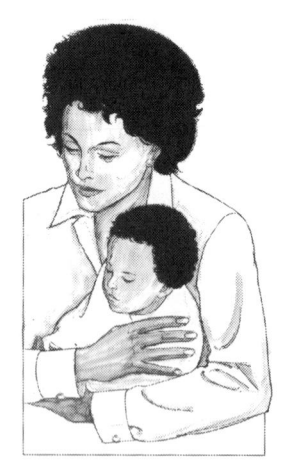

Happy Endings: Through the Maze of Military Adoptions

We'll take an in-depth look at six families who have adopted children while in the military. Some have gone through agencies in the United States; others have done private adoptions. Still others have adopted children from other countries. Each has expended an *enormous amount of energy* and a good deal of money in order to adopt.

The impetus for this story came originally from a *Family* reader who wrote:

My name is Debbie Satterfield. My husband, SSgt. Joe Satterfield, and I are childless with the greatest wish to adopt a baby. We are certified through the state of Arizona, but we're unable to adopt through any agencies because of the cost and the fact that Joe is stationed in Colorado.

I'm presently living in Phoenix because when Joe got his orders, we thought we had a very good chance for a baby; but the girl had a miscarriage. Since that time there have been other possibilities that have fallen through.

We would like to know if there is any kind of information that you could send us regarding adopting in the military......We have been married for five years and are in our late 20's. Four years ago, I lost a son when I was six and a half months along, and was told that I could never carry another child. We have decided that since we are already certified in Arizona, that I will stay and have everything finalized here. Could you write up some kind of article about families wanting to adopt?

We soon discovered that Debbie and Joe's situation is far from unique. There are a great many military families unable to adopt a child because they do not stay in one place long enough to go through the laborious paperwork and waiting process an adoption requires. Recognizing the difficult position military families are in, the Army has begun working with the Department of health and Human Services to make adoption procedures more conducive to military families. William Coffin, Director of the DoD Office of Family Policy says there will be a DoD initiative soon. Measures might include methods of allowing military families to adopt "military" more easily and reciprocal agreements between state agencies for those who start the adoption process in one state and must move.

Nationwide, approximately 25,000 newborn adoptions occur per year, with about half handled by state agencies and charitable organizations. The other half are handled through independent searches. When *Family* sought adoptive families willing to share their stories, we were overwhelmed by the number and the variety of avenues used. As you will see in the family profiles that follow, motivation and means may vary, but *the common denominators are research and perseverance.*

John and Beth Elkins

"Bring size zero girl's clothes," was the message John Elkins received while on TDY in Washington, D.C., from his wife Beth in Iran. When Captain John C. Elkins (USN) talks about the months of paperwork and interviews that had gone before this telegram (and the months yet to follow), he says of their daughter CaroLu: "She's mine -- I went through the labor!"

In early 1976, John was stationed with the U. S. Navy Technical Assistance Field Team in Tehran. He had gotten to know the obstetrician who delivered the Queen's babies and was head of the Tehran General Hospital. At a Christmas party, John mentioned to him, "If you ever find a little girl on your doorstep, think of me." (Children were abandoned at the hospital all of the time.)

John and Beth already had two healthy boys of their own aged six and nine, and had decided that their family was complete, but they found they couldn't stop thinking of adopting a little girl. "Our timing was right because the national legislature had just passed a new law permitting infidels to adopt Moslem children." One day, Beth received a call while John was away. "Today you come choose your baby. Today we got a shipment of babies from the south" (literally a train shipment of babies from the nomad desert area in southwestern Iran).

Beth was allowed to observe 14 babies in ten beds from a window. "In the first room there were two or three *tiny, tiny* babies per crib. They were extremely clean, but everything was so white and sterile. In the second room were the infants that the orphanage head mistress said were six months old. They were just lying still in their beds. There was no crying. The only sound was Iranian music on a radio. The only time the babies were picked up was when the nurses changed shifts. Then each baby was picked up and held under a faucet to wash. A new diaper was put on, and the child was put back on her back. They had lost their sucking ability because they were fed a rice-milk-turnip green mush from a bottle with the nipple cut off."

"You choose," she was told, except for two or three "no can have." Beth drew upon everything she had learned in her professional work as an educator. "My great fear was that the babies might be a product of the 'ideal Moslem marriage' -- the arranged marriage of two first cousins. Many children of such marriages are blind, lame, or mentally retarded. I stood for twenty or thirty minutes, which felt like an eternity, watching. One baby's eyes followed me from the first moment I appeared at the window. There was no movement by any of the other children. On the basis of her eyes and her curly wavy hair, I asked the nurse to bring her to me. CaroLu turned her face from me. She did not want close contact -- she had not been held and loved. But her little finger traced the paisley pattern in my blouse over and over. She was mesmerized by the pattern.

"I tested her hearing by clapping to see if she had a startle reflex. I held my fingers to let her hand grasp and pull up -- to check muscle tone. She could not sit up. She weighed less than ten pounds, but the orphanage said she was ten months old. She looked like six months to me."

Stalling Tactics

After choosing CaroLu, John and Beth were told they could visit daily to hold their child, and to "bring presents." They did so each day, bringing cute clothes and toys, only to return the next day to find her in rags. At first they also held some of the other children, but finally had to stop because they clung so tightly the Elkins could not tear them away.

Bribes were also expected by every office to which John went to formalize the adoption. He literally went to court every day for a month before finally obtaining "the paper." Then, in order to get an identity card for CaroLu, he had to go with two adult Iranians who would claim that he was the father. Her certificate now lists John as the natural father.

Beth and John admit to having doubts when the months dragged on, often wondering if it were the right thing to do. Finally, in their prayers they asked, "God, please make this happen if it is Your will." The very next day, when they went for their daily visit, they noticed for the first time a birthmark on her right arm -- *identical in size, shape, and placement* to a birthmark on their eldest son's right arm. They saw it as a sign that Nassim, CaroLu's Iranian name meaning "the fair evening's breeze," should become a part of their family.

Their departure from Iran was hasty because the orphanage delayed turning her over to them even after the paperwork was complete. Their original contact person literally ordered Beth to take the baby and get in the car while she staved off the head of the orphanage. They lived like hermits until their flight lifted off two weeks later.

Upon their return to Virginia, John was assisted with the United States adoption forms and petition letter by the base legal office. After a case study by a social worker, the adoption was final.

Currently stationed in Guam, Beth and John feel that it is important to respect and appreciate the culture from which an adopted child comes so that parents can share that as she grows -- and not inadvertently pass on a disrespect. And they are very pleased with their daughter -- "She has turned out to be brilliant and beautiful."

Jan and Mark Evans

LCdr. and Mrs. Peter M. Evans are the proud adoptive parents of two little girls, Danielle and Melissa, who are nine months apart in age. Both were received within days after birth through independent (private) adoptions.

Married at 31, and realizing that they were fast entering the danger zone for having their own children or being allowed to adopt through a state agency, they had begun to call OB/GYN doctors and attorneys. They had gone through infertility counseling for some time at the Naval Air Station Jacksonville Hospital, FL, and fertility seemed unlikely. They had heard that they were likely to be discriminated against by state agencies because they were military. As luck would have it, Jan's best friend is an OB/GYN specialist in the southwest and came across someone who was about to give birth and wanted to place the baby up for adoption. She called and said, "You may be a mommy in five weeks!"

At age 36, Jan began the saga that would take six months of paperwork to complete. Before leaving Jacksonville, she contacted attorneys in both states, knowing that an inter-state adoption would be tricky. However, her Florida attorney failed to get the pre-adoption home study started, which was to cause considerable delay in the proceedings. (She recommends that you double-check by contacting your state

Department of Human Resources or Health & Rehabilitation Services [HRS] yourself to make sure what you will need to do.) In order to comply with the Interstate Compact law, which protects children against black-market selling, Jan had to fly back alone to Florida, while the doctor served as custodian of the baby, to get her pre-adoption home study. The HRS in the natural mother's home town waived the home study for placement. Thirty days after the Petition for Placement was filed, Jan could have the baby in her care.

"Danielle was born to a Spanish mother and an Anglo father. Her mother stipulated that she wanted her child to go to an Anglo couple who could not have their own children," says Jan. "Because my doctor friend knew the mother, we could be sure that she was not on drugs, alcohol, or tobacco -- good safety factors. Her hospital bills were covered by her own insurance, so my costs were 'only' my travel and lawyers' fees, obstetrics fees for the mother, and the baby's medical bill."

Within months after her return to Jacksonville, Jan heard through another friend of a mother with a baby on the way. "Simply by talking about your desire to adopt, you run into all sorts of people who have been involved with adoption or may be a connection. They come out of the woodwork." If you are interested in adoption, Jan advises telling *everyone* of your intent.

For their second child, she and Mark worked through an attorney who had the HRS adoption packet ready to fill out on the first visit. The friend relayed the name of the attorney to the birth mother, "so we both dealt with one attorney and he turned in the information to HRS. The social worker who was already working with us for Danielle did the home study. We were able to finalize Melissa's adoption in three months because it was all in-state."

"We paid for the delivery. Because a Caesarean was required, we paid $6,500 for medical expenses. legal fees were on top of that. Between the two children, our total costs have been about $15,000, which is far outweighed by our joy in having two healthy children."

Connie and Jerry Ellison

Connie and Jerry Ellison, who are neighbors of the Evanses, were successful in adopting a child via an adoptive agency. Soon after moving to Jacksonville, they went to the two agencies listed in the phone book. "Children's Home Society said 'within three years,'" remembers Connie. "Catholic Charities said we could go on a list to get on the waiting list, and it could take five years. A couple of years later, we were formally on the waiting list and got an application form." Connie found the home study, "which is a group process until the final meeting when the social worker comes to your home," to be supportive and filled with lots of good information.

"We were lucky, though. When our time for home study finally came, it was also time to get orders. Our home study began two weeks after Jerry started a new job right here. If he had been at sea, it would have had to be postponed -- if he had been transferred, we would have had to start at the bottom of a new list."

Their baby was ten weeks old when adopted. With an agency adoption, the birth mother had read the profiles of families wanting to adopt prior to her baby's birth, chose where to place the child, and took up to a month to sign the paper to allow adoption. Then the father was sought for agreement. "Then you get 24 hours' notice!" says Connie.

"The cost to adopt is 8 1/2% of your annual income, with a maximum of $4,000 plus court and legal fees. Our total was about $3,300."

Connie and Jerry would like to adopt one more child, but must wait from the bottom of the list again (and could not go on the list for the waiting list until the first adoption was finalized after six months. They worry that they will not be able to remain in the area long enough. However, "sometimes, if you have been on the list long enough, the agency will continue with an out-of-state adoption......"

Special Needs Children

Connie and Jan explained that the wait to adopt an older child is the same length as an infant unless he or she is a "special needs" child -- that can mean handicapped, bi-racial, or a sibling group. "Some agencies have top ages of 40 for adoptive parents."

Ray and Joy Aldridge

Suzy Aldridge is a member of Actors' Equity Guild. At age six, she was in *The King and I* with Yul Brenner in Memphis, TN, for six weeks and this past spring, at age ten, she was named Young Miss Camden County, GA. Quite a track record for a young lady who left the Bo Yu Quan Orphanage in Chin Hae, South Korea, under most unusual circumstances.

Suzy's version is "Mama and Daddy were there. They saw me. They liked me. So they got me!" Her mother, Joy, tells the story a little differently. While she and her husband Ray (LCdr., USN) were stationed in Korea, the Officers' Wives' Club supplemented a daily meal at the orphanage. In January 1976, Joy and Ray went to help with a party. "Ray had never been in the baby room, but we had both seen the toddler room. A friend showed Suzy to Ray and said, 'You will adopt her,' but he never told me that. May brought an outbreak of chicken pox, and I wanted to keep the baby from getting chicken pox. We were just going to help her through the outbreak, but we never took her back."

"Our guess is that Suzy was born in August 1975. In November, someone put her in a basket and lowered her over the wall of the orphanage. They had kept her healthy and well-cared for for several months."

Pak Kum Ja. "Golden Daughter," became Suzy with a "Y" because she wanted a "Y" in her name like her little brother Charley and her parents. Joy and Ray had decided not to have their own child in Korea, but were ready when they returned to the States. The explained to Suzy that they had *chosen her*, but they would *have to keep* whatever the baby turned out to be!

Adoption seems to run in the family. This year they all adopted Chester, a puppy who had been abandoned and was found caught with his neck in a fence. As their family portrait shows, they are a happy family. (*My great regret is not being able to show you the photographs of these families -- and dog!*) The Aldridges are now stationed in Stuttgart, Germany, learning to enjoy yet another culture and language.

Neil and Cheryl Rondorf

Cheryl Rondorf chuckles about the arrival of their adopted daughter. "Sean was five and Ryan three when we adopted Kira. When they first saw her, we waiting for reactions to her color -- but do you know what they were concerned about? Her ears! 'Mommy, her ears are very flat! Will she be able to hear?'

"It was a few months later, when I overheard Ryan describing his baby sister to a friend, that color was mentioned. 'I have a new baby. She's a girl. She's got flat ears, she's brown, and sometimes I get to hold her.' If only the rest of the world were so accepting...."

Cheryl and her husband, LCdr. Neil Rondorf, are a family stationed in Orlando, FL. After losing their third son, they decided that they wanted to adopt a bi-racial child. They applied via the Children's Home Society, but also mentioned their hopes to a longtime chaplain friend. "We asked him to pray for us. Well, our prayers (or his) were answered.... a few days after he received our letter, a young military active duty woman walked into his office and asked him to find a home for her baby. She was due shortly.

Normally, chaplains refer these cases elsewhere, but he decided to call us first. We were stunned and amazed, but after a few days of hard thinking, we decided to say yes."

Cheryl describes their next steps. "We then contacted the adoption agency and told them to take us off their lists. As it turned out, the day after Kira was born, the agency received a new bi-racial baby boy -- and we would probably have gotten him because the agency had only two other families waiting -- for girls. So either way, we would have received a baby within three months of our first inquiries. "We found a lawyer, the lawyer contacted HRS and started the process for the home study. Five and a half weeks later, we finally got Kira."

Rondorfs' Adoption Advice

Cheryl and Neil have some recommendations to share with prospective adoptive parents:

- "Make sure that the lawyer you choose is well versed with state laws and *has done private adoptions* (vs. agency adoptions). In Florida, a lawyer may charge only $500 for a fee, and any extra charges have to be explained to the court.
- "Be realistic about costs. We didn't have to pay for hospitalization because our child's natural mother was in the military. A normal hospital bill can run $3,000 - $5,000; lawyers' fees, $500; HRS fees, $280; filing and court fees, $150. Usually the child isn't covered by insurance until formal adoption takes place. Any medical costs incurred by the baby is your responsibility. Again we were fortunate that our child could use military facilities under her mother's social security number.
- "Talk to lots of adoptive families. Sharing time with other people who have your same goals already achieved (i.e., the kids are settled in) will give you a clearer picture of what to expect.
- "Be patient with people who try to give you pats on the back for taking in 'a poor homeless waif.' Smile and tell them you count your blessings all the time. Reserve your right to your family's privacy and dignity."

Phyllis and James Tucci

LCdr. James M. Tucci, the neurologist at NAS Jacksonville Hospital and his wife, Phyllis, knew they were committed to the concept of foreign adoptions, but they could hardly foresee the scenarios that would unfold as they adopted two "tigers" from Central and South America.

"Even before we were married, we had both been interested in the idea of adopting youngsters from countries less fortunate than our own.

Therefore, seven or eight years later, when I was clearly having trouble having a baby, it was easy to make the decision to adopt foreign. You still have to have the home study done, and inter-racial feelings are included. That was easy for me...I felt strongly that kids *die* in orphanages down there."

Direct adoption was the avenue used to adopt Jimmy, now five, from Colombia. "With direct adoption, the home study is done here in the United States, and then you contact specific foreign agencies. (See *Resources and Referrals* on page 392.) *You* must do all of the paperwork (like 40 documents, through nine or ten different levels of hierarchical authentication.) Translations must be done by officially recognized translators. And you must do the immigration work before referral."

Phyllis recommends direct foreign adoption only if you have a good contact, via a church mission, for example, which has an "in"with the orphanage system. Jimmy, who proudly shows off his Superman outfit, was anything but Superman after he spent one and a half months in an orphanage. The Tuccis had first heard of him through the family of a Navy corpsman. A cousin worked in the orphanage system and saw him come in at eleven days of age. She got foster care custody of the baby, so Phyllis was able to see him on her first trip to Colombia.

However, the directress of the orphanage was upset that Phyllis had had direct contact and insisted on his return. Within the one month before Phyllis returned to finalize the adoption, "he got very sick and was emotionally deprived. He was not smiling. He had not been held and loved. "Both Jimmy and Petey (almost three, from Honduras) still are very prone to eczema and skin infections, due to the treatment in their orphanages. Salmonella is common, as are lice. Parasitic infections are common."

Petey was really a happy accident. The Tuccis had gone to Honduras to adopt a three-month-old boy via indirect adoption (they had worked through a mediating agency, Universal Aid for Children). "When we got there, the boy was literally dying." Because of their medical backgrounds, (Phyllis is a nurse), they knew the child was at risk. "He was severely dehydrated, his leg and arm muscles were contracted, and he was being fed with an eye-dropper due to a mouth infection. He should have been in a hospital. The orphanage decided not to release the child for adoption even though we were planning to return for him the following day.

"In the next few days, the judge remembered a child in a hospital further out. We literally went in a pick-up truck with a lawyer and a social worker over the mountain roads to a little town about ten miles from the Nicaraguan border. he had been abandoned at the hospital at about one month of age, and spent his whole first year there. He had been given good care on weekends by the doctors and nurses who took him home. Our first view of Petey was two stubby legs...he was running and walking at 13 months, even though he had been in a crib most of the time!"

Foreign Adoptions

Phyllis says, "There are three major areas for foreign adoption. Korea and India require that you go through the agencies with which they have contracts. In Latin America, one may use the direct or indirect route. The cost for Latin American adoptions runs $5,000 - $8,000, which includes the two trips to the country in question. During the first trip, you start the paperwork which takes four to six weeks to be processed. On the second trip, you must complete the immigration paperwork and visa, clear the child medically, clear the child via the U.S. Consulate, and clear the child via foreign passport. A lawyer usually does the latter.

"When you bring the child home from Latin America, you are the adoptive parents. When a child comes via plane from Korea or India, you are not the adoptive parent in the foreign country; you just have custody. For *all children*, you must readopt, refinalize here in the U.S. because some states do not recognize foreign adoptions, even though the federal government does. Later, the child goes through naturalization."

****

An addition to the resources on page 392:

Los Ninos International
1110 Wm. Cannon Suite 504
Austin, TX 78745-5460
(512) 443-2833

A year after writing, and six months after publishing the article above, I entered Civil Service in the Department of Defense Office of Family Policy. Shortly thereafter, Congress passed legislation that initiated a pilot program that would permit reimbursement for specified adoption expenses within a certain timeframe up to $2,000 per child (for a maximum of $5,000 per calendar year). Because of this article, I was selected to manage that program in its early stages and heard many stories from military families wishing to adopt. Although the pilot program has been discontinued by Congress, there are many families in the right calendar windows to qualify for reimbursement. Check with your post or base Legal Office for details.

Adoption Resources and Referrals

F.A.C.E. Families Adopting Children Everywhere
P.O. Box 28058 Northwood Station
Baltimore, MD 21239 (301) 256-0410
Produces a monthly newsletter "FACE Facts" and refers members to agencies that operate in specific states or overseas. $12 membership per year.

International Concerns Committee for Children
911 Cypress Drive
Boulder, CO 80303
They list information on agencies by country and state in their publication "A Report on Foreign Adoption." Updates are sent automatically nine times a year. A $15 donation is required when you request the book.

Latin America Parents Association
P.O. Box 72
Seaford, NY 11783
National organization with newsletter "La Palabra." $20 membership per year.

Latin America Parents Association
Maryland Region Chapter
P.O. Box 4403
Silver Springs, MD 20904 (301) 384-7467
Lots of good information in their newsletter "Buena Vista." $20 per year includes the national membership and newsletter as well.

National Adoption Center
1218 Chestnut Street, Suite 204
Philadelphia, PA 19107
(215) 925-0200
This federally-privately funded organization acts as a computerized clearinghouse and charges *no fee*. Families desirous of adopting and children who need to be adopted are listed and matched. The children are all "special needs children": older children, young minority children, sibling groups who are not to be separated, and children who are physically and/or emotionally handicapped. Brochures and application forms available.

North American Council on Adoptable Children
P.O. Box 14808
Minneapolis, MN 55414
This is a non-profit coalition of individuals and organizations which focuses on placing "special needs children." Annual conference will be in Orlando, FL, in 1987. Individual or family memberships, including subscription to "Adoptalk," is $25 per year. Send a self-addressed stamped envelope when requesting information.

OURS: Organization for United Response, Inc.
3307 Hwy. 100 North, Suite 203
Minneapolis, MN 55422 (612) 535-4929
A non-profit adoptive parent support organization. Membership, including subscription to "OURS Magazine," is $16 a year.

Universal Aid for Children
P.O. Box 610246
North Miami, FL 33161
This is the adoptive agency through which Tuccis worked. It can serve Florida, Maryland and Virginia families. Those living elsewhere should check with them.

Your base/post chaplain:
May refer you to local agencies, or on a case by case basis, may facilitate linkage.

Your base/post legal officer:
Can prepare all necessary paperwork for an individual to represent himself/herself (military member only) to become stepparent, if natural parent agrees.
Can give list of agencies to whom prospective adoptive parents can turn and can look over legal paperwork.

Your church:
Many of the denominations sponsor orphanages and offer adoption placement services. •

Originally appeared as "Happy Endings: Through the Maze of Military Adoptions" in Family, *October 1986. Chart is from* Family.

55

The ABC's of Toy Buying

Are you feeling *baffled, bothered, and bewildered?* Do you worry about being *bamboozled* or going *bankrupt?* You are suffering from *Toy Trauma* .... a condition commonly experienced by parents in the six unbearable weeks before Christmas.

In the face of the almost overwhelming array of toys, you need some rules of thumb to assess each candidate for purchase. The investments you make are not only important financially. They also can make significant differences educationally. Our ABC's will be easy to remember. A is for Appropriate. B is for Beneficial. C is for Creative. F is for Fun, and S is for Safe.

Appropriate

First on your mental checklist is whether or not the toy is appropriate for your child's stage of development. Our Developmental Chart is based on the common age at which an average child reaches a given physical or intellectual level. Please consider this an approximation. You child may be ahead of the developmental stage listed for a given chronological age due to innate abilities and/or stimulation by parents, brothers and sisters, or friends. On the other hand, children sometimes regress a stage or two during or after a move, or as a result of a parent's deployment or unaccompanied tour of duty, not to mention the birth of a new baby brother or sister!

Toy makers often note the target age of a toy on the package. However, armed with the Developmental Chart and your own observations, you can fine-tune your decision for your own child.

Beneficial

Asking if the toy is beneficial takes your choice to the next level. Will it stretch your child and help him or her gain new skills? Ideally, it will be a challenge that builds on current abilities and moves beyond so that success is guaranteed. If you find that you have overestimated your child's readiness and frustration is the result, put the toy away for a while. Toys, much like clothing, can be saved to "grow into."

You may feel bewildered at first, knowing that toys and activities can enhance so many different skills. But if you consider your child's time his major investment in learning and growing, then your investment becomes more than monetary. For example, as a Girl Scout leader of second and third grade Brownies, I wondered how we could get the greatest benefit out of our two hours together each week. I read up on their developmental needs (in books by researchers such as Gesell, Piaget, Spock, and Ginott), and found that they needed lots of hand/foot-eye activities to strengthen their reading skills. So, we played circle ball games and did imaginative calisthenics for their big or "gross" motor skills.

They also needed to begin to use their fine motor skills, so our crafts allowed cutting, drawing, and tweezer work. As their fingers became more nimble, we did some whittling with jack knives and some basic sewing projects. Their observation skills were enhanced by walking in the woods after a snow or taking their magnifiers to explore what lives under rocks and leaves. We made the time productive by knowing what they could already do and where they needed to go.

A study of mathematically precocious girls by The Johns Hopkins University has shown that they had access to "boys' toys" when they were young. As you select toys and activities for your child, it is important to cross the traditional gender lines. Otherwise, some skill areas may not be developed. For children ages three to seven, you will enjoy Donna Stiscak's book *Lollipops and Parachutes* (McGraw-Hill Book Co., 1984, $10.95). The author gives 120 stimulating learning activities that require only the usual raw materials you tend to have at home. She provides a handy "Educational Skill Reference Guide: which arranges the activities by age and by the major skill developed: analysis, categorizing, counting, communication, concentration and attention, identifying, listening, following directions, memory (auditory and visual), motor (gross and fine), reading, and creativity.

Creative

In the creative category there are two concepts: Does the toy stimulate the child' imagination and does it have multiple uses? For example, a hand puppet not only aids hand movements, but it also allows a child to create a character and endless scenarios, alone or with others. (A hint: give two puppets to stimulate both hands and both sides of the brain.)

Other toys with multiple uses are: *puzzles* whose pieces can stand on their own as cars, trucks, houses, or animals; *blocks* with a variety of shapes (not just a "ranch set"); small *combination car and truck sets* that can be turned into bridges or slopes to teach over and under concepts; and *jacks*, which teach multiplication and division, but also increase hand-eye coordination and wrist dexterity. If you buy sets that add on to others, or are in the *same scale,* you greatly increase the variety of uses to which the toys may be put (e.g., model cars in the same scale as blocks).

Fun

The bottom line is that a toy should be *fun*. All parents hope for a "show-stopper," a toy that is such a success on Christmas morning that all unwrapping comes to a roaring halt. Other eventual successes may take warm-up or learning time, but will bring pleasure over the long haul. Ideally you will find one of each.

Safe

Two components of toy safety are *durability* -- the item does not break easily into sharp pieces -- and selection of toys *appropriate for a given age* -- not giving small, fragile items to young children. The third factor is *safe construction,* and that should be the domain of manufacturers. However, parents must be critical consumers. Some hints:

• Before you purchase an item, check for protruding parts (screws, easily-removed button eyes or nose, sharp corners or edges) and cords, toy collars, or bands that could strangle a child.
• Avoid hinges on boxes or mechanical toys that could pinch or crush. (Check your toy box for safety hinges.)
• Check for small parts that could be removed and put into a child's mouth (wheels, rattle pieces, balloons) or could be poked in an eye.
• Rub your fingers around plastic toys to ensure that the seams are not sharp.
• Make sure that painted toys carry the non-toxic label, and all fabrics are labeled flame-resistant.
• Do not select battery-powered toys for children who still put things in their mouth.

To promote bicycle safety, require your child to wear a helmet. About 650 children under 14 years of age die annually from bicycle injuries.

Developmental Chart

Age	Developmental Needs	Appropriate Toys
Birth - 6 mos.	sees faces & objects follows an object with eyes puts objects in mouth reaches & grasps for things	mobile (remove when your child can reach it) teething ring small stuffed animal (washable) squeaky toy
3 - 6 mos.	learns cause & effect transfers objects from one hand to the other bangs toys together grasps with finger & thumb sits with support & then alone pokes at objects can begin to entertain self likes textures, sounds, color & visual activity	activity ring teething ring bath toys rattle crib gym (remove at 5 mos.) activity center musical/noise toys
6 - 9 mos.	can push buttons with finger can do basic stacking likes color pulls apart & puts back together throws small objects crawls & explores sees self & smiles loves bath	activity center thick bright books with big pictures stacking toy colored blocks two-part toy suctioned rattle (to attach to high chair) small rubber ball (4") to push & see over mirror toy floating toys, plastic funnel, bottle, beater (for suds) rag doll
9 - 12 mos.	can put items in order of size (pre-math skill) learns up/down, inside/out classifies (puts same items together) can open & shut takes first steps	stacking toy—rings on spindle nesting toy sorting toy, blocks activity center/book push toy to encourage walking

Age	Developmental Needs	Appropriate Toys
1 - 2 years	imitates sounds & actions (pre-language & memory)	play telephone
	listens to music & stories	music making toy
	asks identification of items by 18 mos. can turn pages	picture books
	begins using words & mimics inflection	your talk is better than talking doll
	walks & explores	push & pull toy (little wagon)
	can seat self	ride-on toy, chair
	carries & hugs favorite toys	small soft animal
	stacks toys	pots & pans & box
	can go up & down 3 stairs and jump 12"	small slide, little two-step stool
	when 2, can run & kick ball	big ball
	develops large muscles	pounding pegboard
	needs finger manipulation	big stringing beads, screw top bottle
	begins pretend play (tending dolls, pushing cars)	picture books, blocks, sturdy dolls and vehicles
	puts items in & out	toy box, shelves, basket
	reconstructs from memory	simple puzzle
	begins pouring, measuring	shovel, pail, funnel & sieve for water/sand
2 - 3 years	advances pouring, measuring	cooking items
	learns mechanical skills	sturdy record player, magnets, "jewelry" kits (big beads, etc.)
	refines listening	songs, nursery rhymes
	enjoys simple stories	story books
	loves language	important to read aloud to children until they can read comfortably (age 7-8)
	classifies	good blocks—variety of shapes & sizes
	manipulates better	large crayons/markers, easel for drawing
	plays imaginatively makes houses	dolls (for boys, too), old clothes/hats, puppets, small gym set for multi-use

Age	Developmental Needs	Appropriate Toys
3 - 4 years	imitates parent of same gender (ages 3 - 6)	toys to play house, store, doctor
	begins small muscle coordination (girls have better fine motor skills & wrist rotation for turning knobs, dressing & brushing teeth at this age)	small tools, cooking equipment drawing equipment (big pad of paper, liquid paints & wide brushes—small watercolor sets too frustrating)
		modeling clay
	begins to cut	safety scissors, paste & colored paper
	begins group play	houses, forts from boxes, sheets
	continues big muscle development	tricycle, wheelbarrow, small rake, jungle gym
	gains leg strength, balances	small ball to throw/catch
4 - 5 years	builds complex structures	Lincoln Logs
	wants highly realistic miniature toys (ages 4-7)	dollhouse, cars, fire station
	needs hand-eye coordination	Spirograph, Carroms, big needlepoint
		big ball to bounce
	needs foot-eye coordination	sidewalk games
	begins math/science concepts	simple board games with counting (dice or numbered cards)
	by age 5, can tell long story accurately & add fantasy	short fiction and non-fiction in area of interest (dinosaurs)
	asks how things work & meaning of words	
5 - 6 years	has lots of energy	ball game items
	likes complex projects (continues for days)	simple model boat, house
	likes cutting, pasting & folding	paper dolls, activity books, easy Origami
	counts to 30s	Cribbage, games with adding/subtracting

The ABC's of Toy Buying

Age	Developmental Needs	Appropriate Toys
6 - 12	likes heroes, plays roles, fantasizes	history, fiction, & comic books
	likes to learn/make rules and master	formal & informal games with others
	accumulates information, memorizes vast systems, likes to categorize	recall games such as Trivial Pursuit, books, magazine subscription for interest area (ask librarian, teacher for ideas)
	likes collectibles, is intensely interested in specific hobby (teaches valuable commitment)	dolls, cars (have multi-use) & specific hobby
	likes strategy (is necessary for growth to higher thought processes ages 11 - 12)	bias bowling balls, board games, problem solving tasks (with various results)
	likes to invent, experiment	raw materials such as junk boxes
	likes hands-on doing, exploring, begins to think scientifically	Kits for chemistry, electricity, microscope, magnifier, binoculars, compass, jackknife
	likes to make, build	tools, lumber, wheels for vehicles, forts
	needs small muscle refinement	increasingly complex models, block set, sewing, weaving
	needs big muscle refinement	outdoor games such as basketball
	builds computation & spatial relations skills	games that involve multiplication & division (like jacks), mazes, more complex puzzles
	enjoys jokes	joke books, humorous stories
	is the period of refinement of skills for lifetime interests	music, art, sports, science, etc.

Watch your newspaper for the December 1st report on the annual toy survey by the Consumer Affairs Committee of Americans for Democratic Action in Washington, D.C. This citizen group has been pricing and testing the most heavily advertised new toys for five- to ten-year-olds for the last 15 years. If you want your own copy of their report, please send $5 to cover postage and handling to: Toy Price Survey, Americans for Democratic Action, 1411 K Street, N.W., Washington, D.C. 20005.

Originally appeared as "The ABC's of Toy Buying" in Family, November 1986. Chart layouts are from Family.

Parenting, Military Style

Good parenting and good wine making have more in common than you might imagine. Making wine and raising children both require a careful mixture of sugar and acid, coddling and leaving them alone. Too much of any one thing can cause disaster -- vinegar or exploding bottles in the case of wine; neurosis, rebellion, or worse in children. If you keep the proper balance, however, you are rewarded with a superior product (wine or child!) that is a pleasure to be with and to share with friends.

Stages of Development

In order to keep this balance, it is important to know the various stages in children's development, and how best to deal with them as a parent. This is especially true for military families with our unique stresses of frequent moves and deployments or unaccompanied tours.

Stage One: Parents need to help their children achieve some order out of the chaos of their world. In very basic terms, children need to become civilized. They need to learn certain rules of behavior to ensure their survival. (Picture a kindergarten classroom early in the year as classic Stage One.

Stage Two: Children continue to learn rules from authorities such as parents and teachers throughout the elementary school years. They also learn great quantities of information and basic thinking processes, such as reading, writing, and mathematics. This is still a period of great control by authorities. Structure continues to be important as a support for children in this stage. However, it would be ideal to allow children increasing opportunities to analyze and make decisions in the physical, social, emotional, and eventually, intellectual spheres of their lives.

CHART A

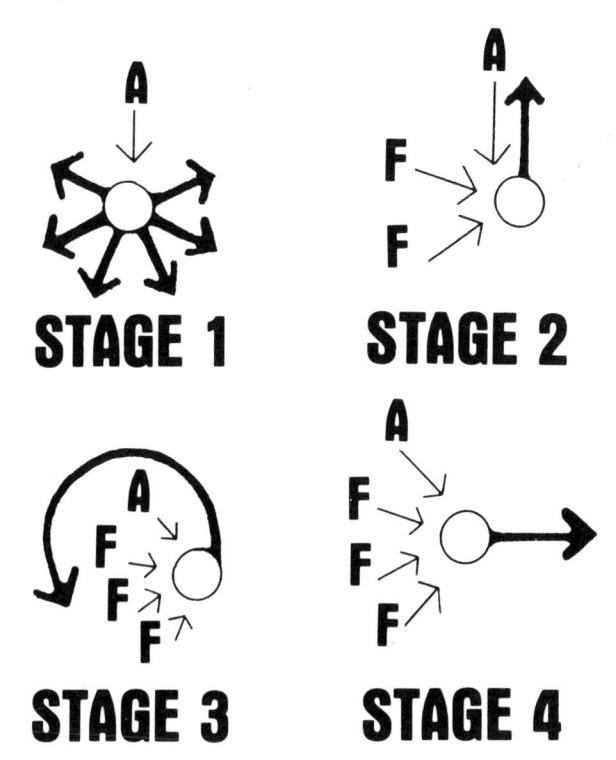

STAGE 1 **STAGE 2**

STAGE 3 **STAGE 4**

Key: O = the child. A = authorities (parents, teachers, etc.). F = friends.

Stage Three: By junior high and the onset of adolescence, *critical thinking* becomes a major activity. Parents of teenagers interpret that phrase in a slightly different way than educators do, but the growth it represents is important. No longer willing to accept the word of authorities as unquestioned absolutes, teens listen more to their friends, but they have simply changed "authorities." These rebels are *still dependents*, reacting to others' rules -- reacting negatively to adults, usually, and positively to their peers. They tend to refuse parental structure of any kind.

Stage Four: The ideal here is to become a *responsible independent*, aware of others' needs and points of view, but capable of making one's own decisions. An internal value system replaces the chaos of Stage Three. A person in this stage is capable of full-fledged membership in a participatory democracy.

There is no guarantee that an individual will reach Stage Four. Depending on many factors, including personality and parenting styles, some people end-stop at Stage Two (*order takers* and *givers*), or at Stage Three (*perpetual adolescents* or *rebels*).

What Makes Military Families Different

While these developmental stages are of concern to all parents, military parents must recognize that our lifestyle brings opportunities and difficulties that are not experienced by most civilian families. Our mobility and parent absence rates are higher than our civilian counterparts; whether they are a bane or a blessing depends on factors under our control.

Chart B diagrams the ideal progression a child would make through all four developmental stages. The usual progression, however, is a zig-zag, moving ahead and regressing now and then. (The teenage years can be full of zags!)

The typical military child has yet a different profile. Moves are harder for some pre-school youngsters than they will be in later elementary school. If a parent, usually the father, goes away on a temporary or unaccompanied duty assignment, a child in Stage Two may regress somewhat. Sometimes parent absence or a move may be a beneficial challenge to a Stage Three youngster who wants to expand horizons or reponsibilities. The danger here is that the returning parents may not be sensitive to the growth that has taken place, and a temporary setback may occur.

As I was researching the coping skills of successful military parents for the new handbook, *Charting Your Life in the United States Coast Guard*, I found two seeming opposites: <u>constants and flexibility</u>. The key word there is <u>and</u>. It shows the mix of two parenting styles of the past: the flexible, sometimes chaotic approach we commonly call *permissive*, and the constant, often *authoritarian* approach in which rules were parents' favorite tool. Stage Two or Stage Three individuals are likely results from these two extremes of parenting. The synthesis of the two is what makes a Stage Four person likely.

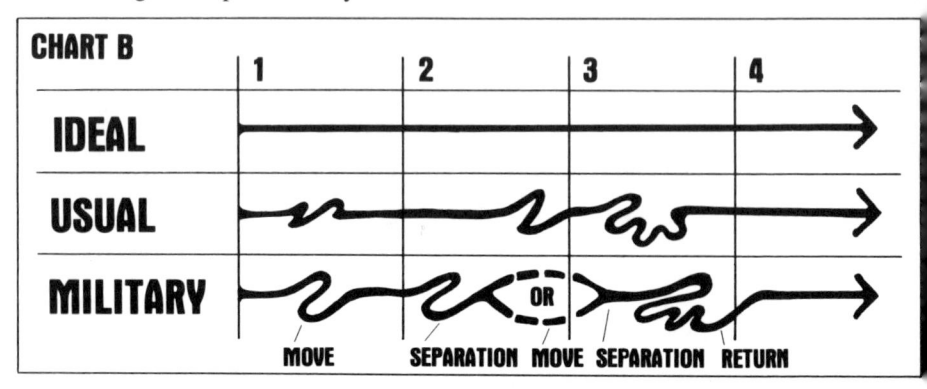

CHART B

	1	2	3	4
IDEAL				→
USUAL				→
MILITARY				→

MOVE   SEPARATION MOVE SEPARATION RETURN

The military Services, by their nature, have accentuated the Stage Two order-giving and order-taking mentality. This kind of control or structure is very *efficient* in the short haul or in crisis situations. Its *effectiveness* for the long haul, however, is being questioned today by everyone from parents and educators to corporate management analysts.

Constants and Flexibility

How do we as parents provide the ideal constants that our children need, and yet allow for their increasing flexibility? Betty J. Johnson, a school psychologist with the Duval County Schools in Florida, who serves many Navy and Coast Guard children, recently shared her personal and professional insights into achieving the delicate balance.

She emphasizes that the most important thing that children need is *confidence in themselves*. They need to know that they are loved and respected by their families before they can relate well to people outside of their family. So the *constant of love should be number one* for parents. Mrs. Johnson suggests complimenting children daily in one or two things they have done well, to accent the positive. Much parenting in the past has been critical or negative, and children have wondered if they could ever live up to their parents' expectations. (Some give up trying.) When children feel successful in their family. they are more likely to have the confidence needed to make new friends and learn from a new teacher when a move is necessary.

One way to build a child's confidence in being loved is to devote a quantity of time on some structured basis to each child alone. Mrs. Johnson suggests: "Do something together that you both enjoy. It is guaranteed time, concentrated time." It could be fishing, boating, or working with tools. It could be gardening, making dinner one night a week, or playing miniature golf. "Don't feel that the child has deserted you if he skips it now and then; the important message is that you have saved that time and it will be available."

Dad's Impact

Fathers often have more impact on their young children than they realize. Studies on father absence when a boy is quite young show that there is a tendency for the child to pick up his mother's learning style. Her style tends to be verbal and global, while a military dad's learning style is usually analytic and visual -- in the sense of ability with spatial relations. There is no *right* learning style, but a father who has been away (either physically or in the sense of being home but too busy to be emotionally present) may sense that his boy is "different than I was." Neighborhood dads and male leaders in sports, church, and Scout activities can provide an important balance when children's fathers must be away. (Interestingly enough, Harvard studies show the the reverse is true, for both boys and girls, if their dad is away for brief periods of time when they are a bit older. Mathematical ability actually shows an increase!)

For parents who wonder what activities would be appropriate for various ages, there are a couple of good resources. *Real Men Enjoy Their Kids*, by Singer, Schechtman, and Singer, gives a nice overview on developmental dimensions and a wide variety of activities. Many parents will remember the pleasure they found in Girl or Boy Scouting, and can turn to those handbooks for ideas -- available in your library or through your local Scout council.

For children one to three years of age, a readable guide is *Good Beginnings: Parenting in the Early Years*, by Judith Evans and Ellen Ilfeld (High/Scope, Ypsilanti, MI 48197). The authors have been active in a number of parenting programs for young military parents.

One of the very special ways that military parents can share with their children is to *show them where they work*. If a parent drives a tank, flies a helicopter, or sails on a ship, the children need to see it. Then, if deployment takes the parent away, they can visualize where dad (or mom) eats and sleeps. Some of the greatest treasures children can receive are unit T-shirts and caps, or photos of "their" ship or plane.

This constant of love shows up in other important ways when deployment or other duty assignments take a parent away temporarily. The idea of *emotional presence* is one that successful military families accomplish even though the father (or mother) is *physically absent*. Communications by mail, phone, or radio play a great role. Many military folks shop for small gifts or cards in advance, and arrange to have them sent to their children on a given schedule if they will not be in port often.

The parent at home is also important in maintaining the emotional presence. Usually that means that Mom must fill in for Dad. She can do it by saying, "Oh, you father will be so proud of you when he hears that you...." And then, she must indeed relay the news so that he can react. Unfortunately, a wife under stress in her husband's absence is more likely to say, "Wait 'til your father gets home!" He is characterized as a Super Disciplinarian, and the children begin to fear his return. Military families must be on guard for this common problem.

Another constant that Mrs. Johnson recommends is that of *discipline*. Discipline has gotten a negative meaning for many of us, but its original meaning is more positive: a system of rules or teachings. Ideally, parents will work out their discipline together, and it will remain the same whether the family moves to a new location or whether one parent must "hold the fort" alone for a while. The children will test to see that the rules are the same, but will be relieved to discover the continuity. "Limits set by parents are important to kids. They need to know that you love them enough to impose restrictions for their well-being," explained Mrs. Johnson.

Another constant that will enhance parenting military style is the *family council*. This is a family meeting at which major decisions are made together which not only allows children to play a responsible part in a decision that will affect them, but also teaches them the skills of decision-making. Children need training for independence. Obviously, when they are quite young, this will be on a very simple level, but the object is to increase the level as they mature. Mrs. Johnson recommends *Raising a Responsible Child: Practical Steps to Successful Family Relations* by Don Dinkmeyer and Gary D. McKay, as a good book on the family council concept.

Parenting for Responsible Children

This style of parenting may not come naturally to military members used to hierarchical units, where orders are given and followed. They may have a tendency to operate their homes on the same "ship shape" basis. Families may need to think this philosophy through carefully. A leader/follower relationship may produce an efficient household, but will it result in individuals who have learned competent independence?

One Navy wife who has not only raised teenagers, but has taught this age group shares her strategy. "I try to build in guaranteed success. With appropriate preparation, by allowing my children or students just enough leeway to feel that they have completed a project on their own, I enable their gradual movement from passive dependents to capable independents. In our household, we call it guided democracy!"

Military families who have coped with frequent moves or deployments are almost unanimous in their recommendation that children be allowed as much responsibility as they can handle on a continuous basis, not just when their father is away. If they have jobs only when dad is gone, they may resent his return to take over their jobs and their niche.

Flexibility

The constants of love, discipline, and family decision-making are the foundation that will allow military children the flexibility they need to mature to Stage Four adults.

Flexibility comes in a variety of guises for military children. Because many have a "fishbowl existence" when they live on a post/base, we as parents need to look carefully at the behavioral absolutes we set down for them. If some normal, acceptable avenues for Stage Three rebellion are not found, a teenager may passively accept all orders and remain a permanent Stage Two; or may experience Stage Three later in life (poor marriage choices or divorces often are really a delayed Stage Three reaction); or may experience an explosive, potentially damaging rebellion. The family council should be a tool for on-going discussion and respect for parents' and children's needs.

**Researchers on cognitive growth have determined that while youth may experience *behavioral repression* and later progress to Stage Three and Four successfully, that is *not true intellectually*. If adolescents are not permitted to progress through the critical thinking stage "on time," they will <u>forever</u> fail to develop the intellectual patterns necessary for Stage Four depth and complexity of thought processes. That is an awesome finding with significant ramifications for all parents.

Frequent moves are taken for granted in most military families. A caution here is that the stress caused by moves (whether positive or negative stress) is *cumulative*. A child who can move every couple of years in elementary school with no ill effects may find frequent moves in high school more than he or she can cope with socially, emotionally, or academically.

Parenting Stages

As you may have gathered, there are parenting (and teaching) stages as well as child and student developmental stages. Stage One parents are characterized by total flexibility. Stage Two parents would allow their teenagers no flexibility at all. Stage Three parents are often characterized by their own rebellion against authorities in their life, and are rarely competent to support Stage Three children through a healthy passage to Stage Four. Stage Four parents are the ideal -- the mix of the constant and the flexible, operating from a core philosophy, but open to new thoughts and ways of doing things.

Happy wine making. May you produce only premium vintages!

Originally appeared as "Parenting, Military Style" in <u>Family</u>, October 1983. Charts are from <u>Family</u>.

The Value of Photographs

Our 17-year-old son bought a rather expensive automatic camera this year, and his father and I wondered where we had erred to make this kid think that he should invest to such a degree in a camera. Erred? Status? Consumption? Those were our first, second, and third reactions. But on calmer reflection, I have realized that he was simply putting into practice what his father and I have preached and practiced for our 23 years of marriage.

How does one share with a submariner the results of the garden he planted or the children he fathered? When he was incommunicado for almost three months at a time, twice a year, photographs had to record important events like birthdays and holidays. When dad was away five out of seven Christmases when the kids were pre-school to fourth and fifth grades, the camera was our ally. It was our mode of communications of the *now* for when-you-can-be-here.

Although we were very conscious of the rapid growth of our children and the need to record it when my husband was at sea, it was only recently that we realized how valuable the photographic documentation had been. Heather, our number two child, had been fortunate to be in a program for mathematically gifted seventh graders. After a marvelous summer session in which she and other area students learned as much as two years of high school math, we received a questionnaire designed to determine how the girls involved had matured mathematically. Questions which asked <u>what</u> kinds of games she had played as a child, and <u>when</u>, would have received guestimate answers had we not had photographs as documentation. When we looked over the photos we had taken as our two followed each other through pre-school, we could pin-point the fact that most of the play time took place in Mike's room with the puzzles, trucks, and hats. We could date the summer I taught them cribbage and they worked their first 100-piece puzzle (when it rained in Maine at a friend's cottage).

Photographs showed that fishing gear was shared equally, as was gardening prowess. Birthday party photos reminded us of the year that Mike had to fulfill the Boy Scout requirements for agility. Heather helped to design the obstacle course for a party game, and her time was close to the boys' best. These are the kinds of activities that educators suspect give boys an edge in some phases of mathematics.

Photographs enabled another kind of documentation: our son's growth pattern and his dad's. When we were worried about Mike's delay in adding his wished-for inches, and his health record has been "cleaned out" by some unknown goblin in the dispensary, we again turned to photographs. The specialist in adolescent growth also wanted to see pictures of his dad as a teenager, so we had some amusing moments seeing the prized car beside which his father and his taller sister posed. Parents' memories need the precision that photographs give to the blurred progression of joys and concerns.

As the children began to go away to camp for a week, or for eight weeks, they needed photographs of their family for themselves ... for moments when internal strength was needed and for moments when friends wanted to share "you family and where you live." I still have the photographs of my parents that I took to college. They were 3000 miles away in Paris, and there were moments when I needed their faces and all that they represented. I suspect that my parents and children still need the same.

Like many families, we have tried to send a family photo each Christmas as a link to our far-flung family and friends. We had not realized how much it meant to people until this past year when we substituted a picture of a ship model that my husband had hand-carved. With holly berries and candles, it was lovely on our mantel. Friends wrote that they liked the ship, but missed seeing our faces; and one submarine captain came to visit saying, "I have to see this model that you think more of than your family!"

Family trips have not always been purely recreational. One year, when I was deeply involved in the preservation of our nineteenth-century community of Mystic, CT, our "vacation" took us to all of the historic preservation areas in New England. We eagerly photographed the newly renovated Quincy Street Market in Boston, Salem, Plymouth, Marblehead, Portsmouth, Strawbery Banke (NH), and Sturbridge Village (MA), as well as Concord and Lexington. The trip convinced me that we in Mystic were forerunners in the art of preserving a living village plus a

The Value of Photographs

museum. No one else had done it as well, except Fort Ticonderoga, which is under private ownership. Those same slides have excited my summer school classes in American literature -- (Emerson, Hawthorne, and Thoreau lived and wrote in these towns). My son has remembered his youthful trips as he has seen them on slides and has incorporated them into his American history and architecture reports.

Other school reports have been recorded on film. When we went to visit my parents in Tucson, we promised their sixth grade teacher that each child would do a report to share with their class. Heather chose the flora of the region, and, Mike, the fauna. We have instamatic records of the special quail, the endlessly fascinating cacti (including a Teddy Bear cactus imbedded in Mike's hand), and the coatimundi.

We also methodically photograph the areas in which we live. Those photographs constitute visual roots for our highly mobile children (and their parents!). Though they would never remember where we lived when they were born, they can "go back" via our slides. They can also share their most recent community with friends when they move.

There are two more uses of photography that are important to military families. One is the careful room-by-room record of the furniture we own for insurance purposes. Insurance companies strongly recommend this practice, and those who have had to fill out claims for fire or travel damage agree that they have found such photos invaluable in triggering their remembrance of all of the items in a room. These should be kept in a safety deposit box or with our hand-carried papers when we move. Foreign Service families suggest leaving a set of these photos in a stateside bank box so that claims for emergency evacuation can be accurate.

For homeowners, pictures of "before" and "after" are helpful verification of our records for capital gains tax deductions. When a house is sold, the owner may deduct certain costs for improvements from taxable profit; visual proof is a nice addition to sometimes erratic record-keeping.

***Little could we know how critical following our own advice would be. Our cabin, with much of my research on military families, was hit by lightning in 1989. Had we not had photos in the bank box (and an article in Family featuring the cabin, we would have missed a lot of items in our claim. One of the first things people asked us over and over was, "Did you lose all of your family photos?" Fortunately, we had some of our collection with grandparents and elsewhere.*

Originally appeared as "On the Younger Side: Lens Appeal" in Army, Navy, Air Force Times, January 10, 1983.

An IOU from Dad

No one knows better than Marine drill instructors how precious time is. In a matter of weeks they are expected to take charge of a group of young men and women and whip their bodies and minds into shape. And when they're though with this group, they start all over again with a new group. But they must also make time for another part of their lives -- the time spent with their own children.

With this in mind, a group of Marines gathered last spring to brainstorm on ways to enrich their time with their kids. The meeting was part of a program sponsored by the Family Service Center, in observance of the Month of the Military Child. They met in an auditorium not far from the fields of Parris Island, SC, where many of them are drill instructors. They spend their days disciplining recruits, shaping other people's children into fighting men and women. Then they go home.

Work vs. Home Life

Sometimes it is hard to separate their work and home environments. At work, orders are given and standards of neatness, dress, and behavior are to be achieved on schedule. If the recruits fall behind, the drill instructors are held accountable. They must live at a level of peak performance -- fault-free in the eyes of their superiors and their recruits.

Modifying those expectations at home can be difficult. Peter H. Neidig, Ph.D., who has done significant work with Parris Island drill instructors and their families, recommends a simple solution: take 15 minutes when you first come home from work to change out of your uniform (or work clothes) into leisure clothes -- and change your mode of behavior in the process. (See also Chapter 20.)

In order to get the drill instructors out of their formal mode in the auditorium and to move to the vacant front seats, I told them that I needed their help -- that I wanted them to develop their own "pleasure profile." (See Chapter 28.) On small pads of paper, they were to list at least 20 activities they enjoyed when they were five to ten years old. I suggested that they think about the places they lived and played, the people they knew, the smells, the food they loved. They began to get comfortable in their seats, crossed their legs, and wrote a few quick things. Bit by bit, smiles began to light up their faces. They nudged each other and pointed something they had just written.

Childhood Memories and Learning Experiences

They began to get faraway looks on their faces and memories came flooding back. I suggested that they also include some of the things they always wanted to do, but didn't, for one reason or another.

When they completed the first rush of ideas, I shared some of my own favorites. Making the point that we don't become the people we are overnight, that we are shaped by our experiences (good and bad), I shared with them my own love of the woods.

Kids learn a great deal from their childhood experiences. And fortunately, we know a lot more today about how children learn than in my parents' era. As it turns out, they did a lot of things right, but most were done unconsciously or by chance. As parents today, we can eliminate some of the guess-work and become conscious, active co-adventurers with our children. Why? Partly because it is *fun*. Children are an excuse to do some of the things that we would look pretty silly doing alone as adults. I used to take my Girl Scout troops into the woods with magnifiers on shoestrings around their necks. We would all sprawl on the ground and investigate the life in front of us from a bug's eye view.

Exploring with Dad

Dads are very important co-adventurers to children. Dads often are the ones who teach the use of tools (big ones for large muscle control, and finer ones for small muscle dexterity). Jack knives, magnifying glasses, and hatchets are often "dad's tools," and mom is usually the one to worry about safety. Calculated, low-risk learning builds competence and self-sufficiency of which children can be proud. This confidence will be the key to being willing to try new situations and new tools. For example, one study showed that adults who gained a "can-do" attitude as children, and a sense that a tool is a tool -- not a mystery, were willing to try their hands at computers while their peers shied away from the frightening new technology.

Building Courage and Abilities Early

As parents, we can enable our children to build their courage (physical, emotional, and intellectual courage) by helping them test themselves under conditions where they are likely to succeed. Courage is an element with which the Marine drill instructors work daily .... their own courage and that of the other people's children they train.

They are often frustrated by the lack of traits or abilities they encounter in their recruits. One such ability is hand-eye coordination. It shows up most readily in the marksmanship exercises. The irony is that by the time these instructors get a recruit, that young man or woman is usually 18 years old or older. At that point, the IQ level and mental skills have been established. Yes, new *facts* can be learned, but *completely new abilities*, no! By the time a child is four years old, 50% of his adult mental abilities have been developed. At eight years of age, 80%, and at age 17, they are 100% developed.

The time to learn hand-eye coordination is the preschool and early elementary school years. Those hours spent throwing and catching a ball or going fishing will pay handsome dividends -- in the ability to read and in ways you can hardly imagine as your arm aches and your child pleads for "just a few more pitches, Dad" (or Mom, especially when Dad is deployed or away on unaccompanied duty).

Kids' IOU's

Several years ago, *Family* worked with two elementary school classes in Groton, CT. (See Chapter 9.) Over 90% of the children in the school had parents in the Navy or Marine Corps, and many were going to be away at Christmas. We asked the first and sixth graders to design IOU coupons for their dads. Their ideas gave clues about what they thought were important activities. The favorites were raking the yard, mowing the lawn, or cleaning the car -- *things they saw as grown up and joint activities with their dad*. Another popular coupon was *a favorite meal* -- again, something to be shared. The third category promised *things they would make*, such as cookies ("gingerbread men with rainbows" or "a snowman with a bird and hat on top"). The fourth category promised "a *big hug*," or "3,000 kisses" -- the illustration showed the child on the pier with the hearts reaching out over the water to his dad on the submarine.

Two Bonuses: Being Specific and Enjoying Anticipation

The children had learned the lesson that parents need to learn for their own IOU's: be as specific as possible, so that your child can visualize the activity that you are offering. Their enjoyment then is doubled, with anticipation being as valuable as the actual event. And remembering afterward, as the Marines remember their own sources of pleasure as children, can be an additional bonus. *(The combination of past, present, and future -- out of order this time.)*

Promises from Dads

So, what did our 100 Marines promise their children in their IOU's?

Trips and Activities:

- IOU a trip to the park to let you swing and enjoy the outdoors.
- IOU a strawberry-picking trip.
- IOU a trip to Nag's Head. We'll go across on the ferry, feed the seagulls, and camp at Cape Hatteras. One day we'll go hang gliding, another, fishing.
- IOU a family picnic.
- IOU playing musical instruments.
- IOU dancing like James Brown.
- IOU watching cartoons together.
- IOU a ten-minute horsey ride around the living and dining rooms.
- IOU one overnight camping trip.
- IOU a ride in a power boat.
- IOU a night fishing trip.
- IOU making and flying a kite.
- IOU a roll of film and letting you take pictures.
- IOU a trip to the library to find some new fantasy books.

How-to Activities:

- IOU learning how to train a bird dog.
- IOU learning how to build a box.
- IOU building a plastic or wooden model together.
- IOU building an obstacle course together.
- IOU building a tree house together.
- IOU letting you teach me to operate the computer (*a nice twist for older children, to value their special skills*).

Physical Activities and Games:

- IOU one field reconnaissance mission to include: watching people without being seen, moving at night, and building/using rope bridges. (*There was laughter when this one was shared with the group, as with others that sounded like their recruit training, but you can imagine how thrilled a daughter or son would be to share such a grown-up activity that is part of dad's job.*)

Parenting

- IOU a chance to do push ups, pull ups, bends and thrusts, leg lifts, and mountain climbers. (*Lucky kid!*)
- IOU two hours of shooting marbles.
- IOU a bike ride in the woods.
- IOU the opportunity to work on a farm/ranch in South Dakota during your summer vacation.
- IOU many flying trips, letting you take the controls occasionally. *(The ideal way to offer this is single flights, multiple coupons.)*
- IOU learning to hunt and track.

- IOU a game of Monopoly.
- IOU a free magic marker tattoo.
- IOU a game of racquetball.
- IOU a day at the beach building sand castles.
- IOU an imaginary shopping trip.

- **IOU an explanation about why Dad is a Marine.**

When I read this last IOU to the group, we all knew that it was the grand finale -- a sharing of what one's life represents, something we need to do over and over with our children, in ways that they can understand, as they grow up in our military families.

Originally appeared as "IOU from Dad" in <u>Family</u>, *February 1988.*

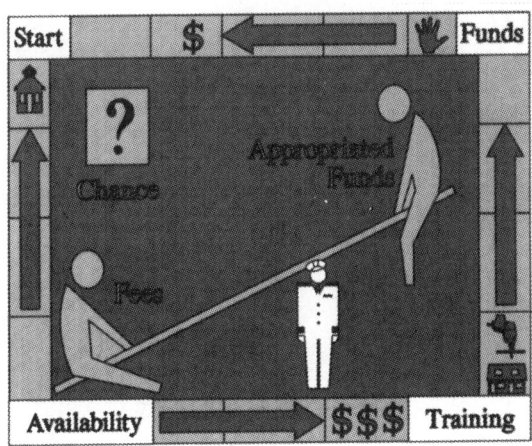

Child Care: 1990's Board Game

Appropriate for children, parents, and military policy makers.

All participants place their child-shaped players at the starting position (the old building with children hanging out of all of the windows and a long line of children and parents waiting to get in the front door).

The object of the game is to progress to the winner's circle (the blueprint drawing shows the old building with a new facade and name: **Child Development Center**. It has two new satellite additions called **Family Home Child Care** and **Drop-In Center**.)

En route, the players pass fragments of the new building under construction. The fragments are entitled **Funds, Quantity, Quality, Availability,** and **Training**. The two columns that support the entry to the new center are labeled **Readiness** and **Retention**.

As players move from block to block, sometimes experiencing slides that propel them backwards, giant leaps that hasten their forward progress, or swings that go back and forth, they pass a chubby child called **Fees** sitting on a seesaw. Up in the air and not balancing his weight is a slender child called **Appropriated Funds**. The fulcrum of the seesaw, the pivotal point, is a uniformed figure called **Installation Commanding Officer**.

Players also pass many child care providers doing flips toward the exit.

416 Parenting

Any new game seems like a puzzle to first time players. Some like to just try it first and read the instructions later. Others methodically research the rules before they begin. They discover a pack of cards from which to draw when it is their turn. These cards stipulate their movement (whether forward, backward, or standing still) and do not permit the players to have total control. While players might like to believe that this is primarily a game of choice and strategy, it is primarily a game of chance.

The cards from which the players may draw bear the symbols: (+), (-), or (+/-). The number of spaces to be moved follows. The (+/-) card, gives the number of spaces forward and then backward that players must move -- a frustrating concept for players of all ages.

Some of the cards that appear in the deck read as follows:

****

Family Home Child Care
+ 10

Military spouses provide care for up to six children in quarters (including their own children under age eight).
They are monitored, trained, and inspected regularly through unannounced visits.
Their hours are more flexible than center hours, therefore more accommodating for irregular duty hours.

****

Family Home Child Care
+/- 3

The Army and Navy provide liability insurance coverage for FHCC providers at little or no cost. The U.S. Marine Corps insurance program costs providers $150.00 per year. The Air Force requires insurance.

****

RIF (Reduction in Force)
+/- ?

Plan to move ahead with child care programs while moving an unknown number of blocks backwards.
Construction of new child care centers or renovations of existing sites proceeds without knowledge of specifics of installation closures anticipated in drawdown of military ordered by Congress.

****

Family Home Child Care Providers Mobilized
- 3

Edwards Air Force Base has experienced drop in child care options as a number of their FHCC providers are themselves Reservists called to active duty.

****

Child Care: 1990's Board Game 417

Parent Advisory Groups
+ 5

The requirement that Child Development Centers appoint a parent advisory group enables parents to play an active role in the support and fine-tuning of services. Parent Advisory Groups are permitted to fundraise to enhance supplies and equipment available under stringent center budgets. (One parent group has designed an enchanting sweatshirt for children touting their center. Funds generated are used for "nice-to have's."

****

The Military Family Assistance Act 1991
+ 10
BONUS: Double points if passed

Senate Bill 334, sponsored by Senator Edward Kennedy, has just been submitted as Family goes to press. It proposes to:

(1) Enable military child care authorities to contract with eligible civilian sector child development centers and Family Home Child Care providers for slots for military families at the same reduced fees charged in military centers. This enables military child care authorities to take advantage of current dropping rates in civilian child development centers (due to lessened demand as people lose jobs in a tight economy). Contracts with civilian centers while spaces are available and less expensive than usual would save the Services money and time (vs. waiting for permission and funds to build their own centers). Waiting lists could become almost non-existent under this Act, where deployed units predominate.

(2) Provide certificates/vouchers directly to families for reduced fee child care in the civilian sector who live too far away to access military centers. To qualify, families must have an active duty member deployed, have an income under a limit to be determined by the Department of Defense, and need child care to permit the parent (or in loco parentis) at home to be employed or have respite care.

*The proposed legislation is not tied directly to Desert Storm, but does stipulate for families of deployed active duty members. Benefit ends for Reserves 60 days beyond active duty.

*Points given even if law not passed because it recognizes the strains on military families.

****

The Military Family Assistance Act 1991
+ 3

Military spouses are given preference to receive grants to correct minor deficiencies in their quarters which would enable them to become Family Home Day Care Providers.

****

Relocation
-/+ 5/ 10/ 15

Your family has orders to move.
(1) If there is no provision at your current location for short-term child care while you arrange to move, go backwards 5 squares.
(2) If you are moving to an installation with a long child care waiting list, go backwards 5 squares.
(3) If the new installation to which you are moving has no short-term, drop-in child care while you house hunt and move in, go back 5 squares.
(4) If a miracle occurs, and you have both long-term and short term options readily available, move forward by leaps and bounds!

****

Family Home Child Care Providers Depart Germany
- 3

As U. S. troops in Germany deployed to Desert Shield/Storm, some of their spouses "went home," leaving a void in FHCC provisions.

****

Military Construction (MILCON) $$$
+ 14

In 1990, Congress authorized and funded construction of 14 child development centers (six more than requested by the Department of Defense!).

BONUS POINTS: + 20

If you are assigned to any of the following installations:
Fort Stewart, GA
Carlisle Barracks, PA
Fort Myer, VA
NAS Miramar, CA
NSB San Diego, CA
NETC Newport, RI
Lowery AFB, CO
Hickham AFB, HI
Scott AFB, IL
Grissom AFB, IN
Andrews AFB, MD
Wurtsmith AFB, MI
Whiteman AFB, MO
Minot AFB, ND

****

Non-Traditional and Junior Enlisted Military Members' Needs Met
+ 10

The variety of child care options readily available at your installation meet the mission-requirements (hours & short notice) and finances of single parents, dual military couples, and junior enlisted families.

Child Care: 1990's Board Game

****
Installation Commanding Officer
+/- 20

Installation commanding officers have the discretion to use some of their appropriated funds for child care or for other services and activities. Move up to 20 squares forward or backward based on your perception of your CO's (and your major command's) commitment to child care as a critical factor in service members' READINESS and RETENTION.

Deficit Points: - 10

In testimony on the proposed Military Child Care Act of 1989, DoD officials opposed concept of "fencing" (protecting) funds to be used at the local level for child care. They argued for flexibility of CO to meet mission requirements. Those in disagreement with this philosophy believe that hardware always comes first, but understanding how child care positively impacts readiness is often in short supply.
****

Family Home Child Care Providers
+ 5

The quantity of providers has increased in most Services, but more importantly, the quality of the providers has improved with the training and support mandated by the Military Child Care Act of 1989. One supervisor can monitor 30 FHCC providers. Additional supervisors may monitor 40 each. So for the salaries of three civil servants, 110 FHCC providers can provide care for 660 children. All are licensed (vs. only 10% of family day care centers nationally).
****

Drop-In or Short-Term Care
+/- 20

Move up to 20 squares forward or backward depending on the availability of this kind of child care at your installation. To determine the degree of your movement, consider whether you must make appointments two weeks in advance (the norm) or whether there are truly "drop-in" slots. Also consider whether the number meets the respite and volunteer needs of your military community.
****

Innovative Contracting for New Centers
+ 5

Use of the authority of 10 USC 2809 permits the Services to enter into long-term contracts for the construction, management, and operation of child development centers. Two centers, at the Pentagon and Tracy Depot, CA, have been built and opened in record time.

Child Abuse Prevention Increased
+ 25

A 1989 Department of Defense Instruction (DoD) increased personal, professional, and educational requirements for child care providers. It requires significant background checks and specified training on a regular basis on child care regulations, child growth and development, child care programming and activities, health practices, first aid, and CPR, nutrition and meal service, design and use of physical space, working with parents, safety and emergency procedures, child guidance techniques, child abuse and/or neglect prevention, detection, and reporting.

Bonus Points: + 10

Establishment of the Family Advocacy Command Assistance Team (FACAT) to respond to allegations of child sexual abuse in DoD-sanctioned activities.

Establishment of <u>DoD Child Abuse and Safety Hotline</u> (expanded to international service in November 1990): The intent is that this is a net above and beyond local family advocacy personnel and safety officials to whom you would still report any alleged incident <u>first.</u>

United States	800-336-4592
Germany	0130-81-2702
Guam	800-164-8003
Italy	1678-70-154
Japan	0031-11-1821
Korea	008-1800947-8278
Panama	800-111-0058
Philippines	800-111-9034
Spain	900-99-1107
United Kingdom	0800-89-7478

Military Child Care Act of 1989
+/- 15

The Act provides that child care centers be closed at the end of a 90-day period if non-life threatening violations are not corrected. Many military centers are located in old, converted buildings that cannot be repaired in 90 days. While they await renovation or replacement, waivers must permit them to function after doing the most practical to diminish the cause of non-life threatening violations. Otherwise, hardship will occur and families may make even less safe/desirable arrangements.

Additional Child Care Services Provided
+ 5/ 10/ 15

Move ahead if your installation provides the following:
(1) Resource and referral services regarding child care
(2) Before and after school programs
(3) Parent Cooperatives

Child Care: 1990's Board Game

****

Higher Pay for Child Development Center Employees
+/- 15

The higher pay scale will be more attractive to the many military spouses who start as child care providers, but move as soon as possible to higher paying jobs. Their increased longevity added to the mandated training will increase the quality of care being given and decrease the likelihood of stress-related child abuse. The increased pay scale should also preclude the occurrence (noted in 1988) of new centers delaying opening or opening with less than their capacity due to lack of staff. The down side is that their salaries must be funded through higher child care fees.

****
*

Military Centers Offer Infant Care
+ 10

Infant care is exceptionally expensive and hard to find in the civilian sector due to the child: caregiver ratio required. It is critical to our active duty personnel who must return to work before many civilian centers accept infants. Military child development centers and FHCC fill this important gap -- when space is available.

****
*

Special Needs Care
+ 10

FHCC providers usually can accommodate night care, care for mildly ill children, and children with special needs.

****

Fees
+ 10/ 20

Most civilian working families expect to spend an average of 10% of their income on child care. Navy testimony in 1988 on the Military Child Care Act stated that a study at West Coast military centers showed that a military single parent of one child paid between 14 - 19% of his annual income for child care; for married couples, child care ranged between 7.3 - 10.8 % of annual income.

Fast mathematics on the new DoD fee scale for child development centers can help you determine what percentage of your annual income you pay. Multiply your fee X 52 weeks and then divide by your income. (Example: You earn $20,000 a year, so pay $41.00 a week per child in high cost of living areas, for a total annually of $2,132 -- or 10.6% of your annual income. FHCC fees are also set, but at a higher rate than the center rate.

Comparison with civilian sector fees for licensed child care makes the military fees look good!

($) Total Family Income	($) Fees Per Week Per Child
$0 -- 27,000	$31 - 41
$27,001 - 42,000	$42 -- 52
$42,001 - 59,000	$53 -- 63
More than $59,000	$64 -- 74

Total family income is your adjusted gross income, verified via your most recent income tax return.

Bonus Points: **+5**

Two tax options offer substantial savings for parents. The first is a tax credit (you may take a credit against taxes you owe for 30% of your child care expenses -- up to $2400 in expenses for one child and $4800 for two or more children. Every dollar of credit reduces your taxes by one dollar). The second option is a "dependent care account," useful to military families only if the non-military spouse can set it up through his/her employer. You may use only one of these options.

****

Military Family and Children Act
+10

On January 29, 1991, Senator Edward Kennedy introduced S. 281, a bill to provide, among other things, comprehensive support services to families of members of the Armed Forces serving on active duty. Part of the proposed legislation would provide grants to non-profit organizations, such as the American Red Cross, YMCA, and USO, to improve support services in areas in which there are no military installations. Among these "support services" are child care and respite care. If passed, this will be especially helpful for those who are family members of mobilized Reserve and National Guard personnel and families of those who have "gone home" to wait out Desert Storm.

****

Just as most games mimic real life and have a not altogether amusing symbolism, our **Child Care 1990's** board game has given us a lot of insights into a very complicated, ever changing area of concern.

Adapted as "Child Care: 1990's Board Game," in Family, April 1991.

Alone After School:
Alternatives for Latchkey Children

Goldilocks was a latchkey kid. While out wandering through the woods one day, she stopped to peer into the window of a nice little cottage. Seeing no one, she peeked through the keyhole of the front door. Still no sign of anyone home, though there was porridge poured in the three bowls at the table. She lifted the latch and found the door unlocked. The rest you know......

Or you think you know! The cottage owners, who had had no reason to fear intruders of any size in the past, had gone for a walk with their baby bear while their porridge cooled. They symbolize the nurturing family. Goldilocks, like many latchkey children in their own homes, took the opportunity to investigate their belongings. This fairy tale is one of the few that ends without a clear lesson for children.

Interestingly enough, modern versions of the story have added the comment that Goldilocks had been sent on an errand by her mother. Other fairy tales of unsupervised children come to mind. **Little Red Riding Hood**, who was specifically told by her mother not to dally on her way to deliver food to her sick grandmother, and not to deviate from the well-traveled path, dallied and deviated and was devoured by the Big Bad Wolf. The wolf, in varying forms, is a real life concern to most parents today.

Add **Hansel and Gretel** to the fairy tale children who wandered unsupervised -- in their case, having been led into the woods by their father and stepmother who talked of no food and too many mouths to feed.

We all know these tales, We heard them as children and now, as adults, have read them to our own children. They figure in our value systems in powerful ways.

Living Next Door to Goldilocks

You may remember that the Three Bears were appalled to find that Goldilocks had tested their food, had damaged Baby Bear's chair, and had fallen asleep in the baby's bed. They were not concerned for her well being; they were critical of her intrusion on their happy, well-ordered household.

They bear a great resemblance to many neighbors of latchkey children. How often have you agreed to be listed as an emergency contact for neighbors' children at school, and the school nurse calls to say you'll have to pick up Susie? She's too sick to stay at school and her mother is "unreachable" at work. (Susie often feels miraculously better once she's home with you, has had a warm blanket, some gingerale, and some one-on-one attention.)

How often have you had a child come for your help in breaking up a fight between siblings at their home? Or how often have you heard the after-school battles through the wall and wondered what your responsibilities are? As a teacher or Scout leader, have you watched children's performance decline? How early do children get dropped off at school and left to wait until it opens, or how often do they come late or not at all? How many come without breakfast, or have been up for hours by the time school starts in order to mesh with working parents' schedules?

Not fair, you say. You're hitting only the negatives. What are some of the positives? you ask. Let's first define latchkey children.

Who are Latchkey Children?

Latchkey refers to those school-aged children who are left unsupervised before and/or after school on a regular basis. Some now refer to them as *children in self-care*, in order to remove the negative connotation of latchkey. Ages range from five to 17, but most concern is focused on those ages five to 15. It is illegal in many states to leave a child under the age of 12 alone or responsible for other younger children. Each military installation has regulations for those in quarters. These vary by Service and by state.

The latchkey issue is, without a doubt, one of the most emotional and pervasive issues of our time. Parents and children struggle with it individually. Schools and organizations that serve families find that it has changed their programs radically. Researchers are trying to learn quickly as they are being overtaken by the phenomenon -- because the long-term results for children, parents, and society at large are unknown. Historically, children helped their parents in home-based work until the family's financial status permitted the mother to remain at home (or to hire others to do so). The extended family took care of children when parents needed to work outside of the home.

While some children in latchkey arrangements existed since World War II, the tidal wave now experienced is estimated conservatively at 25% of school-aged children (with some urban areas reporting 33% -- one of every three children). No longer are they only the children whose parent or parents cannot afford to pay for other childcare arrangements. Latchkey arrangements are found across the socioeconomic scale as women join the labor force for reasons of personal achievement as well as economic gain.

There are two philosophies at work as well. One group of parents believes that children do not need supervision and/or social activities beyond the school day. The other parents regret the deprivation they believe their arrangement represents, but feel they have no alternatives.

Latchkey Kids in Military Families

Military families reflect the statistics of the civilian society around them. The 1985 *Department of Defense Surveys of Officer and Enlisted Personnel and Military Spouses* stated that 48% of officers' wives and 54% of enlisted men's wives whose youngest child was six to 11 years of age were employed. The figures rose to 58% and 64% respectively for mothers whose youngest was a teenager. (These statistics included those outside of the continental United States who are less likely to be employed than their stateside counterparts. These statistics also included those who work full and part-time.)

These DoD Surveys also showed who were the usual caregivers when the youngest child was under 15 and the mother (not a military member herself) worked, looked for work, or was in school. The total percent of officers' children who cared for themselves or were cared for by siblings was 22.4%. Children of enlisted men experienced less self-care and sibling care (13.5%), with more care given by the military member himself or non-relative care (which includes individual or center-based care). A word of caution: these figures are self-reported, and even on anonymous surveys, there is a tendency to be secretive about one's arrangements.

Alternatives for Latchkey Kids

What are the alternatives to latchkey arrangements? Some school systems or individual schools have designed programs for before and after the regular school day. They have various names such as "extended day" or "school-based childcare," but most operate on a sliding scale according to parents' income. In recent Gallup polls reported by the National School

Boards Association, 76% of parents think schools should provide such programs. Federally subsidized school breakfast programs, available on the same criteria as reduced-lunch programs are offered in a number of schools.

If you are interested in starting a school-based childcare program, you have two good resources: the National Parent-Teacher Association and the Wellesley College Center for Research on Women (Wellesley College, 828 Washington Street, Wellesley, MA 02181). The latter has assisted a number of school systems, such as Fairfax County, VA.

The European Parent Teacher Student Association, which covers Department of Defense Schools in the Mediterranean and Atlantic regions, initiated a cooperative effort with the European Red Cross last spring to provide after-school programs. Their goal is to have a uniform latchkey program at all major installations, primarily staffed by volunteers.

Military Latchkey Programs

Recognizing that there are many school systems that do not provide school-based childcare, and that there are often long waiting lists for those programs that do exist, the Department of the Army instituted its School Age/Latchkey program (SA/LK) at all major installations in 1987. The SA/LK coordinator works out of either the Youth Activities or Child Development Services to assess the needs of installation families for child-care and to determine all of the local providers.

For you, as a parent, that means that upon your arrival at your new post, you can call the SA/LK coordinator to request information on all of the school programs, center-based options, such as those offered by the childcare center, youth center under the Division of Recreation Services, YMCA or YWCA, USO, or churches and home-based childcare. "Prime Time," a new program created by the YMCA, currently provides school-based childcare at more than 20 elementary schools in San Antonio, TX. You can find the SA/LK coordinator by calling the child care center, Youth Activities, or the DPCA (Director of Personnel and Community Activities).

Stephen W. Pratt, Chief, Youth Activities, Department of the Army, told *Family* that pieces of the SA/LK program have existed for a number of years, but four years ago, money was sought to unify and strengthen them. The focus of the SA/LK program is *fun*. It should not be seen as an extended school day -- rather an opportunity for enrichment and recreation, learning skills that enhance children's school performance, but are not tutorial in nature (unless requested by the parents).

Depending on the needs and desires expressed by parents at each installation, the SA/LK program incorporates use of post recreational facilities (bowling alley, swimming pool, gymnasium, craft or hobby shop) with instruction in art, dance, and music, and participation in team sports. Where too few kids are interested in a specific area to bring an instructor to the youth center (such as piano lessons or soccer), arrangements are made to take the students to such activities and bring them back to the center.

The periods covered vary by installation and the needs of the families there, but for the most part they include after school (before school as needed), vacation/school conference days, and summer vacation. For the Army program, families must commit to use the program for the school year. No "drop-in" participation is permitted. The summer day camp programs, however, with before and after extensions in many cases are for all children on a first-come basis.

Off-Post Opportunities

While the Army SA/LK program is predominantly for those children who live on post, Pratt indicated that the coordinator may work out an arrangement with the local school system, on a case-by-case basis, to pick up an off-post student whose parent has transported him or her to the youth center on post in the morning and to return him there in the afternoon. Otherwise, the coordinator will help parents find appropriate programs by organizations in the community or neighborhood home-based care.

Navy and Air Force Programs

The Navy and the Air Force offer programs through their equivalents of the child care/development center and youth activities center at all major installations. Mick McAndrews, of the Navy Recreation Services Division, echoed Pratt's emphasis on active fun-oriented programming. After children have sat through a six-or-seven-hour school day, they need a chance to unwind and move their bodies. The Navy has published eleven activity manuals to upgrade their programs for six- to 12-year-olds. Navy and Marine Corps parents can contact Recreation Services for their program and the Family Service Center for other child care options.

The Air Force provides closely supervised latchkey programs for children ages five to 11 at all of its Child Development Centers. According to Beverly Schmalzried, Chief, U.S. Air Force Morale, Welfare and Recreation Operations Policy, about half of the base youth centers offer recreation-oriented after-school programs for children ages five to 14. Check-in is required so that children's presence is accounted for (unlike the drop-in recreations options where children may come and go on their own). She stressed that all youth centers now offer full day summer camps. Survival Skills classes for parents and children are offered through the base youth centers for families who elect self-care.

Teens Help Themselves

In April 1988, the Army began programs with a risk-adventure theme for teens at 24 locations (check your own installation for more information). The Teen or Youth Council, an active body of students, advises the installation youth director on programs and helps with the short- and long-term planning and budgeting. Some may develop Outward Bound-type activities. Others may choose volunteering in public service (on and off the installation), career exploration (internships or entrepreneurial options in conjunction with the Family Member Employment Assistance Program), lifelong sports, and training in life survival skills (e.g. balancing a check book, writing a resume, and filling out job applications).

These programs are not provided just because they are "nice to have." Enough is known about children who are unsupervised after school to know that healthy, preventive programs will lessen the accident rate (fire, personal injury, and sexual abuse), vandalism, and substance abuse. These programs are advantageous in terms of safety, proximity to medical care, social time with peers, and activities that are stimulating intellectually, artistically, and physically -- the major points on which parents and teachers are critical of latchkey arrangements.

There are still other options to restricting your children to staying inside or within one's own yard, often afraid of noises, weather, or sibling fights. Each of the Services has a program to train and certify home/family day care providers at all major installations. For those parents interested in adding to their income while remaining at home with their own children, home day care can be an ideal part-time job. School hours are free for activities of one's own choosing. Contact your SA/LK coordinator (Army), or family service/support center (Navy, USMC, and Air Force) for details. Home day care can provide small group interaction, the freedom to play outside or go to Scouts, music lessons, or county recreation programs.

Form a Kid Co-op

Enterprising parents might consider forming a co-op, with one giving sewing lessons, one doing crafts or art lessons, another cooking, hiking, tutoring, or giving music lessons one afternoon a week. Children can benefit from a variety of scheduled caregivers who are sharing what they do best. This could work as a co-op among five families or five care providers could divide the number of children into age-ability groups and run the enterprise as a home-based business.

If none of the above options is available to you and your children, and you decide to be pioneers in a latchkey arrangement, do your research carefully with some of the resources available to you. Experts say you are least likely to have a successful experience if you initiate a latchkey arrangement by default when other childcare provisions fall through or right after a move. It's a double-whammy for children to lose a known neighborhood and friends *and* a parent on hand after school.

A Successful Latchkey Program

You are most likely to have a successful latchkey experience if:

1   You wait until you have lived in your new neighborhood awhile and have built a good support network of adults and children's friends;

2   You talk through the pitfalls and likely crises with your child or children; and

3   You do some trial runs.

Then assess your program continuously, and be prepared to look for other alternatives if your schedule changes, if you or your children experience ongoing stress, or if their change in age or stage makes your experiment no longer appropriate.

Reading Up on the Latchkey Issue

Here are a few good resources for learning more about childcare after school. Check in your library before purchasing:

After School: Young Adolescents on Their Own by Joan Lipsitz, (The Center for Early Adolescence, University of North Carolina at Chapel Hill, Suite 223, Carr Mill Hall, Carrboro, NC 25710 - 1987). $15.00. This new book addresses the after school needs of all young adolescents, with special chapters on the physical, social, and emotional growth of the ten- to 15-year-olds.

Alone After School: A Self-Care Guide for Latchkey Children and Their Parents by Helen L. Swan and Victoria Houston, (Prentice-Hall, Inc., Route 9, Englewood Cliffs, NJ 07632 - 1985). $8.95. This book provides a good discussion for parents and children in the study of latchkey issues and has good "what if" emergency scenarios to practice.

On My Own: The Kids' Self-Care Book by Lynette Long, Ph.D., (Acropolis Books, 2400 17th Street, N.W., Washington, DC 20009 - 1984). $7.95 plus 50 cents postage and handling. This workbook is ideal for the young latchkey child who appreciates pictures more than words. To help make the emergency pages easier to find, pull them out and put them in a separate, easy-to-reach spot.

School's Out -- Now What? Creative Choices for Your Child by Joan Bergstrom, Ed.D., (Ten Speed Press, P.O. Box 7123, Berkeley, CA 94707 -- 1984). $10.95. The best overall guide for parents on enriching their children's out-of-school activities, whether or not in a latchkey arrangement.

The Handbook for Latchkey Children and Their Parents by Lynette Long, Ph.D. and Thomas Long, Ed.D., (Arbor House Publishing Co., 235 E. 45th Street, New York, NY 10017 - 1983). $7.95. A very complete discussion of the pros and cons, assessment of your child's readiness for self-care, and provisions for successful arrangements. Considered a "classic" in the new field of latchkey children.

Originally appeared as "Alone After School" in Family, *March 1988.*

Section X

Children's Educational Needs

61

A Kid's Eye View of the Military

To celebrate the Month of the Military Child, *Family* asked military sons and daughters to share their perspective on their lifestyle (to *Pass It On!*) Over 70 responses came from all over the world, from all services, and from all ages (including one toddler and one former Army "brat" who is now an Air Force wife.

In some cases, writing letters became a family affair. A pair of friends wrote from Hill AFB, UT, and four classes used the article as an assignment: Mrs. Marcia Reass's fourth-grade class at Seoul American Elementary School, and three of Mrs. Jimmie Melvin's classes at Knob Norster Public School near Whiteman AFB, MO. One parent wrote a special thank you, saying that reading her son's letter helped her understand better what he had experienced in the last move.

Researchers have found that when parents and children talk honestly about their feelings when they move, the adjustment is smoother than if the parents ignore the difficulties and hope they will go away with time. Just as adults resent the insinuation that moving gets easier as they get more experienced, children know that it is harder some times than others.

The <u>frequency</u> with which they move plus <u>their age</u> makes a great deal of difference. As children grow older, they get the hang of the physical move and how to unpack in their new house. But friend-making takes <u>longer</u> and surprisingly enough, requires more <u>skill</u> from a teenager than a five-year-old.

Family did not underestimate the wisdom of our young correspondents. **Let's hear it from the kids!**

On Moving in General

> *It never gets easier, no matter how many times you move. I believe that it gets harder each time you move, but each place you live will always be inside you. (Alytrius Burns, 14)*

> *What's it like moving? Think of yourself as a junior in high school. Locate your home town on a world map. Move one to five inches in any direction. That is where you'll be spending your next school year! Growing up isn't easy and being a military child is even harder. I have been to four elementary schools, one junior high, and at this time, I am enrolled in my third senior high school. Hard, huh? There is no one word to express this educational jigsaw. No one understand you unless he or she has experienced the same mobility. (Inga Hagen, 17)*

> *Living in a military family means moving a lot, and moving means leaving friends and messing up the school year for me. Being in the middle of the school year, I might not be able to join any sports such as basketball, softball, or track. I will have to make new friends, learn different cultures, and start all over again. (Edika Haley, 13)*

> *I am 12 years old and have lived in eight different places...I really think it depends on how you feel about the place you live before you can say how you feel about moving. For instance, I didn't care for Florida much, so I was glad we moved. (Erinn Dempsey, 12)*

> *A military family is like a big moving truck. (Jaime Howell, 9)*

> *For me, moving often is really a great experience. . . I want to see if I will have a larger bedroom! (Tyssha Kelly, 11)*

> *We're moving again! It's not a question, it's a nightmare. The hours of grief and tears some children spend mourning the memories that may never live again.....*
>
> *Has the spouse also had second thoughts? There may be nights filled with arguments about the future. This added to the child's stress is painful. What if the pressure of military life leads to family problems? What happens next? The airman's career could collapse from lack of concentration; a happy home could suffer, or military children could be tormented by civilians and called "brats." ......*
>
> *If you and your family are some of the many people who 'serve your country,' get together (include any children), discuss the topic of military life, and see what everyone thinks. Try to find a solution to any problems. To make the world a better place, you have to start somewhere. Try your own home. (Jennifer Dianand, 13)*

I have moved four times and will be moving again soon. Each time I have to leave somewhere, I know I will miss my home, school, and friends. But I know that I will find new friends, will have a new house and school that will be almost like the one I left. (Chris Santiago, 9)

Hints for Coping with the Move

Chris has shown us one very interesting coping skill: he notices what is the same, and therefore, has a sense of continuity. Most of us accentuate what is different, and that often translates to complaining. Others learn to accentuate the positive.

You get to eat different foods and sleep in other houses. You know who are bullies and who are not. You get to know nice teachers and mean teachers. (Jason Smith, 11). His sister Tashi, 14, adds: *Once in a while you get homesick for your old friends or something special you used to do in the last place you were, but then you just think of all the great times and friends here and forget about it. And even if you don't like where you are now, you know that you'll either get used to it or move soon.*

One of the hardest things is explaining to your friends that you have to move. Part of you is always left behind...but when you think of them (friends), I think of them as someone who added a little extra to my life. (Megan Bruchas, 13)

Children (and adults) leave more than people behind: *It hurts to leave a place that you've grown accustomed to...running away unwillingly from your special places: hideouts, creeks, and a special tree. (Jason Rahm, 13)*

Two of our correspondents have discovered that fantasy can help them bridge a move: *Moving often is like dreams. You're in a whole new environment and you're fantasizing: what am I going to do? How am I going to meet new friends? What's going to happen? (Venus Brown, 13)*

I imagine what my new neighborhood and school will be like. (Angela Hefferman, 10)

Reactions to News of a Move

When my dad was stationed at Walter Reed (Army Hospital in Washington, D.C.), he came home one day with the news, 'We're going to Japan! I was frightened at first and started to cry. I didn't know what it would be like in Japan until I checked out some books at the library. I read and read. I felt a little better. Then I thought about the plane and got scared. Suddenly the time came to go, and the plane ride was fun. (Vanessa Collins, 10)

Plane rides and being scared are often-mentioned experiences. *The first time I moved I felt weird because the airplane was going up and down. It felt like a boat on a waving sea. It was sort of scary. I could never get comfortable, so I slept on my dad's lap. (Nick Lessing, 9)*

I have been through blizzards and deserts, over oceans and through mountains with curves worse than a roller coaster. I've also been on about every commercial airline there is. (Ashley Willemsen, 8th grader)

Moving to a Foreign Country

When I moved to England, I was scared. I didn't know what was going to happen to my family or me. It was hard for me because I didn't fit into their lifestyle and I was scared. (Michael Davis, 13)

Two of our correspondents in Korea commented on "culture shock." *How do I feel when I move? Well, I feel scared because I am shy and it takes time to meet new friends. it's even harder to adjust in a country that does not speak English. in Korea, customs are very different from ours. Blonde-haired children look like little dolls and the Koreans always want to pat them on the head. (Jackie Petty, 9)*

The third time I moved, we moved to Seoul, Korea. It was fun. When I found out, I was uneasy, but since my dad was there, it was okay. My family went to St. Louis and flew to Alaska, to Japan, and to Korea, where I am now in unlikeable, unjoyable, unthinkable (until orders came) Korea!! (Earnest E. Robinson, Jr., 9)

When I moved to Puerto Rico four years ago, everybody spoke Spanish. Imagine moving to a foreign country where you stand out because of your blond or red hair, while everyone else has dark skin and hair...Next time you ask someone what their dad does and they say the military, tell them 'I know how you feel!' (Jason Geck, 15)

Making Friends

Military life is different from civilian life. Friends come and go.... I make a good and close friend and think she's going to be my friend for life, and then she moves. I feel rejected and left out. If my friends don't move, I do, leaving not just friends, but teachers and church members. (Misty Qualls, 13)

Where are we going? To Bitsburg? That's a weird name. What if I don't make any friends there? I guess I'll just have to smile a lot, be talkative, and try not to show how nervous I am. They'll understand because most of them go through the same thing I do. (Laura Hunt, 13)

You're sitting in science talking with your friends when the principal slides in with a new student. You stare at the long red-haired girl. You tell yourself you dislike her. The teacher stands up nice and sweet by the girl, telling the class her name and where she came from, and all that junk the class never listens to. You are about to leave for art when the teacher asks you to show the student around school. You ask yourself why she picked you......As you show her around, you begin to talk. Two months later, you are best friends, telling each other your feelings. A year later, you find out she is moving. You knew this would happen. You have to say goodbye again for the 80th time. You hug each other before she leaves. As they drive away, a sad feeling creeps inside of you. (Kristin Donyl, 14)

Kristin has learned an important lesson: having a good friend is worth the hurt that her departure brings. Most of our older correspondents indicated that it is easier to make friends with other military children -- because they understand.

Friend-Making Techniques

It's easy to make new friends at school and invite them over. (Alexis Beauvais, 6)

When you go to a new school, don't wait for the kids to come to you! Go to them and make them like you...The first week I always bring an extra snack at lunchtime and offer it to share. (Avi Besancon, 11)

When we first get to our new duty station, my sisters and I go over to check out the D.Y.A. (Youth Activities). You can meet a lot of kids there. (Cassandra Brown, 14)

I try to be seen outside; that way, the kids can come over and introduce themselves and welcome me. (Yawanda Brown, 16)

I am rather shy. When I first move, it's pretty much up to the others to make the first move....My dad invites a buddy over who has a kid, and we get to know each other. (Erinn Dempsey, 12)

When I move to a new place, I am always happy and carefree. I don't complain about moving or about how much I miss the places I've come from. I love making people laugh, and I can tell you, a good humor gets you tons of friends. (CaroLu Elkins, 13)

The hardest thing to overcome is the initial loneliness....Moving when you're younger is easier than at my age because now you're dealing with cliques and insecurities. Joining activities is the fastest and easiest way to make friends. (Audrey Flewelling, 16)

I join clubs or start my own. Soon enough, I have friends that are right for me and everything feels A-OK again. (Angela Hefferman, 10)

Join a club that takes teamwork to get things done. I have made many friends in Girl Scouts for the last six years. (Tyssha Kelly, 11)

Keeping in Touch with Friends

Our correspondents are great pen pals. Allonia Brown, 10, echoed the suggestion of many: *Get friends' addresses and phone numbers before moving.* (including the address of friends' grandparents or another relative who doesn't move frequently. A number had their own address labels -- an inexpensive gift from parents that gives identity in a new location and can be sent to friends for easy mailing.

Many correspondents mentioned phone calls and visits to their friends. Cassandra Brown, 14, suggested making a photo album of your friends and teachers. Researchers know that an album brings comfort and a sense of wholeness when people suffer loneliness at a new location. It also helps to combat a normal problem: being able to picture in one's mind people who are not present. A continued exchange of photos among friends is helpful. Jason Rahm, 13, commented, *I have two friends that I haven't seen for two years. it's hard to write again and again when you have to keep picturing what your friend is really like these days.*

Ups and Downs

Our correspondents often referred to the ups and downs of military life. Dean Lister (11), Caryn Murphy (12), and Tiffany Levert (13) made the point that *many civilian kids think that we can get away with murder on military bases. They don't know the half of it -- much is expected out of us by the military and our parents.* The dichotomy is clear in 23-year-old Susan Kornegay's summation: *Growing up as a military dependent was a special, though often trying, experience.*

Being a pioneer is what the military is all about....being independent rather than having the convenience and stability of being among friends and relatives. (Jennifer Spase, 20)

Family is proud of the quality of thought that our young people shared. Perhaps because of their ups and downs, their challenges, they evaluate their lives with a frequency and maturity that is not common among those who do not move. **Let's hear it for the kids!**

Originally appeared as "A Kid's Eye View of the Military" in Family, *April 1988.*

New Kids in School: Passports for Our Lifestyle

Paris, Texas to Paris, France -- as an Army daughter, I lived in these totally different cities, as well as 15 others in between. There were too many high schools attended to fit on the college applications blanks, and far too many addresses for the Civil Service form.

How can we help our children make the frequent and radical adjustments that are a fact of life for military families? As a product of this lifestyle, a teacher of junior high, high school, and college students, and the mother of two Navy children, I have some specific suggestions that will help us prepare our children for the moves that they will experience.

Passport #1: Portable Achievement

Beginning in late elementary school, we should help our children identify, and then, sharpen any particular skill, talent, or interest that they may have. Perhaps more than average, non-moving Americans, our children need to know that they excel in a specific area, whether it be sports, music, dramatics, or art. Both for their own view of themselves and immediate recognition in their new community, being outstanding in one area is important.

Investment of time, energy, and money in excellence will pay particularly portable dividends. Every school is happy to receive a fine pianist or a clever cartoonist for the paper. The allure of a good gymnast, wrestler, or football player is well known. My college physical education department had interesting words of wisdom on the selection of sports for a lifetime: that one should choose at least one sport that can be done alone or in pairs (i.e., golf, tennis, running, or swimming) so that you don't have to wait to get a large group together. This is particularly true for a youngster who moves at the beginning of the summer and must make friends slowly until school starts.

Our children's portable achievement will have two additional benefits.
- It will serve as an emotional outlet; our children experience greater stress than their non-moving counterparts and need to learn healthy ways to work out their inner feelings.

- Another plus is that this hobby or talent may serve as a lead to a job in a new community. Most churches need substitute organists, which I learned as a 15-year-old. Lifesaving training has certainly been an effective passport to a job and friends in a new community.

One can get a copy of the results of the Civil Service general aptitude exam (plus typing) which can be carried to a new area to serve as a passport for summer employment, either in the Civil Service or the civilian sector. Keep a good file or scrapbook for each child's achievements; this will be a ready source of information, plus a source of pride when he is feeling lost after a move.

Passport #2: A Carefully Planned Scholastic Program

When your child is ready to enter junior high, you should make an appointment with his or her school guidance counselor to set up a basic plan for the six remaining years of school. Looking at the catalog of several colleges or technical schools that are typical of what you foresee for your youngster would be helpful. If the counselor does not have the catalogs you are interested in, and they cannot be found in the high school guidance office or the local library, write to two or three colleges/technical schools and request them.

As a student, I attended five schools in grades 7 - 12. Needless to say, requirements and offerings varied. As a teacher, I have seen further evidence of the need to plan some leeway in a teenager's school program. Go heavy on the "solid subjects" and light on the electives, so that he does not move in his junior or senior year and find himself light on credits and faced with a slew of local requisites. I would also suggest choosing French or Spanish as a modern foreign language (Latin 1 & II are usually available). German frequently is not available in stateside high schools. Get as much math and science as you can wherever you are, because many schools can offer highly advanced sections in these subjects for those who have the background.

Get to know your children's teachers well, early in the year. As a teacher and parent, I know that it is human nature for a teacher to give a little extra to those students whose parents visibly care.

Hints for Moving Scholastically

When you must move, there are several hints as far as schoolwork is concerned. If you have been in a state requiring the purchase of texts, take them with you as a help in the transition. Otherwise, copy the name of each text used for each subject -- this is useful at the elementary level as well. Ask for all workbooks, as they usually are not given to another student anyway. As a parent, you may often carry copies of the school testing scores (which are valuable *absolutes* vs. the relative grades given). The school, of course, will send the official copy. These absolute scores on national aptitude and achievement tests will help in the appropriate placement of your child in classes that are homogeneously grouped (grouped according to ability and achievement). Keep a copy of these national test scores in your child's personal file.

If you move at the end of a school year, go register in your new school immediately so that your children will have a better chance of being properly placed, instead of being put in wherever vacancies exist in the schedule in September. Summer school may be a good opportunity to fill holes, do remedial work, take extra courses like typing, and meet friends with whom to enjoy the summer.

Our children should be aware that different areas of our country approach history, not to mention other subjects, in highly different ways. I will never forget moving from Virginia to Kansas in the eighth grade, and proudly answering that in 1861 there was "The War Between the States." I got roundly kidded and told that that was known to the rest of the country as the "Civil War!" Embarrassing though such incidents are, they help us become sensitive to varying points of view.

If a child must move just before or during his senior year, keep a list of the teachers he knew fairly well at the previous school, as well as Scout leaders, minister, and employers. They will be a valuable source of recommendations for a job or further training. A move before my senior year was excruciating, but, I must now admit, a very good preparation socially and scholastically for going off to college. Some families have decided that completion of the senior year in the old school is preferable, so the mother has remained or the child has lived with friends. Each situation requires careful evaluation of the pros and cons of moving.

Passport # 3: Membership in National Organizations

Scouts, 4-H, Keys/Keyettes, and church groups automatically accept boys and girls who have transferred to the area. Their programs teach self-sufficiency, which is especially valuable in our military family lifestyle. Membership in a church provides an extended family when most of us must live away from our own relatives. A strong faith gives our teenagers an inner strength, a communication with God wherever they may move.

Passport #4: A Strong Nuclear Family

Passport #4, which really is first in terms of age and importance, is a strong nuclear family. As highly mobile families, we need *constants*. Our children need continuous evidence of our love for them. We and they need *absolute standards of behavior* -- standards that are the same where we go, that are not relative. Mobile families need constants and consistencies to balance the unsettling changes that moves and shore/sea duty bring.

We need to admit our own feeling of loss when we leave a favorite duty station, so that our children do not feel guilty about hating to leave. At this point we can do several things for them: we can help them maintain their old friends by collecting scrapbooks to cherish, writing, visiting each summer, and maybe even by owning a house to return to. My *home* is Mystic, CT, now, having lived there more years of my life than anywhere else; but I live in Arlington, VA. We must teach our children the dimensions of all of the tenses of living. To be whole, we must be creatures of our *past and present*, with a confident eye toward the *future*. For the present, we can help our children to be confident in themselves as people to be valued. We will have been helping them already by honing their skills or interests, and by planning their scholastics carefully. As very little people, they should learn to amuse themselves (as well as to play with others) for self-sufficiency and inner-direction.

We should give quality time to our children through interest in their activities and concerns. Be a Scout leader or junior choir mother; be part of your children's world, though you also must have adult activities to keep your own interests in balance. Explore your new area together on a regular basis. Familiarity with a new duty station usually leads to a sense of belonging there. It is also a good lifetime habit.

These passports are specifically designed for our children, but perceptive parents will notice that the need to excel in some field, to live confident, inner-directed lives, and to tie the past to the present are not unique to teenagers. Living for the present only is one-dimensional. We can be multi-dimensional people who enrich our own lives and those of our children, as well as the communities in which we live.

Originally appeared as "New Kid in School" in Family, May 1980. Adapted in Making a Home in the Navy: Ideas to Grow On, G/C/T (January-February 1981), and Charting Your Life in the United States Coast Guard.

Parents: Partners in Education

A thought-provoking question appeared on my 25th college reunion questionnaire: Do you *give enough time to your children?* I posed it to my family at dinner time, and we found ourselves in a discussion that probably takes place periodically in your house.

We agreed that different children have different needs at different ages, so the same amount of time at all ages would be inappropriate. We then asked ourselves *what most people really leave behind:* great works? fame? Remembrance by those who have known us -- until they, too, die? We decided that we hope to pass on our values and commitment to society via our children. *Do we operate daily on that proposition?* We agree that children come with personality traits and abilities, but nevertheless, what they become, for good or ill, is determined to a great degree by important adults in their lives -- their parents and their teachers.

The State of our Schools

A great deal of attention has been focused on the state of our schools, thanks to four major reports last year. Those who have read those reports carefully cannot miss the fact that the quality of education attained by our young people results from a three-way partnership: their schools, their parents, and their own investment in their future.

The Advisory Council on Instruction for the Arlington Public Schools in Virginia, a committee I chair, studied one of those reports last fall, entitled *A Nation at Risk,* to determine the implications of the report for our schools. As we worked, it became clear that our next logical step had to be a focus on parents' potential roles in the educational partnership. Because the Arlington schools serve many students from military families, including those who live on Fort Myer and those who live in the community, and because Arlington has been a leader in educating children from a wide variety of socio-economic and ethnic backgrounds, the lessons learned should be helpful to parents everywhere.

Our Experts

In addition to talking with parents, teachers, and principals informally, I asked four educators to share their points of view. Margaret Marston, the mother of three in high school and college, is a member of the Virginia Board of Education and the National Commission on Excellence in Education (which produced *A Nation at Risk*). In the first eight months after the release of the report, Mrs. Marston gave 156 speeches -- a comment on the incredible interest of educators and citizens in the commission's work.

Dennis Hill, the father of two in high school and college, is the principal of Wakefield High School. His previous work at the junior high level adds to his sensitivity on the needs of teenagers.

Brenda Glenn comes to her job as assistant principal of Yorktown High School from the English department. Her accessibility to students and parents is legendary.

Sharon Steindam was selected for her position as principal of Thomas Jefferson Intermediate School by a committee of administrators and parents. The parents at the elementary school that she served for almost six years hated to see her leave, but she feels that she has an especially good beginning when parents care enough to participate in the selection process.

Our experts feel that parents' ideal roles in their children's education vary by school level. Foundations established when the children are young become the cumulative base from which they will continue to grow.

Pre-school Years

Communication with our children should be frequent and descriptive. We are provided the words, the sentence structure, and the expressiveness that they will grow on. We should be delighted when we hear ourselves mimicked as they grow in verbal power; therefore, baby talk is out!

Establishment of the dinner hour as a time of pleasurable exchange with family members should begin at a very young age. Pediatricians recommend that babies can be fed earlier, but should watch and listen from their chairs. It is an important part of the civilizing process.

As they mature, children should be provided with playthings that allow them *manipulative experiences.* Studies of mathematically able girls show that they usually had access to "boys toys" as well as those usually thought of for girls. Educators are increasingly aware that the preferred learning style for one quarter of our students is through "hands-on" activities. Ironically, there are fewer and fewer of these as children progress to higher grade levels, so parents can fill important gaps by insuring these outside of school. (See also Chapters 55, 64, 65, and 66.)

Fathers play an important role in their children's development. While moms tend to be verbal and gentle in their play, dads tend to like more rough and tumble play and like to make things. A high school athletic director adds that fathers need to spend as much time helping their daughters in sports as they spend with their sons. Readiness for reading relies on good hand-eye coordination, so ball-tossing is valuable play.

Reading to and with our children establishes a habit and a skill for a lifetime. A recent *New Yorker* cartoon showed a daughter in bed and her dad in a rocking chair nearby. He was reading his paper and she was listening to a story on her cassette recorder! That qualified as physical presence, but intellectual-emotional absence.

Bruno Bettelheim, in his book *The Uses of Enchantment: The Meaning and Importance of Fairy Tales,* helps parents understand how valuable fairy tales are. Unlike many "real life" stories written for children today, they provide satisfying solutions, happy endings without the heavy moralizing of fables. They allow children four major elements: fantasy, recovery from danger, escape, and consolation. Justice is done to the evil doer and order returns to the world. Bettelheim cautions that parents should not explain the meaning of the fairy tales. Instead, let children understand them at their current level. Throughout their lives, they will return to those tales, consciously or unconsciously, on varying levels of complexity. Children do understand that the tales are fantasy; having parents share the stories with them lets them know that their own anxieties and fantasies are not unique and there are acceptable solutions.

Trips to the library should be a regular experience for pre-schoolers and their parents. The children's sections of most libraries today are a treasure trove of delightful books. Being allowed to select two or five each visit is a cherished experience for little ones who see getting their own library card as a passport to being big.

Monitoring the *quality and quantity of television-watching* by pre-schoolers is another critical role for parents. Most educators feel that some exposure is beneficial. The major criticisms are that television shows for pre-schoolers have so many short segments that the viewers' attention span is shortened rather than lengthened by the experience, and that preschoolers need active learning, not the passive response to television. The temptation for parents is to use television as a babysitter; it would be preferable to help our children learn to be self-entertaining during regularly scheduled quiet time each day. (See also Chapter 69.)

Elementary School

Habits and schedules that are started in pre-school form the foundation for the elementary school years. The mother of a third grader at Fort Belvoir Elementary School (VA), was delighted to receive a questionnaire from her son's teacher. He eagerly explained that he would get special credit if his mother and father could check off four or five of the following:

- Do you have a specific area for your child to do homework?
- Do you have a specific time each day for doing homework?
- Do you assist your child by helping with spelling and multiplication tables?
- Do you look at the graded work your child brings home?
- Do you display your child's work?

In a very nice way, the teacher was reminding parents of what they could do to enhance their children's learning. We parents can structure the environment in terms of a place and time to study so that the regular *routine of learning* becomes a habit in our homes.

A place to study for early elementary schoolers may be in the kitchen or dining room, but their own desk in their room is preferable by the late elementary school years. A place for their projects, such as a table or part of the workbench in the basement is ideal as well. As Brenda Glenn says, "It is important for kids to have a space of their own for whatever they want to do in it. If you don't encourage studying, you're never going to get it; so set a time and clear off the dining room table, if necessary."

The *length of study time* should be adjusted to fit our children's ages. It is not a punishment. It is a tool for increasing their attention span with as few distractions as possible. It should be flexible to the extent that a child could elect to study earlier or later on a special occasion when the opportunity warrants the change.

The best time to study is a time when parents will be accessible. Parents can use the study time to do desk work, such as family finances and letters, or reading; that way we are role models for our children. Margaret Marston says simply, "Learning is hard work. It requires time and effort." In her own household, she found that she would often read in bed during the study time, and bit by bit, her bed would have visitors for help with their studies or just plain company.

Asking about children's work in school should be a routine as well. Part of that discussion can take place at the dinner table. Children can share what they have learned or experiences that they have had. New assignments can be talked about, so parents have an idea when a project will be due and what kind of resources will be necessary. Is a trip to the library in order? Are special supplies needed? Planning in advance is a good habit to learn early.

We should not underestimate the *power of our interest* in our children's work and *our willingness to display it* where all can see. Their efforts gain stature by such a simple act as posting their story or drawing on the refrigerator. Some parents use the walls to the basement as the display gallery for their children's work. Others invest in a handsome frame, and hang their works in a prominent place. Some can be displayed on the all-important bulletin boards that children have in their rooms.

Monitoring their work is another facet of showing interest. Margaret Marston agrees that "the kids may not always like it, but you tend to do a little better when you know you're going to be held accountable. Consistent interest is the key, not sporadic -- not just when there's a problem."

Connecting our children to other sources of education in our communities begins at this time. Museums and nature centers, Scouts, church, sports, and lessons in talent or interest areas all fall in this category. These amenities are harder for dual career parents, but can be accomplished through co-op arrangements (see pages 428-29), hiring a local teenager or college student to chauffeur or instruct, and through establishing work hours that enable us to do it ourselves.

We can introduce our children to the *daily newspaper* by the midelementary years. The comics are not a bad place to begin, but they can progress to news of their school, community, and finally, the front page.

Sharon Steindam and other elementary school principals and teachers added a few more requisites for parents at this level. Make sure children have had a *good breakfast* before they come to school. They are seeing up to one third of their students being left by working parents to get their own breakfasts -- the the children don't follow through. With the bulk of reading and math studied before lunch, many children complain of being "tired" or "not feeling well." They certainly are not capable of doing their best. (The need for breakfast continues through high school and college!)

Parents should attend the *teacher conferences* that many systems offer instead of report cards for the first and fourth marking periods. These one-to-one opportunities to discuss students' strengths and areas needing work are very beneficial for parents, students, and teachers. Parents can share their expectations and concerns, and can ask for guidance and help from their ally, the teacher. Principals are seeing a rise in the number of parents who do not show, using the excuse, "we work." We can arrange to be there if we care enough.

Children are coming to school sick in greater numbers these days. Principals attribute this to the "inconvenience factor" for working parents. By the time parents can be contacted by the school and they actually arrive, children often spend a couple of hours being watched by the school secretaries and children get the message on their parents' priorities. Some resort to attention-seeking devices with either their parents or teacher as the target. We need to listen to these unspoken pleas.

Parents tend to be relatively *involved in their children's school* at this level, attending PTA meetings, baking cookies, and helping out with the school fair, library, and field trips. Dennis Hill, one of our high school principals, sees another trend as children enter junior high. "Parents tend to say, 'You're on your own.'" He sees it partly as a letdown after "having attended so many meetings and having volunteered for everything. I see the phenomenon in other organizations, too, when people have served for six years. It also has to do with students wanting to divorce their mom and dad from school, and the parents are willing to let them assume more responsibility. Toward the end of the child's junior year, though, parents tune back in to school because it's a crucial time in their lives. Where will their children go to college?"

Junior High School

Sharon Steindam urges parents to remain committed to their schools at the secondary level, but perhaps in a new way. "Be involved with the school advisory committee (volunteers appointed by the school board) which has the official responsibility for monitoring school programs. *Keep the schools accountable* -- not in a negative way, but by being interested in the county guidelines and the test results. Help keep principals aware of strengths and weaknesses as you see them so we can say, here's where our school needs to focus."

She sees the need to continue setting aside time daily for homework, asking about what happened in school, and valuing education. "I want to see children pushed." This is meant in the most positive way, that their *abilities should be stretched* both at home and at school.

"Monitor television watching. It can be such a time waster. Reading is becoming a lost art because it cannot compete with the visual medium. Parents should set the maximum number of hours to be watched a week. Let the children circle their *choices* on the weekly schedule, so that they have the choice but must *discipline themselves.*" Neil Postman in *The Disappearance of Childhood* states that parents should provide an on-going critique of the themes and values being presented on television.

Dennis Hill believes that at this level, parents' thrust should be on *communication*. While he agrees that we may not all see eye to eye, we will at least know what each other is thinking, keep the avenues open for discussion, and develop a respect for each other's point of view. He says that *listening* is the most important of all. "The tendency is to jump to a decision. Parents really need to listen...then you can jump!" He is a father, too, so knows that practicing what he preaches is hard.

One of the main times for listening continues to be dinner time. Margaret Marston sees it as a time to learn how to question "in a dignified manner." Parents should set an atmosphere in which questioning is a healthy, not an intimidating endeavor. *Critical thinking skills* are built this way. "Everyone has to rally here at six o'clock -- no excuses. No one spends the night at someone else's house on a school night." Those absolutes ensure the continuity of family discussions.

High School

This brings us to our final role as parents: *perspective keeping*. Dennis Hill first approached this concept when discussing the need to keep the *balance between school work and after-school jobs*. He and Brenda Glenn agree that high school students can learn a great deal through a job, such as "the responsibilities of being on time, completing tasks, working with a boss, and meeting the public. But because a little money can go to their head, and because they are often treated more as an adult on the job than at home or school, they slowly let their job take precedence over their school work. Rather than letting the situation become extreme, and then having to issue an ultimatum, be aware on a daily basis.

"Know your children's guidance counselors and talk with them frequently. That way they can support family expectations and help you nip any problems in the bud. Most parents seem to wait for an invitation to come to school," complained Brenda Glenn. She wishes they would come frequently, when things are going well, just to say thanks to a teacher. She talks of the joy of running into parents and students in the grocery store. "Then there's the potential for familiarity, for the sense of being whole people. It opens up communication and makes it easier for parents to call or visit. We can focus on the kids and reinforce each other as joint educators."

For military families there is an additional sense in which we must maintain the perspective. Unlike those whose children remain in one location with fairly constant friendships and with a school system whose basic emphasis is consistent, we must contend with variables in these domains. We need to have a strong sense of our own goals and values in order to help our children evaluate their changing environments.

The bottom line is that good parenting is hard work and takes time. Although the quality versus quantity of time argument has been popular with parents over the last few years, it bears renewed evaluation. I hold out for an increased quantity of time to be devoted to our children. Warm-up time is required before one reaches one's peak of performance -- whether in playing sports or a musical instrument, learning, or parenting.

Originally appeared as "Parents: Partners in Education" in Family, August 1984., and in the Camden County Tribune as "Foundations Established for Pre-schoolers Can be Base for Growth" and "Parents Can Help Enrich Their Children's Learning Experiences," August 15 and 22, 1985.

Challenging Children:
Their Needs and Roles for Parents

We cannot sufficiently challenge your child in school. You simply will have to keep him busy after school. Your daughter is a troublemaker in class. She's always asking questions, challenging what I've just said. She often finishes her work too rapidly and distracts the other students.

If you have heard variations on these themes, you may have a gifted child in your household, one of an estimated five percent of our population. Many people assume that gifted (academic) or talented children are no different from other youngsters their age, and that no special parenting skills are required. Wrong! However, gifted children do share some of the needs of all children, so some of our basic parenting roles below would be *true for all children.*

Conducive Climate Providers: As parents we should strive to provide an environment in which our children may study, develop interest and skills, and explore creatively. We need to provide an area to work in, supplies, tools, and the encouragement to pursue interests. Studies of mathematically precocious girls show that they had access to "boys' toys" and games when they were little .... games that required strategy, manipulation, and what-if? situations.

Communicators: Discuss daily activities and thoughts about current events at the dinner table. Keep the avenues of communications open, especially with teenagers. Don't require a consensus, but develop a healthy respect for each other's point of view. Model your own respect for learning. Share fairy tales with your children when they are young.

Congratulators: Take a praise-giving vs. negative, perfectionist posture adopted by many parents. Display your children's work.

Caregivers: We can help our children understand that we love them unconditionally, though we may dislike specific actions or products.

Continuity Providers: In a world that is changing as rapidly as ours, and in a country whose citizens move at the rate of one out of five every year, our children need a constancy of rules and values in our families.

The following roles are more specific to parents of gifted children. However, teachers, leaders of youth groups, and parents of all children may find hints they can adapt for their own uses.

Co-adventurers, Catalysts, Explorers: Share your joy, your contagious enthusiasm for your own, as well as your children's specific interests. In our family, we have shared poetry, photography, woodworking, music, gardening, canoeing, and hiking in the woods.

This diversity of interests showed up in the 25th reunion yearbook that I completed recently for my class at Smith College. The 200+ profiles of gifted women show they have not only excelled in areas widely tangential to their undergraduate majors, but they have shared their wealth of interests with their children. For example, a chemistry Ph.D. has had her children's books published, her music performed, and her watercolors sold. She has shared her love of writing and photography with her boys.

As children develop their own specific areas of interest, parents can be fellow journeymen. They often need someone with whom to share ideas learned, and someone to understand the overwhelming compulsion of the creative process when it occurs. Their peers may not be appropriate buddies in this domain because they do not have the intensity of interest or the level of understanding of their gifted friends.

Connectors: As our children's interests progress beyond our capabilities, we can research what is available and link them with mentors, programs, and organizations. We can urge community organizations to provide opportunities for gifted students. For example, churches can allow talented musicians to join the adult choir based on their level of achievement, not age. Young artists could contribute their work to newsletters and booklets. Special musical productions and children's sermons can be given by young people (and enjoyed by the entire congregation). Organizations offering a wide range of ages and tasks are ideal for gifted children.

Collaborators: You can work *with* your children on projects and grow together in ability and sensitivity. My children and I have collaborated on musical performances, articles, illustrations, and photography for church flyers and magazine articles. Collaboration differs from living vicariously through one's children. All of you are growing through joint efforts.

Be prepared for the day that you children's abilities surpass yours in a given field. Be ready to connect your flutist to a better accompanist when she is ready. She will need the experience of working with others, too.

Commentators: Gifted children are more perceptive than their peers, and often more critical thinkers than adults with whom they come in contact. As parents, you can open discussion on the sermon just heard or the plot of the television program just watched. Sharing your honest evaluation is important. Feel free to contradict the message delivered by an "authority." In our family, we have fostered the concept of *earned respect* vs. *automatic respect* for a person or a source of information. For children quick to spot hypocrisy, this is a far healthier position than unquestioning acceptance.

Gifted children often have a heightened sensitivity to others' emotions and thoughts. One game that my daughter has loved playing whenever we are in a theater or on an airplane is to guess what the people we see are really like and to match them with an appropriate first name!

Consolers: We need to be accessible listeners. Build in occasions to have quiet time with each child. Warm-up time is required, so don't scrimp. Our car has been the site of many special sharing times, en route to lessons or activities.

Counselors: There are three basic kinds of counseling you can share with your gifted children: *reactive, preparatory, and career*. In the *reactive* category will be the sharing of their experiences. My daughter once shared her sense of being outside herself, watching herself play a role. When she mentioned it to her friends, they said, "You're weird!" She clearly wanted to know if I had experienced it so that she wouldn't be alone. When I told her I had grown up with that sense, and had always presumed that others did, she felt greatly relieved.

Preparatory counseling is given on the theory that being forewarned is forearmed. Talk with your children about good stress reduction techniques before exams or a performance. Creative people often experience a natural high that bears similarity to a drug-induced state. The body releases endomorphins, and one can feel quite exhilarated but frightened by the experience. Knowing that such an intense sensation may accompany a creative period would allow a child to cope with it appropriately.

Another fairly unusual capability of some gifted children is *directed dreaming*. As the name implies, the dreamer can determine the scenario of a dream much like plugging a software package into a computer. Various strategies or solutions can be tried out as a subconscious problem-solving or creative technique.

Career counseling should be shared with school professionals. Pay close attention to the results of standard tests (e.g. the Strong-Campbell Interest Inventory -- usually given at the tenth or eleventh grade). You also might avail yourselves of an opportunity to take the Myers-Briggs Personality Inventory, which indicates a person's preferred mode of action. Career discovery programs are offered by a number of colleges as summer programs for high school students. They are valuable opportunities for your child to test his or her interest and ability in a given career field before having to commit to a specific major in college. For example, the Harvard Career Discovery program allows people of a wide age range to explore architecture, urban planning, and landscape architecture as potential career fields.

Coordinators: On a more mundane level, parents of gifted children need to help them leave leisure blocks for creative, daydreaming time. Gifted children tend to overbook their waking hours, even though they need less sleep than other children ...not to mention their parents!

Controllers: Although we want to teach service to one's community, we need to help our gifted children choose their involvements carefully. They should consider the offers and requests; we can help them learn how to say "No" graciously. At points, parents need to ensure that community organizations do not "use" their children unfairly. Opportunity is one thing; not paying for professional abilities is another.

Change Agents: As parents we must often be the ones who educate schools and school boards (not to mention other parents) about the abilities and needs of gifted children. The children themselves are powerless and often very vulnerable.

Contributors: When we contribute to our communities, we are role models for our children. Research on children whose parents have been actively involved with their school has shown that the children perform better academically than those of equal ability whose parents are not involved.

Continuous Learners: As a follow-up to the research above, our pursuit of learning in our own areas of interest gives our children a model for a lifetime. This has become especially true for mothers, whose daughters look to them as prototypes as they begin their own search for the appropriate balance of family and career in their lives. Sons are watching, too. A dad's valuing of his children's intellect or talent shows up as a highly positive factor in most studies of achievers, whether they be girls or boys. Our impact is far greater than most of us can imagine.

Originally appeared as "Challenging Children" in <u>Family</u>, *August 1986.*

Precious Play

At a recent Smithsonian Institution seminar, "What is Creativity?" I was reminded of the importance of play, both for children and adults. Jerome Kagan, a professor of psychology at Harvard University, defined play as "having fun...an inner state." He reminded us that it is our state of mind that matters, not our activity or product. What might look like work (or nonsense) to one person might be a special experience for another.

Professor Kagan also talked of the need for creatives to maintain their sense of awe, of wonder. Most children start with this wondrous approach to life; it's only later that we allow the magic to fade. So as we approach the mid-summer "There-Is-Nothing-To-Do" doldrums, let's help our kids create a little magic -- and reinvigorate our own lives while we're at it.

Kids -- Your Excuse to Play, Too!

As adults, we can do lots of things if we have children in tow, that we probably couldn't get away with by ourselves. A grown adult has a hard time explaining why she is stretched out on the ground with a "bug box" or magnifier in hand, examining the flora and fauna within inches of her nose. Add a Girl Scout troop and hardly anyone asks questions!

Imagination

Children are a wonderful excuse to explore a myriad of phases of your personality. You can add in their fantasy and practice your mime skills when they are little and need responses to their attempts. How many "pretend culinary treats" have you requested, and then appreciatively "consumed," as you wiled away hours with your kids at the beach? "I'd like a steak and mashed potatoes and a malted milk, please," and off they go to create the menu out of sand.

Children's Educational Needs

How often have you climbed a jungle gym or pushed your child in a swing and said, "Where shall we go? To Africa? To the ocean? To the zoo? " When a choice is made, you all move in time and space, imagining and describing as you go. "Oh, look at the gorilla. What is he doing?" Your child, who has been joined by a gaggle of children, responds with something astute or absurd, and you move onto the next imagined cage.

Let's never grow too "old" to enjoy and value the make-believe, the curiosity and exploration of children. I hope that blank pieces of paper, a pen, a pair of scissors, and a rainbow of markers will continue to be my favorite tools, promising hours of delight with no need for a companion.

Playtime and Building Skills

Play has its serious side as well...at least it is serious as we have fun helping our children build skills that they may not develop otherwise. For example, we can help our daughters build their math skills through increasing their *field dependence* -- the visual way in which boys traditionally excel because of their games outdoor in which they explore, draw maps, and crawl over obstacles of all sorts. The Cub Scout manual used to require the design and use of an obstacle course. When our son designed one for his birthday party one year, his younger sister was busy testing herself on the ladder run, the garbage can jump, the rope swing, and the swing set climb, so that she could shine when the gang came for the party. Girls need play clothes that allow them the same freedom to explore and climb as the boys, and they need our encouragement to do so.

Strategy is another skill that girls often do not develop because few of the games or sports in which they are traditionally involved require it. Team sports usually have elements of strategy, as do hide and seek, packing the car for a trip, planning a surprise of any sort, or tracking a wild animal.

Observing and Classifying

Animal tracking leads to another pair of skills that we want to accentuate. Children have both the desire and ability to learn very specific information about an area of interest (and huge words, if possible!) At our most recent duty station, the new submarine base at Kings Bay, GA, I walked our black labrador every afternoon along the sandy back roads. I often had several neighborhood children for company, and they learned quickly to keep their eyes peeled on the road for evidence of deer, armadillos, rabbits, and snakes (we saw very few signs of snakes).

In the process, they often found fossils of all sorts: sharks' teeth, shells, the insides of clams, and once in a while, whales' ear bones and horses' teeth. Imagine their parents' amazement when they rushed home saying, "I've found a turitella from the Pleistocene Era!" Sheer joy in accumulating knowledge was the enticement to follow the "Pied Piper" and my dog. And I soon had a few adults in tow.

Testing and Experimenting

Testing and experimenting are two more skills we can share with our children -- hands-on experience without constant evaluation of the product. Boys need time in the kitchen, experimenting with funnel pancakes for breakfast, and girls need time with tools and chemistry sets. We need to provide the cross-gender experiences to fill the usual gaps that occur when children have only the stereotypical experiences of their sex.

Ideas for the Doldrums

A valuable source of ideas is a children's guide to activities in your area. If none exists, you might want to enlist the aid of your wives' club or family service/support center to produce one. Several years ago, I produced such a book with the help of the Kings Bay Officers' Wives' Club: *Let's Go Fly a Kite! Ideas for Kids in NE Florida & SE Georgia.* We listed more than 300 activities for families within an hour's radius of the new submarine base, and our opening chapter focused on kids' favorite low- or -no-cost pastimes:

Dress Up -- save old hats, dresses, belts, jewelry, purses, and have a full-length mirror nearby.
Bug watching -- look at insects (or their own hands) with a magnifier.
Collect -- everything! Shells, postcards, rocks.
Read up -- children should have their own library cards.
Sky watching -- lie on their back and look at the sky for tree top patterns and cloud shapes.
Body Tracing -- trace the outline of their hands, feet, or whole body .
Shadow art -- make silhouettes on the wall with their hands; a slide projector or a strong light source will do.
Shopping by mail -- "order" items from catalogs; this can be a great math game with a set budget.
Paper play -- make paper dolls from clothing catalogs.
Make their own postcards -- from stiff paper cut to regulation size; send to friends and grandparents.
Mold clay -- modeling builds good spatial, hand-eye skills and can be a soothing activity.
Interior decorating -- furnish their cardboard dream house or a single room with catalog and magazine illustrations.
Build -- sand castles, blocks, wood scraps, cartons, blankets over a card table, or a sheet teepee.

Children's Educational Needs

Spatter-paint their own cards -- a toothbrush, a piece of screen, and some water-based powdered paint (tempera) can turn ferns, bugs, and flowers into unique patterns.

Take things apart -- never throw away an old motor or clock!

Keep a list of books they've read -- star the best ones (3x5 cards make a good file).

Treasure hunts -- give simple or complex maps and/or written directions for inside or outside.

Interview -- a doll, statue, puppet, or another child; use a tape recorder to play back their own voices.

Display their art or written work -- on the refrigerator or in a special frame (the big acrylic frames are easy to change displays).

Have their own bulletin board -- for an ever-changing collection of meaningful items.

Make their own flashcards or small books -- out of 3x5 cards; a hole punch and two snap rings will complete the book.

Make up stories -- draw the names of four random items out of a hat and weave a story around them. (For example: a boat, a needle, a full moon, and a gorilla!)

Draw maps -- of their room, house, yard, neighborhood, ideal town, or fantasy world like Pooh Bear's.

Play "Tickle-Rub-Scratch-My-Back" -- on the beach or at bed time -- this takes two people.

Watch big machinery work -- a fascinating thing for you & kids!

Make a puzzle -- make their own jigsaw puzzles with magazine pictures, a glue stick, light cardboard, and scissors.

Cook with you -- peel carrots, grate cheese, choose ingredients or toppings for omelets, make pancakes or funnel cakes of their own designs, make ice cream sundaes, and make ice tray popsicles.

Costuming -- make costumes out of paper bags.

Gardening -- plant, weed, and tend their own garden.

Be "workers" -- like firemen, waitresses, drivers, cooks, or pilots; keep hats or construction paper for hats handy.

Design their own license plates -- they become increasingly symbolic!

Build cities -- with recycled items, blocks, their own small cars, and a large sheet of paper on which to draw the layout.

Sort it out -- sort a collection of odds & ends into categories (such as an assortment of buttons, nuts & bolts, beads, or your junk drawer).

Make jewelry -- out of buttons, bolts, beads, fishing bobbers, lures, snaps, and colored paper clips.

Grow a window garden -- from potatoes, avocado seeds, and carrot tops.

Sculpt with pipe cleaners -- keep away from eyes and ears.
Make puppets -- out of socks, yarn, and felt.
Make musical instruments -- from kitchen and garage utensils -- percussion items are favorites.
Make masks -- little children often don't like their whole face covered or painted, so use glasses and animal noses and ears.

The list goes on and on. Armed with some of these activities, the right supplies, and a truckload of creativity -- yours and your kids' -- you'll have no problems tacking those mid-summer blahs. And don't be surprised if you have as much fun as your kids!

Ammunition for Boring Afternoons

Here are some supplies to keep on hand for those boring summer afternoons:

construction paper
scratch paper
glue stick
safety scissors
stapler
water-based colored pens
pencils & sharpener
rubber bands
paper clips (colored ones are exciting)
pipe cleaners
straws
old magazines to clip
hole punch
string and rope
brads (to make movable pieces on paper sculptures
clip rings (to make small books and other things)
3 x 5 cards (for flashcards, games, or small books)
a scrapbook
a bulletin board
boxes (big and small)
an old lunch box (makes a good carrying case for supplies plus a surface to write on)
shelf paper (for banners, maps, body drawings, murals)
clear Contac paper (to laminate favorite photos or to make table mats from ferns, leaves, etc.)
sketch pad (one with a spiral binding is easy to use)
plastic milk bottle tops (for Tiddly Winks & other games)
old purses, hats, shoes, belts, jewelry for dress-up (yard sales and thrift shops are good sources)
old keys
tennis balls
plastic berry baskets
paper towel cylinders
PVC scrap piping (can be used for horns, tunnels)—get from plumbing supply store
plastic bowls
old thread spools
scrap materials
old blankets and sheets (to build tents)
box of nuts & bolts, screws, old locks, motors
old wheels—to build own vehicle
own hammer, screw driver, and pliers
clay or Playdough
tape (masking usually doesn't leave as bad marks on walls as the clear variety)
first-aid kit
sense of humor! •

Good Books on Kids' Activities:

The Anti-Coloring Books by Susan Striker and Edward Kimmel (Holt, Rinehart and Winston, New York: 1978 -- plus updated versions). These paperback "coloring books" allow your children to draw imaginative responses to fanciful situations.

Please Touch, also by Susan Striker (Simon & Schuster, Inc., New York). This book emphasizes ways to stimulate your child's creative development (with good charts on tools and activities for specific ages).

Boy Scout and Girl Scout manuals -- most public libraries have copies of the current versions. Use the badges and required activities as triggers for age-appropriate experiences.

Bringing Out the Best by Jacqulyn Saunders and Pamela Espeland (Free Spirit Publishing, 123 N. Third St., Suite 716, Minneapolis, MN 55401 -- 1986). Their sections on activities to do with your child and toys are especially good.

Family Times, developed by the Cooperative Extension Service, University of Wisconsin, to help families build family strengths through working and playing together: $6 ppd. payable to Wisconsin Clearinghouse. Send to: Wisconsin Clearinghouse, Dept. Family, P.O. Box 1468, Madison, WI 53701.

Lollipops & Parachutes by Donna Stiscak (McGraw-Hill Book Company, New York: 1984). The author lists 120 stimulating learning activities by age group and by educational skills.

Smart Girls, Gifted Women by Barbara A. Kerr, Ph.D. (Ohio Psychology Publishing Co., 131 N. High St., Suite 300, Columbus, OH 43215 --- 1985). This book has insights on the special needs of girls as they grow up.

What Works, by William J. Bennett, Secretary of the U. S. Dept. of Education (1986). A summary of ideas for helping our children learn. Available from Consumer Information Center, Pueblo, CO 81009.

Let's Go Fly a Kite! Activities for Kids in NE Florida & SE Georgia. To order a copy, send $7.50 ppd. to Lifescape Enterprises, P. O. Box 218, West Mystic, CT 06388.

Originally appeared as "Precious Play" in Family, July 1988. The chart is from Family.

Summer Fun

Recently I opened a package of bath soap and found myself transported to Camp Turkey Creek. It was amazing what memories the scent of citronella brought back -- that much despised mosquito repellant that all good Girl Scouts took to camp -- that I adored! Those visions of tents, latrines, lashed wash stands, and "log cabin fires" reminded me that many survival skills and a lifetime love of the woods had resulted from those all-too-brief Scout camps. I had also learned how to get along with three other girls in a tent, how to conquer fears of the unknown at night, and to do my fair share of the unpleasant tasks that are part of group living.

Summer will soon be upon us, and whether or not it will be citronella-scented for us and for our children, it should be seen as an opportunity for special experiences. What is special for each of us will vary widely but the need to plan ahead is greater than in years past. Pressures on existing summer options will be heavy due to economic factors and the need of dual career families for formal programs.

Some parents resist over-planning their children's summer schedule, believing that the school year is structured enough and kids need a vacation. Three weeks into a summer without some special plans will find these folks in a vacuum, not knee deep in recreation. There are super possibilities for your kids this summer, from elementary school through high school Knowing *where to look* and *when* is the key. The answer to *when* is NOW.

Resources

Where? Three easy resources will give you an overview of what is generally available in your community: *your school system, your public library, and your city/county recreation department.*

Children's Educational Needs

Public Schools

Secondary school guidance offices receive flyers for local and non-local offerings. Most keep a file or box of all the materials. Some post the information regularly in display windows or give lists in PTA newsletters. A lunch hour spent perusing this file could be very productive for you and your teenager.

The school system itself will generally have summer school offerings in three basic categories: make-up and strengthening, courses for new credit (acceleration), and enrichment. Generally, elementary school provisions are enrichment and basic review only, while secondary school students have more options. You need to sign up shortly after brochures on these programs are available in order to be sure of a slot. Bus transportation is often included in the usually reasonable fee.

Arlington County Public Schools (VA) not only offer the traditional remedial courses, but offer opportunities for students to accelerate their studies in math, English, and government. Typing is also a new credit course, and quite young students may petition into it based on their academic record and interest. Students may enroll in instrumental and vocal music at three levels of proficiency, and art at two levels. Driver's education can be taken so that school year course time is freed up.

Arlington's Career Center, which is the vocational arm of our school system, offers three-week mini-courses in automobile tune-up, auto body repair, television production, photography, carpentry, commercial art, computer programming, animal sciences, speed reading, and think skills. (I wish I were a kid with three summers to spare!)

For grades 5-7, the Outdoor Lab course takes students for a Monday - Friday residential session. Geology, astronomy, botany, zoology, and tents are all part of the $80 price tag.

Special education students also have the option of an Outdoor Lab week plus a myriad of other summer programs. You will be amazed what public schools offer.

Public Library

Your library can serve you in your search in three ways.

1   It will post or file the announcements of local summer programs.

2   Many library systems initiate their own summer series, ranging from craft and movie sessions to summer book clubs. It's always more fun to

Summer Fun   463

read when you can share your discoveries and reactions with people of your own age. If your library doesn't offer a mystery club or Great Books, you might suggest a trial run. A Nancy Drew Club might be a big attraction for 5th - 7th graders, or an Agatha Christie Clan might attract the Nancy Drew graduates.

3   Your library also serves as a resource for information on non-local summer opportunities. The best reference material I know of is Porter-Sargent's *Guide to Summer Camps and Summer Schools*. It is updated annually, and most libraries put it in their reference section under #R373. It gives a full listing of offerings by subject, talent, and sport categories.

City or County Recreation Department

Your city or county recreation department may offer courses and day camps for people aged three to 103! In addition to the usual art, music, and dance classes, you may find that there are travelling tennis teams, summer theater productions for kids and adults to participate in or attend, and open studio arrangements. Read the registration date and time carefully. We four O'Beirnes have stood in huge lines to get our first choices. *Go early*, especially for the day camp session slots.

Organizations that Have Summer Programs

Beyond these super sources, you have a variety of other possibilities:

• Obviously as a former Girl Scout and leader, I feel that the local Girl and Boy Scout Councils are good resources. Many offer reasonable day camps as well as the residential camp sessions. You children *do not* have to be Scouts to participate.
• The YMCA and YWCA have similar programs, as does 4-H in some areas. To find information on 4-H, contact your county Cooperative Extension Service (listed in the Yellow Pages under Gov't, State.")
• Your local churches often sponsor summer Bible schools and have ties to camp facilities. Some churches even give camperships to deserving youngsters.
• Your American Red Cross chapter will be able to tell you where and when courses in junior and senior lifesaving, first aid, CPR, boating and water safety, and "Tending Our Tots" will be given. Pool management is a valuable course for teens to take for future employment options.
• Your post or base youth activities division will have summer offerings. Some, such as the West Point Youth Camp, plan extensive residential programs. While family members at West Point have priority, there often is room for additional youngers ages 7-15. For further information, write Youth Activities, Bldg. 693, West Point, NY 10996.

Children's Educational Needs

Educational-Career-Talent Programs

Nationwide opportunities for exploring and honing talents include programs at the National Music Camp (Interlochen, Michigan) in dance, music, art, and theater; Northwestern University in the performing arts and journalism; Rhode Island School of Design in the visual arts; Middlebury College Language Schools; and Chautauqua Summer School (NY) in music, art, theater, and dance. These are all open to high school students. Your teenager also should be aware of the opportunities for rising seniors to attend Boys' and Girls' State. Some states sponsor a Governor's School for the Gifted (especially VA and NC), and there are varying summer provisions for All State Band members. Most of these are free or almost. School guidance counselors have this information.

Other kinds of career exploration can take place at universities. Arlington schools have arranged one-week credit courses in architecture and engineering with the University of Virginia for 9th-12th graders. After enjoying that experience immensely several years ago, our son went to the Harvard Graduate School of Design Career Discover Program two summers ago. It is a six-week-long design program for rising high school seniors plus college undergraduates and graduates. Living in a dormitory away from home is fine preparation for high schoolers; emotional, financial, and laundry management lessons are learned, too!

Alternatives to Formal Learning

Some alternatives include buying a ping pong or pool table. Keep a stock of cold punch in your refrigerator, and you'll know where your kids are -- and everybody else's. You can organize a "Not Ready for Prime Time Trio" for your budding musicians. Perhaps music could be borrowed from your school music library.

You could arrange a kid-swap with friends who have moved away. Each family could have the kids one week, freeing up the other parents. The kids benefit from the change of scene and households.

Rent a series of simple to complex tents from Recreation Services. Your own back yard can be quite an adventure after dark. Rent a canoe or row boat to explore nearby ponds, rivers, or swamps. Use flora and fauna books from your library. Whatever your choices, summer can be our most humane season if we balance continued learning with fun, and structured activities with contemplative, creative time.

Originally appeared as "Summer Vacation, or What to do with the kids" in Army, Navy, Air Force Times, *May 16, 1983 and "Summer Fun for Children of All Ages" in* Family, *March 1984.*

Summer Job Strategies for Teens

(Clap your hands!)

Want a job?
And leisure, too?
Even though
You're in Timbuktu?
Want some cash?
Some clothes with dash?
Want to do more
Than slingin' hash?
Want some work that's "meaningful?"
Not just grim, demeaningful?
Then pack it in and listen up...
<u>Family's</u> cup is steaming-full.

(Clap your hands!)

Military teens,
Like their civilian friends,
Want to.......
Need to......
Try their wings,
Strut their stuff,
Join the workforce,
Though the goin's tough.

    Cadence aside, teens want to use their summer productively. That generally translates to being out of mom's hair and having the magical mix of work they enjoy (paid or unpaid) and some leisure time.

Even though the nationwide labor force statistics say that teens are in big demand, you may live overseas or at isolated stateside installations where employment is rough, or you may feel that employment will come soon enough, and the teen years are critical years to explore career options, pursue academic- or talent-related training, or travel. *Family*, therefore, has collected a wide variety of options, hoping that one will be "just right" for the teen(s) in your household. We hope parents will share this article (*Pass It On!*) with their teens who need to be part of the research-and-decision-making team.

Where to Search for Ideal Summer Opportunities

Your library: Books suggested throughout this article can be found in either the reference or stack section. Look in the card catalog under *summer employment, employment, teens, summer programs, and summer camps*. If your library and the other resources listed below are short on good references, you may need to purchase some of our recommended books. Additional titles can be found in *Books in Print* in the reference section of your library.

Your installation newspaper: It may carry notices of teen volunteer and employment opportunities.

Your installation education center: This center should have materials on local and non-local education programs in which teens may participate.

Your installation youth activities coordinator: He or she will have information on programs offered and opportunities for teens to work as staff counselors or assistants.

Your community recreation department: It will have summer program offering s and work opportunities (paid and unpaid). For example, many town and country recreation departments hire lifeguards, park maintenance crew members, ticket takers, fast-food concession operators, and instructors for crafts and sport programs.

Your installation Civilian Personnel Office: It announces positions with Appropriated Fun and Non-Appropriated Fund (NAF) activities. The latter include the swimming pool, bowling alley, clubs, and the exchange. NAF activities tend to hire a fair number of teens and continue their hiring throughout the spring (and sometimes continually over the summer) so that those of you who move this summer still stand a chance at your new location. The Appropriated Fund jobs tend to be highly competitive and applications close in March or early April.

Summer Job Opportunities for Teens

Your installation family member employment coordinator and the volunteer coordinator: Many recruit summer positions for teens and maintain a listing. Call Army Community Services, Air Force Family Support Center, or Navy/Marine Corps Family Service Center.

Your installation chapel or local church: Most churches conduct vacation Bible schools, and some have music and religious drama or puppetry programs. Many are affiliated with regional camps that might interest you as a camper or counselor-in-training. Some churches sponsor teen job banks. You also might find that your church would be interested in you as a summer intern -- in the office, in maintenance/repairs, or youth activities. If you have office or musical skills, you might contact a number of churches to serve as a substitute secretary or organist while the regular employees go on vacation.

Your school counselors and teachers or your college vocational office: They can direct you to established programs such as Boys' and Girls' State, Governor's School, gifted and talented options, educational-talent programs, and internships. (See Chapter 66.) Also possible are summer jobs in construction and automotive repair via your high school vocational and distributive education programs.

Your city or state employment service: this service, listed in the blue pages of your telephone book under city or state agencies, assists youths seeking employment. There are a number of programs designed to assist teens from families with low incomes. (Military pay rates do fall within the guidelines in several programs, and some of these jobs continue into the school year as well, so they are well worth investigating.)

Your volunteer action center: It maintains job listings for several hundred agencies in your community. Also called the Volunteer Center or Bureau, its job is to match volunteers with jobs/internships that need to be done. Look in the white pages of your phone book under *Volunteer*....

Your local Chamber of Commerce: Ask what they have in the way of a teen job bank, and ask whom you should contact to work in the career field of your choice. (Listed in the white pages of the phone book.)

The service clubs in your community (such as Rotary, Kiwanis, and Business and Professional Women): They may offer summer work opportunities or internships. The Chamber of Commerce can direct you to the current leaders of these organizations.

Boy Scouts, Girl Scouts, 4-H, YMCA and YWCA: These organizations offer summer camp programs that are appropriate for teens either as campers, counselors-in-training, or counselors.

American Red Cross: Your local chapter offers courses to qualify you for lifesaving, CPR, and babysitting. The chapter may also know of prospective employers eager for your services once qualified.

Your state parks and forest division: They hold the keys to many summer positions, ranging from lifeguards, ticket takers, and interpretive guides to graphic or landscape workers and engineering assistants. (Look in your phone book under State government.)

Other Options

If you live in areas where teen job opportunities are limited, work with your installation family support and youth activities programs to carve out innovative options. When we lived at the new Naval Submarine Base Kings Bay, GA, our two college teenagers were desperate for meaningful use of the weeks or months they spent in a community where they had not gone to high school. (They were precluded from any work on base due to the nepotism regulations -- and were excluded from any employers in the private sector who had contracts with the base. That made it rough!) Through my contacts with the Camden County Business and Professional Women's organization, I was able to link my daughter with the editor of one of the weekly newspapers. Even in the three weeks she was home, she was able to write feature stories, take a photo that was published, and learn to operate the typesetting machine.

Other teens on base worked with an archaeological team. The possibilities were as broad as their imagination. Volunteer internships with professionals on base could have provided career explorations in such fields as forestry and animal management, architecture, engineering, and printing. The USO, American Red Cross, and Navy Relief welcomed responsible teens in office support as well as program arenas.

Help Your Library Help You: Your installation library would probably be grateful for offers to establish special focus collections (such as summer crafts and play ideas for children, places to visit locally, military family literature, or youth employment) and special exhibits (shells collected in the area, fossil artifacts, stamps, etc.) Your library might also like you to plan reading sessions for different age groups throughout the summer.

Volunteer Apprenticeships: Last year the New London Submarine Base, CT, advertised for teen volunteers at the hospital and VET clinic. Another avenue: seek out experts in your community and offer your assistance (paid or unpaid). Serve as an apprentice to a wallpaper hanger, a graphic artist, an automobile mechanic, a cake decorator, or a picture framer. You can develop skills that will be very marketable.

You can also select *places* you would like to work and offer your services, such as your local science center, pet store, art museum, or landscape firm. For example, last summer, the Smithsonian Institution in Washington, D.C. offered "Discover Graphics," a free program for talented area public high school junior and seniors and their teachers. Participants learned etching and lithography on museum equipment. And some have gone on to win awards and scholarships to art schools and universities. One can also be a volunteer docent in museums -- one particularly popular spot has been the Insect Zoo in the Museum of Natural History!

Your Own Business

If you elect to go into business for yourself, to provide a product or a service, advertising your availability will be very important. Use your installation newspaper, public bulletin boards, and flyers or 3x5 cards that you deliver door to door. (Your installation employment assistance coordinator and the USO maintain lists of military family members providing services.) Two boys in our neighborhood had their names and phone numbers printed on a stiff card which advertised their services, including lawn mowing, pet-sitting, house-sitting, and general attic-garage clean up. Because their card was attractive and easily posted on a refrigerator or bulletin board for reference, they soon had more work than they could handle and had to hire additional friends.

Be imaginative in your offering. Grow your own vegetables and establish regular sales routes. Offer classes in computers, art, calligraphy, or musical instruments. Offer classes in basic sewing and crafts for children in your neighborhood. Run a puppet-making and show "camp" in your garage. Offer a two-hour game session every afternoon from 4:00 - 6:00 p.m. -- the parents in your neighborhood will love you!

Another market ripe for enterprising students is working mothers. What kinds of services do they need? One young man in the Washington, D.C. area who enjoys cooking has started his own cookie route. He has about ten specialties and takes orders for the following week as he delivers this week's batch. (Variations on this include casseroles, salads, children's birthday cakes and party favors, etc.). You would also build a clientele quickly if you offered to paint woodwork, hem dresses, mend children's clothes, or clean kitchen appliances!

Share the things you enjoy doing and you will be an enthusiastic instructor. A great book to trigger your thoughts on your own business is *The Teenage Entrepreneur's Guide: 50 Money-Making Businesses Ideas* ($8.95 paperback from: Surrey Books, 500 North Michigan Avenue, Suite 1940, Chicago, IL 60661l).

Children's Educational Needs

Resources:

Participating in formal camp, academic, or travel programs can be a very productive use of your summer. One of the most complete listings is found in *The Guide to Summer Camps and Summer Schools* (in the reference section of your library or from Porter-Sargent Publishers, 11 Beacon Street, Boston, MA 02108). *The 1990-91 version is $21.00 in paperback.* It will amaze you to find over 1,100 options, ranging from the National Audubon Camp in Maine, the Center for Creative Youth in Connecticut, and the National Music Camp in Michigan to credit and non-credit courses for high school juniors and seniors at the University of Arizona and Southern Methodist University.

Three other fine sources of information are:

Summer Opportunities for Kids and Teenagers (Peterson's Guides): available in your library reference section or at book stores. This book lists programs that offer financial assistance, those with jobs, and very specific interest categories such as pack animal trips, clowning, rappelling, robotics, and windsurfing.

The Directory of American Youth Organizations: A Guide to Over 400 Clubs, Groups, Troops, Teams, Societies, Lodges, and More for Young People is indexed by interest area and gives addresses to contact. It is available in paperback for $14.95 from Free Spirit Publishing Co., 123 North Third St., Suite 716, Minneapolis, MN 55401.

Internships lists thousands of on-the-job training opportunities, including international options. It is available in paperback for $21.95 from Writer's Digest Books, 9933 Alliance Road, Cincinnati, OH 45242.

Military teens often end up with an assortment of commitments -- especially if most local employment opportunities are part-time, if your family has a move or vacation on the horizon, or if your plans include a segment away at camp, school, or traveling. Don't despair! These sometimes frustrating segments do add up. Enjoy the pieces you put together this summer that will help to make you a very interest multi-faceted young adult.

Originally appeared in <u>Family</u> as "Summer Jobs" (March 1984) and "Summer Work" (April 1989).

Hints for the College-Bound

How many parents have wished that they could have done a trial run on the college search and application process before it "counted for real?" Our two children were both high school seniors this past year, so we had the experience in spades. The "we" is all four of the O'Beirnes -- both parents and both kids. Make no mistake -- choosing a college and gaining acceptance is a family affair.

It is also time to tap the wisdom of your friends, school guidance counselors, and teachers. The information in this chapter is the result of things we did right (and wrong), plus hints from four generous experts: Evelyn E. Wilson, Director of Guidance, Wakefield High School Arlington, Virginia; Timothy B. Evers, Counselor, East Lyme High School, Connecticut, and past admissions officer for Connecticut College and Case Western Reserve University (Tim also has a private service to aid students outside of his school); Happy B. Esty, Admission Alumnae Coordinator, Smith College, Northampton, Massachusetts; and Cate Mueller, Admissions Evaluator (10 years) George Washington University, Washington, D.C.

While students can be responsible for many of the sections below, they will need help from their parents, so the "you" referred to can be an individual or group, depending on how your family divides these tasks.

[ ] Take the most demanding schedule you can manage from 9th grade on. Colleges weight the honors and Advanced Placement (AP) classes heavily. Don't wait until 12th grade to start earning your best grades. *Grades are the most important factor for admission.*

[ ] Keep a file of all activities in which you participate plus dates. You will need this data later.

[ ] Spring, 10th grade, take the practice SAT or ACT exam. Check the block indicating you would like to be part of the Talent Search. Then you will receive brochures from many institutions.

[ ] Many students take short courses in the math or verbal skills to be tested by the SAT exam. Just knowing the types of questions to be asked and some helpful test-taking techniques can make a student feel more at ease and ready to do his or her best. For example, it helps to know that in each section of the SAT, questions are arranged from the least to the most difficult.

[ ] October, 11th grade, take the PSAT exam. This is the only test that qualifies you for the National Merit Scholarships.

[ ] Attend College Night at your high school; it is a good opportunity to collect information and talk with alumni or admissions officers.

[ ] Attend group sessions when college admissions officers visit your high school. (Repeat this senior year; you will be remembered.)

[ ] Have a parent-student-guidance counselor discussion of your student's cumulative record. Results of interest inventories and standardized aptitude and achievement tests will be helpful as potential career areas are explored.

[ ] Begin to read college catalogs in the guidance office or school library. *The Index of Majors* will enable you to know which colleges offer the major fields that interest you. For special major fields such as architecture and engineering, *Peterson's Guides* have separate catalogs.

[ ] Determine the qualities of your ideal college.
- Offers your major interest field?
- Location: urban/rural? residential/commuter?
- Size: ratio of faculty to students?
- Cost: is admission "aid-blind?"
- 2 - 4 year or university? Is there sufficient "top" for your field?
- Co-ed or single sex? To evaluate options for women, use *Everywoman's Guide to Colleges and Universities* (Feminist Press).
- Housing: % in dorms; % off campus? single, double rooms? single-sex or co-ed dorms?
- Student body -- make sure this college is compatible with your breadth of experience.
- Types of programs: work/study, honors, study abroad?
- Social and religious activities?
- Sports?

[ ] Some high schools have access to computers which will pool the above information and list possible choices.

[ ] Read catalogs for those choices carefully. If the ones you want to look at are not in your guidance office, send a postcard to the colleges requesting information. Your name and address should be clear.

[ ] Check *The College Handbook, Lovejoy's College Guide, Barron's Profiles of American Colleges,* or *Peterson's Guide to Under-Graduate Study* to see if your SAT or ACT scores are near the range of the most recent freshman class.

[ ] Spring, 11th grade: If you think you might major in a visual or performing art or creative writing, or that you want colleges to consider your talent in one of these areas:
  • Talk with your instructors about taping your music or preparing a portfolio of your work.
  • Take a workshop on portfolio preparation.
  • Read the catalog/application description of what your portfolio or tape will have to cover.
  • Get busy creating your sketches and pottery, or learning the music required.
  • Write to the Arts Recognition and Talent Search (ARTS, Box 2876, Princeton, NJ 08541) for their Prospectus. The music, art, and English curriculum specialists in your school system probably have the previous year's information on file for guidelines.

[ ] April or May, 11th grade: take SAT exam again. If you apply for early decision in the fall of your 12th grade year, you will need this score. Have the score sent to your top three college choices.

[ ] May, take the AP exams. If you have taken Advanced Placement courses, take the exams for potential college credit or advanced standing in college. Send scores to your top three college choices.

[ ] Establish a file for each of your major college choices. This can be a box. All brochures and copies of your letters and application will go in here.

[ ] During April or May, some colleges offer Pre-college Day to 11th grade students. This is a good introduction to the total college search.

[ ] June, 11th grade: take ACHievement test. 11th graders need to take three ACH tests at this point (English & two other subject areas). Choose subjects that you are strong in, are completing junior year

and will not take again your 12th grade year (e.g. chemistry, or the final year of a language). Students who anticipate applying for early decision absolutely need these now.

[ ] Write the admissions office of the four or five colleges of your choice to arrange a visit and interview.
- Check their brochures or catalog in the guidance office to make sure that they grant interviews. Most highly selective colleges require them or say they are highly desirable.
- Plan to visit your last choice colleges first. Save the interviews for your first choices until last, when you have gained experience and confidence.
- Write six weeks in advance of your visit, if it is to be in the summer, or even further ahead, if early fall dates are desired. The appointments fill quickly!

[ ] Prepare your resume.
- Using the information you've been collecting in your file since 9th grade, determine three to four broad categories in which to group your activities. You might choose *special awards, talents and training*, and *extracurricular activities* as your groups, or *scholastic achievements and extracurricular courses, sports, interest/talent areas, community activities,* and *employment*. (Be sure to include Scout awards -- First Class for girls, Eagle for boys.)
- Try to place your strongest area first, and within any given section of your resume, place your strengths first. (Dates or grade level should be given.)
- Type your resume. Put your name and address at the top left. Leave healthy margins for visual appeal (and so admissions personnel have room to make notes). Leave spaces between groups so that you can add additional awards or activities without having to retype the whole thing (unless you are lucky enough to have it on a computer!) Copies are acceptable, so save your original.

[ ] Tim Evers shares these hints on admission interviews:
- Dress counts here. Boys should wear a suit or sports jacket and tie. (If summer heat precludes, a nice shirt will do.) Girls need the equivalent -- a tailored outfit, moderate heels on shoes. Hair should be trim. Your appearance needs to say, "I care about how I look, and this interview is important to me."
- Be punctual. Arrive ahead of time so you will have time to check in with the receptionist and collect your thoughts.
- Be assertive. A firm handshake (boys and girls), eye contact, and attentive posture give a positive impression.

- Give the interviewer a copy of your resume so that he/she has a quick review of your interests - accomplishments for discussion. He or she will probably keep it for your file.
- If you haven't applied yet, bring with you an unofficial transcript of your grades and test scores (from your registrar or guidance counselor) in order to get a more realistic picture of your chances for admission.
- Be informed. Read the catalog before your campus visit, so that your questions do not duplicate easily available information.
- Have a small note pad with questions you want answered (e.g. May you participate in theatrical or performing arts groups even if you do not intend to major in these fields? What percentage of graduates who major in your intended area go on to graduate school, and what are their career fields? Do senior faculty members teach undergraduates, especially introductory level courses, or are junior faculty and fellows given these assignments? Do they want a portfolio or tape of your art or music?)
- Be yourself. Be willing to talk about your personal strengths and weaknesses as a student and as an individual (but try to turn a weakness into a strength by showing what you have learned for the future).
- Share your impressions with your parents. Often the interviewer will close the session by returning you to your parents and asking if they have any questions. (Mom and Dad, the hints are the same for you as for your student. You need to be spiffy, confident, and informed. Wear comfortable shoes. You will walk on tours!)

[ ] Take a tour of the campus.
- Tours arranged by the admissions office and conducted by an enrolled student give the fullest view of the college.
- Make sure you see classrooms, dining facilities, sample dormitory rooms, and other facilities related to your major academic and extracurricular interests. It helps in the future decision process to be able to visualize the whole lifestyle.
- Really look at the campus neighborhood. Can students go off campus safely? Is it a pedestrian, bicycle, or car campus? Is it a weekday-only campus? When is the library open?
- If possible, plan to stay overnight in a dormitory and attend classes. Many colleges offer this opportunity in the fall. Some make special arrangements between your notification of acceptance and your decision date.

[ ] Write a brief thank you letter to each interviewer -- typewritten or by hand on *formal* stationery.

[ ] Determine your four - five college choices. Pick one sure acceptance, one dubious, and three middle of the road. Beware: many public colleges are getting better students than in years past due to their lower fees.

[ ] <u>Fall, 12th grade:</u> Write for applications in *early* fall.

[ ] Take SAT/ACH exams as necessary in fall.

[ ] Application hint: make a copy of the blank application to use as as trial run.

[ ] Read *total* application immediately.
- You may find you need to take additional tests.
- Note the information you will have to obtain.
- If essay questions are involved, begin to think about them. Jot down ideas. Having time to mull over the essays will improve their quality.

[ ] Write the ideal and absolute mailing deadlines on your calendar.

[ ] Type your application. Admissions officers must read so many forms that a handwritten application can have a negative impact. If you must write, use black ink.

[ ] Use your resume to help you list all activities and awards. If the form does not request these, attach a copy of your resume to the application.

[ ] Tim Evers advises avoiding mention of your name in commercial publications like *Who's Who in American High Schools*. He suggests including summer and part-time jobs, volunteer work, and hobbies.

[ ] Some applications have *optional* essays. Admissions counselors advise writing these. It is your opportunity to present yourself; failure to do so is interpreted as lack of interest or inability to write.

[ ] Essay techniques: write your rough draft. Recheck for spelling, grammar, and logical flow. If it looks like the measles, rewrite. Underline the beginning words of the sentences. Variety of structure will enhance your essay. Some can be direct statements: "My most challenging experiences have been..." Others can begin with clauses: "Because I have not decided on a major, a college that provides a wide exploration...." Ask your parents or English teacher to critique. Rewrite. Type on practice form to ensure that it fits.

Hints for the College-Bound

Happy Esty says, "Don't be afraid to add an extra page (not ten!). Fill in gaps. If your grades went down junior year because you had mono, tell the college. Your counselor may forget. Don't be afraid to be creative in your essay. Don't lose sight of your sense of humor."

[ ] If the application to your home state university doesn't have adequate space for you to explain permanent address vs. current address due to military orders, attach an explanation of your resident status.

[ ] Recommendations: Unless the college specifies individuals, try to ask people who know you well and can write well. Provide them with a copy of your resume, the college form, and a pre-addressed and stamped envelope. Attach the deadline date on a brightly colored piece of paper. Explain why you have selected given colleges. On your own calendar, note a date a week ahead of the deadline to check back with them and ask if they are willing to provide a copy for your file.

[ ] Transcripts:
- Turn in requests and addresses of colleges to school registrar or counselor *early*.
- Note dates due on your calendar and check registrar one week before due.
- Cate Mueller suggests that if you move senior year, have your previous high school send your official transcript for work done there to colleges because your current high school may fail to translate your course descriptions, grades, or class rank accurately.
- Be aware that transcripts sent prior to the end of the first semester of 12th grade do not include any senior grades.

[ ] Have SAT or ACH scores sent to any additional colleges to whom you have not already had them sent.

[ ] Research all college-based, local, and national scholarship and financial aid options. Mid-March is deadline for filing Financial Aid Form.

[ ] Alumni contacts: Take advantage of interviews and receptions offered by local alumni. See and be seen.

[ ] May -- take AP exams for advanced placement and/or credit.

[ ] June -- take ACH exams for proper placement.

478   Children's Educational Needs

[ ] Maintain high level grades throughout senior year. Colleges look at final semester and reject some whose grades decline.

[ ] Rejection: If you believe the college's decision was made prior to receipt of latest grades or test scores, ensure that they have your official transcript and request a review of your application.

[ ] Acceptance: Notify all of your colleges, graciously, of your decision by their deadline.

[ ] Wait-listed: If you still would really like to attend this college, go ahead and accept another and put down the necessary fees to ensure your enrollment. But, write your preferred choice, let them know that if they offer you the chance, *you will come!* Provide any additional information on awards or internships or summer employment that they may not already have. There are instances in which colleges keep track of your responses (by phone and in writing) once you have been wait-listed -- as evidence of your perseverance.

Resources:

For further information regarding placement tests, contact the College Entrance Examination Board (for SAT and ACH). Eastern states: CEEB, Box 592, Princeton, NJ 08540. Western states, territories, and Pacific: CEEB, Box 1025, Berkeley, CA 94701. American College Testing Program (for ACT): P.O. Box 168, Iowa City, IA 52240.

Additional references and workbooks recommended:

30 Days to a More Powerful Vocabulary, by Dr. Wilfred Funk and Norman Lewis (Pocket Book: New York, 1971). This workbook is designed for corporate executives who want to move ahead, and asks only 15 minutes a day of your time.

Everywoman's Guide to Colleges and Universities (The Feminist Press). Look for this in your guidance office. Colleges are rated on their provisions for women (i.e. opportunities for leadership, role models on the faculty, intercollegiate and intramural sports, security provisions, career-oriented programs, etc.)

Originally appeared as "Hints for the College-Bound" in Family Magazine Scholarship Handbook, July 1983. It has been used by high schools in Arlington, Virginia and Jacksonville, Florida, as well as Smith College.

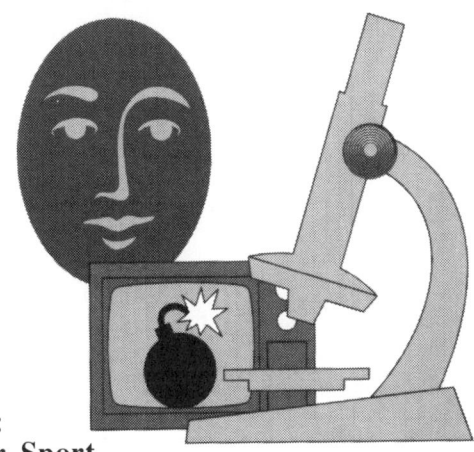

Television Viewing:
A Participator Sport

Television is perceived by its viewers as a form of relaxation, of entertainment. But insofar as TV forms an important part of their consciousness, insofar as it can be regarded as their collective daydream, and insofar as the denizens of that daydream, through their omnipresence and their continuous existence over long periods of time, become the equivalent of mythic archetypes, ultimately all that world of fiction, that realm of entertainment, assumes a highly concrete reality. It is real because it shapes people's actions: the heroes of its sagas become models of human conduct....

The Age of Television by Martin Esslin

Military families can be more vulnerable to the negative aspects of television than their civilian counterparts if they allow "friends" in soap operas or sitcoms to substitute for the harder task of making new real friends with each move.

Reports of Americans everywhere tending to "cocoon," to retreat into their homes and families, could be received as a positive trend, <u>if they are using the opportunity to pursue creative, participatory activities.</u> Television <u>viewing</u> vs. <u>watching</u> can be a participator vs. a spectator experience for all ages. The key is to remember that television is a tool to be manipulated by the user.

Dangers

Most of us have read of the dangers of endless passive television watching. **Time** spent by various age groups in front of the "boob tube" is often cited. A recent advertisement for a calculator stated that a third grader spends an average of 900 hours a year in class and 1170 hours watching television. And *Cable Guide* (October 1990) reported that "the average American child spends more time with TV than with parents or in school (the 11,000 hours he or she will sit in classes through high school compares with 15,000 hours sitting in front of the TV)."

To put these cold statistics in perspective, the *PTA TV Trainer's Manual* says, "Even before the typical American child reaches first grade, he has compiled more hours watching TV than he would need to earn a college degree."

Sitting and **eating** in front of the television are twin evils that have been seen as key elements in the decline of physical fitness and the increase in obesity for both adults and children. These are valid issues of concern, but even more insidious is the failure to spend enough time during childhood "playing," learning the skills that translate to hand-eye coordination (for readiness to read) and exploring the outdoors (for spatial relations and mathematical skills).

Passivity and **inappropriate learning processes** are potential negative results, as is **overstimulation**. Many parents know the short-tempered child who emerges from a Saturday morning diet of cartoons. That same child may be hard to engage in activities such as cleaning his room or playing a game after his brain has been in the "receive mode" for so long.

Neil Postman, in *The Disappearance of Childhood*, developed the thesis that television can be the most destructive force in childhood because it is basically a right-brain, visual activity that requires very little left-brain activity -- sequential, logical, linguistic, critical thought.

Constructive Television Viewing

How, then, can we use the very remarkable attributes of the medium of television in positive ways? *Family* turned to Kay Janney, Professor of Dramatic Arts at the University of Connecticut, for suggestions on how to approach television viewing as a participatory sport, a critical-thinking activity.

While some of what follows is fairly sophisticated, you can adapt it as appropriate, because one of the primary recommendations is to view television with family members and <u>comment</u> on the fare -- <u>before, during, and after each program.</u>

Types of Programs

Prof. Janney, who not only teaches drama and communications courses, but has had the experience of raising three children in the television era, suggests that viewers understand the different types/genres of programs and their typical structures.

For example, **soap operas** that air on weekdays have a daily pattern and a weekly pattern. The daily mini-crises peak before commercials to keep you tuned, and Fridays bring larger cliff-hanger events to lure you back on Mondays. Once you are aware of the repetitive "peaks," you may find the manipulation of your emotions all-too-obvious.

Prof. Janney credits some soap operas with dealing with some of the major social, medical, and ethical issues of our day. (Some university-level courses are taught on soap operas as contemporary literature!) However, current story lines veer to the more sensational, with exotic themes, locations, and "good guys - bad guys" characters.

She also suggests noting some very interesting visual techniques being used to move from one scene or story line to another (fading through glass or via the camera focused on a common object). Once you start observing in this way, you are well on your way to an observational approach to the medium.

Observe the close-ups. How do they affect the viewer? Do you see people in real life that closely?

Combine the intimate closeness of view with the fact that you may watch soap opera characters everyday over a period of years. They can become so familiar that it is hard to remember that they are characters/actors vs. "real people." A classic example of this phenomenon is the fact that Murphy Brown, a fictional character, placed second in a newspaper poll of readers on who should replace Diane Sawyer, a real reporter on *60 Minutes*.

The longevity of a soap opera allows a complexity of character development that one finds in other long-running types of programs such as a series or situation-comedies ("sitcoms").

In a **series** such as "Hunter" or "Murder, She Wrote," the viewer has the mix of known characters plus a new situation or challenge and new characters. The focus is on action, and, unlike the soap opera, each segment is complete. (Hence, your annoyance when one of your favorite weekly shows pulls the dirty trick of being "Part I of II.")

Hour-long series have begun to adapt the technique of soap operas to run parallel, seemingly-unconnected stories. An analytical exercise suggested by Prof. Janney that would enhance your awareness of the intricacy of some of these structures would be to chart each mini-story in an overall block.

	Plot line I	Plot line II	Plot line III
Character A			
Character B			
Character C			
Character D			

Which characters (if any) are present in all plot/story lines? In only one?

When and how do the plots/characters intersect?

When and how is each conflict resolved? Do some story lines finish before others? Is there any attempt to bring all of the story lines to a unified (simultaneous) ending? (For example, Shakespeare's plot lines and characters are complex, yet all have some common thread or character.)

Can you forecast the chase scene?

Note how you are moved from one mini-story to the other. Do commercial breaks serve this purpose, or are four other transition devices used: the cut, the dissolve, the fade, or the wipe?

In his book, *Television Production Handbook*, Herbert Zettle describes the **cut** as an "instantaneous change from one image to another. It is the most common and least obtrusive" of the transition devices because it "most closely resembles the human eye changing its field of vision."

The cut can change local, time, impact, pace, rhythm, and intensity. For example, if the camera cuts from a long distance shot of a place or character to a close up, the result is to intensify the viewer's involvement. The reverse brings a reduction. (Viewers of home video productions often feel yanked around -- the result of too-frequent cuts.)

The **fade** signals the definite end of a scene and the beginning of a new one. It functions just as a curtain does in a theater, bringing a period of black screen.

The **dissolve**, on the other hand, is an actual overlapping of two shots. Artful directors can indicate a connection between events or people through use of this device.

Other types of shows continue to move us from the realm of fiction toward reality. In addition to a series, we also have the **single show**, usually drama, and increasingly we are having made-for-television productions of more than one hour in length. (Some of these are prototypes for new series, so the producers go to great effort to present both characters and situations of potential on-going interest to viewers. Often the prototype is far better than the follow-on episodes.)

Game shows and **talk shows** are highly structured in spite of their surface informality. Can you spot the rhythms and segments in each?

News and **documentaries** bring us closer to reality, but a caution is in order here. Viewers need to be aware how carefully crafted and how selective these programs are. Rarely do we see absolutely "live" television. Most footage has been carefully selected, taped, and edited prior to the show. As protestors are well aware, some events have been created/staged for the primary purpose of being taped and shown on television. The reality may be that there were few protestors present, but the camera angle can make the few seem like only a portion of a larger group. The reverse can also be true.

The documentary, by its length, has the advantage missing in most evening news programs: the luxury of time to investigate the issue or event in some depth. Viewers of evening newscasts should also look to daily newspapers to give more information than is possible in 60-second or three minute "bites." For military families who want information about world events (vs. just local news), purchase of the Sunday edition of a major newspaper and a weekly news magazine will help to put global issues in perspective.

Live **sports** events are the most "real" shows on television. Even so, a critical viewer needs to provide his or her own assessment as a reality check against that of the official commentator.

Our reality - fiction scale brings us to the one type of show that we have not discussed: the **commercial**, the most carefully crafted "show" of all! Martin Esslin, in *The Age of Television*, points out the three patterns most often used in commercials. In the first, the "three-beat pattern," the model is the Greek drama format. (1) The sufferer is near despair and appeals to a friend or relative for help. The helper tells the sufferer about the commercial product. (2) The sufferer experiences an "aha!" -- a moment of insight. (3) The sufferer experiences a reversal of fortune (is restored to good health, clean clothes, etc.)

Esslin calls the second pattern the "analytical pattern." A presently pretty girl shows how she was ugly or suffered until she discovered the product. We then see the trademark and hear the accompanying tune (we are being instructed through at least two senses).

The third pattern is the "testimonial." A real star or athlete of folk hero dimensions endorses the product. The star is <u>acting</u> and using a text composed by skillful writers -- and the star is not performing out of the goodness of his or her heart!

In order to be a critical viewer of commercials, you should look at what the actors are wearing, what the set tells you about what advertiser thinks is the target audience, and what role music plays. Most commercials use drama rather than "talking heads" to <u>indoctrinate</u> their viewers -- not too harsh a word for this most manipulative of all genres on television.

Placement of commercials is also something to notice. Gregor Goethals in his book, *The TV Ritual: Worship at the Video Altar*, gives the example of the evening news (often full of "dismal, tragic events without easy solution or resolution"). Then commercials break in and break the mood of irresolution by offering comforting solutions to headaches, dirty dishes, etc.

Tricks of the Trade

Now that many Americans are beginning to take their own videos, a critical eye on techniques will bring the double benefit of enabling viewers to understand how techniques affect their reactions to a program and how to do it themselves.

Picture composition and lighting are two major techniques to notice. The length of the shot and the movement of the camera toward or away from a person or object have emotional impact on the viewer. The five lengths of shots are: the extreme closeup (showing only a portion of an object or a person's face), the closeup (showing not only the head but also the top of the chest), the medium shot, long shot, and extreme long shot. The closer the shot, the more intense the reaction. Think of the amount of distance from a person that you usually find comfortable in real life, and then you will understand why the extreme closeup of a stranger makes you feel uncomfortable.

Another source of comfort or discomfort is the angle of the camera. If it is tilted differently from our ordinary visual experience, we feel a heightened response and a sense of instability. This is a highly manipulative technique that can be effective for short spans, but will turn a viewer off if it is prolonged, because it is too uncomfortable.

Lighting

Lighting can create mood. We know this intuitively when we turn up or down the lighting in our homes. The source of light makes a difference. If there is intense lighting from the back, there are no shadows on the background. The effect is to glamorize the model in a fashion shot, or to give a larger-than-life quality to a newscaster. Long shadows, on the other hand, suggest danger.

We expect most lighting to occur from above (sunlight and room lights). If lighting is from below eye level, a mysterious mood is created.

Two special effects are becoming more common in all types of shows. The split screen allows viewers to see an event from two different viewpoints at the same time. This effect should not be used for a prolonged period, however, as the viewer will have a hard time after awhile switching back and forth. Newscasters sometimes use this technique in order to keep their presence on screen in one corner while previously-taped footage is aired. (The viewer will tend to think of the newscaster as being at the event, when in truth, he or she is just as distanced geographically as the viewer.)

Superimposition, the overlaying of one scene on another, can add information or can create the effect of allowing viewers to experience a character's thoughts or dreams. The symbolic value of this technique can be remarkable. The clash between the present and past or between reality and one's perceptions can be illustrated visually by an artful director.

One of the major deficits of television has been the overuse of stereotypes -- characters who represent one emotion or ethnic group or social class. They move through their fictional stories as shallow, cardboard figures, lacking the complexity and richness of fully developed human beings. One of the dangers of stereotypes is that viewers subjected to this unreality may, over time, come to interact with real human beings based on limited perceptions. Instead of looking beneath the surface and understanding the kaleidoscopic nature of fully developed people, they narrow their intellectual, social, and emotional ranges.

Conversely, television viewers are given the opportunity to "know" characters who may broaden their experience and expectations. Viewers who have not travelled extensively or known people from diverse backgrounds, can be enriched by portrayals of complex characters beyond their ken.

Commentators often enhance their stature by a number of production techniques. Newscasters can use props to increase their credibility factor. For example, if they sit at a high desk or podium, and the camera looks at them from below, they take on the majesty of a courtroom. If they want to establish friendliness (and credibility of a different sort), the camera will approach them at eye view level with a waist- or chest-up shot -- just like a neighbor talking over the fence.

On talk shows, the placement of the host and guests will signal the viewers what the anticipated interchange will be. If the host and guest sit at right angles to each other, the interchange is likely to be relaxed and friendly. If the two sit side-by-side and don't look at each other much, there is a coldness built in. If the two are face-to-face, you will see tension, debate, and conflict.

Main Fiction Themes

The five main fictional themes found on American television today (with many variations) have been popular in literature and movies as well. The Western is not as popular as it used to be, with its easily distinguishable heroes and villains, its conquest of difficult territories and peoples, and its resolution of law and order.

Today we see far more spy, detective, and police stories, some still operating with stereotypical characters of good/white and evil/black, but many providing more complex/gray characters who are closer to the reality of the world we live in. Issues and situations are also more "gray," and need analysis by the viewer instead of passive consumption. The spy/detective/police story still assures us of the victory of right over wrong, but crime and violence are provided for entertainment. Children, particularly, have a hard time separating this so-called entertainment from the reality of injury and death.

A third theme, the science fiction program, salutes the power of technology. Mere mortals can escape from their inadequacies through machinery. Superman and all of his spinoffs ensure that good triumphs over evil, but viewers need to underscore the role of human motivations and not just the technical tools involved. Viewers' creativity can be enhanced if they use the scientific fictions as stimuli for their own ideas and inventions.

The family has become a prevalent theme on television today -- the family in almost every imaginable form possible. We see not only the traditional family with father, mother, and children, but single parents, live-ins or perpetually present neighbors, the-local-bar-as-family, and one's co-workers-as-family. We are seeing a wide spread of ethnicity and socio-economic-educational backgrounds as well. Viewers need to sort out what behavior and value systems they cherish as programs are targeted at different segments of the American population (translate that as buying public!). Children may have a hard time understanding why their wise-cracking counterparts on television are not acceptable models to emulate at home. Parents' commentary and family discussion of issues and behavior patterns can be highly beneficial.

This leads us to the fifth and final television theme, the cartoon. Not only for children, cartoons provide viewers with all sorts of fictional-mythical creatures -- including animals, demons, and all-powerful children. Esslin, in his book *The Age of Television*, cautions that cartoons have replaced the traditional fairy tales and better children's fiction, which had "fine language, poetic imagery, and an underlying tenderness absent from today's cartoons." He believes that cartoons can debase children's taste, imagination, and language.

As in all media, there are outstanding, beautifully crafted programs and there are unadulterated trash. Parents can enhance their children's intellectual, artistic, and moral development by helping them select only the best programs and learning how to show their distaste by turning off the set when the programming does not live up to their standards (rather than feeling that the turning off is a punishment of the viewers!).

Now that you have had the equivalent of Basic Television Viewing 101, you will be in a position to recognize when a production is terrific or terrible. You will be able to recognize the quality of a production like Ken Burns' "The Civil War," which became the most-watched PBS series ever. The fact that it aired at a time when Americans were being mobilized for Desert Shield heightened its impact, even though the parallel to the present was never alluded to. You are now prepared to be a new participatory viewer, a critic, discussing with your family what you and they view: before, during, and after each program.
****
Special thanks to Professor Kay Janney. Her military connections include her son, LT Brooke H. Janney, USA, and his wife Wendy.

Originally appeared as "Family TV Viewing: It's a Participator Sport" in Family, *March 1991.*

Glossary of Acronyms

AAFES	Army & Air Force Exchange Service
ACS	Army Community Services
AUSA	Association of the U. S. Army
BAQ	Basic Allowance for Quarters
BAS	Basic Allowance for Subsistence
CAAC	Counseling and Assistance Center
CACO	Casualty Assistance Calls Officer
CEU's	Continuing Education Units
CHAMPUS	Civilian Health and Medical Program of the Uniformed Services
CLEP	College-Level Examination Program
CLO	Community Liaison Office
CO	Commanding Officer
COB	Chief of the Boat
COLA	Cost of Living Allowance
CONUS	Continental United States
CPO	Chief Petty Officer
CPO	Civilian Personnel Office
DANTES	Defense Activity for Non-Traditional Education
DEERS	Defense Eligibility Enrollment Reporting System
DoD	Department of Defense
DODDS	Department of Defense Dependent Schools
DoT	Department of Transportation (under which the Coast Guard serves except in wartime)
EERC	Employment and Education Resource Center
ERC	Employment Resource Center
EX-POSE	Ex-Partners of Servicemen/Women for Equality
FBM	Fleet Ballistic Missile submarine
FHCC	Family Home Child Care
FLO	Family Liaison Office
FSC	Family Service or Support Center

GED	General Education Degree
ICAF	Industrial College of the Armed Forces
JAG	Judge Advocate General
LES	Leave and Earning Statement
MCAS	Marine Corps Air Station
MFRC	Military Family Resource Center
NAF	Non-Appropriated Funds
NAS	Naval Air Station
NCO	Non-Commissioned Officer
NMFA	National Military Family Association
NMWA	National Military Wives Association (former name of NMFA)
NSB	Naval Submarine Base
NWCA	Navy Wives Club of America
OCONUS	Outside Continental United States
OTIS	Overseas Transfer Information Service
PCS	Permanent Change of Station
PX	Exchange (Army)
ROTC	Reserve Officers Training Corps
R & R	Rest and Relaxation
RSVP	*Respondez, sil vou plait* (reply, if you please)
SA/LK	School Age/Latchkey Program
SEAP	Spouse Employment Assistance Program
SBP	Survivor Benefit Plan
SF-171	Standard Form- 171 (Civil Service application)
SGLI	Servicemen's Group Life Insurance
TAD	Temporary Additional Duty (Army & Air Force)
TDY	Temporary Duty (Navy and Marine Corps)
USMA	United States Military Academy (West Point)
USNA	United States Naval Academy (Annapolis)
USAREUR	U. S. Army Europe
USO	United Services Organization
VHA	Variable Housing Allowance
WEAL	Women's Equity Action League
XO	Executive Officer

Index

AAA, 16
AAFES (Army & Air Force Exchange), 82
absence (parent), 140-41
abuse (child), 47, 86
abuse (spouse), 47, 86, 132-39
accidents (car), 86
accountability, 68
achievement, 223-4, 285, 334-35, 439-40, 452, 454, 474
activities, 42-44
accomplishments, 36, 69, 171, 259, 285, 439-40
acquaintances, 171, 175, 230, 252-53
Adak (AK), 95
Adams, John, 259
adaptation, 19
Adderholt-Elliott, Miriam, Ph.D., 150
address, 86, 94, 189, 192
Adler, Sandy, 342
admirals, 70
admirals' wives (see also generals' wives), 263
adolescence (See teenagers)
perpetual, 30
age stage, 123, 200
adoption, 318, 382-92
advance pay, 29
Advisory Council on Instruction, 443
advance shipment, 11
advocates, 258, 260
After School: Young Adolescents on Their Own, 429
Age of Television, 479, 483, 487
ages, 32, 34, 36, 123, 125-27, 142, 152-3, 156, 159-60, 172, 433, 452
age-stage, 68-69, 140-50, 235, 263,

aging (See parents)
aircraft carrier, 53
Air Force, 3, 7, 21, 20, 22, 24, 41, 78-80, 91-93, 107, 113, 117, 121, 126-27,155, 158,170,175,228, 230, 233, 259-61, 263, 270, 273, 280, 298-300, 303-5, 308-9, 316-18, 351, 355, 416, 427-28
Air Force Aid, 93
Air Force Blue Ribbon Panel, 259-60
Air Force Family Service, 270
Air Force Family Symposia, 117, 259
Air Force Military Spouse Skills and Resource Center, 127, 301-305
alcohol (abuse), 47, 92, 137-8
Aldridge, Joy & Ray (LCDR), 387-88
alienation (See isolation), 29
All Hands, 93
allotments, 74, 119, 187
allowances, 90, 95
allowances (moving), 8
alone (See loneliness), 38
Alone After School, 429
amalgam (See diversity), 298, 470
American Assn. of University Women (AAUW), 228
American Cancer Society, 159-60
American Planning Association, 104
American Red Cross, 92, 121, 128-9, 171, 228, 252, 279-80, 283, 374, 376, 381, 422, 463, 468
Anacostia Naval Station (DC), 125, 128, 304
anger, 52, 135-36
Annenberg School of Communications, 345
anniversary, 53, 55

anomie (See isolation), 34
anorexia, 140-42, 144-46, 150
Anti-Coloring Books, 460
appliances, 6, 131, 187, 189-90
Aquarian Conspiracy, The, 173, 271
architecture, 328-29, 331
arguments, 67-68
Arlington (VA), 61, 172, 210-11, 255, 288, 329, 332-40, 443-50, 462, 464, 471, 478
Armed Forces Hostess Association, 191
Armed Services YMCA, 92, 127-29, 228
Armstrong, Lynne, 304-06
Army, 3, 20-22, 24, 41, 51, 69-70, 73-75, 88, 91-93, 94-100, 109-, 110, 117-22, 126-27, 129, 171, 173, 228, 230, 245, 259-60, 270, 273, 284, 299, 303-06, 308-09, 331, 335, 339-40, 351, 355-60, 363, 416, 426-28, 433, 439, 487
Army Community & Family Support Center, 93
Army Community Services (ACS), 23, 73, 75, 92, 121-22, 126, 129, 228, 251, 270, 280, 283, 305, 374
Army Emergency Relief, 93
Army Family Action Plan, 22, 97
Army Family Action Plan Conference, 22, 97
Army Family Liaison Office, 23, 261, 284
Army Family Symposium, 97, 99, 117, 173, 259, 265, 273, 284, 289, 303-4, 332
Army, Navy, Air Force Times, 409, 464
Army Wives' Club of the Greater Washington Area (AWOCGWA), 289
Army Reserve, 22, 361, 416
Arthur, Jack, iv
Ashworth, M.D. (MAJ), 50
assertiveness, 128
Assessment of Prior Learning, 343-44
Association of Foreign Service Women, 222, 302
Association of the U. S. Army (AUSA), 120, 270, 273
auto (See car)

automatic teller machine (ATM), 75, 82, 84
Autovon, 22, 99
Awalt, Suzanne (MAJ), 360
awards, 188

babies, 16, 33, 120, 313, 375-81
Babino, Dorita & Lucius (SFC), 319
babysitters, 20, 21, 30, 35, 77, 128, 185, 188, 286, 335, 372, 463
bachelors (See also geographic bachelors), 8
Bachelor of General Studies (BGS), 342-43
Bacon, Joan, 157-8
balance, 67-69, 117, 134, 172-73, 220, 223-4, 279-86, 449, 454
Banister, Linda & Roger, 344
banking, 82-84, 106-7, 119-20, 131, 188-89
baptism, 189
Barnett, Rosalind, 223
barrier, 50
Barthell, Pamela & Joe (CAPT), 317, 320
Baruch, Grace, 223
Basic Allowance for Quarters (BAQ), 95, 99, 119
bathrooms, 97
Beauvais, Alexis, 437
becoming, 228
Becraft, Carolyn, 358
beds, 16
behavior, 86, 133-35, 137, 442, 487
Behavioral Science Associates, 133, 139
Behind Closed Doors, 137
Beirut, 222, 237-39
Beller, Abbie, 328
Belleville (IL), 20
Bellevue Navy Housing (DC), 124-5, 128
belonging, 35, 37, 48, 60, 69, 169-70
benefits, 49, 85, 88-93, 259
Benford, Dorothy, 125
Bennett, Wm. J., 373-74, 460
Bergstrom, Joan, Ed.D., 430
Bermudes, Robert W. (Rev.), 40
Besacon, Avi, 437

Index

Bethesda Naval Hospital (MD), 151-52, 154-55
Bettelheim, Bruno, 445
Better Times....., 193
Bey, Douglas R., M.D., 40
bills, 130-31
birth certificate, 102, 131, 188-89
birthday, 53, 55, 77, 187, 192
Blain, Tonya & Greg (SSGT), 319
Bloxham, Leslie, 312
Bohannon, Lillian, 342-43, 345
Bolling AFB (DC), 125-26, 298, 351
bond (See camaraderie), 48, 170, 177
bonding, 371-72
bonds, 188
Bonnie's Household Organizer, 193
Boone, David & Kathy, 21
Boorda, Michael (VADM), iii
Boswell, Day (LT) & Chip, 53, 314-15
Bott, Bobbie, 328
Boyette, Marsha & David, 22
Boy Scouts, 403, 408, 428, 441-42, 447, 456, 460, 463, 474
brainstorming, 266-71, 339
"brats," 20, 434
Brazelton, T. Berry, M.D., 371-72, 374
breakfast, 447
breast cancer, 151-60
Brenton, Bobbie, 128
brides, 123-31
Bringing Out the Best, 460
Brothers, Joyce, Dr., 133
Brown, Allonia, Cassandra, Venus, & Yawanda, 435, 437-38
Brown, Pattie, 124
Brown, Peggy, 50
Brown, Harold, 8
Brown, Mrs. George S., 7
Bruchas, Megan, 435
Buck, Pearl, 171
buddy system (See friends), 35, 36, 337
budget (See finances), 29, 32, 75-77, 128-29, 194
Buell, David G. (MAJ), 45, 48, 50
bulimia, 140, 142-45, 149
Bunton, Wilett, 305
Burger, Ninki Hart, 254
burial allowances, 90

Burnett, Carol, 255
burnout, 217-20
Burns, Alytrius, 434
Business & Professional Women (BPW), 228, 312, 467-68
businesses (See home-based), 88
busyness, 36

cabin fever, 177
caging (one's wife), 30, 35, 48-49, 118, 121, 129, 137, 171, 177
calendar, 76-77, 131, 185-86, 221
Callahan, Bruce L., 41
camaraderie (See cohesion), 35-37
Camden County Tribune, 327-28, 366, 450, 468
camera, 52
Campbell, Bonnie, 153, 156
Campbell, Kay (LCDR), 362-63
Camp Lejeune (NC), 237-39, 349
camps, 461, 463, 467, 470
cancer (See breast cancer), 151-60
CAPSTONE course, 263
captain's wife, 28, 33, 35, 126
car:
  insurance: 188
  purchase: 119
  registration: 87, 189
  repairs: 131, 188
  shipping: 11
career, 68-69, 178, 223, 298, 332, 454
Carey, Beth, 124
Carlon, Gerry, 24
Carnahan, Ralph H. (RADM, USN, Ret.), 122
car pools, 20
car (travelling), 13-17
Carr, Justin, iv, 62
Carr, Helen M., iv, 510
car seat, 16
Casualty Assistance Calls Officer (CACO), 90, 238
catalysts, 265, 452
Catholic, 79
Cavanaugh, Tammy & Larry (SGT), 24, 319
challenges, 174, 177, 179, 184, 193, 226, 249, 339, 341
Chamber of Commerce, 13, 107, 270, 301, 330, 467

Index   493

CHAMPUS (See medical), 89-90, 92-93
chance, 171, 177
change, iii, 454
chaplains, 28, 29, 33, 37, 44, 92, 118, 121, 127, 136, 230, 388-89, 392
charity, 77
Charleston (SC), 4, 20, 29, 126, 156, 257
Charleston Naval Hospital (SC), 126
Charleston Family Service Center, 126
Charting Your Life in the U. S. Coast Guard, 9, 41, 44, 63-64, 70, 402, 442
checking account, 74, 119
checklist, 12
Cherry Point MCAS (NC), 45-50, 176, 346, 348-49
Chestnut, Sherry, 17
Chief of the Boat's (COB's) wife, 34, 35, 126, 283
child abuse, 138, 420
child care, 50, 87, 118, 124-25, 127, 149, 262, 299, 309, 314-15, 318-24, 415-22, 423-30
child development, 125, 128, 393-99, 400-06, 407-8, 410-14, 426-27
children, 43-44, 47, 57-62, 64, 123-25, 127-28, 133-36, 169-70, 176, 178, 187-89, 192, 194, 199-200, 228-29, 233, 334, 367-87
Childwise Catalog, The, 381
Chirinko, Ann Marie, 20
choice, 38, 171, 173, 177, 201-10, 221, 249-55, 262, 272, 280, 282
Choosing the Right Plants for SE Georgia and NE Florida, 327
Christmas (See holidays), ii, 56, 57-62, 75-7, 218, 221, 231, 270, 412
church, 37, 128, 171, 321, 333, 373, 436, 441-42, 447, 452, 464
Cilley, Richard N., Ed.D., 350
citizenship, 130, 189
City University, 352
civilian community (See community), 36, 64, 67, 70, 170-73, 252-53, 259, 262, 272, 438
Civilian Personnel Office (CPO), 87-88, 91, 330-31, 466

Civil Service, 85, 87-88, 298, 302, 318, 331, 333, 351, 363, 439-40
Civjan, Becky & Ralph, 21
climate, 101, 177-78
clothing, 33
clubs, 92, 121,
Coast Guard, 41, 54, 63-64, 70, 91, 93, 94, 96, 175, 228, 230, 255-56, 260, 290-94, 303, 314-15, 402- 03
Coffin, William, 383
cohesion (See camaraderie), 35-37, 63, 65, 68
college, 87, 89, 190, 212, 325-29, 331, 332-340, 341-45, 346-52, 440-41, 454, 464, 470, 471-78
College-Level Examination Program (CLEP), 334, 340, 347
Collins, Barbara, 133-34
Collins, Vanessa, 435
Color Me Beautiful, 229
Columbus College, 351
"Coming Home -- Again," 63
Commander's Conference, 48
Commanding Officer (CO), 19, 40-47, 49-50, 64, 89, 178, 238, 264, 288, 415, 419
Commanding Officer's wife (See captain's wife), 28, 33, 35, 46-47, 54, 254, 260, 263
command-sponsored, 127
command support, 122
commissary, 18, 75, 87, 91, 121, 124, 127, 185-86, 194, 199, 229-30, 238, 289
commitment, 173, 200, 236, 280
communications (family), 28, 36, 128-29, 135-36, 404, 407, 444, 449-50
communications (official/network), 35, 49
community (See civilian community), 36, 44, 68, 95-96, 99-100, 124, 222, 228, 282
Community Liaison Office (CLO), 302
companionate marriage, 222, 250
complaints (consumer), 32, 83-4, 185
Complete Guide to Self-Publishing, 311
confidentiality, 138
conflict, 128, 132-39

Connecticut College, 343
constants and flexibility (See
  consistent), 402-03, 442, 450
constitutional rights, 85-86
consumer (See complaints), 83-84,
  104
Consumer Affairs Office, 104, 107,
  130-31
Consumer's Guide to Baby Equipment..
  381
Consumer Information Center, 460
Consumer's Resource Handbook, 131
Continuing Education Units (CEU's),
  351
continuity (See traditions), 49, 57,
  65, 122, 177, 435, 442, 447,
  452
contracts, 8, 32, 130-31
contributions (See charity), 77
control, 79, 86, 117, 137, 141-50,
  186, 193, 223-24
CONUS, 24
Cook, Kaye, 311
Cooperative Extension Service/
  System, 121, 311, 374, 460
coping skills, i, ii, 47, 57, 135-36,
  199-200, 219-20, 369
Cormier, Judith & Larry (SSGT),
  317, 324
corporate wives, 8, 9, 39, 41, 169,
  249-51, 254, 259
*Corporate Wives - Corporate
  Casualties?* 8, 39, 41
correspondence schools, 344-45
cottage industries (See home-based
  businesses)
Council for Advancement of
  Experiential Learning, 344
Council for Adult and Experiential
  Learning, 352
Council on Military Education
  (GA), 341
counseling, 33, 88, 90, 92, 117,
  121, 136, 138, 334, 339-40,
  453-54
Counseling and Assistance Center
  (CAAC), 366
counselor, guidance, 440-41, 449,
  454, 467
coupons (IOU), 53, 57, 410-14
courage, 6, 237-39, 263

CPR, 121
crafts, 121, 229, 252
Cranford, Kathryn, 347
Crawford, Jacie & John (SGT),
  316, 320
creative balance, 172-73, 280
creativity, 51, 54, 68, 236, 265-71,
  394-95, 453-54, 455-56, 459-60,
  479, 486
credentials, 222, 334, 343-44
credit, 77, 79, 82, 130-31
credit/charge card, 75, 79, 81-84,
  119-20, 188
credit unions, 82, 130-31
crew wives (See enlisted wives),
  34
crisis, 29, 33, 117, 122, 129-31
critical thinking, 401, 449, 452-53,
  480
criticism, 226
Crowley, Karen, 351
Crump, Sheila, 316
Cuba, 95
cultural adaptation, 120
culture shock, 436
culturgram, 101
cumulative, 134, 140, 218, 406
currency, 20
Curtin, Cara (LCDR), 12
cushion, 79

dad's roles (See fathers), 372-73,
  403-4, 410-14, 444, 454
Dahl, Barbara B., 67
Defense Activity for Non-Traditional Education, 347
daughters, 140-50
Davis, Michael, 436
Davis-Monthan AFB (AZ), 316-18
Davis, Virgil L., III, 22
death, 237-39
death gratuity, 90
debit cards, 81, 84
decision-making, 128, 238-39, 271
decorating, 189-190
deed, 189
Defense '90, iii
Defense, Secretary of, 8
Delta Dental Plan, 93
DeMille, Agnes, 236

Index   495

demographics (See ages), iv, 121-24, 240, 358-61
Dempsey, Erinn, 434, 437
dental care, 89-90, 93, 189, 191
Department of Defense (DoD), iii, 88-89, 109, 229, 260, 306, 308-9, 330, 346, 383, 391, 417-18, 420, 425
Department of Housing and Urban Development (HUD), 10
Department of Defense Dependent Schools, (DODDS), 102
Department of Education, 373
Department of Human Resources 386
Department of State, 303, 305, 331
departure, 150
dependence, 5, 31, 65, 67-68, 137
dependent daughter, 29
deployment (See separation), 27, 39, 42-44, 45-62, 119, 176, 179-83, 190, 204, 227, 412
Dependence and Indemnity Compensation, 90
deployment, 27-70, 123, 126, 128-29, 130-31, 135, 176, 179, 187, 192, 240, 262
deposits (rental, utility), 8, 118-19
depression, 68, 145, 148-49, 217-220, 224
Desert Storm, iii, 417-18, 487
detachment, 30, 31
Dianand, Jennifer, 434
difference, ii, 173, 199, 205
Dinkmeyer, Don, 405
dinner (See meal times), 37, 186, 444, 447, 449, 451
direct-deposit, 119-20
Directory of American Youth Organizations, 470
Directory: Opportunities for Prior Learning Credit, 344
Disappearance of Childhood, The, 449, 480
discharge (military), 133, 138
discipline (child), 47, 66, 79 86, 128, 143, 404-05
distance (See separation, geographic), 28-29, 32, 169, 176-77
diversity, 262, 452

divorce, 37, 47, 91-92, 132, 262
doctor, 189
Dolphin, 39, 41
domicile (See State of Record), 87
domineering, 30
Don't Panic, 189, 191
Donyl, Kristin, 437
Dornsife, Pamela, 21
Douglas, William, 251, 254
dreams, 36
Dresdow, Elke, 120
drill instructors (DI), 134-35, 150
driver's license, 6, 21, 87
drug abuse, 47, 86, 92, 137-38
dual career military (See Jasitt), iv, 52, 78-79, 259, 262, 299, 360, 418, 447, 461
durability, 395

East Ocean View (VA), 129
eating disorders, 140-50, 480
Ebbert, Jean, 40
education (See college), 89, 91, 117, 127, 189, 200, 229, 443-50, 451-54, 455-60, 480
Education Center, 89, 345, 466
Edwards AFB (CA), 416
Effman, Virginia, 58
elder-care (See aging parents), 269
Elkins, Beth & John (CAPT), 383-85
Elkins, CaroLu, 383-85, 437
Ellison, Connie &Jerry, 386-87
El Toro MCAS (CA), 346
embassy, 19
emergency, 45, 82, 119, 123, 138, 164, 169-71, 186-87, 199, 228, 429
Emerson, Ralph Waldo, 226
Emily Post's Etiquette, 291
emotional presence (See deployment), 404
emotional stages:
  deployment: 30-31, 170
  moving: 3-9, 10-12
  shore duty: 65-70
employment, 5, 67, 87-88, 94, 102, 118, 121, 126-27, 188-89, 201, 204, 208, 221, 259, 262, 280, 297-300, 301-6, 307-13, 314-24,

employment (cont.) 325-31, 334, 344, 351-52, 371, 421, 428, 449, 465-70, 478
Employment and Education Resource Center (EERC), 304-6, 309
enlisted personnel (See junior enlisted personnel), 29, 64, 73-80, 96, 98, 120, 123-24, 127, 129, 133-35, 170, 176, 365-66, 425
enlisted wives (i.e. spouses of enlisted personnel), 34, 45-47, 50, 63, 126, 164, 177, 260-61, 316-19
entertainment, 74, 77-79
Espeland, Pamela, 460
Esslin, Martin, 479, 483, 487
Esty, Happy B., 471, 477
ethnicity, 178, 228
etiquette, 290-94
evacuation, 22
Evans, Jan & Mark (LCDR), 385-86
Evans, Judith, 404
Evers, Timothy B., 471, 474, 476
Everywoman's Guide to Colleges and Universities, 472, 478
evolution, 259
exams, 334, 338-39, 453, 472
Exchange (See AAFES), 55, 75, 81-82, 91, 119-21, 186, 289
executive officer's wife, 34, 35, 46-47, 254, 260
Executive's Wife, The, 254
exercise disorders, 140, 145-46, 149
experiential learning, 346-52
EX-POSE, 91-92, 132, 139
ex-spouses (See former spouses), 91-92
extended family (See relatives), 61, 169, 175-83
extra-marital affairs, 29
Exxon's Touring Service, 13

fairy tales, 14, 140-41, 255-58, 423-24, 445, 487
Families Adopting Children Everywhere (F.A.C.E.), 392
Families: What Makes Them Work, 199-200, 236
Families in the Military System, 67
family (See extended family and unit/ship family), 16, 17, 23, 40, 50, 52, 56, 61, 62, 73, 75, 84, 85, 92-93, 94, 100, 102-5, 107, 110, 120, 122-24, 139, 146, 149-50, 153, 157, 160, 166, 169-73, 174-183, 186, 193, 200, 220, 224, 230, 236, 237, 239, 240, 246, 271, 278, 286, 289-90, 300, 306, 307, 309-13, 314-15, 319-20, 324-26, 331, 340, 346, 357, 366, 374, 375, 381-83, 406, 409, 412, 417, 422, 430, 433, 438, 442, 450, 454, 460, 464, 466, 470, 478, 480, 487
Family Advocacy Program, 121, 134, 420
family council, 405
familygrams, 28, 54
family home child care (FHCC), 416-19, 421, 427-29
Family Liaison Office (State Dept.), 302-3
Family Readiness Program, 45-50
family service/support centers (FSC), 48, 85, 92-93, 117-22, 123, 125-26, 128-29, 136, 138, 149, 176, 178, 228, 239, 261, 316-18, 343-44, 346-47, 350-52, 374, 378, 410-14, 467, 469
Family Times, 460
family (unit/ship), 60, 121-137
fantasy, 435, 445
FBM submarine, 27-29, 31-32, 34, 43, 63, 65-66
fear, 133, 341
Fellman, Pat, 12-21
female military members, 20, 85, 120, 353-66
Ferguson, Marilyn, 173
Ferguson, Mike & Marilyn, 193, 271
field duty, 121, 123
fights, 65-66
finances, 29, 32, 33, 67-69, 73-84, 85, 118-19, 123, 125, 130-31, 137, 186-87, 204, 314-24, 340, 344, 375-81, 421-22
fire, 33, 37, 104-9
fire department, 105-6, 109
first aid, 186
First Three Years of Life, The, 374, 381
fishbowl existence, 140, 148, 176
fitness, 149, 480
flag, 292

Flatley, Janet, 48-49
Flewelling, Audrey, 437
flexibility, 31, 49, 73, 177, 184,
  186-87, 192-93, 200, 204, 299,
  306, 307, 344, 402-3, 405-6
Florida Times-Union, 12
food, 77
Ford, Barbara (LT), 234, 363-64
foreign-born spouses, 120, 132,
  137, 175, 178, 289, 365
Foreign Service wives, 278, 302-3,
  409
former spouses (See ex-spouses),
  91-92, 132, 138-39
Fort Belvoir (VA), 119, 304-5,
  309-10, 446
Fort Benjamin Harrison (IN), 315,
  365
Fort Benning (GA), 119, 227-28,
  351
Fort Bragg (NC), 98, 119
Fort Campbell (KY), 119
Fort Hood (TX), 119-20, 332
Fort Huachuca (AZ), 320
Fort Jackson (SC), 119
Fort McClellan (AL), 73, 75
Fort McNair (VA), 249-50
Fort Monmouth (NJ), 21
Fort Myer (VA), 24, 51, 153,
  172, 309, 318-19, 331,
  418, 444
Fort Polk (LA), 119
Fort Richardson (AK), 119
Fort Sill (OK), 22
Fort Stewart (GA), 96, 119-22, 418
Four-H (4-H), 441, 464, 467
Franklin, Benjamin, 233
freedom (personal), 68, 85-86,
  201-210, 211-16, 272
frequency, 433
friction (See arguments, fights,
  rank), 63, 65, 68-70, 260-61
Friedman, Dale H., 135-37, 139
friends, 7, 37, 38, 44, 49, 56, 64,
  65, 124-28, 137, 169-71, 177-
  78, 185, 192, 199, 221-24,
  225-30, 232,251-55, 320, 479
friends (children), 10, 433-38,
  440-41, 450
Frischkorn, Cheryl & Kenneth
  (SSGT), 24, 319

fun, 42-44, 394-95, 411, 426, 428,
  455-60, 461-64
Frank, Wilfred, Dr., 478
furniture, 18, 131, 270
Future Shock, 299-300, 332

Gabower, G., 39
Gager, Barbara, 343-44
games, 14-15, 189, 455-60
G/C/T *(Gifted, Creative, Talented)*,
  442
Geck, Jason, 436
GED (General Education Degree),
  350, 358
generals' wives (See admirals' wives),
  46, 48, 55, 263, 283
geographic bachelors, 262, 360, 363
George Washington University, 334,
  336-37, 339-40, 361, 471
Germany, 18, 21, 23, 79, 120, 127,
  313, 328, 388, 418, 436
Giammettei, Helen, 9
GI Bill: 363
  education: 91
  home loan: 91
gifted students, 11, 451-54, 460, 467
Gilligan, Carol, 148-49, 219
Girl Scouts, 171, 184, 217, 228-29
  252, 280, 283, 301, 411, 428, 438,
  441-42, 447, 455, 461, 463, 474
Given, Sharon & Jim, 332-33, 336-38
Glenn, Brenda, 444, 446, 449
goals, 6, 67, 77, 172, 204-7, 249
Goethals, Gregor, 484
"going home," 29, 124-25, 176,
  214-15, 219, 238
Golden Gate University, 349
Goldhammer, Teri & Gordon (SSGT),
  319
*Good Beginnings: Parenting in the
  Early Years*, 404
Good-bye, House, 101
Goodman, Ellen, 235
gossip, 29
Goulart, Artis (CDR), 152
Gracey, Randy, 290-94
Graziano, Linda, 309
grade (See rank, rate), 47-48
grandparents, 11, 61, 172, 192,
  423, 438
grants (educational), 89, 127

grass-roots, 49
Great Lakes Naval Station (IL), 63, 301
Grenada, 238
Grimes, Shari & Robert (SP4), 319
grocery shopping (See commissary), 77
Groton (CT), 27-41, 57-59, 412
growth (personal), 68, 178
LPH GUADALCANAL, 129
Guam, 29, 365
Guantanamo Bay (Cuba), 95
Guerra, Esther & Nicolas (AMN), 317, 320
Guertin, Mary, 339-40
Guidelines for the Wives of Commanding and Executive Officers, 254
Guide to Summer Camps and Summer Schools, 463, 470
guilt, 30, 31, 52-53, 321
Guiness, Jeanne, 18
Gutheil, Thomas G., M.D., 41

Hagen, Donald (RADM), 155
Hagen, Inga, 434
Haley, Edika, 434
halfway (through tour), 36, 43, 54
Hall, Brenda, 290
Hamilton, Nancy Greer, 298-300
Hampton Roads (VA), 306
Handbook for Latchkey Children... 430
Handel, Marvin, 82
harassment, 359
Harmond-Early, Cherry, 18
Harris, Fannie, 351
Harvard University, 328, 371, 377, 404, 454, 455, 464
Hastings, C. Rick, 331
Hatch Act, 85
Hatten, Cherry (CAPT), 156
Hawaii, 17, 27, 157, 263, 306, 365-66
Hawes, Gene, 345
Headstart, 89
health (See wellness)
Health Benefits Advisor (See CHAMPUS), 85, 89-90, 92-93

health plan, 92
Hefferman, Angela, 435, 438
Helton, Lynda, 309-11
Henn, Katy, 149-50
heroes/heroic, 174, 179
Hibbert, Richard, 109
hierarchy, 34
high chairs, 16
high school (See teenager), 332, 336-39, 471-78
High Scope, 125
Hill, Dennis, 444, 448-49
hiring priorities, 87-88
historic, 94, 96
Hite, Barbara, 45
hobbies, 68, 92, 200, 219, 229, 252, 440
holidays, 43-44, 56, 57-62, 163-64, 170-71, 202
Holt, Marge, 20
home-based businesses, 89, 234-35, 307-13, 324, 428-29, 469
homemaker, 73, 221, 223
homeowner, 97
HOMES, 98
home visitors, 125
Honolulu (HI), 27, 228
Hooper, LexaLynn & Lynn C. (BG), 240-43
hospital, 126, 468
hostess, 34, 292-94
hotels, 101
hotline, 129
Household Goods Transportation Office, 107
househunting, 4, 17, 21
housing (See military housing, quarters), 27-28, 75-76, 78, 89, 91, 94-102, 103-114, 128, 164, 178, 345-46, 267-70, 307-10
Housing Referral Office, 98, 103-5, 270
Howe, Harriet ("Trink"), 127, 324
Howell, Jaime, 434
How to Care for Your Parents, 245
Hulse, Lisa S., 330
humor, 16, 60, 184, 199, 223, 239, 437
Hunter, Edna Jo, 67
hurricane, 106, 114
Hunt, Laura, 436

Index 499

Iceland, 20
ideascope, 266
identification card (ID), 87, 90-92, 192
Ilfeld, Ellen, 404
imagination (See creativity), 16
improvements, 96-97
In a Different Voice, 219
income tax, 187
independence (See personal freedom), 31, 66, 137, 176, 400-6, 438
India, 21-22
Industrial College of the Armed Forces (ICAF), 174-76, 249-51
information and referral (I&R), 92, 117, 126, 132, 149
inner-directed, 36, 442
Innis, Pauline, 291
innovation, 265-71
insurance, 74, 76, 79, 89-90, 107 119, 130-31, 187-89, 239, 322-23
intercultural programs, 162-63
Internal Revenue Service (IRS), 106, 310, 323
International Concerns Committee for Children, 392
internship, 325-31, 350-51, 467-69, 478
Internships, 330, 470
interviews, 474-75
introductions, 36
invasive, 141
inventory, 131
invitations, 35
IOU's (See coupons), 57-62, 174-83
IQ, 412
Iran, 383-85
Isay, Richard A., M.D., 30 ff., 39
isolation, 5, 30, 32, 34, 49, 123- 24, 126-29, 137, 171, 174-83, 249
Italy, 263
Iwakuni, Japan, 346

Jacksonville, (FL), 75, 133-34, 231, 234, 375, 386, 478
Jacksonville (NC), 346
Janney, Kay (Prof.), 40-82,487
Janney, Wendy & Brooke H. (LT)
Japan, 22, 120, 164, 319, 435

Jasitt, Donna (LT) & Lance (LT), 52, 55, 366, 370-71, 375-80
job (See employment, skill/job bank), 298, 340, 341
Johns, John H. (Ph.D. & BG, USA, Ret.) & Barbara, 195-97
Johns Hopkins University, The, 394, 407-8
Johnson, Margie & Al (CDR), 10-11
Johnson, Betty J., 403-5
Joint Employment Management System (JEMS), 300
Jones, Betty, 126-27
Jones, Edwin S. (CDR), 29, 39
journal, 36
Jovero, Dale, 24, 319
juggle, 234-35, 249-55, 335-36, 339
junior enlisted personnel, 50, 96, 98, 123-24, 127, 129, 164, 176- 78, 267-70, 283, 317-18, 418
junior enlisted spouses, 123-30, 287
Junker, Linda (MA2), 366

Kagan, Jerome, 455
kaleidoscope, 265-66
Keflavik (Iceland), 20, 164, 347
Kelly, Tyssha, 434, 438
Kennedy, Edward (Senator), 417, 422
kerosene heater, 105
Kerr, Barbara A. (Ph.D.), 460
Kersh, Joyce & John M. (RADM), 243-44
Keys/Keyettes, 441
Key Wives, 45-50, 176
Kidd, Jerome, 109
King, Christie, 24
Kings Bay NSB (GA), 10, 12, 51, 53, 75-76, 105-7, 114, 118, 212, 231-36, 326-29, 363-66, 456, 468
Kingsland (GA), 105-6
kitchen, 96
Knob Norster Public School, 433
Korea, 75, 120, 124, 387-88, 433, 436
Kornegay, Susan, 438
Kroesen, F. J., (GEN), 98

Lacy, Lee, 19
Ladycom (See *Military Lifestyle*), 9, 40, 254

500   Index

Lange, Jean, 40
latchkey children, 164, 423-30
Latin American Parents Assn., 392
Laws, Theresa (JOC), 365
lawyer (See legal assistance), 189
layettes, 33
Leach, Arden, 160
leaders (See natural leaders), 34, 49-50, 127
leadership strategies, 258-59, 272-78, 361
League of Women Voters, 228
Learningames for the First Three Years, 374
learning styles, 337
leases (rental), 8, 108
legal age (See minor), 130-31
legal assistance, 32, 75, 82, 85, 87, 92, 105, 108, 130-31, 132-33, 188, 385, 391-92
legal protection, 85-86
Lengyel, Elizabeth, 40
Leonard, Gloria, 305
Lessing, Nick, 436
Let's Go Fly a Kite!..., 16, 457, 460
letters (See mail), 192
Levenkron, Steven, 150
Levert, Tiffany, 438
Levin, Nora Jean, 240
Lewis, Suzanne & Benjamin (SFC), 319
library, 330, 333, 345, 435, 440, 445, 461-63, 466
licenses (See driver's license), 16, 89
Lifelong Learning Program, 348-49
Lifeprints, 223
Lifescape Enterprises, 460
lifescaping, 279-286
lifestyle, i-ii, 167, 176-77, 179, 184, 195, 228, 332, 341, 345, 441
Lipsitz, Joan, 429
listening skills, 48, 449
Lister, Dean, 438
livability, 96-97
loans, 106
lobby, 49, 132
locator services, 230
Locke, Rosemary, 152-60
Lollipops and Parachutes, 394, 460

loneliness (See isolation, solitude), 7, 125, 128, 177, 179
Lord, Sharon (Ph.D.), 332
Long, Lynette (Ph.D.), 430
Loring AFB (ME), 263
Los Ninos International, 391
lovaholic, 223
love, 30, 51, 53, 59
Lunsford, Kathy, 128

MacIntosh, Houston, M.D., 40
mail, 43, 53-55, 192
maintenance, 96-97, 190
make a difference (See difference)
Making a Home in the Navy:..., 9, 41, 44, 69, 184, 223, 325, 442
Malcolm Grow USAF Medical Center (MD), 155
map, 185, 189
Marine Corps, 18, 22, 45-50, 93, 94, 112, 117, 121, 123-25, 127, 134-36, 175-76, 221-22, 228, 230, 270, 280, 300, 306, 308, 328, 346-49, 351, 355, 361, 372, 410-14, 416, 427-28
marital communications, 128
marital difficulties, 30, 47, 65, 92, 128, 132-39, 142, 147
marriage certificate, 131, 189
marriage enrichment, 135-36
Marston, Margaret, 444, 446-47, 449
Martinez, Francesco, 24
Mary Morrisson Elementary School, 58-62
Maslow, Abraham, 287-88
Maslow's Hierarchy, 174-83, 196-200, 204-7, 212-16, 232-34, 287-88, 369-73
Master Chief Petty Officer of the Navy (MCPON), 95-96
matriarchy, 34, 273
maturity, 30, 36, 219
mayor (Army), 121
McCaffree, Mary Jane, 291
meal times (See dinner), 37
Mayport Naval Station (FL), 51
McAndrews, Mick, 427
McCleskey, Kathleen, 261
McClintock, Susan, 302
McCubbin, Hamilton I.(Ph.D.), 69, 199-20, 236

Index 501

McDaniel, Jan, 124-25
McGinty, Thomas J. (CDR), 96, 100
McGlothin, Gail & Hubert J. (HMCS), 54, 75-77
McKay, Gary D., 405
McPherson, Jane, 312-13
mechanical failures, 32
medical care, 32, 33, 89-91, 124, 132-38, 189, 191-92, 199, 229, 238
meeting places, 121
Melvin, Jimmie, 433
Merkle, Candice & Raymond (LTC), 318, 320
messages, 28, 33, 53-55
midlife, 68-69, 147
Military Child Care Act, 419-20
military clause (rental), 8
Military Construction (MILCON), 418
Military Family Resource Center (MFRC), 123, 127, 360
Military Family Studies, 174, 325-27, 375
military housing (See housing), 27-28, 86, 89-90, 94-100, 118, 121, 123-24, 176
military juniors (See "brats"), 433-38
Military Lifestyle (See *Ladycom*)
Military Living, 193
Military Marketing, 123
Military Spouse Day, 262
Military Spouse Business and Professional Assn., 263, 311
Military Spouse Skills Resource Center, 303
Military Travel Guide, 193
Miller, Becky Juett, 20
mine sweeper, 54
Ministers' Wives, 251, 254
minor, 130-31
mirror, 225-27, 259
Misawa AB (Japan)
Mitchell, Brenda, 371, 373
mobile homes (See trailer), 29, 48, 75-76, 103-14
Mobile Travel Routing Service, 13
mobility (See moving), 140, 171, 222, 262, 297-300, 406, 434

mobilization (See deployment and unaccompanied tours), 111, 27, 39, 42-44, 45-62, 119, 417, 422
Model Installation Program, 109
Mohegan Community College, 343-44
Montreal Children's Research Institute, 369
Moody AFB (GA), 119
morale, 52
Morehouse, Laurence (Ph.D.), 197-98
Morgan, Steven (Dr.), 351
mothering workshop, 126
Mother's (See "going home"), 29
motivation, 282, 334, 342-43
moving, 3-24, 39, 57, 68-69, 87-88, 119, 131, 141, 146-47, 189-93, 205, 211-12, 232-33, 406, 418, 429, 433-38, 439-42
Moving American, The, 8, 39, 41, 254
multi-gifted, 227, 452
Murray, Sandra, 45, 47-48
museums, 267, 447, 455, 469
Myers-Briggs Personality Inventory, 454
Mystic (CT), 4, 60, 160, 408, 442
myths, 32, 33, 132-39
Mueller, Cate, 471, 477
Munn, Gail, 58
Murphy, Caryn, 438
mutual aid, 91
My Image, 151-60

NAS Cecil Field (FL), 365
NAS Jacksonville (FL), 133-34, 231, 234, 371-73
NAS Patuxent River (MD), 151-52
National Adoption Center, 392
National Alliance of Homebased Businesswomen, 312
National Cancer Institute, 155, 160
National Commission on Excellence in Education, 444
National Defense University (See Industrial College of the Armed Forces), 361
National Guard, iii, 261, 422

502 Index

National Home Study Council Directory of Home Study Schools, 345
National Military Family Assn. (NMFA), 93, 154, 263
National Music Camp, 464, 470
National Oceanographic and Atmospheric Agency (NOAA), 91
National Park Service, 329
National Register of Historic Places, 96
National Trust for Historic Preservation, 329
Nation at Risk, A, 443-44
Nation of Strangers, A, 8, 39, 41, 254
natural leaders, 34, 35
nature, 14
Naval Institute *Proceedings,* 14
Naval Station Orlando (FL), 378, 388
Navy, i-ii, 3, 10, 22, 24, 27-41, 51-54, 57-60, 63, 65-67, 75-77, 90-91, 93, 94-100, 107, 109-10, 113, 117-22, 123-26, 128-29, 130-31, 132-33, 150-60, 170-71, 175, 223, 228, 230, 240-45, 256-57, 260, 264, 270, 272, 284, 287-89, 291-93, 301, 305, 308, 311, 325-28, 333, 335-36, 342-44, 349-50, 355-61, 362-66, 375, 382-92, 412, 416, 421, 427-28, 439, 456, 468
Navy Family Awareness Conferences, 22, 117, 259, 272
Navy Family Service Center (See family service/support centers), 20
Navy Family Support Program, 184, 240, 272, 304, 325, 327
Navy Judge Advocate General (JAG), 130-31
Navy Leader's Family Manual, 170
Navy League, The, 270
Navy Overseas Transfer Information (See OTIS)
Navy and Marine Corps Relief Society, 32, 33, 37, 38, 40, 52, 77, 93, 122, 126, 129, 251, 270, 272, 280, 283, 301, 340, 468
Navy Spouse Employment Assistance (SEAP) (See employment), 311
Navy Times (See *Army, Navy, Air Force Times*), 41

Navy Wifeline Association, The, 39-40, 93, 254, 291
Navy Wives Club of America, 118, 228, 287
NCO wives, 45-47, 283, 287-88
needs, 204-6
Neidig, Peter (Ph.D.), 133-39, 372, 410-14
neighborhood, ii, 36, 37, 44, 60-61, 64, 67, 124, 137, 169-71, 175, 177-83, 189, 211, 221, 227, 230, 333, 403-4, 424
Nellis AFB (NV), 24
Nelson, Kathy, 237, 239
Nepal, 19
Nettleingham, Jo, 50
newcomers (See sponsors), 17-24, 86, 231-32, 263
New London (CT), ii, 27, 57, 96, 149-50, 160, 228, 263-64, 284, 287-89, 314-15, 341-45, 349-50, 468
New London DAY, 40
New Orleans (LA), 76, 261
newsletters, 327
newspaper, 49, 124, 176, 326-27, 447, 466
newspaper (ship's), 55
New Yorker, 445
non-appropriated fund (NAF), 87-88
Norfolk Navy Family Services Center, 128-29
Norfolk (VA) area, 128-29, 256, 284
North American Council on Adoptable Children, 392
Northern Virginia Community College, 333, 340
notice (rental), 8
nuclear family (See family), 169, 174, 177, 442
nurse (See Navy Relief), 33, 36, 126, 152, 154, 156, 280
nutrition, 128, 150, 187, 198-99
Nutting, Maureen, 303, 305-6

O'Beirne, Heather, 327-28, 330, 407-9
O'Beirne, Michael, 328-30, 407-9
obligations, 65-66
O'Connell, Brian J. (CAPT), 95, 97, 99
O'Donnell, David (MAJ), 304

Office of Family Policy and Support (DoD), 88, 260-61, 306, 330, 383, 391
officers' wives (See wardroom), 29, 34, 45-47, 64, 126-27, 164, 260-61, 287, 304, 326, 387
Offutt AFB (NB), 158
Ohio University, 348-49, 352
O'Keefe, Georgia, 225, 230
Olander, Ed (CAPT, USN, CC), 237-39
Olson, David (Ph.D.), 236
ombudsman (See Key Wives), 41, 93, 129, 132, 134, 251, 259-60, 264
Once Over....Lightly, 291
Once Upon a Mattress, 255
On My Own...., 430
Ono, Allen K. (LTG), 22-23
Orbach, Susie, 150
orders, 4, 101, 224
Organization for United Response, Inc. (OURS), 392
organized, 76-77, 184-93
orientations, 19, 86, 163
Orthner, Dennis (Ph.D.), 148
OTIS (Navy Overseas Transfer Information Service), 24, 101-2
Ouimette, Rodney A. (TSGT) and Susan (TSGT), 78-80
Our Town, 233
outer-directed, 36
outreach, 122, 124, 128, 164
overseas, 19-21, 53, 85-89, 98, 101-2, 120, 127, 161-66, 176, 178, 189, 215, 302-3, 309, 331, 365-66, 435-36, 466
Overseas Briefing Center, 303
overseas travel, 15

Pachkoski, Janet, 54
Packard, Vance, 8, 39, 41, 254
Panama, 22
parade, 292
parasites, 172
parenting (See child development), 118, 125-28, 136, 400-06, 410-14, 424, 442-50
parents (aging), 240-46
Parker, Nina and Theodore W. (GEN, USA, Ret.), 55, 244
Parris Island (SC), 134-39, 372, 410-14

Parry, Jon, 128-29
partnership, 118, 443-50
Pascagoula (MS), 114
Passages, 66
Pass It On!, i-iv, 20, 22, 125-26, 129, 220, 223, 237, 433, 466
passports, 12, 439-42
past/present/future, i, 60-62, 223, 231-35, 413, 442
patience, 16
patrol cycle, 27-28, 31, 36, 54
pay (See finances), iii
Pearlman, Chester A. (M.D.), 30 ff., 40
Peebles, Fire Chief, 105-6
Pegnam, John W. (LT), 29, 39
Penning, Janis, 24
Pentagon, 79
perfection, 134, 141, 145-46, 150
permanent change of station (PCS) (See moving), 22, 119
perseverance, 349, 383, 478
personal property, 107
personnel office (See Civilian Personnel Office), 102
Peterson, Katherine, 244
Peterson's Guides, 470, 472-73
pets, 21, 135, 231, 469
Petty, Jackie, 436
Pfeffer, Kasue & Leslie (SSGT), 316, 320
Philippines, 10, 11, 21
Phillips, Mopsy, 307
phone tree (See telephone), 35
photographs, 20, 52, 55, 131, 189, 192, 407-9, 438, 452
Piaget, Jean, 394
pictures (See photographs)
Pierson, George W., 8, 39, 41, 254
pilot program, 46
pioneer (See Isolation Matrix), 438
Platte, Ronald J., 67-68
play, 455-60
Please Touch, 374, 460
pleasure, 201-10, 223-24, 411-14
Plummer, Gina, 156-57
police, 106, 109, 133
policy, 177, 272
Poriss, Martin, 8
portable (See home-based), 222, 297-300, 439-42

Porter-Sargent, 463, 470
portfolio, 327-28, 344, 349, 351, 373, 375
Portsmouth (NH), 96
Portsmouth Naval Hospital (VA), 126
poseidon (See submarine), 27, 31
Postman, Neil, 449, 480
potluck, 42-43
Powell, Colin L. (GEN, USA), 161
power-of-attorney, 18, 32, 92, 120, 130-31, 188-89
Pratt, Stephen W., 426-27
predictable crises, 66, 249
preference (hiring), 87-88
pregnancy, 78
pressures, 6, 47, 49, 201-10
prevention, 33, 34, 37, 68, 122, 130-31, 132, 190, 195, 428
preventive (repairs), 52
Princess and the Pea, 255-58
Prince William County (VA), 104, 113
prisoners-of-war (POW/MIA), 199-200
privacy, 205
privileges, 86
problem-solving, 48, 266, 271
promotion, 132, 150
protocol, 290-94, 307
psychiatrists, 30, 33, 37
psychologists, 121-22
PTA, 333, 426, 448
Public Health Service, 89, 91
Puerto Rico, 436
Puget Sound Naval Shipyard (WA), 351-52
Pulaski, Mary Ann (Ph.D.), 374
puppets, 121

quality of life, 121-22
Qualls, Misty, 436
Quantico (VA), 18, 346-47
quarters (See military housing), 89, 94-100
questionnaire (See survey), 40

R & R (rest and relaxation), 31
Racinowski, Barbara, 312
Rahm, Jason, 435, 438
Raising a Responsible Child, 405
Raising Children in a Difficult Time, 374

Rand Report, 298
rank (See grade, rate), 47-48, 95, 260-61
Reach to Recovery, 160
readiness, iii, 19, 38, 49, 170, 178, 262, 264, 415, 419
Reagan, President and Mrs. Ronald, 164
real estate (See housing), 76
Real Men Enjoy Their Kids, 404
Reass, Marcia, 433
rebellion, 141, 144, 146
recipe, 45, 221-24
records, 184-93
recreation services, 118, 426-28, 461, 463-64, 466
recruiting, 356-60
Red Cross (See American Red Cross)
Redo, John (JO1), 56
re-entry, 178
referral (See information and referral), 129
Regents College, 345, 348-49, 352
rehabilitation (See alcohol/drug abuse), 92
Reifenberger, Marlene, 351-52
relatives (See extended family, parents), 61
relationships, 219, 223
religion, 79, 178, 200
relocation (See moving)
relocation assistance, 22, 418
rental, 107, 188
rental deposits (security deposits), 8
repairs, 29, 32, 96-97, 131, 188, 190
research, iv, 11, 19, 27, 58, 63, 69-70, 127, 132-39, 140-50, 153, 170, 195, 219, 223-24, 226, 236, 240, 261, 297-99, 302, 308, 341, 344, 369, 371, 404, 406, 412, 424-26, 433, 438, 451-52, 454, 480
Reserves, iii, 22, 361, 416-17, 422
residence (legal) (See domicile)
responsibilities, 65-66, 118, 137
resolutions (New Year's), 217, 235
respect, 264, 453
restraints (car), 16
resume, 303, 328-39, 474
retention, iii, 19, 49, 68-69, 98, 138, 170, 178, 262, 264, 271, 272, 309, 415, 419

Index 505

retirement, iii, 63, 65, 67-68, 85, 89-91, 133, 204, 303
reunion, 30, 31, 36, 63-64, 227
revolution, 259
Reynard, Bibs, 291
Reynolds, Kim, 127
Rhode Island School of Design (RISD), 329, 464
Rich, Glynda, 291-93
Richardson, Eliot, 280,
rights, 85-88, 259
risk ("at risk"), 125, 135-36, 140, 146, 200
rituals (See traditions)
Rivers, Caryl, 223
Roach, Pam & Elizabeth, 332-34, 336-38
Roberts, Debra (LCDR)
Robinson, Earnest E., Jr., 436
Rogers, Patricia (SKC), 362
role models, 127-28, 134, 154, 160, 249-254, 255-58, 334, 451, 454
roles, 31, 32, 65-68, 133, 135, 171-73, 177, 247, 249-54, 255-64, 265-71, 314-15, 341, 369-73, 443-50
Rondorf, Cheryl & Neil (LCDR), 388-89
Ross, Tom & Marilyn, 311
Rota (Spain), 20
ROTC, 363
Rountree, Steven, 316
R.S.V.P., 292
rumor, 28

safety, 66, 86, 103-10, 123, 395
safety deposit box, 131, 188-89
safety net, 86, 123-30
Salyer, Samuel C., 101-02
Samuels, Mike (M.D.), 200
Sanders, Billy C. (MCPON), 95-96, 99-100
San Antonio (TX), 426
San Diego (CA), 27, 95, 109, 228, 263, 306, 418
Sandman, Sonya, 302-03, 306
San Francisco (CA), 109, 260
Santa, 61-62, 171
Santiago, Chris, 435
Satterfield, Debbie & Joe (SSGT), 382-83

Savannah News-Press, 366
savings account, 29, 74-79, 187
scared, 436
Schaefer, Earl S. (Dr.), 371
Schaffer, Richard (RADM), 154
Schmalzried, Beverly, 427-28
scholarships, 89, 164, 340, 477
school (See education), 79, 185, 189, 191, 439-42, 443-50, 454, 463
School Age-Latch Key program (SA/LK), 426-27
school board, 178
School's Out -- Now What?, 430
Scotland, 29
Scouts (See Boy or Girl Scouts)
scrapbook, 192
Sears, Barbara, 54
Sears, H. J. T. (RADM), 155
Sears, Joan, 53
"seasoned wives," 129, 154
Secretary of Defense, 259
Secretary of Navy, 68
security, 94, 171, 184
security deposits, 8, 105
Seesholtz, Marylee & J. Richard (RADM), 244-45
Seidenberg, Robert (M.D.), 8, 39, 41, 254
self-discovery, 6, 201-10, 211-16, 279-86
self-esteem, 47-48, 128, 141, 147, 179, 222-24, 264
selfish, 31, 234
self-sufficiency, 428-30, 441-42
senior enlisted personnel, 19
senior wives, 38, 259
separation (See deployment), 27, 39, 42-44, 45-50, 51-56, 64, 67, 123, 129, 190, 233
separation, geographic (See distance), 29, 39, 135, 187
separation (marital), 47, 91-92
serendipity, 268
Serviceman's Group Life Insurance (SGLI), 239
sex, 30
sexual abuse, 145, 428
Sharp, Pat, 121
Sheehy, Gail, 66
shelter, 138

shore duty, 63-69, 204
Shusko, Valerie, 125
sickness, 32-33, 448
Singer/Schectman, 404
singles, 20, 118, 120, 169, 172
single parents, 125, 259, 262, 366, 418
skill/job bank, 300, 301-06, 312
Slaughter, Katherine, 8
sleep disturbances, 31
Small Business Administration, 311
Smart Girls, Gifted Women, 460
Smith Barbara, 48
Smith College, 452, 471, 478, 509
Smith, Heidi, 326-27
Smith, Jason & Tashi, 435
Smith, Shirley & Keith A. (MAJGEN), 46, 49
Smithsonian, Institution, 455, 469
Social Security, 90-91, 188, 322-33
social workers, 121-22
Soldiers' and Sailors' Relief Act, 87
solitude, 5, 177
Southern Illinois University (SIU), 349-50
Spain (See Rota), 20, 29
Sparling, Joseph, 374
Spase, Jennifer, 438
special education, 462
Spock, Benjamin (M.D.), 374, 394
sponsor (military member), 86, 176
sponsors (relocation), 7, 8, 11, 17-24, 99, 102
sports, 439
spouse (See wife), iv
spouse centers, 120-21
spouse employment assistance, 87-88
spouse rights/benefits, 85-93
squadron, 45-50
stages, 400-02, 406
Standish, Kay, 129
Stars and Stripes, 313
State, Department of, 19, 102
State of Record (See domicile), 74, 87
stationery, 52
Status of Forces Agreement (SOFA), 86
steering committee, 46, 48
Steindam, Sharon, 444, 447
Stephens, Kim, 21

stereotypes, 260-61, 283
St. Marys (GA), 11, 105, 231-33
Stewart, Bonnie, 335-36
Stewart, Marlene, 107
Stiscak, Donna, 394, 460
stocks, 188-89
Stone, Bonnie, 41
Storm, Linda, 313
Strategic Air Command (SAC), 263
strategies, 274-78, 279-86, 287-89, 456
Strawn, Lynne (SSGT), iv
stresses, emotional, 31, 47, 57, 117, 125, 134-38, 140-50, 184, 321, 339, 429
stress, financial, 6, 47, 147, 184, 321-24
Striker, Susan, 374, 460
Strong-Campbell Interest Inventory, 454
structure (See organization), 73
students, 58-59, 332-40, 341-45, 346-52, 439-42, 443-50, 451-54, 471-78
students, foreign, 21
study skills, 335-39, 446-47, 449
submarine, 27-41, 51, 54, 57, 60, 63, 65, 123, 178, 204, 227, 366, 407, 412, 468
subsistence allowance, 29
substandard quarters, 95, 125
success (See achievement), 7, 48, 79, 122
suicide, 117, 136
summer (See vacation), 440-41, 455-60, 461-64, 465-70
Summer Opportunities for Kids and Teenagers, 470
Sumrall, George (LTC), 119-20
Superwoman, 281
support centers (See family service/support centers), 117-22
support groups (See ship wives and family/unit), 63, 121, 127
Sure-Pay (See direct deposit), 79, 119-20
survey (See questionnaire), 40, 46-47, 49, 95, 118-19, 123
Survival Kit for Overseas Living, 101
survivor benefits, 90
Swan, Helen L., 429

syndrome:
  shore duty: 67-68
  submarine wives: 30-32

tapes (audio-video), 52-53, 55
taxes, 74, 77, 83, 87, 131, 187-88, 191, 310, 321, 409
teachers, 36, 185, 440, 443-50
Teenage Entrepreneur's Guide, 469
teenagers, 7, 64, 95-96, 123-31, 132, 140-50, 172, 178, 401-3, 406, 427-29, 433-38, 439-42, 447-50, 461-64, 465-70, 471-78
teleidoscope, 266
telephone, 53, 124, 176, 185-86, 189, 336
telephone tree (See phone tree), 35, 46
television, 178, 345, 445, 449, 479-87
Television Production Handbook, 482
temporary duty (TDY), 121, 135, 204, 227
Temporary Military Lodging, 193
temporary positions, 302
Terry, Cassandra & Duane L. (SGT), 73-74
Thanatos, 237-39
30 Days to a More Powerful Vocabulary, 478
Thoman, Mark (CPT), 49
Thomas Jefferson Intermediate School, 444
thrift shop, 252, 270
thrive, i-ii, 117, 225
time, 222, 227, 231-36
time management, 233, 235-36, 336
Time Out, 124-25
Toffler, Alvin, 299-300, 332
tools, 185, 190, 192
Torma, Ann, 158
tornados, 106, 114
Total Fitness, 197-98
Toynbee, Arnold, 179, 193
toys, 393-99, 407-8, 445, 451
traditions, family, 57, 59-62, 178, 192
traditions, military (See protocol, Pass It On!)
trailer (See mobile homes), 29, 48, 103-14, 121, 124, 176

trainers, professional, 49-50
training, 37-39, 46, 48-50, 125-27, 129, 260, 263
transiency (See moving), 68
transportation, 20, 21, 35, 127, 176, 322-23, 334, 339
traveler's checks, 119
traveling, 13-15, 82, 119, 161-62, 191
Tripler Army Hospital (HI), 157
Trull, Rhonda, 233
Tucci, Phyllis & James (LCDR), 389-91
Tucker, Everett L., Jr. (COL), 96-99
Tucson (AZ), 316-18, 409
tuition, 340, 472
TV Ritual: Worship at the Video Altar, 484
Twentynine Palms (CA), 351

unaccompanied tour, 27-69, 75, 86, 121, 130-31, 204, 227, 233, 240, 412
under-employed, 321
Understanding Piaget, 374
unfaithful, 47
uniforms, 360, 375
unit family (See family/unit-ship and support groups), 169-72, 175-83, 200, 227, 229, 264
Universal Aid for Children, 392
University of Connecticut (UCONN), 342-43
unpatriotic, 31
Upson, Norma, 8
Urda, Brenda, 151-52
USAREUR, 98
U. S. Consumer Product Safety Commission, 377, 381
U. S. Military Academy, 51, 359, 463
Uses of Enchantment, The, 445
USO, 24, 75, 92, 101, 120, 124-25, 128, 161-66, 172, 228, 270, 318-19, 327-28, 340, 374, 381, 422, 426, 468-69
USS G. W. CARVER, 40, 169-71
USS PATRICK HENRY, 27, 40
USS SARATOGA, 56
USS SIMON LAKE, 114, 366
USS THRESHER, 28
USS VON STEUBEN, 40

utility bills, 76-77, 97, 187-88
utility deposits, 8, 118-19
vacation, 74, 76, 327-30, 427
Vail, Doris R. (CAPT), 361
Valdosta State College, 326-27
Variable Housing Allowance (VHA), 99-100
Veterans Administration (VA), 90-91, 106, 108
Vickroy, Grace, 107
Vincent, Michael (CDR), 152
visiting nurse (See Navy Relief), 126
Voluntary Action Center, 285
volunteer force, 28
Volunteer Income Tax Assistance, 187
volunteer management, 229, 346
volunteers, 6, 21, 50, 67-68, 76, 120-22, 124-26, 155-57, 159, 172, 208, 221, 249-55, 259-60, 272, 279-86, 305, 316-17, 324, 325-30, 341, 344, 428, 466-70
VOLUNTEER - The National Center, 260-61, 352
voting, 85, 190
vulnerable, 48, 237-39

Wakefield High School, 444, 471
Walker, Lea Ann, 304-5
Walker, Lenore, 135
Walter Reed Army Hospital (DC), 155, 435
wardroom, 29, 34, 60, 64
Warner Robins AFB (GA), 21, 119
warranties, 189
Washburn, Susan & Gary E. (LTC), 346-49, 351-52
Washington, D.C. area, 63-65, 95, 164, 201, 228, 240, 263, 265, 298, 300, 311, 314, 333, 435
Washington Post, 297
weight, 140-50
Weisensee, Nancy & Wm. J. (CAPT), 349-50
Welcome Aboard, 40
Welcome, Baby, 126
Well Child Book, 200
Wellesley College Center for Research on Women, 224, 426
wellness, 194-200
Wells, Larry & Kathy, 22
welcome aboard packet, 20

Werkman, Sidney (M.D.), 222
Wesleyan University, 212, 216
WESTPAC, 52, 55, 336
What Works: Research About Teaching & Learning, 373-74, 460
Wheeler, Dan (Chaplain), 238
Wheeler, Kelly Ann, 22
White, Clara, 52
White, Burton L., 374, 377, 381
Whiteman AFB (MO), 433
Whitworth, Shauna, 22-23, 123, 127-28, 261
Wickham, John A., (GEN), 118, 196
widows, 83, 85, 89-91, 237-39
Wifeline (Navy), 44
Wilder, Thornton, 233
Willemsen, Ashley, 436
Willett, Nongyow (EM1), 365
wills, 32, 92, 130, 188-89
Wilson, Evelyn E., 471
Wise, Wendy, 305
wives' clubs (See support groups), 118, 121, 127, 129, 172, 194, 208, 229, 233, 239, 251-55, 261-62, 265, 287-89, 304, 307, 321, 326, 387-88
wives' fund, 43
wives' night, 31, 35
women's centers, 120
Women's Equity Action League (WEAL), 93, 358, 361
women's liberation movement, 67, 137, 249, 272, 279, 361
women, military, 85, 353-66
work (See employment), 86
workaholic, 223, 234
workshops, 118
Wright, Duard & Caroline, 18
Wright, Steven E. (CDR), 130-31

Yankee Magazine Internship, 329
YMCA (See Armed Services YMCA), 9, 127-29, 228, 270, 373, 381, 422, 426, 463, 465
Y-ME, 156, 160
YWCA, 221, 426, 463, 467
Yokota AFB (Japan), 120
Yorktown High School, 444
youth activities, 426-28, 437, 463, 466

Zumwalt, Elmo (ADM), 260

# About the Author

Kathleen P. O'Beirne -- Army daughter, Navy wife, and long-time advocate for military families.

As the Associate Editor of *Family* and author of two Services' official family handbooks, she is the most published author in the field of military families. She wrote <u>Making a Home in the Navy: Ideas to Grow On</u> for the U. S. Navy Family Support Program in 1980 and revised it in 1985. In 1983, she wrote and published <u>Charting Your Life in the United States Coast Guard</u> for the U. S. Coast Guard Family Programs.

As a teacher, Mrs. O'Beirne designed and taught her course, "Military Family Studies," at the Industrial College of the Armed Forces of the National Defense University in Washington, D.C. She later offered it at Jacksonville University in Jacksonville, Florida and Valdosta State College, Georgia. Other work in the field of education includes teaching English at the junior high, high school, and college levels and serving as the chairman of the Gifted and Talented Advisory Committee and the Council on Instruction for Arlington Public Schools in Virginia.

Mrs. O'Beirne has served as a consultant, trainer, and speaker for the Army, Navy, Air Force, Marine Corps, and Coast Guard. She serves currently as a member of the World Board of Directors of the USO. Formerly, she worked as Family Programs Information Coordinator, Office of Family Policy and Support, Department of Defense (1987 - 89) where she was responsible not only for public affairs and publications, but also for spouse employment, volunteer management training, and adoption issues.

A graduate of Smith College and Wesleyan University, she serves on the Board of Directors of the Alumnae Association of Smith College.

About the Illustrator

Helen M. Carr --

My love-hate relationship with the Navy began in Jan 76, when I enlisted in the Navy .... young, naive, with a lost dream and no plans. I married an enlisted man on 18 Nov 78, who inspired a plan for the future, and brought the lost dream back to life. Started taking college classes using Navy benefits.

Became pregnant, the center of controversy at work. Had just re-enlisted and received bonus. Was told I could get out because I was pregnant and did not have to pay the money back. Stayed in because it was the right thing to do. Had a son on 14 Jan 81 and thus began the juggling between our military and family lives.

In 82, was in the Navy still, working mid-shift, going to school for commercial art in the morning after work (following my dream), going home to take care of my son after school until my Navy husband got home from work, and then sleep, heavenly sleep.

Got out of the Navy in 84. Went to school full-time using the GI Bill. Took my finals same week we packed out, got my associate's degree, and moved in 85. Career and life in limbo, not in one spot for more than three months for next year. Finally in one spot. Got first full-time commercial art job in 87. Husband went to sea.

In 88, husband's fun at sea interrupted in mine field and fun really began. In 89, husband came home safe, no worse for the wear. I felt ready to return to college, but discovered I had lost my remaining G.I.Bill benefits!

In 90, shore duty and move. Opportunity to leave secure job to hunt for a new job during recession and time of layoffs.

In 91, working, whew! Still following my dream, whew! Husband still in Navy, whew!

Me, I'm a Navy wife. I have a love-hate relationship still with the Navy: am thankful for opportunities gained and resentful of opportunities lost.

To order additional copies of Pass It On!

Name_____

Street Address_____

City_____State_____Zip_____

Send $14.95 (includes sales tax, postage & handling) per copy desired. Make check payable to Lifescape Enterprises.

Number of copies desired:_____

Total amount enclosed:_____

If address to which book is to be sent is different from above, please check here [ ] and indicate on back of form.

Send order to: Lifescape Enterprises
P. O. Box 218
West Mystic, CT 06388

- -

To order additional copies of Pass It On!

Name_____

Street Address_____

City_____State_____Zip_____

Send $14.95 (includes sales tax, postage & handling) per copy desired. Make check payable to Lifescape Enterprises.

Number of copies desired:_____

Total amount enclosed:_____

If address to which book is to be sent is different from above, please check here [ ] and indicate on back of form.

Send order to: Lifescape Enterprises
P. O. Box 218
West Mystic, CT 06388

To order additional copies of Pass It On!

Name_____

Street Address_____

City_____State_____Zip_____

Send $14.95 (includes sales tax, postage & handling) per copy desired. Make check payable to Lifescape Enterprises.

Number of copies desired:_____

Total amount enclosed:_____

If address to which book is to be sent is different from above, please check here [ ] and indicate on back of form.

Send order to: Lifescape Enterprises
                   P. O. Box 218
                   West Mystic, CT 06388

▫ ▫

To order additional copies of Pass It On!

Name_____

Street Address_____

City_____State_____Zip_____

Send $14.95 (includes sales tax, postage & handling) per copy desired. Make check payable to Lifescape Enterprises.

Number of copies desired:_____

Total amount enclosed:_____

If address to which book is to be sent is different from above, please check here [ ] and indicate on back of form.

Send order to: Lifescape Enterprises
                   P. O. Box 218
                   West Mystic, CT 06388

To order additional copies of Pass It On!

Name __Daphne B. Latimore_____

Street Address __P. O. Box 3645_____

City __Ft. Polk_____ State __LA____ Zip __71459__

Send $14.95 (includes sales tax, postage & handling) per copy desired. Make check payable to Lifescape Enterprises.

Number of copies desired: __2_____

Total amount enclosed: __$29.90_____

If address to which book is to be sent is different from above, please check here [ ] and indicate on back of form.

Send order to: Lifescape Enterprises
P. O. Box 218
West Mystic, CT 06388

To order additional copies of Pass It On!

Name _____

Street Address _____

City _____State_____Zip_____

Send $14.95 (includes sales tax, postage & handling) per copy desired. Make check payable to Lifescape Enterprises.

Number of copies desired: _____

Total amount enclosed: _____

If address to which book is to be sent is different from above, please check here [ ] and indicate on back of form.

Send order to: Lifescape Enterprises
P. O. Box 218
West Mystic, CT 06388